SMALL STATE CONSTITUTIONALISM

This volume addresses the important, but under-noticed, question of the impact of state size and scale for constitutional law and governance.

Often, the best way to understand the effect of scale is to examine states where scale is demonstrably lacking. Doing so allows for a form of 'reflective' comparison that provides greater insight and clarity into the significance of state size, and constitutional scale, as factors affecting a range of constitutional outcomes.

As such, the collection brings together scholars from a wide range of jurisdictions, living and working across the Global South and North, to focus on the lessons from a range of small states and jurisdictions in this context. Attention is devoted to the constitutional experiences of such states and jurisdictions in Europe, Africa, Asia, South America, the Caribbean and Oceania. The volume also explicitly invites critical reflection on, and problematisation, of the issues of line-drawing and boundary definition around notions of state and jurisdictional size.

It will be of interest to audiences working in and interested in small states generally, as well as a broader comparative audience interested in issues of scale in constitutional design and implementation.

Small State Constitutionalism

Edited by
Elisabeth Perham
Maartje De Visser
and
Rosalind Dixon

•HART•
OXFORD • LONDON • NEW YORK • NEW DELHI • SYDNEY

HART PUBLISHING

Bloomsbury Publishing Plc

Kemp House, Chawley Park, Cumnor Hill, Oxford, OX2 9PH, UK

1385 Broadway, New York, NY 10018, USA

Bloomsbury Publishing Ireland Limited, 29 Earlsfort Terrace, Dublin 2, D02 AY28, Ireland

HART PUBLISHING, the Hart/Stag logo, BLOOMSBURY and the Diana logo are trademarks of Bloomsbury Publishing Plc

First published in Great Britain 2025

A catalogue record for this book is available from the British Library.

A catalogue record for this book is available from the Library of Congress.

Library of Congress Control Number: 2025945687

ISBN: HB: 978-1-50997-976-9
ePDF: 978-1-50997-978-3
ePub: 978-1-50997-977-6

Typeset by Compuscript Ltd, Shannon

For product safety related questions contact productsafety@bloomsbury.com

To find out more about our authors and books visit www.hartpublishing.co.uk. Here you will find extracts, author information, details of forthcoming events and the option to sign up for our newsletters.

CONTENTS

Part IC
Citizenship, Belonging and Regional Integration

PART II
STATE DESIGN AND OPERATION

Part IIA
Separation of Powers, and Checks and Balances

Part IIB
Mediating Division

LIST OF CONTRIBUTORS

Victor T Amadi is a postdoctoral research fellow at the Centre for Comparative Law in Africa at the University of Cape Town, South Africa. He holds an LLD degree in mercantile and labour law from the University of the Western Cape, South Africa. His research focuses on international trade and comparative regional integration and development in Africa.

Tony Angelo KC is Professor Emeritus at Victoria University of Wellington, New Zealand. His main research interests are in small states' law, and Pacific legal studies, and he has published extensively on the laws of Mauritius, Seychelles, and the small nations of the Pacific.

Ine Apapoe is senior lecturer and former head of the Department of Public Administration (Policy and Government) of the Faculty of Social Sciences of the Anton de Kom University of Suriname. She has a PhD from the Vrije Universiteit in Amsterdam, the Netherlands, which focuses on traditional, modern and dual governance in Suriname's maroon communities. Ine has been involved in several research projects in the field of (local) governance, small-scale gold mining, traditional governance and livelihood, land rights, gender and gender mainstreaming.

Joelle Barnes is a lecturer for the Judicial Institute for Africa based in the Democratic Governance and Rights Unit at the University of Cape Town. She has a wide expertise in public law and judicial studies. Joelle's research in judicial decision-making crosses multiple jurisdictions and includes seven years working directly in apex courts in the Constitutional Court of South Africa and the office of the Chief Justice of the Seychelles Supreme Court.

Elisa Bertolini is Associate Professor of Comparative Public Law at Bocconi University, Milan. Her fields of research include Japanese constitutional law, constitutional systems of microstates, African constitutional systems, freedom of expression and Internet governance. She is the author of monographs, essays, and articles in Italian, French, Spanish, and English.

Ann Black is a Professor of Law at the TC Beirne School of Law, the University of Queensland, and Executive Director (Comparative Law) of its Centre for Public, International and Comparative Law. Her research analyses the intersection of law, religion and secularism, in particular the operation of *Syariah* in Southeast Asia. She has over 100 publications, with monographs on *Modern Perspectives on Islamic Law* (with Nadirsyah Hosen and Hossein Esmaeili – Edward Elgar Publishing, 2013), *Law and Legal Institutions of Asia* (with Gary Bell – Cambridge University Press, 2011), and

Religious Freedom in Secular States (Brill, 2022) and *Freedom of Religion and Religious Diversity* (Routledge, 2024) (both with Jahid Hossain Bhuiyan).

Petra Butler is Professor and Executive Dean at the University of Canterbury's Faculty of Law in New Zealand. She specialises in human rights and international commercial law, and has led law reform studies for the Commonwealth Secretariat, on judicial diversity in small Commonwealth states and international commercial arbitration. As Director of the Institute of Small and Micro States, Petra works to establish small states law as a distinct field, co-organising the annual Small States conference with WilmerHale and the British Institute of International and Comparative Law.

Conor Casey is a Senior Lecturer at the University of Surrey School of Law in the UK. Conor's research specialises in administrative law, constitutional law, and legal theory. His current research interests include studying the influence of government lawyers on law and policymaking and the influence of natural law theory in public law thought and practice. He is the co-editor of the *Dublin University Law Journal* and co-founder of *the New Digest* legal theory blog.

Jennifer Corrin is Professor Emerita at The University of Queensland and a Fellow of the Centre for Public, International and Comparative Law. She is an Honorary Professor at the University of Sydney. Jennifer's research focuses on law reform and development in plural legal regimes and legal issues affecting small states. Jennifer is the author of several books, including *Introduction to South Pacific Law* (with Vergil Narokobi – Intersentia, 2022), which is in its fifth edition.

Maartje De Visser is a Professor of Law at the Yong Pung How School of Law and College of Integrative Studies, Singapore Management University. Her research is centred on how a state's courts and non-judicial actors engage with its constitution, including to reap legitimacy benefits, as well as transnational judicial dialogues. She also has an abiding interest in comparative methodology, including the role of language, and in the study of how size may affect constitutional design and performance.

Rosalind Dixon is a Scientia Professor at the Faculty of Law & Justice at the University of New South Wales Sydney, and the former Director of the Gilbert + Tobin Centre of Public Law. She is a Fellow of the Australian Academy of Law and Australian Academy of Social Sciences, and is past co-president of the International Society of Public Law. Her work focuses on comparative constitutional law and constitutional design, constitutional democracy, theories of constitutional dialogue and amendment, and socio-economic rights.

Anna Dziedzic researches and practises in the field of comparative constitutional law. She is an Honorary Fellow of Melbourne Law School, University of Melbourne. She was a founding Convenor of the Constitution Transformation Network at Melbourne Law School from 2016–23 and a Programme Officer for Constitution Building Processes at the Asia Pacific Office of the International Institute for Democracy and Electoral Assistance (International IDEA) from 2023–25. Her scholarship examines the constitutional systems of the Oceania region from a comparative perspective, with a focus on constitution making, courts and judges, citizenship and legal pluralism. She is the author of *Foreign Judges in the Pacific* (Hart Publishing, 2021) and co-editor of *The Cambridge Handbook of Foreign Judges on Domestic Courts* (Cambridge University Press, 2023).

Sabir Kadel is the CEO of the Mauritius Law Reform Commission. Specialising in criminal law, he is a member of the editorial committee of the *Mauritius Criminal Law Review*, as well as the Spanish translation review *Transletters*. He taught at the University of Mauritius and the Institute for Judicial and Legal Studies in Mauritius. He has given lectures in France, Italy, Spain, the Netherlands and the USA. He has authored articles published in journals in Mauritius, Germany, New Zealand and France.

Dr Hervé Raimana Lallemant-Moe is an associate member of the Governance and Insular Development Research Team (University of French Polynesia) and the Centre of International Law (Jean Moulin University Lyon III). His research interests include environmental law, international law, and French overseas communities' legal issues, as well as climate change. He teaches law at the University of French Polynesia, Tahiti, where he is an alumnus. He also graduated from the University of Western Brittany (France) and the University of South Pacific.

Sam Macintosh is an admitted Barrister and Solicitor of the High Court of New Zealand, specialising in complex civil dispute resolution and arbitration. Sam previously practised in a well-known New Zealand full-service firm, and is currently practising as an Associate in the litigation and arbitration team at Cooke, Young & Keidan in London. Sam graduated from Victoria University of Wellington with a Bachelor of Laws, and a Bachelor of Arts (International Relations and Mandarin).

Sinethemba Memela is a PhD candidate at the University of New South Wales Sydney. She holds a Master of Laws in Human Rights from the University of California, Los Angeles where she was a Health and Human Rights Fellow, and a Bachelor of Laws from the University of the Witwatersrand, Johannesburg. Before her PhD studies, she spent several years working as a researcher in social and economic rights at the South African Human Rights Commission.

Ada Ordor is the director of the Centre for Comparative Law in Africa (University of Cape Town) and is the convener of the LLM course 'Law, Regional Integration and Development in Africa' and the 'Comparative Business Law in Africa' programme at the University of Cape Town Faculty of Law. Her research and postgraduate supervision explore the interconnectedness of development processes and their enabling laws. She is editor of the *Journal of Comparative Law in Africa* and was Henry Steiner Visiting Professor at Harvard Law School in 2024.

Christos Papastylianos is an Associate Professor at the School of Law of the University of Nicosia, Cyprus. He holds a PhD in Law from the European University Institute (Florence). His research currently focuses on constitution making and constitutional change through amendment and informal changes of the Constitution, on Greek and Cypriot constitutional history, and on immigration and asylum law. His publications have appeared, among others, in the *Cyprus Review*, *Religions* and the *Vienna Journal on International Constitutional Law*.

Elisabeth Perham is Lecturer at the Faculty of Law & Justice, University of New South Wales Sydney, and Deputy Director of the Gilbert + Tobin Centre of Public Law. She is a comparative constitutional law scholar with interests in constitution making, constitutional transfers, small state constitutionalism, and gender and constitutions, as well as in public law in Australia and Aotearoa New Zealand more generally.

Tracy Robinson is Professor of Law at the Faculty of Law, The University of the West Indies, Mona (Jamaica). Her interdisciplinary research spans constitutional law, family law, human rights law and gender, sexuality and the law. She is the co-author, with Arif Bulkan and Adrian Saunders, of *Fundamentals of Caribbean Constitutional Law* (2nd edn, Sweet & Maxwell, 2021).

John Stanton is an Associate Professor in Law at City St George's, University of London and Affiliate Associate Professor in Law, University of Malta. John is an expert in Maltese Constitutional Law and has written widely on the subject. Most notably, in 2024, John co-edited (with Tonio Borg) *The Constitution of Malta at Sixty* (Kite Group, 2024), a book published to mark the sixtieth anniversary of Maltese independence.

Mele Tupou Vaitohi is a Senior Lecturer at the Faculty of Law at Te Herenga Waka – Victoria University of Wellington. She hails from the Kingdom of Tonga. She is a leading scholar in Tonga's constitutional law and was formerly lead researcher for the 'Improving Pasifika Legal Education' project in Aotearoa New Zealand.

Janine Ubink is Professor of Law, Governance and Development at the Van Vollenhoven Institute for Law, Governance and Society, Leiden University. Her research centres around legal pluralism, customary law, traditional authorities, natural resource management and gender. She has a regional focus on Africa, particularly Ghana, Namibia, South Sudan and South Africa. Janine is the President of the International Commission on Legal Pluralism.

Se-shauna Wheatle is a Professor of Constitutional Law at Durham Law School, in the UK. Her research interests include unwritten constitutional principles, common law constitutionalism and Commonwealth Caribbean constitutional law. Se-shauna is author of *Principled Reasoning in Human Rights Adjudication* (Hart Publishing, 2017). She is co-editor of the *Oxford Handbook of Caribbean Constitutions* (Oxford University Press, 2020), series editor (with Jonathan Herring) of the Bristol University Press *Diverse Voices* book series, and editor (with Elizabeth O'Loughlin) of *Diverse Voices in Public Law* (Bristol University Press, 2023). Se-shauna is also Project Lead of the 'Unwritten Constitutional Norms and Principles' research project.

1

On Small State Constitutionalism

ELISABETH PERHAM, MAARTJE DE VISSER AND ROSALIND DIXON

I. Introduction

Constitutional self-government takes place across a wide variety of terrains and settings. It occurs in new, fragile and consolidated democracies, unitary and federal systems, and in developed and developing as well as former colonising and colonised states. It involves many different 'we the peoples', each with their own ideas, preferences and aspirations as regards the composition and functioning of the state. One pertinent, but not always reflected upon, characteristic is that in some constitutional contexts, the people are many, whereas in others, they are few. The focus of this volume is on this latter context, where constitutional self-government takes place within a 'small state' – understood, for our purposes, as a state (or – as discussed shortly – jurisdiction) with a population under 1.5 million people.[1]

This volume builds on a rich and growing scholarly literature on small states and territories, and their internal organisation and external relations in both law and, more expansively, political science and international relations.[2] It agrees with the appreciation in that literature that 'small states are simply too numerous and – sometimes individually, and certainly collectively – too important to ignore'.[3] As compared to existing works, our focus is, however, quite distinct, namely: the implications of state

[1] This is, for example, the definition of small state adopted by the World Bank: 'The World Bank in Small States' (*World Bank*), www.worldbank.org/en/country/smallstates/overview.

[2] In law, see eg P Butler and C Morris (eds), *Small States in a Legal World* (Cham, Springer, 2017); T Angelo and J Corrin (eds), 'Small States: A Collection of Essays' (2019) XXIII *Comparative Law Journal of the Pacific* (Hors Series Special Issue); C Morris (ed), *Making and Changing Law in Small Jurisdictions* (Cham, Springer, 2024). In political science, see eg G Baldacchino, 'Mainstreaming the Study of Small States and Territories' (2018) 1 *Small States & Territories* 3; J Corbett and W Veenendaal, *Democracy in Small States: Persisting Against All Odds* (Oxford, Oxford University Press, 2018). There is also a literature in international relations, see eg, C Ingebritsen, I Neumann, S Gstöhl and J Beyer (eds), *Small States in International Relations* (Seattle WA, University of Washington Press, 2006).

[3] I Neumann and S Gstöhl, 'Introduction: Lilliputians in Gulliver's World?' in C Ingebritsen, I Neumann, S Gstöhl and J Beyer (eds), *Small States in International Relations* (Seattle WA, University of Washington Press, 2006) 3; cited and affirmed in G Baldacchino and A Wivel, 'Small States: Concepts and Theories' in G Baldacchino and A Wivel (eds), *Handbook on the Politics of Small States* (Cheltenham, Edward Elgar Publishing, 2020) 2. See also J Corbett and W Veenendaal, 'Why Small States Are Beautiful' (2019) 10(1) *Political Insight* 4.

size – and specifically a small population – for the design and operation of a system of *constitutional* self-government.

Small jurisdictions often have comparatively fewer resources with which to engage in processes of democratic self-government, which may be exacerbated by the developmental nature of many of their economies (which in turn may be caused or amplified by their size). They typically have smaller and more inter-connected legal and political elites in ways that may increase the difficulty of creating an effective system of constitutional checks and balances – especially one involving truly independent and impartial courts and 'fourth branch institutions'.[4] This then points to the need to explore a range of constitutional design solutions and innovations, including the idea of constitutional 'multi-tasking'[5] and a mix of internal self-government and external involvement in government. It may also mean that the understanding ascribed to classic notions of separation of powers and independence may have to be rethought in the context of small jurisdictions.

Furthermore, small states and jurisdictions offer a window into the challenges of postcoloniality in constitutional self-government. Small states have frequently emerged out of a process of decolonisation. More generally, whether or not they had antecedents in pre-colonial government, they are deeply shaped by processes of colonisation and decolonisation, with at times enduring informal as well as formal, legal linkages to the former (or ongoing, in the case of many small jurisdictions) colonising power.[6] The experience of small states, therefore, can offer valuable insights into the features of post-colonial constitutionalism and how this can be profitably studied.

Linked to this postcolonial identity is often a commitment to legal pluralism, given the realities of pre-colonial, customary forms of law and government that have endured alongside more modern forms of constitutional rule. This pluralist challenge is also deeply important on its own terms, and worthy of much greater attention within the field of comparative constitutional studies. A focus on small states provides a natural opportunity for comparative constitutional scholars to adjust their attention in this direction.

At the same time, it should be acknowledged that scale is a question of degree, and depends on an intersection of population, geography and economic development. Many of the constitutional challenges facing small states are also common to states with much larger populations, although their regulation may be impacted by the size question. Conversely, there is such wide variation among small states that, in some contexts, it is artificial to treat them as a coherent category of constitutional system. Their positioning and engagement with other forms of law and other states or organisations can vary

[4] See generally M Tushnet, *The New Fourth Branch: Institutions for Protecting Constitutional Democracy* (Cambridge, Cambridge University Press, 2021). And more specifically, see J Barnes, 'Not the Usual Suspects – Executive Dominance in Seychelles and the Developing Institutions that Could Counter it', Chapter 15 in this volume.

[5] See A Dziedzic, 'Multitasked Office in Pacific Constitutions', Chapter 13 in this volume.

[6] See T Robinson, M De Visser and E Perham, HR Lallemant-Moe, and T Angelo and J Corrin (Chapters 2, 3, 4 and 14 respectively) in this volume on small territories and their ongoing constitutional relationships with their administering (colonial) power. On the impact of colonial heritage on regime choice in independent states with 1 million inhabitants or fewer, see D Anckar, 'Regime Choices in Microstates: The Cultural Constraint' (2004) 42 *Commonwealth & Comparative Politics* 206.

significantly, as can their population and territory size, such that it may be possible to speak of microstates.[7]

This internal heterogeneity notwithstanding, there are still benefits to giving renewed attention to small states as a distinct set of constitutional systems. Our focus on democracies reflects our view that democracy and constitutionalism are closely intertwined, though we also include several jurisdictions that are not (fully) democratic, and in doing so explore the porous nature of this divide or relationship. But what is most important is that these are a distinctive sub-class of constitutional systems which, because of their small size, are often overlooked in constitutional scholarship. Hence, turning our attention to these countries draws attention to a broader set of constitutional cases beyond the 'usual suspects' in comparative constitutional studies.

This expanded focus can help question prior assumptions in the field, and point to new constitutional models and patterns that can help refine our existing understandings along the lines sketched out above.[8] Indeed, this is what Dann, Riegner and Bönnemann call the 'double turn' in comparative constitutional studies – the insights to be gained from a shift from the traditional Global North suspects to a broader collection of Global South countries, as the focus of the field.[9] While not all small states are in the Global South, many are, thus naturally re-directing our focus. Moreover, it does not matter, for this purpose, that the countries selected for comparison are themselves internally diverse, or somewhat randomly selected. In inviting authors to contribute to this collection, we were cognisant of ensuring both a geographic diversity of small jurisdictions (as discussed below – largely states, but also some non-state jurisdictions), and of more junior and more senior scholars, as well as the inclusion of some authors who spend more time in practice than in universities but who deeply understand their jurisdictions. Beyond that, there is some randomness to the case selection, but the very fact of this randomness may be generative in some settings.[10] It can help us get beyond cognitive or behavioural biases that take us back to the 'usual suspects'.[11]

The remainder of this chapter is divided into five sections. Section II explores definitional questions surrounding the boundaries of what counts as a 'small state' for the purposes of the comparative constitutional analysis undertaken in this volume, and briefly surveys some of the differences as well as similarities between small states. Section III considers some of the constitutional design and implementation challenges inherent in small state size, including challenges of resources and independence and impartiality. Section IV explores associated challenges, including the challenges of

[7] See eg, W Veenendaal, *Politics and Democracy in Microstates* (London, Routledge, 2015) 40–43, treating microstates as those states with a population of fewer than 250,000 people. However, these definitions and classifications are by no means settled. For example, Anckar classifies any state with a population below 1 million people as a microstate: Anckar, 'Regime Choices in Microstates' (n 6).

[8] Cf Commonwealth Secretariat, 'Law Reform in Small States' (2018) 44 *Commonwealth Law Bulletin* 721 (noting that small states have made 'very considerable contributions' to law reform).

[9] P Dann, M Riegner and M Bönnemann,'The Southern Turn in Comparative Constitutional Law: An Introduction' in P Dann, M Riegner and M Bönnemann (eds), *The Global South and Comparative Constitutional Law* (Oxford, Oxford University Press, 2020) 1.

[10] R Dixon, 'Review of "Constitutional Interpretation in Singapore: Theory and Practice"'(2016) 11 *Asian Journal of Comparative Law* 337.

[11] Social scientists call this tendency a form of 'anchoring' or 'confirmation' bias. See eg, A Tversky and D Kahneman, 'Judgment under Uncertainty: Heuristics and Biases' (1974) 185 *Science* 1124.

constructing a postcolonial and pluralist constitutional order, while section V notes just one of the serendipitous patterns within the global constitutional community revealed by attention to small states (that of monarchy). Section VI offers brief concluding remarks and sets out the structure of the remainder of the volume.

II. Definitions and Variations

The definition of small states has a somewhat received global meaning: it tends to refer to states with a population of under either 1 million or 1.5 million people. The latter definition is used in a wide variety of official inter-governmental contexts,[12] and has also been adopted by some legal scholars focusing on small states.[13] Almost all the jurisdictions included in the volume also belong to this definition or category of small states.[14]

But smallness is a question of degree, and involves a range of overlapping vectors – including population size, economic and territorial scale, and resources.[15] Suriname, for example, has a small population but a relatively large territory, in ways that introduce distinctive challenges of distance between the government and many of those governed by the state – as demonstrated by Ine Apapoe and Janine Ubink in their contribution to this volume.[16] Suriname further has large mineral resource deposits that help contribute to its middle-income status. In contrast, a jurisdiction such as Niue – discussed by Tony Angelo and Jennifer Corrin in Chapter fourteen of this volume – or the jurisdictions of the Marshall Islands, Nauru and Kiribati– discussed by Anna Dziedzic in Chapter thirteen of this volume – have a small geographic size, relatively low average income and small total population. Many other jurisdictions included in the volume fall somewhere in between these two poles. Against these types of measures, smallness can also change over time. A country may gain or lose population, territory, or economic resources. Climate change and its effects on many low-lying small states are also likely to accelerate

[12] See eg, 'The World Bank in Small States' (n 1); 'Small States' (*The Commonwealth* website) thecommonwealth.org/our-work/small-states (although the Commonwealth of Nations also includes in its definition some larger states that 'share many of the same characteristics' as small states).

[13] Butler and Morris (n 2) v. We note, however, that others employ a different definition: for example, Angelo and Corrin adopted the criteria of 'fewer than 1 million inhabitants or a state with a land area of less than 20,000 km[2]': see T Angelo and J Corrin, 'Editorial Note/Avant-Propos' in AH Angelo and J Corrin (eds), 'Small States: A Collection of Essays' (2019) XXIII *Comparative Law Journal of the Pacific* (Hors Series Special Issue) 3.

[14] Other definitions related to population size are employed in some contexts, however, particularly in relation to international relations. See eg, B Thorhallson, 'Studying Small States: A Review' (2018) 1 *Small States & Territories* 17, 18.

[15] See eg, B Benedict, 'Sociological Aspects of Smallness' in B Benedict (ed), *Problems of Smaller Territories* (London, The Athlone Press, 1967) 45–47; M Jugl, *Country Size and Public Administration* (Cambridge, Cambridge University Press, 2022) 5–6; Baldacchino and Wivel (n 3) 3–6; BF Gussen, 'On the Classification of Small States' in T Angelo and J Corrin (eds), 'Small States: A Collection of Essays' (2019) XXIII *Comparative Law Journal of the Pacific* (Hors Series Special Issue).

[16] I Apapoe and J Ubink, 'Small-state Constitutionalism and Legal Pluralism: Logging and Mining Governance in Suriname', Chapter 7 in this volume; cf, TE Smith, 'Demographic Aspects of Smallness' in B Benedict (ed), *Problems of Smaller Territories* (London, The Athlone Press, 1967).

this kind of change: many small states are islands that face an existential threat to their territory, and hence, distinct challenges of emigration and economic survival.[17]

In a global or comparative context, 'smallness' is also a product of, or way of describing, a relative lack of economic and political power globally.[18] Small states in Europe, for example, often have significant global influence – both historically by virtue of their wealth and contemporaneously due to their proximity to global centres of power. Chapter six in this volume, by Conor Casey, for example, points out the disproportionate influence that the Vatican City State has had, and continues to have, both in the development of the ideas of constitutionalism that we are now so familiar with, and in an ongoing diplomatic sense. In a modern context, the power of some European small states is also augmented by their membership of or relationship to the European Union and, to a lesser extent, the Council of Europe, which may enable them to augment their geopolitical and economic clout, although they are in turn also subject to strong pressures in terms of democratic values and constitutional expectations attendant on such regional membership, as outlined in Chapter five by Elisa Bertolini in this volume (focusing on Andorra, Liechtenstein, Monaco and San Marino).

Compared to the small states of Europe, Caribbean states are more distant from traditional global power centres but have a long history of trade and economic connections – for good and, arguably largely, for bad – with the United States and Europe. Small states in Oceania could be viewed as lying at the other end of the spectrum: they are geographically distant from Europe and the United States, and hence from traditional global centres of power. The move toward constitutional independence has also reduced the reach of their global networks, without any accompanying rise of regional groupings or bodies with equivalent geo-political or economic power, at least for the moment.[19]

Nonetheless, the global influence of some of these small states is amplified by their membership of inter-governmental organisations. For example, many small states (26 of them meeting our criteria for classification as small states) – including many in both the Caribbean and Oceania – are members of the Commonwealth of Nations,[20] and their global power and influence is therefore arguably somewhat tied to the power and sphere of influence of that organisation. Small independent states have also strategically leveraged their numbers, or simply their formal equal access to and standing in global institutions, to exert influence.[21] For example, in the chapter by Tony Angelo

[17] See eg, J Topsfield and B Preiss, 'Tuvalu Is Being Swallowed by the Ocean. Its People Face a Difficult Choice' *The Sydney Morning Herald* (19 May 2024), www.smh.com.au/world/oceania/tuvalu-is-being-swallowed-by-the-ocean-its-people-face-a-difficult-choice-20240516-p5jea1.html. While there is not a standalone chapter on Tuvalu in this volume, this fact and related challenges are briefly addressed in Chapter 3, 'Spectrums of "Stateness": Constitutional Relations among the Constituent Countries of the Kingdom of The Netherlands' by M De Visser and E Perham.

[18] See eg, Baldacchino and Wivel (n 3) 4.

[19] See discussion of strengthening Pacific regionalism in Chapter 11, 'A European Union-style Pacific Common Market' by P Butler and S Macintosh in this volume.

[20] The Commonwealth website states that 33 small states are members of the organisation, but of that list, seven have a population over 1.5 million (Botswana, Gabon, Jamaica, Lesotho, Namibia, Papua New Guinea, The Gambia). See 'Small States' (n 12).

[21] See eg, D Guilfoyle, 'Litigation as Statecraft: Small States and the Law of the Sea' [2023] *British Yearbook of International Law* brad009.

and Sabir Kadel in this volume, the authors discuss how Mauritius took on the United Kingdom in both the United Nations General Assembly and the International Court of Justice in a dispute over the sovereignty of the Chagos Islands, ultimately prevailing and, in the process, galvanising the identity of its small but heterogenous population (see Chapter eighteen).

Smallness can also be understood in more episodic, subjective terms: states may attract a small or large amount of global attention, in ways that vary over time. Many small states will have domestic constitutional arrangements that exist 'below the radar' in the global community. But the peculiarities of global politics and media attention can also put small states in the temporary spotlight, which changes global perceptions of a state's 'smallness'. A good example is how various small states and jurisdictions have approached the recognition and protection of LGBTQI+ rights. In Oceania, there has been very limited litigation around these issues, in part because of the small size of the legal profession and domestic civil society sector working on legal and constitutional issues in these jurisdictions.[22] In the Caribbean, in contrast, there has been a much greater recent history of LGBTQI+ rights litigation.[23] Yet, compared to the equivalent litigation in larger states, it has received far less global notice. Instead, small states have tended to be prominent in global debates on LGBTQI+ rights only where they are seen as adopting egregious practices – or are global 'outliers' or worst offenders.[24]

Another example of smaller states gaining temporary prominence, this time for perceived innovation, involves the process of popular constitution making in Iceland. While popular participation in constitution making is on the rise worldwide, Iceland is widely seen as a leading exemplar of a 'crowd-sourced' constitution-making process, with all the promise and pitfalls that can entail.[25] And a further example is when small states or jurisdictions come into the spotlight because of geopolitical tensions: as for example when the Solomon Islands decided it would cease diplomatic recognition of Taiwan in favour of diplomatic recognition of China and subsequently signed security agreements with China,[26] or when President Trump suggested he would 'buy' Greenland.[27]

Indeed, one danger in using the language of 'smallness' is that it could be understood as having a negative or pejorative valence, or as signifying unimportance

[22] R Dixon, 'A Democratic Theory of Constitutional Comparison' (2008) 56 *American Journal of Comparative Law* 947, 981–82.

[23] See eg, discussion in Tracy Robinson's Chapter 2 in this volume, 'Dyadic Caribbean Constitutions', focusingon the British Overseas Territories in the Caribbean region.

[24] See eg, the world media reaction to Brunei's laws about anal sex and extra-marital affairs: Y Tan, 'Brunei Implements Stoning to Death under Anti-LGBT Laws' *BBC News* (3 April 2019), www.bbc.com/news/world-asia-47769964.

[25] For a positive view, see H Landemore, *Open Democracy: Reinventing Popular Rule for the Twenty-First Century* (Princeton NJ, Princeton University Press, 2020); for a more sceptical view, see D Landau and R Dixon, 'Utopian Constitutionalism in Chile' (2024) 13 *Global Constitutionalism* 228.

[26] 'Solomon Islands Breaks Ties with Taiwan after Chinese "Dollar Diplomacy"' *ABC News (Australia)* (16 September 2019), www.abc.net.au/news/2019-09-16/solomon-islands-cuts-taiwan-ties-after-china-dollar-diplomacy/11510898; K Lyons and D Wickham, 'The Deal That Shocked the World: Inside the China-Solomons Security Pact' *The Guardian* (20 April 2022), www.theguardian.com/world/2022/apr/20/the-deal-that-shocked-the-world-inside-the-china-solomons-security-pact.

[27] I Aikman, 'Donald Trump Says He Believes the US Will "Get Greenland"' *BBC News* (26 January 2025), www.bbc.com/news/articles/crkezj07rzro.

or insignificance. During the decolonisation era, when many of the states discussed in this volume were emerging, smallness was treated as a challenge to be overcome.[28] And even today, some constitutional scholars suggest that states can 'be too small'.[29] But the premise of this book is just the opposite: paying attention to the states in the volume helps bring new insights, patterns and possibilities to the surface that are of deep importance to the global constitutional community. That is, to the extent that 'smallness' is a question of psychology or perception, we suggest that smallness can be understood as a signifier of importance.

There are also myriad ways in which small state jurisdictions may be 'large' in a geographic and cultural sense – that is, in their oceans, traditions and cultural heritage. This is for instance the case, as Hervé Raimana Lallemant-Moe points out in his contribution to this volume, with the states and territories of Oceania, which conceive of themselves as large in territory on account of the vast parts of the ocean that are considered as belonging to the state in addition to their land mass (see Chapter four). As the scholar Epeli Hau'ofa famously explained in the early 1990s, the peoples of Oceania perceive themselves as living in a sea of islands, rather than on islands in a sea.[30] This language resonates so strongly with the states in the region that it was picked up by the regional intergovernmental body, the Pacific Islands Forum, in 2017 in the publicity for its 2050 Strategy for the Blue Pacific Continent: 'Blue Pacific – Our Sea of Islands, Our Livelihoods, Our Oceania'.[31] And smallness can present benefits and opportunities as well as challenges: for example, it can increase 'innovative, nimble and flexible' policy responses to global challenges.[32] It can likewise expand opportunities for direct democracy, and democratic deliberation.[33] As Joelle Barnes notes in her chapter in this volume on Seychelles, a 'key benefit of smallness is the ability to harness the active political climate and create dialogue between those who vote and those who are elected' (see Chapter fifteen).

The notion of a 'state' is itself also open to different interpretations. One might employ the criteria contained in the Montevideo Convention, namely '(a) a permanent population; (b) a defined territory; (c) government; and (d) capacity to enter into relations

[28] See eg, discussion in B Burton, 'Introduction' in B Benedict (ed), *Problems of Smaller Territories* (London, The Athlone Press, 1967).

[29] NW Barber, *The Principles of Constitutionalism* (Oxford, Oxford University Press, 2018) 34. Barber goes on to say 'micro-states are unjust' because their neighbouring states decide 'questions relating to domestic and foreign policy' and because of this, the citizens of these states are not allowed to 'take responsibility for these decisions'.

[30] E Hau'ofa, 'Our Sea of Islands' (1994) 6 *The Contemporary Pacific* 148.

[31] D Salesa, 'Introduction: Alāva'a: Seaways across an Indigenous Ocean' in D Salesa, *An Indigenous Ocean: Pacific Essays* (Wellington, Bridget Williams Books, 2023) 4.

[32] Thorhallson (n 14) 20.

[33] See eg, J Corbett, 'Democratic Innovations and the Challenges of Parliamentary Oversight in a Small State: Is Small Really Beautiful' (2018) 1 *Small States & Territories* 35. See also D Ott, *Small Is Democratic: An Examination of State Size and Democratic Development* (London, Routledge, 2000); as discussed in D O'Brien, 'Small States, Colonial Rule and Democracy' in P Butler and C Morris (eds), *Small States in a Legal World* (Cham, Springer, 2017). On direct democracy in small states, see also S Wolf and P Bussjaeger, 'Law, Small State Theory and the Case of Liechtenstein' (2018) 1 *Small States & Territories* 183; and on participatory constitution making in small states, see M De Visser and E Perham, 'Variables Shaping Participatory Constitution-Making: Insights from the Experiences of Small States' (2022) 20 *International Journal of Constitutional Law* 1216.

with other states'.[34] These are now commonly agreed to form part of customary international law. Of course, there are well-rehearsed problems with the Convention criteria.[35] Thus, it is difficult to establish, using the Convention criteria, what precisely a state *is*. Other definitions, therefore, adopt a more functional conception, for example, the presence of some level of self-government.

The volume focuses primarily on formally independent states recognised as states within the international law system (largely, but not exclusively, through United Nations membership). But it also includes consideration of some small semi-autonomous or dependent territories, such as French Polynesia and New Caledonia, Niue, countries in the Dutch Caribbean, and some British Overseas Territories in the Caribbean. By expanding our focus in this way, we seek to problematise the line between statehood and non-statehood, and question the significance of statehood (as opposed to smallness) to the questions of constitutional design and construction that animate the volume. This specific problematisation is picked up further in the chapter by two of us exploring 'spectrums of stateness' (De Visser and Perham – Chapter three), and the justification for (and importance of) looking beyond formally independent states is explained there.

III. Inherent Challenges: The Challenges of Closeness and Scale

Political theorists have been thinking about the question of size for millennia, starting with Plato and Aristotle.[36] Perhaps the most famous writing on constitutionalism and scale was that by James Madison in *The Federalist* Number 51: Madison suggested that there were inherent dangers for republican forms of government in having too small and homogeneous a community. The danger, he argued, was that in small societies governments could readily overcome the formal separation of powers, and exercise unconstrained public power.[37] In larger, more diverse societies – in contrast – different factions and officeholders were more likely to compete, so that '[a]mbition [could] be made to counteract ambition'. Because of this, he argued that 'the larger the society, provided it lie within a practical sphere, the more duly capable it will be of self-government'.[38] More recently, political scientists Robert Dahl and Edward Tufte, in their seminal work *Size and Democracy*, have picked up on this line of political thought, exploring the relationship between size and democracy. Much subsequent work in

[34] Convention on Rights and Duties of States adopted by the Seventh International Conference of American States (opened for signature 26 December 1933, entered into force 26 December 1934) 165 LNTS 19.

[35] TD Grant, 'Defining Statehood: The Montevideo Convention and Its Discontents' (1999) 37 *Columbia Journal of Transnational Law* 403, 453.

[36] See eg, discussion in chapter 1 of RA Dahl and ER Tufte, *Size and Democracy* (Stanford CA, Stanford University Press, 1973).

[37] J Madison, '*The Federalist*, No 51: The Structure of the Government Must Furnish the Proper Checks and Balances Between the Different Departments' (New York, 6 February 1788): 'Whilst all authority in it will be derived from and dependent on the society, the society itself will be broken into so many parts, interests, and classes of citizens, that the rights of individuals, or of the minority, will be in little danger from interested combinations of the majority'.

[38] ibid.

political science has also interrogated this relationship – with earlier large-N studies suggesting a positive relationship between small size and democracy (somewhat in opposition to Madison's claims),[39] and later more fine-grained studies nuancing these findings.[40]

This ongoing interest of political scientists in questions of size and democracy can be explained by the fact that Madison's concerns live on in many contemporary small states and jurisdictions. While smallness can have many benefits (including, as noted in the previous section, theoretically promoting dialogue between those who vote and those who are elected), small population size can make the practice of constitutional self-government challenging in several ways. For example, a jurisdiction may have too small and close-knit a society to easily create an effective system of checks and balances (at least in the way these systems are commonly designed for larger jurisdictions).[41] For one example, judges and fourth-branch actors may have many personal and professional connections to political elites in ways that make it difficult for them to maintain true independence and impartiality.[42] For another, there may be pressure to maintain harmonious personal relationships, in ways that militate against the formation of key 'proximate' or supporting constitutional institutions, such as political parties.[43]

Of course, on the flip side, a high degree of social interconnection, and kinship, can have a range of social and political benefits: for example, it can assist in the preservation of traditional or customary norms and authority. And it can help promote social harmony, stability and cohesion. But it can sometimes shade into corruption, cronyism and clientelism, as discussed particularly in John Stanton's contribution to this volume (though these problems are far from unique to small states).[44] And, while the assumption is that small societies are more likely to be homogenous 'with respect to beliefs, values and goals', this is certainly not always the case. Tony Angelo and Sabir Kadel's contribution on Mauritius in this volume highlights the heterogeneity of that small state, but Mauritius is far from the only heterogenous small state (Chapter eighteen). For example, Christos Papastylianos' contribution, focusing on Cyprus,

[39] See eg, Ott (n 33).

[40] See eg, J Erk and W Veenendaal, 'Is Small Really Beautiful?: The Microstate Mistake' (2014) 25 *Journal of Democracy* 135. For a general treatment of this body of literature, see Corbett and Veenendaal, *Democracy in Small States: Persisting Against All Odds* (n 2).

[41] See eg, J Corbett, '"Everybody Knows Everybody": Practising Politics in the Pacific Islands' (2015) 22 *Democratization* 51.

[42] Burton (n 28) 8. See also R Dixon and VC Jackson, 'Constitutions Inside Out: Outsider Interventions in Domestic Constitutional Contests' (2013) 48 *Wake Forest Law Review* 149; R Dixon and V Jackson, 'Hybrid Constitutional Courts: Foreign Judges on National Constitutional Courts' (2018) 57 *Columbia Journal of Transnational Law* 283.

[43] On proximate institutions, see A Dziedzic and D Samararatne, 'Asking the Woman Question of Constitutions: Insights from Sri Lanka' (2023) 56 *World Comparative Law* 127. On the importance of political parties to democracy, see S Issacharoff, *Democracy Unmoored: Populism and the Corruption of Popular Sovereignty* (Oxford, Oxford University Press, 2023). On the absence of political parties in (some) small states, see eg HR Lallemant-Moe in this volume, and J Corbett and W Veenendaal, 'Westminster in Small States: Comparing the Caribbean and Pacific Experience' (2016) 22 *Contemporary Politics* 432, 437–438.

[44] J Stanton, 'The Struggle for Democratic Government in Malta', Chapter 17 in this volume. See also eg, A Saati and T Bergman, 'Democracy, Façade or Somewhere in between? An Exploration of Vanuatu, Kiribati and São Tomé and Príncipe' (2022) 5 *Small States & Territories* 141 (exploring these dynamics in several small states); G Baldacchino, 'Islands and Despots' (2012) 50 *Commonwealth & Comparative Politics* 103; Dahl and Tufte (n 36) 92–93.

a divided society, looks at the role smallness played in the constitutional breakdown in 1963 (Chapter nineteen). And there are many others.[45]

An additional challenge is that a state may be too small socially and economically to sustain a range of institutions staffed by full-time, qualified office holders. This is particularly the case when size is not taken into account (or 'ignored') in constitutional design, as outlined by Tony Angelo and Jennifer Corrin in their discussion of Niue in this collection (Chapter fourteen). There may be few qualified local lawyers both able and willing to serve as judges or bring cases before a court (in Niue, for example, there is only one lawyer in private practice). Those qualified to do so may also have been trained overseas, in ways that limit their knowledge of the local constitutional system and context or their willingness to return to a jurisdiction to play this role. There may likewise be few citizens with training and experience in higher level public administration in ways that make it difficult to staff the civil service or fourth-branch institutions.[46]

Further, the size of the population may be too small to sustain a vibrant civil society.[47] The absence of civil society organisations can affect constitutional self-government in two ways. Social movements and civil society often play a crucial role in bringing constitutional complaints before courts and fourth-branch institutions.[48] Hence, their absence can undermine the capacity for key state institutions to uphold and enforce constitutional norms. Social movements likewise typically play a central role in the enforcement and implementation of the decisions of courts and fourth-branch bodies.[49] Again, therefore, their relative absence can weaken processes of constitutional implementation. Taken together, this can contribute both to breaches of constitutional norms, and to more subtle failures of democratic responsiveness – in the form of what one of us (Dixon) has called persistent *democratic burdens of inertia*.[50] It should be noted, however that where civil society is present in a small state, it can have conversely have a big impact: for example, in Chapter eighteen, Tony Angelo and Sabir Kadel highlight the role of civil society in recent LGBTQI+ rights litigation in Mauritius.

Economic pressures facing many small states may also make it difficult to justify the cost of maintaining a range of public institutions, none of which are likely to have anything like a full-time workload, which in turn can impact on available levels of

[45] See eg, W Veenendaal and J Corbett, 'Navigating Hyper-Fragmentation in Small States: A Comparison of Solomon Islands and Vanuatu' in L Briguglio and others (eds), *Handbook of Governance in Small States* (London, Routledge, 2021); S Wilson, *Politics of Identity in Small Plural Societies: Guyana, the Fiji Islands, and Trinidad and Tobago* (Cham, Springer, 2012).

[46] For a useful exploration of these challenges, see Jugl (n 15).

[47] Dixon, 'A Democratic Theory of Constitutional Comparison' (n 22) 981–82. For a rich and comprehensive exploration of the role of civil society and social movements in small states, see L Briguglio, S Bunwaree and C Slatter (eds), *Handbook of Civil Society and Social Movements in Small States* (London, Routledge, 2023).

[48] See eg, CR Epp, *The Rights Revolution: Lawyers, Activists, and Supreme Courts in Comparative Perspective* (Chicago IL, The University of Chicago Press, 1998); MW McCann, 'How Does Law Matter for Social Movements?' in B Garth, F Levine and A Sarat (eds), *How Does Law Matter?* (Chicago IL, Northwestern University Press, 1998); and discussion in R Dixon, *Responsive Judicial Review* (Oxford, Oxford University Press, 2023) 171–75.

[49] See also R Dixon and R Chowdhury, 'A Case for Qualified Hope? The Supreme Court of India and the Midday Meal Decision' in GN Rosenberg, S Krishnaswamy and S Bail (eds), *A Qualified Hope: The Indian Supreme Court and Progressive Social Change* (Cambridge, Cambridge University Press, 2019); and R Dixon and J Lavery, 'Commissioning Economic Equality? Lessons from Scotland' (2023) 51 *Federal Law Review* 315.

[50] See Dixon, *Responsive Judicial Review* (n 48) chapter 3.

expertise and experience. And even in relatively wealthier small states, the expense is likely to be significant, given the absence of economies of scale in the operation of public institutions. Indeed, neo-classical economics points to two key benefits to larger firm or state size: first, economies of scope (the efficiency gains from a firm or state doing multiple activities at once, or within the same production process) and second, economies of scale (or the efficiency gains from larger-scale production processes). Economies of scale are also an especially important implication of state size: as Alberto Alesina and Enrico Spolaore have noted, small states face far greater resource challenges in large part because of their inability to exploit economies of scale in their internal organisation, and service and programme delivery.[51]

In addition, small states often have less diversified economies, which make them more vulnerable to exogenous shocks.[52] Shocks of this kind are proliferating in many parts of the world: the interconnected nature of the global economy increases the risk of global economic contagion. Climate change also poses increasing environmental, humanitarian and economic risks for all countries, but especially low-lying island nations – many of which are small states.

This is one reason why Alesina and Spolaore suggest a trade-off, between exploiting these benefits and creating 'unmanageable' levels of pluralism or heterogeneity, in the design of 'optimal' state size.[53] For constitutional lawyers, manageability is ultimately an endogenous question – linked to our capacity to design and adopt institutional innovations capable of managing social and political pluralism. But even with constant innovation and re-imagination of prevailing constitutional models, there may be limits to how much diversity a democratic constitutional system can manage without facing threats of violence or civil war.

Similar challenges can be seen across the design and implementation of an entire legal system – including the trajectory of legal education. To achieve true self-government, small states must be able to train local lawyers to understand, interpret and enforce domestic constitutional norms in a way that reflects global knowledge and principles, but also local knowledge – especially about the traditional elements of a constitutional system. Yet in many small states, there are huge challenges of personnel, funding and scale which get in the way of creating a law school staffed entirely by local lawyers: Tonga and Seychelles are just two examples, as outlined in the contributions by Mele Tupou Vaitohi and Joelle Barnes (Chapters eight and fifteen respectively) in this volume.

A state's relative, not just absolute, economic power may be another factor limiting the effectiveness of national-level constitutional arrangements: for instance, a state may be too small in relative economic terms to succeed in facing off challenges from traditional (or new) forms of colonial or imperial influence. This includes global economic actors, such as multi-national corporations, and states with greater economic and military power. Indeed, military power – or a lack of it – is often identified as one of the key international or external challenges facing small states. It is also one of several factors militating against some autonomous territories seeking independence, and

[51] A Alesina and E Spolaore, *The Size of Nations* (Cambridge MA, MIT Press, 2003).
[52] ibid.
[53] ibid.

instead choosing to maintain constitutional links with their administering powers,[54] and encouraging independent small states to enter into regional or international groupings and alliances, or to engage in 'shelter-seeking' alliances.[55] Two of us (De Visser and Perham) suggest in our chapter that more attention should be paid by constitutional scholars to a potential new suite of international law arrangements between small states and larger states, such as the recent Falepili Union Treaty between Australia and Tuvalu (see Chapter three). The international aspects of this agreement were closely watched by observers in both countries, and around the world, but the constitutional dimension to Tuvalu's decision to enter the treaty – both in terms of its sovereignty implications and its identity implications – was largely overlooked.

IV. Constitutional Design Responses: Multi-tasking and Regionalism

A. Constitutional Multi-tasking or Abusive Small State Constitutionalism?

One response to some of these challenges, identified in Chapter thirteen by Anna Dziedzic, is the idea of 'multi-tasked' office – or the combination of different constitutional roles, which in larger states would be allocated to different officials, in a single constitutional office. This could be viewed as the opposite of what Jake Gersen calls the 'unbundling' of constitutional powers: it is a form of reverse bundling or re-bundling.[56]

A design of this kind has several potential advantages. It can help solve problems of scarcity in the pool of potentially qualified applicants for high constitutional office. It can amplify the influence of qualified and impartial officeholders on the constitutional system. It offers cost advantages, and it could allow small states to build on a range of formal and informal precedents in Indigenous, colonial and postcolonial constitutional government within their territory.[57]

Of course, it also carries potential dangers and limitations. Some forms of multi-tasking may make a constitutional office extremely onerous, and hence unattractive even to the most qualified applicants, or too onerous for candidates who might otherwise be qualified to occupy a more unbundled, singular role. It may also increase what comparative constitutional scholars have called the 'second period' problem, or problems of

[54] W Veenendaal and G Oostindie, 'Head versus Heart: The Ambiguities of Non-Sovereignty in the Dutch Caribbean' (2018) 28 *Regional & Federal Studies* 25, 35–36.

[55] Thorhallson (n 14) 19, citing R Väyrynen, 'On the Definition and Measurement of Small Power Status' (1971) 6 *Cooperation and Conflict* 91; MI Handel, *Weak States in the International System* (London, Routledge 1991); B Thorhallson and AJK Bailes, 'Do Small States Need "Alliance Shelter"? Scotland and the Nordic Nations' in AW Neal (ed), *Security in a Small Nation: Scotland, Democracy, Politics* (Cambridge, Open Book Publishers, 2017).

[56] Cf, JE Gersen, 'Unbundled Powers' (2010) 96 *Virginia Law Review* 301.

[57] See eg, D Anckar, 'Bicameralism, Small States Style' (2018) 1(1) *Small States & Territories* 55.

constitutional transition:[58] the risks to constitutional stability and continuity when a successful constitutional officeholder steps down. Such risks always exist, but they go up substantially when a single person holds multiple constitutional offices.

Constitutional multi-tasking may also pose real risks to structural constitutional commitments and related values. Multi-tasking necessarily involves modifying our understanding of the separation of powers, and the embrace of a more flexible, dynamic account of this foundational constitutional idea.[59] But even with modifications, there is a need for any small state constitution to preserve commitments to accountability, independence and impartiality and ensure their effective operation in practice. We should also realise that some forms of multi-tasking, for example involving sitting as opposed to retired judges in executive functions, will have much higher risks than others in this regard.

Constitutional multi-tasking may also increase the risk to democratic constitutional values, including the capacity for a constitutional system to protect and maintain what one of us (Rosalind Dixon, with David Landau) has called the 'democratic minimum core'.[60] Since not all small states are democratic, not all face this same risk from constitutional multi-tasking. Brunei Darussalam is a leading example, as Ann Black outlines in Chapter sixteen in this collection, where power is concentrated in the hands of the Sultan. But those that are dependent for their endurance on three interdependent sets of institutional arrangements, namely: (i) a system of regular, free and fair, multi-party elections; (ii) political rights and freedoms; and (iii) institutional checks and balances, will need to take care that recourse to multi-tasking – often for practical reasons – does not come at the expense of respect for that democratic minimum core.[61] In this regard, we should be mindful that constitutional multi-tasking can increase the ability of a single would-be authoritarian actor to adopt legal and political changes that undermine all three of those arrangements, especially the freedom of the press, opposition and civil society, and the independence of courts and other key oversight institutions.[62] At the very least, it reduces the costs to a would-be authoritarian seeking to capture or co-opt these institutions.

Small state size may also itself already heighten the risk of 'abusive' constitutional change of this kind. For instance, it means that there are fewer independent institutions and officeholders that a would-be authoritarian must capture, or coerce, in order to exert complete control over the state.[63] It reduces the number of press outlets, and hence the difficulty of capturing or co-opting a free press. And it means that there are fewer civil society actors willing and able to challenge practices of democratic backsliding. In small states with small territories, it also reduces the costs of monitoring opposition

[58] See R Dixon and T Roux, 'Marking Constitutional Transitions: The Law and Politics of Constitutional Implementation in South Africa' in AZ Huq and T Ginsburg (eds), *From Parchment to Practice: Implementing New Constitutions* (Cambridge, Cambridge University Press, 2020).

[59] See eg, D Bilchitz and D Landau (eds), *The Evolution of the Separation of Powers: Between the Global North and the Global South* (Cheltenham, Edward Elgar Publishing, 2018).

[60] R Dixon and D Landau, *Abusive Constitutional Borrowing* (Oxford, Oxford University Press, 2021).

[61] ibid.

[62] D Landau and R Dixon, 'Constraining Constitutional Change' (2015) 50 *Wake Forest Law Review* 859.

[63] On capturing and coercing as abusive tactics, see D Landau and R Dixon, 'Abusive Judicial Review: Courts Against Democracy' (2020) 53 *UC Davis Law Review* 1313; D Kosar and K Sipulova, 'How to Fight Court-Packing?' (2020) 6 *Constitutional Studies* 133.

groups and opponents of a regime. One can see this play out in the forms of democratic backsliding that have occurred in Malta and Seychelles, as described in the chapters by John Stanton and Joelle Barnes in this collection – in ways that point to the complex nature of the democratic design challenge in many small states.[64]

It is important, however, to note the likely alternative to formal constitutional multi-tasking of this kind. Often, it can mean that constitutional officeholders combine public office with private work, which may be even less compatible with their independent and impartial performance of public office. It can also mean that there is a lack of suitably qualified domestic candidates to fill various public offices, and therefore that a country must turn to constitutional 'outsiders' to perform the role.[65]

'Outsider' constitutional actors have several advantages: they can expand capacity and can increase impartiality in the performance of various public offices.[66] In some cases, they can also serve as a useful bridge between external and internal constitutional perspectives. But they also carry clear risks or downsides, including that depending on whence they originate, and how they are structured and funded, they may be perceived by citizens as lacking basic sociological legitimacy. Further, they increase the risk of decisions that lack sensitivity to local traditions and understandings, and the local social and political context.[67] In her chapter proposing a new framework for understanding Tongan constitutionalism, for example, Mele Tupou Vaitohi notes that existing (outsider) theoretical frameworks, such as legal pluralism, have struggled to explain the Tongan system (see Chapter eight).

Constitutional multi-tasking, in this sense, is one of a suite of potential responses to the challenge of constitutional scale; and must be assessed against a backdrop where most responses involve much heavier reliance on outsider influences.

B. Regionalism

Another important constitutional design response to small state size is often a move toward regional forms of government, or a mix of national and transnational models of constitutionalism. That is, smallness in state size can be a key driver toward – as well as reflection of – regional groupings and arrangements with constitutional implications.

For instance, in the Caribbean, there was a range of quasi-federal arrangements that were a product of inter-colonial organisation and power sharing. But another early source of regional solidarity was a desire to resist formal British and French colonial rule.[68] In a contemporary context, another driver for regionalism in the Caribbean

[64] See J Stanton, 'The Struggle for Democratic Government in Malta' and J Barnes, 'Not the Usual Suspects – Executive Dominance in Seychelles and the Developing Institutions that Could Counter it' (Chapters 17 and 15 respectively) in this volume.

[65] Dixon and Jackson (n 42).

[66] ibid; though note that Dziedzic is somewhat sceptical of the impartiality claim: A Dziedzic, *Foreign Judges in the Pacific* (Oxford, Hart Publishing, 2021) chapter 6; and see also T Robinson, 'Foreign Judging and Securing Judicial Independence in the Anglo Caribbean' in A Dziedzic and SNM Young (eds), *The Cambridge Handbook of Foreign Judges on Domestic Courts* (Cambridge, Cambridge University Press, 2023) 324.

[67] Dixon and Jackson (n 42); Dziedzic (n 66) 113–25.

[68] SS Ramphal, 'Federalism in the West Indies' (1960) 6 *Caribbean Quarterly* 210.

has arguably been a desire, with strong domestic support, to establish a postcolonial constitutional order in the face of a long tradition of Privy Council adjudicative authority. This authority has posed a source of jurisdictional competition for any truly national constitutional order, and one response to this has been the creation of a regional constitutional court – the Caribbean Court of Justice (CCJ) – with greater capacity to offer a credible and powerful alternative to the Privy Council.

This context helps explain the link between small state identity and regionalism in the Caribbean. As Se-shauna Wheatle notes, it informs the ways in which constitutional identity has been produced and reproduced in the Caribbean.[69] And it also has potential normative advantages: it offers a way of balancing commitments to impartiality with context-sensitivity in a way that exemplifies the best model of democratic *and* rights-protective constitutionalism in small states. At the same time, the impact or effectiveness of regional institutions can vary across countries and contexts. Some regional groupings have grown quickly in size and influence, whereas others have been much slower to develop. And some small states have been quick to adopt and implement regional norms and rulings, whereas others have adopted a posture of 'resistance' that has muted regional norms and influences.[70]

At the same time, issues of scale can undermine the effectiveness of regionalism itself as a solution. In the Caribbean, for example, this is exemplified in the limited supply of cases to the CCJ. To achieve a coherent regional jurisprudence, the Court requires cases that raise and ventilate a range of constitutional issues. Yet the relatively small number of jurisdictions that have acceded to the Court's jurisdiction, alongside the small size of those jurisdictions, mean that relatively few cases have come before the Court: this probably reflects the limited funding for litigation, the potentially smaller economic stakes involved in litigation, and the relatively small number of lawyers and civil society actors pushing for public interest litigation, in each jurisdiction (as discussed above). In Oceania, as Petra Butler and Sam Macintosh demonstrate, while proposals for a 'common market' have recently been mooted and may yield economic, security and other benefits, the realisation thereof will require a significant reimagining of existing frameworks and principles, including respect for national sovereignty and non-interference.[71] As they note, meaningful integration will presumably require an 'EU-style' transfer of powers to regional bodies – something that the small states concerned may be uneasy about, also given their colonial histories – while they would also need to contend with the clout that other, larger states in such a common market (Australia and New Zealand) would likely have. The desire to retain control is also brought up in the contribution by Ada Ordor and Victor T Amadi focusing on the free movement of people in Africa, who note that Seychelles and Mauritius have refrained from signing up to regional plans to foster freer movement of persons, and prefer to keep

[69] S Wheatle, 'The Construction of Constitutional Identity(ies) by the Caribbean Court of Justice', Chapter 10 in this volume.

[70] Suriname, for example, might fall into this category in the context of the Inter-American Commission.

[71] P Butler and S Macintosh. 'A European Union-style Pacific Common Market?', Chapter 11 in this volume.

the initiative to themselves, to ensure that incoming mobility flows do not overwhelm what their territory and population can manage.[72]

A further dimension to size or 'smallness' that can also pose an obstacle to effective regional co-operation or external/internal models of constitutional government is geographic distance, such as in Oceania in particular, or more generally when the small states are island nations. The challenge of geographic distance influences both the cost and feasibility of movement in ways that affect the plausibility of high degrees of regional integration. And while some of this distance could be closed, over time, through technology, limits to connectivity mean that those solutions remain very far off in many small states, while it also is often difficult to cultivate a coherent regional identity that can undergird integration initiatives.

V. Associated Difficulties: The Challenge of Plural, Postcolonial Government

A. Postcolonial Identity

For states with a history of colonial rule, perhaps the greatest contemporary constitutional challenge is to craft a form of *postcolonial* constitutionalism[73] – including a postcolonial constitutional approach to constitutional design and implementation, and to the construction of constitutional identity.

The notion of 'constitutional identity' is complex and contested: in Europe, it is often understood in quite 'defensive' terms, which involve national and supranational courts enforcing limits on the scope of legitimate constitutional change.[74] But in many small states, it has a more positive, constructive quality: a postcolonial constitutional identity is a near universal aspiration of independent, self-governing states (and also those jurisdictions which are not fully independent – as highlighted particularly in the chapters about Niue (Chapter fourteen) and French Polynesia and New Caledonia (Chapter four) in this volume). The process of constructing this identity can also help to bind postcolonial systems together at a national and regional level.[75]

In the Caribbean for instance, as Se-shauna Wheatle discusses in her chapter, questions of postcolonial identity have played out in the jurisprudence of the CCJ. That Court's jurisprudence also provides a window into the constitutional identity of the 12 (mostly) small states within the scope of the Court's jurisdiction. Identity, in this context, emerges through experience and dialogue. It is not fixed at founding, and the text alone is not the only source or indication of constitutional identity. Constitutional jurisprudence is also an important site of constitutional identity construction, and an archive

[72] A Ordor and VT Amadi 'Freeing Up the Movement of People: An Incremental Strategy for African Citizenship', Chapter 12 in this volume.

[73] See O'Brien (n 33).

[74] See discussion in Dixon and Landau (n 60) 144–50.

[75] See S Wheatle, 'The Construction of Constitutional Identity(ies) by the Caribbean Court of Justice', Chapter 10 in this volume.

that allows us a window into understanding constitutional identity. In the case of the CCJ, that archive also points to the dual construction of identity through backward- and forward-looking narratives, and local and more universal narratives and identities. focusing in her chapter specifically on the Anglo Caribbean sub-region and developing an account of the dyadic constitutions in three small jurisdictions in that sub-region, Tracy Robinson similarly understands the ongoing process of collaborative constitution making in those jurisdictions as somewhat dialogic, but it is a dialogue where there is active contestation over identity not as a response to the '*aftermath* of colonialism', but rather as a 'reflection on the imperial constitutional *present*' (Chapter two).

How does state size inform this pattern? State size, as discussed in the immediately preceding section, has important connections to the formation of regional bodies and networks. A regional focus for identity-formation is also necessarily post- or trans-textual in character: it is based on a common sense of regional belonging, rather than on any distinctive set of textual commitments or within particular national constitutional systems.

More broadly, and in a different context, Tony Angelo and Sabir Kadel also highlight how state size can interact with postcoloniality, international law and identity formation in multiple ways. For example, they describe how the fight by Mauritius for sovereignty over the Chagos Islands, though a contest taking place on the terrain of international law, played an important role in Mauritius asserting its identity as an independent and self-determined postcolonial state, and – in that context – played an important function as a 'unifying issue' rallying the diverse groups of Mauritius around a shared cause. They also highlight the importance that Mauritius, as a small state, places on the embedding of human rights locally in order to enhance its international standing as a postcolonial, independent nation (see Chapter eighteen). Of course, this latter choice can cut both ways – the direction taken to assert identity may rather be to assert a distinct identity as a postcolonial small state by rejecting international norms: in her chapter on Eswatini, Sinethemba Memela explains how the size, as well as location and culture, of the Kingdom allows the King to exercise essentially absolute power, and to reject any form of resistance as 'unSwazi' and foreign (see Chapter nine).

Somewhat relatedly, another challenge for any postcolonial constitutional project is the risk of new forms of coloniality. On the one hand, networks of mutual learning and support can be a critical part of building a successful model of small state constitutionalism. In Eswatini, for example, South African constitutional ideas have been a (limited) positive influence on the development of a more rights-protective constitutional order, as also noted in the contribution by Sinethemba Memela. But these same networks come with risks of new forms of coloniality: for instance, as Hervé Lallemant-Moe notes in his Chapter four, in French Polynesia, there are parts of the territory that see Tahiti as replicating a form of new colonial governance, and they have sought their own form of autonomy or self-government. In this context, Larmour has noted that the 'smallness of South Pacific states has not reduced demands for decentralisation' – and local-level governments in these states and territories are important 'expressions of local identity'.[76]

[76] P Larmour, 'Scale and Governance in the South Pacific' in M Turner (ed), *Central-Local Relations in Asia-Pacific* (Basingstoke, MacMillan Press Ltd, 1999) 149.

And – of course – some modes of external constitutional regulation linger, as Tracy Robinson describes in relation to the authoritative use of the European Convention on Human Rights by the Judicial Committee of the Privy Council in the Anglo Caribbean jurisdictions still subject to that Court's jurisdiction, with the potential attendant issues of sociological legitimacy and context-sensitivity discussed in the last section in relation to constitutional outsiders (Chapter two).

B. Legal Pluralism

Also flowing from the fact that most small states were at one time colonised by European powers (or if not colonised, then otherwise influenced by European legal ideas – as in Tonga, for example) is the reality that most small states are legally pluralistic to some greater or lesser degree. A legally pluralist jurisdiction is classically understood as one in which 'two or more legal systems coexist in the same social field'.[77] Many, if not all, colonised or formerly colonised territories are understood to be legally pluralist, because in the process of colonisation it was common for colonisers to 'superimpose' their legal systems onto Indigenous legal systems.[78] Of course, depending on how broadly a 'legal system' is defined (and on this there is not agreement in the literature), all jurisdictions, whether postcolonial or not, may be understood to be legally pluralist.[79]

In some cases, legal pluralism – while empirically present – is not reflected in the legal order of the state (that is, it is informal or unofficial). This is very often the case in the 'Global North'. Or where such pluralism is recognised – as in many settler societies – Indigenous or customary forms of law are only regarded as law to the extent that 'they can be understood to derive from state sovereignty by being "recognized" by the legislative or judicial branches of settler governments'.[80] In other cases, however, and very often in the 'Global South', the fact of legal pluralism is formally recognised or endorsed by law and state policy, and rules are put in place to establish hierarchies of laws (often in Constitutions), and to manage the inevitable conflict between legal systems.[81] Official recognition and/or endorsement of legal pluralism has many virtues: it can provide a means of accommodating diverse world views (for example, in states such as Mauritius where there are diverse communities practising different religions, as noted in Chapter eighteen by Tony Angelo and Sabir Kadel) and, often, the rights of Indigenous peoples within a modern constitutional state – at least to some extent.

At the same time, it can raise a range of challenges – including for individual rights. One of the longstanding objections to the state endorsement of legal pluralism is the

[77] SE Merry, 'Legal Pluralism' (1988) 22 *Law & Society Review* 869, 870. In his synthesis of the literature on legal pluralism, Gebeye notes 'that there is neither agreement about what law is nor a consensus on the definition of legal pluralism itself within the legal pluralism scholarship': BA Gebeye, *A Theory of African Constitutionalism* (Oxford, Oxford University Press, 2021) 18.

[78] Merry (n 77) 870.

[79] See classically, ibid 869.

[80] K Gover, 'Legal Pluralism and Indigenous Legal Traditions' in PS Berman (ed), *The Oxford Handbook of Global Legal Pluralism* (Oxford, Oxford University Press, 2020) 848.

[81] G Corradi, 'Introduction – Human Rights and Legal Pluralism: Four Research Agendas' in G Corradi, E Brems and M Goodale (eds), *Human Rights Encounter Legal Pluralism: Normative and Empirical Approaches* (London, Bloomsbury Publishing, 2017) 1, 3.

potentially antagonistic relationship of certain legal orders to individual rights, and especially the rights of women[82] and sexual minorities. In other cases, 'colonial and postcolonial policies on legal pluralism [have] sought to co-opt customary law institutions as instruments of domination'.[83] As Corradi notes, human rights law has long had to grapple with questions – on the one hand – about whether 'human rights law recognise[s] a right to "one's own law"', and – on the other hand – about 'how states should respond to legal pluralism in order to protect human rights'.[84]

Another is the capacity of legal pluralist orders to respond to pressing social and economic challenges. We live in an age of increasing corporate power. Private actors are gaining power through the sheer scale of their activities, their multilateral character and their increasing control of online and digital domains. This poses a threat to the regulatory capacity of all states, but especially smaller states, with limited regulatory capacity and global economic power. Legal pluralism can increase these risks: pluralism, by definition, involves overlapping and distinctive legal norms and approaches. This can create regulatory gaps and loopholes ripe for exploitation by powerful private actors.

In their chapter on logging and mining governance in Suriname,[85] for example, Ine Apapoe and Janine Ubink note the development of a de facto system of legal pluralism in the regulation of resource extraction: they note that in some more remote areas (such as Tapanahony) 'traditional leaders firmly reject the authority of state institutions over what they regard as *their* natural resources',[86] whereas in less remote areas (such as the Cottica) the relationship between modern and traditional authorities is much more cooperative. In these areas, the state has established and is involved in an effective system of resource permits, and dispute resolution, while in the more remote areas, there is much more 'local self-regulation'.

This difference in regulation also has clear downsides for Suriname's economic development: it means that in areas such as Tapanohony, the state recovers little tax or revenue from international resource extraction. In addition, the relative lack of regulation in these areas poses clear environmental and social challenges: it means that traditional communities are left to impose restrictions on extraction that, often, they have no power to enforce against powerful multinational corporations.

Apapoe and Ubink also note that state size plays a paradoxical role in this context: the *large* geographic size of the country relative to its population is part of what explains the decision of (or necessity for) the state to cede regulatory authority to traditional leaders in remote areas. But, as they note 'it is also the *small* size of the population, and the tax base this generates, that means that the state has limited *capacity* to reach remote areas' (emphasis added).[87] And smallness also reduces the *willingness* of the state to engage in regulation of this kind – because it means there is a strong overlap between legal, economic and political elites. Indeed, as they also note, many traditional and

[82] One example is where, in some states 'customary laws [related to male primogeniture] are officially applicable but exempted from the constitutional prohibition of discrimination on the basis of gender': ibid 7.
[83] ibid.
[84] ibid 5.
[85] I Apapoe and J Ubink, 'Small-state Constitutionalism and Legal Pluralism: Logging and Mining Governance in Suriname', Chapter 7 in this volume.
[86] ibid section V.A.
[87] ibid section VII.

elected political leaders have direct personal interests in the gold and logging industries, in ways that undermine the prospects for effective regulation of these industries.

One response to this ambivalent character to legal pluralism in small states is to abandon a commitment to legal pluralism, and adopt either a more thorough-going form of traditional rule and authority, or else a modern, formal approach to law and state authority. Both approaches, however, face principled as well as practical objections.[88] Indeed, in Suriname, Apapoe and Ubink stress the informal or de facto nature of what is in fact a strong form of legal pluralism – and, as just noted, the role that size plays in its strength. A more plausible path lies in an attempt to reconcile or synthesise these different legal systems, in ways that can generate a more consistent and effective regulatory response, which is still sensitive to the relevant local context and traditions. Prior work on African constitutionalism explores the idea of 'syncretic' constitutionalism as offering a reconciliation of this kind.[89] Along somewhat similar lines, but in an entirely different (and small state) context, Mele Tupou Vaitohi in Chapter eight in this volume introduces the idea of 'constitutional weaving' as a framework for understanding Tongan constitutionalism.[90] She argues that instead of understanding the mix of formal and traditional authority as two separate legal systems operating in parallel, one needs to understand the Tongan constitutional system as one system – both in terms of process and in terms of result. And there is a growing literature from small states suggesting the need for this kind of nuanced synthesis of local custom and context and 'Weberian' formal constitutional authority.[91]

C. Constitutional Dualism or Pluralism

Another, related, theme that emerges from attention to small states is the importance of attention to the many dualities within constitutionalism itself. This includes the significance of both formal, written and more informal, unwritten norms to practices of constitutional self-government. This duality is already a clear theme in comparative constitutional scholarship.[92] But attention to small states reveals how this dynamic may be amplified beyond the basic idea that constitutional systems that follow the Westminster model embody features of unwritten constitutionalism, while also allowing us to draw out different permutations or aspects of this duality.

Unwritten norms and principles are pervasive in many small states and often have serious practical relevance. This can be accounted for on several grounds. Informality is often easier to achieve and operate in smaller settings as compared to larger groups

[88] See eg, N Oppong, 'The Twists and Turns of Institutional Innovation in Small Island Developing States: The Case of Tuvalu' (2016) 54 *Commonwealth & Comparative Politics* 23.

[89] Gebeye (n 77).

[90] M Tupou Vaitohi, 'Constitutional Weaving in Tonga, a Small State with Traditional Authority: A Theoretical Framework for Tonga's Constitutionalism', Chapter 8 in this volume.

[91] Oppong (n 88).

[92] See eg, A Kavanagh, 'The Ubiquity of Unwritten Constitutionalism' (2023) 21 *International Journal of Constitutional Law* 968; VA MacDonnell, 'Rethinking the Invisible Constitution: How Unwritten Constitutional Principles Shape Political Decision-Making' (2021) 65 *McGill Law Journal* 175; B Galligan and S Brenton (eds), *Constitutional Conventions in Westminster Systems: Controversies, Changes and Challenges* (Cambridge, Cambridge University Press, 2015).

or states, as it seems comparatively more straightforward to identify and take account of all affected interests through reliance on pre-existing relations and close linkages between the rulers and the ruled, thus obviating the need for voting or relying on official decision-making processes laid down in the written constitution. Unwritten norms may also be considered more appropriate than formal rules, as the latter may create the perception of 'winners' and 'losers' that do not mesh well with traditional, Indigenous approaches to governance and a belief that arriving at a consensus would make for a more legitimate, and effective, decision.[93] This may also explain why certain institutional structures, such as legislatures, are perceived differently in some small states as compared to larger states. It also evokes the earlier discussion about (de)colonisation and legal pluralism: formerly colonised small states were not a legal *terra nullius* when Western powers arrived, but rather had customary rule-making processes and governing structures in place that endured or were revived upon independence. In several small states, for instance, rulers relied on a religious or customary claim to power and status to govern, and this explains why we still see monarchs or traditional leaders with greater informal authority than a bare reading of the constitution would suggest (as is discussed further in the next section of this chapter). It also bears remembering that constitutions are always incomplete, with unregulated aspects that nevertheless need to be addressed to enable the constitutional order to function well. As alluded to earlier, the role of courts in small states may be limited as a matter of practice, which means that other institutions – including those of a customary nature that often can lay claim to a strong sociological legitimacy – take the lead in gap-filling and devising, interpreting and applying unwritten norms and principles, with such norms and principles in turn assuming a great deal of daily significance.

A further dualism that emerges from small states is the idea of dual or multi-track processes for formal constitutional amendment. There is still a notable tendency for small state constitutions to prescribe fairly rigid processes for constitutional amendment.[94] There are also interesting variants of multi-track constitutional amendment in certain small states. In Cyprus, for example, Christos Papastylianos notes the existence of ordinary amendment processes within the Cypriot Constitution, but also the *imposition* of a form of super-entrenchment or 'unconstitutional amendment doctrine' (UCA).[95] This UCA or 'basic structure' doctrine was part of the negotiated settlement between Greek- and Turkish-Cypriot communities and was designed to protect the terms of that settlement. But while settling or reducing political conflict, it has also raised distinctive challenges of democratic legitimacy, or challenges to the legitimacy of a system of external–internal self-government that involves very limited

[93] In Oceania, in many small states, governance decisions would traditionally be made by way of consensus. See, for example, in relation to Kiribati: I Tabai, 'The First Twelve Years' in H Van Trease (ed), *Atoll Politics: The Republic of Kiribati* (Suva and Christchurch, University of the South Pacific and University of Canterbury, Macmillan Brown Centre for Pacific Studies, 1993) 315; and in relation to the Melanesia region: L Marai, 'The Psychology of Consensus in Melanesia' (2007) 1 *Journal of Pacific Rim Psychology* 54.

[94] D Anckar, 'Constitutional Amendment Methods in Twenty One Small Island Democracies' (2012) 7(2) *Island Studies Journal* 259.

[95] See C Papastylianos, 'A Tale of Self-Fulfilling Constitutional Failure: The Role of "Smallness" in the Cyprus Constitutional Breakdown of 1963', Chapter 19 in this volume. On imposed constitutionalism, see eg, R Albert, X Contiades and A Fotiadou (eds), *The Law and Legitimacy of Imposed Constitutions* (London, Routledge, 2018).

forms of local consent. The Cypriot experience is by no means unique in this context: the German Basic Law and its eternity clause were in part the product of imposed constitutional norms, as too is the well-known example of the role of foreign drafters in relation to the Japanese Constitution. But paying attention to the Cypriot experience helps return our gaze to the democratic 'trouble' associated with a model of external–internal constitutional self-government that comes from a top-down rather than bottom-up process of constitutional change.

VI. Ad Hoc Insights: Looking Beyond the 'Usual Suspects'

Devoting attention to small states offers a window into a wide range of issues that are not necessarily unique to small states, but nonetheless are raised by the constitutional experiences of at least some small states. There are a number of these that become apparent throughout the chapters in this collection, including, for example, issues of executive dominance in postcolonial 'Westminster' systems, questions of the place and role of the diaspora in a constitutional democracy, and questions around the enduring relevance of traditional forms of authority. We do not have the space to address all of these issues here, so we highlight the last in this list by way of illustration.

Several small states covered in this volume are monarchies, which reflects the more general pattern of almost a quarter of the world's small states having a royal head of state, making this a more common regime arrangement within such jurisdictions as compared to larger ones. This fact alone serves to counter the conventional wisdom that 'monarchy has become a political anomaly' and instead suggests that small states may offer valuable insights into the design and operation of this regime arrangement, thereby also expanding our wisdom about available forms of government, their features and desirability from a democratic perspective.

In this regard, it has been observed that 'the combination of smallness and monarchy leads to dissimilar outcomes across small states'.[96] In some instances, like in Andorra, we find constitutional monarchies in which the royal function is mainly ceremonial and real governmental power is exercised by democratically-elected institutions. In other places, absolute monarchies continue to exist, such as in Brunei or Eswatini, with the ruler's political and legal power unchecked by other state institutions. In yet other small states we find an 'intermediate' breed of government: the quasi-constitutional monarchy, in which the constitution formally purports to follow the ceremonial model, but with a monarch capable of exerting 'a large measure of political influence'[97] and enjoying some discretionary constitutional powers alongside extensive informal powers that give them the ability to shape the country's public life. This conception of the monarchy can, for instance, be found in Bhutan, Monaco and Tonga, where the monarch is

[96] W Veenendaal, 'Monarchy and Democracy in Small States: An Ambiguous Symbiosis' in S Wolf (ed), *State Size Matters* (Wiesbaden, Springer Fachmedien, 2016).

[97] J Corbett, W Veenendaal and L Ugyel, 'Why Monarchy Persists in Small States: The Cases of Tonga, Bhutan and Liechtenstein' (2017) 24 *Democratization* 689, 691.

generally revered and trusted, at times more so than the conventional elements of a democratic regime.

Consideration of the small state experience, then, helps to highlight that the model of the constitutional monarchy, as it has played out in several large(r) European jurisdictions,[98] should not be taken as having a universal value or degree of general representativeness, even within continental Europe. The reality of quasi-constitutional monarchical government in particular serves as a powerful reminder to pluralise understandings of 'the monarchy', accepting that 'the various abilities of monarchies to affect national affairs may be best conceived in shades of grey',[99] while the informal power wielded by the royal head of state under that form of government, coupled with the endurance of absolute monarchies, suggests that royal powers have not always or inevitably given way to fully-fledged democratic arrangements.

In making sense of the comparatively outsized role of the monarchy, the size of the state may be a relevant factor, albeit not the only one. There may be an important sense in which the monarch and the people stand in a relationship of mutual respect towards one another, which may be amplified in small states in view of the closer linkages between the ruler and the ruled. The size of the community may also mean that it is relatively easier to engage in repressive practices, as seems to have been the case in Eswatini (as described in Chapter nine by Sinethemba Memela), that limit freedom of expression that could otherwise have enabled critical societal reflections on the desirability of retaining a particular form of monarchical rule. In this regard, recall also the typically small size of civil society as well as the low number of legal professionals whose role it is to take the lead in questioning the existence or exercise of royal power. More generally, constitutional culture and history have explanatory value too, in that importance may be ascribed to retaining traditional forms of governance, for instance because the state in question has never been colonised (as in Tonga) or precisely because such forms of governance pre-date colonisation and are thus seen as valuable to preserve precisely on account of their indigenous character. A further factor relates to tradition and religion, with monarchs conceived as the guardian of the country's official faith or customs – and therefore often attributing their formal power to this role, as is the case in Brunei and Bhutan, for instance.[100] Especially if the relevant society continues to care deeply about heeding religious or customary norms, this augments the social legitimacy of the monarch, who may accordingly be viewed as entitled to respect, if not reverence. In these circumstances, the monarch is also typically conceived as embodying part of the country's constitutional and national identity, which further entrenches his or her position and authority, including the ability to exercise informal powers.

[98] R Hazell and B Morris (eds), *The Role of Monarchy in Modern Democracy: European Monarchies Compared* (Oxford, Hart Publishing, 2022).

[99] M De Visser and A Harding, 'Monarchical Constitutional Guardianship and Legal Métissage in Asia' (2022) 9 *Asian Journal of Law and Society* 345, 347.

[100] See eg, N Dorji, 'The Progressive Monarchy of Bhutan: A Not-So-Absolute Monarchy to a Democratic Constitutional Monarchy' (2022) 9 *Asian Journal of Law and Society* 440; DM Müller, 'Beyond the Sharia State: Public Celebrations and Everyday State-Making in the Malay Islamic Monarchy of Brunei Darussalam' (2022) 9 *Asian Journal of Law and Society* 418.

VII. Concluding Thoughts and Brief Outline of this Volume

In this chapter we have not sought to provide any conclusions as such, but rather to highlight some of the constitutional issues either caused by, or often encountered in conjunction, with the small size of a jurisdiction. In doing so, we have drawn on the case study chapters to illustrate the issues we have raised. The rest of the volume comprises these 18 case study chapters, and is organised into two broad thematic parts, further organised into 'sub-themes'. The first broad part focuses on issues of *identity, culture and belonging*.

Part IA covers the first sub-theme in this part, focusing on questions of *identity, creation, survival and stateness*, and includes a chapter by Tracy Robinson that explores the dyadic constitutions of the Anglo Caribbean; a chapter by two of us (Maartje De Visser and Elisabeth Perham) focusing on constitutional relations in the Kingdom of the Netherlands by way of spotlighting why constitutional lawyers need to pay more attention to the international law relationships between sub-national jurisdictions and their administering states, as well as between smaller and larger states; a chapter by Hervé Raimana Lallemant-Moe discussing the constitutional issues that may arise should the small non-self-governing jurisdictions of New Caledonia and French Polynesia take further steps towards independent statehood; a chapter by Elisa Bertolini discussing the role of tradition in the design of the separation of powers in the continental European micro jurisdictions; and a chapter by Conor Casey highlighting the unique constitutional history and identity of the Vatican City State.

Part IB deals with the second sub-theme in this part, focusing on questions of *legal culture and pluralism*, and includes a chapter by Ine Apapoe and Janine Ubink exploring the relationship between Suriname's small population size and the strong, but largely informal, legally pluralist regulation of national resources in that state; a chapter by Mele Tupou Vaitohi setting out a new framework for understanding constitutionalism in Tonga – a weaving of traditional and modern forms of constitutionalism; and a chapter by Sinethemba Memela discussing the role of custom in the operation of the Constitution of Eswatini.

Part IC addresses the third sub-theme in this part, focusing on questions of *citizenship, belonging and regional integration* and features a chapter by Se-shauna Wheatle explaining the role of a regional constitutional court, the Caribbean Court of Justice, in constructing constitutional identity or identities; a chapter by Petra Butler and Sam Macintosh exploring what it would take to advance regionalism in Oceania (as called for by some Pacific leaders, partly in response to the small size of the states) by creating a European Union-style Pacific common market; and a chapter by Ada Ordor and Victor T Amadi explaining how moves towards enhanced African regionalism through increasing the free movement of people on the continent are being received by small states in the region

Part II features chapters that zoom in more squarely on questions of *state design and operation* in small polities. The first set of chapters (Part IIA) focuses on the sub-theme of *separation of powers, and checks and balances* in small state contexts where, as described above, there are small political and legal elites, perhaps fewer resources, and fewer personnel to staff constitutional offices. It includes a chapter by Anna Dziedzic examining the phenomenon of the 'multi-tasked office' apparent in the Constitutions of Kiribati, the Marshall Islands and Nauru; a chapter by Tony Angelo and Jennifer Corrin examining the role of smallness in the constitutional design of Niue and the challenges it presents for achieving aspirations such as the separation of powers; a chapter by Joelle Barnes highlighting the role that fourth-branch institutions could play in countering executive dominance in Seychelles; a chapter by Ann Black describing the role of the Sultan in the governance of Brunei Darussalam and exploring how smallness both allows for a personalised style of rule in that state, and is used to justify illiberal practices; and a chapter by John Stanton arguing that Malta's small size has played an important role in the perpetuation of autocratic practices in that state since its independence.

The second set of chapters (Part IIB) addresses the sub-theme of *mediating division* and features two chapters addressing small states with so-called divided societies: the chapter by Tony Angelo and Sabir Kadel focuses on how the multi-communal state of Mauritius has mediated division and developed a unified identity through the implementation of a 'Best Loser' electoral system and strategic engagement with international law; while the chapter by Christos Papastylianos examines the role smallness played in the failure of the attempted constitutional settlement between the two communities on Cyprus.

As can be seen, the case studies cover a large number and wide range of jurisdictions, selected – as described at the beginning of the chapter – through a mixture of randomness and design. And, as is probably also apparent, many of the chapters cut across the thematic divisions.

We have conceived of this volume as the beginning, not the end, of a broader conversation about questions of whether and how scale (here understood as small population size) should or does impact on issues of constitutional design and operation, including questions of sovereignty, identity, culture, and transnational legal norms and relationships. That discussion is somewhat more advanced in the fields of political science and international relations (in relation to the questions those disciplines seek to answer) than it is in comparative constitutional law in relation to these more legal questions. Of course, if we understand our field as one that is broader than law,[101] we should – as academic lawyers contributing to that field – embrace and build on the insights brought to bear by our colleagues in cognate disciplines, while bringing to the conversation our unique disciplinary insights as lawyers. It is our hope that this volume provides a useful jumping-off point for this broader conversation.

[101] R Hirschl, *Comparative Matters: The Renaissance of Comparative Constitutional Law* (Oxford, Oxford University Press, 2014); though perhaps this depends on the precise questions being asked: see T Roux, 'Comparative Constitutional Studies: Two Fields or One?' (2017) 13 *Annual Review of Law and Social Science* 123.

PART I

Identity, Culture and Belonging

Part IA
Identity, Creation, Survival and Stateness

2

Dyadic Caribbean Constitutions

TRACY ROBINSON*

I. Introduction

The 'nation-state' is the grist for constitutional law studies, and 'the most recognizable organizing principle of modern political order'.[1] It is also the site of contestation in small polities because their constitutional practices and cultures typically 'avoid a strictly sovereign form of life'.[2] In the Caribbean, which has the largest concentration of small jurisdictions in the world,[3] the dichotomy between formally independent small states and small non-sovereign subnational jurisdictions is somewhat overdrawn. Some affluent, small non-independent territories assume 'a state-like identity which allows them to play with and … possibly modify the institution of sovereignty'.[4] Additionally, sovereignty is asserted and spectral 'in the wake of' decolonisation,[5] which produced small state formations that are still 'being worked over by colonialism',[6] and struggling to 'close the circle of independence'.[7] Accordingly, the Caribbean region, including states that have achieved 'flag independence', has been described as 'non-sovereign' or characterised by 'constrained sovereignty'.[8]

The Anglo Caribbean sub-region, which extends across the Caribbean archipelago and into the Atlantic, and includes the mainland countries of Belize and Guyana,

* I am grateful to Oliver Ray for his excellent research assistance in the preparation of this chapter.

[1] S Torres-Saillant, 'Paradoxical Sovereignty Imagining Caribbean Futures' in L Lewis (ed), *Caribbean Sovereignty, Development and Democracy in an Age of Globalization* (New York, Routledge, 2012) 140.

[2] U Pram Gad and R Adler-Nissen, 'Postcolonial Sovereignty Games' in R Adler-Nissen and U Pram Gad (eds), *European Integration and Postcolonial Sovereignty Games: The EU Overseas Countries and Territories* (Oxford, Routledge, 2013) 1, 4.

[3] G Baldacchino, 'Island Versus Region: The Politics of Small States in the Caribbean' in G Baldacchino, and A Wivel (eds), *Handbook on the Politics of Small States* (Cheltenham, Edward Elgar Publishing, 2020) 279, 279.

[4] Gad and Adler-Nissen (n 2) 8.

[5] Y Bonilla, 'Freedom, Sovereignty and other Entanglements' (2017) 53 *Small Axe* 201, 201, 204.

[6] G Prakash, M Laffan and N Menon, 'Introduction: The Postcolonial Moment' in G Prakash, M Laffan and N Menon (eds), *The Postcolonial Moment in South and Southeast Asia* (London, Bloomsbury Academic, 2018) 1.

[7] See D Pollard, *The Caribbean Court of Justice: Closing the Circle of Independence* (Kingston, Ian Randle Publishers, 2004).

[8] Y Bonilla, *Non-sovereign Futures: French Caribbean Politics in the Wake of Disenchantment* (Chicago IL, University of Chicago Press, 2015) 10.

comprises 18 small jurisdictions, a dozen of which are former UK colonies and now independent states[9] and the smallest six of which are British Overseas Territories (BOTs).[10] Only two, the oldest states, have populations that exceed 1.5 million people.[11] Today, two-thirds of Anglo Caribbean jurisdictions have populations of less than 200,000, and four of the six non-independent territories have populations below 40,000. With the failure and formal end of the 1958 West Indies Federation in 1962,[12] the most populated colonies were the first to proceed to independence that year. During their colonial histories, the smallest territories, several of which are now BOTs, were either administratively governed from a larger British Caribbean colony or through a colonial federation.[13] Bermuda, the oldest overseas territory, is a notable exception.

The constitutions of small Anglo Caribbeans states and territories reflect 'the vocabulary and grammar of modern constitutionalism' – they identify 'the people' and distinct political communities, say who are citizens, secure fundamental rights, establish a form of democratic governance and treat the constitution as the fundamental law.[14] However, the incomplete and disrupted paths to decolonisation in these jurisdictions trouble the notion that the end of empire is a precondition for modern constitutionalism.[15] Small jurisdictions in the Caribbean, and elsewhere, bring the neglected analytical frame of *empire* to the fore in comparative constitutional studies. They make more visible the imbricated constitutional lives of metropoles, colonies and postcolonies, as such. They also draw attention to the constitutional animation generated as small jurisdictions that fall well short of the ideal of a sovereign state, as Lee Cabatingan puts it, *cite* the nation-state, claiming relatedness to it and acknowledging an 'irreducible distance' from it.[16]

The distinction between the independent nation-states and non-sovereign overseas territories is frequently the point of departure for Anglo Caribbean constitutional

[9] The following 12 Caribbean countries obtained their independence from the UK between 1962 and 1983: Antigua and Barbuda 1981, Bahamas 1973, Barbados 1966, Belize 1981, Dominica 1978, Grenada 1974, Guyana 1966, Jamaica 1962, St Christopher-Nevis (St Kitts-Nevis) 1983, St Lucia 1979, St Vincent and the Grenadines 1979, and Trinidad and Tobago 1962.

[10] Anguilla, Bermuda, British Virgin Islands, Cayman Islands, Montserrat, and Turks and Caicos Islands are British Overseas Territories under the UK British Overseas Territories Act 2002, c 8. Bermuda and Turks and Caicos Islands are located in the Atlantic Ocean, north of the Caribbean Sea. Although the UK does not describe Bermuda as a Caribbean BOT, Bermuda is routinely included in descriptions of Anglo Caribbean legal systems. See R-M Antoine, *Commonwealth Caribbean Law and Legal Systems* (London, Cavendish Publishing, 1999).

[11] Jamaica (2.8 million) and Trinidad and Tobago (1.56 million). See M De Visser and E Perham, 'Variables Shaping Participatory Constitution-Making: Insights from the Experiences of Small States' (2022) 20 *International Journal of Constitutional Law* 1216, 1218, on using 1.5 million people as a threshold for small states.

[12] West Indies Act 1962, c 19 (UK).

[13] S Dickson, 'The British Overseas Territories of Anguilla, British Virgin Islands, Cayman Islands, Montserrat, and Turks and Caicos Islands: A Modern Approach to a Traditional Relationship' in R Albert, D O'Brien and S Wheatle, *The Oxford Handbook of Caribbean Constitutions* (Oxford, Oxford University Press, 2020) 190.

[14] D Bonilla Maldonado and M Riegner, 'Decolonization' in R Grote, F Lachenmann, and R Wolfrum (eds), *Max Planck Encyclopedia of Comparative Constitutional Law* (Oxford, Oxford University Press, 2020).

[15] ibid.

[16] L Cabatingan, *A Region Among States: Law and Non-sovereignty in the Caribbean* (Chicago IL, University of Chicago Press, 2023) 13–14.

studies.[17] This chapter highlights the operation of a dyadic constitutionalism in non-independent and most independent Anglo Caribbean countries, in which the formal or large-c constitution references, is entangled with, and may owe its existence to an external constitution that is British and, in good measure, imperial. The scaffolding for dyadic Anglo Caribbean constitutions is UK imperial laws and policies, with the latter often less visible than the former. Dyadic Caribbean constitutional infrastructure interpolates British institutions in Caribbean governance, including the Judicial Committee of the Privy Council (JCPC), His Majesty and his representatives, the UK Parliament and the UK Government. The strong relevance of an imperial constitution to BOTs, which are part of the British realm, is to be expected. The dyadic constitution is also a feature of many small *independent* states in the Anglo Caribbean. Most have prototypical constitutions that were 'tailored' or refined in London; most were inaugurated by a UK Order in Council and establish the British King as head of the independent state, and several still provide for the London-based JCPC as the final court of appeal.

Dyadic constitutionalism reflects formal structural features of governance and dynamic relationships of power. Internal and external institutions are tensely yoked in dyadic constitutions as nationalism, imperialism, globalisation and geopolitics interact. The *citation of the nation-state* is very pronounced in disputes about gender and sexuality in small Caribbean jurisdictions. Gay marriage has become a 'pivotal issue for indexing sovereignty when questions of political independence are being debated' across the Caribbean.[18] Consequently, gender/sexuality debates are an important site for the operation of and tensions within dyadic constitutionalism. This illustrates how relations and representations of gender, sexuality and family are foundational to discourses about the nation-state, the national body and imperialism.[19]

This chapter focuses on the three affluent small Caribbean jurisdictions, the Bahamas, Bermuda and the Cayman Islands, a state and two BOTs in the northwest Caribbean/Atlantic. I use contentions about gender and 'legitimate' intimacies as a mode of feminist constitutional comparison to explore principles and practices that are shaping dyadic Caribbean constitutionalism.[20] These gender/sexuality controversies have become key questions in constitutional reform, and some have made their way to the extraterritorial appellate jurisdiction of the JCPC based in London. In 2022, in appeals from the overseas territories of Bermuda and the Cayman Islands, the Privy Council ruled that there was no constitutional right to same-sex marriage in either territory.[21] In a 2023 appeal from the Bahamas, the Privy Council held that the right to citizenship of

[17] See, eg: F Phillips, *Commonwealth Caribbean Constitutional Law* (London, Cavendish Publishing, 2002); Dickson (n 13) 188.

[18] V Agard Jones, 'Le Jue de Qui? Sexual Politics at Play in French Caribbean' in F Smith (ed), *Sex and the Citizen: Interrogating the Caribbean* (Charlottesville VA, University of Virginia Press, 2011) 181, 182, fn 8 (referring to personal correspondence with Dutch Caribbean human rights activist and LGBTQ leader, Mario Kleinmoedig). See also F Smith, 'Crosses/Crossroads/Crossings' (2007) 11 *Small Axe* 130, 136.

[19] See A McClintock, 'Family Feuds: Gender, Nationalism and the Family' (1993) 44 *Feminist Review* 61; R Rubio-Marin, 'Gendered Nationalism and Constitutionalism' (2020) 18 *International Journal of Constitutional Law* 441.

[20] R Dixon, 'Feminism and Comparative Constitutional Studies' (2023) 1 *Comparative Constitutional Studies* 310.

[21] *Attorney-General for Bermuda v Ferguson* [2022] UKPC 5, [2022] 3 LRC 579 (PC Bermuda); *Day v Governor of the Cayman Islands* [2022] UKPC 6, [2022] 3 LRC 557 (PC Cayman Islands).

persons born in the Bahamas, of a Bahamian 'parent', included persons born outside of marriage to a Bahamian father and a non-Bahamian mother, notwithstanding language in the Constitution that restricted citizenship acquisition from unmarried fathers.[22]

Section II briefly discusses features of dyadic Caribbean constitutions. With the three northwest Caribbean jurisdictions in sharper focus, section III looks at 'cooperative' constitution making, its products and its gendered subjects. Section IV explores the growing significance of collaboration and consensus in setting the boundaries for constitutionally acceptable intimacies. The final section, section V looks at the authoritative use of the European Convention on Human Rights (ECHR) by the Privy Council as a form of external constitutional regulation in the Caribbean that is within its interpretative reins.

II. The Dyadic Caribbean Constitution

With the substantial decline of the British Empire by the mid-twentieth century, analyses of British imperial constitutionalism have been mostly consigned to history.[23] However, the post-WW2 period produced distinct intimacies of decolonisation, including political negotiations and constitution making.[24] It inaugurated a new era of asymmetrical cooperative constitutionalism,[25] as the UK and the colonised negotiated scores of new 'modern' independence and intermediate constitutions.[26] In the small jurisdictions in the Anglo Caribbean where decolonisation was neither linear nor inescapable, the ebb in the British Empire *animated* imperial constitutionalism and its longstanding project of conceptualising measured or quasi-sovereignty in colonial realms – weaving modern and imperial constitutionalism.[27] Randolph Hahn notes that 'more constitutions have been written in London than anywhere else in the world'.[28] Between the 1950s and the early twenty-first century, UK law brought into effect over 30 new constitutions in the Caribbean, as the British Government recalibrated degrees of sovereignty for small territories, parsimoniously offered increments of constitutional reform toward self-government or independence, and carefully managed its responsibilities towards Caribbean colonies and new states.[29]

[22] *Attorney-General v Rolle* [2023] UKPC 13, [2023] 5 LRC 439 (PC Bahamas).

[23] See, eg RW Kostal, *A Jurisprudence of Power: Victorian Empire and the Rule of Law* (Oxford, Oxford University Press, 2008) 20; L Benton and L Ford, 'Island Despotism: Trinidad, The British Imperial Constitution and Global Legal Order' (2018) 46 *Journal of Imperial and Commonwealth History* 21.

[24] T Robinson, 'A Trace of Law: State Building and the Criminalization of Buggery in Jamaica' in D Herzog and C Schields (eds), *The Routledge Companion to Sexuality and Colonialism* (Oxford, Routledge, 2021) 305, 310.

[25] See M Blackhawk, 'Foreword, The Constitution of American Colonialism' (2023) 137(1) *Harvard Law Review* 1, 105–10.

[26] W Dale, 'The Making and Remaking of Commonwealth Constitutions' (1993) 42 *International & Comparative Law Quarterly* 67.

[27] L Benton, 'From International Law to Imperial Constitutions: The Problem of Quasi-Sovereignty, 1870–1900' (2008) 26 *Law and History Review* 595.

[28] RK Hahn, 'The British Influence on the Initiation and Introduction of Commonwealth Bills of Rights' (1988) 26 *Journal of Commonwealth & Comparative Politics* 54, 64.

[29] S Mawby, *Ordering Independence: The End of Empire in the Anglophone Caribbean, 1947–69* (Basingstoke, Palgrave Macmillan, 2012) 245.

Dyadic constitutionalism is a form of plural constitutionalism. Theories of constitutional pluralism move beyond state-centred constitutionalism and acknowledge that multiple 'sites of constitutional authority' can operate in tandem.[30] They have been particularly valuable in understanding postnational community regimes like the EU, and the relationship between its national and supranational legal systems.[31] In the US context, Maggie Blackhawk discusses a less considered plural constitutionalism, a dual system with a hyper-visible internal framework relevant to 'We the People', and an external one which created and regulates colonies, which she calls the 'constitutional law of colonialism'.[32] She contends that there has been an erasure of American colonialism from conventional accounts of US constitutional law.

The coloniality of constitutionalism is plainer in the colonised Caribbean. Here, the imperial constitution, to borrow from Ann Laura Stoler, *haunts* and 'indelibly permeate[s]' the constitutional texts and is 'a force that not always bares a proper name'.[33] This may be because the dyadic Caribbean constitution is 'out of time'.[34] The constitutional law of British colonialism is alive in small Caribbean jurisdictions at a time when the British empire is thought to be long dead. Constitutional structures that integrate exogenous, imperial institutions are not unique to small states and non-independent jurisdictions. For example, the British monarch is still the head of state in some large Commonwealth states like Australia and Canada. The difference in small jurisdictions is typically scale, and the import of the external constitution. In the Anglo Caribbean, the exogenous institutions, laws and policies are consequential and expressive, producing an imperial guardianship that contributes materially to the Caribbean's 'constrained sovereignty'.

The powers of the Crown, with their origins in the royal prerogative to make laws for the colonies and to be petitioned by colonial subjects, are the 'lifeblood' of the imperial constitution.[35] The JCPC is a creature of royal prerogative whose arrangements are now determined by UK law,[36] and its judges primarily sit in the UK Supreme Court. It has a commanding role as a final appellate court in seven states and all six BOTs in the Anglo Caribbean region. The global overseas jurisdiction of the once dominant Privy Council is now miniscule, with appeals arising from just 11 independent states, most of which are in the Caribbean.[37] The imperial Court's judicial oversight in the newly independent states then carried considerable heft because of its entrenchment in

[30] See N Walker, 'Constitutional Pluralism Revisited' (2016) 22 *European Law Journal* 333, 334.

[31] ibid.

[32] See Blackhawk (n 25) 8, 116. See also H Yusuf and T Chowdhury, 'The Persistence of Colonial Constitutionalism in British Overseas Territories' (2019) 8 *Global Constitutionalism* 157; J Cross, 'The Vestiges of Colonial Constitutionalism' in R Albert, D O'Brien and S Wheatle, *The Oxford Handbook of Caribbean Constitutions* (Oxford, Oxford University Press, 2020) 631.

[33] AL Stoler, 'Intimidations of Empire: Predicaments of the Tactile and Unseen' in AL Stoler (ed), *Haunted by Empire: Geographies of Intimacy in North American History* (Durham NC, Duke University Press, 2006) 1, 1.

[34] R Rao, *Out of Time: The Queer Politics of Postcoloniality* (Oxford, Oxford University Press, 2020) 9.

[35] K Roberts-Wray, *Commonwealth and Colonial Law* (London, Stevens & Sons, 1966) 150.

[36] See Judicial Committee Act 1833, c 41 (UK).

[37] Appeals lie from the following independent states within the Commonwealth: Antigua and Barbuda, The Bahamas, Grenada, Jamaica, Kiribati, Mauritius, St Kitts and Nevis, St. Vincent and the Grenadines, Tuvalu, and Trinidad and Tobago, as well as from the Cook Islands and Niue (self-governing countries in a relationship of free association with New Zealand).

Caribbean constitutions. Terminating appeals to the Privy Council in the six smallest Anglo Caribbean nations, all in the eastern Caribbean, required referenda.[38] In four, their independence constitutions provided an alternative route. They require qualified parliamentary majorities *and* the post-independence agreement of the UK Government to constitutional change.[39]

In constitution making, the imperial constitutional framework brings about the formal Caribbean constitution. UK Acts of Parliament authorised the making of Caribbean constitutions by Orders in Council, a statutory instrument made by the monarch on the advice of her or his Privy Council.[40] The tension is plain in an independence constitution like that of the Bahamas. The Constitution begins by declaring it is the supreme law and establishes a sovereign democratic state.[41] Yet that supreme Constitution is a schedule to the Bahamas Independence Order 1973, which was made by the UK Crown, and the Order is subordinate legislation to the UK Bahamas Islands (Constitution) Act 1963.[42]

The Order in Council is a powerful tool of imperial governance and intervention in the BOTs, which are distinct legal jurisdictions with written constitutions, authorised by UK law, establishing their form of democratic government and degree of autonomy.[43] The UK Parliament is supreme and has unlimited power to make laws for the territories.[44] A UK-appointed governor represents His Majesty and retains substantive executive functions to ensure good governance in the territories.[45] In some territories, the governor has reserve legislative powers.[46] Except in Bermuda, the UK can legislate directly for the overseas territories by Order in Council.[47] This route for the UK Government to impose legal change on the territories has been described in the Cayman Islands as the 'nuclear option'.[48] When consultations in the 1990s by the UK

[38] Antigua and Barbuda Constitution (1981), s 47; Dominica Constitution, s 42 (amended by Constitution of Dominica (Amendment) Act 2014, which terminated appeals to the Privy Council and acceded to the appellate jurisdiction of the Caribbean Court of Justice (CCJ)); Grenada Constitution (1973), s 39; St Lucia Constitution (1979), s 41 (amended by Constitution of Saint Lucia (Amendment) Act 2023, which terminated appeals to the Privy Council and acceded to the appellate jurisdiction of the CCJ); St Kitts and Nevis Constitution (1983), s 38; St Vincent and the Grenadines Constitution (1979), s 38. See also *Independent Jamaica Council for Human Rights (1998) Ltd v Marshall-Burnett* [2005] UKPC 3, [2005] 2 AC 356 (PC Jamaica).

[39] Dominica, St Kitts and Nevis, St Lucia, and St Vincent and the Grenadines Constitutions (n 38 above). See also *Attorney General's Reference* (2013) 83 WIR 228 (CA SLU). Dominica and St Lucia have terminated appeals to the Privy Council with the agreement of the UK Government and there have been four failed constitutional referenda in Antigua and Barbuda (2018), Grenada (2016, 2018) and St Vincent and the Grenadines (2009) as others attempt to conclude the reign of the imperial Court.

[40] West Indies Act 1962, c 19 (for the Cayman Islands); Bahamas Islands (Constitution) Act 1963, c 56; Bermuda Constitution Act 1967, c 63 (UK).

[41] See, eg Bahamas Constitution (1973), ss 1, 2.

[42] Bahamas Islands (Constitution) Act 1963, c 56, Bahamas Independence Order 1973 (SI 1080) (UK).

[43] I Hendry and S Dickson, *British Overseas Territory Law*, 2nd edn (Oxford, Hart Publishing, 2018) 14.

[44] ibid 57–59.

[45] D O'Brien and P Clegg, 'Roles and Responsibilities of Governors in the UK Overseas Territories: Prerogative Power and Democratic Accountability' (2023) 6 *Small States and Territories* 135.

[46] See, eg Cayman Islands Constitution (2009), s 81. The Cayman Islands Governor exercised his reserve legislative powers to introduce the Civil Partnerships Act 2020, a version of which had been rejected by the Legislative Assembly.

[47] Cayman Islands Constitution 2009, s 125. Hendry and Dickson (n 43) 60–62.

[48] W Vlcek, 'Crafting Human Rights in a Constitution: Gay Rights in the Cayman Islands and the Limits to Global Norm Diffusion' (2013) 2 *Global Constitutionalism* 345, 352.

Government on decriminalising consensual homosexual sex between adults met with strong resistance in Caribbean overseas territories, and thus did not lead to the repeal of the criminalisation by local legislatures, a 2000 UK Order in Council achieved this result.[49] The UK's outsider law-making generated 'tremendous ill feeling' in the territories, as BOTs strongly asserted a right to non-intervention by the UK on matters deeply tied to the cultural identity of the territories.[50]

The modern post-1960 Caribbean constitution – written with constitutional bills of rights and enabling constitutional judicial review[51] – is soldered onto external constitutionalism. While many constitutions made or finalised by the UK Government in London 'have been unmade',[52] in the Anglo Caribbean, exogenous imperial statutory instruments are the primary legal foundation for 15 of the 18 extant constitutions, and the British King is the head of state in 14 of these 18 states and territories. The inclusion of justiciable bills of rights in Caribbean constitutional design from 1961 onward reflected a shift in UK imperial policy from objecting to constitutional bills of rights to expecting or insisting on them.[53] The JCPC's imperial jurisdiction 'modernised' during decolonisation in the Caribbean, as the Court assumed the role of an extraterritorial apex Supreme Court with a power of constitutional review, and ultimate judicial oversight of constitutional change in both self-governing and newly independent polities.

The structural features of the dyadic Caribbean constitution – imperial law authorising constitutions, imperial policy shaping how constitutions are made and their substance, and the integration of British institutions into Caribbean governance – do not negate its flexibility. The dyadic constitution is dynamic, involving 'constitutional conversation and contestation'.[54] Its parameters are manipulable and changing force fields. Dynamism in the dyadic constitution is especially strong in the small multi-island polities in the northwestern Caribbean and Atlantic Ocean – the state of the Bahamas, and the territories of Bermuda and the Cayman Islands – where economic wealth affords 'non-sovereign' Caribbean jurisdictions more 'practical autonomy'.[55] Small states tend to be classified as middle-income or high-income economies, despite their social and economic inequalities.[56] The Bahamas, Bermuda and the Cayman Islands have the highest per capita GDPs in the Anglo Caribbean.[57] Indeed, the per capita GDPs of the two territories are among the highest in the world, well exceed their metropole, the UK, and are higher than that of their close neighbour, the US.[58]

[49] The Caribbean Territories (Criminal Law) Order 2000 (UK). In Bermuda, partial decriminalisation was achieved by the enactment of a private member's bill in 1994.

[50] P Clegg, F Dunwoodie-Stirton and P Cole, 'Human Rights in the Overseas Territories: In Policy but not in Practice? (2016) 54 *Commonwealth & Comparative Politics* 46, 52.

[51] J Weinrib, 'The Modern Constitutional State: A Defence' (2014) 40 *Queen's Law Journal* 165, 165.

[52] Dale (n 26) 67.

[53] COH Parkinson, *Bills of Rights and Decolonization: The Emergence of Domestic Human Rights Instruments in Britain's Overseas Territories* (Oxford, Oxford University Press, 2008) 265.

[54] Blackhawk (n 25) 54; V Carter, C Ku, and AP Morriss, 'Evolving Sovereignty Relationships Between Affiliated Jurisdictions: Lessons for Native American Jurisdictions' (2023) 40 *Arizona Journal of International & Comparative Law* 411, 421.

[55] MW Sybblis, 'Corporate Law as Decolonization' (2024) 71(3) *UCLA Law Review* 798, 805.

[56] 'GDP Per Capita (Current US$)' (*World Bank Group*), data.worldbank.org/indicator/NY.GDP.PCAP.CD.

[57] ibid.

[58] ibid. The World Bank estimates the per capita GDPs of Bermuda and Cayman Islands as $123,091.10 USD and $96,073.80 USD respectively, that of the UK as $48,866.60 USD, and that of the US as $81,695.20 USD.

The Bahamas became an independent state in 1973 and has a population of about 400,000 people. Like most Anglo Caribbean states, it retains its independence constitution negotiated with the UK. Bermuda is the oldest and most sovereign self-governing overseas territory, with a population of about 64,000 people. Its legislature, dating back to 1620, is oft described as the oldest in the Commonwealth, outside of Westminster.[59] Its 1968 Constitution is also one of the oldest in the Anglo Caribbean. The Cayman Islands has a population of approximately 71,000 people. It was colonially administered from Jamaica until the latter's independence in 1962. Its 2009 Constitution is one of the most recent in the Anglo Caribbean and it included, for the first time, a bill of rights.

The economies of all three northwestern Caribbean countries are built around offshore financial services and tourism, which has meant that foreign markets, foreign investors, foreign visitors and workers are critical to their small-state economic survival. With substantial mixed migration flows and large numbers of non-citizens living in, transiting and visiting the islands, the three countries have each generated strong claims about their small-state identity and sharp definitions of the boundaries of the polity and who belongs to it. Jacqui Alexander explains that small, affluent Caribbean polities like the Bahamas have opened their borders to 'the massive entry of transnational capital' and bodies through tourism and financial services, and that this incites 'a legitimation crisis for the state which moves to restore its legitimacy by recouping heterosexuality'.[60] In this milieu, 'particular [gendered] bodies' are 'offered up' in the struggle for national legitimacy in the Caribbean as globalisation changes 'the ways that nations [and territories] constitute and imagine themselves'.[61]

III. Constitution Making and its Gendered Subjects

The Constitutions of the Bahamas, Bermuda and the Cayman Islands are the product of asymmetrical 'cooperative' constitution making in different phases of imperial governance. Caribbean constitution making involved vertical collaboration between the metropole and the colonised people, which was governed by imperial policies that called for some horizontal political consensus among the colonised about constitutional change. The antagonistic and strongly paternalistic constitution-making processes during decolonisation in the 1960s and 1970s brought about a body of evolutionary, genetically-related and durable constitutions that include the self-governing Bermuda Constitution 1968 and the independence Bahamas Constitution 1973. At the end of the twentieth century, there were a handful of small non-independent territories that, on balance, wanted to retain their status as part of the British realm, some of them prosperous and financially independent like Bermuda and the Cayman Islands. In 1999, the UK Government called for a 'renewed contract' and 'modern and effective partnership'

[59] Commonwealth Parliamentary Association, 'Parliament of Bermuda celebrates its 400th Anniversary' (2020) 101 *Parliamentarian* 304, 304.

[60] M Jacqui Alexander, 'Not Just (Any) Body Can Be a Citizen: The Politics of Law, Sexuality and Postcoloniality in Trinidad and Tobago and the Bahamas' (1994) 48 *Feminist Review* 5, 6–7.

[61] ibid.

between it and its overseas territories, and proposed revised, modern BOT constitutions that promoted good governance, the rule of law and human rights.[62] The Cayman Islands Constitution 2009 is the product of 'constitutional modernisation' during this period.

Constitution making in the Caribbean called for inter-'state' negotiations, borrowing from the 'vocabulary of the law of nations'.[63] Through its products (the constitutions) and a process calling for colonials to be state-like, constitution making was a new domain to become (more) sovereign and, as I have argued borrowing from Belinda Edmondson, for 'making men'.[64] The negotiations between the UK Government and Caribbean nationalist politicians in constitution making during the late twentieth century operated within sustained 'hostility between nationalism and late imperialism'.[65] Debates on the readiness of Caribbean colonies for independence often turned to questions of black Caribbean masculinity.[66] Alexander explains that conjugal heterosexuality was essential to 'constituting respectable masculinity'.[67] Black male nationalist leaders demonstrated their sophistication and ability to lead new nation-states, conservatively, by claiming British and colonial constitutionalism as their heritage and as the framework for their new sovereign states.[68]

Distrustful of the emergent black and brown nationalist male leaders calling for greater political autonomy and pressing for an expeditious transfer of power, UK officials prolonged the process with increments of reform toward self-government and independence.[69] Between 1963 and 1973, the Bahamas saw three new constitutions introduced by UK Orders in Council, moving the colony through stages of self-government and responsible government to independence, all containing justiciable bills of rights just like the Jamaica Constitution 1962. Once local politicians formally called for greater self-government or independence and the UK Government agreed in principle to constitutional reform, imperial policy for finalising new constitutions in the 1960s and 1970s focused on realising consensus 'between representatives of the various shades of political opinion' in the territory.[70] The UK government convened constitutional conferences in London to negotiate the details with government and opposition politicians and civil servants from the territory. These closed-door negotiations in London, chaired by UK officials and politicians, were the capstone in the constitution-making process.[71]

[62] Secretary of State for Foreign and Commonwealth Affairs, *Partnership for Progress and Prosperity: Britain and the Overseas Territories* (Cm 4264, 1999) 4.

[63] Blackhawk (n 25) 20.

[64] T Robinson, 'Gender, Nation and the Common Law Constitution' (2008) 28 *Oxford Journal of Legal Studies* 735, 739, borrowing from B Edmondson, *Making Men: Gender, Literary Authority, and Women's Writing in Caribbean Narrative* (Durham NC, Duke University Press, 1999).

[65] Mawby (n 29) 22.

[66] Edmondson (n 64) 8.

[67] Alexander (n 60) 11.

[68] Robinson (n 64) 740.

[69] Mawby (n 29) 245.

[70] *Hinds v R* [1977] AC 195, 212 (PC Jamaica).

[71] See, eg Secretary of State for Foreign and Commonwealth Affairs, *Report of the Bahamas Independence Conference 1972* (Cmnd 5196, 1973); Secretary of State for the Colonies, *Report of the Bermuda Constitutional Conference 1966* (Cmnd 3174, 1967).

Constitution making connected the territories to their past constitutional developments and those of their neighbours. Bermuda's 1968 Constitution, for example, was modelled on the 1963 self-government Constitution of the Bahamas. While there are differences between the products of constitution-making processes for self-governing and newly independent Caribbean jurisdictions between the 1960s and the early 1980s, the constitutional texts emerged as related instruments, including carrying common 'genetic defects',[72] like the codification of gender inequality in the chapters dealing with citizenship and fundamental rights in the Bahamas Constitution. Both are chapters which are subject to the highest level of constitutional entrenchment – namely, amendment can occur only following a referendum.[73] The Bahamas Constitution established married men as the preeminent citizens, and secondary rights to citizenship for women.[74] Bahamian women face restrictions in passing on Bahamian nationality to their children born outside the country and to their non-Bahamian husbands.[75] In addition, 'sex' is not included as a prohibited ground of discrimination in the Constitution's anti-discrimination provision.[76] These were defects of the Jamaica Constitution 1962, reproduced in the Bahamas Constitutions of 1963, 1969 and 1973. Since the Bermuda Constitution 1968 was modelled on the 1963 Bahamas Constitution, it also replicated the limited anti-discrimination provision.[77]

The defects in these early constitutions were substantive and procedural. There was little public participation in their finalisation; their negotiations were mostly confidential and the reports on the constitutional conferences prepared by the UK Government were sanitised and thin. As a result, there has been sustained criticism of constitution making during this period as elitist and producing texts that are not 'our own'.[78] To be 'our own', the constitution must also be *distinguishably* ours. The expansion of sovereignty and acknowledgment of self-determination embodied in these independence constitutions were undermined by the pronouncement by the Privy Council that they were 'Westminster modelled' and 'evolutionary not revolutionary', with similar styles of drafting.[79]

Accordingly, these early constitutions took on a prototypical cast, as planned, conventional outputs of cooperative imperial constitution making for small places, and as common law constitutions with thin distinctiveness. As Se-shauna Wheatle notes, the methodological practices of common law constitutionalism travel well and can neutralise claims of distinct national and constitutional identity.[80] The outsider constitutional

[72] L Henkin, 'A New Birth of Constitutionalism: Genetic Influences and Genetic Defects' (1992) 14 *Cardozo Law Review* 533, 534.

[73] Bahamas Constitution (1973), art 54.

[74] T Robinson, 'Gender, Feminism and Constitutional Reform in the Caribbean' in B Bailey and E Leo-Rhynie (eds), *Gender in the 21st Century: Caribbean Perspectives, Visions and Possibilities* (Kingston, Ian Randle Publishers, 2004) 592, 601.

[75] Bahamas Constitution (1973), arts 8, 9, 10.

[76] ibid, art 26.

[77] Bermuda Constitution (1968), s 12.

[78] See S McIntosh, *Caribbean Constitutional Reform: Rethinking the West Indian Polity* (Kingston, Caribbean Law Publishing, 2002) 42.

[79] *Hinds v R* [1977] AC 195 (PC Jamaica) 212.

[80] S Wheatle, 'Common Law Constitutionalism Through Methodology' (2019) 65 *McGill Law Journal* 341, 343.

interpretation by the Privy Council has shaped Caribbean constitutional identities and, conversely, as seen in *Attorney-General v Rolle*,[81] assumptions about constitutional identity influence interpretation.[82] The five applicants in that case were born in the Bahamas to unmarried Haitian and Jamaican nationals, two of the largest immigrant groups in the Bahamas, and asserted that they had Bahamian fathers. Article 6 of Bahamas Constitution grants *ius soli* citizenship acquisition automatically at birth if one of the 'parents' is a Bahamian citizen. The question before the Privy Council was whether 'parents' included the father of a child born outside a marriage. Article 14(1) of the Constitution incorporates the patriarchal common law doctrine of *filius nullius*. It provides that any reference in the citizenship chapter to 'the father of a person shall, in relation to any person born out of wedlock … be construed as a reference to the mother of that person'.[83] A similar provision is found in all six Caribbean independence constitutions made between 1962 and 1973.[84]

In *Rolle*, the Privy Council resolved the interpretation question about qualification for birthright citizenship 'entirely [using] conventional principles of statutory interpretation'.[85] The Privy Council looked at the 'natural meaning' of Article 6 and utilised the statutory presumption that where different words are used, – 'parent' in Article 6 and 'father' in Article 14 – they carry different meanings, and the restrictive definition of 'father' was not intended to apply beyond instances where the citizenship chapter referred to 'fathers'.[86] The Privy Council acknowledged that the issue before it was 'a matter of considerable sensitivity and controversy in The Bahamas'.[87] The Bahamas Constitutional Commission described citizenship, in which thorny migration issues are implicated, as the 'most singularly difficult subject the Commission had to consider'.[88] In 2002 and 2016, proposals to amend the discriminatory provisions in the Bahamas Constitution failed at constitutionally required referenda. Yet in *Rolle*, the Privy Council concluded that there was no need to address the submissions on appropriate principles of *constitutional* interpretation. The contested moral issues about citizenship, migration, gender and the Bahamas Constitution that undergirded the case were flattened, as the 1973 Constitution featured as a prototypical legal instrument which could be made sense of using conventional rules of statutory interpretation.

IV. Collaboration, Consensus and Constitutional Sex

The twenty-first century framing of constitutional reform in overseas territories as a 'modern [colonial] relationship' based on a 'partnership' between the UK and

[81] *Attorney-General v Rolle* [2023] UKPC 13, [2023] 5 LRC 439 (PC Bahamas) (*Rolle*).
[82] M Rosenfeld, 'Constitutional Identity' in M Rosenfeld and A Sajó (eds), *The Oxford Handbook of Comparative Constitutional Law* (Oxford, Oxford University Press, 2012) 756, 771.
[83] Bahamas Constitution (1973), s 14.
[84] *Attorney-General v Rolle* (SC Bahamas, 3 December 2019) [30] (Winder J).
[85] *Rolle* (n 81) [52].
[86] ibid [33], [46].
[87] ibid [19].
[88] Constitutional Commission, *Report of the Constitutional Commission into a Review of the Bahamas Constitution* (Government of The Bahamas, 2013) 22.

territories[89] offered a revision of the terms of collaborative constitution making, giving territories like the Cayman Islands more negotiating power in the process than was enjoyed by their predecessors in the independence movement decades earlier.[90] The Cayman Islands delegation comprised Government and Opposition politicians, and representatives from the churches, Chamber of Commerce and the Cayman Islands Human Rights Committee. Unlike the earlier single constitutional conferences, there were three negotiating rounds between the UK and Cayman Islands, and these were held in both London and the Cayman Islands in 2008 and 2009.[91] Generally, the results generated more autonomy for overseas territories, but within a more defined human rights and rule-of-law framework.[92]

Same-sex marriage emerged as the most controversial issue in debates about the human rights provisions in modernised constitutions in Caribbean overseas territories,[93] and has featured prominently in constitutional reform processes in the independent states.[94] The disputes about same-sex marriage are foregrounded by protracted debates about the criminalisation of consensual same-sex sex in the Anglo Caribbean.[95] Decriminalisation of consensual same-sex sex between adults in 2000 in five Caribbean BOTs by UK Order in Council represented emasculating imperial intervention for those overseas territories. In his ethnographic research in Barbados, David Murray observed that many Barbadians represented their small state as 'feminized, submissive and subordinated' and under threat of violation and penetration by the global economy and the sexual values of the Global North.[96]

Jack Corbett and Wouter Veenendaal argue that the way elites frame external threats is critical because smallness contributes to 'a powerful sensitivity to external threats'; they warn that the elites can mobilise and exploit these threats in electoral processes.[97] Christian leaders have become influential elites who duel over religious freedom and identity in constitutional processes in the Anglophone Caribbean, strongly opposing

[89] *Partnership for Progress and Prosperity* (n 62) 7.

[90] Vlcek (n 48) 361.

[91] Constitutional Commission Cayman Islands, *Promotion of Public Understanding and Awareness of the Constitution and Its Values: Providing Advice on Constitutional Status and Development*, www.constitutionalcommission.ky/upimages/commonfiles/CCInfoBrochure_updated17122_1642798579.pdf.

[92] J Connell and R Aldrich, *The Ends of Empire: The Last Colonies Revisited* (Singapore, Palgrave Macmillan, 2020) 66.

[93] Hendry and Dickson (n 43) 166. See British Virgin Islands Constitution (2007), s 20(1); Montserrat Constitution (2010), s 10(1); The Cayman Islands Constitution (2009), s 10(4).

[94] D O'Brien and S Wheatle, 'Post-independence Constitutional Reform in the Commonwealth Caribbean and a New Charter of Fundamental Rights and Freedoms for Jamaica (2012) *Public Law* 683, 697; W Grenade, 'Direct Democracy and Party Politics in the Commonwealth Caribbean: An Analysis of the 2016 Referendum on Constitutional Reform in Grenada' (2020) 58 *Commonwealth & Comparative Politics* 1, 11–12.

[95] See L Lazarus, 'Heteronationalism, Human Rights, and the Nation-State: Positioning Sexuality in the Jamaican Constitutional Reform Process' (2011) 36 *Canadian Journal of Latin American and Caribbean Studies* 71; J Gaskins, '"Buggery" and the Commonwealth Caribbean: A Comparative Examination of the Bahamas, Jamaica, and Trinidad and Tobago' in C Lennox and M Waites (eds), *Human Rights, Sexual Orientation and Gender Identity in The Commonwealth* (London, University of London Press, 2013) 429; A Novak, *Transnational Human Rights Litigation: Challenging the Death Penalty and Criminalization of Homosexuality in the Commonwealth* (Cham, Springer, 2020).

[96] D Murray, *Flaming Souls: Homosexuality, Homophobia, and Social Change in Barbados* (Toronto, University of Toronto Press, 2012) 19–20.

[97] J Corbett and W Veenendaal, *Democracy in Small States: Persisting Against All Odds* (Oxford, Oxford University Press, 2018) 122.

queer Caribbean subjectivities. There has been a rise of what Latoya Lazarus terms 'church law', which is a system of norms, influence and power 'operating in conjunction with and influencing the formal legal system', and which defines the nation-body-state as fundamentally Christian.[98] The cross-border influence of the US evangelic movement in the Caribbean has encouraged the growth of church law.[99] The 'nonnegotiable' positions of Christian groups in the Caymanian negotiations, supporting a 'traditional ideal of marriage and the family' and the preservation of Caymanian values, were decisive in shaping the final position of the Caymanian delegation presented to the UK Government.[100]

In the referendum on the draft Cayman Islands Constitution, held in May 2009, 73 per cent of eligible voters participated and 62.7 per cent of those voting said yes to the new Constitution.[101] The democratically approved Constitution, which was introduced by a UK Order in Council, begins by speaking about the territory's 'distinct history, culture and Christian heritage' and its Bill of Rights, Freedoms and Responsibilities 'recognises the distinct history, culture, Christian values and socio-economic framework of the Cayman Islands'.[102] The marriage rights provision, section 14, provides that the 'Government shall respect the right of every unmarried man and woman of marriageable age (as determined by law) freely to marry a person *of the opposite sex* and found a family' (emphasis added).[103]

The referendum, an emblem of participatory constitutional change, did decisive boundary-work in the Cayman Islands constitution-making process. Members of the negotiating team for the Cayman Islands successfully deployed the islands' 'national' identity as a 'strategic resource' both in negotiations between themselves and with the UK.[104] The referendum anchored aversive constitution making, or what Kim Lane Scheppele describes as 'a nation-making sense of rejection of a particular constitutional possibility' (emphasis removed).[105] Civil unions had been permitted in the UK since 2004, but same-sex marriage was legalised only in 2013, years after the conclusion of the Cayman Islands Constitution 2009.[106] Nevertheless, many Caymanians

[98] L Lazarus, 'This is a Christian Nation: Gender and Sexuality in Processes of Constitutional and Legal Reform in Jamaica' (2012) 61 *Social and Economic Studies* 117. See also A Johns, 'Public Morals Versus Private Rights: Examining the Influence of Christian Norms and Institutions on the Development of LGBT Rights in Jamaica' (2020) 58 *Commonwealth & Comparative Politics* 387.

[99] See M Jackman, '*Living in Sodom's Shadow:* Essays on attitudes towards gay men and lesbians in the Commonwealth Caribbean' (PhD thesis, University of Manchester, 2016) 63.

[100] Pastor Al Ebanks, quoted in 'Formal Negotiations on a New Cayman Islands Constitution: Second Round between the Cayman Islands Delegation and the United Kingdom Delegation, Tuesday, 13 January – Friday, 16 January 2009, Grand Cayman', p 13, www.constitutionalcommission.ky/upimages/educationdoc/SecondRound-13-6anuary009_1490094518_14900945231_1606146274_1606146275.pdf.

[101] Government of the Cayman Islands, 'Report of the Supervisor of Elections: Referendum 2009', portal.elections.ky/files/downloads/ge2009/COUNT_for_Referendum_Command_Centre_2009.pdf.

[102] Cayman Islands Constitution (2009), preamble, s 1(2).

[103] ibid s 14.

[104] P Bárd, N Chronowski and Z Fleck, 'Use, Misuse and Abuse of Constitutional Identity in Europe' in M Tushnet and D Kochenov (eds), *Research Handbook on the Politics of Constitutional Law* (Cheltenham, Edward Elgar Publishing, 2023) 611, 612, 628.

[105] K Lane Scheppele, 'Aspirational and Aversive Constitutionalism: The Case for Studying Cross-Constitutional Influence through Negative Models' (2003) 1 *International Journal of Constitutional Law* 296, 300.

[106] Civil Partnership Act 2004, c 33; Marriage (Same-sex Couples) Act 2013, c 30 (UK).

took note of the trend in Western Europe toward same-sex marriage, and the UK's insistence that the ECHR should be a floor for Caribbean constitutional reforms. The referendum was constitutional and political fortification against the possibility of the UK using the 'nuclear option' of an Order in Council in the future to legislate for same-sex marriage.[107] This form of aversive constitution making is used to anticipate future threats to Caribbean jurisdictions that highlight their smallness as a form of endemic vulnerability.[108] The referendum also served to delimit and empower those deemed to be a part of the 'legitimate' political community in the Cayman Islands. Just 59 per cent of the resident population in 2009 was Caymanian, the basis for eligibility to vote.[109] There were many non-Caymanians living and working in the islands who could not participate in the referendum. Thus, the referendum constructed this group of non-Caymanian residents, who appeared to have more liberal views on the rights of LGBTQ+ persons, as an outgroup.[110]

Consensus and cooperation in the constitution making heightened the legitimacy of the Cayman Islands Constitution. In *Day v Governor of the Cayman Islands*[111] the Privy Council gave special regard to the adoption of the Constitution 'pursuant to a process involving a vote by the public',[112] and described that Constitution as 'a self-contained legal instrument drafted in terms specifically chosen as appropriate for the Cayman Islands'.[113] In comparison to the Bahamas Constitution, the Caymans Islands Constitution in *Day* was regarded as value-laden, and ordinary legal rules were important but under-determinative of the outcome the case.[114] Unlike *Rolle*, the Privy Council in *Day* gave strong consideration to the 'principles of construction applicable in relation to the Constitution and the Bill of Rights' in deciding whether that Constitution guaranteed a right to same-sex marriage.[115] It held that section 14 was a *lex specialis* in relation to the right to marry. The Board said that invoking a generous approach to constitutional rights and the living tree principle were misplaced because the Constitution clearly wished to provide constitutional protection for different sex marriage only, and this was confirmed by its repeated references to the cultural and religious values of the islands.[116]

The 2009 Constitution is the only Anglo Caribbean constitution that has successfully been put to a referendum vote. Constitutionally required referenda in Anglo Caribbean states have consistently failed in ushering constitutional changes.[117] The 2016 proposed Bahamian constitutional reforms promoting gender equality were a symbol of

[107] Vlcek (n 48) 355.

[108] See M Mos, 'The Anticipatory Politics of Homophobia: Explaining Constitutional Bans on Same-Sex Marriage in Post-Communist Europe' (2020) 36 *East European Politics* 395.

[109] Economic and Statistical Office, *Statistical Compendium 2009: Population and Vital Statistics* (Government of the Cayman Islands) 109.

[110] Vlcek (n 48) 364.

[111] *Day v Governor of the Cayman Islands* [2022] UKPC 6, [2022] 3 LRC 557 (PC Cayman Islands) (*Day*).

[112] ibid [57].

[113] ibid [44].

[114] T Gyofry, 'The Politics of Constitutional Interpretation' in M Tushnet and D Kochenov, (eds), *Research Handbook on the Politics of Constitutional Law* (Cheltenham, Edward Elgar Publishing, 2023) 199, 199–200.

[115] ibid [33].

[116] Cayman Islands Constitution (2009), preamble, s 1(2).

[117] C Barrow-Giles and RRF Yearwood, 'Mandatory Constitutional Referendums in Commonwealth Caribbean Constitutions: Placing 'People' at the Centre of the Constitution?' (2023) 34 *King's Law Journal* 215.

postcolonial progress that came into conflict with the heteropatriarchal underpinnings of the small state, and generated dissensus. Many Bahamians feared that the proposed prohibition of sex discrimination in the Bahamas Constitution 'would open the door for constitutional interpretations to embrace other collateral rights' – particularly a right to same-sex marriage.[118] The referendum question recommended that the Constitution define 'sex' in limited binary terms as 'being male or female', to ward off concerns about the expansion of rights for LGBTQ+ persons. The Constitution would also retain an exception to the application of the anti-discrimination clause for laws with respect to marriage.[119] With a strong 'Save the Bahamas' campaign mounted by religious leaders and activists, Bahamians said no to all the gender-related constitutional reforms, with the change to the anti-discrimination provision garnering the least support.[120]

The recent Privy Council cases have sharpened the value associated with consensus and political compromise in deciphering constitutional meaning in the Anglo Caribbean and as markers of collective self-determination and self-definition. Fifty years after the introduction of the Bermuda Constitution, the 2018 Bermuda Domestic Partnership Act (DPA) made provision for *domestic partnerships* entered into by any two persons, but limited *marriage* to heterosexual unions. The enactment of the law followed a 2016 referendum on same-sex marriage with a strong no vote, but which lacked validity because of the low voter turnout. Soon after, the Bermuda Supreme Court held that a restrictive definition of marriage violated the Bermuda Human Rights Act 1981, which guarantees a right to non-discrimination on the basis of sexual orientation and provides for judicial review of legislation.[121] Recognition of same-sex relationships formed part of the election manifesto of the political party that gained power in 2017, and it introduced the DPA 2018 as a political compromise between non-recognition and a right to same-sex marriage. The supervisory Human Rights Act did not apply to the limits placed on marriage in the DPA.[122] In *Attorney-General v Ferguson*,[123] a majority of the Privy Council upheld the constitutionality of the DPA 2018, which it described as fulfilling an electoral promise and bringing about 'a democratic solution to a divisive debate … and [doing] so in a way which accommodated the position of both sides to the debate'.[124]

Referenda results can give rise to very different interpretations in the context of the Caribbean's dyadic constitutions. In the 2016 Bahamas referendum, 66 per cent of voters said no to a constitutional amendment that would have settled the constitutional equality between men and women in passing on citizenship to children born in the Bahamas, the subject of the *Rolle* litigation brought a year later. This outcome may have signalled that the people of the Bahamas *did not* support non-discriminatory citizenship provisions. In *Rolle*, the referendum outcome was not particularly relevant to the Privy Council's interpretation of Article 6 of the Bahamas Constitution, which coincided with the failed 'yes' option. Referenda may be decisive acts of self-determination, as in the

[118] *Report of the Bahamas Constitutional Commission* (n 88) 113.
[119] Bahamas Constitution (1973), art 26(4)(c).
[120] International Foundation for Electoral Systems, 'Election Guide: Commonwealth of the Bahamas Referendum, June 7, 2016' (IFES), www.electionguide.org/elections/id/2970/.
[121] Human Rights Act 1981 ss 2, 29 (Bermuda).
[122] Domestic Partnerships Act 2018, s 53 (Bermuda).
[123] *Attorney-General v Ferguson* [2022] UKPC 5, [2022] 3 LRC 579 (PC Bermuda) (*Ferguson*).
[124] ibid [56], [58].

Cayman Islands, or neutralised democratic stalemates on matters of 'considerable sensitivity', as seen in the Bahamas.[125] Worse still, they may be regarded as evidence of political immaturity and 'backward peoples'.[126] The last is particularly salient in the independent Caribbean states, where constitutionally required referenda – a form of entrenchment negotiated during decolonisation – have become 'constitutional handcuffs'[127] in ongoing constitutional reforms.

V. Constitutional Convergence, the JCPC and the ECHR

The rich scholarship on constitutional convergence and foreign and international sources of constitutional law tends to assume a state that can make the choice to use exogenous sources of law 'even though … not legally compelled to do so'.[128] Less attention has been given to constitutional borrowing in small states and small non-sovereign subnational jurisdictions where sovereignty is constrained by outsider judicial constitutional interpretation, which has been an incubator for constitutional convergence. The JCPC assumed new significance by the end of the twentieth century as a powerful supranational constitutional court for the small emerging decolonised and self-governing jurisdictions in the Caribbean. Comparisons between the constitutions of polities that are or were within the jurisdiction of the JCPC, deploying its own decisions as binding precedents across multiple jurisdictions, became a conventional route through which the Court expanded its authority and legitimacy.[129] Additionally, the application of international law across several jurisdictions operates as a form of extra-constitutional and supranational regulation that is within the control of the extraterritorial Court, as it is the JCPC that decides which sources of international law count, in what way and when. In general, the JCPC has been described as a 'strong selling point' for affluent Caribbean countries.[130] It held its first sitting outside London in the Bahamas in 2006 and made its fourth visit in 2017 at the invitation of the state. The Cayman Islands is also one of three countries in which it has conducted working visits.

The chapter dealing with fundamental rights and freedoms in the Constitutions of the Bahamas and Bermuda, and most independent Caribbean states, is a variant of that drafted by the British Colonial Office for the Nigeria Constitution 1960,

[125] *Rolle* (n 81) [19].

[126] A Wallace, 'Policymaking in a "Christian Nation": Women's and LGBT+ Rights in The Bahamas' 2016 Referendum' (2017) 25 *Gender & Development* 69, 79, quoting former Governor-General, Sir Arthur Foulkes.

[127] R Albert, 'Constitutional Handcuffs' (2017) 3 *Intergenerational Justice Review* 18; Barrow-Giles and Yearwood (n 117).

[128] S Choudhry, 'Globalization in Search of Justification: Towards a Theory of Comparative Constitutional Interpretation' (1999) 74 *Indiana Law Journal* 819, 831 fn 21.

[129] See T Robinson and A Bulkan, 'Constitutional Comparisons by A Supranational Court in Flux: The Privy Council and Caribbean Bills of Rights' (2017) 80 *Modern Law Review* 379, 383.

[130] 'The Judicial Committee of the Privy Council: A Strong Selling Point for Bermuda, the British Virgin Islands and the Cayman Islands' (*Conyers*, September 2022), www.conyers.com/publications/view/the-judicial-committee-of-the-privy-council/. See also S Voigt, M Ebeling and L Blume, 'Improving Credibility by Delegating Judicial Competence: The Case of the Judicial Committee of the Privy Council' (2007) 82 *Journal of Development Economics* 348.

influenced by the ECHR. The drafters in the Colonial Office of the Nigeria bill of rights were unfamiliar with drafting constitutional bills of rights and used the ECHR as 'a practical template'.[131] The distinctive shape of the 1960 bill of rights – of a wide-ranging opening section describing rights, followed by about a dozen detailed provisions with ponderous exceptions to the rights – flowed from imperial sentiment that the habits of constitutionalism were not well established in Africa and that judicial review would be less effective if rights were framed in very general terms like the ECHR.[132] It was the lumbering 'neo-Nigerian bill of rights', as SA de Smith termed it, that was repeatedly exported throughout the British empire during decolonisation in the second half of the twentieth century, including to the Bahamas and Bermuda.[133] The position of the ECHR in the Cayman Islands Constitution was different. It was drafted in the wake of the UK's policy that its territories should comply with the same international obligations to which Britain was subject, highlighting just two instances of the UK's international human rights obligations, the ECHR and the International Covenant on Civil and Political Rights (ICCPR).[134]

The majority in *Ferguson* gave two reasons why the ECHR was relevant to the interpretation of the Bermuda Constitution 1968. First, because it was 'binding on the UK in relation to Bermuda on the international plane', and secondly, that it inspired provisions in the Constitution.[135] The majority added that it was 'the policy of the UK to negotiate with representatives of each country for rights which corresponded with Convention rights', and that it was '[m]anifestly … the intention of the Constitution' to make Strasbourg jurisprudence 'particularly relevant' in interpreting constitutional rights 'that could be traced back to the Convention'.[136] This reasoning has also been offered by the JCPC in constitutional cases from independent Caribbean states. Since 2000, the JCPC has consistently attributed the relevance of Strasbourg jurisprudence in interpreting these Constitutions to the application of the Convention to the state *before* it became independent, and to the ECHR being an antecedent of their constitutional bills of rights.[137] The implication that the application of the ECHR to colonial Caribbean jurisdictions, without any incorporation in domestic law, has embedded norms in their postcolonial legal regimes is not credible;[138] that is, except within the frame of dyadic Caribbean constitutionalism which achieves imperial oversight through multiple routes, including the supervisory constitutional court jurisdiction of the Privy Council. By the 2000s, the metropole's treaty obligations under the ECHR, through sleight of interpretation, were presumed to have bled into postcolonial Caribbean common law constitutions.

[131] Parkinson (n 53) 269.
[132] SA de Smith, *The New Commonwealth and its Constitutions* (London, Stevens & Sons, 1964) 210.
[133] ibid 193.
[134] *Partnership for Progress and Prosperity* (n 62) 20.
[135] *Ferguson* (n 123) [15].
[136] ibid [14], [16].
[137] See, eg *Reyes v R* [2002] UKPC 13, [2002] 2 AC 235 (PC Belize) [24]; *Grant v R* [2006] UKPC 2, [2007] 1 AC 1 (PC Jamaica) [20].
[138] D Berry, 'The Use of International Law by Domestic Tribunals in the Caribbean in Death Penalty Cases' in D Berry and T Robinson (eds), *Transitions in Caribbean Law: Law-making, Constitutionalism and the Convergence of National and International Law* (Kingston, Caribbean Law Publishing, 2013) 103, 114.

Charles Parkinson has noted that the argument that the ECHR was 'a valued instrument whereby the civilizing mission of British colonization could be perpetuated in the post-colonial world',[139] was amplified *after* the British legal community began to regard the European Convention as a seminal constitutional development in the UK, a shift reflected in the enactment of the Human Rights Act 1998.[140] As already noted, the early Caribbean constitutional bills of rights most closely resemble their African constitutional counterparts of the 1960s, and Parkinson has established that the drafters of the 1960 Nigeria Constitution did not use the ECHR with the intention of extending its operation after independence, but rather relied on it as a practical guide.[141] It is important to take into account not only changing British regard for the ECHR, but greater British ease in its interpretation, as the judges of the UK Supreme Court, who also sit on the Privy Council, grew accustomed to interpreting the Convention as part of UK law. It is also possible that reliance on the well-known ECHR and its jurisprudence in colonial contexts may reduce the outlay of imperial judicial administration across multiple jurisdictions, and function as a 'shorthand' that reduces 'how much of certain kinds of information one needed to operate'.[142]

The extension of the ECHR to the Caribbean as a supranational layer of regulation energised the dyadic constitution in the overseas territories in a less anticipated way. As an agreement between states, the Convention generated a form of *equivalence to* or *recognition as a state* for the Caribbean's non-sovereign territories. Although several Western European states have moved towards marriage equality, Europe is divided on this and other sexual rights issues.[143] To date, the European Court of Human Rights (ECtHR) has given a wide margin of appreciation to European states in respecting the Convention right of LGBTQ+ persons to a private and family life.[144] It has insisted that civil unions with similar rights and responsibilities to marriage must be available to all. However, given the lack of European consensus on marriage equality, the ECtHR has respected the sovereignty of Member States to regulate marriage according to notions of the traditional family.[145]

Bermuda and the Cayman Islands hedged against the uncertainty of the ECHR's future interpretation of sexual rights with aversive lawmaking and constitution making, and they mined the margin of appreciation as an opportunity to exercise 'sovereign' national decision-making like a Member State. Bermuda's compromise Domestic Partnership Act 2018, recognising civil partnerships and excluding same-sex marriage, fit within acceptable regulation under the ECHR at that date, and locked

[139] AW Brian Simpson, *Human Rights and the End of Empire: Britain and the Genesis of the European Convention* (Oxford, Oxford University Press, 2001) 873.

[140] Human Rights Act 1998 c 42 (UK). Parkinson (n 53) 10–11.

[141] Parkinson (n 53) 269.

[142] AL Stoler, *Carnal Knowledge and Imperial Power: Race and the Intimate in Colonial Rule* (Berkeley CA, University of California Press, 2002) 207.

[143] A Tryfonidou, 'The Politics of Sexual Identity and the Emerging Constitutional Battles in Europe' in M Tushnet and D Kochenov (eds), *Research Handbook on the Politics of Constitutional Law* (Cheltenham, Edward Elgar Publishing, 2023) 532, 547.

[144] Convention for the Protection of Human Rights and Fundamental Freedoms (European Convention on Human Rights, as amended) (ECHR) art 8.

[145] *Schalk v Austria* App no 30141/04 (ECtHR, 24 June 2010).

in the conservative approach of the ECtHR in its seminal 2010 decision in *Schalk v Austria*.[146] The Cayman Islands Constitution 2009 was negotiated before *Schalk* and the UK's recognition of same-sex marriage in 2013. Section 14 of the Constitution hedged against the uncertainty of future interpretations of the Convention by replicating the ECHR's Article 12 right to marry – '*men and women* of marriageable age have the right to marry and to found a family' (emphasis added) – with plainer heterosexual emphasis. The 2009 Constitution speaks of right of 'every unmarried man and woman', in the singular, and sharpens its meaning by adding, 'to marry a person of the *opposite sex*' (emphasis added).[147]

Deference to the decisions of overseas territories on same-sex marriage also kept at bay more liberal approaches adopted in foreign and international law jurisprudence by non-European courts and tribunals.[148] The majority in *Ferguson* said the texts considered in those cases were not analogous to the Bermuda Constitution or, if in the form of a treaty, did not bind the UK or the territory. The Privy Council added that there was 'no international consensus on the way in which committed same-sex relationships should be recognised in law'.[149] The UK's departure from the EU has not affected its obligations under the ECHR, and it is not yet clear whether the regard for the Strasbourg jurisprudence in the UK courts will evolve post Brexit. It if does, those currents are likely to affect the interpretation of Caribbean constitutions by the JCPC.

VI. Conclusion

It is customary to perceive the Anglo Caribbean's constitutional terrain as marked by imperial debris.[150] The dyadic Caribbean constitution, however, is oriented less toward the notion of an *aftermath* of colonialism and what is left behind, than it is toward reflecting on the imperial constitutional *present* in small Anglo Caribbean jurisdictions. By design, imperial constitutional regulation of small Caribbean states persisted after dates of independence. That regulation has become locked in by the prototypical products of asymmetrical cooperative constitution making between the metropole and the colonised in the second half of the twentieth century. *Men were made*, but subject to imperial supervision. The more 'modern relationship' between the UK and its overseas territories in the twenty-first century retains imperial oversight. However, it has redefined collaborative constitution making in the Caribbean and the role of consensus, and, consequently, sharpened the self-determination and political identity of territories

[146] ibid.

[147] Cayman Islands Constitution (2009), s 14.

[148] See, eg Gender Identity and Equality and Non-discrimination of Same-Sex Couples (IACtHR Advisory Opinion OC-24/17) (24 November 2019).

[149] *Ferguson* (n 123) [93]. See D O'Brien, 'The Judicial Committee of the Privy Council, Constitutional Interpretation, and the Right to Same-Sex Marriage' (2023) 21 *International Journal of Constitutional Law* 1140.

[150] See Cross (n 32).

like Bermuda and the Cayman Islands. That gendered and sexed bodies are the 'site of performances of sovereign power'[151] and constitutional contestations around the dyadic constitution in shared Caribbean and British constitutional spaces offers a sober reflection on the schema of modern constitutionalism. In small states, and beyond, the modern constitution is 'simultaneously politically essential and politically regressive'[152] and is sustained through the abjection of others.[153]

[151] T Blom Hansen and F Stepputat, 'Sovereignty Revisited' (2006) 35 *Annual Review of Anthropology* 295, 297.
[152] W Brown 'Suffering Rights as Paradoxes' (2000) 7 *Constellations* 230, 239.
[153] R Rao, 'Queer Questions' (2014) 16 *International Feminist Journal of Politics* 199, 213.

3

Spectrums of 'Stateness'

Constitutional Relations Among the Constituent Countries of the Kingdom of the Netherlands

MAARTJE DE VISSER AND ELISABETH PERHAM

I. Introduction

The title of this volume is 'small *state* constitutionalism' but, as is known to scholars of comparative constitutional law, many political units that are not formally independent states also have their own constitutions, as well as being in constitutional relationships with other political units including formally independent states. Going one level down from the state, one well-known example is the constitutions and constitutional relations of States in a federal unit, on which there already exists a reasonably large literature addressing what is often discussed as subnational constitutionalism, or federal constitutionalism.[1] And going one level up from the state, another well-known and oft-discussed example is supranational constitutionalism, particularly in the context of the constitutional order of the European Union.[2]

However, less well-known, and certainly less discussed in the realm of comparative constitutional studies, are the constitutional arrangements of numerous small countries and territories with varying levels of autonomy but with some constitutional ties with larger (and often unitary) states. Political scientists have given such countries

[1] See eg, P Popelier, G Delledonne and N Aroney (eds), *Routledge Handbook of Subnational Constitutions and Constitutionalism* (London, Routledge, 2021); J Marshfield, 'Models of Subnational Constitutionalism' (2011) 115 *Penn State Law Review* 1151.

[2] See eg, the titles of leading textbooks, such as K Lenaerts and P van Nuffel, *EU Constitutional Law* (Oxford, Oxford University Press, 2021) or A Rosas and L Armati, *EU Constitutional Law – An Introduction* (Oxford, Hart Publishing, 2018) or of one of the leading European law journals: the European Constitutional Law Review, as well as A Stone Sweet, 'Constructing a Supranational Constitution' in A Stone Sweet, *Governing with Judges: Constitutional Politics in Europe* (Oxford, Oxford University Press, 2000); E de Wet, 'The International Constitutional Order' (2006) 55 *International and Comparative Law Quarterly* 51.

and territories a range of labels – including partially independent territories,[3] non-sovereign island territories,[4] and subnational island jurisdictions[5] – and categorised them according to a range of criteria. Taking Ferdinand et al as an example, there are 55 such jurisdictions.[6] As is evident from the labels just mentioned, most of these jurisdictions are insular (ie, they are islands or archipelagos).[7] Additionally, most have small populations,[8] making them relevant to this collection focused on the constitutional arrangements of political entities with populations under 1.5 million people. Examples include the constituent countries in the Kingdom of the Netherlands located in the Caribbean (on which this chapter focuses), as well as countries and territories within the Realm of New Zealand,[9] the Danish Realm,[10] overseas France,[11] the UK overseas territories,[12] and the US insular territories.[13] Going up a level, legal scholars have perhaps primarily paid attention to these in a comparative sense as international law arrangements – most of these jurisdictions have constitutional ties with a large independent state as a result of colonisation, and international law scholars have therefore been interested in asking questions such as what their international legal status *is* (including what is the line between formal statehood vs some other status),[14] and whether and how their international legal status meets the requirements of the United Nations (UN) Charter and the UN General Assembly's various resolutions on decolonisation and self-determination.[15] And, going down a level, where constitutional law scholars have paid attention to these jurisdictions, they have focused on them in a non-comparative sense as domestic constitutional law arrangements, although, as will be discussed in

[3] See eg, D Rezvani, *Surpassing the Sovereign State: The Wealth, Self-Determination, and Security Advantages of Partially Independent Territories* (Oxford, Oxford University Press, 2014).

[4] eg, M Ferdinand, G Oostindie and W Veenendaal, 'A Global Comparison of Non-Sovereign Island Territories: The Search for "True Equality"' (2020) 15 *Island Studies Journal* 43.

[5] See eg, G Baldacchino and D Milne (eds), *The Case for Non-Sovereignty: Lessons from Sub-National Island Jurisdictions* (London, Routledge, 2009).

[6] Ferdinand, Oostindie and Veenendaal (n 4) 50.

[7] ibid 46.

[8] ibid 50. Of their list, only two have populations of more than half a million people: Puerto Rico and La Réunion.

[9] See further, eg, A Quentin-Baxter, 'The Cook Islands, Niue and Tokelau as Parts of the Realm of New Zealand' (2021) 52 *Victoria University of Wellington Law Review* 579; ER Perham, 'Citizenship Laws in the Realm of New Zealand' (2011) 9 *New Zealand Yearbook of International Law* 219; as well as Tony Angelo and Jennifer Corrin's 'Niue: The Constitutional Journey', Chapter 14 in this volume.

[10] See eg, UP Gad, 'Greenland, the Faroe Islands, and Denmark: Unity or Community?' in P Munk Christiansen, J Elklit and P Nedergaard (eds), *The Oxford Handbook of Danish Politics* (Oxford, Oxford University Press, 2020).

[11] See the discussion in Hervé Raimana Lallemant-Moe's 'Potential future small States: the case of New Caledonia and French Polynesia', Chapter 4 in this volume.

[12] See some discussion in Tracy Robinson's 'Dyadic Caribbean Constitutions', Chapter 2 in this volume on the English-speaking Caribbean.

[13] See eg, GL Neuman and T Brown-Nagin, *Reconsidering the Insular Cases: The Past and Future of the American Empire* (Cambridge MA, Harvard University Press, 2015).

[14] See eg, generally on statehood, J Crawford, *The Creation of States in International Law*, 2nd edn (Oxford, Oxford University Press, 2007); and more specifically on the status of the Cook Islands and Puerto Rico vs Tuvalu: A Green and D Guilfoyle, 'The Australia-Tuvalu Falepili Union Treaty: Statehood and Security in the Face of Anthropogenic Climate Change' (2024) 118 *American Journal of International Law* 684, 698–702.

[15] See eg, S Hillebrink, *The Right to Self-Determination and Post-Colonial Governance: The Case of the Netherland Antilles and Aruba* (The Hague, TMC Asser Press, 2008).

section II, these jurisdictions very often slip from the gaze of even the domestic constitutional law scholars in the relevant parts of the world.

Our basic argument in this chapter is that comparative constitutional law scholars need to extend their gaze both up and down. In section II of this chapter, we briefly interrogate the idea of 'stateness' to explain why we think comparative constitutional lawyers need to look beyond the state when thinking about constitutional arrangements – noting that these lawyers have often paid limited attention to what are often treated as international law arrangements between larger and smaller political entities, despite the fact that they often are – whether in form or just in function – primarily constitutional arrangements. We then turn in section III to explore the constitutional arrangements in the Kingdom of the Netherlands, in order to illustrate some of what we can see if we extend our gaze both up and down. In section IV, we conclude, briefly highlighting some of the questions that this shifting of our gaze to often neglected arrangements throws up.

II. On Smallness and Stateness

As outlined in the Introduction to this book, in determining its scope, there was a need to draw lines somewhere. One line that was drawn was what political units we would define as *small* for the purposes of inclusion – and the widely-used (though also criticised) choice of political units with a population of fewer than 1.5 million people was chosen as a bright line. But we did not draw such a bright line in respect of what types of political entities we would include in the collection. Though the title includes the word *state*, the collection ventures beyond states, including as it does chapters on Niue, on French Polynesia and New Caledonia, the Anglo-Caribbean – both independent and not, and this chapter.

Constitutional law focuses overwhelmingly on formally independent states. Normally, discussions about the formal definition for a state begin with a discussion of the criteria contained in the Montevideo Convention, which is now commonly agreed to form part of customary international law.[16] But there are well-rehearsed problems with the Convention and its criteria: not least that it 'includes elements that are clearly not prerequisite to statehood, and it excludes elements that writers now widely regard as indispensable to the definition of a state'.[17] More broadly, it has long been recognised that a 'statist' view of the world is less useful than it once was – at least, as Tierney points out, as far as the 'viability of the nation-State … conceptualized to represent a "Westphalian" mode of absolute sovereignty' is concerned.[18] Furthermore, it is a definition, as are many, developed for the purposes of international law.

Following World War II, many new states (including very small states) emerged, particularly as the UN pursued an agenda of decolonisation – before World War II there

[16] Convention on Rights and Duties of States adopted by the Seventh International Conference of American States (opened for signature 26 December 1933, entered into force 26 December 1934) 165 LNTS 19.

[17] TD Grant, 'Defining Statehood: The Montevideo Convention and Its Discontents' (1999) 37 *Columbia Journal of Transnational Law* 403, 453.

[18] S Tierney, 'Reframing Sovereignty? Sub-State National Societies and Contemporary Challenges to the Nation-State' (2005) 54 *International and Comparative Law Quarterly* 161.

were around 75 states in the world,[19] while by 2025 there are 193.[20] In 1960, the UN General Assembly (UNGA) adopted the Declaration on the Granting of Independence to Colonial Countries and Peoples, noting the principle of self-determination and requiring 'immediate steps' to be taken to transfer independence to non-self-governing territories.[21] For a long time, it was assumed that the most desirable outcome of decolonisation for non-self-governing territories was independence and the emergence of a new state (with the options of integration and free association also clearly on the table as 'modes of implementing the right to self-determination' following a 1970 UNGA Resolution, as well as 'any other political status freely determined by a people').[22]

However, after an initial explosion, the number of new states has now slowed to a trickle, and many non-sovereign territories have actively chosen a non-sovereign legal status. Indeed, some scholars have labelled as 'upside-down decolonisation' the phenomenon whereby the metropole wants its non-sovereign territories to become independent, while the territories reject independence.[23] Veenendaal notes that 'non-sovereignty has increasingly come to be seen as an acceptable or even favourable political outcome for small island territories',[24] and there is a reasonably large literature exploring why that is the case.[25] For their part, Veenendaal and Oostindie have concluded, based on survey data in the Dutch Caribbean which they believe to be broadly generalisable, that the preference for a non-sovereign status among the people of the non-sovereign entities has pragmatic drivers ('military and judicial protection, nationality and the right of abode [in the state of the Netherlands], economic development and financial support')[26] – related to the 'awareness of the vulnerability that comes with smallness'[27] – but that there are nonetheless 'apparently widespread feelings of disenfranchisement and relative deprivation' – making the choice for non-sovereignty 'a painful trade-off

[19] Crawford (n 14) 4.

[20] If one only counts UN Member States. On other counts, there are more.

[21] Declaration on the Granting of Independence to Colonial Countries and People, UNGA Res 1514 (XV) (14 December 1960).

[22] Declaration on Principles of International Law Concerning Friendly Relations and Co-Operation among States in Accordance with the Charter of the United Nations, UNGA Res 2625 (XXV), UN Doc A/RES/2625(XXV) (24 October 1970) annex; see also eg, E Perham, 'A Solution for the Third International Decade for the Eradication of Colonialism: A "fourth" Option to Obviate the Need for a Fourth Decade?' (2013) 11 *New Zealand Yearbook of International Law* 3.

[23] R Hoefte and G Oostindie, 'The Netherlands and the Dutch Caribbean: Dilemmas of Decolonization' in P Sutton (ed), *Europe and the Caribbean* (London, MacMillan, 1991) 93. The Dutch Parliament, for example, adopted the position in the late 1960s that sovereignty over Suriname and the Netherlands Antilles should be transferred as soon as possible, but independence was rejected by the Netherlands Antilles and for the last 30 years Dutch governments have accepted that independence is not an option the people of the (now dissolved) Netherlands Antilles will accept: G Oostindie, 'Postcolonial Sovereignty Games in the Margins of Europe: The Netherlands, the Antilles and Europe' in R Adler-Nissen and UP Gad (eds), *European Integration and Postcolonial Sovereignty Games: The EU Overseas Countries and Territories* (London, Routledge, 2013) 203, 205.

[24] W Veenendaal, 'Smallness and Status Debates in Overseas Territories: Evidence from the Dutch Caribbean' (2016) 21 *Geopolitics* 148, 148.

[25] See eg, J Connell and R Aldrich, *The Ends of Empire: The Last Colonies Revisited* (Singapore, Palgrave MacMillan, 2020); Rezvani (n 3); Baldacchino and Milne (n 5).

[26] W Veenendaal and G Oostindie, 'Head versus Heart: The Ambiguities of Non-Sovereignty in the Dutch Caribbean' (2018) 28 *Regional & Federal Studies* 25, 35.

[27] Ferdinand, Oostindie and Veenendaal (n 4) 60.

between head and heart'.[28] The fact remains, however, that there are a dozens of such entities, and most are small islands[29] with small populations.[30]

In the context of thinking about small states, then, there are scholars who treat all 'political entities' as states.[31] One argument for widening the definition of small states to include such non-state entities is that, even if certain political entities might not be recognised as states by the international community, the distinction between states and non-states might not serve a useful purpose, depending on the questions one is asking.[32] For example, if one is seeking to inform policy interventions in a particular political entity by reference to other similar entities, smallness will be the main criterion for comparison, and status at international law may become irrelevant, or much less relevant.

Further complicating things is the fact, as noted by Robinson in her chapter in this volume, that, while all formally independent states are – as a matter of international law – enjoying sovereign equality, 'the dichotomy between formally independent small states and small non-sovereign subnational jurisdictions is somewhat overdrawn'.[33] In her chapter, she highlights the claim of Bonilla, writing with a focus on Guadeloupe – formally an overseas department of France located in the Caribbean – that that region is 'non-sovereign' or characterised by 'constrained sovereignty', despite the presence of many formally independent states.[34] So, not only is adopting a formal definition of a state not always helpful, depending on the question asked, but function does not always follow form.

In terms of independence and dependence – and taking into account this more functional position on stateness/ sovereignty vs non-stateness/ non-sovereignty – it is also important to note that there are formally independent states in relationships of what might be called 'dependence' with other states.[35] This is not a new phenomenon by any means, but is perhaps one that we may see re-emerging as geopolitics continue to reconfigure, and 'sovereignty games' play out across regions such as Oceania and the Caribbean that are characterised by small states and jurisdictions.

Taking just one example, in 2022, a parliamentary select committee of the Australian Parliament recommended that the Australian Government 'start dialogue with Pacific Island countries about compact of association considerations'.[36] This recommendation is – as the Committee noted – controversial: 'The Committee acknowledges the

[28] Veenendaal and Oostindie (n 26) 41.

[29] Ferdinand, Oostindie and Veenendaal (n 4) 44–46, 50.

[30] ibid 50.

[31] See eg, BF Gussen, 'On the Classification of Small States' in T Angelo and J Corrin (eds), 'Small States: A Collection of Essays' (2019) XXIII *Comparative Law Journal of the Pacific* (Hors Series Special Issue) 227, 233.

[32] ibid.

[33] Robinson, 'Dyadic Caribbean Constitutions', Chapter 2 in this volume.

[34] Y Bonilla, *Non-Sovereign Futures: French Caribbean Politics in the Wake of Disenchantment* (Chicago IL, University of Chicago Press, 2015) 10, as cited in Robinson, Chapter 2 in this volume.

[35] Crawford distinguishes these from 'entities lacking statehood by virtue of their dependence': Crawford (n 14) 287.

[36] Commonwealth of Australia, 'Strengthening Australia's Relationships in the Pacific' (Parliament of Australia Joint Standing Committee on Foreign Affairs, Defence and Trade 2022) [4.114], parlinfo.aph.gov.au/parlInfo/download/committees/reportjnt/024684/toc_pdf/StrengtheningAustralia%E2%80%99srelationshipsinthePacific.pdf. A similar idea had been floated some years earlier: G Colton, 'Time for Australia to Forge Free Compact Agreements in the Pacific' (*The Interpreter*, 24 November 2017), www.lowyinstitute.org/the-interpreter/time-australia-forge-free-compact-agreements-pacific.

sensitivities around proposals of regional integration, in particular compacts of free association which may impact (usually hard won) state sovereignty'. It has definitively neo-colonial undertones. Fast forward to 2024 and Australia – a state of nearly 27 million people – and Tuvalu – a state of nearly 12,000 people under imminent threat of disappearing under the ocean due to climate change[37] – ratified the Falepili Union Treaty. The ratification was accompanied by both fanfare and controversy – fanfare because of the agreement of both states that Tuvalu's statehood will continue even if its territory does not, and because of the pathway for 'mobility with dignity' it creates for Tuvaluans to move to Australia;[38] and controversy because of concerns about the potential for the Treaty to 'compromis[e] Tuvalu's sovereignty' despite perceived insufficiency of public consultation with 'Tuvaluan communities' – no version of the Treaty was released before it was signed.[39] The concern about sovereignty relates to Article 4(4) of the Treaty, which has been described as the *quid pro quo*, stipulating that 'Tuvalu shall mutually agree with Australia any partnership, arrangement or engagement with any other State or entity on security and defence-related matters' – providing Australia 'on its face … with a veto over a wide range of issues in Tuvalu's foreign relations'.[40] In a very careful analysis of the provisions, and of what the governments have both said about the treaty, Green and Guilfoyle conclude that – in relation to its impact on sovereignty – 'Tuvalu's basic status must be presumed unaltered notwithstanding art 4(4)', but they do seem to suggest that, at least functionally though not in form, the Treaty does look somewhat like a treaty of association.[41]

Taking all this together – ie, as a matter of form, not all small political entities are states, and as a matter of function, they may nonetheless share very similar issues – as the title of this chapter indicates, it makes sense to think of 'stateness' as a spectrum. This is not a revolutionary claim by any means, but perhaps one which constitutional lawyers should pay more attention to – particularly as it relates to the legal relationships between non-sovereign entities and metropole states, and perhaps also between small states and larger states. These are relationships which have largely been left to colleagues in political science and, where they have been taken up by legal scholars, it is often

[37] S Yeo, 'Tuvalu: The Disappearing Island Nation Recreating Itself in the Metaverse' *BBC* (22 November 2024), www.bbc.com/future/article/20241121-tuvalu-the-pacific-islands-creating-a-digital-nation-in-the-metaverse-due-to-climate-change.

[38] P Conroy, 'The Falepili Union: A Pacific Response to the Greatest Global ChallengesLowy Institute' (*The Interpreter*, 28 August 2024), www.lowyinstitute.org/the-interpreter/falepili-union-pacific-response-greatest-global-challenges (note that the author of this blog post was at the time Australia's Minister for International Development and the Pacific).

[39] E Sopoaga, 'Australia-Tuvalu Falepili Union "shameful" – Former Tuvalu PM' *Radio New Zealand* (27 November 2023), www.rnz.co.nz/international/pacific-news/503354/australia-tuvalu-falepili-union-shameful-former-tuvalu-pm; J Marinaccio, 'Tuvalu's Parliament Debates the Falepili Union' (*Devpolicy Blog*, 28 November 2023), devpolicy.org/tuvalus-parliament-debates-the-falepili-union-20231129/. See also J Marinaccio, 'The Australia-Tuvalu Falepili Union: Tuvaluan Values or Australian Interests?' *Radio New Zealand* (15 November 2023), www.rnz.co.nz/international/pacific-news/502493/the-australia-tuvalu-falepili-union-tuvaluan-values-or-australian-interests; and, more positively, Richard Herr, 'The Falepili Union and the Question of Pacific Sovereignty' (*The Strategist*, 23 November 2023), www.aspistrategist.org.au/the-falepili-union-and-the-question-of-pacific-sovereignty/.

[40] Green and Guilfoyle (n 14) 696–97, and see this article more generally for an excellent analysis of the Treaty and its impact on Tuvalu's sovereignty as a matter of international law.

[41] ibid 699–701.

those in international law.[42] Constitutional lawyers have shown more interest in what might be called 'sub-state national societies' in developed liberal democracies asserting some distinctiveness – such as Quebec, Catalonia, and Scotland – and recognised these as cases requiring constitutional law and international law to speak to each other. But, to take another example, the standard US American law degree contains no mention of the insular cases[43] (relating to the constitutional status of Puerto Rico, and other insular territories of the US). Both of the authors of this chapter received their first law degrees in countries with constitutional arrangements with geographically distinct non-independent political entities (New Zealand and the Netherlands), but for Perham the first time she remembers the Realm of New Zealand (and the constitutional relationship between the state of New Zealand, and the Cook Islands, Niue and Tokelau) being mentioned was in a final-year public international law elective, and the key constitutional law textbook makes only a few passing mentions of the Realm.[44] In De Visser's recollection, references to the Kingdom during the foundational course on constitutional law were similarly sparse and focused mainly on the unavailability of the legal instrument regulating the relationship between the various entities (the Charter) as a benchmark against which Dutch courts can assess statutes. While leading Dutch textbooks devote separate chapters to the Kingdom,[45] these typically appear at the end of the volume and are not often assigned as mandatory reading. The corollary is that, even as exceptions exist, there often is a general sense that non-independence entities are, both literally and figuratively, far removed from the metropole state.

III. Case Study: The Kingdom of the Netherlands in the Caribbean

Having made the case for comparative constitutional law scholars to expand their attention up a level and down a level, in this section we provide a (necessarily brief) description of the constitutional arrangements within the Kingdom of the Netherlands to illustrate what important questions might arise when one expands one's focus in this way. We could have chosen any number of examples for this illustration, but we have chosen to focus on the Kingdom of the Netherlands, because little attention has been paid to these arrangements in the English-language constitutional law literature.[46] Indeed, as comparative constitutional scholars, we should be mindful of the role of

[42] eg, Green and Guilfoyle (n 14); Hillebrink (n 15).

[43] S Levinson, 'Why the Canon Should Be Expanded to Include the Insular Cases and the Saga of American Expansionism' (2000) 17 *Constitutional Commentary* 241.

[44] PA Joseph, *Joseph on Constitutional and Administrative Law in New Zealand*, 5th edn (Wellington, Thomson Reuters, 2021) [18.3.4], [20.2].

[45] AD Belinfante and JL de Reede, *Beginselen van het Nederlandse Staatsrecht*, 20th edn (Deventer, Kluwer, 2023); DJ Elzinga, R de Lange and HG Hoogers, *Van Der Pot Handbook van het Nederlandse Staatsrecht*, 16th edn (Deventer, Kluwer, 2014).

[46] With the exception of I Broekhuijse, E Hirsch Ballin and S Ranchordás, 'The Constitutions of the Dutch Caribbean: A Study of the Countries of Aruba, Curaçao and Sint Maarten and the Public Entities of Bonaire, Sint Eustatius and Saba' in R Albert, D O'Brien and S Wheatle (eds), *The Oxford Handbook of Caribbean Constitutions* (Oxford, Oxford University Press, 2020).

language in steering the selection of jurisdictions for exploration as well as in shaping decisions as to what count as worthwhile questions to interrogate, with English often exerting hegemonic pressures in this regard, resulting in a concomitant lack of engagement with materials and discourses in other languages that limits the intellectual development of our field.[47]

A. Historical Background

The Netherlands, a constitutional monarchy with a parliamentary system of government and a population of over 17 million people, is located in north-western Europe.[48] It is the largest entity within the Kingdom of the Netherlands, which also comprises six small islands in the Caribbean that came under Dutch colonial control from the seventeenth century onwards.[49] These islands are, in alphabetical order: Aruba (110,000 inhabitants), Bonaire (16,000 inhabitants), Curaçao (150,000 inhabitants), Saba (2,000 inhabitants), Sint Eustatius (4,000 inhabitants) and Sint Maarten (40,000 inhabitants).[50]

As Sharpe puts it, these 'are multicultural and multiracial societies with historical influence from Africa, indigenous peoples, Latin America, the Netherlands, other European countries, North America and Asia'.[51] While historically administered in various configurations as Dutch colonies, the islands as a unit did not develop 'any social, economic [or] cultural infrastructures, or shared interests'.[52] For example, Aruba, Curaçao and Bonaire are all located close to each other, and very close to the coast of Venezuela. The language predominantly spoken on those islands is Papiamento, a Portuguese-based creole. English is the predominant language on Sint Maarten, Sint Eustasius and Saba – which are located towards the north of the Caribbean Sea. The histories of the islands differ too: for example, although located close to each other, the Papamiento-speaking Curaçao and Bonaire have a shared history of slavery, while Aruba does not.[53]

During the decolonisation era in the aftermath of World War II, there was a general sentiment within the Netherlands as well as the Caribbean islands (known then as the Netherlands Antilles) – and in Suriname, on the north-eastern coast of South America and at the time also a colony of the Netherlands – that the latter territories should

[47] On this, see M De Visser, 'Constitutional Comparisons and Language' in M Khosla and VC Jackson (eds), *Redefining Comparative Constitutional Law: Essays for Mark Tushnet* (Oxford, Oxford University Press, 2025).

[48] On the constitutional framework of the Netherlands (in English) see, eg, P Bovend'Eert and C Kortmann, *Constitutional Law in the Netherlands*, 3rd edn (Deventer, Wolters Kluwer, 2018); M De Visser, 'Nonjudicial Constitutional Interpretation: The Netherlands' in DS Law (ed), *Constitutionalism in Context* (Cambridge, Cambridge University Press, 2022).

[49] The islands were initially administered by the West-Indian Company (WIC) before they came under constitutional control of the government in the Netherlands in 1813.

[50] Only the southern part of this island is part of the Kingdom of the Netherlands; the northern portion is an overseas collectivity of France.

[51] MO Sharpe, 'Extending Postcolonial Sovereignty Games: The Multilevel Negotiation of Autonomy and Integration in the 2010 Dissolution of the Netherlands Antilles and Dutch Kingdom Relations' (2022) 21 *Ethnopolitics* 299, 301.

[52] N Quik-Schuijt and I Broekhuijse, 'A Case Study: Law and Emotions Within the Kingdom of the Netherlands' (2016) 4 *University of Baltimore Journal of International Law* 55, 62.

[53] ibid 63.

remain part of the Kingdom of the Netherlands.[54] The approach chosen to give effect to this outlook, while at the same time paying due regard to the right to self-determination as encapsulated in the UN Charter and developed through the UNGA resolutions mentioned in section II, consisted of the adoption of a new constitutional framework. This constitutional framework was initially conceptualised by the Netherlands as also intended to include Indonesia, a much larger and economically important part of the Dutch Empire. The idea for colonial reform was offered during the war with Indonesia following its declaration of independence in 1945. It was, as Oostindie puts it, 'too little and too late for the Indonesian nationalists', but '[a]ble Dutch Caribbean politicians made sure that Dutch promises intended to lure Indonesia to remain within the Kingdom now materialized for their nascent micro-states. Matters of scale were turned on their head'.[55]

On 15 December 1954, after eight years of negotiation, a new Charter for the Kingdom of the Netherlands (*Statuut voor het Koninkrijk der Nederlanden*) was signed by the Netherlands (ie, the country in Europe) and the Netherlands Antilles and Suriname as newly autonomous countries.[56] The main principles of this Charter have stood the test of time; they have not fundamentally changed. The internal composition of the Kingdom, however, has been altered on several occasions since 1954. Suriname became independent in 1975 following political negotiations, while Aruba was granted a '*status aparte*' as compared to the other Caribbean islands in 1986[57] and became an autonomous country.[58] At the time Aruba was granted *status aparte*, the Dutch government required it to accept that this was a transitional status that would lead to its independence in 1996, although independence was never desired by Aruba (and ultimately not forced on it).[59]

This change to Aruba's status can be seen as the start of a process that culminated in the dissolution of the country of the Netherlands Antilles – not least because it taught the other islands the viability of pursuing a strategy of separate autonomy.[60] Curaçao – the most populous island – had begun to be perceived as 'too dominant' by the other islands and there was a growing disinclination for the islands to cooperate together on a range of affairs.[61] In the early 2000s, referendums were accordingly held on the other five islands to determine whether the Netherlands Antilles should be dissolved in favour of a different type of constitutional settlement. The populations on Curaçao and Sint Maarten voted for their islands to also become autonomous countries within the

[54] The institutions in the Netherlands envisaged a similar solution for 'Netherlands-India' (present-day Indonesia), which had also been part of the Dutch colonial empire. Indonesia, however, declared itself independent following the Japanese surrender at the end of World War II.

[55] Oostindie (n 23) 204; see also Sharpe (n 51) 303.

[56] Charter for the Kindom of the Netherlands, https://wetten.overheid.nl/BWBR0002154/2024-01-01. On the Charter, see C Borman, *Het Statuut Voor Het Koninkrijk*, 3rd edn (Deventer, Wolters Kluwer, 2012).

[57] This status came about after lengthy negotiations, with a 1977 consultative referendum on secession and subsequent local unrest providing an important impetus for the Dutch government to open discussions with the island about its constitutional future.

[58] This was originally envisaged as a preliminary step to Aruba's ultimate independence on 1 January 1996, but in the early 1990s the island let it be known that it no longer had this intention.

[59] Sharpe (n 51) 305–6.

[60] ibid 305.

[61] AW Heringa, J van der Velde, LFM Verhey and W van der Woude, *Staatsrecht*, 12th edn (Deventer, Wolters Kluwer, 2015) 320.

Kingdom, while the other islands opted for a direct link to the Netherlands.[62] Following a host of constitutional and legislative changes, the new arrangement entered into effect on 10 October 2010. Since that date, the Kingdom of the Netherlands has consisted of four autonomous countries – the Netherlands, Aruba, Curaçao, and Sint Maarten – while the remaining three Caribbean islands enjoy the status of special public bodies and are treated like Dutch municipalities, ie, units of local government (with some slight adjustments to account for their geographical distance from the rest of the Netherlands).[63] The rest of this section focuses on the constituent countries of the Kingdom, because the other islands have now effectively integrated into the country of the Netherlands.

B. The Constitutional Framework

Each of the constituent countries has its own constitution. That of the country of the Netherlands was adopted in 1815, making it one of the oldest in the world. The Constitution of Aruba was adopted in 1985, and those of Curaçao and Sint Maarten, in 2010, by the legislative bodies of these countries by a two-thirds majority vote, without popular involvement in the form of a referendum or otherwise.[64] The government of the Kingdom (the arrangements for which are discussed in subsection III.C. below) also had a role to play as far as the enactment of the latter two constitutions was concerned. The Bill containing the proposal could only be presented to the municipal legislature after 'the sentiments' of this government has been solicited, while it also had to give its assent before the Bill could take legal effect.[65] A similar preventive approval role for the government of the Kingdom is envisaged when it comes to amendments to the Constitutions of the Caribbean countries that concern the bill of rights, the competences of the Governor[66] or the representative institutions or the judiciary. These amendments must also be presented to this government for input and can only enter into force after governmental assent has been obtained, thereby limiting the constitutional autonomy of the Caribbean countries.[67]

In terms of their substance, the Constitutions of Aruba, Curaçao and Sint Maarten resemble in important respects that of the country of the Netherlands. They each have

[62] The inhabitants of Sint Eustatius voted, by a majority, to retain the status quo, but were effectively overruled by the results on the other Caribbean islands. Some scholars have suggested this means the changed status may be a breach of the right of the people of Sint Eustasius to self-determination: WP Veenendaal, 'The Dutch Caribbean Municipalities in Comparative Perspective' (2015) 10 *Island Studies Journal* 15, 21.

[63] Constitution of the Netherlands, art 134. Before 2010, the Charter expressly declared that those three islands were part of the constitutional order of the country of the Netherlands. For a discussion of this new arrangement, see HG Hoogers, 'De Herstructurering van Het Koninkrijk Als Lakmoesproef: Kanttekeningen Vanuit Constitutioneel Perspectief Bij de Opheffing van de Nederlandse Antillen, Deel 2' [2010] *Tijdschrift voor constitutioneel recht* 376. See also Veenendaal (n 62).

[64] Cf Charter, art 42(2).

[65] Charter, art 60a.

[66] The Governor has a dual mandate: she represents the King as the head of state in the Caribbean countries and in this capacity she needs to act in accordance with the instructions issued by the government of the Kingdom, and also represents the King as the part of the municipal government, in which capacity she acts as an inviolable head of state of the country. On this combined role, see LJJ Rogier, 'De gouverneur, landsorgaan én koninkrijksorgaan' (2020) 9(2) *Caribisch Juristenblad* 138.

[67] Charter, art 44. This is especially true since no similar arrangements are in place in relation to the Constitution of the Netherlands.

a catalogue of fundamental rights and liberties and a familiar-looking institutional structure, with a parliament, government (composed of the King, as represented by the Governor and the ministers), a council of ministers, a Council of Advice (comparable to the Dutch Council of State), a court of audits, an Ombudsman, courts, and a public prosecutor. The most notable difference concerns the availability of judicial review. According to Article 120 of the Dutch Constitution, Dutch judges are prohibited from pronouncing on the constitutionality of statutes. However, the constitutions of the Caribbean countries recognise the power of the regular local judiciary to check local legislation against their constitution.[68] The Constitution of Sint Maarten even creates a Constitutional Court that can assess the validity of Acts adopted by the island legislature before these enter into force, at the exclusive request of the country's Ombudsman.[69]

Above all the country Constitutions, including that of the Netherlands, stands the Charter. The Charter is the highest legal norm within the Kingdom and can be considered a type of 'super-constitution'. It exhaustively enumerates which topics can be considered affairs of the Kingdom that can, or should, be regulated by the institutions of the Kingdom.[70] These are rather limited and include defence, foreign affairs,[71] citizenship, and extradition, as well as rules referring to the monarchy and the exercise of royal and legislative powers in relation to Kingdom affairs.[72] Importantly, the people of all constituent countries have rights to equal Dutch citizenship.[73]

Article 41, first paragraph of the Charter affirms that the four countries are entitled to regulate all their own affairs independently. This safeguard of local autonomy covers a wide range of areas, from internal affairs to education and from economic affairs to public health, with the Caribbean countries and the Netherlands having enacted their own legal frameworks in this regard. More generally, it has been noted that the nature of the relationship established by the Charter among the countries is one that is focused on 'differentiation and autonomy, not one that is focused on unity and collaboration', as is evident in the fact that there is, for instance, no monetary or customs union or unrestricted free movement of persons among the constituent countries.[74]

Article 43, first paragraph further charges each country with ensuring the realisation of 'fundamental human rights and liberties, legal certainty and the soundness of governance'. This last notion is understood in a twofold manner as far as the Caribbean

[68] Constitution of Aruba, art I.22 read together with art VI.4; Constitution of Curaçao, art 101; Constitution of Sint Maarten, art 119.

[69] Constitution of Sint Maarten, chapter 8. This is an unusual design, as countries with a constitutional court tend to grant access to a wider range of actors.

[70] Charter, art 5(2).

[71] This, inter alia, means that only the Kingdom concludes treaties, with art 27 of the Charter stipulating that the Caribbean countries will be 'involved in the preparations of agreements with other entities that affect them at the earliest possible stage'. The geographical scope of treaties is a matter for internal negotiation and discussion among the countries, with art 25 of the Charter stipulating that a country can oppose being bound by a treaty regulating economic or financial matters.

[72] Charter, art 3.

[73] Cf art 3 of the Kingdom Law pertaining to Dutch Citizenship.

[74] HG Hoogers and G Karapetian, *Het Koninkrijk Tegen Het Licht: Rechtsvergelijkend Onderzoek in Opdracht van de Tweede Kamer Der Staten-Generaal Naar de Staatsrechtelijke Overzeese Verhoudingen in Het Koninkrijk Der Nederlanden, de Franse Republiek, Het Koninkrijk Denemarken En Het Verenigd Koninkrijk van Groot-Brittannië En Noord-Ierland* (Rijksuniversiteit Groningen, April 2019), www.tweedekamer.nl/sites/default/files/atoms/files/hoogers_karapetian_het_koninkrijk_tegen_het_licht_3_mei_definitief.pdf.

countries are concerned.[75] On the one hand, their finances must be in good order. On the other hand, they must abide by the ideals of a democratic state based on the rule of law, which, inter alia, entails that measures are taken to avoid corruption, nepotism and clientelism affecting the integrity of public governance. At the same time, the second paragraph declares that safeguarding the rights and principles listed in the first paragraph comes within the purview of the Kingdom, which is able to intervene in the case of structural inadequacies,[76] thereby blurring the line between affairs of the Kingdom and those of the countries. Heringa and others have observed that the government of the Kingdom has displayed a greater willingness to intervene in the affairs of the Caribbean countries since the constitutional reform of 2010 with reference to Article 43,[77] although the number of interventions has remained relatively small overall.

The revision of the Charter is regulated in Article 55, according to which amendments shall be adopted by way of Kingdom legislation, again without making provision for public participation. The regular procedure for the enactment of such legislation is followed, albeit with the difference that the elected bodies of Aruba, Curaçao and Sint Maarten each have the right of assent. Failure to secure the approval of the Caribbean legislatures accordingly prevents the adoption of a Charter amendment. Their assent is given through the adoption of a municipal law, which must be passed in two readings unless the proposal was passed by a two-thirds majority of votes cast during the first reading, in which case approval is immediate.[78]

Interestingly, the Charter stipulates that for certain topics, such as the exercise of legislative competences regarding Kingdom affairs, the arrangements as laid down in the Dutch Constitution shall be followed.[79] This last document thus also functions as a partial constitution for the Kingdom as a whole, as we shall see in greater detail below.[80]

C. Institutional Relationships and Power Dynamics

The Charter formally treats all the countries equally, with the preamble stating that the countries have declared that they will 'safeguard the common interests on an equal footing'. In reality, however, the country of the Netherlands and this country's Constitution are very much the *primus inter pares*.[81] Many of the institutions established by the Dutch Constitution – including the monarch, the Council of State, the council of ministers and

[75] GAK Bakhuis, 'Autonomie, Toezicht En Interventie in de Caribische Landen van Het Koninkrijk Der Nederlanden' (PhD thesis, Erasmus University Rotterdam, 2020) 240.

[76] This intervention needs to be based on art 51 of the Charter (on which, see below) or a legal basis contained in Kingdom legislation or municipal law.

[77] Heringa and others (n 61) 330. This has not systematically culminated in an Order in Council as per art 51, but has more often taken the form of a direction issued to the Governor of the country concerned.

[78] This process is procedurally less demanding than that for revising the Dutch Constitution, which requires the dissolution of Parliament and intervening elections between the first and second readings, while proposals must further be passed by a two-thirds majority of votes cast during the second reading. This enhanced voting requirement is, however, not applied to changes to the Charter that would deviate from the Dutch Constitution: in such cases a simple majority at the second reading suffices.

[79] Charter, art 5(1).

[80] See also Charter, art 14(1), according to which rules pertaining to Kingdom affairs can be regulated in the Dutch Constitution (or international rules).

[81] Oostindie describes the idea of mutual assistance in the Charter as 'fictitious' – 'support has been a one-way street for the past 60 years': Oostindie (n 23) 207.

the Houses of Parliament – are double-hatting to discharge Kingdom affairs, albeit with some adjustments to ensure representation of or the possibility to provide input for the other countries. The choice for 'double-hatting' was taken deliberately at the time of the Charter's adoption in 1954 for reasons of political efficiency. On the one hand, the number of decisions that would have to be taken at the level of the Kingdom seemed sufficiently small that the creation of an entirely new and dedicated institutional framework would not be warranted. On the other hand, an arrangement whereby the institutions of the various countries would act together would presumably result in a cumbersome lawmaking process, while it would also give rise to an inequitable distribution of influence, given the marked differences in population size.[82]

In practice, double-hatting results in the following arrangements. The Dutch council of ministers is supplemented with an 'authorised minister'[83] for each Caribbean country, nominated by the governments of Aruba, Curaçao, and Sint Maarten to constitute the council of ministers of the Kingdom.[84] The composition of the Dutch Council of State, which acts as the government's official legal advisor, is expanded with a member from each of the Caribbean countries when rendering advice on Kingdom legislation and Orders in Council.[85] The highest court within the Kingdom as far as civil and criminal cases are concerned is the Dutch Supreme Court,[86] which can hear appeals in cassation of the Common Court of Justice that operates for Aruba, Curaçao and Sint Maarten.[87] Although the possibility exists for the Caribbean governments to request the addition of a justice, none had made use thereof as of early 2025.

The arrangements for the Houses of Parliament are slightly different in that their composition remains unaltered. Statutes for the Kingdom are deliberated and adopted by the Dutch Parliament following the arrangements set out in the Dutch Constitution, with the democratically elected organs of the other countries having the right to make written observations[88] and also the entitlement to representation during the oral proceedings by special delegates who can provide explanations, propose amendments and adopt a position on the Bill without, however, having the right to vote.[89] The authorised ministers are similarly entitled to participate in the oral proceedings in the Houses of Parliament.[90] If, when taking a stance on the Bill, the representatives of the Caribbean countries object to the proposal, they can ask for the deliberations to be

[82] Cf Heringa and others (n 61) 325.

[83] These individuals are in practice more akin to senior level civil servants who must follow the instructions of their government: unlike Ministers, they do not have a direct relationship with the respective Caribbean parliaments.

[84] Charter, art 7. These authorised ministers only participate in discussions that concern Kingdom affairs 'that affect the country involved': art 10(1). What qualifies as such affairs is set out mainly in arts 11 and 45 of the Charter.

[85] Charter, art 13(2). This institution is also one of the highest administrative courts in the Netherlands, but it fulfils no judicial role in relation to Kingdom matters.

[86] Charter, art 23.

[87] This Common Court of Justice is instituted based on one of the consensus Kingdom laws mentioned below. It is the final instance court within the Caribbean and hears appeals from the four Caribbean courts of first instance (one for each of the countries as well as one for the three special municipalities).

[88] Charter, art 16.

[89] Charter, arts 17(2) and (4) and art 18(2). As a rule, inhabitants of the Caribbean countries similarly do not have the right to vote in elections for the Dutch Houses of Parliament, even though these also act as the legislature for the Kingdom, giving rise to a 'democratic deficit'.

[90] Charter, art 17(1) and (4) and art 18(1).

suspended – allowing for renewed deliberations and possibly changes to the Bill. If the Bill is nevertheless passed but with less than three-fifths of the total number of votes cast, the proceedings will be halted so that discussions can continue in the council of ministers of the Kingdom. If those discussions do not yield a different outcome, then the Bill will continue to make its way through the rest of the legislative process.

It should be clear that the institutions or representatives of the other countries do not have the power to ultimately prevent the enactment of Kingdom legislation or policy.[91] In addition to what already has been mentioned, we also wish to draw attention to Article 12 of the Charter, which contains a political dispute settlement clause. During discussions in the council of ministers of the Kingdom, the authorised ministers of Aruba, Curaçao or Sint Maarten can formally object to a proposed Bill on the ground that its application could result in a 'severe negative effect' for their country or raise any other conflict. If the full council of ministers disagrees with the objection, the authorised minister can trigger an internal appeal mechanism. Conversations regarding the contentious issue will then continue among a small subset of the full council of ministers, comprising an equal number of representatives of the Caribbean country/ies and Dutch ministers and chaired by the (Dutch) Prime Minister, who has the deciding vote if no consensus can be found. As Bovend'Eert and others accordingly point out, the decision of the Dutch ministers will carry the day in the event of a disagreement, as they are in the majority.[92]

Other than affairs of the Kingdom that require the enactment of Kingdom legislation, the Charter also envisages the possibility of collaboration regarding municipal matters that 'affect the interests of two of more of the countries'.[93] These include (among others) fostering cultural and social relations, questions regarding currencies and banking policies, promoting economic resilience, transport arrangements, and the operation of business and professions of citizens of the Kingdom. To deal with municipal matters in a concerted manner the countries can also adopt Kingdom legislation, in the form of what are called 'consensus Kingdom laws'[94] – with the nomenclature indicating that the countries involved need to agree as to the substance of these laws, given that this involves an exercise of their autonomy. Several consensus Kingdom laws have been adopted, largely pertaining to the administration of justice[95] and law enforcement[96] as well as financial supervision.[97] These laws are controversial in the Caribbean countries due to the impression that they were 'de facto imposed in 2010 by the Netherlands as conditions for securing the status of autonomous country and debt relief'.[98]

[91] As we have seen, this is only different for Kingdom Bills that seek to change the Charter itself: for such Bills, the legislative assemblies of Aruba, Curaçao and Sint Maarten have the right of assent, see Charter, art 55(2).

[92] JLW Broeksteeg and others, *Constitutioneel Recht*, 7th edn (Deventer, Wolters Kluwer, 2016) 104.

[93] Charter, art 37(1).

[94] Charter, art 38(2). The procedure to be followed for the adoption of such laws is not set out in the Charter itself, but in a declaration adopted by the four countries on 12 November 2007 (signed on 22 January 2008 in Sint Maarten).

[95] Kingdom Law Common Court of Justice (2010).

[96] Kingdom Law Council for Law Enforcement (2010); Kingdom Law Public Prosecutor (2010); Kingdom Law Police (2010).

[97] Kingdom Law Financial Supervision (2010).

[98] Heringa and others (n 61) 329.

There are further administrative supervisory mechanisms in place for the Caribbean countries under the Charter. According to Article 50, first paragraph, the government of the Kingdom can annul legislative and administrative measures of those countries that are contrary to higher law (the Charter, international rules or Kingdom legal measures) or at odds with 'interests the regulation or safeguarding of which are an affair of the Kingdom'. Although the second paragraph of this provision states that this matter will be regulated by the Dutch Constitution for the Netherlands 'in so far as necessary', no such provisions has been adopted. As of early 2025, Article 50 has not been used, with some arguing that this is due to the high political cost this would entail.[99] In addition, Article 51 first paragraph gives the government of the Kingdom the right to intervene by a (Kingdom) Order in Council if one of the Caribbean countries does not (adequately) ensure that which is required by higher law. Again, there is a possibility to provide for a similar arrangement in the Dutch Constitution, which again has not come to pass. Article 51 is often read together with Article 43, which, it will be recalled, requires the realisation of 'fundamental human rights and liberties, legal certainty and the soundness of governance'. Systemic failures in this regard on the part of one of the countries can engage the responsibility of the Kingdom, potentially triggering the use of the power to issue a (Kingdom) governmental decree. Finally, there exists the possibility of financial supervision for the Caribbean countries: a special board can render advice to their municipal institutions regarding their budgets. If its advice is not heeded, the board can recommend that the council of ministers of the Kingdom issues an Order in Council (of the Kingdom) to the country concerned.

D. Evaluation

The arrangement in place in the Kingdom of the Netherlands has been described as constitutionally *sui generis*.[100] One can, at first blush, identify features of a federation: the Kingdom has its own organs that exercise competences in domains exhaustively listed in the Charter, which ranks above all other legal norms in the Kingdom, and that can create norms that outrank those adopted by the autonomous countries. At the same time, we have seen that the institutions of one of the countries, ie the Netherlands, also operate as part of the overarching institutional infrastructure, which is unusual in classic federations. There is, moreover, no role for the judiciary in resolving disputes between the Kingdom and the countries: in a famous ruling in 1989, in the so-called *Harmonisatiewet* case,[101] the Dutch Supreme Court held that legislation adopted within the Netherlands could not be reviewed for compliance with the Charter, and the general view is that the same must be true for municipal laws enacted by the Caribbean countries.[102] Another atypical feature is that cooperation within the Kingdom is based

[99] Bakhuis (n 75) 241. In practice, diplomacy is used to manage difficulties that arise in this regard.

[100] Heringa and others (n 61) 323.

[101] Dutch Supreme Court, 14 April 1989, NJ 1989, 469. This is despite art 49 of the Charter, which indicates that the Kingdom legislature can set rules regarding the validity of laws that contravene the Charter, international rules, or Kingdom legislation. The legislature has, however, never exercised this competence.

[102] Following the constitutional reform of 2010, a new dispute settlement clause pertaining to such matters was added to the Charter. This article 12a provides for the enactment of Kingdom legislation in this regard.

on the voluntary agreement of the countries; as the preamble notes, they accept its legal order 'freely'. This means that secession is possible, and even explicitly acknowledged as a legal right as far as Aruba is concerned.[103] In a similar vein, Hoogers and Karapetian observe that the legal order of the Kingdom also has confederal aspects (as is evident, inter alia, in the fact that changes to the Charter require the unanimous consent of each of the countries) as well as elements of a unitary state (particularly as far as the competences to exercise administrative supervision under Articles 50 and 51 of the Charter are concerned).[104]

Turning to the relationship among the countries, it should be clear from the preceding discussion that there is a legal and institutional imbalance between the position in which Aruba, Curaçao and Sint Maarten find themselves as compared to that of the Netherlands. The latter occupies a privileged position, as its Constitution and state bodies also play a role as far as the governance of the Caribbean part of the Kingdom is concerned, without there being any reciprocity. The autonomy of each country, which is the 'basic idea that undergirds the Charter',[105] is thus partially qualified for the Caribbean countries,[106] and so too is the notion of the formal equality of all constituent parts of the Kingdom of the Netherlands. One could, however, argue that this design has been voluntarily accepted by each of the countries; whether this is problematic is then largely contingent on how the institutions of the Kingdom use their competences.

IV. Concluding Thoughts

We began this chapter with a call for constitutional law scholars to shift their gaze – and to turn their focus both up a level and down a level, before doing that ourselves. In this final section, we do not propose to draw a conclusion as such, but rather seek to highlight some of the questions and issues that come to the fore as a result of this shift of gaze. Going up a level, we reiterate the importance of conceiving of the relationship of the various non-sovereign entities and territories with large(r) independent administering states as constitutional in nature, with the relevant legal arrangements as an integral part of the constitutional settlement of the independent state concerned. Relatedly, but in less depth, we also raise the broader question of whether there are some treaty-like relationships between independent states that are not conceived of as constitutional in nature, but perhaps should be – pointing to the recent Falepili Union treaty between Tuvalu and Australia as one such relationship (bringing to the fore, as it does, questions around sovereignty, identity and migration).

The Caribbean countries favoured a role for the Supreme Court of the Netherlands in this regard, but the Dutch government preferred a more administrative approach. A Bill that envisaged an advisory role for the Council of State for the Kingdom was withdrawn in 2021, following objections from the special delegates from the Caribbean countries regarding the possibility for the council of ministers for the Kingdom to deviate from the advice rendered.

[103] Charter, art 58.

[104] Hoogers and Karapetian (n 74) 7.

[105] Bakhuis (n 75) 236.

[106] We also recall that there are no legally enforceable constitutional safeguards for this autonomy.

To be fair, these relationships may certainly also be important to study from an international level status perspective, but this should not obscure the fact that, ultimately, we are dealing with decidedly *constitutional* designs that should be appreciated and analysed as such (as well as some designs that perhaps should be, though their categorisation as constitutional in nature may be more contested, or at least contestable). Doing so against the backdrop of the wider comparative constitutional law discourse and focusing on the arrangements in the Kingdom of the Netherlands as our case study, at least three areas for exploration emerge.

First, subnational constitutionalism should not be associated exclusively with states that have explicitly adopted federalism, devolution or regionalisation; a special version thereof can also be found in some broadly unitary states like the Kingdom of the Netherlands, which suggests that our thinking about this concept deserves to be nuanced. This is true, by extension, for the descriptors used for and expectations regarding the various legal documents: the Charter, as we have seen, can be considered a sort of 'super-constitution' that nevertheless lacks certain attributes that we would normally associate with such a text, like a bill of rights or identity-affirming provisions.

Second, the existence of a constitutional 'master text' directs attention to how it came into being and, in line with the focus in much of the contemporary literature and practice,[107] whether the people had a role to play in the process. The making of the Charter appears to have been a largely elite-driven process, although popular input was provided for in the 2010 restructuring of the Kingdom, in the form of a referendum being held in each of the affected islands. The need for participation opportunities is particularly important in light of the warning that smallness often 'obstructs and distorts the formation of an informed public debate about non-sovereignty and political status options', due to a combination of factors such as weak news media and lack of transparency as well as personalistic politics, patron-client relations and governmental dominance.[108]

Third is the design of the arrangements governing the relations between the non-sovereign entities and the independent state, particularly the extent to which the interests and concerns of the former are respected and protected. In this regard, the Kingdom of the Netherlands offers a cautionary tale. It suffers from a democratic deficit, as the Dutch Parliament essentially doubles up as the Kingdom Parliament, but citizens living in the Caribbean countries cannot vote in the Dutch parliamentary elections, with the authorised ministers of those countries further having more limited opportunities to influence the content and adoption of Kingdom legislation as compared to their Dutch counterparts.[109] Moreover, while the four countries are nominally considered to

[107] See eg, A Saati, 'Participatory Constitution-Making as a Transnational Legal Norm: Why Does It "Stick" in Some Contexts and Not in Others?' (2017) 2 *UC Irvine Journal of International, Transnational, and Comparative Law* 113; C Saunders, 'Constitution Making in the 21st Century' (2012) 4 *International Review of Law* 4; UN Secretary General, 'Guidance Note of the Secretary-General on United Nations Constitutional Assistance' (2020), peacemaker.un.org/sites/default/files/document/files/2022/11/sg-guidance-note-constitutional-assistance.pdf, 4.

[108] Veenendaal (n 24) 149.

[109] Rapport van de Commissie Democratisch Deficiet, 'Kiezen voor het Koninkrijk: Democratische Legitimiteit van Besluitvorming en Controle op Koninkrijksniveau (11 November 2009); S Otje and J van der Heijden, 'Staatsburgers zonder volksvertegenwoordigers: het democratisch tekort van het Koninkrijk der Nederlanden' (*Stuk Rood Vlees*, 13 November 2020).

be equals according to the Charter, the composition of institutions and the structuring of procedures envisage a dominant role for the Netherlands. This has caused significant tension between the country in north-western Europe and the Caribbean islands, with the Prime Minister of Aruba even going on a hunger strike in 2014 to protest a perceived infringement of his country's autonomy, as he also considered the dispute settlement mechanism for inter-country disputes to be 'useless'.[110] Sentiments of inequality have endured and perhaps even deepened over the years, and have also shaped perceptions of identity and belonging among the inhabitants of the Dutch Caribbean.[111] The need to address such sentiments, including through a dynamic interpretation of the Charter, was recognised by the Dutch Council of State in a 2024 unsolicited opinion as symbolically important to enhance the legitimacy of the Kingdom.[112]

Going down a level, there could be interesting innovations that exist within the non-sovereign entities that might merit closer scrutiny, including possibly as providing inspiration for constitutional engineering elsewhere. A good example is the creation of a Constitutional Court in Sint Maarten, the experience with which could offer food for thought in the current debates in the Netherlands about the possible removal or qualification of its prohibition on judicial review of legislation. On this view, the non-sovereign entities could perhaps be viewed and function as 'constitutional sandboxes' precisely on account of their small scale, possibly coupled with their (often) geographic remoteness from the larger administering state. More broadly, such entities and their constitutional arrangements could serve as fruitful comparators for small states, and arguably would be a more natural choice than using say, large 'usual suspect' countries like the United States, Germany or India precisely on account of similarities in population size and associated governance challenges.

It should be clear, then, that studying arrangements between non-sovereign entities and independent states is a valuable enterprise for comparative constitutional scholars as these provide sites to test and finesse our understanding of contemporary tropes. Our hope is that this chapter will help raise awareness of the latent potential in exploring these arrangements and provide an instructive roadmap for identifying some of the most pertinent questions to think about in this regard.

[110] Quik-Schuijt and Broekhuijse (n 52).
[111] Ferdinand, Oostindie and Veenendaal (n 4).
[112] Council of State, '70 Years Charter of the Kingdom – Collaboration on the basis of mutual understanding' (2 October 2024) ch 4.

4

Potential Future Small States

The Case of New Caledonia and French Polynesia

HERVÉ RAIMANA LALLEMANT-MOE

I. Introduction

France is not a small state by any means. However, like many other countries (New Zealand, United Kingdom, United States of America, Netherlands, etc), there are overseas territories legally bonded to the French Republic, that can potentially transform themselves in 'small States'[1] in the future.

These are French Polynesia, New Caledonia, and Wallis and Futuna (Pacific Ocean),[2] Saint Pierre and Miquelon (North America), French Guiana (Latin America), Martinique, Guadeloupe, Saint Martin, and Saint Barthélemy (Caribbean), Réunion and Mayotte (Indian Ocean), and the French Southern and Antarctic Lands (Terres australes et antarctiques françaises (TAAF) – five different territories in the Indian Ocean) and the inhabited island of Clipperton (Pacific Ocean). The French overseas territories represent a population of over 2.6 million inhabitants, with a total land area of almost 560,000 km^2 and a maritime area of 10 million km^2.

Remnants of a previous colonial era or other historical events, these territories are geographically differentiated from continental France.[3] For some of them, the contrast in terms of ethnicity, culture and history is quite important. They benefit from constitutional arrangements in the French legal framework (mainly found in Articles 72, 73, 74, 76 and 77 of the French Constitution).

The French Constitution of 27 October 1946, put an end to the legal colonial system, erasing the notion of a French 'Empire'. Nevertheless, some legal principles remained. The current 1958 French Constitution did not wipe out the distinction between 'legislative identity' and 'legislative specialty', which remains the *summa divisio* of French overseas territories' legal system. The French Constitutional Act of 28 March 2003, on

[1] T Angelo and J Corrin (eds), 'Small States: A Collection of Essays' (2019) XXIII *Comparative Law Journal of the Pacific* (Hors Series. Special Issue).

[2] P-Y Le Meur and A Mawyer, 'France and Oceanian Sovereignties' (2022) 92 *Oceania* 9.

[3] P de Deckker, 'Decolonisation Processes in the South Pacific Islands: A Comparative Analysis between Metropolitan Powers' (1996) 26 *Victoria University of Wellington Law Review* 355.

the decentralised organisation of the Republic, brought many changes but safeguarded this dual separation:

- Article 73 of the French Constitution sets out the constitutional status of overseas departments and regions (*départements et régions d'outre-mer* – DROMs) and unique collectivities (CUs), governed by the principle of legislative identity, which means the automatic extension of French law with greater adaptability.
- Article 74 of the French Constitution sets out the constitutional status of the category known generically as '*collectivités d'outre-mer*' (COMs), which replaces that of the '*territoires d'outre-mer*' (TOMs) but brings together within the same constitutional framework all those collectivities governed wholly or partially by the principle of legislative specialty, which is characterised by the absence of automatic extension of French law in these territories.

Today, some of the French overseas territories are closely linked to France, but others are more distinct and internationally recognised, like New Caledonia and French Polynesia.[4] The spectrum is therefore quite large, ranging between integration and association with the French State.

French Polynesia and New Caledonia are still French territories today due to a combination of historical, political, and strategic factors. France has had a major presence in the Indo-Pacific ever since it colonised New Caledonia in 1853. New Caledonia has held three votes on independence since 2018. The second poll saw an increase in the pro-independence vote from the first, but the final referendum in 2021 was boycotted by pro-independence parties due to the impact of Covid on the Indigenous Kanak population. Because of the boycott, the result showed overwhelming support for New Caledonia to remain in France. However, the issue of self-determination remains at the forefront of minds for many in the French territory. French Polynesia's status as a French territory is partly due to historical factors, with a French annexation that began in 1880. Atomic testing on the atolls of Moruroa and Fangataufa enabled France to develop the nuclear arsenal it needed to remain one of the world's leading powers.

These two territories are particularly important for France today because of its will to develop an 'Indo-Pacific Strategy'. This geopolitical strategy, launched in 2018, addresses issues of sovereignty: France is an Indo-Pacific nation, with seven of its 13 overseas Departments, Regions and Communities situated in either the Indian Ocean or the South Pacific. Moreover, France, as well as the European Union, has its own economic, political, and strategic interests to defend in the region. Ongoing shifts in the Indo-Pacific region have direct consequences for the prosperity and security of the different people living in the Pacific. The main objective is to maintain an open region, free of any form of coercion and based on the rule of international law and multilateralism.[5]

Sometimes referred as 'quasi small states', New Caledonia and French Polynesia are usually acting on their own, surfing on a complex framework of statute law and

[4] H Leslie and G Prinsen, 'French territories in the Forum: Trojan horse or paddles for the Pacific canoe?' (2018) 59 *Asia Pacific Viewpoint* 384.

[5] A Karambelkar, 'An analysis of the French strategy in the Indo-Pacific' (2021) 17 *Maritime Affairs: Journal of the National Maritime Foundation of India* 92.

constitutional provisions. As French territories, they are nevertheless members of the Pacific Islands Forum (a regional inter-governmental organisation), are recognised as Non-Self-Governing Territories (NSGTs) under Chapter XI of the Charter of the United Nations, and negotiate international agreements, especially with the sovereign states in the Pacific region.[6]

Identical to the independent states of the Pacific region, New Caledonia and especially French Polynesia dismiss the notion of themselves as 'small states', calling themselves 'Big oceanic states/ territories' or 'Large Ocean States' due to their large maritime spaces and the will to express their sovereignty through maritime spaces.[7]

France's territories in the Pacific have historically been isolated from the rest of the region by a linguistic barrier – these groups of islands are the only francophone territories in a sea of English-speaking countries – and by their unique trading relationship with Europe due to colonial history and economic relationships. The linguistic divide (shared by the French-speaking territory of Wallis and Futuna, also in the South Pacific) has hindered diplomatic relations and regional cooperation in the past, especially for French Polynesia, as cultural and communication barriers limited the engagement with other Pacific islands nations.[8] The French state also limited its own opportunities to engage the independent states of the Pacific by directing aid exclusively to its territories. This situation began to change in 1996 with France's decision to cease nuclear testing in the Pacific and with the desire of New Caledonia and French Polynesia to become more active players in the region and to reconnect with their neighbours, although they are not sovereign states.[9] Moreover, there is a renewed interest by the anglophone Pacific world in the French territories, especially following the 2024 New Caledonian crisis.[10]

French Polynesia and New Caledonia are also integrated into the European Union Overseas Countries and Territories (OCTs) status. They are associated under Part Four of the Treaty on the Functioning of the European Union (TFEU). For these overseas countries and territories, which are not part of the European territory, the main challenge is to maintain and strengthen the support for economic development provided by the European Union, under Article 198 of the TFEU, which underpins the association of these territories with the European Union. Until 31 January 2020, there were 25 OCTs, 12 of which belonged to the United Kingdom. Since Brexit, there are now only 13 OCTs in the EU. The OCTs are members of the European Union Overseas Countries and Territories Association (OCTA).[11]

[6] M Joyau, 'The External Relations of the Territory of French Polynesia' (2003) 9 *Revue Juridique Polynésienne* 35.

[7] A Hume, J Leape, KLL Oleson, E Polk, K Chand and R Dunbar, 'Towards an ocean-based large ocean states country classification' (2021) 134 *Marine Policy* 104766.

[8] 'Regional exchanges between New Caledonia and French Polynesia: limiting factors and support: Express note No 28' (*IEOM*, January 2011), www.ieom.fr/IMG/pdf/ne28_eclairage_echanges_regionaux_nc_et_pf_version_anglaise.pdf.

[9] N Maclellan, 'France and the Blue Pacific' (2018) 5(3) *Asia and the Pacific Policy Studies* 426.

[10] A Pearse, 'Pacific forum head disappointed by failed New Caledonia mission but vows to try again' *The New Zealand Herald* (25 August 2024), www.nzherald.co.nz/nz/politics/pacific-forum-head-disappointed-by-failed-new-caledonia-mission-but-vows-to-try-again.

[11] S André, 'L'Union Europeenne et la Zone du Pacifique/The European Union and the South Pacific' (1998) 28 *Victoria University of Wellington Law Review* 595.

The fact that New Caledonia and French Polynesia are part of one of the more unitary system-oriented states in the world creates a lot of challenges for these small territories to follow a path to full sovereignty, or even simply to implement a decolonisation process (that could also lead to full integration with France). These challenges are created by the complexity of their respective legal status in the French Constitution and the numerous differences (social, cultural, historical, etc) between them and continental France. In summary, we need to understand these challenges that are facing these small territories integrated to France on the road to potential statehood. In this context, smallness makes French Polynesia and New Caledonia quite hard to comprehend to the other territories in the Pacific. Smallness could also be a limiting factor in their journey to obtaining sovereignty, faced with the will of a powerful State, France, their administrative power.

In the following parts of the chapter, I will outline briefly some aspects of the complex legal status of both French Polynesia (section II) and New Caledonia (section III), as well as highlight some important aspects of the history and distinctiveness of the territories. In section IV, the decolonisation pathway for French Polynesia and New Caledonia will be presented, as well as the present crisis occurring in New Caledonia, blurring the statutory future of this territory.

II. French Polynesia

Beginning with French Polynesia, I briefly outline the name and geography of the territory, its political history and institutions.

A. Name and Geography

Since Act no 57-836 of 26 July 1957, on the composition and formation of the Territorial Assembly of French Polynesia, the collectivity's identity has become 'French Polynesia', following its renaming as an overseas territory and a colony of French establishments in Oceania. The collectivity's name is currently present in Article 72-3 of the Constitution.

French Polynesia has had a flag since deliberation no 84-1030 AT of 23 November 1984, and an anthem since deliberation no 93-60 AT of 10 June 1993. Today, these symbols are based on Article 1 of Organic Law no 2004-192 of 27 February 2004.

The only legally recognised identification today, the notion of 'French Polynesia' is rivalled by different names in Reo Tahiti (the Tahitian language), for example: Tahiti Nui, Porinetia, Te Fenua, Te Ao Maohi. Today, Maohi Nui is the name most often used by politicians and the media.

French Polynesia is around 16,000 km from France. Article 1 of Organic Law no 2004-192 of 27 February 2004 states that: 'French Polynesia comprises the Windward Islands, the Leeward Islands, the Tuamotu Islands, the Gambier Islands, the Marquesas Islands and the Austral Islands, as well as the adjacent maritime areas', and the territory comprises approximately 5.5 million square kilometres of maritime space, 3,500 square kilometres of land (half the size of Corsica) in its 118 islands.

The estimated population of French Polynesia in 2020 was 280,908. Tahiti, located in the Society Islands, is the most populous island, with close to 69 per cent of the total population according to the 2017 census. 78 per cent of the population is Polynesian, 12 per cent is Chinese, and the remaining 10 per cent is made up of local and metropolitan French. French and Tahitian are the official languages of French Polynesia.

It should be noted that under deliberation no 64-27 AT of 6 February 1964, Polynesia ceded full ownership of the Moruroa and Fangataufa atolls to the French Government, free of charge, for the purposes of the Pacific Nuclear Experimentation Centre (CEP).

B. Political History

Polynesia's institutional history is quite the roller-coaster ride.[12] It seems that a collection of social and moral laws, mainly customary and known as the 'Tetuna'e Code', existed before the arrival of Europeans. However, it was the arrival of missionaries from the London Missionary Society (LMS) in 1797 that led to the first written legal codifications, such as the Pomare Code of 1819. Other texts were subsequently developed, such as the 'Book of Laws of Tahiti and Moorea' of 1842. Institutions were also established, with an assembly of legislators made up of elected representatives from each district acting as a counterweight to royal power. At that time, part of Polynesia was clearly unified as a state in the sense of international law, with full sovereignty.

This qualification was confirmed by the treaty of 9 September 1842, concluded between Admiral Dupetit-Thouars and Queen Pōmare IV, instituting a protectorate over the Kingdom of Tahiti (without the consent of the King of France). However, this agreement was obviously imposed by the French representatives, and the sovereign quickly denounced the treaty, leading to the annexation of the Kingdom and a war. The result was a rapid transition from the highest degree of autonomy to no autonomy at all. Fortunately, the Queen was reinstalled on 6 February 1847 by the King of France, but the Kingdom's powers were gradually and rapidly reduced in favour of the French state.[13]

On 29 June 1880, King Pōmare V abdicated and ceded the Kingdom of Tahiti to France. The Tahitian state disappeared and was transformed into the colony of 'French Establishments in Oceania' (EFO). This marked the start of the annexation and unification of all the Polynesian archipelagos not yet incorporated (the unification was completed in 1903). All powers were concentrated in the hands of a French Governor (appointed by the President of the Republic), and it was not until 1930 that an assembly was created.

It wasn't until the Fourth Republic, on 27 October 1946, that things began to change in Polynesia. The category of TOMs and the principle of legislative specialty (the principle that French standards can only be applied overseas if there is an express mention of their applicability) were introduced.

[12] B Gille, 'Du Royaume Pomare au Pays d'Outre-Mer: Gouvernance et Institutions à Tahiti de 1767 à 2009' (2010) 16 *Revue Juridique Polynésienne* 69.

[13] S Tcherkézoff, 'The French Pacific in 2019: from the Colonies to Autonomy' (Sovereignty, Autonomy and Diversity in the French Pacific, Wellington, 14 March 2019), hal.science/hal-03563011.

After a period of stagnation, the *Defferre Loi-Cadre* (framework law) of 23 June 1956, and the decree of 22 July 1957, gave Polynesia considerable autonomy, with very extensive powers. The community became French Polynesia. There was still a Governor, but there was also a Government Council headed by a Vice-President, and a territorial assembly with enhanced powers. Unfortunately, the prospect of the installation of the CEP and concerns about a shift from autonomy to independence led to a sharp decline in Polynesian autonomy. It was at this time (11 November 1958) that Pouvana'a a Oopa (the Vice-President of the Council and French Parliament representative) was arrested. He was charged with arson in Papeete (the capital, located on Tahiti) and sentenced to 8 years in prison and 15 years' exile in France, a conviction widely seen as politically motivated due to his opposition to the French state. Pouvana'a a Oopa was an important Tahitian politician and advocate for broader French Polynesian autonomy or independence. He is considered as the '*metua*' (father) of French Polynesia's independence movement and his conviction was quashed in 2018 by the French Cour de Cassation after new evidence showed that French police had fabricated evidence against him. Some commentators believe his arrest was planned to protect the scheduled nuclear testing in French Polynesia.[14]

It was the statute of 12 July 1977 (known as the *Autonomie de Gestion*) that represented the starting point for contemporary autonomy in French Polynesia, and for the progress of ever-increasing decentralisation in the community. It saw the emergence of the High Commissioner (still the official head of the executive) and a Government Council that rapidly grew in importance (with the Vice-President of the Council becoming, in practice, its leader). This was also the time when Polynesia was granted jurisdiction in principle, while the French state was only competent in a limited list of areas.

Autonomy was further strengthened with the statutory law of 6 September 1984, which gave the territory 'internal autonomy'. The most important change is that the head of the executive is now elected (a member of the Assembly elected by his or her peers). He or she is called the President of the Government. The High Commissioner is now no more than a delegate of the central government.

The Organic Law of 12 April 1996 slightly altered the local status, and new powers were transferred to French Polynesia, but overall, it wasn't a revolution.

Currently, French Polynesia is an 'autonomous' overseas collectivity (COM) – in accordance with the Constitutional Law of 28 March 2003, based on Article 74 of the Constitution. Autonomy is not defined in the French Constitution. Under Article 74, it potentially allows: special control by the State Council (*Conseil d'État*) over texts adopted locally, protection of competences (declassification), protection of local employment and property, and participation in French state jurisdiction linked to public freedoms.[15] The organisation and functioning of COMs are determined by specific statutory laws. In contrast with other French overseas territories, their legal status is thus more flexible and specific to each territory. French Polynesia is a more advanced territory regarding

[14] J-M Regnault, *Pouvana'a et de Gaulle, la candeur et la grandeur* (CreateSpace Independent Publishing Platform, 2016).

[15] S Al Wardi, 'Twenty Years of Politics in French Polynesia' (2009) 44 *The Journal of Pacific History* 195.

self-governing issues – it is possible to find other territories classified as a COM like Saint Pierre and Miquelon with almost no autonomy whatsoever.

This decentralisation process, which began in 1977, followed the transformation of the French state to a more decentralised state, which is now clearly stated in the first article of the Constitution. It also followed the fight of several French Polynesian politicians (especially Mr Gaston Flosse) to obtain more autonomy and self-governance. This fight was ultimately a success, arguably in part a reward for the fact that French Polynesia was used as a nuclear testing ground.

Despite increasing levels of autonomy, however, in international law French Polynesia is a non-self-governing territory attached to the French administering power (since 2013) and based on United Nations General Assembly Resolutions 66 (I) dated 14 December 1946, and 67/265 dated 17 May 2013.

C. The Institutions and Legal Regime

As noted earlier, based on Article 74 of the Constitution, Organic Law no 2004-192 of 27 February 2004 on the autonomous status of French Polynesia was adopted, and French Polynesia became an autonomous overseas collectivity. The notion of country or '*Pays*' is used locally, based on the first article of the Organic Law (LOPF).

Since the 1977 statute, French Polynesia's powers have ceased to be listed exhaustively. Henceforth, French Polynesia has general jurisdiction, while the French state only has powers attributed. As a result, when a matter is not listed in the state's competencies, it falls under the jurisdiction of French Polynesia.[16]

French Polynesia exercises its jurisdiction through:

- Decrees issued by the Council of Ministers,
- Deliberations (autonomous regulatory power of the Assembly of French Polynesia), and
- Laws of the Country/ '*Lois du pays*' (regulatory acts with legislative force).[17]

State powers are listed in Article 14 of the LOPF and the French state possesses jurisdiction in limited domains like nationality; civil rights; electoral law; civil rights, status and capacity of persons, in particular civil status certificates, absence, marriage, divorce, filiation; parental authority; matrimonial property, etc. The cities ('*communes*') also only have the powers that are attributed to them, which are listed in Article 43 of the LOPF.

Because of the legislative specialty principle, in respect of the domains in which the French state has jurisdiction, French Laws are only valid in French Polynesia if they include a special mention of applicability. There are, of course, exceptions for some sectors (Article 7 of the LOPF) like national defence, judicial procedures and French state public servants' status. Consequently, if a French Law or Decree does not include

[16] J Peres, 'Application des Lois et Règlements en Polynésie Française : Répartition des Compétences' (2004) 11 *Revue Juridique Polynésienne* 23.

[17] A Moyrand and AH Angelo, 'Cancelling a Loi du Pays' (2023) 29 *Comparative Law Journal of the Pacific* 131.

an express mention of applicability to French Polynesia, it is inapplicable, and you cannot invoke it before the judge.

Article 5 of the LOPF specifies that French Polynesia comprises four institutions: The President, the government, the Assembly of French Polynesia (APF) and the Economic, Social, Environmental and Cultural Council (CESEC).[18]

The structure of Polynesian institutions is classic, with powers distributed as follows: executive power is vested in the President and the government; deliberative and legislative power is vested in a single chamber, the APF; and consultative power is exercised by the CESEC.

The APF is a classic parliamentary chamber comprising 57 representatives elected for five years by universal suffrage. From these 57 representatives will be chosen the President of French Polynesia, who in turn will choose the members of the government. The APF may pass laws of the country (administrative acts that are materially legislative), deliberations (which fall under the autonomous regulatory power of the APF) and possibly resolutions (requests to the French state). Moreover, the President of the Country and the government can be removed through the intermediary of a motion of no-confidence (difficult to achieve as it requires a vote of three-fifths of the members of the APF). Neither the President nor the local government has a similar direct weapon of deterrence.

The Presidents of French Polynesia represent the collectivity and head its administration and government. They are elected for a five-year term by their APF peers. As they appoint the members of the government, they are clearly the most important element of the Polynesian executive, combining, in a way, the attributes of the French President of the Republic and the French Prime Minister.

For the government, the number of ministers must be between 7 and 10 and the responsibilities of each minister are freely determined by the President of French Polynesia according to the priorities the President intends to put forward. The Council of Ministers has normative powers to apply the norms of the Assembly of French Polynesia (Article 89 paragraph 3 of the LOPF) and is autonomous (Articles 90 and 91 of the LOPF). Although it has no weapon against the APF, it can ask the French President of the Republic to call early elections for the APF (Article 157-1). However, this is a far cry from the parliamentary system, where the executive and legislative branches can threaten each other. The institutional system in place in French Polynesia is quite close to the one in place in classic decentralised French territories like 'Départements' or 'Régions' with an executive and a deliberative branch, but without the means to politically function fully without the intervention of the French state. For example, the dissolution of the French Polynesian Assembly cannot be enforced by the President of French Polynesia but only by the French President.[19]

Finally, the CESEC is a consultative institution that contributes to local legislative, deliberative, and executive power by involving civil society. It can include a maximum of 51 representatives appointed for four years by the French Polynesian government,

[18] J Corrin and T Angelo (eds), *Legal Systems of the Pacific: Introducing Sixteen Gems* (Cambridge, Intersentia, 2021).

[19] Loi organique no 2004-192 of 27 February 2004, art 157.

who are divided into different colleges. The CESEC must be consulted on all draft or proposed legislation in the country of an economic or social nature.

It is interesting to note that, unlike other Pacific island territories, legal pluralism and customary law widely disappeared in French Polynesia. The centralisation pursued by the Kingdom of Tahiti in the nineteenth century, and the French colonisation that ensued, completely wiped out Polynesian legal pluralism, apart from some environmental mechanisms still used today.[20]

The next section turns to a brief outline of the history and political status of the special territory of New Caledonia. Before doing that, it is worth noting that New Caledonia and French Polynesia both hold unique positions within the French Republic, characterised by varying degrees of autonomy and self-governance. The French Polynesian level of autonomy is quite comparable to New Caledonia except for a few key elements. Apart from the political and institutional differences, the statutory legal framework of New Caledonia is protected by the French Constitution (Articles 76 and 77 of the French Constitution) which is not the case for French Polynesia. Moreover, the *Loi du pays* in New Caledonia is considered a law, equal to French law, which is not the case for its French Polynesian counterpart, which is an administrative act – as noted above. Finally, the New Caledonian legal jurisdiction is a little bit more developed. For example, the whole of the French civil code was transferred to New Caledonia, but in French Polynesia, the status and legal capacity of persons is still in the hands of the French state.

III. New Caledonia

This brief outline of New Caledonia will follow the same structure as that of French Polynesia, discussing the name and geography of the territory, its political history, and institutions.

A. Name and Geography

New Caledonia's status is 'governed by Title XIII' of the French Constitution (Constitution, Article 72-3, paragraph 2). By distinguishing it from the 'overseas collectivities governed by article 74', Articles 13, paragraph 3 and 74-1, paragraph 1 make clear that New Caledonia is not a COM. The country is also known as 'Kanaky' (land of the Kanak people) by pro-independence political parties' members.[21]

New Caledonia sits 18,000 km from France. It is an archipelago comprising 'Grande Terre' (which is 400 km long and 42 km wide on average), the Loyalty Islands to the north, and many other islands and islets, only a few of which are inhabited. Coral reefs, several parts of which have been inscribed by UNESCO on its World Heritage List, border lagoons.

[20] T Bambridge (ed), *The Rahui: Legal pluralism in Polynesian traditional management of resources and territories* (Canberra, ANU Press, 2016).

[21] C David, 'The road to sovereignty for New Caledonia? Analysis of the November 2018 consultation on self-determination' (2019) 2(2) *Small States and Territories* 141, https://hal.science/hal-02540822v1.

The Indigenous people are called 'Kanak'. The Kanak culture is marked by the importance of the land, which gives identity to those who come from it, the organisation of clans and tribes, and the rites of exchange. From the time when New Caledonia's 'Grande Terre' was occupied by France on 24 September 1853 (the Loyalty Islands were not occupied by France until 1869), almost 80 years after their discovery by James Cook in 1774, colonisation began – at first mainly by prison settlers, then by free settlers – from France, Asia, and Oceania. As a result, by the 1970s the Kanak population was in the minority. Today, the Kanak people represent between 40 and 45 per cent of the population of New Caledonia.[22]

The Kanak are governed by custom: a set of rules governing their social life, in particular concerning filiation, marriage, property, and inheritance, which vary according to the customary areas to which the chiefdoms grouping their clans belong. The colonial regime recognised these specific rules as bestowing what was defined as a civil status under special law. Citizens with special civil status are thus exempt from most of the provisions of the Civil Code.

Political organisations representing most of the Kanak population have been demanding independence since the mid-1970s. From 1984 onwards, these demands became more radical, leading to clashes and a quasi-insurrectionary situation. Successive statutes signed between 1984 and 1988 attempted to respond to certain aspects of these demands: participation in political power, land reform and recognition of cultural identity.[23] With the Matignon (26 June 1988) and Nouméa (5 May 1998) Accords, New Caledonia's status became temporary, with a self-determination ballot as its deadline.

B. Political History

New Caledonia became a separate colony of 'Oceania French Establishments' by a decree of 17 March 1862. It was headed by a Governor. A decree of 2 April 1885, set up a 16-member general council, which elected a colonial commission from among its members.[24]

The French Constitution of 27 October 1946 created the overseas territories (TOMs), endowed, under Article 60, 'with a special status taking account of their specific interests within the overall interests of the Republic'. Law no 56-619 of 23 June 1956 was made applicable to New Caledonia by Decree no 57-812 of 22 July 1957. The general council became a territorial assembly.

[22] 'Un mosaïque pluriethnique' (Institute of Statistics and Economic Studies of New Caledonia), www.isee.nc/population/recensement/communautes.

[23] C Fontaine, 'Kanak's quest for identity: the influence of citizenship on the construction of customary law in New Caledonia' (L'Institut international de recherche sur la conflictualité (*IiRCO*), Université de Limoges, 5 December 2020), www.unilim.fr/iirco/2020/12/05/kanaks-quest-for-identity-the-influence-of-citizenship-on-the-construction-of-customary-law-in-new-caledonia/.

[24] A Muckle and I Merle, *The Indigénat and France's Empire in New Caledonia: Origins, Practices and Legacies* (Cham, Palgrave Macmillan, 2022).

The desire to maintain a French presence in the Pacific to ensure the safety of nuclear experiments, followed by the need to control the mining sector at a time when the nickel economy was expanding, led to laws reducing the territory's autonomy. However, and much later, Law no 76-1222 of 28 December 1976, gave the territory of New Caledonia greater autonomy, with jurisdiction under ordinary law. The French state's powers are listed exhaustively.

A new statute was adopted by the Law of 6 September 1984. The French state retained the powers it had acquired under the Law of 28 December 1976, with a few adjustments. Six 'customary territories' were recognised. An assembly of customary territories, made up of 24 representatives of custom and 24 representatives of the communes, was set up. A vote on self-determination was scheduled to be held within five years, but it was postponed.

The Law on the development of New Caledonia was promulgated on 23 August 1985. It provided for the creation of four new local authorities, distinct from both the territory and cities, known as 'regions' (that would later be transformed into 'Provinces'). These assemblies come together to form the Congress of New Caledonia, which has jurisdiction over the entire territory. Following a change in the parliamentary majority, Law no 86-844 of 17 July 1986 maintained the regions, but reduced their powers.

Following violent events in New Caledonia in 1984–88, the French Prime Minister decided to send a peace mission to New Caledonia. Subsequently, two delegations, led by Jean-Marie Tjibaou for the pro-independence '*Front National de Libération Kanak Socialiste* (FLNKS)' and Jacques Lafleur for the non-independence '*Rassemblement pour la Calédonie dans la République* (RPCR)', agreed to come to Paris for talks. The discussions resulted in a general declaration and two texts on 26 June 1988. The Matignon Accords were to culminate in a referendum on self-determination to be held between 1 March and 31 December 1998. As early as 1991, the president of the main non-independence party, the RPCR, Jacques Lafleur, put forward the idea of a 'consensual solution' to extend the referendum date, which the signatories of the Matignon Accords would propose together to the electorate. Negotiations therefore began between the two local partners and with the French Government. On 5 May 1998, the Nouméa Accord was signed by the Prime Minister, Lionel Jospin, on behalf of the state, and by members of the RPCR and FLNKS delegations, led respectively by Lafleur and Roch Wamytan.

This agreement was confirmed by Constitutional Act no 98-610 of 20 July 1998 on New Caledonia, adopted by the French National Assembly on June 16, by the French Senate on 30 June and by the Congress of the French Parliament on 6 July re-establishing a Title XIII entitled 'Transitional provisions relating to New Caledonia', to mark the time-limited nature of the Nouméa Accord (between 15 and 20 years), which includes two new Articles 76 and 77 and provides for a process of self-determination. The Nouméa Accord was implemented by Organic Law no 99-209 of 19 March 1999 relating to New Caledonia, and by Ordinary Law no 99-210 of the same date and bearing the same title.

In international law, New Caledonia is still a non-self-governing territory attached to the French administering power by General Assembly Resolutions 66 (I) of 14 December 1946 and 41/41 of 2 December 1986, even though three referendums were organised in New Caledonia in 2018, 2020 and 2021.

C. The Institutions and Legal Regime

As noted earlier, in practice, the status of New Caledonia within French law is quite close to the status of French Polynesia, albeit with an apparent shift from merely administrative autonomy to political autonomy for New Caledonia due to the constitutional protection of the institutional framework of this territory. The structure of New Caledonia is more complex and unusual than French Polynesia, with many more institutions and political subdivisions.[25]

Since Law no 88-1028 of 9 November 1988, the Congress has been the name of New Caledonia's deliberative assembly. It brings together all the members of the provincial assemblies. The Congress comprises 54 members. The proportion of representatives of the three provinces (North Province, South Province and The Loyalty Islands) in the Congress may therefore not be too far removed from the population distribution. In application of the Nouméa Accord, the members of the Congress are elected by a restricted electorate, made up exclusively of the 'citizens' of New Caledonia. Voters eligible to take part in these elections are entered on a special electoral list, drawn up by a special administrative commission, which is also responsible for drawing up the supplementary list of voters not eligible to take part. Article 83 of Organic Law no 99-209 of 19 March 1999 lays down the principle that the powers of New Caledonia are exercised by the Congress, except where they are assigned to the government of New Caledonia or its President.

New Caledonia, of all the French oversea territories, possesses an unusual political subdivision: the Province. Created by law no 88-1028 of 9 November 1988, the three provinces succeeded the regions. Competences that are not devolved to the state or New Caledonia by Organic Law no 99-209 of 19 March 1999, or to the communes by the legislation applicable to New Caledonia, fall within the remit of the provinces. In New Caledonia, the provinces thus have jurisdiction in principle. They comprise provincial assemblies and a local executive, the '*Président de Province*'.

New Caledonia's executive is an elected government. It is elected by Congress and is accountable to it. The Nouméa Accord stipulated that the government would be collegial, so that none of the signatory parties would be excluded and consensus would be sought in relation to the government's actions. Composed of between five and 11 members, the number being determined by a deliberation of the Congress, the executive is elected by the Congress. The government meets under the chairmanship of its President or Vice-President, or a member of the government designated by the President or Vice-President. The High Commissioner (the representative of France) attends government meetings by right and may consultatively speak. The government adopts the bills of the country or deliberations, executes the decisions of the Congress, and takes decisions in matters falling within the competence of New Caledonia.

The President of the Government of New Caledonia represents New Caledonia, notably in legal proceedings. He exercises administrative police powers and the power

[25] C David, 'The status of New Caledonia in the French Constitutional context' (France in the Pacific: An Update, Canberra, 2012), https://hal.science/hal-03387402v1.

of requisition in matters falling within the jurisdiction of New Caledonia. He directs the administration and makes appointments to public posts which are not filled by decisions of the government.

The Customary Senate is made up of 16 members appointed for six years, for the first term, and for five years for subsequent terms, two from each of the customary councils, 'according to the practices recognised by custom',[26] ie, according to the rules that the customary authorities decide to adopt, with the President of the Government simply recording these appointments by decree published in the *Official Journal of New Caledonia and Dependencies*. The President of the Customary Senate is appointed annually. He organises and directs the services of the Customary Senate. He is consulted on draft and proposed deliberations relating to identity signs (flag and local hymn), customary civil status, customary land tenure (including customary leases and palavers), the boundaries of customary areas, and election procedures for the Customary Senate and Customary Councils. For *Lois du pays* regarding Kanak Customs, the Customary Senate is regarded as a co-legislator with the New Caledonian Congress. Customary Councils are appointed in each of New Caledonia's eight customary areas, in accordance with the practices specific to each customary group. Their number is not fixed. The Customary Senate serves as a significant institution within this system of legal pluralism. It acts as a consultative body and co-legislator on issues related to Kanak customs and identity, thereby influencing the legislative process and ensuring that Melanesian values are represented in local laws.[27]

In contrast with French Polynesia, which had already centralised its legal system even before French annexation, customary law is still strongly present in New Caledonia, as well as many other parts of Melanesia. Indeed, New Caledonia exhibits a unique form of legal pluralism that integrates French law with local customs and customary law, particularly reflecting the Kanak culture. The Kanak people have their own customs that govern personal status and land rights, which are recognised by the legal system. This is facilitated through the establishment of customary assessors who assist civil courts by providing insights into customary practices relevant to specific cases. This mechanism allows judges to incorporate traditional rules into their decisions, particularly in matters involving Kanak identity and land.[28] Different legal systems co-exist within the same geographic area in this territory. For example, the civil law in New Caledonia may be different from that in force in the French national law. This is due to the *sui generis* legal status of New Caledonia. Moreover, in New Caledonia, two personal statuses exist, and each one is governed by a different legal corpus. The first is called ordinary civil status and is regulated by common civil law. The second, as noted earlier, is called customary civil status and is regulated by Kanak custom.[29]

[26] H Gire, 'La coutume en Nouvelle-Calédonie' (2001) 32 *Victoria University of Wellington Law Review* 751.

[27] C Bidaud-Garon, 'New Caledonia: Legal Pluralism and Diversity of Interpretation of Fundamental Rights (Common Law, Customary Law, Reservation Related to Indigenous Rights): The Example of New Caledonia' in M Brinig (ed), *International Survey of Family Law 2019* (Cambridge, Intersentia, 2019).

[28] E Cornut and P Deumier (eds), *La Coutume Kanak dans le pluralisme juridique calédonien* (Nouméa, Presses universitaires de Nouvelle-Calédonie, 2016).

[29] ibid.

Finally, the Economic, Social and Environmental Council has, since the Organic Law was amended in 2013, comprised 41 members. Within a period of one month (reduced to 15 days in the event of an emergency) the Economic, Social and Environmental Council gives its opinion, which is made public, on draft and proposed *Lois du pays* and deliberations of the Congress 'of an economic, social or environmental nature'.

IV. The Road to Sovereign States?

From far away, it appears that there might be a parallel path for New Caledonia and French Polynesia toward decolonisation, as discussed in section IV.A below, but a crisis in New Caledonia may have altered that path, or at least delayed the journey along it, as discussed in section IV.B.

A. A Parallel Path?

Despite their differences, New Caledonia and French Polynesia share similar political situations that highlight the possibility to break from the French Republic in the future, especially the fact that their own institutions, local legal structure, and laws are quite unusual in the French Republic system.[30] And, importantly, New Caledonia and French Polynesia are the only French overseas territories listed as Non-Self-Governing Territories by the United Nations.

An NSGT is a territory deemed by the United Nations General Assembly to be 'non-self-governing' for the purposes of Chapter XI of the UN Charter. The UN defines an NSGT as 'a territory whose people have not yet attained a full measure of self-government' (Article 73 of the UN Charter). The main consequences of being inscribed on the UN list of NSGTs are that the administering state (the country responsible for the territory) must submit annual reports to the UN on the political, economic, social and educational status of the territory; the UN Special Committee on Decolonisation (known as C-24) monitors the situation in NSGTs and makes recommendations for the political development of the territories; and NSGTs are eligible for assistance from UN specialised agencies and international institutions to promote their development. The UN General Assembly passes resolutions each year affirming the right to self-determination for NSGTs and calling for decolonisation.[31]

> The decolonisation efforts of the UN derive from the principle of 'equal rights and self-determination of peoples' as stipulated in Article 1(2) of the Charter of the United Nations, as well as from three specific chapters in the Charter which are devoted to the interests of dependent peoples [Articles 73–74, 75–85 and 86–91] … In 1960, the UN General Assembly adopted the Declaration on the Granting of Independence to Colonial Countries and Peoples

[30] A Moyrand and AH Angelo, 'International Law Perspectives on the Evolution in Status of the French Overseas Territories' (1999) 5 *Revue Juridique Polynésienne* 49.

[31] 'Resolution on the question of New Caledonia, Implementation of the Declaration on the Granting of Independence to Colonial Countries and Peoples' GA Res 78/94, UN Doc A/RES/78/94 (7 December 2023); 'Resolution on the question of French Polynesia, Implementation of the Declaration on the Granting of Independence to Colonial Countries and Peoples' GA Res 78/91, UN Doc A/RES/78/91 (7 December 2023).

(General Assembly resolution 1514 (XV)), known also as the Declaration on Decolonization. By this resolution, the General Assembly, considering the important role of the UN in assisting the movement for independence in Trust and Non-Self-Governing Territories, solemnly proclaimed the necessity of bringing colonialism in all its forms and manifestations to a speedy and unconditional end, and in this context, declared, inter alia, that all people had a right to self-determination … A Non-Self-Governing Territory can be said to have reached a full measure of self-government through

- Emergence as a sovereign independent State,
- Free association with an independent State, or
- Integration with an independent State.[32]

On 17 May 2013, by General Assembly Resolution 67/265, French Polynesia was re-listed as a NSGT as one of the 17 remaining on the agenda of C-24 under Chapter XI of the UN Charter. It was initially inscribed by UN General Assembly Resolution 66 (I) of 14 December 1946 but quickly removed (one year later) following a request from the French state.

French Polynesia is a less known and understood territory in the UN or even the regional ecosystem for three main reasons: it is the territory most recently added to the list of NSGTs; it is a francophone territory (as noted, one of the few in the Pacific region); and its legal framework and autonomy system within the Administering power (France) is quite complex, even for local legal experts.

Nevertheless, we can easily summarise the situation of French Polynesia toward the decolonisation process in a few points:

- The French Polynesian government and elected institutions traditionally wanted to be removed from the NSGTs list, because the local government was against the independence of the territory,
- The French Polynesian opposition (the independence party, for a long time) wanted the help of the United Nations to influence the Administering power into accepting the basis of a self-determination process,
- France, the Administering power, decided to not participate in this debate.

Since 2013 this status quo has not evolved, but in 2023 France did participate in the decolonisation debate at the United Nations for the first time regarding French Polynesia, and the local government called for strengthening the process.[33]

This situation can be explained by the fact that 30 April 2023 marked the first time that the pro-independence party *Tavini huira'atira* won the most seats in Assembly, and is now able to form a stable government. *Tavini huira'atira* won 38 seats with 44.3 per cent of the votes in the second round, defeating *Tapura huira'atira*, led by then President, Édouard Fritch, which won 16 seats with 38.5 per cent of the votes. The third party, *A here ia Porinetia*, another anti-independence party, won three seats with 17.2 per cent of the votes. The turnout was quite high, with almost 70 per cent of electors voting. Moetai

[32] UN website: 'The United Nations and Decolonization', https://www.un.org/dppa/decolonization/en/about#.

[33] HR Lallemant-Moe, 'The French Polynesian Elections of 2023: The Rise to Power of the Tavini Huira'atira' (2023) 29 *Comparative Law Journal of the Pacific* 43.

Brotherson became the French Polynesian President and now leads a pro-independence government.[34]

New Caledonia has a longer history with the United Nations decolonisation process. It was on the list of NSGTs from 1946 to 1947, following the transmission of information on New Caledonia and Dependencies by France under Article 73e of the UN Charter. In 1986, the General Assembly re-inscribed New Caledonia on that list. Moreover, and unlike when French Polynesia was re-inscribed in 2013, France participated in this process at the UN.

Politically speaking, New Caledonia is also marked by the majority held in its Congress by pro-independence parties and has a FLNKS President. The 17th government of New Caledonia was elected on 17 February 2021 by the elected members of the Congress and comprises 11 members from all the local political groups. The President of the Government, Louis Mapou, was elected on 8 July 2021.

One interesting point is the near institutional future of New Caledonia. On 12 December 2021, New Caledonia held its third and final independence referendum as foreseen by the 1998 Nouméa Accord. With a voter turnout of just 43.87 per cent, the official answer to the question 'Do you want New Caledonia to accede to full sovereignty and become independent?' was 3.5 per cent in favour and 96.5 per cent opposed.

This differs drastically from the first two referenda in terms of both turnout and results. In 2020, with a turnout rate of 85.69 per cent, the results were 46.74 per cent in favour of independence and 53.26 per cent opposed. Before that, the 2018 turnout rate was 81.01 per cent, with 43.33 per cent in favour of independence and 56.67 per cent opposed. This situation can be explained by the international COVID-19 pandemic situation and the fact that pro-independence parties called for a postponement of the voting date, which was unfruitful. As a result, they called on their members to abstain from voting.

After this process described in the Nouméa Accord, there is now a legal obligation for the French state to modify the French Constitution to consider these referendums and create a new status for New Caledonia. By the middle of 2024, the negotiations were stalling between the French Government and all the New Caledonian political parties, and so the question of what the future will hold for this territory is quite unclear, as is the question of whether French Polynesia will follow suit and be included in the next French constitutional reform.[35]

B. The New Caledonian Crisis

As already discussed, the last independence referendum in New Caledonia was deemed illegitimate by the local independence party. It was also deemed so by many observers, including the Pacific Islands Forum.[36]

[34] HR Lallemant-Moe, 'Clearing the Path to Decolonisation with Pragmatism and Agility in a Global Pandemic Context: The Case of French Polynesia' (2022) 27 *Comparative Law Journal of the Pacific* 13.

[35] A Moyrand and AH Angelo, 'Some Perspectives on the Development of the Status of New Caledonia and French Polynesia to Non-self-governing Territories within the Republic of France' (2022) 28 *Comparative Law Journal of the Pacific* 15.

[36] N Maclellan, 'Crisis in New Caledonia' (*DevPolicyBlog*, 17 May 2024), devpolicy.org/crisis-in-new-caledonia.

Nonetheless, the beginning of a proposed multiple-step constitutional reform concerning New Caledonia to transform the local institutions was recently promoted by President Emmanuel Macron. Under the proposal, the reform aims first to expand the electorate for local elections in the territory (for the 'Provinces' and a fortiori the local Congress). The constitutional Bill modifying the electoral body for the elections to the Congress and provincial assemblies of New Caledonia was voted on by the National Assembly and the Senate in identical terms on 14 May 2024. This constitutional reform project has the peculiar characteristic of being conditional. It was intended to come into effect on 1 July 2024, unless an agreement was reached among the partners to the Nouméa Accord, and it could even be rendered void if an agreement were made after the reform but before the elections. The aim of this first step in the constitutional reform is to create Article 77-1 of the Constitution and thereby to include in the electors to the Congress and Provinces those voters registered on the general electoral list of New Caledonia who were born there or have been domiciled there for at least 10 years (ie, to widen the franchise).

This step was perceived by many groups of Indigenous people in New Caledonia as a direct threat to their political power and identity (because it would result in an expansion of the non-Kanak proportion of electors), leading to violent protests that erupted on 13 May 2024. The unrest resulted in several fatalities, and billions in property damage. The French authorities declared a state of emergency and sent more than 1000 police personnel to New Caledonia.[37]

The French President, Emmanuel Macron, travelled to New Caledonia and called for dialogue among the different political factions but now faces significant challenges in bridging the divide between pro-independence and pro-France sentiments, especially because he is seen as taking the side of the latter.

Moreover, following a significant defeat in the European Parliament elections, President Macron announced the dissolution of the French National Assembly on 9 June 2024. Following the subsequent elections, the French National Assembly is now divided into three roughly equal groups (representing the left, centre and extreme right), and no group has a clear majority. Prime Minister, Gabriel Attal, and his cabinet resigned following these elections, and by August 2024 there was still no new Prime Minister or Cabinet.

This situation postponed any progress in relation to the political situation in New Caledonia. On 25 July, the President of the French Republic received four New Caledonian parliamentarians at the Élysée Palace. It was seen as a first step for the resumption of political dialogue between pro-independence and anti-independence supporters. The four New Caledonian parliamentarians consist of two pro-independence and two anti-independence members, including Emmanuel Tjibaou, a pro-independence representative elected in the last elections and considered as one of the first New Caledonian pro-independence '*Députés*' elected.[38] However, the state

[37] K Needham and C Raynaud, '"Massive" French police deployment arrives to secure New Caledonia', *Radio New Zealand* (17 May 2024), www.rnz.co.nz/news/world/517093/massive-french-police-deployment-arrives-to-secure-new-caledonia.

[38] J Péru-Gelly, 'Avenir institutionnel de la Nouvelle-Calédonie : Emmanuel Macron espère une reprise des discussions politiques en septembre' *FranceInfo* (25 July 2024), la1ere.francetvinfo.fr/avenir-institutionnel-de-la-nouvelle-caledonie-emmanuel-macron-espere-une-reprise-des-discussions-politiques-en-septembre-1508573.html.

of emergency in New Caledonia, combined with the political situation in France, will certainly push any modifications of the Constitution much further into the future. Ideally, for the political crisis to be resolved, the French state will need to stop any kind of national legislation agenda tending to modify the New Caledonian status, and begin new negotiations with all the local parties. Collaborating more with the region is also vital for France to detach itself from its colonial image. With a never-before-seen governmental crisis in France regarding the Prime Minister nomination, it will certainly be a long and difficult process, especially given that outbursts of violence are still occurring in New Caledonia.

The NSGTs includes several small island territories like French Polynesia and New Caledonia, the American Samoa, the Falkland Islands (*Islas Malvinas*), Guam, Pitcairn Islands, Saint Helena, Tokelau, the United States Virgin Islands, Montserrat, Anguilla, Bermuda, the British Virgin Islands, Cayman Islands, and Turks and Caicos Islands. New Caledonia was considered to be the most advanced NSGT pursuing the decolonisation process. It was scheduled to be the first territory to exit this list since the creation of the NSGTs, becoming a full sovereign state or being self-governing in association with (or within) France. The recent crisis in New Caledonia seemed to have completely reset the process. As the territory considered to be a good example, this failure may prove to be a new obstacle for all the NSGT small island territories in their path to decolonisation with their respective administrative powers, proving, in a sense, that smallness is indeed a complex challenge in the face of a decolonisation process. The cases of French Polynesia and New Caledonia imply that smallness is creating challenges for these two territories to be fully understood and heard on the regional and international stage, as well as keeping the helm toward a decolonisation process that does not completely fit into the French legal structure. This situation can definitely be translated to other NSGTs, also experiencing these effects from smallness generally induced by their small island territory status.

5

Traditional Constitutional Arrangements and the Separation of Powers

A Difficult Relationship in Continental Europe Micro Jurisdictions

ELISA BERTOLINI

I. Premise

All continental Europe micro jurisdictions – the Principalities of Andorra, Liechtenstein and Monaco, the Republic of San Marino, and the Vatican City State[1] – are geographical enclaves.[2] Their diminutive size has allowed them to develop, throughout the centuries, original legal solutions with respect to their state architecture, while entertaining close relations with their neighbouring macro states, whose constitutional arrangements were meant to have, sooner or later, an influence on theirs. To be an enclave does not mean that these states are impervious to the circulation of ideas from other jurisdictions that followed the French Revolution.

The present chapter analyses the impact that the diminutive size of these micro jurisdictions has upon their constitutional arrangements, in particular when it comes to the balance of powers between the different branches of government.[3] This focus is of particular interest from the microstates' perspective, because it allows one carefully to

[1] The Vatican City State will not be analysed here, due to its peculiar relationship with the Holy See, the implications of this relationship in terms of the State's aims (being instrumental to the Holy See) and its character of absolute monarchy. See C Casey, 'The Fundamental Law of Vatican City State: Hidden Treasures in the Constitution of the World's Smallest State', Chapter 6 in this volume.

[2] For the purposes of the present analysis, I consider micro jurisdictions to be those states having a territorial size of maximum 1,000 km^2 and 1 million inhabitants. Malta would fit within the classification; however, being an island and a decolonised state, it will not be discussed. I discuss the classificatory criteria more exhaustively in E Bertolini, 'The Constitutional Identity of European Micro States and the Continental Integration Mechanisms. The Influence of the Diminutive Size' (2020) 14(2) *Vienna Journal of International Constitutional Law* 133.

[3] Diminutive size impacts on every aspect of a micro jurisdiction's life. For a broader look at small (and not just micro) jurisdictions, see P Butler and C Morris (eds), *Small States in a Legal World* (Berlin, Springer, 2017); for an even broader look, reference is made to the Springer book series The World of Small States.

reflect on the difficulty of balancing the maintenance of their traditional institutions, on the one hand, with the need to be receptive to the development of European constitutionalism, on the other hand. Indeed, these constitutional systems are quite unusual from a comparative perspective, being anchored in a distinctive legal and historical tradition, influenced by their diminutive size. At the same time, these legal systems had to reform their distinctive institutional arrangements from the moment they aspired to integrate into regional integration mechanisms, such as the Council of Europe (CoE).[4] The input of the CoE, together with the will to be part of the international community, has driven all constitutional reform in these micro jurisdictions since the 1970s.

It is widely claimed that micro jurisdictions tend to incorporate foreign law[5] and are particularly likely to depend on external legal support,[6] because of their diminutive size and lack of sufficient resources and expertise. European micro jurisdictions fit the pattern; nevertheless, the attachment to their constitutional identity and tradition has prevented substantive changes in these states' architecture.

Indeed, opening these systems to the core pillars of constitutionalism – rule of law, separation of powers – may be critical in terms of preservation of the traditional institutional arrangements embodied in their traditional state architecture.[7] The traditional arrangements, as will be discussed in the chapter, were designed to function efficiently in a diminutive context, which faces distinct problems and challenges. Hence, the social, economic and political conflict that brought about the development of constitutionalism did not characterise these micro jurisdictions. Nevertheless, the close ties that these jurisdictions have with their neighbours have constantly worked as a stimulus to introduce some social, economic and institutional reforms. The core point turns out to be the extent of reform, because micro jurisdictions are not a replica of ordinary-sized jurisdictions and feel the need to protect their uniqueness. Their constitutional identity is hence a limit to any reform process, which explains why these jurisdictions are characterised by a weaker implementation of the rule of law and of the principle of the separation of powers.

Since the nineteenth century, these jurisdictions have carried out a cautious policy of 'guarded openness'. When examining their openness to the circulation of constitutionalism, two main models are identified. The reception *en bloc* of constitutionalism, with the enactment of a rigid and codified constitution, on the one hand, and abidance by the principle of institutional continuity, on the other hand. The three principalities (Andorra, Liechtenstein and Monaco) belong to the former model, whilst San

[4] I discuss the topic in 'The Constitutional Identity of European Micro States' (n 1).

[5] W Marxer and ZT Pállinger, 'Die politischen Systeme Andorras, Liechtensteins, Monacos, San Marinos und des Vatikan' in W Ismayr (ed), *Die politischen Systeme Westeuropas* (Wiesbaden, VS Verlag für Sozialwissenschaften, 2009); C Frommelt, 'Liechtenstein's tailor-made arrangements in the EEA: a small state's creative solutions in European integration' in S Wolf (ed), *State Size Matters: Politik und Recht im Kontext von Kleinstaatlichkeit und Monarchie* (Berlin, Springer, 2016).

[6] The best example is the fact that micro jurisdictions tend to select Constitutional/ Supreme Court judges from neighbouring jurisdictions. See E Bertolini, 'The Independence of Constitutional Judges in Microstates: the Challenge of the Diminutive Size' (2023) 34 *Revista General de Derecho Público Comparado* 294; R Dixson and V Jackson, 'Hybrid Constitutional Courts: Foreign Judges on National Constitutional Courts' (2019) 57 *Columbia Journal of Transnational Law* 283.

[7] P-A Blevin, *Les micro-états européens: Étude historique, juridique et fiscal (Andorre, Liechtenstein, Monaco, Saint-Marin, Vatican)* (Paris, L'Harmattan, 2016) 290.

Marino follows the latter. Still, the principalities did not all follow an identical pattern, because their opening to constitutionalism happened in significantly different historical moments across the nineteenth and the twentieth centuries and had differing impacts on their traditional institutional arrangements. Nevertheless, the analysis of the four jurisdictions' constitutions will show that their legal systems are still centred upon a dominant constitutional body – either the Prince (Liechtenstein and Monaco) or the Parliament (Andorra and San Marino).

The analysis of the constitutional arrangements of the four selected microstates has a twofold aim. The first is to examine the interaction between their traditional arrangements, highly influenced by their diminutive size, and one of the core principles of constitutionalism – the separation of powers – so as to identify a sort of breaking point, namely the point where the traditional arrangements cannot be modified anymore without risking an implosion of the whole system. To that aim, section II will briefly discuss the micro jurisdictions' opening to constitutionalism and section III their constitutional arrangements in terms of separation of powers. Finally, some conclusions are drawn in section IV).

II. The European Micro Jurisdictions: A Constitutional Overview

This section aims to provide a general understanding of the complexity of the constitutional history of the four micro jurisdictions, briefly discussing when and how they inaugurated the progressive reforms of their traditional institutional arrangements by introducing the separation of powers, the main reason being to integrate into international organisations (the Council of Europe in particular).

A. The Principality of Andorra

The Principality of Andorra has undergone a series of important reforms since the second half of the nineteenth century; nonetheless, the apex of the reform process was the enactment of the Constitution in 1993, which was considered to be a real revolution.[8]

It was following the enactment of the Constitution that Andorra ceased to be '*un objet étatique mal identifié*' (unidentified state-like object).[9] Indeed, until 1993, the Andorran legal system faced two main issues that had to be addressed, one related to the international dimension and the other to feudality. Andorra didn't enjoy a real international dimension, because it was not regarded as considered to be a person in international law. The reason derived from the fact that the two-headed head of

[8] O Gassiot, 'Une révolution juridique dans les vallées d'Andorre: la Constitution du 14 mars 1993' in M Hecquard-Théron and J Krynen (eds), *Regards critiques sur quelques (r)évolutions récentes du droit, tome II, Réformes-Révolutions* (Toulouse, Presses de l'Université Toulouse Capitole, 2005) 685.

[9] J-C Colliard, 'L'État d'Andorre' (1993) 39 *Annuaire français de droit international* 377; F de Saint-Sernin, 'Le Président de la République française, Coprince d'Andorre' (2001) *Revue des Deux Mondes*, Numéro spécial hors série: *Visages de l'Andorre* 18.

state – the two Coprinces, ie, the Catalan Bishop of Urgell and the French President of the Republic – is foreign and therefore, Andorra was considered a protectorate, whose foreign policy was almost entirely handled by France.[10] This explains, for instance, why Andorra did not apply for League of Nations membership in the 1920s.

The 1993 Constitution clarifies the nature of the relationship with the two neighbouring macro states and, under the first additional provision, gives a mandate to the Parliament and the government, jointly with the Coprinces, to negotiate an international tripartite treaty with France and Spain, based on respect for the sovereignty, independence, and territorial integrity of Andorra.[11]

Furthermore, Andorra was still a feudal system[12] and it was the Constitution that officially turned it into a constitutional state, with a legal system highly influenced by the 1978 Spanish Constitution. Although the Coprinces remained the head(s) of state under the 1993 Constitution, sovereign power was re-assigned to the people, along the lines of twentieth century constitutionalism.

The form of government of the parliamentary Coprincipality remains unique from a comparative perspective, though it is a perfect example of compromise between maintaining a traditional distinctive identity and the reception of new constitutional principles. Indeed, under Article 44(1), the Coprinces are the symbol and guarantee of the permanence and continuity of Andorra. Hence, despite the reception *en bloc* of constitutionalism in 1993, the Andorran Constitution also marked the importance of institutional continuity, considered to be essential to the distinctiveness of the Principality. To reform the head of state would not only have significantly affected the principle of institutional continuity but also altered the balance between the different branches of government, which had been in place for centuries and allowed Andorra to maintain her independence from her two powerful neighbours.

B. The Principality of Liechtenstein

The Principality of Liechtenstein enjoys the longest constitutional tradition among the four micro jurisdictions under consideration in this chapter, with three constitutions in the span of a century: the 1818 *landständische Verfassung*; the 1862 *konstitutionelle Verfassung* (KonV); and the 1921 *Verfassung* (LV).

The constitutional development of the Principality was influenced by its membership first of the Holy Roman Empire and then of the *deutscher Bund*. The Austrian influence, mainly through the Constitution of the *Land* of Vorarlberg, apparent in the text of the KonV, declined after the 1866 defeat of the Austrian Empire by Prussia at Sadowa, in favour of German constitutionalism. The 1862 Constitution was certainly a turning point for Lichtenstein, shifting the Principality from monarchical absolutism to constitutionalism.

[10] See B Bérlinguier, *La condition juridique des Vallées d'Andorre* (Paris, Éditions A Pedone 1970) 223–34.

[11] The Treaty of Good Neighbourliness, Friendship and Co-operation between the Principality of Andorra, the Kingdom of Spain and the French Republic was signed in Paris and Madrid on 1 June 1993 and in Andorra la Vella on 3 June 1993 (1872 UNTS 31980).

[12] C Mondou, 'La Constitution andorrane du 28 avril 1993: la disparition de la dernière institution féodale d'Europe' (1996) 1 *Revue de la recherche juridique* 83.

The 1862 KonV was almost entirely changed in 1921, when the LV entered into force. The LV, despite the various influences of the 1874 Swiss Federal Constitution, the 1890 Constitution of St Gallen (Switzerland) and the 1920 Austrian Constitution, is the result of an independent constitutional debate.[13]

Due to this significant constitutional tradition, none of the constitutional reforms that Liechtenstein underwent modified the foundations of the country, ie, the Prince and the people. Indeed, the most distinctive constitutional element is this double sovereignty of the Prince and the people, which makes Liechtenstein a bifocal or elliptical form of state.[14] Hence, the Prince still exercises significant executive powers, and the people are given significant powers of control vis-a-vis both the Prince (ie the personified head of state) and the monarchy (the institution). Moreover, any constitutional reform altering the status quo would be considered out of line with both the tradition of the country and good governance principles. To insert non-autochthonous constitutional elements would be detrimental to the good functioning of the institutions and, moreover, unnecessary. Therefore, the unicameral Parliament (*Landtag*) and the government (*Regierung*) are squeezed between these two strong poles, which are reciprocal balancing powers. This explains why it is possible to classify qualify the system as a semi-direct democracy, and also explains the significant extent of powers enjoyed by the Monarch and the people.

The 2003 constitutional reform strengthened further the powers of the Prince, giving him the power to dismiss the government, nominate judges and veto legislation. To rebalance the constitutional architecture, the amendment introduced the option of a vote of no-confidence in the Prince as well as the citizens' right to vote by referendum for the abolition of the monarchy.[15]

C. The Principality of Monaco

The Principality of Monaco traditionally has shared a close bond with France, since the 1643 Treaty of Péronne.[16] In 1918 a Treaty of Protective Friendship was signed: France committed herself to protect the Monegasque territory as if it were her own (Article 1). Therefore, a question arose as to the location of the real sovereignty over Monaco,[17] which also affected the constituent power of the Principality.

Under Article 1 of the 1962 Constitution (Article 2 of the 1911 Constitution), Monaco is a sovereign and independent state within general principles of international law and

[13] G Batliner, 'Einführung in das liechtensteinische Verfassungsrecht (1. Teil)' in G Batliner (ed), *Die liechtensteinische Verfassung 1921, Elemente der staatlichen Organisation* (1994) 21 *Lichtenstein Politsche Schriften* 41 (Vaduz, Verlag der Liechtensteinischen Akademischen Gesellschaft).

[14] A Ignor, 'Monarchisches und demokratisches Prinzip in der liechtensteinischen Verfassungsentwicklung' in V Press and D Willoweit (eds), *Liechtenstein-Fürstliches Haus und staatliche Ordnung* (Vaduz, Verlag der Liechtensteinischen Akademischen Gesellschaft, 1988) 482.

[15] This reform was heavily criticised by the Venice Commission. European Commission for Democracy through Law, 'Opinion no 227/2002 CDL-AD (2002) 32 on the Amendments to the Constitution of Liechtenstein Proposed by the Princely House of Liechtenstein' (16 December 2002), www.venice.coe.int/webforms/documents/default.aspx?pdffile=CDL-AD(2002)032-e.

[16] A list of all the agreements between Monaco and France can be found at: www.ambassade-en-france.gouv.mc/Relations-avec-la-France/Traites-bilateraux-avec-la-France.

[17] P Costanzo, *La Costituzione del Principato di Monaco* (Torino, Giappichelli, 2006) 64–68.

conventions agreed upon with France. After 1911, the year Monaco adopted her first constitution, some scholars supported the idea that the Monegasque Constitution could not be revised unilaterally; rather, an accord with France would be necessary, thus qualifying the relations between the two countries as a synallagmatic contract.[18] However, the Prince, when proceeding with a 1917 constitutional amendment, affirmed his full constituent power, justifying notification of the amendment to France as a matter of simple courtesy. Despite this, both the 1918 Treaty and the 1930 Convention on the Access to Public Offices in France and on the Recruitment of Public Officials in the Principality of Monaco seem to support a different interpretation. The main problem is that neither of the two states' constitutions have made clear the position of international law within the system of the legal sources. The issue is far from trivial, because international conventions and covenants with France set the margins for Monegasque independence. A 2001 decision of the Supreme Tribunal of Monaco seems to clarify the issue, concluding that international law provisions do not have a constitutional ranking.[19]

The year 2002 was a turning point for the Principality, because both the 1918 Treaty and the 1962 Constitution were amended to clarify the relationship with France and to democratise further the form of government. The significant amendment of the 1918 Treaty has put an end to the protective friendship, thus introducing full equality between the two parties. Nonetheless, the relationship is still very close, because of the procedure for appointment of the *Ministre d'État* (Minister of State, who can be considered a sort of Prime Minister responsible for implementing the directives of the Prince). The Minister of State is appointed by the Prince from a pool of three names of French high officials proposed by France. Furthermore, they are not responsible to the legislative body, the *Conseil National* (National Council), but exclusively to the Prince (Article 43). This provision is one of the main traits of the so-called Monegasque specificity, upon which the 1962 Constitution is still built, resulting in the predominance of the Prince as the pivotal constitutional body. Furthermore, it is not only the Minister of State, but also the Prince, which is the body exercising the executive power, who is not responsible to the legislative body, because no relationship of confidence exists.

Monaco, alongside Liechtenstein, is still a constitutional monarchy, a distinction considered by the Monegasques to be beyond amendment. The position of the Prince within the constitutional architecture is strengthened by the fact that the Constitution is completely silent with respect to the legal nature of the *ordonnance souveraine*, the main source of law: namely, whether it is a legislative or a regulatory act. However, according to the jurisprudence of the Supreme Tribunal, the *ordonnance souveraine* is an act that cannot be scrutinised by any constitutional body.[20] Furthermore, no real constitutional review exists, even though a Supreme Tribunal has been in operation since 1911 as the protector of Monegasques' rights and freedoms.[21]

Another major consequence is the character of the Constitution, which still adheres to the model of nineteenth century liberal constitutions, being both flexible and *octroyée*

[18] M Torelli, 'La révision de la Constitution et les relations internationales' (2003) 5 *Revue de droit monégasque* 103, 128.

[19] ibid, 131–32.

[20] See the treatment of the 1975 *Corruble Case*, in M Torelli, 'La révision de la Constitution' (n 18) 124.

[21] R Drago, 'Le Tribunal Suprême de la Principauté de Monaco' (1999) 1 *Revue de droit monégasque* 29.

(ie granted by the Prince), despite the association of the *Conseil National* – which has to agree with any amendment Bill – to the amendment process.

D. The Republic of San Marino

The Republic of San Marino for a long time resisted the adoption of both a rigid constitution and a system of constitutional justice, two main pillars of contemporary constitutionalism. Indeed, the Republic had opted, at least until 1974, for a series of specific and careful reforms, abiding by the principle of institutional continuity, whose purpose was to avoid any reform that could prove disruptive to the whole state architecture.

Traditionally, San Marino has been an oligarchic system, whose pivotal body was (and still is) the legislative body, the *Consiglio Grande e Generale* (Grand and General Council). The two *Capitani Reggenti/ Reggenza* (Captains Regent/ Regency), with a six-month term of office, represent the head of state; this short term must be explained by San Marino's diminutive size (it has a population of 35,436) and the subsequent need to prevent any family from becoming more powerful than others.

The cautious Sammarinese approach to reform, abiding by the principle of institutional continuity, first suffered a blow in 1974. Until that moment, the most important Sammarinese sources of law were the Ancient Customs and the 1600 Statutes and subsequent amendments, and the *ius commune*.[22]

1974 was the turning point because of the adoption of the *Dichiarazione dei diritti dei cittadini e dei princìpi fondamentali dell'ordinamento sammarinese* (Declaration of Citizens' Rights and of the Principles of the Sammarinese System (DD)). Because names are important, it seems worth noting the choice of the word declaration rather than constitution, even though, as will be discussed, the DD works as a true constitution for San Marino.

The DD is a recognition of the historical development and of the very general principles regulating the Sammarinese legal system. However, under Article 16(1), the DD is qualified as a supreme top and rigid source. The major drift from institutional continuity is marked by the 2002 amendment, which, in Article 16, establishes the review of legislation by the *Collegio garante della costituzionalità delle norme* (Guarantors' Panel on the Constitutionality of Norms),[23] the only Sammarinese body not going back to the Renaissance and not provided for by the *Leges Statutae* of the seventeenth century. Despite the organising efforts of the DD, the system of legal sources remains characterised by a plurality of sources,[24] though the *ius commune* is pulling back progressively receding, because of the increasing codification of the law.

[22] On the Sammarinese sources of law, see G Guidi, *Le fonti scritte nella Repubblica di San Marino* (Torino, Giappichelli, 2004).

[23] E Bertolini, 'Constitutional Justice in the Republic of San Marino' (2019) 23 *Comparative Law Journal of the Pacific* 53.

[24] M Mularoni, 'Il sistema giuridico sammarinese nell'orizzonte del diritto uniforme europeo' (2012) *Identità sammarinese* 139, 150–53.

III. The Separation of Powers and the Traditional Constitutional Arrangements

When the branches of government operate in the context of a diminutive population, they must face challenges that significantly differ from those characterising medium/large jurisdictions.[25] The main issue is that in micro jurisdictions everybody knows everybody.[26] Personal connections, clientelism, factionalism, and political patronage, though not exclusive to micro jurisdictions, are much more relevant because of the small population.

Clearly, there is a relevant consequence with respect to the independence of the constitutional bodies and their respective checks and balances, their term of office, the procedure for their selection, and the impossibility to hold other offices (known as an incompatibility regime), as well as with respect to the function of monitoring and controlling that should be exercised by Parliaments upon the executive power. Furthermore, legislative bodies in micro jurisdictions – whether unicameral or bicameral – are also micro sized, which again affects their functioning and their capability to effectively scrutinise the executive power (especially in Liechtenstein and Monaco).[27]

The constitutional arrangements of the four micro jurisdictions, because of those places' diminutive size and their historical background and despite the recent reforms, still provide for a dominant branch of government which has no proper counter-power, thus weakening the separation of powers.

From a diachronic perspective, the principle of the separation of powers emerged from the conflicting Crown–Parliament dialectic, where the latter aimed at circumscribing the powers of the former. However, as the previous paragraph discussed, this conflicting relationship never truly existed, either in the monarchical or in the oligarchic jurisdictions, which resulted in a continued prevalence of either the Monarch or the Parliament.[28] This conflict did not exist mainly due to the small size of the demographic conditions of the state, which implied a more homogeneous society characterised by fewer conflicting interests. Hence, there was no keenly felt need to proceed with a strict division of powers.

The relationship between the different branches of government still relies on traditional dynamics, which allow the whole system to function. A weaker separation of powers principle is thus incorporated into these traditional constitutional arrangements. Indeed, as this section will discuss, either one of the two branches is predominant over the other because of the constitutional design or because they are not fully distinct and separate. Indeed, in all four jurisdictions there is a predominant constitutional body,

[25] A comparative analysis of the forms of government of microstates is in E Bertolini, *I micro Stati. La sfida della micro dimensione e la sua ricaduta costituzionale* (Bologna, Bononia University Press 2019).

[26] J Corbett, '"Everybody Knows Everybody": Practising Politics in the Pacific Islands' (2015) 22 *Democratization* 51, 55.

[27] The unicameral Monegasque legislature comprises 24 members, whilst in Liechtenstein there are 25 members of Parliament.

[28] It is of particular interest also to frame the two micro monarchical experiences within European monarchies. See R Hazell and B Morris (eds), *The Role of Monarchy in Modern Democracy: European Monarchies Compared* (Oxford, Hart Publishing, 2020).

though not necessarily the same in each: it is the Prince in the two Principalities, and the Parliament in San Marino and Andorra.

Hence, the important constitutional reforms of the last decades all aimed to strengthen the rule of law by introducing more balance between the different constitutional bodies. Nevertheless, none opted for a limitation of powers of the predominant body; rather, they either strengthened the powers of the legislative body (Monaco, Andorra) or the instrument of direct democracy (Liechtenstein), or they introduced a new body competent to scrutinise legislation (San Marino).

A. The Principality of Andorra

The Andorran parliamentary Coprincipality structure (Article 1 Constitution) is unique because of the head(s) of state. The distinctive feature, which clearly affects the entire institutional architecture, is represented by the fact that the office is held by foreign citizens, who acquire functional citizenship for the duration of their term. Nevertheless, the two Coprinces remain alien to the effective functioning of the Andorran government, also because of the Andorran choice of a parliamentary regime, which significantly limits the powers and prerogatives of the head of state.

In line with a typical characteristic of parliamentarism, the head of government is formally appointed by the head of state (Article 68), following election by the *Consell General* (General Council, the legislative body) by majority and, if a second vote is necessary, the run-off is between the two candidates with the highest number of votes. Also in line with the parliamentary regime, the Coprinces are responsible for the promulgation of the law, and they must consent to the signing of international treaties, in respect of which they can ask for the *Tribunal Constitucional*'s opinion on their constitutionality; in the event of a positive judgment, at least one of them must sign. A single signature is sufficient, but exclusively when one of the Coprinces fails to implement the act within the constitutionally required time. They are not politically responsible, although they can be held responsible for the acts adopted in the exercise of their own powers, pursuant to Article 46 Constitution, which do not require a countersignature. However, this provision has a low probability of ever being enforced in practice, both because these powers have little impact on a political level and, above all, because no removal mechanisms are foreseen; nor even are there provisions to deal with the event of a vacancy in the office. Rather, there are provisions that regulate it, but they are those provided for by the original legislation (Article 49); in this case, the vacancy of the Coprinces is of second degree, in the sense that it derives from the vacancy of the original office (Bishop of Urgell or President of the French Republic). As further confirmation of the concrete difficulty and low probability, the Charter does not even provide for the possibility of criminal liability.

The constitutional role of the Coprinces is therefore strongly limited. In full respect of the parliamentary tradition, they sign a lot but decide little.[29] The pivotal role in the constitutional architecture falls to the *Consell*.

[29] J-C Colliard, 'L'État d'Andorre' (n 9) 386.

Concerning the government, similarly to San Marino, the Constitution regulates the term limit for the head of government, specifying that one person can hold that position for a maximum of two full terms, which is a total of eight years (Article 78(1)). The link with the micro dimension and the desire to discourage the personalisation of institutions characterising micro jurisdictions emerges clearly. Another provision typical of micro jurisdictions relates to the size of the government. While Ministers are chosen and appointed by the head of government, the number of Ministers (currently 10) is determined by primary legislation (Article 72(1)). Further, to avoid any partial overlap between the government of the *Consell*, the Constitution provides for a strict incompatibility regime, as in San Marino (Article 78(2)).

The government and the *Consell* are in a relationship of confidence (Article 69), which can be interrupted by resignation, death, supervening incapacity (though there are no clues as to the body competent to ascertain this), vote of no confidence, failure to approve the question of confidence, or dissolution of the Parliament. Confidence is characterised by a variable rationalisation: it is key to the selection of the head of government and to the approval of a motion of no confidence, whereas it is attenuated for the dissolution and very simplified for the question of confidence. A motion of no confidence must be presented by at least one-fifth of the councillors, and they cannot present another one in the same year; it is discussed between three and five days after filing and must be approved by an absolute majority open vote. It cannot be presented in the first six months of government. The question of confidence is regulated in a very concise way, is at the exclusive initiative of the head of government, and must be approved by a simple majority (Article 70). The power of dissolution (Article 41) lies only with the head of government (therefore without the obligation to consult the Coprinces), but it is not very rationalised; it may not be exercised when a motion of no confidence is underway, in the first year following the elections, or during a state of emergency.

The predominance of the *Consell* is also achieved through the important powers held by the *Síndic General* who presides over it. In fact, the *Síndic General*, and not the head of government, has the task of informing the Coprinces on state affairs (Article 44(2)), of transmitting to them the laws approved for promulgation (Article 63) and above all the power to countersign some of their documents. For this reason, he or she is informed before the government if one of the Coprinces is unable to exercise their powers within the terms established by the Constitution and in such a way as to be able to replace the incapacitated Coprince (Article 45(3)). The *Síndic General* also participates in the government formation process, countersigning the appointment of the head of government (Article 68(5)). Again, regarding the power of appointment, he or she participates, together with the Coprinces and the head of government, in the appointment of the members of the *Consell Superior de la Justícia* and the *Tribunal Constitucional*. Due to the importance that the *Síndic General* assumes in the Andorran government balance, the Constitution provides for a limit of two terms for this position also (Article 55(3)).

However, it is worth noting that, among the four micro jurisdiction experiences, Andorra's is the one where the separation of powers is most effective, both in terms of design and of operation.

B. The Principality of Liechtenstein

Liechtenstein's experience offers similarities to the Monegasque one, because of the centrality of the Prince; nevertheless, the importance of direct democracy has made Liechtenstein very distinctive.

The Prince shares sovereign power with the people, thus giving rise to a double sovereignty that each of the two poles exercises towards the other; this feature, translated into terms of separation of powers, means that each of them is the counter-power of the other, because they must act in a consensual manner, even though it may be difficult to appraise the real extent of this reciprocal counter-power. On this basis, the Principality can be defined as an elliptical state (Article 2), because it combines two elements generally not associated in any system: the hereditary constitutional monarchy on the one hand and the fully expanded direct democracy on the other – the former typical of nineteenth-century constitutionalism, the latter of twentieth-century constitutionalism.

The system is of a dualist parliamentarism, as the government must enjoy double confidence, from the Prince and from the *Landtag*. The appointment of the government (composed of the head of government and four Ministers, all nationals) is up to the Prince upon the proposal and in agreement with the *Landtag* (Article 79); in the event of resignation of the government, the Prince is responsible for appointing a transitional government (without any countersignature), which cannot last longer than four months (Article 80). However, the expiry of the deadline does not cause the resignation of the transitional government, or in any case not automatically, as it must request the confidence of the *Landtag*. This provision serves a dual purpose: to restore the political control of the *Landtag* and, in the event of a lack of confidence, to proceed towards new elections. If the *Landtag* is unable to propose a new government and decides not to support the one proposed by the Prince, dissolution is the only possible option.

From a formal point of view, the functioning of the double confidence puts the Prince and the *Landtag* on an equal footing, but doubts remain from a more substantive perspective, namely whether the situation of a government forced to resign because it does not enjoy the Prince's confidence could occur. To answer the question, it must be considered which body between the Prince and the government holds the political control. Hypothesising the autonomy of the Prince, not responsible to the *Landtag*, would shift the form of government towards semi-presidentialism, with the difference that the head of state would not be elected. Furthermore, the Prince, as co-sovereign, ensures that the government acts in accordance with the will of the parliamentary majority and, if not, in agreement with the *Landtag*, dismisses the government or forces it to resign. The power of dissolution, which the Prince holds, must also include a form of control over the *Landtag*, although the assessment of the opportunity falls exclusively on the Prince.

The Prince holds the power of legislative initiative, although it must always pass through the government (Article 64). Even when he it exercises the power of emergency legislation or adopts secondary regulatory acts, it is the government that proceeds and the Prince countersigns.

Despite the pivotal role in the executive, the Prince is not responsible to anyone and is not even covered by the government's responsibility (Article 7). This is one of the major problems of the system, because it excludes the Prince from being subject to any control, and considering, too, the approval power he has, any amendment seems difficult. Indeed, the Prince is responsible for approving the laws and thus also enjoys a veto power. The veto presents critical issues with respect to the democratic principle for two reasons: it cannot be overcome by a second vote of the House, and it can also be applied even if the law is approved by the *Landtag* and then by referendum as well as by referendum following a rejected popular initiative project by the *Landtag* (Article 66). Furthermore, the veto can also be placed on constitutional laws. The only law that does not require princely approval is that of abolition of the monarchy (Article 113). According to Article 65(1), if six months pass without the Prince having approved a law, the law is considered rejected. The comparison with the other European monarchies, where the veto power is always formal, is certainly striking. However, the already mentioned possibility for the people to remove the Prince, pursuant to Article 13ter, can be considered a counterbalance, being a deterrent to the opening of an institutional crisis. Whether this possibility is a realistic one is far from certain.

Another deterrent is Article 113(1), according to which at least 1,500 citizens can present an initiative for constitutional amendment aimed at abolishing the monarchy. In the case of approval, the *Landtag* and the Monarch prepare a constitutional draft (for the former there is the rather obvious obligation to provide for the republican form of state, while the latter has the right but not the obligation to present his own text) to be subjected to a referendum. If only one proposal is presented, an absolute majority is sufficient for approval; if two texts are presented, voters can choose between one of these and the LV. The procedure is divided into two rounds; in the first, voters have two votes available to vote for the two drafts they want to put on the ballot (namely, the two texts that have received the most first and second votes); in contrast, in the run-off there is only one vote available and the text that obtains the absolute majority will be the new Constitution.

The dialogue that the procedure pursuant to Article 113 establishes between the Prince and the people is also reflected in the regulation of the maintenance of the Constitution (Articles 112, 64 and 66), a discipline which, despite the participation of all the constitutional bodies, nevertheless sees in its final phase a predominant role for the Prince, who can refuse approval. The fact that only on very rare occasions has the Prince refused approval does not diminish the problem with the provision in terms of the democratic principle. Nevertheless, it is convenient to contextualise the princely powers in the balance that the constitutional architecture attempts to achieve and in the deterrent effect that certain provisions can exert when implemented.

An interesting connection that introduces a triangulation between the Prince, the *Landtag* and the people is represented by the procedure for appointing judges (Article 96), which is divided into three steps, each of which is characterised by the predominance of one of the three bodies. The first step takes place within a special commission, responsible for selecting and proposing candidates. That commission is composed of an equal number of representatives of the *Landtag* (one for each parliamentary group) and of the Prince. The Prince again prevails, since he chairs the commission and enjoys the prevailing vote in the event of a tie. The second step sees the *Landtag* vote on the proposed candidates, whom it can reject. The third step, in case of a lack of agreement between the *Landtag* and the commission, sees the calling of a referendum. Once again, therefore, the two sovereigns play a dominant role in a fundamental procedure for the rule of law – namely that of the selection of judges.

To conclude, it is worth noting that both sovereigns, and not just the Prince, are actually predominant, leaving to both the government and the *Landtag* (especially the latter) a very narrow window for action or control. Nevertheless, to what extent the people can be a real counter-power to the Prince remains unclear.

C. The Principality of Monaco

The 2002 Monegasque reform focuses mainly on strengthening the democratically elected body, the *Conseil National*, and in fact the revision of the Constitution was also accompanied by a general revision of the electoral law. The amendment altered the balance of powers, though not significantly; therefore, a discrepancy remains between the main objective of the reform, ie, the rebalancing of powers, and the result. Though the state is defined as liberal by law (*État de droit attaché au respect des libertés et droits fondamentaux*, ex Article 2(2)) and the separation of the three traditional powers is affirmed (Article 6), the role assigned to the representative body is still circumscribed, as the letter of the Constitution proves. The Constitution itself leaves little room for the interpretation of the ultimate source of each one of the three traditional powers: the Prince, who is inviolable and holds sovereign power. He is the titular executive power (Article 3) and co-legislator together with the *Conseil National* (Article 4). The combined reading of these provisions signals a fully-fledged constitutional monarchy.

The key element of the Monegasque system is in fact not the non-elective nature of the head of state, but rather the fact that the assignment of governmental power is not accompanied by any real counter-powers. Indeed, no relationship of confidence between the executive and the legislative power exists. The former is exercised, under the guidance of the Prince, by the *Ministre d'État* – assisted by the *Conseil de Gouvernement* (Government Council) (Article 43) – who is responsible towards the Prince alone (Article 50). If the 2002 reform had introduced a relationship of confidence between the executive and the legislature, that would have undermined the centrality of the Prince and would have required a complete rethinking of the entire constitutional architecture, as the Prince explained when Monaco joined the CoE.[30] Furthermore, the Prince still holds the power of dissolution of the *Conseil National* (Article 74) upon receipt of formal advice from the *Conseil de la Couronne* (Crown Council). The latter creates a mechanism of partial coordination between the Prince and the *Conseil National*, due to both its composition and role of advisory body on specific matters. Regarding the composition, four out of seven members (including the President) are appointed by the Prince and the remaining three, although always appointed by the Monarch, are of parliamentary designation. The connection with the *Conseil National* is weak for three reasons: first, because the parliamentary appointees are in the minority, due to the preference for an odd-numbered composition capable of guaranteeing the princely preponderance; secondly, due to the rule of incompatibility between the position of MP (as well as the government) and membership of the *Conseil de la Couronne*; and finally, as the initiative of convocation lies with the Prince and the President. It follows that

[30] The Prince stressed that the 2002 reform (requested by the CoE) should have been performed '*dans la limite de nos équilibres fondamentaux … et que nous ne pouvons compromettre sans danger pour la stabilité de notre Pays*'. In (2003) 5 *Revue de droit monégasque* 15.

even the newly introduced obligation to consult cannot have a significant impact on the determination of the political direction (Article 77).

Moreover, the ministerial countersignature is not provided for the purpose of the validity and effectiveness of the Prince's acts. In contrast to contemporary parliamentarism, the signature of the Prince is the final act of the process of perfection of the ordonnance which becomes executory with the princely signature.

The exercise of the legislative power also perpetuates the subordination of the *Conseil National* to the Prince and his government: first, because the law must be the result of the common will of the Prince and the *Conseil*; and secondly, the legislative initiative is not fully enjoyed by the Parliament, because it remains subordinated to the government. The drafting of a Bill by the *Conseil* does not automatically start the legislative process but it must be transmitted to the *Ministre d'État* who decides whether to have the draft discussed (not necessarily in the version originally presented, as the government has the right to amend it). The fact that, in the latter case, the Constitution provides for an obligation to report to Parliament does not reduce the limitation in the exercise of the legislative power by the *Conseil*. The same applies to the regulation of the legislative process, since the right to present amendments is limited both by the specification that a direct link must be evident between the proposed amendment and the provision – and the government will be the judge of that – and because the government always enjoys the possibility of withdrawing the project before the final vote (Article 67).

The extension of the Parliament's competence to include budgetary and foreign policy has increased the role of the *Conseil National* in the institutional framework, but not so as to make it a real counterbalance. In fact, although the *Conseil National* can now vote on finance and budget laws, it cannot propose any amendment. Furthermore, the provision according to which certain international treaties (Article 14) cannot be ratified except by virtue of a legislative provision has little impact on foreign policy – that remains within the hands of the Prince (however, he is required to report to the *Conseil National*).

Finally, the centrality of the Prince is further confirmed by the already mentioned character of the *octroyée* and partially flexible Constitution. Indeed, any constitutional amendment requires the mutual agreement of the Prince and the *Conseil National*, and if the initiative comes from the latter, a quorum of two-thirds is required for approval (Article 95).

To conclude, the government is a mere emanation of the Prince, and the *Conseil National* cannot yet be classified as a body of political control, as all its actions must be in concert with the Prince, on whose political conduct it can only exercise an indirect influence.

D. The Republic of San Marino

The Sammarinese issues in terms of separation of powers stem from the predominance of the legislative branch, the Great and General Council, thus marking a significant difference with respect to the previously analysed experiences.

The separation of powers is incorporated in Article 3 DD, according to which the Captains Regent exercise the functions of head of state, the Great and General Council has the legislative and political direction function,[31] the Congress of State has the power of government, and the judiciary has the judicial power. The powers of the state act according to respect for mutual autonomy and independence.

San Marino, being historically an oligarchy, was neither characterised by the Crown–Parliament conflict nor was the legislative branch created through a top-down self-limitation of executive power. Rather, it was created following a bottom-up process, from the *Arengo*,[32] which progressively transferred its powers to the Great and General Council,[33] which became the sovereign (Rubrica III, Book I *Leges Statutae*).

The 2005 reform tries to better reallocate power; however, this happened within the Great and General Council, which still is the pivotal body within the Sammarinese government. It is as if the separation of powers has been realised *within* the Grand and General Council, rather than between the Council and the other constitutional branches of government. Nevertheless, the reforms were never meant to establish an effective system of counter-powers.

The original conferral of the executive power to the Captains Regent must be read from this perspective. The Regency, since its origins, has represented a weak counter-power to the Great and General Council for two reasons: the six-month term; and the prohibition of re-election before three years have passed. Even the provision, unique in a comparative context, whereby the Regency presides over the Council, does not in any way undermine the latter's primacy. The will to preserve the primacy of the Council emerges also when considering the genesis of the Congress of State, which was originally attributed very limited powers until the 1945 reform. It is only since then that the Congress has been transformed into a fully-fledged governing body, in a relationship of political responsibility (collegial and individual) with the Council.

The Captains Regent are elected by a majority of voters by the Council (Article 1 qualified law n⁰ 186/2005), in order to guarantee political homogeneity between the two bodies. Constitutional law n⁰ 185/2005 reconfirms them as the guardians of the San Marino constitutional order (Article 1(2)) and as such they supervise the functioning of the public powers and of the state, ensure the balance between the bodies, and are entitled to raise the conflict of jurisdiction with other constitutional bodies before the Guarantors' Panel (Article 2). The Captains Regent preside over the Council and, above all, it is their responsibility to convene it (Article 3); hence, no power of self-convocation belongs to the Council. They can send legislation back to the Council if they find elements of formal and substantive illegitimacy, with precise reference to the provisions and principles that are presumed to have been violated; however, if the Council reapproves it, the Captains are required to proceed with the promulgation of that legislation (Article 7 qualified law n⁰ 186/2005). The Regency presides over the formation process of the new government (Article 14 qualified law n⁰ 186/2005). The Council is responsible for approving the government programme and electing the Congress (Article 1

[31] See G Crescentini, 'Il Consiglio Grande e Generale' (2015) *Identità Sammarinese* 91.

[32] This is the assembly that ruled San Marino from the fifth century until 1243. It constituted an intermediate body between the electoral body and the Great and General Council. See C Buscarini, 'Corpo elettorale, Arengo, Consiglio dei Sessanta' (2017) *Identità Sammarinese* 15, 16.

[33] F Balsimelli, *Elementi di diritto pubblico sammarinese* (San Marino, Gruppo Poligrafico Editoriale, 1966) 56–58.

Constitutional law n⁰ 184/2005), by majority. The Congress can have up to 10 members, and they are normally elected from among the members of the Council. It is interesting to note, with respect to the problem of a possible overlapping between the two branches, that, once appointed, the incompatibility of Congress membership with the office of councillor arises and therefore the new Secretary (ie a member of the Congress of State) is replaced with the first of the non-elected councillors from the same list (Article 7 Constitutional law n⁰ 183/2005).

The Council and the Congress are in a relationship of confidence, characterised by a weak rationalisation, in the sense that no particular mechanisms (such as the constructive vote of no confidence) have been designed in order the make this relationship as stable as possible. Any motion of no confidence must be presented by at least one-fifth of the members of the Council, discussed between three and seven days from filing, and voted on by open ballot by roll call with an absolute majority, but cannot be presented in the first six months of the appointment. A very interesting provision that must be highlighted, especially because it is clearly connected to the diminutive size of the state, is the regime of mandate of the Secretaries of State, who cannot hold office for more than 10 years. However, the ban is not absolute, as the law provides for the possibility of being able to hold the office again, but only after the passage of at least another 10 years (Article 1 qualified law n⁰ 184/2005, as amended in 2011).

The weak position of the Congress is confirmed by the fact that the sessions are convened by the Regency, and it was the Congress itself, with its own regulation (Article 5 qualified law n⁰ 184/2005 and regulation n⁰ 4/2007) that provided for this. The agenda is also set by the Regency, albeit on the proposal of the Secretaries of State. A further anomaly, also from a comparative perspective, is the lack of a real presidency: which Secretary should represent the Congress externally is decided from time to time (Article 7 qualified law n⁰ 184/2005), because formally, the presidency falls to the Regency, which is discontinuous, being re-elected every six months.

Hence, the distinctive elements of the San Marino system are both its weak separation of powers and the internal structure of the constitutional bodies. These elements are particularly evident in the accumulation of functions that are attributed to the Regency which, even if only formally, presides over both the Great and General Council and the State Congress. This also creates a curious incompatibility between the DD and the *Leges Statutae*, as the former attributes the office of head of state to the Regency, whereas the latter attributes the *iura regalia* (ie the rights belonging to the sovereign) to the Council. This discrepancy is perpetuated by the fact that some powers which are traditionally associated with the head of state, such as that of pardon, belong to the Council. The Regency presiding over the Council tends to undermine the function of guarantee and mediation and to involve the Regency in the political conflict. Upon conferring the office of head of state it would have been more appropriate to deprive the Regency of tasks and functions incompatible with it. Rotation certainly does not contribute to the efficiency of the body, as it no longer responds to institutional needs; on the contrary, it almost seems that it is preserved for party-related reasons.

To conclude, the progressive rebalancing of powers, always in line with the principle of institutional continuity – except for the Guarantors' Panel on the Constitutionality of Rules – has preserved the centrality of the Council, which is exemplified in the fact that the Regency, the Congress, and the Guarantors' Panel emanate from it, as they are elected by it.

IV. Conclusion

Micro jurisdictions are not found on the European continent only. The phenomenon of decolonisation led to the emergence of several new states, a great number of which, mainly in the Caribbean and in the Pacific, are also of diminutive size. There are, however, obvious differences between European and decolonised micro jurisdictions due to their different historical backgrounds and geographical locations.[34] But, although the particular circumstances and mechanisms may differ, diminutive size typically means that micro jurisdictions are all confronted with the same difficulty, ie, the implementation of the separation of powers.

Micro jurisdictions globally have in many cases employed similar solutions to address this shared problem: for example, the lack of resources and expertise is solved by outsourcing recruitment (mainly in relation to the staffing of the judiciary). However, when it comes to structure of the government and the separation of the three branches, a substantive difference emerges between continental European and decolonised micro jurisdictions (with Tonga falling a bit in-between, having maintained a form of traditional government[35]). The decolonisation process, mainly of the former British colonies, has been highly centralised at Whitehall, generally leading to a fully-fledged transplant of the Westminster model,[36] with almost no adjustments to take account of diminutive size.[37]

Especially in the Caribbean,[38] the predominance of the executive is so evident that the Westminster model has been renamed by some 'Westmonster', whose distinctive traits are: the overwhelming predominance of the executive power; a non-efficient bicameral Parliament; and an almost non-existent resort to direct democracy. The most

[34] D O'Brien, 'Small States, Colonial Rule and Democracy' in P Butler and C Morris (eds), *Small States in a Legal World* (Berlin, Springer, 2017).

[35] Indeed, Tonga shares significant similarities with the two European micro monarchies, being a constitutional monarchy. I compare these three experiences in E Bertolini, 'La Costituzione del Liechtenstein nel diritto comparato' (2022) 52(2) *DPCE online* 847. Besides, Tonga has never be fully colonised by the British.

[36] For the definition of the model, see SA de Smith, *The New Commonwealth and its Constitutions* (London, Stevens and Sons, 1964) and *Hinds v R* (1975) 24 WIR 326; [1977] AC 195 (PC Jamaica), where Lord Diplock discusses the main features of the model. The divergence from the model consists of the constitutionalisation of the bill of rights, and of the main constitutional conventions on the one hand and the principle of the supremacy of the constitution – which implies a compression of the prerogatives of Parliament – on the other hand.

[37] W Dale, 'The Making and Remaking of Commonwealth Constitutions' (1993) 42(1) *International & Comparative Law Quarterly* 67.

[38] RA Carnegie, '*Floreat* the Westminster Model? A Commonwealth Caribbean Perspective' (1996) 6 *The Caribbean Law Review* 1; J Corbett and WP Veenendaal, 'Westminster in Small States: Comparing the Caribbean and Pacific Experience' (2016) 22 *Journal of Contemporary Politics* 432; H Ghany, 'The Myth of the Westminster Model' (1994) 7 *Caribbean Affairs* 62; P Larmour, 'Westminster Constitutions in the South Pacific: A "Policy Transfer" Approach' (2002) 10 *Asian Journal of Political Science* 39.

relevant element is the first, resulting from a series of factors: the predominant role of the Prime Minister; the possible absence of an Opposition;[39] cabinet ministers being MPs; the possible absence of backbenchers; the small size of Parliament;[40] use of the First-Past-the-Post electoral formula; and the social and political background (being more homogeneous and less adversarial than in the UK).

A comparative analysis suggests that there is a prevalence of the executive over the legislative branch. There are three possible reasons that may account for this state of affairs. The first is a constitution that expressly sanctions such supremacy, as is the case in Monaco, Liechtenstein, and Tonga, thus crystallising their tradition. The second is an almost total overlap in personnel between the executive and the legislative branches, as is the case in the Caribbean 'Westmonster'. The third – which is present in all micro jurisdictions – is the diminutive size of Parliament, which may prevent that institution from properly functioning as a monitoring body.[41]

At the same time, the analysis carried out in this chapter suggests that there is an exception, ie, the prevalence of the legislative over the executive branch, which can be observed in Andorra and San Marino. The reason is again to be found in the historical experiences of these jurisdictions. Nevertheless, either way, the common element is the prevalence of one state power over the other.

These jurisdictions, therefore, are not fully aligned with the common model of the separation of powers, not because they do not accept the principle, but because they incorporate it in a weakened manner, still basing the relationship among the different branches of government on traditional relational dynamics that continue to endure and are considered too distinctive and fragile to be amended. In fact, it is important to underline that intervention concerning an institutional structure so strongly rooted in the social context can call into question the fundamental balances between the different constitutional bodies without being able to establish equally adequate new ones. Indeed, as this chapter has discussed, micro jurisdictions do *not* face the same exact problems as ordinary-sized ones. The low population causes these institutions to function in a very distinctive way – social control together with social proximity deriving from the 'everybody knows everybody' environment. Hence, a centuries-old balance between the different institutions must be recalibrated very carefully. It is not impossible to establish a new balance; nevertheless, the peculiarities connected to diminutive size mean that it is advisable to proceed with special care. Micro jurisdictions are not special in the sense

[39] H Ghany, 'The Office of the Leader of the Opposition: An Examination of the Whitehall Version in the Commonwealth Caribbean' (2001) 7(2) *Journal of Legislative Studies* 105.

[40] D Anckar, 'Westminster Lilliputs? Parliaments in Former Small British Colonies' (2007) 60 *Parliamentary Affairs* 637; H Ghany, 'The Commonwealth Caribbean. Legislatures and democracy' in NDJ Baldwin (ed), *Legislatures of Small States. A comparative study* (New York, Routledge, 2013).

[41] This is particularly relevant in those microstates of the Commonwealth, where the Westminster model is implemented, without specific arrangements in the light of the diminutive size. On the issues characterising mainly the Commonwealth Caribbean, see: D O'Brien, *The Constitutional Systems of the Commonwealth Caribbean. A Contextual Analysis* (Oxford, Hart Publishing, 2014); T Robinson, A Bulkan and A Saunders, *Fundamentals of Caribbean Constitutional Law* (London, Sweet & Maxwell, 2015); J Corbett and WP Veenendaal, 'Westminster in Small States: Comparing the Caribbean and Pacific Experience' (2016) 22 *Journal of Contemporary Politics* 432; H Ghany, 'The Myth of the Westminster Model' (1994) 7 *Caribbean Affairs* 62; D Hinds, 'Beyond Formal Democracy: The Discourse on Democracy and Governance in the Anglophone Caribbean' (2008) 46 *Commonwealth & Comparative Politics* 388.

that they are not fit to implement the rule of law or international standards; they require special adjustments, because of the peculiarities of their constitutional architecture. This explains why reforms may not have a significant impact or may miss the target in the end.

Even those jurisdictions, ie Andorra and San Marino, which seem to have been more concerned by both the concentration of powers and the issue of proximity, and which have proposed solutions, have partially missed the target. Oligarchic San Marino, during the Renaissance, was concerned about too much power concentrated in the hands of one family (as had happened in Florence for instance) and a bicephalous short-termed head of state has been the solution to that concern; however, no counterbalance to the Council has been designed. Similarly, though for different reasons, Andorra provided for a foreign bicephalous head of state, to balance the influence of the conterminous jurisdictions (previously the Kingdoms of Aragon and of France, and later of the Kingdom of Spain, and the Kingdom and then the Republic of France), but again, the legislative body remains predominant – although less so than in San Marino.

Indeed, in contrast to micro jurisdictions outside Europe, which are characterised by the phenomenon of fully-fledged transplants/ legal borrowings (with some adjustments, mainly in the Pacific) from the former colonial powers, the four European jurisdictions have not suffered a true colonial experience. They had a special/ protective friendship with their conterminous macro states and they have been influenced by those states constitutional developments; however, never to the point that the influence has led to an alteration of their traditional institutional foundations. Even the most relevant trigger of reforms, membership of the CoE, has not been able to alter these foundations. These jurisdictions are open to external suggestions and requirements to a certain extent, ie, until they demand an alteration of traditional institutions and relationships between bodies which represent their core identity. The outsourcing of judges is a good example of this openness, but even that is not free of concerns.

To conclude, as the present analysis suggests, the peculiar arrangements of the European micro jurisdictions demand further reflection by comparative constitutional scholars, mainly with respect to the viability of international and regional standards for the separation of powers or judicial independence. The peculiarity of constitutional arrangements of micro jurisdictions is the result of the interplay of multiple factors; however, all of them can, in the end, be traced back to their diminutive size. This is the reason why micro jurisdictions cannot and must not be approached in the same way as larger jurisdictions. They are not miniatures of larger jurisdictions: they have their own distinctive traits, and this distinctiveness has specific reasons than cannot and must not be overlooked. Therefore, international or regional standards for separation of powers need to be adjusted for micro jurisdictions. This should not entail that international organisations make use of some sort of double standard when assessing micro jurisdictions. Rather, it is important for these organisations to adapt their international standards to the peculiarities of micro jurisdictions, mainly those related to the diminutive population. In other words, international and regional organisations must be ready to consider the possibility of having concurrent solutions, depending on the jurisdiction's size, to effectively implement those standards.

6

The Fundamental Law of Vatican City State

Hidden Treasures in the Constitution of the World's Smallest State

CONOR CASEY

I. Introduction

The constitutional history of Vatican City State is distinctive in many ways. It is intertwined with the broader history of the rise of Christianity as a world religion, the transformation of the Roman Empire and the emergence of Christendom, conflicts between temporal and spiritual authority within Christendom about their proper ordering and relationship, disputes over the spiritual and temporal authority of the Roman Pontiff, and much more besides. This chapter offers an introduction to its Fundamental Law and suggests some lessons public law scholars can take away from studying the constitution of this unique micro-state.

Section II offers a brief account of the constitutional history of Vatican City State and its predecessor, the Papal States. Here I examine the fascinating question of why the spiritual head of one of the world's largest religions exercises temporal sovereignty over a state in the first place. The intellectual underpinning motivating the creation of the Papal States and Vatican City State is deeply linked to how the Church has historically understood its own identity and role vis-à-vis temporal authority, and its need for total independence from political control. Section III provides an outline of the main features of Vatican City State's Fundamental Law. The Fundamental Law has gone through three iterations since the establishment of Vatican City State in 1929, and I focus on the Fundamental Law promulgated in May 2023 by Pope Francis. Section IV engages with this volume's theme of 'smallness'. I highlight how one can readily and starkly contrast aspects of the smallness of Vatican City State, with the role of its head of state in world affairs. Despite being the world's smallest state, the social, political, and spiritual influence of its sovereign – the Roman Pontiff – has been extensive for much of human history. I focus on how the papacy has had a subtle but important influence on the formation of concepts making up the building blocks of modern public law thought, in particular upon the concept of sovereignty. I argue that the Fundamental

Law of the tiny Vatican City State offers public lawyers a fascinating window into the deep, but often forgotten, early intellectual scaffolding of contemporary Western public law thought – namely, a rich admixture of Roman law, canon law, and more generally, the influence of political theological concepts that underpinned assertions of legitimate temporal and spiritual power.

II. The Constitutional History of Vatican City State

A. Why Does the Pope Exercise Temporal Authority?

The occupants of the Holy See have exercised temporal authority in the Italian peninsular for over 1500 years. From the eighth to the late nineteenth century, the papacy was the temporal ruler of a territory in Italy known as the Papal States. The lands that would eventually make up the Papal States first came to the Church from donations of land made by wealthy Christian families and successive Eastern Roman Emperors – grants made after Christianity gained the toleration, and then favour, of the Roman state in the fourth and fifth centuries.[1] Until the eighth century these lands, known as the Patrimony of St Peter, remained under the de jure temporal rule of the Eastern Roman Empire.[2] However, as the Eastern Roman Empire's effective control of the Italian peninsular became increasingly tenuous and came under pressure from Lombard aggression, the papacy itself began to exercise temporal authority over the Patrimony, including organising the feeding and defence of the citizenry.[3] The papacy turned to Pepin, King of the Franks, for protection and support against the Lombards, finding in him a stalwart protector and benefactor of the Holy See.[4] Eventually, Pope Leo III would bestow the title of Emperor of the Romans on Pepin's son Charlemagne on Christmas day in 800, a consequential moment that, inter alia, signalled the papacy's autonomy from the Eastern Roman Emperor. Pepin and Charlemagne would give generous donations of land to the Pope, who began to exercise effective temporal rule over them, heralding the beginning of the Papal States[5] – states which would endure, waxing and waning in strength and territorial size, for over a millennium.

These donations, and the (often grudging) recognition of the papacy's dominion of these lands by the Holy Roman Empire, all proved critical to the papacy and Church establishing effective independence from temporal authority over its internal affairs and execution of its mission.[6] They were critical to the papacy largely prevailing in disputes with temporal authority over issues like the appointment of Bishops and the mode of electing the Pope, both of which became vested in the papacy and newly established College of Cardinals respectively. Asserting and securing its own temporal

[1] J Woods, 'The Rise of the Papal States up to Charlemagne's Coronation' (1921) 7 *The Catholic Historical Review* 44, 45–46.

[2] ibid.

[3] ibid 47.

[4] ibid 50–52.

[5] ibid 45, 54.

[6] ibid.

independence and authority, along with other developments like the systemisation of Canon law, the growth of a skilled central Curia that was for many centuries without equal in its bureaucratic competence,[7] and the cultivation of a deep reservoir of highly educated and skilled human capital, all helped to lay the groundwork for the Church, through the papacy, to assert and exercise an enormous level of influence and authority across Christendom for much of the High Middle Ages and pre-Reformation period.[8]

The importance of temporal authority to papal independence also explains the extreme concern displayed by the Church at the eventual loss of the Papal States in the latter half of the nineteenth century, following their annexation during Italian Unification. Not long before the fall of the Papal States to Italian nationalists, an increasingly concerned Pope Pius IX stressed the importance to the faithful, in his 1859 encyclical *Qui Nuper*, of the papal exercise of civil authority, and how it was bestowed by Divine Providence so that they 'might enjoy the political liberty so necessary for them to exercise their spiritual power, authority and jurisdiction throughout the whole world, without any impediment'.[9] Pope Pius IX's worst fears were eventually realised when, in 1870, the Papal States were annexed to the newly unified Kingdom of Italy, following unsuccessful attempts by King Emmanuel I to persuade the Pope to surrender his territories. The long history of the Papal States was finally ended when the Italian army took the Vatican at the point of a bayonet.

Several years later, the same Pope's fury at the loss of the Papal States was on full display in his 1873 encyclical *Esti Multa*. Pope Pius IX's lament was based squarely on his concerns for what the loss of temporal authority meant for the Church's spiritual functions. He argued that the 'defences and instruments by which We are able to rule and direct the universal Church' had been 'nefariously taken away from Us' by the Italian Kingdom, and was emphatic that the 'purpose of the sacrilegious usurpation of Our rule is the destruction of the force and efficacy of the papal primacy and eventually the Catholic religion itself'.[10] Such was their hostility to being under the temporal authority of another ruler that Popes began to refer to themselves as political prisoners, and refused to leave the Vatican. These papal pronouncements are all testament to the Church's longstanding emphasis on the importance of territorial and political independence.

The Italian King Emmanuel I offered unilateral terms to the indignant Pope, which were passed by the Italian Parliament as the Law of Guarantees.[11] This law offered legal protections to the person of the Pontiff and secured property rights over Church buildings, freedom of assembly, and an annual annuity to compensate for the loss of territory.[12] Pope Pius IX refused to accept the validity or legitimacy of the Law and flatly rejected its terms. As a sign of his displeasure the Pope issued his famous '*non expedit*'

[7] A Grzymała-Busse, *Sacred Foundations: The Religious and Medieval Roots of the European State* (Princeton NJ, Princeton University Press, 2023) 78–79.

[8] ibid 28–29.

[9] Pope Pius IX, *Qui Nuper* (1859), www.vatican.va/content/pius-ix/it/documents/enciclica-qui-nuper-18-giugno-1859.html.

[10] Pope Pius IX, *Esti Multa* (1873), www.papalencyclicals.net/pius09/p9etsimu.htm.

[11] Law of Papal Guarantees, Law No 214 (13 May 1871) (Italy).

[12] SW Halperin, 'Church and State in Italy during the Last Years of Pius IX' (1936) 5 *Church History* 71, 72.

decree, which forbade Italian Catholics to vote in parliamentary elections lest they be seen as ratifying the actions of the Italian authorities.[13]

Between 1870 and 1929 subsequent Popes, as just noted, referred to themselves as 'prisoners in the Vatican' and considered themselves to be under illegal occupation. This long-running political and theological dispute over the territory of the former Papal States became known as the 'Roman Question' and was not resolved until the Kingdom of Italy and the Holy See agreed the Lateran Treaty in 1929 (the Treaty). This Treaty, however, did not restore to the papacy the lands of the former Papal States, which by 1870 included a not insignificant chunk of central Italy. Rather, the Treaty affirmed the full ownership, exclusive dominion, and sovereign authority and jurisdiction of the Holy See over the small piece of territory now comprising Vatican City State, as well as several additional buildings within Rome.[14]

Vatican City State was established as a distinct juridical entity from the Holy See, which is the spiritual and canonical office occupied by the Pope as Bishop of Rome. Vatican City State is, rather, the juridical entity through which the occupant of the Holy See exercises temporal authority over the territory mentioned in the 1929 Treaty. Reference to the Lateran Treaty is explicitly made in Article 7 of the Constitution of the Italian Republic, which provides that:

> The State and the Catholic Church are independent and sovereign, each within its own sphere. Their relations are regulated by the Lateran pacts. Amendments to such Pacts which are accepted by both parties shall not require the procedure of constitutional amendments.

The importance of the 1929 Lateran Treaty, from the perspective of the papacy, is that it once again provided it with an independent territorial base from which the Pontiff could administer the Church free of any secular power. It also ensured that, as a matter of international law, Vatican City State is considered juridically equal to other temporal authorities and sovereign states. Like the creation and maintenance of the Papal States, the creation of Vatican City State was a direct result of the Church's consistent self-understanding that a level of temporal authority was essential to the performance of its divine commission.[15]

As of 2024, this remains the understanding of the papacy under Pope Francis. On the official website of Vatican City State, for example, the state is described as having the 'singular characteristic of being an instrument of the independence of the Holy See and of the Catholic Church from any established power in this world'.[16] Moreover, the

[13] M Larkin, 'The Vatican, France and the Roman Question, 1898–1903: New Archival Evidence' (1984) 27 *The Historical Journal* 177, 178–79.

[14] Article 3 of the Treaty.

[15] For the sake of clarity, I note that the account of the intellectual underpinnings of Vatican City State's existence I offer here is one that is deeply internally grounded in Catholic political and juristic thought. My aim is to immerse the reader in the internal perspective of those working within, and dedicated to, the Church and its magisterial teachings. For practising Roman Catholics – and I include myself here – many of these claims may be considered persuasive or even authoritative. But readers clearly do not have to accept in any way the coherence – let alone validity – of the many metaphysical and theological truth assertions of this account in order to grasp how they might have motivated the actions of those that *did* over two millennia of Church history.

[16] 'Origins and Characteristics' (*Vatican City State*, 23 May 2019), www.vaticanstate.va/en/state-and-government/general-informations/origins-and-characteristic.html.

preamble to the 2023 Fundamental Law issued by Pope Francis reiterates that the Pope has been 'called to exercise sovereign powers' over Vatican City State by virtue of the 'Petrine office' to guarantee the 'Holy See's absolute and visible independence' and its 'sovereignty also in the international arena'.[17]

B. Vatican City State Today

As of 2024, Vatican City State is the smallest independent state in the world, both in terms of its number of inhabitants and the expanse of its territory.[18] The state's territory encompasses little more than 44 hectares of land. Of its boasted 618 citizens, only 246 (including the 104 who are members of the Swiss Guard) live within its territory.[19] Vatican City State issues its own postage stamps, publishes a daily newspaper, *L'Osservatore Romano*,[20] founded in 1861, and, since 1931, there has been a radio station, Vatican Radio,[21] which broadcasts throughout the world. The security needs of the Pope and the state are met by the famous Swiss Guard Corps and the Gendarmerie Corps, who are responsible for all police and state security. Vatican City State is a UNESCO World Heritage Site and boasts some of the world's most famed and treasured art works, architecture, and Holy relics.[22] The birth-rate in the state is around one child a year, which is invariably born to the family of a Swiss Guardsman or Gendarme.

Acquisition of citizenship is governed by Law n^{0} CXXXI 22 February 2011, which was promulgated by Pope Benedict XVI.[23] The Law provides for quite a unique system for granting citizenship, as it eschews reliance on the two main ways of granting citizenship – the principles of *jus soli* (right to citizenship through birth in the territory) and *jus sanguinis* (right to citizenship through blood relationship to an existing citizen). Citizenship in Vatican City State is, rather, closely linked to the occupation of a particular office or to discharging a service within the state. Citizenship can be acquired by law or through administrative decision. Citizenship is granted by law to three classes of persons: (a) the Cardinals resident in Vatican City State or in Rome; (b) the Holy See's diplomats; and (c) the persons who reside in Vatican City State by reason of their office or service. This last class includes the members of the Swiss Guard.[24] Citizenship can also be acquired by an administrative decision following a request in three situations: (a) by residents of Vatican City State when they are authorised by reason of their office or service; (b) by persons who have obtained papal authorisation to reside in the state, independently of any other conditions; and (c) by the spouses and children of current citizens, who are also residents, of Vatican City State.[25]

[17] Fundamental Law of the Vatican City State (13 May 2023) (Fundamental Law), preamble.
[18] ibid.
[19] 'Population' (*Vatican State*, 26 June 2023), www.vaticanstate.va/en/state-and-government/general-informations/population.html.
[20] '*L'Osservatore Romano*', www.osservatoreromano.va/en.html.
[21] *Vatican News*, www.vaticannews.va/en.html.
[22] 'Vatican City' (*UNESCO World Heritage Convention*), whc.unesco.org/en/list/286/.
[23] Legge sulla cittadinanza, la residenza e l'accesso, N^{0} CXXXI (22 February 2011), www.vaticanstate.va/phocadownload/leggi-decreti/Leggesullacittadinanzalaresidenzaelaccesso.pdf.
[24] ibid.
[25] ibid.

III. The Fundamental Law of Vatican City State

The Fundamental Law of Vatican City State is promulgated by the Pope, who exercises sovereign power over the territory. The Fundamental Law outlines how Vatican City State is to be governed and the offices through which *public power* can be exercised in the name of the Pontiff. The Fundamental Law is the foundation of all laws and regulations of Vatican City State, which are different from the legal regime applicable to the Roman Curia, which is the office through which the Pope exercises *spiritual authority*, and which is ruled by the Code of Canon Law.[26] There have been three iterations of the Fundamental Law: the first promulgated by Pope Pius XI in 1929, the second in 2000 by Pope St John Paul II, and the third by Pope Francis in May 2023. The current Fundamental Law came into effect in June 2023. There is considerable continuity between each of these documents, and I will focus on the Fundamental Law currently in force.

In the preamble to the 2023 Fundamental Law the Pope asserts that he has been 'called to exercise sovereign powers' over Vatican City State by virtue of the 'Petrine office' in order to guarantee the 'Holy See's absolute and visible independence' and its 'sovereignty also in the international arena'.[27] Another purpose of the Fundamental Law mentioned in the preamble is to constitute governing bodies to exercise functions and powers in service of the state. The preamble stipulates that the Pope, when promulgating the Fundamental Law, does so pursuant to his enjoying the 'fullness of sovereign authority' over the territory.

The Fundamental Law comprises five parts and 24 articles. Aside from guaranteeing fair procedures and natural justice during the judicial process, the Fundamental Law is solely concerned with the 'nuts and bolts' of the governance of the state, by constituting institutions to exercise legislative, executive, and judicial functions on behalf of the Supreme Pontiff and structurally demarcating how each institution should interact with the others. As such, it lacks the inclusion of any kind of bill of rights now very common to contemporary constitutional systems. Part I is entitled 'General Provisions'; Part II deals with legislative functions; Part III concerns executive functions; Part IV concerns judicial functions; and Part V concludes with two miscellaneous articles that address the commencement of the Fundamental Law. In the next few paragraphs, I sketch the most consequential articles of the Fundamental Law.

A. General Provisions

Article 1 makes clear that the structure of the state's government is centred around a very robust form of monarchical authority. In legal terms, the Pontiff is an elected absolute monarch vested, as 'Sovereign of Vatican City State' with the 'fullness of the power of government, which includes legislative, executive and judicial power'. Article 2.1 affirms the purpose of the state as ensuring 'the absolute and visible independence of the Holy

[26] 'Code of Canon Law', www.vatican.va/archive/cod-iuris-canonici/cic_index_en.html.
[27] ibid.

See for the fulfilment of its lofty mission' and guarantees its 'indisputable sovereignty also in the international arena'. Article 2.2 states that the temporal and spiritual authority of the Roman Pontiff are to be considered separate, noting that the 'State and its system are distinct from the Roman Curia and the other institutions of the Holy See'. Although the fullness of sovereign power is firmly vested in the office of the Pontiff, Article 2.3 ensures that his powers can be exercised in his name by subordinate governmental bodies, providing that 'functions proper to the State system are exercised by the Governorate of Vatican City State in conformity with laws and other normative provisions'.

Article 6.1 provides that representation of Vatican City State in relations with states and other subjects of international law, in diplomatic relations and for the conclusion of treaties, is reserved to the Supreme Pontiff who exercises them through his Secretariat of State. Article 6.3. provides that the Governorate (the executive branch) participates in international institutions of which the Holy See is a member in the name and on behalf of the state.

Article 3.1 provides for the continuity of government of Vatican City State when the papal throne is vacant. It states that during the 'period of Sede Vacante, the College of Cardinals ensures the continuity of the functions of the State and exercises its powers'. The College's legislative powers are restricted to issuing 'legislative provisions only in cases of necessity and urgency and with effectiveness limited to the duration' of the vacancy, unless they are 'subsequently confirmed by the Supreme Pontiff'.

B. Legislative Power – The Pontifical Commission and Councillors of the State

Article 7 provides that 'except in cases that the Supreme Pontiff intends to reserve for himself' the legislative power is exercised by the Pontifical Commission for Vatican City State (the Commission). The Commission is, according to Article 8, composed of Cardinals appointed by the Pope for five-year terms. There are six commissioners at present, including the President.[28] Significantly, the President of the Commission appointed by the Pontiff also serves as head of the Governorate, and so wields both legislative and executive powers.

Article 9 permits other members of the Governorate to participate in Commission meetings in an advisory capacity. Article 10.2 requires that all draft laws must be submitted for the direct consideration of the Pope prior to promulgation. Article 10.3 provides that the 'authentic interpretation of the laws of the State' is reserved to the Commission. Article 11 provides that the President can issue ordinances and decrees which implement general laws issued by the Commission. Article 13 vests the Commission with responsibility for setting the annual budget of the state, and approving a three-year financial plan that will ensure a balance 'between revenue and expenditure and … guided by the principles of clarity, transparency and fairness'. Both the annual budget and financial plan must be submitted to the Pontiff for approval. The budget is subject

[28] 'Organization Chart' (*Vatican City State*, 11 July 2018), www.vaticanstate.va/en/state-and-government/structure-of-the-government/organization-chart.html#vatican-city-state.

to the control and audit of a college composed of three members appointed for a three-year term by the Commission, to which it reports.

Article 12 constitutes the offices of General Councillor and College of the Councillors of the State, which both perform 'advisory functions in the drafting of laws, other regulatory acts and executive functions'. Article 12.3 provides that the President of the Governorate may submit to the College a 'request for an opinion on a doubt of law, such as not to require an authentic interpretation. Such opinions may take the form of statements or explanatory notes'. There are currently four Councillors of the State and the current General Councillor, who leads the College, is a former President of the Italian Constitutional Court.[29]

C. Executive Power – The Governorate

Article 15 provides that the President of the Commission is also the President of the Governorate and exercises the executive function of the state in the name of the Pontiff. The President exercises the executive function through the Directorates of the Governorate[30] and is assisted by a Secretary-General[31] and Deputy Secretary-General.[32] The Directorates assist the Governorate in an analogous way to how Departments of a permanent civil service assist their Ministers. Article 19 provides that the Governorate, through the Directorates, is responsible for the following functions, and any additional ones provided by law:

- security, public order and civil protection;
- the protection of health, healthcare, public hygiene, the environment and ecology;
- economic activities; postal, philatelic and customs services;
- connectivity and network infrastructure; construction activity; technical, hydraulic and electrical systems; and their supervision and maintenance;
- the conservation, enhancement and use of the artistic complex of the Vatican Museums, as well as superintendence over the assets of the entire artistic, historical, archaeological and ethnographic heritage.

D. Judicial Power

Article 21.1 provides that the judicial function is exercised, in the name of the Supreme Pontiff, by the bodies constituted by law. Under a law promulgated by Pope

[29] ibid.

[30] ibid. There are currently seven Directorates: Directorate for Infrastructure and Services; Directorate of Telecommunications and Information Systems; Directorate of the Economy; Directorate of Security and Civil Protection Services; Directorate of Health and Hygiene; Directorate of Vatican Museum and Cultural Heritage; Directorate of the Pontifical Villas.

[31] Fundamental Law, art 16.

[32] Fundamental Law, art 17.

Francis *motu proprio*, the court system is now composed of three layers: the Tribunal, the Court of Appeal and the Court of Cassation.[33] The Tribunal consists of both lay and clergy, and its members are entitled to hold other legal posts. Its members are appointed by the Supreme Pontiff and are 'preferably' to be chosen from among 'tenured or retired university professors' and 'renowned jurists'.[34] The Court of Appeal is composed of a President and at least three ordinary judges, appointed by the Pontiff for five-year terms. An interesting feature of membership of the Court of Cassation is that its President occupies the post *ex officio* because of his role as Cardinal Prefect of the Apostolic Signatura, the highest canonical law body within the Church. At least two other members of the Court must also be cardinals and members of the Signatura and are appointed by the President. Two or more non-cardinal judges may be appointed by the Pontiff. All judges hold office at the pleasure of the Pontiff.

Article 21.2 provides that the Supreme Pontiff, in any civil or criminal case, may refer the investigation and decision to any instance of the judicial hierarchy that he sees fit, with the exclusion of any other appeal. Article 21.3 provides for interpretative principles that govern judicial proceedings, stating that 'judges shall be guided by the principle of equity, shall work for the restoration of justice and shall promote conciliation between the parties'. In criminal cases, moreover, the court is obliged to impose the 'penalty seeking the rehabilitation of the offender, his reintegration and the restoration of the violated legal order'. Article 21.4 stresses the importance of fair procedures and natural justice, providing that in 'every trial, the impartiality of the judge, the right of defence and the adversarial procedure between the parties shall be guaranteed'.

E. Papal Supervisory Authority

The Pontiff enjoys authority to appoint and remove – entirely at will – all the officials who populate the legislative, executive, and judicial branches of the state. There are no tenure protections for any of these officials. It is increasingly unusual in comparative constitutional experience for an unelected monarch to enjoy authority to dismiss members of the legislative branch and remove judges from office without first receiving advice from a democratically accountable government. Indeed, it is increasingly unusual in many constitutional systems for the executive to enjoy authority to dismiss civil servants at will and without cause.[35] This is, then, more evidence of the comparatively enormous extent of the Pope's constitutional authority.

[33] Legge sull'ordinamento giudiziario dello Stato della Città del Vaticano, N° CCCLI (16 March 2020), www.vaticanstate.va/phocadownload/leggi-decreti/normativa-generale/legge%20CCCLI%20All.%203.pdf.

[34] Fundamental Law, art 8.

[35] C Casey, 'Political Executive Control of the Administrative State: How Much is Too Much?' (2021) 81 *Maryland Law Review* 257, 258–59.

F. Additional Sources of Law

Although not mentioned in the Fundamental Law itself, one of the most significant legislative enactments issued by the Pontiff is the Law on the Source of Laws.[36] Perhaps unsurprisingly given Vatican City State's location, this enactment provides that the laws of the Italian state are to be observed by Vatican City citizens and officials and treated as having binding force, *subject* to their consistency with divine law, principles of canon law, and the norms of the Lateran Pacts. The Italian Civil and Criminal Codes therefore make up the bulk of the applicable legal obligations operative within the state.

G. The Constitution-in-Action

In many constitutional systems, there is a considerable gap between the formal 'large-C' Constitution elaborated in canonical codified texts, and how constitutional power is actually allocated and exercised in practice.[37] This gap is often very wide when it comes to the place of the executive branch. In Anglo-American legal systems, for instance, the formal legal boundaries of executive power tend to emphasise both the importance of controlling executive authority and its duty as a faithful *law-executor*. The constitutional traditions of many of these legal systems all share core understandings of the boundaries of executive power linked to this conception: namely, subordination of the executive to the rule of legislation, the executive's duty to faithfully execute the law even if it disagrees with it, and prohibitions on unilateral executive suspension or abrogation of law.[38] This modest formal place of the executive in each system contrasts with legislative pre-eminence. But such accounts alone do not, of course, offer anywhere near an accurate or persuasive conceptual account of the executive in these systems, whose role is characterised by predominance over the political process and policy formation, both domestic and foreign.[39]

The mismatch between the formal position of certain constitutional actors, and how public power is exercised in practice, is also a very common feature of constitutional monarchies. In the United Kingdom for instance, as a matter of formal constitutional principle, the heart of public power is the Crown, from which flows all the powers we tend to associate with a state.[40] The Crown is 'life, the head, and the authority of all things that be done in the realm'.[41] However, over the course of British history, the Crown's authority to legislate, execute policy, and to render justice according to law all

[36] Legge sulle fonti del diritto, N° LXXI (1 October 2008), www.vaticanstate.va/it/stato-governo/legislazione-e-normativa/norm-general.html?download=10:legge-sulle-fonti-del-diritto-1-ottobre-2008-n-lxxi.

[37] A Kavanagh, 'The ubiquity of unwritten constitutionalism' (2023) 21 *International Journal of Constitutional Law* 968, 974–75.

[38] See, in the context of the United Kingdom: *R v Miller* [2017] UKSC 5, [2018] AC 61; in the context of Ireland: *Duggan v An Taoiseach* [1989] ILRM 720 and *NHV v Minister for Justice & Equality* [2017] IESC 35; and of the United States: *Youngstown Sheet & Tube Co v Sawyer* 343 US 579 (1952).

[39] C Casey and D Kenny, 'The Resilience of Executive Dominance in Westminster Systems: Ireland 2016–2019' (2021) *Public Law* 356.

[40] *R v Miller* (n 38) para 41.

[41] H Berman, 'Origins of Historical Jurisprudence: Coke, Selden, Hale' (1994) 103 *Yale Law Journal* 1651, 1660.

became functionally vested in other actors, in the form of the Crown-in-Parliament, HM Government, and the judiciary respectively. To borrow a well-known phrase from Bagehot, the UK Constitution (as with many other constitutional monarchies) has a dignified and efficient aspect,[42] with the King exercising a largely ceremonial function in the sense that all his formal powers either cannot be used (the authority of the courts to render justice for instance) or, by constitutional convention, are only exercisable with the advice and consent of a democratically accountable government.

A fascinating feature of the constitutional order of Vatican City State is, I suggest, the extent to which its large-C Constitution and small-c constitution *do not diverge*. The Popes are not only formally vested with the 'fullness of the power of government, which includes legislative, executive and judicial power', but also regularly use those powers on their own initiative. This is not to say the Pope is the sole font of policy-making for the state. Day-to-day governance of Vatican City State – the management of its buildings and facilities, tourist attractions, waste collection, security and so forth – is invariably conducted in the name of the Pontiff via the institutions discussed above. Nor are all the important policy issues facing Vatican City dealt with solely by the Pontiff. For instance, during the COVID-19 crisis the public health emergency was dealt with by a series of ordinances issued by the Pontifical Commission.[43]

But Vatican City State *is* unique amongst the monarchies of Europe since the Popes directly exercise their constitutional authority to address important policy issues. The three most recent Pontiffs, for instance, engaged in significant law-making activity. St Pope John Paul II introduced a new Fundamental Law in 2000 with a view to giving 'systematic and organic form to the changes introduced by successive stages into the legal system of Vatican City State' since its foundation in 1929. His successor, Pope Benedict XVI issued consequential statutes like the Law on the Source of Laws, discussed above. Pope Benedict also issued statutes bolstering Vatican City State's anti-money laundering initiatives. As noted above, in 2023 Pope Francis issued significant statutes reforming the structure of and eligibility criteria for the judiciary.

In constitutional terms, then, the Pontiff's ability to unilaterally exercise legislative, executive, and judicial power on his own initiative not only makes him the only remaining absolute monarch in Europe, but one of the most powerful executive offices in the world. We can say that in the Constitution of Vatican City State, the dignified and efficient are decisively co-mingled.

Another interesting feature of Vatican City State is how the Pontiff's relatively unmatched constitutional powers do not attract any (vocal or visible) concern from its citizenry. This is doubtless linked to the extremely small size of Vatican City State, its miniscule population, and to very high levels of religious and ideological uniformity. As noted earlier, out of the tiny number of Vatican City State citizens, only 246 reside within its territory. Of these residents, nine are cardinals, 104 are members of the Swiss Guard, and the rest are largely the families of the guardsmen and other religious personnel.[44] All, therefore, are Roman Catholic and deeply loyal to the papacy. Indeed,

[42] See W Bagehot, *The English Constitution* (1867).

[43] See 'Normativa Emergena Sanitaria' (*Vatican City State*), www.vaticanstate.va/it/stato-governo/legislazione-e-normativa/norm-sanitaria.html.

[44] 'Population' (n 19).

most citizens will have personally sworn a vow or oath to the Pontiff. All citizens that are in religious life will have taken, during their ordination, a vow of obedience to their superiors – which of course includes the Pope. Each member of the Swiss Guard will also have sworn an oath to 'serve faithfully, loyally and honourably the reigning Pontiff and his legitimate successors' and 'if necessary' give his life 'in their defence'.[45] In other words, the lack of political debate over the relatively unmatched breadth of papal *temporal* authority in Vatican City State, is closely linked to its citizens' unusually high levels of religious homogeneity and deference to papal *spiritual* authority.

IV. On the 'Smallness' of Vatican City State

Vatican City State is tiny, boasting the population of a small village, and one can walk the length and breadth of the state's territory in well under an hour. One can, however, readily contrast these aspects of the smallness of Vatican City State, with the role of its head of state in world affairs. Despite being the world's smallest state, the influence of its sovereign is nearly unrivalled in human history. Although the Pope does not command divisions of troops,[46] tanks or planes,[47] and even with the increasing secularisation of much of the world – the social, political, and spiritual influence of the sovereign of Vatican City State remains unmatched by other state leaders, even those whose countries' military and economic might dwarf the Vatican's.

We can see this in a visible manner in the way that the encyclicals, exhortations, and statements of modern Pontiffs still exercise considerable influence on the lives and actions of clergy, lay Catholics, civil society groups and political actors the world over. In recent decades, the Popes have been an important voice and source of moral authority (even if controversially so to some) on a range of issues, including questions of peace, justice, inequality, climate change, religious freedom, and human rights.[48] Their positions on these issues do not merely generate discussion within the Church itself, but regularly spark debate, reflection, and responses from non-Catholics. To invoke a term in vogue in political parlance, Vatican City State exercises a high level of 'soft power' in world affairs that belies its smallness.[49] But here I focus most of my attention on a more subtle, even hidden, instance of influence by considering how the papacy has impacted the development of public law concepts now central to contemporary political systems and constitutional theory.

[45] 'Swiss Papal Guard Recruits Oath' (*Swiss Federalism*, 4 May 2022), swissfederalism.ch/en/swiss-papal-guard-recruits-oath/. The oath is sworn by new guardsmen on 6 May, a date which commemorates the date of the Sack of Rome by Holy Roman imperial troops in 1527. Dozens of Swiss Guards died defending then Pope Clement VII during the sack. See 'Press Release, Pontifical Swiss Guard Oath Ceremony 2024' (*Vatican Press Office*, 17 April 2024), press.vatican.va/content/salastampa/en/info/2024/04/17/240417a.html.

[46] As already noted, the security of Vatican City State is provided by the Papal Swiss Guard, which consists of just over 100 men.

[47] As famously, and possibly apocryphally, pointed out by Josef Stalin to Winston Churchill.

[48] See RB Shelledy, 'The Vatican's Role in Global Politics' (2004) 24 *The SAIS Review of International Affairs* 149.

[49] 'Soft power' has been defined as 'the ability to affect others to obtain the outcomes one wants through attraction rather than coercion or payment': JS Nye Jr, 'Public Diplomacy and Soft Power' (2008) 616 *The Annals of the American Academy of Political and Social Science* 94.

Many articles in the Fundamental Law of Vatican City State will look familiar to comparative constitutional scholars, framed as they are using text and concepts that are now standard fare for a modern large-C constitutional document. But in fact, some of these seemingly bog-standard articles reflect concepts and ideas first honed and developed by the Catholic Church and papacy itself, in the precursor to Vatican City State, during their long running contests with temporal authorities. Consider Article 1 of the Fundamental Law, which provides that the 'Supreme Pontiff, Sovereign of the Vatican City State has the full power of government, which includes the legislative, executive and judicial powers'. Elsewhere, in the preamble, the Fundamental Law refers to the Pontiff enjoying the 'fullness of sovereign authority' as the source of his ability to repeal the 2000 Fundamental Law and replace it with a new one. The idea expressed in these provisions – of a juridical entity having power to make or unmake any law, to bind or unbind legal subjects – is of course now a settled (if constantly debated) part of constitutional theory.[50] In perhaps most constitutions, sovereignty is declared to be vested in 'the People', or a body corporate representing different elements of a people of a given territory, like the Crown-in-Parliament for the United Kingdom.

The precursor to this idea in Western political thought, of an entity enjoying the fullness of authority to set or vary legal obligations, comes to us in large part from the Church via Roman law. In Roman law, the *lex regia*[51] was used by jurists as a compendious legal concept to capture the effect and consequence of wholesale transfer to the office of Roman Emperor of the Roman people's natural power to govern themselves.[52] The *lex regia* was the font of other famous precepts like whatever pleased the Prince had the force of a statute (*quod principi placuit legis habet vigorem*);[53] and the Emperor not being bound by the laws or answerable to any higher authority in the exercise of his functions (*princep legibus solutus*).[54]

After the disintegration of the Western Roman Empire, the Church was key to the European rediscovery and revival of Roman law in the eleventh century, most notably in its recovery of the *Corpus Juris Civilis*, and to the adaption and translation of its key legal concepts to articulate its own positions on important issues of authority and power.[55] Alongside scriptural arguments for papal primacy over the

[50] J Habermas, 'Human Rights and Popular Sovereignty: The Liberal and Republican Versions' (1994) 7 *Ratio Juris* 1.

[51] There is, of course, heated debate about what is the precise nature of the *lex regia*. As Canning puts it, 'One school of thought has seen it as an ex post facto legal construction to justify the transition from the republic to the empire. Such a law in fact never existed, but was postulated by later classical jurists to explain the transfer of sovereignty from the Roman people to the first princeps, Augustus, a device, in short, to legitimise the imperial power. The other view identifies the lex regia with the leges de imperio by which the popular assembly gave power to each emperor at the beginning of his reign'. J Canning, *A History of Medieval Political Thought: 300–1450* (London, Routledge, 2003) 8, 18.

[52] According to Ulpian: 'A decision given by the emperor has the force of a statute. This is because the populace commits to him and into him its own entire authority and power, doing this by the lex regia which is passed anent his authority. Therefore, whatever the emperor has determined by a letter over his signature or has decreed on judicial investigation or has pronounced in an interlocutory matter or has prescribed by an edict is undoubtedly a law. These are what we commonly call constitutiones (enactments)'. A Watson (ed), *Digest of Justinian* (Philadelphia PA, University of Pennsylvania Press, 1985) Book 1.4.1.

[53] *Digest of Justinian* (n 52) Book 1.4.1.

[54] *Digest of Justinian* (n 52) Book 1.3.31.

[55] The *Corpus Juris Civilis* is a set of several different set of legal sources assembled at the command of Emperor Justinian in the sixth century. They include Emperor Justinian's *Digest*, which is a codification and

Church and faithful in spiritual matters, concepts drawn from Roman jurisprudence provided an additional powerful conceptual tool.[56] One of the ideas adapted from Roman law was that the Church, as the body of the faithful, could be conceived in corporeal terms, and that when it came to its internal governance and leadership, the Pope inherited,[57] by divine ordination as the 'unworthy heir of St Peter', the fullness of authority given to Peter over this body by Christ.[58] The natural person of the Pope was not vested with these powers, but the divinely empowered Petrine *officium* which he unworthily occupied until his death, and which outlasted him.[59] The Pope, as the immediate successor to Peter, enjoyed the fullness of power – *plenitudo potestatis* – over the Church; which encompassed power to make and enforce any law and adjudicate legal questions without being answerable to any other authority save God.[60] Popes and supportive canonists and jurists also invoked Roman law precepts associated with imperial power – including those referring to the Emperor's plenary law-making power (*quod principi placuit*) and the fact he is not bound by the positive law (*legibus solutus*) – alongside arguments from scripture and tradition, to anchor their very active role in shaping and clarifying canon law and magisterial teaching, making uniform rules of behaviour for clergy across the whole of Christendom, disciplining and exhorting temporal rulers to abide by natural and divine law, and claiming ultimate say over the appointment and removal of clergy – all while claiming complete liberty from temporal direction.[61]

Papal invocation of Roman law concepts and the fullness of power was a significant development in juridical thinking in the West for several reasons. First, it promoted the idea that law was not merely something that was customary, or something discovered or developed. Rather, it could also be created, altered and repealed for the good of the body politic by an office with appropriate authority; an idea seized upon enthusiastically by Popes in issuing decretals[62] on a wide array of issues concerning canon or natural law and their adjudication of disputes from across Christendom, during which they acted as a kind of proto-supranational court of final appeal. Second, the fullness of power doctrine meant that the Pope was not answerable to anyone on this earth for exercise of his authority. In other words, like the Roman Emperor, he admitted no juridical equal

systemisation of the juristic opinions of the most important jurists; the *Institutes of Justinian*, which is a highly simplified version of the *Digest*, designed as a manual for the instruction of new law students; the *Code*, or the laws and enactments of previous Emperors; and finally, the *Novelle Code*, or new laws made by Justinian and his successors.

[56] H Berman, *Law and Revolution: The Formation of the Western Legal Tradition* (Cambridge MA, Harvard University Press, 1983) 204–6.

[57] Popes like Leo I (440–61), when elaborating on the impact of Christ's Petrine commission, explicitly drew on Roman law concepts of inheritance, where the inheritor succeeds to the rights and duties of the testator. W Ullman, 'Leo I and the Theme of Papal Primacy' (1960) 11 *The Journal of Theological Studies* 25, 34.

[58] ibid 47.

[59] ibid.

[60] These were not arguments for arbitrary power, however, as it was universally accepted that Popes were bound by divine and natural law. A Larson, 'Popes and Canon Law' in K Sisson and A Larson (eds), *A Companion to the Medieval Papacy: Growth of an Ideology and Institution* (Leiden, Brill, 2016) 149.

[61] BF Deutsch, 'Ancient Roman Law and Modern Canon Law' (1971) 31 *Jurist* 478, 480.

[62] A decretal is a decision, usually contained in a letter, issued by the Pontiff in respect of issues concerning canon law.

that could coercively call him to account for his use of power, his *potestas*. Of course, it was universally accepted that the Pope was answerable to God for his tenure and decisions and to the directive force of natural and divine law; but there was no temporal force that could sit in judgment of him – *papa a nemine iudicatur*.[63]

These concepts and the Roman law sources that helped buttress them were eagerly embraced and translated by temporal rulers, who were keen to shore up their own authority. Holy Roman Emperors and their supporters, who could chafe at papal assertions of authority to intervene in temporal affairs for reasons of faith and morals, would themselves heavily invoke Roman law concepts like the *lex regia*, indeed the concept of *plenitudo potestatis* itself, to describe their own unassailable authority in the temporal realm.[64] Kings, eager to centralise their authority within their own dominion and over their noble class, began to claim enhanced law-making and tax-levying powers within their realm based on precepts drawn from the *Corpus Juris Civilis*. Kings across Christendom also began to resist the idea they were de jure subject to the Holy Roman Emperor's authority by asserting that, within the bounds of their kingdom, they exercised the fullness of temporal power of the kind enjoyed by the Emperor.[65] In other words, rulers of powerful kingdoms like England and France, that were never really de facto subject to the Holy Roman Emperor's control to begin with, began to assert that they were de jure akin to Emperors within their own domain – *Rex in regno suo est imperator* – and not subject to the jurisdiction of other rulers.[66] Like the Emperor, they claimed to enjoy the *lex regia* from their people and the fullness of law-making power that came with it, acknowledging no temporal superior.[67] They were even helped in this pursuit by canonist arguments building on the decretal *Per Venerabilem* issued in 1202 by Pope Innocent III, which observed without criticism that the 'king of France recognises no temporal superior'.[68] The legal transfer by the Roman people of their natural authority to the Roman Emperor in perpetuity was the prototype, but came to be regarded as 'universally applicable to the conditions of any *regnum* and every people' and ubiquitous

[63] T Pink, 'Papal Authority and the Limits of Official Theology' (2022) 13 *The Lamp: A Catholic Journal of Literature, Science, the Fine Arts etc.* 27, 30–31.

[64] JA Watt, 'The Theory of Papal Monarchy in the Thirteenth Century: the Contribution of the Canonists' (1964) 20 *Traditio* 179, 258–59.

[65] To be sure, this was not the same as an assertion of the power to act arbitrarily. Assertions of absolute power were vanishingly rare, and Kings were expected to act according to reason, natural and divine law and for the common good. The point was rather that there was no juristic power superior to the King that could compel him or sanction him for his actions. They were subject to the directive but not coercive force of law. This was how Roman lawyers reconciled precepts of the *Corpus Juris Civille* like 'the prince is not bound by the laws' with others like 'it is a statement worthy of the majesty of the ruler for the Prince to profess himself bound by the laws'. See A Vermeule, 'Echoes of the Ius Commune' (2021) 66 *American Journal of Jurisprudence* 85, 93.

[66] JM Kelly, *A Short History of Western Legal Theory* (Oxford, Oxford University Press, 1992) 127. To be sure, the interpretation of Roman law concepts could vary wildly in different legal systems as jurists attempted to reconcile precepts of the *Corpus Civilis* that seemed to pull in conflicting directions. For example, jurists would debate the extent to which the King was bound by positive law or not, whether he could lose the *lex regia* by becoming a tyrant, and so forth.

[67] G Post, 'Two Notes on Nationalism in the Middle Ages' (1953) 9 *Traditio* 281, 320.

[68] 'Decretal Letters of Pope Innocent III touching on Church and State' (*Legal History Sources*), www.legalhistorysources.com/ChurchHistory220/Lecture%20Four/InnocentIIIChurchState.html.

in the legal writings of all European countries.[69] In time, many European rulers would go one step further, and make the definitive break with the cosmological framing of the medieval world by arguing that, in the exercise of their governmental power, they were not subject to the direction of *any* higher authority, including the *spiritual* authority of the Church and papacy.[70]

In contemporary liberal constitutional theory, the idea of political life being nested within and disciplined by reference to a broader cosmological and metaphysical hierarchy is a dim memory at best; and temporal authority in Western Europe decisively rejects any subordination to the spiritual direction of the Catholic Church. Religion, says Loughlin, is simply 'no longer … the basic structuring force of collective organisation'.[71] That said, the ideas just canvassed continue to find expression in some of the most fundamental and foundational elements of public law thought. For instance, in the proposition that the People of a given state governing a territory enjoy the fullness of sovereign power to give to themselves, or to change, their form of government.[72] Put in Romanist terms, as a juristic entity 'the People' in modern public law thought are Emperors within their own territory, enjoying full and binding authority (*auctoritas*) to establish standing offices of government capable of channelling *potestas* to uphold the infrastructure of the state and its political right to pursue collective ends for the good of that People.[73] Article 6 of the 1937 Irish Constitution offers a neat example of how this claim can be framed, providing that:

> All powers of government legislative, executive and judicial, derive, under God, from the people, whose right it is to designate the rulers of the State and, in final appeal, to decide all questions of national policy, according to the requirements of the common good.

They also find expression in the idea that this sovereign entity within a state, whether it be the People or Crown-in-Parliament, is not de jure answerable to anyone else outside of its territory for the exercise of its *auctoritas* or *potestas*, whether they be spiritual or other temporal powers.[74] In other words, in juristic terms, each sovereign was to be regarded as on equal footing with, and free of the de jure direction of, another, an idea which evolved to be considered a bedrock principle of international public law.[75]

[69] E Kantorowicz, *The King's Two Bodies: A Study in Medieval Political Theology* (Princeton NJ, Princeton University Press, 1997) 298–300.

[70] A famous example being Henry VIII's Act of Supremacy enacted in 1534. Henry VIII declared the realm of England to have an 'imperial crown' and himself as supreme head on earth of the Church of England, a ringing declaration in Romanist terms of the temporal and spiritual independence of his realm. See W Ulmann, 'This Realm of England is an Empire' (1979) 30 *Journal of Ecclesiastical History* 175.

[71] M Loughlin, *Foundations of Public Law* (Oxford, Oxford University Press, 2011) 8.

[72] As Wilkinson and Somek put it, in modern constitutionalism 'authority derives ultimately from the constituent power of the people. Popular sovereignty can then be understood as representing nothing less than the autonomy of the political realm'. A Somek and M Wilkinson, 'Unpopular Sovereignty' (2020) 83 *Modern Law Review* 955, 959.

[73] Loughlin (n 71) 6–7.

[74] Consider the sweep of AV Dicey's classic definition of parliamentary sovereignty as: 'the right to make or unmake any law whatever; and further, that no person or body is recognised by the law of England as having a right to override or set aside the legislation of Parliament'. AV Dicey, *An Introduction to the Study of the Law of the Constitution*, 10th edn (London, Macmillan, 1959) 39–40.

[75] H Kelsen, 'The Principle of Sovereign Equality of States as a Basis for International Organization' (1944) 53 *Yale Law Journal* 207, 208.

V. Conclusion

The development of the authority of the papacy, the creative mingling by the Pontiffs and their supporters of scriptural exegesis, Roman law precepts and sophisticated political-theological argumentation, and the enthusiastic aping of these moves by temporal authorities, all helped to provide some of the 'basic grammar' of key concepts of modern public law.[76] To invoke Schmitt, the history of Vatican City State highlights the extent to which many of the 'significant concepts of the modern theory of the state' are best understood as 'secularized theological concepts' that long pre-date the onset modernity and rise of liberalism.[77] These kind of insights are just some of the, doubtless many, hidden treasures nestled within the terms of the Fundamental Law of the world's smallest state.

[76] Loughlin (n 71) 18.

[77] C Schmitt, *Political Theology: Four Chapters on the Concept of Sovereignty* (George Schwab trans, Chicago IL, University of Chicago Press, 2005) 36.

Part IB
Legal Culture and Pluralism

7

Small-state Constitutionalism and Legal Pluralism

Logging and Mining Governance in Suriname

INE APAPOE AND JANINE UBINK

I. Introduction

Constitutionalism is the principle that the authority of government derives from and is limited by a body of fundamental law. Tribal and indigenous groups, however, have their own fundamental laws and often contest claims of state supremacy in their territories. This poses inherently constitutional questions regarding the governance of legal pluralism. This chapter contributes to the volume's theme of constitutionalism in small states, by studying the design and operation of the governance of legal pluralism in Suriname. Suriname is a natural-resource-rich, upper-middle-income country with a small population, whose economy is highly dependent on its abundant natural resources.[1] While small in terms of its population size, Suriname has a relatively large territory. The geographical as well as cultural distance between the government and tribal and indigenous groups living in the interior is wide, and the reach of the government into the interior areas is limited. The country's history of divided rule constitutes an explanatory factor in this relationship.

Suriname's Constitution (1987) has no provisions that indicate the presence or recognition of law and governance structures of indigenous people and tribal groups (maroons).[2] The state does not officially recognise or regulate legal pluralism. Indigenous people and maroon groups, however, continue to claim authority to govern their own territories. As these habitats contain large reserves of natural resources that are of great economic importance to the country, unclarity and disagreements about the applicable legal system, and the authority of governance actors particularly, centre around the regulation of logging and extractive resource mining. Focusing on the logging and gold mining sectors in Suriname, this chapter analyses how the state[3] and traditional

[1] 'The World Bank in Suriname' (*World Bank Group*), www.worldbank.org/en/country/suriname.

[2] In this chapter, the words 'tribal' and 'maroon' are used interchangeably.

[3] While we recognise that anthropological literature has increasingly shown that institutions and persons who are not officially associated with the state may be de facto involved in the execution of public authority

authorities engage with each other and appeal to different legal registers – foremost statutory law and customary law but also international law – to position themselves. Against the background of the worldwide fight of indigenous people and tribal groups for recognition of land rights, this chapter gives insight into the implications of state size for how governmental and tribal actors engage with each other via complex processes of contestation, negotiation and positioning to gain or maintain authority over governance processes and decisions in tribal habitats, and to defend the authority, supremacy and relevance of their legal register in the make-up of the nation-state of Suriname.

This chapter proceeds as follows: the next section will discuss literature that connects constitutionalism to the governance of legal pluralism. Then we will describe relevant aspects of the history, population, and governmental system of the state of Suriname, the governance systems of maroon communities, and the role of both state and traditional institutions in the governance of natural resources situated in Suriname's tribal habitats. This will be followed by a deeper dive into two sectors of natural resource governance: logging and gold mining, where we show the interplay between state and traditional authorities and the underlying legal registers. The chapter will end with a conclusion on the governance of legal pluralism in small states.

This chapter is based on data that have been collected as part of a wider research project on the quality of modern, traditional, and dual governance in Suriname, with a particular emphasis on the Ndyuka maroons.[4] This research combined desk study of relevant literature and policy documents with semi-structured interviews conducted with government officials, traditional leaders, and representatives from indigenous and maroon communities.

II. Constitutionalism and the Governance of Legal Pluralism

There are many different definitions of constitutionalism. Notwithstanding this definitional diversity, constitutionalism is squarely centred around questions of the organisation of legal norms and the defence of normative hierarchies.[5] Within scholarship focusing on constitutionalism, the impact of plurality is a recurring topic. Febbrajo, for instance, in a chapter on constitutionalism and legal pluralism, poses the question of how a hierarchically organised normative world can be reconciled with the idea of a polyarchy of different sets of norms.[6] Constitutionalism and legal pluralism seem most often debated in relation to international, supranational, or global law.[7] This

and as such 'perform *stateness*' (C Lund, 'Twilight institutions: An introduction' (2006) 37(4) *Development and Change* 673, 676), for this chapter we equate state institutions with governmental institutions.

[4] See IR Apapoe, 'Governing Apart Together. The Structure, Process and Quality of Modern, Traditional and Dual Governance of Traditional Societies in Suriname' (PhD thesis, Vrije Universiteit Amsterdam, November 2024), https://research.vu.nl/en/publications/governing-apart-together-the-structure-process-and-quality-of-mod.

[5] Cf AS Sweet, 'Constitutionalism, Legal Pluralism, and International Regimes (2009) 16(2) *Indiana Journal of Global Legal Studies* 621, 623.

[6] A Febbrajo, 'Constitutionalism and Legal Pluralism' in A Febbrajo and G Corsi (eds) *Sociology of Constitutions: A Paradoxical Perspective* (Abingdon, Routledge, 2016) 68.

[7] See for instance Sweet (n 5); PS Berman, *Global Legal Pluralism* (Cambridge, Cambridge University Press, 2012).

is intimately connected to the absence of an agreed-upon ultimate authority in the international arena. Krisch, for instance, describes how in the EU, the Member States and the Union can each be seen as having their own 'internally plausible claim to ultimate authority', based on a different ultimate point of reference: national constitutions or the EU Treaty.[8]

These debates on global legal pluralism[9] hark back to older debates in legal anthropology, where the term legal pluralism was coined as a response to a legal centralist ideology that law is and should be the law of the state and that other normative orderings are hierarchically subordinate to state law.[10] Instead, it put the issue of competing legal orders centre-stage.[11] Legal pluralism was defined as the presence of 'more than one legal order or mechanism within one socio-political space, based on different sources of ultimate validity and maintained by forms of organisation other than the state'.[12] Here, the distinction between weak and strong legal pluralism is helpful. In situations of weak legal pluralism,[13] the state formally recognises other legal orders, such as customary law. Strong legal pluralism,[14] on the other hand, describes a situation in which multiple legal orders exist and exert authority over people's lives, irrespective of state recognition.[15] In many countries, the state claims the ultimate authority to recognise other legal systems (or not to do so). This does not change the fact that the empirical reality in many countries is one of strong legal pluralism.[16] In countries with strong legal pluralism, various legal systems are meaningful, are in dialogue with each other, and have authority over different groups of people who engage with them via complex processes of negotiation, positioning, and creation.[17] Irrespective of the presence or absence of state recognition, groups of people may perceive other normative registers as more authoritative

[8] N Krisch, 'Who is Afraid of Radical Pluralism? Legal Order and Political Stability in the Postnational Space' (2011) 14(4) *Ratio Juris* 386, 387. Arguing against the idea that any measure of legal pluralism is inversely proportional to any measure of constitutional order, Sweet (n 5) 635 posits that legal pluralism can serve as a catalyser for constitutionalisation: 'Confronting and managing the friction inherent in plural environments allows constitutionalization to proceed'.

[9] Berman (n 7).

[10] F Von Benda-Beckmann, 'Who's Afraid of Legal Pluralism?' (2002) 34(47) *Journal of Legal Pluralism and Unofficial Law* 37, 37.

[11] JM Ubink, 'Legal Pluralism in a Globalized World' (2018) 8 *UC Irvine Law Review* 141, 142.

[12] Von Benda-Beckmann (n 10) 37.

[13] Also called state law legal pluralism, see GR Woodman, 'Ideological Combat and Social Observation: Recent Debate about Legal Pluralism (1998) 30(42) *Journal of Legal Pluralism and Unofficial Law* 21, 34.

[14] Also called 'deep legal pluralism', see ibid 34, or 'social, empirical legal pluralism', see AJ Hoekema, 'European Legal Encounters between Minority and Majority Culture: Cases of Interlegality' (2005) 51 *Journal of Legal Pluralism and Unofficial Law* 1, 4.

[15] J Griffiths, 'What is Legal Pluralism?' (1986) 24 *Journal of Legal Pluralism and Unofficial Law* 1, 5–8; J Vanderlinden, 'Return to Legal Pluralism: Twenty Years Later' (1989) 28 *Journal of Legal Pluralism and Unofficial Law* 149, 150–51; GR Woodman, 'Legal Pluralism and the Search for Justice' (1996) 40(2) *Journal of African Law* 152, 158.

[16] G Corradi, 'Advancing Human Rights in Legally Plural Africa: The Role of Development Actors in the Justice Sector' (2013) 26(1) *Afrika Focus* 89, 90.

[17] M de Theije et al, 'Engaging Legal Systems in Small-scale Gold Mining Conflicts in three South American Countries' in M Bavinck, L Pellegrini and E Mostert (eds), *Conflicts over Natural Resources in the Global South. Conceptual Approaches* (London, CRC Press, 2014) 129, 131–33. M Simon Thomas, 'The Challenge of Legal Pluralism: Local Dispute Settlement and the Indian–State Relationship in Ecuador' (PhD thesis, Utrecht University 2013) 35 points out that the interaction and contact between different legal orders makes it hard to delineate the boundaries between the various legal systems. B de Sousa Santos, *Toward a New Legal Common Sense: Law, Globalization, and Emancipation*, 2nd edn (London, Butterworths, 2002) 437 finds that legal plurality results in situations of 'interlegality', in which people experience the various normative orders as 'different legal spaces superimposed, interpenetrated and mixed in our minds, as much as in our actions'.

than state law in certain fields. The extent to which states have the power to impose norms and determine the normative hierarchy is an empirical question, one that may be impacted by the size of a country's population as well as its territory. The case of Suriname provides an illustrative example here.

III. Suriname: Population and History

Suriname is a former Dutch colony located on the Atlantic coast of South America, neighbouring French Guiana to the East, (formerly British) Guyana to the West and Brazil to the South. The country gained its independence on 25 November 1975. It has a land surface of 163,820 square kilometres and its total population is estimated at 623,000 people. About 85 per cent of the Surinamese population live in the Northern coastal plains, with 67 per cent in the capital, Paramaribo, and the district of Wanica.[18] In 1983, the district of Sipaliwini was created, and it is four times as large as the other districts combined.[19] It spans almost 80 per cent of the total territory of Suriname, is completely covered with tropical rainforest, and has a population density of less than two people per square kilometre. In this district, the majority of the tribal groups are located, and it is the most deprived area of the country, characterised by low accessibility. The few roads are often poorly maintained, and some parts of the district can only be reached by small propeller plane from Paramaribo, or by boat, which depends on the water level in the river and can sometimes take days.

The country is characterised by a population of various ethnic groups, of which all but the indigenous people have colonial roots. After the colonisation of Suriname in 1650, the colonisers first tried to put the native population to work on the plantations, but many did not survive the harsh work there. In response, enslaved Africans were brought to the country to replace the indigenous people as plantation workers. The hazardous work and bad treatment by plantation owners resulted in groups of these enslaved people fleeing the plantations for the remote interior. From there, they organised guerilla-led warfare to help others escape and obtain food, which wrought economic damage on the colonial power. This induced the colonisers to sign peace treaties with the formerly enslaved people, called maroons, in the seventeenth and eighteenth centuries.[20] In the run-up to the abolition of slavery (which transpired in 1863), the colonial government foresaw a serious decrease in workforce at the plantations and began to hire contract workers from Asia. After a relatively small number of migrant workers was brought over from China (1858–74), a much larger stream of indentured labourers was brought to Suriname, first from British India, and then from the Dutch East Indies. These groups were called Hindustani (1873–90) and Javanese (1890–1939).

[18] 'The World Bank in Suriname' (n 1).

[19] Decreet Districtenindeling 1983, Decreet 17, *Staatsblad van de Republiek Suriname* [District Organisation Decree 1983, Decree 17, *Government Gazette of the Republic of Suriname*] 1983 no 24, www.sris.sr/wp-content/uploads/2022/10/SB-1985-No-2-WEt-RiS.pdf.

[20] The first peace treaty was signed in 1760 with the Ndyuka Maroons, followed by treaties with the Saamaka and Matawai Maroons in 1762 and 1767 respectively.

Although some of these indentured labourers returned to their home country later, the majority stayed in Suriname and contributed to the ethnic diversity of the country.

The conclusion of peace treaties between the maroons and the colonisers allowed the maroons to live in freedom in the interior of the country, in relatively closed communities that they governed on the basis of their own customary laws, traditional authority structures, and religion and kinship systems, without Dutch colonial interference.[21] As a result of the peace treaties, the maroons enjoyed a level of legally recognised autonomy that ensured they would not be re-enslaved,[22] but they had limited freedom of movement within the country. According to Mitrasingh and Mitrasingh, the interior area where the maroons lived was not considered an inhabited area by the colonial government and as such did not fall within the geographical area of the Colony and under the authority of the colonial state.[23] The colonial government intended to isolate the maroon population as much as possible in the interior and inhibited their freedom of movement, for instance by requiring a pass for maroons to visit Paramaribo.[24] After the Emancipation of 1863, there was a gradual increase in government intervention and changes in policy towards the interior. Instead of isolation, integration of the maroons was now pursued, and the pass system was revoked.[25] The discovery of large deposits of natural resources, mainly gold and bauxite, in the habitat of the tribal groups further increased the interest of the government in the interior. From the period leading up to independence (in 1975), Suriname has taken a '*verzorgingsgebied aanpak*' (area of care approach),[26] whereby state authorities assumed responsibility for providing the most essential social facilities to the residential areas of the maroon groups. Schools were built, drinking water facilities installed, and medical facilities arranged. However, the interior war that was fought between 1986 and 1992[27] led to the destruction of many of these facilities. Although after the war several initiatives, plans and projects have been undertaken, low budgets and the state's limited implementation capacity continue to result in the poor development of facilities in the interior. Despite this underperformance, many maroon communities continue to believe it is the state's responsibility to provide basic services in their habitat. Unable to set up these facilities themselves due

[21] B Scholtens, *Bosnegers en Overheid in Suriname, De ontwikkeling van de politieke Verhouding 1651–1992* (Paramaribo, Ministerie van Onderwijs en Volksontwikkeling afdeling Cultuurstudies, 1994) 40.

[22] ibid 22; SW de Groot, *Agents of their own Emancipation: Topics in the History of Suriname Maroons* (Amsterdam, 2009).

[23] JC Mitrasing and FEM Mitrasing, *Compendium van het Surinaams Regionaal Recht, Verleden en Heden en de Wet op Regionale Organen* (Paramaribo, Vaco Press, 1992) 16–24. They draw this conclusion based on the introduction of a new 15-district structure for the Colony. This idea was piloted in 1936 and the division of the new districts was established by *Koninklijk Besluit* [Royal Decree] of 21 December 1862 no 26. Article 1 of the *Koninklijk Besluit* stipulated that this division only applied to the inhabited area. The boundaries drawn for the new districts show that the interior, where the indigenous people and maroons lived, was not considered inhabited territory and as such did not fall under the authority of the colonial government.

[24] Scholtens (n 21) 41.

[25] ibid 49.

[26] *Rapport van de Surinaams-Nederlandse Commissie van Deskundigen:Programma voor de Sociaaleconomische ontwikkeling van Suriname* (Paramaribo, Surinaams-Nederlandse Commissie van Deskundigen, 1975).

[27] In this period, the country went through an eight-year civil war between the national army and a guerilla group, the Jungle Commando, led by Ronny Brunswijk. The brunt of this war was borne in the interior of the country. For more information on the interior war, see E de Vries, *Suriname na de Binnenlandse Oorlog* (Amsterdam, Koninklijk Instituut voor de Tropen, 2005).

to lack of financial means and know-how, they often have no choice but to wait for the government or other organisations to establish these facilities.

Besides some basic service provision and some involvement in mineral resource governance, state engagement with the interior has thus remained minimal, and traditional leaders have continued to be the main governing authorities.[28]

IV. Suriname's Governance System

A. State Governance

Political governance in Suriname has its origins in the establishment of the Colonial States in 1937, which were headed by a Dutch Governor appointed by the Netherlands. In 1942, the Dutch overseas territories, including Suriname, were given internal self-government.[29] Gradually the political landscape in Suriname changed, with growing influence of Surinamese politicians on the governance of the country. The political-administrative role of the former mother country gradually decreased, and the Surinamese population increasingly had the opportunity to choose its own government. In 1948, general suffrage for men and women was introduced and the number of representatives in The States (ie, the parliament) was increased from 13 to 21. In 1975 the country became independent and in 1987 a new Constitution was adopted. This document provided for a parliamentary democracy headed by a President accountable to a parliament, the Surinamese people's representative body (*De Nationale Assemblée*, DNA).[30] The Constitution also established regional governance authorities (*district- en ressortraden*). At the district and sub-district levels[31] the government is divided into representative and executive branches. The District Councils (*Districtsraden*) form the representative branch, and the District Administrations (*Districtsbesturen*) the executive branch. District Councils are responsible for law-making and formulating regulations for all districts. If a district ordinance contravenes the Constitution, national public policy, or existing legal regulations, the National Assembly can repeal it. At the sub-district level, a branch of representation consisting of Resort Councils (*Ressortraden*) advises the district government on all matters regarding their sub-district, including issues regarding the traditional societies living in these districts. The districts are led by one or more District Commissioners, appointed by the President. The District Commissioner chairs both the District Council and the District Administration. District and Resort Councils are elected every five years in general elections.

[28] Scholtens (n 21) 55.

[29] J Sedney, *De Toekomst van ons Verleden: Democratie, Etniciteit en Politieke Machtsvorming in Suriname* (Paramaribo, Vaco Press, 2017) 23.

[30] The DNA consists of 51 members, who are chosen every five years via general elections.

[31] The passage of the *Wet Regionale Organen* [Law of Regional Bodies] (*Staatsblad* 1989 No 44) was aimed at enabling district governments to begin managing their revenues and budgets and to deliver simple public services.

According to the 1987 Constitution, Suriname is a decentralised unitary state.[32] In 2002 the Decentralization and Local Government Strengthening Program was introduced and implemented, which aimed to strengthen local government by providing a legal framework and implementing fiscal and administrative institutions in the districts.[33] During the implementation of this programme, the districts in which the traditional communities reside were unable to adequately cope with the requirements of the programme, because their role was not explicitly defined. Research by Kambel 2006 recommended, among other things, the legal recognition of traditional authority and the establishment of an effective, participatory body to coordinate and mainstream indigenous and maroon issues in government policies and programmes and to ensure the effective participation of indigenous and maroon communities in planning and programmatic decision-making and service provision. According to the recommendation, this body should consist of representatives of indigenous peoples, maroons and government.[34] Until now, no concrete action has been taken to implement this recommendation, except for the drafting of a law on traditional authority.

B. Maroon Governance

Four main groups of indigenous people and six maroon groups inhabit the country, with maroons constituting the second largest ethnic group in the country. Parallel to state institutions, traditional authorities continue to play an important role in the governance of tribal communities. The maroon tribes are led by a paramount chief, the *gaanman*. The paramount chief is assisted by *ede kabitens*, *kabitens*, and *basiyas* (head-captains, captains, and their assistants) who belong to one of the 12 *los* (clans) and who, like the *gaanman*, are appointed for life. The matrilineal kinship system affects many aspects of maroon society, including succession patterns, land ownership, and the distribution of political and religious functions.[35]

The governance of maroon society is ascribed to traditional leaders, who must execute this function in accordance with customary law and culture. The daily governance of the villages is the responsibility of the *kabitens* and *ede kabitens* and the councils of elders. These leaders make decisions and try to resolve problems and disputes in maroon society.[36] Topics that surpass the responsibility of the *(ede)kabitens* are submitted to the *gaanman*, who takes a final decision after consulting all parties involved. When issues concern the whole tribe, a *gaankuutu*, a tribe-wide meeting, can be held, chaired by the *gaanman*. These governance rules of tribal society are not stipulated in

[32] ibid art 52, para 1.

[33] B Ahmadali 'Leidraad Decentralisatie 2003–2007' (Paramaribo Decentralization and Local Government Strengthening Program, 2007) 5–6.

[34] E Kambel, 'Indigenous Peoples and Maroons in Suriname' (Inter-American Development Bank Economic and Sector Study Series, RE3-06-035, September 2006) 35, publications.iadb.org/en/publications/english/viewer/Indigenous-Peoples-and-Maroons-in-Suriname.pdf.

[35] HR Libretto, *Het Gezags- en Bestuurssysteem in het Binnenland van Suriname* (Paramaribo, Vaco Press, 1990).

[36] TH Polimé, 'Het Traditioneel Gezag op een Tweesprong: De Ndyuka Marrons' in P Meel and H Ramsoedh (eds), *Ik ben een Haan met een Kroon op mijn Hoofd: Pacificatie en Verzet in Koloniaal en Post-Koloniaal Suriname. Opstellen voor Wim Hoogbergen* (Amsterdam, Bert Bakker, 2007) 55–75.

any written document, but rather captured in orally transmitted maroon customary rules. New rules are often made by consensus and presented to the ancestors before they come into force.

Indigenous and maroon governance authorities are not formally acknowledged or mentioned in any statutory law. Despite this, there are myriad small manifestations of informal dual governance between state institutions and traditional leadership, who communicate, consult, and address topics of concern for the interior population together – for instance, regarding land rights or the quality of education, health facilities and drinking water. We will see below that the cooperation between state actors and traditional authorities becomes more challenging, however, when there are large economic interests at stake.

V. Governance of Natural Resources: State and Traditional Authority

In the year 2000, the World Bank ranked Suriname as the 17th richest country in the world based on its large quantity of natural resources. Suriname's economy has traditionally been dependent on extractive industries, which play a dominant role in driving growth, exports, employment, and government revenue. Gold, oil, and bauxite have historically accounted for around 30 per cent of Suriname's Gross Domestic Product (GDP) and as much as 90 per cent of exports.[37]

Almost 90 per cent of these natural resources are located in the residential areas of the tribal maroon groups of Suriname. The existence of valuable natural resources in tribal habitats, and the question of who has governance and decision-making power over them, are the main sources of conflict between state authorities and the tribal groups. The answers to that question differ significantly depending on the source of law applied to it. Surinamese statutory law places the power to govern natural resources squarely with the state's governance institutions;[38] customary law, on the other hand, defines tribal communities and their governance institutions as entitled to make decisions about and reap the benefits from natural resources in tribal habitats, a position supported by international law.[39] Ultimately, this is a constitutional question about the governance of legal pluralism and whether it is based on 'a conversation among equals'[40] or results from a situation where state authorities, laws, and courts determine the breadth, scope, and validity of customary law concerning the state. The state and traditional leaders each make their own 'internally plausible claim to ultimate authority'[41] to regulate the use and commercial exploitation of natural resources in tribal habitats, each referring to a different ultimate point of reference: the Constitution or customary law. In the next

[37] *Note on Minerals Institute Suriname* (Ministry of Natural Resources of Suriname, February 2019), documents1.worldbank.org/curated/en/715551576654339922/text/Note-on-Minerals-Institute-Suriname.txt.

[38] The Constitution of the Republic of Suriname (1987) art 4.

[39] See section VI of this chapter for a discussion of several relevant international court decisions.

[40] R Gargarella, *The Law as a Conversation Among Equals* (Cambridge, Cambridge University Press, 2022).

[41] Cf Krisch (n 8) 387.

sections we will zoom in on Suriname's logging and gold mining sectors to show the ambiguous interaction – sometimes cooperative, sometimes conflictual – between state and traditional governance institutions, and analyse these differing modalities.

A. A Tale of Two Resources: Logging

While the logging sector currently accounts for only 1.4 per cent of Suriname's GDP, it is believed to have the potential to become a much larger contributor to the state treasury.[42] According to statutory law, state institutions are responsible for the governance of logging in Suriname. State institutions may issue permits for commercial logging projects in the country, including within tribal habitats. In addition, they can issue special logging concessions to tribal groups by designating land areas in their habitats as community forests.[43] The Maroons, in turn, have a long history of governing the natural resources in their habitat, including the regulation of logging, based on unwritten customary rules and verbal agreements. According to these rules, actors interested in logging within the tribal habitat can approach the traditional authority of the appropriate *lo*. If the concession does not conflict with existing concessions in the area and there are no objections from tribal members, the *lo*'s traditional leaders can permit logging activities. If the logging area exceeds the territory of one *lo*, the *gaanman* needs to be involved, who can decide after consulting the traditional leaders of the areas involved.

How traditional authorities and communities react to the claim that state institutions (also) have authority over natural resources in their tribal habitat differs considerably from area to area. In the remote inland area of Tapanahony, traditional leaders firmly reject the authority of state institutions over what they regard as *their* natural resources. The limited accessibility of the area makes commercial logging unprofitable, which results in a lack of interest to apply for and exploit community forests and little enticement for the tribal authority to cooperate with the government in the field of logging. Likewise, the remoteness of the area and the limited viability of commercial logging induces little interest of the government in this area's logging. As a result, the tribal authority continues to govern the logging sector based on customary law with minimal interest and involvement from state governance structures and little impact of state law.

In less remote areas, such as in the Cottica and Commewijne, located in the coastal area, maroon communities *do* have an active interest in commercial logging and the establishment of community forests, which results in frequent contact between state and traditional authorities. Our field research showed that in this geographical area, state and traditional governance structures work together quite amicably in the governance of community forests. As maroon groups often lack the knowledge to exploit their community forests, lower-level policy officers of the Village Development Department

[42] *Forestry Sector Analysis* (Paramaribo, Stichting Bosbeheer en Bostoezich, 2022).

[43] *Wet Bosbeheer* [Forest Management Act] (*Staatsblad* 1992 no 80). This Act replaced the *Verordening Houtkapvergunningen* [Timber Ordinance] of 1947 that introduced special logging permits to give tribal people the opportunity to gain an income from the logging sector and to protect them from concession holders. While these permits were issued to the village, they were in the name of the *kabiten*. As a result, in some areas it was mainly or only the traditional leaders and their relatives who benefited from logging activities. In 1992 these permits were transformed into community forest permits by the *Wet Bosbeheer* to enable the whole village community to benefit from the earnings from this sector.

play an important and useful role in assisting communities with the exploitation of these forests. They help explain the application procedures, regulations, and functioning of community forests to the villagers. Furthermore, they assist communities with setting up agreements with third parties as well as with devising management structures and transparent financial accounting structures. State authorities were also found to intervene in disputes between villagers and their leaders – mostly about the allocation of revenues accruing from the community forests – or between traditional authorities and external entrepreneurs. While they seemed to be largely well-meaning, these policy officers operate without a legal mandate or detailed regulations and have limited implementation capacity, and the informality of their help complicates their activities. Sometimes decisions taken by these policy officers can be overruled by a higher policy officer because they lack legal foundation.

The cooperative relationship between state institutions and traditional governance structures regarding community forests, described above, contrasts starkly with the relationship between traditional and state authorities when large commercial logging concessions are involved. Here state authorities regularly clash with tribal communities, typically when the government grants large commercial logging concessions in tribal habitats to outsiders, without much consultation with, let alone consent of, the maroon communities. One such conflict arose in what became known as the Berjaya case, in which the state prepared to allocate a huge logging concession to the Asian logging multinational Berjaya Berhad in the living area of several maroon groups, without their knowledge and consent. Despite national and international protests against the issuance of the concession and promises by state representatives that the concerns of the tribal groups would be taken into account, the government continued preparations for granting the concession. When parliamentary approval was withheld for the concession of 1,150,000 hectares, the executive proceeded by dividing the concession into several smaller ones, thereby circumventing the requirement of parliamentary approval – which only exists for areas larger than 150,000 hectares.

This analysis of logging governance in Suriname highlights two things about the way state institutions and traditional authorities relate to each other and to one another's claim over natural resources situated in tribal habitats. The first is that we need to distinguish between remote tribal areas and other tribal areas situated closer to governmental and commercial actors. The size of the country and the distance between communities and the capital, as well as the distance from remote inland areas to the main transport arteries, all strongly impact the degree of interaction between state institutions and tribal communities.

This analysis, secondly, teaches us that we need to open the black box of 'the state' to distinguish different governance institutions and actors and realise that these engage with tribal communities and authorities in very different circumstances involving interests of varied proportions. In local affairs, we see a genuine interest on the part of 'street-level'[44] civil servants of the Village Development Department to engage with maroon communities, solve their disputes, and help them organise effective and transparent

[44] M Lipsky, *Street-level Bureaucracy: Dilemmas of the Individual in Public Service* (New York, Russell Sage Foundation, 2010).

exploitation of community forests to the benefit of all community members. Despite limited guidance in the law and a lack of detailed regulation, state governance actors are proactive in creating and applying measures to support tribal groups in exploiting their community forests. However, when logging governance involves large-scale economic interests of importance to the nation as a whole, and possibly also lucrative interests for individual politicians or senior civil servants, a different picture emerges – one where maroon interests are largely ignored and maroon voices often are not even included in the debate. Decisions in these cases are taken by senior government officials who have little contact with the communities and seemingly little affinity and sympathy for the tribal societies. In these cases, the informal character of dual governance practices becomes a burden, as Surinamese law does not provide much protection for maroon communities. The Forest Management Act merely mentions that customary rights must be respected 'as much as possible' when concessions are issued. What this means has not been elaborated and in cases where maroon communities have made a formal complaint the government has not even deigned to respond.

B. A Tale of Two Resources: Gold Mining

The governance structure for the gold sector in many ways resembles what we described for the logging sector. The Surinamese Mining Decree of 1986[45] stipulates that all extractive resources are state-owned and thus state institutions are formally responsible for governing the gold mining sector.[46] This includes the formulation and implementation of policies and laws and the issuance of large-scale and small-scale gold mining concessions. Maroon traditional leaders, in turn, generally hold the opinion that customary law grants *them* the authority to govern small-scale gold mining. Maroon communities largely ignore the state's claim to govern mining resources within their habitat and generally undertake their small-scale mining activities without reference to the government. According to customary law, the traditional leaders representing the *lo* have the legitimate authority to grant outsiders permission for gold mining on the *lo*'s land. Since the end of the 1980s, gold mining has become the main source of income for the maroons. Such permissions, given by a *kabiten* or *ede kabiten*, have resulted in several external investments in gold mining in tribal areas. These investors pay the traditional leaders a percentage of the revenues from their gold mining. There is little transparency around the use of these revenues, and this is a common source of conflict between traditional leaders and villagers.

State authorities, who, according to their own laws, are entitled to issue mining concessions, also allow external parties to mine gold in tribal habitats. The Mining Decree stipulates that 'rightsholders and third-party stakeholders' have to allow concession holders into their territory as long as they have been duly notified and financially compensated.[47] Article 46(c) of this Decree defines third-party stakeholders as 'those whose interests arising from a personal right of enjoyment of private land may be

[45] *Decreet Mijnbouw* [Mining Decree] (*Staatsblad* 1986 no 28, last amended by *bij Staatsblad* 1997 no 44).
[46] ibid arts 2, 3.
[47] ibid art 47(1)(a), (b).

harmed by the exploration or extraction of minerals' (unofficial translation). While this already provides minimal rights to third-party stakeholders, state authorities argue that tribal communities do not qualify as such. They claim that, according to the Surinamese Constitution, all land that does not qualify as private property of an individual is state land and that since maroon communities do not have proof of ownership, the land in their habitat belongs to the domain of the state.[48] This far-reaching interpretation – which is in direct opposition to international obligations to protect indigenous land rights – would mean that tribal communities would not be considered as having *any* rights in their own tribal land and thus would not even be entitled to notification and financial compensation when external concessionaires undertook mining activities in their habitat. In contradiction to this view, Kambel and Mackay conclude that traditional groups *do* qualify as third-party stakeholders under the law.[49]

The above displays that the outdated mining laws and regulations are open to multiple interpretations and that state authorities apply the law in such a way that it does not effectively protect the rights of tribal communities. The fact that successive governments have never responded to any of the complaints by maroon communities regarding the issuance of mining concessions indicates that the government exploits the vagueness of the law to continue to disregard the rights and interests of tribal societies.

Tribal communities often only find out that a concession has been issued on their land when gold mining activities begin. External concessionaires show up unexpectedly in tribal lands and this leads to conflict with local communities and with small-scale miners already operating in the area. This is what happened, for instance, in the village of Nieuw Koffiekamp, a maroon village located in the District of Brokopondo, where a gold mining concession that included their tribal territory was issued to a multinational in the early 1990s. This conflict has been examined by several authors,[50] who describe that, as a result of the concession, the villagers were limited in their freedom of movement and their economic activities. They were not allowed to clear land for agricultural plots without permission from the company and parts of their traditional living area were no longer accessible to them. Also, small-scale gold miners from the village were not allowed to continue their mining activities. This situation led to constant tension between the multinational, the government, and the villagers. After several attempts to solve this problem, in 2017, an agreement was finally reached between the government, the multinational, and the Nieuw Koffiekamp miners' group called *Makamboa*, which allowed *Makamboa* members to carry out gold mining in part of the multinational's gold mining concession. Although this agreement has resolved some of the problems of those small-scale gold miners who are *Makamboa* members, other gold miners from

[48] Constitution of Suriname, art 41 reads: 'Natural riches and resources are property of the nation and shall be used to promote economic, social and cultural development. The nation has the inalienable right to take complete possession of its natural resources in order to utilize them to the benefit of the economic, social and cultural development of Suriname'.

[49] ER Kambel and F MacKay, *De rechten van inheemse volken en marrons in Suriname* (Leiden, KITLV Press, 2003); see also M Heemskerk and C Duijves, 'Small-scale Gold Mining and Conflict in Suriname' in L Cremers, J Kolen and M de Theije (eds), *Small-scale Gold Mining in the Amazon. The Cases of Bolivia, Brazil, Colombia, Peru and Suriname* (Amsterdam, Cedla, 2003) 88.

[50] M Heemskerk and C Duijves (n 49) 88; de Theije et al (n 17) 141.

surrounding villages and outsiders did not benefit from this agreement and are illegally continuing their activities in the area of this gold mining concession.

While large-scale gold mining concessions can have significant consequences for tribal communities, it is the small-scale gold mining sector that has most impact on them due to the relatively high income that can be earned in the sector. For the state also, this is an important sector, which accounts for approximately 47 per cent of state income.[51] Successive governments have therefore attempted to develop new policies for the regulation of small-scale gold mining, but these efforts have largely not brought the desired results.

With the state and the tribes each claiming the right to govern gold resources in tribal habitats, there are no formal mechanisms of cooperation between state and traditional governance structures. State institutions and traditional authorities hardly inform or consult each other about concessions granted, which sometimes results in overlapping concessions. There are very few incentives for tribal communities and authorities to accept the governance claims of state authorities regarding the gold resources within their habitat. Sporadically, traditional leaders apply for formal gold mining concessions, but there is no possibility to apply for a community concession, so these applications are undertaken on personal title. Maroon leaders who apply for such concessions claim they do this to preserve maroon tribal habitat for future generations – making sure that a mining concession is granted to a community member and not to a third party. This seems to be mere rhetoric, though, as in practice it appears that they allow third parties to mine for gold under these concessions and often keep the revenue for themselves.

Occasionally, cooperation between state institutions and traditional governance actors does happen, in an informal and ad hoc way. In such instances, tribal and state governance structures work together to try and find mutually acceptable solutions for conflicts or to discuss certain issues regarding the gold mining sector. One example of such cooperation concerns mining activities in the Mama Ndyuka area. Several *kabitens* were allowing gold mining prospectors to operate in this area with strong cultural significance for the Ndyuka maroon community. The *gaanman* approached the government to assist him in stopping the gold mining activities in this most sacred area of the tribe. Governmental and Ndyuka authorities consulted and jointly decided that the gold mining activities should be stopped. While that indeed happened temporarily, today there is new gold mining activity in parts of this area.[52]

All in all, the outdated mining law, deliberately restrictive interpretation of the Mining Decree, lack of a clear gold mining policy, poor implementation and enforcement mechanisms, and the antagonistic relationship between state and traditional governance institutions, all contribute to a sector still marked by an informal and chaotic character.

[51] *Inzicht in de Overheidsfinanciën over 2021 Ontwikkelingen met Betrekking tot de Overheidsontvangsten, Overheidsuitgaven en Financiering* (Republiek Suriname Ministerie van Financiën en Planning, 2023), gov.sr/wp-content/uploads/2023/12/nota-overheidsfinancien-2021_final.pdf.

[52] A politician who is a member of the Ndyuka tribe was granted a concession in this area by the state after arguing that he had the permission of the traditional authority. Community members are not convinced that the late *gaanman* signed a document that permits mining in the Mama Ndyuka area and his successor has not yet decided how to deal with this issue. In the meantime, gold mining activities are ongoing.

VI. Different Legal Registers: Customary Law, State Law, International Law

Analysing logging and gold mining governance in tribal habitats in Suriname sheds light on the contestation of authority between tribal and state authorities over the right to govern natural resources, and where statutory law and customary law each assign authority. The two sectors tell us somewhat different stories. In the logging sector, state regulation takes the interests of tribal communities into account to a certain extent. Communities can apply for a community forest designation and state agents play a helpful role in setting up and advising on the governance of such forests. In the gold mining sector, on the other hand, the state recognises no rights of tribal communities to the gold resources within their habitat.

As a result, in the logging sector there is some positive cooperation between tribal and state governance structures. This is particularly the case in those geographical areas where liaising with state institutions can bring gain to the tribal communities through increased opportunities for commercial logging activities. Maroon communities in such areas are willing to work with state actors and accept their claim of authority to govern logging, particularly in areas where the creation of community forests could open up new business opportunities. Areas that are more remote have less to gain from cooperation with state institutions, and their distance from the administrative and commercial centre of the country at the same time gives them more leeway to continue as they used to without much governmental interference.

In contrast to the logging sector, in the gold mining sector statutory law does not offer any benefits to the tribal communities, and these communities do not regard state authorities as beneficial partners. This results in a virtual absence of consultation or cooperation between traditional and state governance authorities in the exploitation of gold. State institutions and traditional authorities each attempt to govern the sector without the involvement of the other, resulting in fully parallel and often conflicting governance actions. The maroon communities and governmental institutions largely ignore each other. Community members generally undertake their small-scale mining activities without reference to the state (or its concessionaires) and both traditional and governmental authorities grant external actors mining rights on tribal lands against certain payments. This results in a largely antagonistic relationship and a sector that is chaotic and difficult to regulate, where the rights of the surrounding community are under constant threat.

When large economic interests are at stake, possibly also entwined with political or economic interests of senior policy-makers or politicians, the relationship between the government and tribes becomes largely antagonistic in both sectors. In such circumstances, governmental authorities seem to mostly ignore the maroons and pay no attention to the already minimal protections contained in the laws. They grant concessions that cover tribal habitats without consultation with tribal communities or consideration of their interests. These communities try to resist, and they protest that natural resources on their land belong to the tribal communities, but often with limited impact on the government.

Another legal register that increasingly plays a role in disputes regarding land rights of indigenous and tribal groups is international law, and Suriname's tribal peoples have been quite successful with their protests in the Inter-American Court of

Human Rights (IACtHR). International law provides legal protection for tribal maroon groups, as became clear in the landmark *Saramaka People v Suriname* case.[53] In this case, the *Saramaka* people[54] petitioned the Inter-American Commission for Human Rights (IACHR) because their tribal lands had been invaded by multinational mining and logging companies who were granted permits by the government. The case was later transferred to the IACtHR, which in 2007 considered the people's claim to rights 'asserted as alleged tribal peoples, that is, not indigenous to the region, but that share similar characteristics with indigenous peoples'[55] and concluded that

> the members of the Saramaka people make up a tribal community whose social, cultural and economic characteristics are different from other sections of the national community, particularly because of their special relationship with their ancestral territories, and because they regulate themselves, at least partially, by their own norms, customs, and/or traditions.[56]

This decision stipulated that, henceforth, maroon groups throughout the Americas would be treated as equivalent to indigenous peoples in international law and subject to the United Nations Declaration on the Rights of Indigenous Peoples. The Court furthermore ordered the state to 'delimit, demarcate, and grant collective title over the territory of the members of the Saramaka people, in accordance with their customary laws, and through previous, effective and fully informed consultations with the Saramaka people'.[57] Activities of multinational corporations operating with licences from the state also led to tribal groups petitioning the IACHR in the *Kaliña and Lokoño* case.[58] This case was also transferred to the IACtHR, which again ruled in favour of the tribal groups, and ordered the Surinamese state to legally recognise the land rights of these communities. Despite these rulings[59] from the IACtHR and tireless efforts of several tribal groups, the Surinamese state still has not legally acknowledged tribal land rights.

VII. Discussion and Conclusion: Gold Mining, Logging, and Legal Pluralism in a Small State

States generally assert the authority to decide whether and to what extent to recognise other legal registers and governance institutions within their territory. Indigenous

[53] *Case of the Saramaka People v Suriname* (Preliminary Objections, Merits, Reparations and Costs) Inter-American Court of Human Rights Series C No 172 (28 November 2007), https://corteidh.or.cr/docs/casos/articulos/seriec_172_ing.pdf.

[54] This group began calling themselves '*Saamaka*' in official documents from mid-2010, to conform to their own pronunciation, see R Price, 'Saramaka People v Suriname: A Human Rights Victory and its Messy Aftermath' (*Cultural Survival*, 30 July 2012), www.culturalsurvival.org/news/saramaka-people-v-suriname-human-rights-victory-and-its-messy-aftermath.

[55] *Saramaka People v Suriname* (n 53) [79].

[56] ibid [84].

[57] ibid [194]. For detailed discussions of this case, see R Price, *Rainforest Warriors: Human Rights on Trial* (Philadelphia, University of Pennsylvania Press, 2010) and F MacKay, *Saramaka. De Strijd om het Bos* (Amsterdam, KIT Publishers, 2010).

[58] *Case of the Kaliña and Lokono Peoples v Suriname* (Merits, Reparations and Costs) Inter-American Court of Human Rights Series C No 309 (25 November 2015).

[59] See also *Case of Moiwana Village v Suriname* Inter-American Court of Human Rights Series C No 124 (15 June 2005), in which case the IACtHR came to a similar pronouncement on the land rights of one of Suriname's tribal peoples.

and tribal communities often have very different views and may perceive customary normative registers and traditional authority structures as more legitimate and authoritative than those of the state. Colonial histories often have explanatory power here. In Suriname, runaway maroons were able to establish themselves outside the boundaries of the Colony proper. The Peace Treaties guaranteed that these people would be left in peace, while such instruments also formed part of an isolationist colonial policy that aimed to keep the maroons, as much as possible, separated from the colonial state. While this policy was reversed in the second half of the nineteenth century, the interest of the state in the interior remained limited and was for a long time largely confined to the extraction of natural resources available in the tribal habitats. The interior's inhabitants continued to be governed by their own traditional authorities and the state held limited relevance and legitimacy for them. This factual isolationism lingers in the present, with multinationals invading tribal habitats and revenues mainly flowing to international companies and the state, giving endurance to the predatory image of the state, and communities continuing their struggle to hold on to (or regain) the authority and power to govern the natural resources in their habitats.

State size plays a paradoxical role in the relationship between the state and its governance institutions and tribal communities. The *large* geographic size of the country partly explains the decision of the government to de facto cede regulatory authority to traditional leaders in remote areas such as Tapanahony. The physical distance between the centre and the periphery complicates state regulation and gives more leeway for local self-regulation. Furthermore, the lack of infrastructure in the interior of the country significantly reduces the likelihood of viable business opportunities, which decreases interest in beneficial cooperation on both sides. But it is also the *small* size of the population, and the tax base this generates, that means that the state has limited capacity to reach remote areas such as Tapanohany, and that explains the state's dependency on the revenues generated by natural resource extraction. Combined with the historicity of the governance of Suriname's interior and the challenges of post-coloniality, geographical and cultural distance between the tribes and the government explain the enduring relevance of traditional forms of authority and the continuation of strong legal pluralism in the country.

Struggles between indigenous and maroon communities on the one hand and the national government (and multinational corporations) on the other are no longer confined to the national domain. International law and organisations increasingly play a pivotal role. While the state of Suriname still seems to be striving to complete the journey from separate groups with their own legal systems to a unitary interconnected nation with one overarching legal system (determined by the state), the world – and indigenous and tribal groups within it – has moved on, in two main ways. First, it has moved towards an increasing perception of the legal ordering of states and the world in general as inherently legally pluralistic;[60] and second, towards a growing recognition

[60] General acceptance of the concept of legal pluralism (and of seeing customary justice systems as *legal* systems and customary norms as law) among lawyers and social scientists only happened at the end of the twentieth century, when the expansion of globalisation and the proliferation of international and transnational law started to take on dimensions that clearly refuted the argument that nation-states were the only legitimate source of law-making. As a corollary, opposition to the notion of legal pluralism within national

of the rights of indigenous and tribal communities to manage and control their own territories in accordance with their customary laws and tenure systems. The limited implementation capacity of the international legal system, however, enables states to ignore, or drag their feet with the implementation of, progressive decisions of international courts. This perhaps demonstrates that the fight should be diverted to, or at least also be fought in the national legislative arena. In Latin America, struggles for land rights and autonomy of indigenous and tribal groups have been fought both publicly and behind the scenes during constitutional conferences and sessions of the legislature, resulting in numerous new provisions in the countries' constitutions and laws. Lobbying for legal recognition of the pluralist character of the state might be a logical next step in the fight for the protection of maroon (and indigenous peoples') land rights in Suriname.

legal systems and at sub-national levels also dissolved (see Ubink (n 11) 143; K Von Benda-Beckmann and B Turner, 'Legal Pluralism, Social Theory, and the State' (2018) 50(3) *Journal of Legal Pluralism and Unofficial Law* 255, 265–66).

8

Constitutional Weaving in Tonga, a Small State with Traditional Authority

A Theoretical Framework for Tonga's Constitutionalism

MELE TUPOU VAITOHI

I. Introduction

For many Pacific islands, constitutions and constitutionalism emerged as postcolonial phenomena, but not for Tonga, as it was never formally colonised.[1] Unlike the other Pacific islands, the essence of Tonga's constitutionalism is twofold. First, it embodies the political principle that the nation should be bound together by and unified under a supreme constitution, a set of established principles that should be adhered to by all persons within Tonga either expressly or impliedly. The Constitution of Tonga serves as the supreme source of political power and authority in the country. Second, the Constitution acts as a political instrument that Tonga crafted to acknowledge and incorporate external influences while safeguarding its sovereignty during the colonial period. This process intricately weaves together Tongan and European customs, resulting in a distinct constitutional framework that reflects both traditions.

In Tonga, there is only one constitutional system, and the Constitution is an important document that is like a fine Tongan mat – it is a system of Tongan tapestry of culture, kinship, and identity. Guy Powles made this helpful observation in 1987 about the history of the 1875 Constitution of Tonga: 'The remarkable *Constitution of Tonga* 1875 tied together [the] threads of Tongan and English legal cultures and initiated a process of law-making which subsequently acknowledged that Constitution as the source of its legitimacy'.[2] Powles saw the 1875 Constitution as an amalgamation of elements of

[1] However, it is important to note that while Tonga was never formally colonised, it became a British protectorate from 1900, a status it had until 1970. This formal agreement between Tonga and Britain allowed Tonga to maintain independence and control over its internal affairs, while Britain assumed responsibility for Tonga's foreign affairs.

[2] G Powles, 'The early accommodation of traditional and English law in Tonga' in P Herda, J Terrell and N Gunson (eds), *Tongan Culture and History: Papers from the 1st Tongan History Conference held in Canberra 14–17 January 1987* (Canberra, ANU Printing and Publishing Service, 1990) 145.

two social systems – Tongan and British. It is a social interaction that creates a unique system and context where formal laws are underlaid by unwritten cultural values and traditional powers that go beyond the limits of the Constitution. This relationship orders the Tongan society and polity. It is necessary when trying to understand Tonga's constitutionalism to appreciate the fact that before European colonisation arrived in Tonga, there was already a traditional system of governance and political order in Tonga. To this end, one must address how the Constitution was developed using the English and Tongan legal cultures and the impact on Tonga's constitutionalism. These require a theoretical framework that adequately captures and explains the idea of constitution and constitutionalism in Tonga across time and space.

This chapter suggests constitutional weaving as a theoretical framework capable of capturing and explaining Tonga's constitutionalism. Constitutional weaving is both a process, and the result, of interlacing two cultures with seemingly distinct legal rules, principles, and practices to form balanced and reciprocal relationships between different systems and cultures rather than a true/ false dynamic of conflict or competition. The conceptual framework of constitutional weaving is based on the notion of the relationship as key to the understanding of Tongan society and the complex web of 'networks that operate at all levels'.[3]

The objective of this chapter is to justify the necessity of developing a theoretical framework for Tonga's constitutionalism and to present constitutional weaving as a theoretical framework for Tonga's constitutional culture and order. It explores the seamless fabric of kinship, practice, and traditions. It concerns not only finding the legal recognition of that arrangement but also the fuzzy lines to this arrangement. The interaction shades into co-option which is a stance on principle that shades into mere weaving. It becomes clear that the legal recognition promotes the rule of law. And the fuzziness of these lines is not just the nature of social interaction; it is fostered by the Westminster heritage of law, even constitutional law, being 'unwritten'. That heritage is not only alive in Tonga, despite the adoption of the written Constitution in 1875, it is also the 'backdoor' for traditional authority and unwritten executive powers in Tonga.

II. The Notion of Constitutionalism

In his 1995 book *Strange Multiplicity*, the legal philosopher James Tully draws out what he takes to be the seven conventions of modern constitutionalist doctrine.[4] Tully claims that the doctrine of modern constitutionalism constitutes an orthodoxy that is adhered to in varying ways by contemporary liberals, nationalists, and communitarians, who make up a substantial part of contemporary schools of political and legal thought. He says that each of these schools of thought has slightly different yet similar versions of popular sovereignty based on modern constitutionalist doctrine.[5]

[3] M Tupou, 'The Process and outcomes of the 2010 Constitutional Reform in Tonga' (PhD Thesis, University of Otago, 2020) 72.

[4] J Tully, *Strange Multiplicity: Constitutionalism in an Age of Diversity* (Cambridge, Cambridge University Press, 1995).

[5] ibid 63.

Tully claims that it is these seven features that enabled adherents of modern constitutional theory to suppress alternative conceptions of a constitution based, for example, on historical principles relying on tradition and custom. In summary, these seven conventions are as follows:[6]

1. Adherence to the basic notion of sovereignty as a modern principle of statehood. This is the idea that each nation is recognised by other nations as being in control of its own territory.
2. The modern constitution is defined in contrast to ancient or historically earlier constitutional types which are sometimes treated as 'earlier' and belong to a lower phase of historical development. It also sets up a distinction between that which is distinctly European and that which is not. Ancient or traditional constitutions are also most often treated as implying irregularity or disorder. According to modern constitutionalism, the traditional and the customary become something pre-modern but more significantly also primitive, underdeveloped, and incompletely formed. Hence there is an imperialist element in the argument.
3. There is a contrast between the modern constitution with its features of unity, uniformity, and order, and ancient constitutions which have features of disunity, differentiation, plurality, multiplicity, localness, and perhaps disorder.
4. Then there is the recognition of custom within a general theory of progress. It appears as a lower phase of historical development and, more especially as something which is overtaken or rendered irrelevant by progress in society. We see this tension in the Pacific islands, where the power of courts and parliaments often conflicts with the traditional power of custom owners and chiefs for example.[7]
5. Modern constitutionalism becomes identified with a particular set of European values as essential features. These include ideas like of rule of law, separation of powers, representative government, equal citizenship with fundamental rights, and a distinctive public realm.
6. [A] constitutional state possesses an individual identity as a 'nation', an imaginary community to which all nationals belong and in which they enjoy equal dignity as citizens. Although the nation is interpreted differently in each society … it engenders a sense of belonging and allegiance using the nation's name, national historical narrative, and public symbols. By naming the constitutional association and giving it a historical narrative, the nation and its citizens, who take on its name when they become members, possess a corporate identity or personality.[8]

   This corporate identity of a nation and nationals in a state can be seen in Tonga and other Pacific islands. In many cases, what was once a series of very independent islands and language groups has been combined to form one sovereign nation in which all people are said to be bound together, as Tongans or ni-Vanuatu or Samoans.

[6] ibid.

[7] See, eg J Corrin, 'Resolving land disputes in Samoa' in T Levantis, M Sullivan, P O'Connor, J Munro and S Wawrzonek (eds), *Making Land Work Volume 2: Case studies on customary land and development in the Pacific* (Canberra, AusAID Pacific Land Programme, 2008).

[8] Tully (n 4) 68.

7. The final convention is that which aligns or assimilates modern constitutions and democracy. As Tully puts it, the 'modern constitution comes into being at some founding moment and stands behind – and provides the rules – for democratic politics'.[9] The modern constitution appears as a precondition rather than a part of democratic politics. It lays the ground and prescribes the domain of debate on democratic politics, at the same time excluding the classical dimensions of democratic debate.

As is evident from Powles' examination of Pacific island nation constitutions in 'Changing Pacific Island Constitutions: Methods and Philosophies', published slightly earlier than *Strange Multiplicity*, Tully's seven characteristics of modern constitutionalism resonate in the structural designs and normative foundations of post-independence constitutions across the Pacific islands region.[10] As Powles articulated, 'Pacific Island constitutions have sought to strike a balance between the sovereignty of elected representatives as legislators and the supremacy of the constitution as the expression of "higher law"'.[11] This observation reveals a conceptual tension, underscoring the need for a 'supreme law' to coexist, accommodate, and negotiate with various aspects of customs and tradition in Pacific constitutions. Notably, Tully recognised that legal pluralists challenge the assumed uniformity within modern states, as conceptualised within the prevailing discourse of modern constitutionalism.[12]

A significant issue with the concept of Tully's modern constitutionalism is that it assumes the desirability of dividing the world into nation-states, each with stable constitutions and legal systems, and of the presence of specific principles of constitutional governance in all societies. While this vision of modern constitutionalism reflects how most nations currently participate in international affairs, it distinctly represents a European perspective. This perspective is deeply rooted in the history of European colonisation during the eighteenth and nineteenth centuries. Before European colonisation, many regions had different and stable systems of governance that did not resemble the constitutionalist model, a reality particularly evident in the South Pacific.

According to Tully, modern constitutionalists continue to exclude the voices of diverse minority interests and intercultural groups from political and constitutional discourse. The principles of modern constitutional theory advocate for the universal applicability of these principles, asserting their validity regardless of individual cultures or differing ethical and moral beliefs. This approach diverts the constitutional thinker's attention away from intercultural and regional diversity on a global scale, thereby devaluing and debasing local customs as well as cultural and social diversity. This approach often undermines alternative concepts of the state that are founded on principles recognising and respecting diversity. This is consistent with the principles of modernity, which, while appearing rational, tend to marginalise customs, traditions,

[9] ibid 69.

[10] G Powles, 'Changing Pacific Island Constitutions: Methods and Philosophies' (1992) 22(3) *Victoria University of Wellington Law Review* 63.

[11] ibid 69.

[12] R Hughes, 'Legal Pluralism and the Problem of Identity' in A Jowitt and T Newton Cain, *Passage of Change: Law, Society and Governance in the Pacific* (Canberra, ANU Press, 2010) 339.

and the inherent diversity they represent, both at the domestic and global levels.[13] This discourse is shaped by the forces of modernity and the pursuit of universalism and uniformity, which, on a global scale, seem to diminish and undermine cultural and social diversity.[14]

This issue represents one of the core political challenges faced by nations in designing their own constitutions. The challenge lies in developing a constitution that enables the nation to participate effectively in the international community, build a robust economy, and establish a sound legal system, all while preserving and respecting the diverse local customs and traditions of its people.

III. The Need for a Theoretical Framework for Tonga's Constitutionalism

Before examining the concept of constitutional weaving, it is essential to understand the anatomy of Tongan culture for several reasons. First, the constitutional weaving took place in a polity with a constitutional monarchy where the king held and exercised absolute power, which impacted the process and the substance of constitutional weaving. Second, the constitutional weaving was specific to Tonga, a small state with a structured society under a kinship system, a feature that has important implications for constitutional design and the process.

The understanding of the nature and practice of constitutionalism in Tonga in its normative and empirical forms requires a theoretical framework such as constitutional weaving. Constitutional weaving offers a view on constitutionalism in Tonga that enables examination of constitutionalism from two distinct angles – first, through the lens of the state, and secondly, from the perspective of society itself.

The history of modern Tonga reveals a tapestry made by the Tongan traditional leader and king, Tupou I (1797–1893), who wove Tongan laws to escape the direct rule of colonialism. Tupou I is known as the architect and the protagonist of modern Tonga because he was determined to adapt the concepts and institutions of British-style monarchy to fit the requirements of Tonga's chiefly leadership.[15] The formalised Tongan legal system was developed during his rule in response to threats of colonisation. It was a process whereby the Tongan legal tradition was developed using the advice and experience of Christian missionaries who arrived in Tonga from Britain.[16] So, written law was initially a weaving of religion and politics, before the international socio-political landscape of this era influenced how the constitutional weaving was done in Tonga.

Tongan culture can be understood as 'the total way of life of a society', including 'the society's material possessions, technology and economy, social organisation, its regular daily and ceremonial behaviour system, value and belief system, an expressive system

[13] ibid.
[14] ibid.
[15] Tupou (n 3) 115.
[16] ibid.

including language and art, social control and thought pattern'.[17] These blueprints are embodied in the Tongan social structure, traditional political organisation, kinship, and the Tongan way of life (often referred to as '*anga faka-Tonga*', and including practices like commoners serving the chiefs, and society placing a high value on families),[18] which form the basis of social harmony and stability in Tonga. These embodiments define a person's place in the society, and also constitute the legal tradition which was formalised in a formal law regime when the 1875 Constitution was enacted.

The process of constitution-making leading to the 1875 Constitution was Tongan-led, and the outcome of this process resulted in a 'woven' formal law system where legal tradition was not regarded as 'custom' or 'customary law' operating alongside the formal law regime, but only as the law of Tonga. As a result, despite the theoretical limitations imposed by the written Constitution, the King's traditional and executive roles and powers remained nearly absolute. It is Tonga's legacy from the colonial period, illustrating how Tonga's legal tradition was woven with European ideas when Tonga's independence was threatened during this period. It was important during this time to weave laws that reflected values and principles that were acceptable to European countries. So, as noted above, Tongan leaders used European religious texts and written legal codes as the framework for the development of the Tongan legal traditions.

The historical accounts of the development of the 1875 Constitution show how the Tongan legal tradition evolved in response to the religious, social, and political change in Tonga. The 1875 Constitution reflects Tongan legal tradition, which continues to be grounded in the tenets of Tongan social structure, traditional political organisation, kinship, and the Tongan way.[19] Despite its form as a written Constitution and its similarity to other similar documents, since its inception the 1875 Constitution has been seen as the law of the land and has never been understood in Tonga as an imported Western law, or as regarding customary law as a subordinate form of law. Both were made one in the 1875 Constitution, and all political powers and laws were expected to be exercised within the limits and confines of this new constitutional framework. There is therefore often a misconception when applying a pluralist lens to Tonga: those who are not familiar with the Tongan legal system view colonialism as creating societies with plural legal systems co-existing in the same social field,[20] while others believe that customary law is not recognised in Tonga.[21] The framework of constitutional weaving has thus been developed to provide a way to understand the nature of Tongan constitutionalism.

[17] S Latukefu, 'The Definition of Authentic Oceanic Cultures with Particular Reference to Tongan Culture' (1980) 4 *Journal of Pacific Studies* 60.

[18] See Tupou (n 3) 79–83.

[19] George E Marcus calls this weaving approach a 'compromise culture', referring to the unique combination of Tongan and European customs, see: GE Marcus, 'The Ancient Regime in the Modern Kingdom of Tonga: Conflict and Change among the Nobility of a Polynesian Constitutional Monarchy' (PhD Thesis, Harvard University, 1975).

[20] S Engle Merry, 'Legal Pluralism' (1988) 22(5) *Law & Society Review* 869, 870.

[21] Tonga's Minister of Justice in 2020 submitted a Bill (Act of Constitution of Tonga (Amendment) Bill 2020) to recognise and apply customary law in Tonga. The Bill was passed in the Legislative Assembly but the King has not assented to the Bill to date.

IV. The Nature of Constitutional Weaving

I developed the concept of 'constitutional weaving' in an attempt to signify how traditional constitution-making and the elements of modern constitution-making were woven together. Constitutional weaving is both a process, and the outcome, of interlacing and synthesising distinct strands of diverse and seemingly opposing legal rules, principles, and practices, to form the fine mat of the Constitution.[22]

To appreciate the relevance of 'constitutional weaving' in understanding Tongan constitutionalism, it is essential to understand the broader notion of 'weaving'. The weaving of the mat is a powerful metaphor that stretches across Tonga (and indeed, across many parts of the Pacific). The use of the concept here draws an analogy with the way a group of Pasifika women gather and interlace distinct sets of strands at right angles to form a fine mat.

Now, when we apply the concept of 'weaving' to the Tongan context, we see that it operates within dynamic cultural settings where diverse cultural, political, or religious ideas and practices co-exist within a specific social sphere. The interaction and contact between these divergent ideas and practices triggers weaving, leading to conflict, tension, exchange, and interaction. Depending on power dynamics, such encounters can result in various outcomes, including symbiotic relationships, fusion, adaptation, assimilation, metamorphosis, or even isolation and dissolution. This interplay represents a delicate balance between acceptance and resistance, integration and accommodation, unity and diversity.

In Tongan constitutionalism, 'constitutional weaving' is particularly relevant as it encompasses the collaborative process of blending and interlacing international law, colonial laws, indigenous laws, and positivist liberal constitutional norms and practices. This process gave birth to the Constitution of Tonga in 1875 and also its reform in 2010. These constitutional developments are the products of syncretic configurations, merging international law from above with Pacific indigenous laws from below. As international law, especially Eurocentric international 'customary' law, integrated many Pacific island nations into the global society as colonial territories in the late nineteenth century, and later, in the late twentieth century, recognised them as equal sovereign entities, it facilitated their transition into European-style territorial states. This recognition granted territorial states – both colonial and postcolonial – formal internal autonomy and external protection through the doctrine of sovereignty.[23]

The experience of other Pacific islands during the colonial period was different from Tonga's experience. Though constitutional weaving is a Pacific phenomenon, within the boundaries of the other Pacific territorial states, Pacific indigenous laws underwent reconfiguration to provide the state with the necessary infrastructure and resources for its international operations. Written constitutions, operating within the context of international law from above and Pacific indigenous laws from below, primarily offer legitimacy and the institutional and normative framework for constitutionalism. Despite the diverse origins of these legal components, the Pacific state incorporates

[22] See, eg HE Young Leslie, '… Like a mat Being Woven' (2007) 3/5 *Pacific Arts* 115.
[23] Powles, 'Changing Pacific Island Constitutions' (n 10).

syncretic forms of morality, justice, and rationality, establishing and sustaining itself within its territory. As a result, the written constitutions were declared supreme legal instruments within these states, and the customary laws were officially subordinated to laws introduced by the colonial powers. Comparatively, because of colonialism, the other Pacific island states ended up with two constitutional systems, with one based on a written constitution and the other based on customary laws, hence the explanatory force of pluralism in those states.[24]

In contrast, then, as noted above, Tonga's constitutional system should be understood as a single unified constitutional system. 'Constitutional weaving' thus emerges as a potential analytical framework for understanding Tonga's constitutionalism and not the whole of the Pacific. It accounts for the complex process of blending diverse legal systems, offering insights into the historical, cultural, and political dynamics that shape the constitutional fabric of this country. By embracing 'constitutional weaving', we potentially gain a deeper appreciation of the intricate interplay of legal norms, values, and practices in the Tongan context, shedding light on how the society has navigated the challenges posed by its unique historical legacy and unique cultural landscape.

I now turn to examine the nature of Tonga's traditional concepts of governance prior to the promulgation of its Constitution in 1875, aiming to elucidate the political landscape in Tonga before contact with colonial powers. This analysis seeks to understand the underlying cultural forms that shaped the constitutional framework in Tonga, providing it with meaning and relevance.

V. Key Traditional and Cultural Concepts of Governance in Tongan Society

An understanding of kinship relationships based on the traditional and cultural concepts of governance in Tongan society is key to understanding the context for Tongan political behaviour.[25] These kinship relationships form the basis or blueprints of the social structure of Tongan society.[26]

Kinship is concerned primarily with roles, functions, and relationships.[27] The internal operations of a kinship group may demand not simply formal compliance with the rules of behaviour, but an allocation of power to those leaders who make decisions and give directions. This is an important aspect of Tonga's traditions that needs magnifying because, as shown in Tonga's history, the larger the kinship group, the greater the social distance between the leader and those who are led. Ritual and deference indicators define and perpetuate status.[28] This classification system of kinship relates to the

[24] D McKenzie, 'Challenging the Binary of Custom and Law: A consideration of legal change in the Kingdom of Tonga' (PhD Thesis, Victoria University of Wellington, 2017) 14.

[25] Tupou (n 3) 78.

[26] 'Eiki Nopele Tu'ivakano, 'Eseta Fusitu'a, 'Ana Taufe'ulungaki, Siotame Havea and Mele Lupeha'amoa 'Ilaiu, *Tonga: Fonua 'a Kāinga – Land of Kinship* (UN Development Programme, 2016) 4–8.

[27] Tupou (n 3) 81.

[28] ibid.

system of rank where an individual is entitled to a special type of respectful behaviour from those below him on the scale.

Tongan society, both pre-nineteenth century and post-nineteenth century, is structured into a hierarchy of three 'successive layers of strata of people each with their code of behaviour, rights, and duties and accepted living standards'.[29] This hierarchical structure has at its peak the royalty, followed by the chiefs and the commoners. Within each layer, rank is based on a person's linkage to the most superior kingly line, the *Tu'i Tonga*[30] (the King of Tonga). Societal arrangements are stratified and pay a lot of formal respect to the *Tu'i Tonga* and the chiefs. Consequently, this is not an egalitarian society. The *Tu'i Tonga* is to be served in all respects and he is not allowed to do any work. In that era, in political matters, the *Tu'i Tonga* was the law and he had the right to dictate to the populace on all matters.[31]

In the period immediately before contact with the West, the political organisation of Tonga operated in two spheres in which rank was the dynamic determinant of status and power. As rank was relative, the concept of chiefliness – to be like a chief – permeated society from the top to the bottom. In the first sphere, the ideology was one of kinship in which status, in terms of rank, as ascribed by kinship rules, was the paramount consideration.[32]

Kinship was a check on the exercise of chiefly power. It was the kinship or family image – projected down from the chief or *'eiki* lineage, to the kinship or *kāinga* and below – which on the arrival of Western influences constituted the single principle that bound together, respectively and independently, the Tongan groups of islands.[33]

In the second sphere, the ideology was one of authority founded on the chiefly rank. Even though the two spheres overlapped and interacted, the political organisation and government were based on the public exercise of authority.[34] For example, traditionally Tongans were polytheistic and possessed a hierarchy of gods. Tonga's polytheistic religious belief system appeared to complement the socio-political hierarchy.[35] The chiefs were believed to possess some degree of power or *mana* that was derived directly from the gods, and the higher the chiefly position, the greater the *mana*. There was also a system of taboos that surrounded the chiefs, and the higher the chief the more complex the taboo. The higher one's chiefly rank, the greater one's freedom to violate taboos without causing supernatural anger.

Additionally, the chiefs were regarded as political leaders, and they relied upon priests as their mediators with the gods. Therefore, there was a close alliance that existed between the chiefs and the religious leaders to maintain their mutual interests.

[29] EA Crane, *The Tongan Way* (Auckland, Heinemann Educational Books Ltd, 1978) 33.

[30] This was the first dynasty in Tonga and therefore the first royal title. The first *Tu'i Tonga* was considered to have a semi-divine origin; hence God's representative on earth.

[31] F Helu, 'Democracy Bug Bites Tonga' in R Crocombe et al (eds), *Culture and Democracy in the South Pacific* (Suva, Institute of Pacific Studies, University of the South Pacific, 1992) 144.

[32] IC Campbell, *Island Kingdom: Tonga Ancient and Modern*, 2nd edn (Christchurch NZ, Canterbury University Press, 2001) 68–79.

[33] Crane (n 29) 3.

[34] Helu (n 31).

[35] S Lawson, *Tradition versus Democracy in the South Pacific* (Cambridge, Cambridge University Press, 1996) 86.

The religious belief system was closely interwoven with politics, and the powers of the priests were second only to those of the chiefs.

VI. The Weaving of the Constitution of Tonga

Constitutional weaving provides a compelling analytical framework for understanding Tongan constitutionalism. It accounts for the multifaceted historical and cultural dynamics that have shaped Tonga's legal and constitutional landscape to date. Constitutional weaving, characterised by the process of blending diverse and seemingly divergent legal rules, principles, and practices into a constitutional state, provides valuable insights into the transformation of Tonga's constitutional framework from its pre-Constitution origins to the many developments that it had to undergo to the present day. Weaving is appropriate for analysing Tonga's constitutional evolution due to the intricate interplay of Tonga's values and principles, religious legacies, and international influences in the formation of its legal system. So, the weaving process will be analysed by discussing the different facets of constitutional weaving and how diverse elements and strands have been woven together to shape Tonga's constitutional landscape.

A. Traditional Governance and Cultural Norms of Kinship

The concept of constitutional weaving encompasses the complex process of amalgamating a diverse array of legal rules, principles, customs, and traditional practices into a cohesive constitutional framework. As outlined earlier in the chapter, Tongan society has long adhered to its traditional and cultural legal norms, which are deeply rooted in its cultural heritage. These norms govern various facets of life, ranging from the dynamics of family relationships to matters of land tenure and mechanisms for resolving disputes. The chiefly system, which exerts a profound influence over land laws and the broader governance structure, is of particular significance within this cultural legal framework.

King Tupou I introduced the 1875 Constitution to transform Tonga from an era of 'darkness' to an 'era of light'.[36] The new era coincided with the increasing conversions of Tongans to Christianity by missionaries, spurred by expected ideological shifts that developed with European contact, such as the desire for European material goods, new technologies, and literacy, as well as a certain disillusionment with the comparative failure of Tongan gods to enact physical protection in war and ensure against introduced diseases.[37]

The concept of kinship was woven into clause 1 of the 1875 Constitution, which set out the basic human rights that Tonga as a state was required to respect and enforce. It captured much of the Western philosophy that missionaries and other advisers had

[36] Cited in S Latukefu, *The Tongan Constitution: A Brief History to Celebrate Its Centenary* (Nuku'alofa, Tonga Traditions Committee, 1975) 41.

[37] Campbell (n 32) 68–79.

been seeking to promote in Tonga.[38] However, no means of enforcement accompanied the various 'freedoms' and 'rights'. Further, in respect of the 'equality' clause,[39] the Constitution in which the clause appeared was itself a recognition of traditional inequality.

The Constitution promised unprecedented rights to the commoners, who had been until then fully subject to the absolute rule of their chiefs. The declaration of rights proclaimed that all Tongans – both chiefs and commoners – would be equally subject to the rule of law and that everyone had the right to their property, religious practice, and freedom of speech. Further, although the duties of nobility towards the general commoners are not mentioned in the Constitution, the new patriarchal role of the nobility was outlined by Tupou I, who ordered the chiefs to 'show love to the people you have under you'.[40] Hau'ofa argues that 'little did people know then, or consciously know even today, that they were released from one form of bondage only to be subjected to another, relatively benign, form of subordination'.[41] In other words, the power structure shifted from one that was implemented through open force and severe traditional religious *tapu* or taboos, to a hegemonical form of nationalism, incorporating pride, Christian obedience, and indoctrinated gratitude to the 'benevolent' Tongan Monarch for 'liberating' the Tongan people from the old system. This idea fortified the Monarch's position, because in contrast to the liberation processes in Europe and North America a century before, 'freedom' had been gifted peacefully, rather than through a violent overhaul by the oppressed commoners.

B. Interactions with Outside Laws and Experiences and the Introduced Democratic Principles

By the nineteenth century, Tonga had developed a distinct national and cultural identity. However, the unity of the country was threatened by internal dissent. External threats in the latter half of the nineteenth century added a new dimension to the political quandary. It was against this backdrop that the need for strong national leadership emerged. So, before becoming the King of Tonga, Tupou I, with the guidance of the missionaries, had begun to use Western political institutions alongside traditional measures to change

[38] Clauses 1–32. The Hawaiian Constitution of 1852, which the Tongan drafters had before them, contained a Declaration of Rights of 21 articles (HE Chambers, *Constitutional History of Hawaii* (Baltimore MD, Johns Hopkins Press, 1896) 17). This configuration was not changed during the 2010 reform.

[39] Regarding Clause 4 of the Constitution of Tonga, its wording has evolved over time, reflecting Tonga's unique constitutional weaving. Clause 4 of the original 1875 Constitution, stated 'There shall be but one law in Tonga, for the Chiefs, and commoners, and Europeans and Tongese. No laws shall be enacted for any special class to the detriment of another class; but one law equally the same for all persons residing in this land'. This original text can be found in Appendix A of S Latukefu, *The Tongan Constitution*, (Tonga, Government Printer, 1975). The official translation (2020 Revised Edition) now reads: 'There shall be but one law in Tonga for chiefs and commoners for non-Tongans and Tongans. No laws shall be enacted for one class and not for another class but the law shall be the same for all the people of this land'. (Amended by Act 3 of 1976), https://ago.gov.to/cms/images/LEGISLATION/PRINCIPAL/1988/1988-0002/ConstitutionofTonga.pdf_3.pdf.

[40] Vava'u Law Code, as cited in Latukefu (n 36) 22.

[41] E Hau"ofa, 'Thy Kingdom Come: The Democratization for Aristocratic Tonga' (1994) 6(2) *The Contemporary Pacific* 416.

the basis of legitimacy to reinforce his position and to prevent his rivals from assuming power as he had done. In this regard, the role of Christianity and his affiliation with Wesleyan missionaries were critical.

The missionaries brought with them to Tonga the conservative views of Wesleyan Methodism, with a political philosophy that viewed the Tongan King as a spokesman of God and that people should not be allowed to take part in government.[42] In other words, the view was that rulers have full powers from God and they are accountable for their actions to God alone and not to the people. The views of these missionaries were conservative, and they did not trust democracy.[43] However, converting people to Christianity was hampered by the civil unrest in Tonga in the early nineteenth century.[44] So the missionaries supported Aleamotu'a (1781–1830)[45] and Tupou I because they saw the political system of the *Tu'i Kanokupolu* as similar to the constitutional monarchy practised in European countries.[46]

One of the influential missionaries who helped Tupou I was Shirley Baker, who arrived in Tonga from England in 1860. Baker worked for the church in Tonga, initially from 1860 until 1866, where he became an associate and adviser to the Monarch, assisting in drafting the 1862 Code[47] and drafting some municipal laws.[48] Baker then returned to Tonga in 1869 and Tupou I began to rely on him not only for political, financial, and spiritual guidance but also as a physician.[49] Baker was willing to help Tupou I to establish a structure of government to maintain Tonga's sovereignty, as well as a framework that served to stabilise the government.[50] In this regard, he helped Tupou I to draw up the 1875 Constitution and he negotiated a treaty with Germany in 1876.

Due to the strength of his Christian conviction, Tupou I continued allowing the guidance from the missionaries, and based on advice from Charles St Julian[51] and Thomas West,[52] Tupou I was convinced that the only way to preserve the independence of Tonga and gain recognition by the main powers was to establish an efficient system of government which would be acceptable to the civilised countries of the world.[53] Moreover,

[42] See WJ Warner, The Wesleyan Movement in the Industrial Revolution (London, Longmans, 1930) chapter IV.

[43] See JW Etheridge, *Life of Adam Clarke* (London, 1858) 311.

[44] Latukefu (n 36) 16.

[45] Aleamotu'a was Tupou I's uncle and he was the *Tu'i Kanokupolu* before Tupou I.

[46] See S Latukefu, 'Church and state in Tonga: the influence of the Wesleyan Methodist missionaries on the political development of Tonga, 1826–1875' (PhD Thesis, Australian National University 1967). When missionaries arrived in the 18th century, Tonga was politically divided and in political turmoil due to civil war, and the powers were in the chiefs' hands. The Wesleyan missionaries felt the efforts by Tupou I to unite the country under his rule as King resonated with their political philosophy where the King was a representative of God and not of the people.

[47] The 1862 Code was Tupou I's third written set of laws and is referred to as the 'Emancipation Edict'. It was a significant political reform in Tonga because it was the 'first time a Tongan monarch was seen to limit his own authority': Tupou (n 3) 100.

[48] E Gifford, *Tongan Society* (Honolulu, Bishop Museum, 1929) x–xii.

[49] See N Rutherford, *Shirley Baker and the King of Tonga* (Melbourne, Oxford University Press, 1971).

[50] ibid.

[51] Charles St Julian was a law reporter of the *Sydney Morning Herald*, and later the Hawaiian Consul to Sydney and the Western Pacific. As will be seen later in the chapter, Tupou I first met him in 1854 while in Sydney on a trip that was organised by the missionaries. St Julian sent a copy of the Constitution of Hawaii to one of the missionaries in Tonga in 1854 (Thomas West) to translate and present to Tupou I.

[52] Thomas West was a missionary in Tonga.

[53] Rutherford (n 49).

after he learned about the issues the Māori had with their land in New Zealand through his consultations with the Wesleyan missionaries, he ensured that it would not happen in Tonga by creating a system of land tenure that prevented alienation of land, to hold off any occupation by Europeans.[54]

C. The Political Development and the 2010 Constitution and Political Reform

In examining the process of constitution-weaving and the roles of the Monarch in this process, it is necessary to mention the significant modern-day upheaval and civil unrest that took place on 16 November 2006. The 2006 riot exposed many longstanding issues that culminated in the pressure and push by the people for a more democratic form of government in Tonga. Some view the significant 2010 reform of the Constitution as being a result of the unrest caused partly by concerns about government accountability.[55] From this perspective, the 2006 riot was a culmination of the pro-democracy movement's pressure for change. In a similar vein, it suggests that it was the riot that compelled the Monarch to introduce constitutional and political reforms.

By the early twenty-first century, several factors had paved the way for upheaval in Tonga, including emigration, education, economic stagnation, youth unemployment, media, and a Constitution that was becoming outdated.[56] The modernisation process introduced during Tupou IV's reign (1965–2006) brought changes in the political dynamic as more common people began to question the government policies and people began to demand more accountability. Educated people were well represented in the churches. They had experience from abroad about how democracy works. Stephanie Lawson has explained that it was these educated returnees to Tonga who were instrumental in the establishment of the pro-democracy movement in the 1970s.[57]

Public dissatisfaction with the status quo emerged in 2005 when members of the public service went on strikes and organised protest marches to voice their concerns over several issues (involving public service reforms and utility costs) as well as calling for political change. This public service strike prompted the commissioning of the National Committee for Political Reform by the Legislative Assembly, which was endorsed by the King in October 2005.

Tupou V (1948–2012) knew the importance of constitution-building and the need for it to be representative. Nonetheless, the first indication of changes from the Monarch took place on 10 November 2004, when the then-Prime Minister, Prince 'Ulukalala Lavaka Ata (now Tupou VI), announced that Tupou IV had agreed to changes to be made to the political system.

[54] See Latukefu (n 36).

[55] See 'Tonga: constitution and politics' (*The Commonwealth*), thecommonwealth.org/our-member-countries/tonga/consttitution-politics; G Powles, *Political and Constitutional Reform Opens the Door: The Kingdom of Tonga's Path to Democracy*, 2nd edn (Suva, University of the South Pacific Press, 2013) ss V (H, I and J).

[56] P Langa'oi, 'The Roots of Instability: Administrative and Political Reform in Tonga' (2009) 25 *Ritsumeikan Journal of Asia Pacific Studies* 21.

[57] Lawson (n 35) 100.

However, when the 2006 riot occurred, the late Tupou V (then newly crowned) revealed that he wanted to form a new relationship with the people,[58] and the riot vindicated' his 'belief in the systems approach to change – which compartmentalised each stage of the revolution, putting each under the charge of different groups in the society and government'.[59] The late Tupou V, as the main architect of the reform in 2010, focused the reform work on changing the functions and powers mainly of the Monarch and the Executive branch of Government.

D. The Outcome – The Woven Mat of the Constitution of Tonga

The original Constitution of Tonga 1875 is a document with 132 clauses and is divided into three parts. Part I provides for the declaration of rights; Part II provides the form of government; and Part III regulates the land. Tupou I was strategic in his approach, so each part of the Constitution represents elements that were important for Tupou I to entrench his power in Tonga and to maintain Tonga's political independence, as expressed in the popular Tongan phrase '*Kei Tonga pe 'a Tonga*' or 'Tonga is still Tonga'.[60]

By the early twenty-first century, the style of government adopted in the nineteenth century was no longer suited to the needs and aspirations of the people of Tonga. As a result, major constitutional and political reform took place in 2010, and the introduced democratic principles of responsible government, inclusive participation, free and fair elections, and use of institutional checks on the executive have been further woven into Tonga's constitutional landscape.

The constitutional weaving has produced a multifaceted tapestry of outcomes revealing symbiotic relationships between Tongan norms and international laws and experiences as thoughtfully reflected in the Constitution of Tonga both in 1875 and 2010. This constitutional framework demonstrates a harmonious co-existence of traditional customs and democratic principles, embodying the intricate balance achieved through constitutional weaving.

Illustrating this balance, the Constitution of Tonga recognises the pivotal role of the King, an institution shaped by British and Westminster systems. It demonstrates the intricate interweaving of Tongan customs and democratic principles. This tapestry reflects the ongoing evolution of Tonga's legal landscape, embodying the delicate balance struck between diverse legal traditions and cultural heritage.

The outcome of the constitutional weaving is the Constitution of Tonga, which entrenches the foundation of the Tongan structured society with a uniting sense of morality, justice, and rationality. The framework of constitutional weaving brings together Western principles, customary values, and traditional authorities as pillars of Tonga as a sovereign state.

58 Tupou (n 3).

59 B Hill, 'Interview of Tupou V' (*Australian Broadcasting Commission*, 22 November 2010), www.abc.net.au/news/2010-11-22/king-tupou-v-speaks-to-radio-australia/2346566.

60 Cited in Tupou (n 3) 108.

VII. Conclusion

In conclusion, in Tonga, most constitutional issues stem from not understanding the Constitution and its application, rather than from a contest between custom versus rights or freedoms. Tonga's constitutionalism serves as an illustration of the dynamic nature of constitutional weaving. It showcases how diverse legal rules, principles, and practices have been harmonised, adapted, and interlaced to shape a constitutional framework uniquely woven into Tonga's historical legacies and cultural landscapes. Tonga's woven mat continues to evolve, and this underscores the enduring relevance of constitutional weaving, offering profound insights into the intricate interplay of legal norms, values, and practices in the Pacific region.

The practical impact of constitutional weaving on the constitutional behaviour of state actors can be a source of contentment when interpreting and enforcing constitutional standards. For instance, in February 2024, a Memorandum from the Tongan Lord Privy Seal[61] was addressed to Tonga's Chief Secretary and Secretary to Cabinet advising of the King's decision to 'withdraw His confidence and consent to the appointment of the Hon. [Prime Minister] Hu'akavameiliku [as Minister for Armed Forces] … and Fekita 'Utoikamanu [as Foreign Affairs Minister and Tourism Minister]' 'with the advice from his Privy Council'.[62] No reasons were given for the King's decision and the Memorandum was considered by some people as unconstitutional,[63] as the Constitution is silent on this issue; this issue was even referred to as 'uncharted waters' where if the Prime Minister opposes the King's decision, the King by Constitution can dissolve parliament and new elections can be called.[64] However, by cultural protocol of apology, the Prime Minister and some of the Cabinet Ministers went and met the King on 6 March 2024 as the first step to resolve their differences.[65] Since this meeting, the Prime Minister has resigned from his defence portfolio and 'Utoikamanu has resigned from her foreign affairs portfolio. What can be seen from this recent event is how rational-legal authority has incorporated elements of the customary and traditional conceptions of power, and in so doing, has changed the nature and configuration of Western understanding of power and authority. The customary and traditional conceptions of power go beyond the simple constitutional recognitions and include their manifestations.

It is important to recognise that in Tonga there are two distinct legal systems, and they cannot simply be combined for one system to swallow up another. Weaving the two and keeping them distinct but pushing them in the same direction is important.

[61] PC 17/2024 (2 February 2024).

[62] ibid.

[63] Government of Tonga media release on 6 February 2024, stating that the decision of the King in Council was contrary to clause 51(3)(a) of the Constitution, which specifies that a minister shall retain his or her position as minister until his or her appointment is revoked by the King on the recommendation of the Prime Minister.

[64] L Senituli, 'Uncharted waters: the standoff between Tonga's King and government' (*Devpolicy Blog*, 13 February 2024), devpolicy.org/uncharted-waters-the-standoff-between-tongas-king-and-government-20240213/.

[65] 'Tongan King and Prime Minister take steps to resolve differences' (*Radio New Zealand*, 12 March 2024), www.rnz.co.nz/international/pacific-news/511415/tongan-kingand-prime-minister-take-steps-to-resolve-differences.

For a considerable time, the state and customary systems in Tonga were not regarded as separate normative orders, as legal theories such as pluralism presuppose. For instance, this arrangement conceals a profound impasse that legal pluralism, within its accounts of constitutionalism, struggles to elucidate in a non-Western setting. The reliance of the theoretical framework on disparate epistemological, historical, and legal accounts complicates the understanding of the concept and practice of constitutionalism in both its normative and empirical forms. This impasse usually restricts the range of theoretically coherent and practically viable constitutional solutions for addressing governance challenges in many Pacific island countries. Against this backdrop, we should consider what constitutes the normative framework, or constitutionalism, in Pacific island countries like Tonga. Such an approach will consider expression in both formal and informal ways shaped by diverse narratives stemming from various sources such as customs, religions, and foreign and international agreements. These narratives will be interpreted, woven, and given meaning by different communities in distinct ways. As seen in the case of Tonga, decisions involve intricate amalgamations of these narratives, none of which originate from entirely self-contained and pure legal systems. This unique context, influenced by Tongan indigeneity, the spread of Christianity, and Western democratic principles, alongside their accompanying historical, epistemological, methodological, and ideological aspects, results in plural and sometimes conflicting interpretations of the Constitution and constitutionalism in Tonga.

9

The Authoritarian Swazi King, Custom and the Constitution of Eswatini

SINETHEMBA MEMELA

I. Introduction

The Kingdom of Eswatini is a small, landlocked country in Southern Africa, surrounded by South Africa and Mozambique. It has a population of 1,093,238, with women accounting for 562,127 of the total population.[1] Approximately 43 per cent of the population is under the age of 15, and only 3 per cent is over the age of 65. The life expectancy at birth improved from 58.3 in 2019 to 62.9 in 2021, and the government attributes this to an increase in the number of people benefiting from its social grant for the elderly.[2] The racial and ethnic makeup of the country is homogenous, with 84 per cent of the population being ethnically Swazi. The official languages are SiSwati and English, and Christianity is the main religion. Approximately 77 per cent of Eswatini's population is estimated to reside in rural areas, while only 23 per cent lives in urban areas.[3] Eswatini is not only a small state but also a state that endures challenging socio-economic conditions. An estimated 59 per cent of the Swazi population lives in poverty and 29 per cent lives in extreme poverty.[4] A large proportion of Eswatini's population faces food insecurity.[5] The levels of unemployment in Eswatini are unsustainably high.[6] The challenge of poverty is compounded by a high HIV/ AIDS rate, with 27 per cent of

[1] Kingdom of Eswatini Central Statistical Office 'The 2017 Population and Housing Census Volume 3' (2019) 2, gov.sz/images/FinanceDocuments/Volume-3.pdf.

[2] Kingdom of Eswatini Ministry of Economic Planning and Development, 'Second Voluntary Nationl Review Report' (July 2022), https://eswatini.un.org/sites/default/files/2023-02/Eswatini%20VNR%20Main%20Report%2008072022%20Final%20and%20submitted%20to%20UNDESA.pdf.

[3] ibid.

[4] ibid and 'Poverty and Equity Brief Africa Eastern and Southern: Eswatini October 2020' (*World Bank*, 2020), databankfiles.worldbank.org/public/ddpext_download/poverty/987B9C90-CB9F-4D93-AE8C-750588BF00QA/SM2020/Global_POVEQ_SWZ.pdf. The poverty rate is based on the national poverty line which was set at SZL975.3 per adult per month in 2017.

[5] ibid.

[6] ibid.

adults in the country having contracted the virus, the highest percentage in the world.[7] These socio-economic conditions are particularly acute for women, as Swazi women are disproportionately affected by poverty and unemployment and generally have poorer health outcomes.[8] It is a small, rural and traditional country governed by a monarch.

In 2005, Eswatini adopted a new Constitution with a preamble that states that

> it is necessary to blend the good institutions of traditional law and custom with those of an open and democratic society so as to promote transparency and the social, economic, and cultural development of our Nation.

This preambular statement details the country's commitment to legal pluralism and a blended society that uses both traditional governance and Western democratic and economic mechanisms. Section 2(1) of the Swazi Constitution further provides for the supremacy of the Constitution and states that any law inconsistent with the Constitution is void to the extent of that inconsistency. This section may appear to create constitutional supremacy; however, it will be illustrated that in matters concerning the King, the Constitution appears to be on the back foot. As will be explored in this chapter, tension arises from the co-existence of these norms as Swazi law, and custom has been interpreted in ways which prohibit dissent and effectively make the actions of the King beyond question. Liberal democratic norms demand transparency, accountability and the rule of law – all of which have been rejected by the King, his Cabinet and the courts of Eswatini.

King Mswati III, the *iNgwenyama* and sovereign of Eswatini, on his 50th Birthday, through Legal Notice No 80 of 2018, unilaterally declared that the Kingdom of Swaziland would have its name changed to the Kingdom of Eswatini, effective immediately. The King's decision to unilaterally change the name of the country through Legal Notice No 80 was challenged before the High Court by a prominent human rights activist and lawyer, Thulani Maseko, who was later assassinated in 2023,[9] and an NGO operating in Eswatini called the Institute of Democracy and Leadership. Maseko argued that the King acted unconstitutionally as the decision to change the name of the country should have been made through a participatory legislative process because 'the name change has constitutional implications'; Swaziland is the name used in various provisions of the Swazi Constitution, and therefore changing the country's name amounted to a constitutional amendment.[10] The High Court never heard the matter; therefore, it is possible

[7] World Health Organization, 'Prevalence of HIV among adults aged 15–49 (%)' (July 2024), https://www.who.int/data/gho/data/indicators/indicator-details/GHO/prevalence-of-hiv-among-adults-aged-15-to-49-(-). ABM Kharsany and QA Karim, 'HIV Infection and AIDS in Sub-Saharan Africa: Current Status, Challenges and Opportunities' (2016) 10 *Open AIDS Journal* 34.

[8] 'At a glance: HIV in Eswatini' (*Be in the Know*, 7 May 2024) www.beintheknow.org/understanding-hiv-epidemic/data/glance-hiv-eswatini.

[9] Maseko was shot in his home. It remains unknown who killed him or for what purpose. However, *Human Rights Watch* notes that hours before Maseko was killed King Mswati had issued an address warning 'those calling for democratic reforms that mercenaries would deal with them'. See 'Eswatini: Activist, Rights Lawyer Brutally Killed' (*Human Rights Watch*, 25 January 2023), www.hrw.org/news/2023/01/25/eswatini-activist-rights-lawyer-brutally-killed.

[10] See N Mabuza, 'Swaziland's name change challenged in court' *amaBhungane* (28 August 2018), www.amabhungane.org/swazilands-name-change-challenged-in-court/ and S Nkosi, 'King Mswati III faces court challenge over Swaziland name change' *City Press* (9 July 2018), www.news24.com/citypress/news/king-mswati-iii-faces-court-challenge-over-swaziland-name-change-20180709.

that the Registrar did not admit it onto the Court Roll, in compliance with the Chief Justice's Practice Directive not to admit legal proceedings against the King.[11] It may be difficult to imagine a context where an individual, even a Head of State, can unilaterally change the name of the country they lead without consultation or ratification, but Eswatini has become the exception.

This chapter proceeds as follows: section II provides a brief explanation of Eswatini's constitutional history. Section III then proceeds to assess the constitutional drafting process undertaken to adopt the 2005 Constitution and its political governance and fundamental rights provisions. This section also discusses the country's political party ban, the recent pro-democracy protests and reasons for their limited success. Section IV discusses the relationship between the monarchy and the judiciary and its implications for judicial independence. Section V explores custom governing the monarchy, a human rights challenge to executive action, and the extent to which South African constitutional culture has had an impact on Swazi constitutionalism. The conclusion (section VI) explores some of the reasons for the monarchy's resilience in Eswatini and the impact that the size of the country has had on the continuation of the monarchy.

II. A Brief Constitutional History of Eswatini

Eswatini dates back to the Stone Age. It was first inhabited by the Khoi and San people, then later by Bantu people who, under Kings Sobhuza I and Mswati II during the late eighteenth to mid-nineteenth century, expanded and consolidated the territory into what is now modern Eswatini.[12] During King Mswati II's reign the Swazi, seeking protection from Zulu raiders, began an exploitative system of land concessions with the British and Dutch which culminated in Eswatini becoming a British High Commission Territory.[13] Following the death of Mswati II, Queen Regent Gwamile Labotsibeni held the throne for King Sobhuza II, who was a minor, and her role was to administer native affairs, exercise jurisdiction on matters concerning 'native law and custom' between 'natives' and oversee the different chiefdoms, though the Colonial Office had the final say on all decisions by 'traditional authorities'.[14] The parameters of her powers and functions also applied to King Sobhuza upon his attainment of majority status. When the Union of South Africa was formed in 1910, unifying the four self-governing colonies

[11] Chief Justice of Eswatini, High Court of Swaziland Practice Directive No 4/2011 (16 June 2011). This Practice Directive is addressed to all judicial officers and their supporting staff, the Law Society of Swaziland and all legal practitioners. Paragraph 1.2 states:

'(1) Summonses or applications for civil claims against His Majesty the King and iNgwenyama, either directly or indirectly, shall not be accepted in the High Court or any other Court in the country.

(2) The Registrar of the High Court and/or all those entrusted with receipt of court processes in this country are hereby directed to refuse to accept any summons or application specified in 2(1) above'. Paragraph 1.1 of the Practice Directive cites section 11 of the Constitution: '11. The King and iNgwenyama shall be immune from – (a) suit or legal process in any cause in respect of all things done or omitted to be done by him'.

[12] DH Gillis *The Kingdom of Swaziland: Studies in Political History* (Westport CT, Greenwood Press, 1999) 19–29.

[13] H Kuper, *Southern Africa Part 1: The Swazi* (Abingdon, Routledge, 1952) 5–7.

[14] Gillis (n 12) 131–39.

(Cape, Natal, Transvaal, and Orange River) in Southern Africa, Eswatini did not join the Union. This is because it was not a self-governing territory, it was not directly involved in the Anglo-Boer Wars, and the Swazi did not wish to join the Union.[15]

Eswatini was among the last British colonies in Africa to be granted independence. In the early 1960s, the United Kingdom (UK) initiated constitutional talks in the lead-up to the country's first democratic elections. As negotiations concerning the abolition of colonialism and British control took place, progressive and educated Swazi people began forming political parties in anticipation of elections. They called for the implementation of a Westminster-style constitutional framework coupled with ideologies based on Kwame Nkrumah's African nationalism.[16] Their main concern was the abolition of the monarchy and the entrenchment of constitutional democracy.

Upon the conclusion of constitutional negotiations and the attainment of independence from the UK, a Constitution that was reminiscent of other independence Constitutions imposed by the UK on former colonies was imposed on Eswatini in 1963. Under this constitutional framework, the primary function of the monarchy would be the administration of culture and tradition. King Sobhuza II responded by creating his own political party, the Imbokodvo National Movement, to contest the 1964 election, though he maintained that political parties were 'unSwazi'.[17] The King's political party won the election by 85 per cent. The newly elected legislature, which comprised members of Imbokodvo and white Swazis who were elected through a separate process, began the process of drafting a new Constitution in 1965. A Constitutional Review Committee, led entirely by members of the legislature, adopted a new Constitution in 1967, which affirmed the King as the Head of State. The adoption of a new Constitution was followed by elections in April 1967, which were again won by the King's Imbokodvo National Movement. In 1972, another election was held and an opposition party, the Ngwane National Liberatory Congress, won three out of 24 parliamentary seats.[18] This prompted a swift response by the King, resulting in him repealing the 1967 Constitution, assuming all the powers of the government, dissolving Parliament, and banning all political parties. He provided the following reasons as his justification:

(a) the Constitution has indeed failed to provide the machinery for good government and for the maintenance of peace and order;

[15] A Keppel-Jones, 'South Africa and the High Commission Territories' (1951) 6 *International Journal* 85, 86–88. The South Africa Act, 1909 (9 Edw VII, c 9), in s 151, provided that: 'The King, with the advice of the Privy Council, may, on addresses from the Houses of Parliament of the Union, transfer to the Union the government of any territories, other than the territories administered by the British South Africa Company, belonging to or under the protection of His Majesty, and inhabited wholly or in part by natives, and upon such transfer the Governor-General in Council may undertake the government of such territory upon the terms and conditions embodied in the Schedule to this Act'.

However, the transfer of these territories (Eswatini, Lesotho and Botswana) never took place. It is reported that the Union of South Africa made numerous attempts to annex Eswatini. These attempts began in 1910 and continued until Eswatini gained independence from the British. See PH Bischoff, 'Why Swaziland is Different: an Explanation of the Kingdom's Political Position in Southern Africa' (1988) 26 *Journal of Modern African Studies* 457, 459.

[16] HP Dlamini, *A Constitutional History of the Kingdom of Eswatini (Swaziland), 1960–1982* (Cham, Palgrave Macmillan, 2019) 75–76. Ideas concerning rebuilding Swaziland as a state based on African nationalist ideals such as political freedom, land reform and African unity were promoted by Western-educated Swazis.

[17] ibid 112.

[18] ibid 309.

(b) the Constitution is indeed the cause of growing unrest, insecurity, dissatisfaction with the state of affairs in our country and an impediment to free and progressive development in all spheres of life;

(c) the Constitution has permitted the importation into our country of highly undesirable political practices alien to, and incompatible with the way of life in our society, designed to disrupt and destroy our own peaceful and constructive and essentially democratic methods of political activity; increasingly, this element engenders hostility, bitterness and unrest in our peaceful society.[19]

The King then issued the following decree

> I hereby reaffirm that in terms of Swazi law and custom, the King holds the supreme power in the Kingdom of Swaziland and as such all executive, legislative and judicial powers vest in the King who may from time to time by decree delegate certain powers and functions as he may deem fit.[20]

The primary argument advanced by the King was that practices such as political rivalry and electioneering did not conform with Swazi tradition and culture and would, therefore, be the importation of an alien culture and its imposition on the Swazi people. However, it has been opined that the purpose of the King's proclamation was to 'transform Swaziland into an absolute monarchy with the King wielding absolute powers'.[21] The King's consolidation of political power seemed out of touch with the contemporary events taking place in the continent at the time that resulted in several Southern African countries becoming constitutional democracies. Academics wondered what place Swaziland would take on the world stage and whether returning to absolute monarchism would effectively alienate the country.[22]

III. The Introduction of the 2005 Constitution

In 2005, Eswatini adopted a new Constitution following a Constitutional Review Process that began in 1996. The preamble of the Constitution states that the 2005 Constitution was enacted following 'various *vusela* consultations, economic and constitutional commissions, political experiments and *Sibaya* meeting … established and undertaken … in search of a sustainable home-grown political order'.[23] A Constitutional Review Commission (CRC), appointed by King Mswati III and chaired by Prince Mangaliso Dlamini, the King's brother, drafted the Constitution. Maseko and Abdulraufargued that the Constitution was not democratically adopted because members of the CRC

[19] 'Proclamation by his Majesty King Sobhuza II' (12 April 1973), recitals 2(a), (b) and (c). https://www.icj.org/wp-content/uploads/2014/06/sz1973proclamation.pdf.

[20] ibid.

[21] CM Fombad, 'The Swaziland Constitution of 2005: Can absolutism be reconciled with modern constitutionalism?' (2007) 23 *South African Journal on Human Rights* 93, 95.

[22] Dlamini (n 16).

[23] *Vusela* is defined in s 261(1) of the Constitution as 'a consultative process whereby a person or group of persons or community is visited and addressed with a view to soliciting opinion or consensus on some public matter' and *Sibaya* is defined under the same section as 'the nation meeting as the Swazi National Council at the Ndlovukazi's [mother of the King's] official residence for the purpose of deliberating or deciding on important national matters'.

were appointed by the King in their individual capacities.[24] The Decree which established the CRC prohibited submissions by organised groups, therefore preventing meaningful and effective participation, and further provided that persons who 'insult, disparage or belittle' members of the CRC may be subjected to a fine or imprisonment for a period not exceeding five years, or both.[25] Individuals were permitted to make submissions to the CRC but the submissions were essentially made in secret, as no one other than members of the CRC were permitted to hear those submissions.[26]

Additionally, of the 30 members of the CRC appointed by the King, four resigned, four died and two disappeared, leaving the Commission with a substantial reduction in capacity as they were never replaced.[27] It is reported that 'internal debates and bad blood within the commission' were the reasons for the resignations of respected academics and legal professionals.[28] Another important member of the CRC, Mario Masuku, who was the president of the opposition party Peoples United Democratic Movement – which was described by the CRC as 'one of the political organizations operating illegally in the country' – also resigned.[29]

The conditions created by the CRC are not in conformity with accepted constitutional drafting practices where popular participation, especially through organisational formations, is encouraged in order to promote constitutional legitimacy.[30] Group-based participation in constitution-making would no doubt create better outcomes as individual citizens are not well versed in constitutional language and therefore do not have the skills necessary to articulate the kind of Constitution they want for their country. Additionally, acts as benign as questioning the competence, commitment or political allegiances of a member of the CRC may have had the impact of leading to a fine or imprisonment, so those who were critical of the constitution-making process could not have been able to participate freely. A legal challenge seeking to strike down the 2005 Constitution on the basis of a lack of transparency and a failure to engage a wide range of stakeholders, including members of civil society, was presented before the Swazi Supreme Court, but ultimately failed.[31] The extent of public participation in the constitutional drafting process was abysmally low and under these conditions, it becomes difficult to classify Eswatini's Constitution as democratically drafted. The Constitution was tabled in Parliament, debated and ultimately signed by the King.

Chapter I of the Constitution establishes Eswatini as a 'unitary, sovereign and democratic Kingdom'. It further provides that the Constitution 'is the supreme law of

[24] TR Maseko and L Abdulrauf, 'Constitutional Implementation: The Swaziland Experience' in CM Fombad, *The implementation of modern African Constitutions: Challenges and prospects* (Pretoria, Pretoria University Law Press, 2016) 58.

[25] ibid 58, quoting s 3(1) of Decree No 2 of 1996.

[26] ibid 59.

[27] Section 2(2) of the Constitutional Review Commission Decree No 2 of 1996, read with Constitutional Review Commission, *The Final Report of the Constitutional Review Commission* (2001), www.web.archive.org/web/20110728012957/http://www.ecs.co.sz/crc/crc_report.htm.

[28] JB Mzizi, 'The Dominance of the Swazi Monarchy and the Moral Dynamics of Democratisation of the Swazi State' (2004) 3 *Journal of African Elections* 94, 105.

[29] Constitutional Review Commission (n 27).

[30] See eg W Wahiu, 'A Practical Guide to Constitution Building: An Introduction' in M Böckenförde, N Hedling and W Wahiu (eds), *A Practical Guide to Constitution Building* (Stockholm, International Institute for Democracy and Electoral Assistance, 2011).

[31] *Sithole N.O. and Others v The Prime Minister and Others* (35 of 2007) [2008] SZSC 22 (23 May 2008).

Swaziland' and that any law inconsistent with it is void. Chapter II outlines the powers of the King, which are derived from both the Constitution and Swazi law and custom, and the King is said to be a 'symbol of unity and the eternity of the Swazi nation'. Section 4(4) provides that

> The King and *iNgwenyama* has such rights, prerogatives and obligations as are conferred on him by this Constitution or any other law, including Swazi law and custom, and shall exercise those rights, prerogatives and obligations in terms and in the spirit of this Constitution.

Section 2(2) states, 'The King and *iNgwenyama* and all the citizens of Swaziland have the right and duty at all times to uphold and defend this Constitution'. However, the Constitution does not explicitly state that the King is *subject* to the Constitution. This chapter also provides for the various royal titles and councils that assist the King in fulfilling his duties. Chapter III of the Swazi Constitution concerns the 'protection and promotion of fundamental rights and freedoms'. The Constitution is elaborate and comprehensive in its rights provisions and their limitations. Section 14(1) provides that

> The fundamental human rights and freedoms of the individual enshrined in this Chapter are hereby declared and guaranteed, namely –
>
> (a) respect for life, liberty, right to fair hearing, equality before the law and equal protection of the law;
> (b) freedom of conscience, of expression and of peaceful assembly and association and of movement;
> (c) protection of the privacy of the home and other property rights of the individual;
> (d) protection from deprivation of property without compensation;
> (e) protection from inhuman or degrading treatment, slavery and forced labour, arbitrary search and entry; and
> (f) respect for rights of the family, women, children, workers and persons with disabilities.

Subsection 2 of section 14 states that the rights guaranteed under Chapter III apply vertically and therefore must be respected and upheld by the organs of state and are justiciable and may also apply horizontally in respect of natural and legal persons 'where applicable'. Subsection 3 further states that entitlement to the rights contained is 'subject to respect for the rights and freedoms of others and for the public interest'. The Swazi Constitution does not include socio-economic rights, but has 'directive principles of state policy and duties of the citizen' in Chapter V which are 'not enforceable in any court or tribunal'.[32] In earlier sections, the Constitution provides that 'subject to available resources, the Government shall provide facilities and opportunities to enhance the welfare of the needy and elderly',[33] and has the same provision in the section on the rights and freedom of women, 'to enable them to realise their full potential and advancement'.[34]

[32] The Constitution of the Kingdom of Swaziland (2005), s 56(3). Included in the directive principles of state policy are free compulsory basic education, basic health care services (s 60(8)), welfare and maintenance for the aged (s 60(5)) and a commitment to issue land concessions (s 59(6)).

[33] ibid s 27(6).

[34] ibid s 28(2).

Chapter VI begins by stating that 'the executive authority … vests in the King as Head of State'[35] and outlines the parameters of the King's executive authority. A detailed discussion of the King's executive power and his use and misuse of his powers is beyond the scope of this chapter. Chapter VII under its first section states that

> The system of government for Swaziland is a democratic, participatory, *tinkhundla*-based system which emphasises devolution of state power from central government to *tinkhundla* areas and individual merit as a basis for election or appointment to public office.[36]

Section 87(5) of the Constitution provides that 'there shall be no canvassing for votes as persons are nominated (that is, invited to serve) based on their being known to the community'. This effectively makes King Sobhuza II's 1973 ban on political parties, electoral campaigning or any of the activities commonly associated with a political democracy a constitutional prohibition. The candidates who are invited to serve as *Tinkhundla* representatives are invited to serve by the King and then voted for by the people residing in their *Inkhundla*.[37] Lawyers for Human Rights, an NGO based in Eswatini, approached the African Commission on Human and Peoples' Rights (African Commission)[38] with an allegation that the political party ban was a violation of the African Charter on Human and Peoples' Rights (African Charter), to which Eswatini is party.[39] The African Commission found (at paragraph 63) that

> In the present communication, the King's Proclamation clearly outlaws the formation of political parties or any similar structure. Political parties are one means through which citizens can participate in governance either directly or through elected representatives of their choice. By prohibiting the formation of political parties, the King's Proclamation seriously undermined the ability of the Swaziland people to participate in the government of their country and thus violated Article 13 of the Charter.

Eswatini was then issued with recommendations that it bring the laws used to prohibit political parties into line with the African Charter and engage members of civil society and other stakeholders in drafting a new Constitution. Eswatini has not implemented these recommendations.

AfroBarometer conducted a survey in 2023 in Eswatini, which was available in both English and SiSwati, concerning a number of issues affecting Eswatini, including the political landscape. In both rural and urban areas, at least 60 per cent of the respondents

[35] ibid s 64(1).

[36] ibid s 79.

[37] Eswatini is divided into various *Tinkhundla* (constituencies). Section 80(3) of the Constitution defines *Tinkhundla* as 'units or areas inspired by a policy of decentralised state power, [which] are the engines of development and the central pillars underpinning the political organisation and economic infrastructure of the country through which social services to the different parts of the Swazi community are facilitated and facilitated'. *Tinkhundla* is the plural of *Inkhundla*.

[38] The African Commission on Human and Peoples' Rights is established under art 30 of the African Charter on Human and Peoples' Rights (adopted 27 June 1981, entered into force 21 October 1986) (1982) 21 ILM 58 (African Charter) to promote and promote human and peoples' rights in Africa. The mandate of the African Commission is outlined in art 45 of the African Charter as being 'to hear legal challenges concerning human rights, to conduct research on human rights and cooperate with other bodies to protect and promote human rights'. Eswatini became a signatory to the African Charter in September 1968 and is thus subject to its jurisdiction.

[39] *Lawyers for Human Rights v Swaziland* (Merits) African Commission on Human and Peoples' Rights, Communication No 251/2002 (2005).

surveyed disapproved of the ban on political parties.[40] The survey found very low levels of 'satisfaction with democracy', with only an estimated 11 per cent of the population reporting as being satisfied with how democracy works in the country.[41] This study illustrates that the perception of the Swazi people about the political landscape has not changed since the protests for democracy that took place in 2021.

The 2021 protests followed the death in June that year of a student, Thabani Nkomonye, at the hands of the police. The protests engulfed Eswatini, with the protestors calling for meaningful democratic change, the legalisation of political parties, and respect for human rights. In the same month, the Prime Minister issued a decree banning all protests and submission of in-person petitions to their local *Tinkhundlas*.[42] Members of Parliament were arrested under the Suppression of Terrorism Act for expressing support for the protests.[43] Police and security forces responded with force, and dozens of people were killed.[44] Roadblocks were set up throughout the country in order to restrict the movement of citizens, tear-gas was indiscriminately thrown at peaceful protesters, and an overnight curfew was imposed.[45] The Eswatini Commission on Human Rights and Public Administration, which is a constitutional body established by section 163 of the Constitution, also reported that a large number of people were subjected to lengthy and arbitrary arrests following the protests.[46] The King's response to protests was a message that dissent is not permitted in his kingdom and that the monarchy will remain no matter the consequences.

IV. Judicial Independence under the Monarchy

Section 62(1) of the 2005 Constitution guarantees the independence of judges and places a duty on all government and other institutions 'to respect and observe the independence of the judiciary'. The independence of the judiciary is guaranteed in section 141, where both the King and Parliament are expressly forbidden from interfering with judges in the exercise of their powers and functions.

The relationship between the Swazi monarchy and the judiciary has historically been challenging to manage. Before adopting the 2005 Constitution, the Swazi government had verbally expressed its disapproval of the judiciary and explicitly refused to abide

[40] Afrobarometer, 'Afrobarometer Round 9 Survey in Eswatini, 2023' (QA Strategic Information, November 2023) 25.

[41] ibid 28.

[42] V Laterza and C Golomski, 'Customary nationalism in crisis: protest, identity and politics in eSwatini' (2023) 41 *Journal of Contemporary African Studies* 119–40.

[43] 'Eswatini the System is Broken' (*Amnesty International*, 16 November 2021), www.amnesty.org/en/latest/campaigns/2021/11/eswatini-the-system-is-broken/.

[44] Eswatini Commission on Human Rights and Public Administration found that at least 46 people died during the June 2021 protests. See Eswatini Commission on Human Rights and Public Administration, 'Preliminary Assessment Report on Civil Unrest in the Kingdom of Eswatini June 2021' (2021) p 4 and 'Eswatini: No Justice for June Protester Killings' (*Human Rights Watch*, 2 November 2021), www.hrw.org/news/2021/11/02/eswatini-no-justice-june-protester-killings.

[45] Staff and agencies in Manzini, 'Armed forces open fire in crackdown on anti-monarchy protests in Eswatini' *The Guardian* (29 June 2021), www.theguardian.com/world/2021/jun/29/soldiers-deployed-eswatini-crackdown-protests.

[46] ibid.

by court decisions, prompting the resignation of six senior judges in the country.[47] The mass resignation of the judges was a strong message to the monarchy that respect for the judiciary is an essential component of any government. However, the judiciary continues to be subjected to the monarchy's incursion into its functions, as will be further detailed below.

Chapter VIII of the Constitution provides for the appointment and removal of Superior Court Justices. Section 153(1) provides that superior court judges (Supreme Court and High Court), including the Chief Justice, are appointed by the King on the advice of the Judicial Service Commission (JSC). The JSC is composed of the Chief Justice, two senior legal practitioners appointed by the King, the chairman of the Civil Service Commission (who is appointed to that position by the King), and two other persons appointed by the King.[48] Most of the members who make up the JSC are chosen by the King: four of the six members are selected solely by the King, and there are no specifications at all on the qualifications of two of the four JSC members the King may choose. This broad discretionary power of the King to control the composition of the JSC demonstrates that he has a significant influence on the decisions of the JSC. The JSC plays a critical role in all matters concerning the judiciary as it advises the King and government not only on the appointment of judges, but also on the terms and conditions of service for judges, the disciplining of judges and the administration of justice generally.[49]

The King is empowered by section 158 of the Constitution to remove judges, after an investigation by the JSC and a recommendation from the JSC, based on 'serious misbehaviour or inability to perform the functions of office'. In 2022, when removing Judge Sipho Nkosi of the High Court of Eswatini, he wrote 'I, King Mswati III and *Ingwenyama* of Eswatini hereby remove Sipho Anthony Nkosi as a judge of the High Court for serious misbehaviour with effect from the date of notice'.[50] This notice of dismissal came after the JSC conducted a hearing where it called only two witnesses, before concluding that Judge Nkosi was guilty.[51]

Justice Thomas Masuku, formerly a judge of the High Court of Eswatini, approached the African Commission on 11 April 2013 following his dismissal from his position by the King. He was dismissed after being found guilty of misconduct by the JSC on 11 charges including failing to deliver judgments on time, insulting the King by referring to him as having a 'forked tongue' in a written judgment, defying the Chief Justice's directives, touting himself to be appointed Chief Justice, absenteeism without permission, and threatening the Chief Justice with resignation, among other things.[52] He submitted to the African Commission that his Communication resulted from the exhaustion of

[47] 'Judges quit op Swazi court' *News24* (30 November 2002), www.news24.com/news24/judges-quit-top-swazi-court-20021130.

[48] Constitution (n 32) s 159(1).

[49] ibid s 160.

[50] E Dube, 'King Fired Most Educated Judge Who Wanted To Expose The Judiciary Corruption' *The Newsweek* (17 March 2022), www.sdnewsweek.wordpress.com/2022/03/17/king-fired-most-educated-judge-who-wanted-to-expose-the-judiciary-corruption/.

[51] M Ndzimandze and K Dlamini, 'Sipho Nkosi Removed As High Court Judge' *Times of Swaziland* (17 March 2022), www.times.co.sz/news/135178-sipho-nkosi-removed-as-high-court-judge.htm.

[52] *Justice Thomas S Masuku v The Kingdom of Swaziland*, African Commission on Human and Peoples' Rights, Communication 444/13 (19 July 2021) para 7.

local remedies, as required by Article 56(5) of the African Charter, by virtue of their total unavailability.

The Chief Justice had issued a Practice Directive on 16 June 2011 effectively banning the institution of legal proceedings against the King and *iNgwenyama*.[53] The African Commission held that the 'local remedies required to be exhausted [by Article 56(5)] must be (a) available, (b) effective, and (c) sufficient'.[54] After assessing the merits of Masuku's case, the African Commission found Eswatini to have violated Articles 1, 7 and 26 of the African Charter on Human and Peoples Rights.[55] Article 1 concerns the obligations of Member States to recognise and give effect to the rights, duties and freedoms in the Charter. Article 7 provides for the right to a fair trial, and Article 26 concerns the obligation to respect the independence of the judiciary.[56] The African Commission found a violation of these rights based primarily on observations that the JSC which found Masuku guilty of misconduct was not independent and impartial, as six of the charges he was found guilty of concerned the Chief Justice; therefore the Chief Justice should not have chaired the JSC proceedings.

The African Commission further found that the use by Masuku of certain words in a written judgment did not constitute 'serious misbehaviour' and in fact charging him for that amounted to interfering with Maseko's judicial independence as it 'amounts to exerting influence or pressure on the Victim' and threatened both Maseko and the judiciary broadly, in violation of Article 26.[57] The African Commission then concluded its inquiry by recommending redress to Maseko in the form of compensation and a review of the charges he was found guilty of.

The African Commission also issued broader recommendations which 'urged' Eswatini to review the legal framework regulating the JSC, to permit judicial review of the JSC's proceedings and to include provisions which would entitle judges to object to the participation of certain members of the JSC in their disciplinary hearings on the grounds of bias.[58] The decisions of the African Commission are non-binding in nature but remain important because they can persuade a country to change course, facilitate dialogue among different parties, which may lead to change, or shame a country into compliance with the African Charter.[59]

In April 2015, warrants of arrest were issued by the Anti-Corruption Commission against the then Chief Justice of Eswatini, Michael Ramodibedi, as well as against Judge Simelane on charges which included abuse of power and defeating the ends of justice.[60] Ramodibedi instituted a judicial review of the warrant of arrest against him, and the review was heard before Judge Jacobus Annandale, who set aside the warrant.

[53] Chief Justice of Eswatini, High Court of Swaziland Practice Directive No 4/2011 (1) 'Summonses or applications for civil claims against His Majesty the King and *iNgwenyama*, either directly or indirectly, shall not be accepted in the High Court or any other Court in the country'.

[54] *Justice Thomas S Masuku v The Kingdom of Swaziland* (n 52) para 61.

[55] ibid para 196.

[56] ibid.

[57] ibid paras 187 and 191.

[58] bid.

[59] See F Viljoen and L Louw, 'State Compliance with the Recommendations of The African Commission on Human and Peoples' Rights, 1994–2004' (2007) 101(1) *American Journal of International Law* 1.

[60] International Commission for Jurists, 'Justice Locked Out: Swaziland's Rule of Law Crisis' (International Fact-finding Mission Report 2016) 8–9.

Judge Annandale was later arrested together with the Minister of Justice and his Registrar. Ramodibedi evaded arrest by locking himself inside his home. However, he was later suspended from office and ultimately dismissed by the King on three charges of abuse of power following an inquiry of the JSC.[61]

These events all took place after the adoption of the 2005 Constitution, which – as noted above – guarantees the independence of judges. They provide evidence to suggest that the Constitution cannot protect judicial independence and the rule of law from interference by the King. The International Commission of Jurists conducted a Fact-finding Mission on the Rule of Law Crisis in Swaziland in May 2015 and found that the constitutional and legislative framework in Eswatini does not respect the separation of powers and, therefore, cannot safeguard the independence of the judiciary. The Mission also concluded that former Chief Justice Ramodibedi had failed to protect and defend the judiciary and its independence, the executive was unable to respect the independence of the judiciary, and all these factors then led to the abuse of the legal system for personal gain by the Chief Justice.[62]

In the *Law Society of Swaziland v Simelane N.O. and Others*[63] case, the applicants challenged the King's decision to appoint Justices Nkambule and Shabangu to the High Court as well as the appointment of Acting Chief Justice Annandale. They applied for the appointment of Judge Simelane to be declared unconstitutional and therefore set aside as he did not meet the criteria for judicial appointment. The Court dismissed their case on the basis that the appointment of judges was the prerogative of the King, on the advice of the JSC. In coming to this decision, the Court relied first on section 11 of the Constitution, which states that the King is immune from legal action in respect of his decisions, a Swazi law and custom idiom which provides that *umlomo longacalii manga* (which translates to 'the King's mouth does not lie') and secondly on the failure of the applicant to join the JSC in the legal action.[64]

Dube and Nhlabatsi critique the Court's reliance on section 11 and *umlomo longacali manga* on the basis that the Court failed to consider the context in which they apply.[65] The Court failed to consider whether public power was being exercised and also failed to consider other relevant Swazi law and custom idioms such as *inkhosi yinkhosi ngebantfu*, which translates to 'a King is a King through the people' and thus requires checks and balances, and the social legitimacy of the King.[66] The Court's choice of idiom as evidence of the existence of a customary rule, and the exclusion of another relevant customary rule is not necessarily an indication that Swazi law and custom cannot constrain the powers of the King, but rather that Swazi courts are partial toward the King.

[61] N Twala, 'Mswati sacks humiliated chief justice' *IOL* (21 June 2015), www.iol.co.za/news/africa/mswati-sacks-humiliated-chief-justice-1874127.

[62] International Commission for Jurists (n 60).

[63] *Law Society of Swaziland v Simelane N.O. and Others* [2014] SZHC 179 (1 August 2014).

[64] ibid para 2.

[65] A Dube and S Nhlabatsi, 'The King can do no wrong: The impact of *The Law Society of Swaziland v Simelane N.O. & Others* on constitutionalism' (2016) 16 *African Human Rights Law Journal* 265, 274.

[66] ibid.

V. Swazi Law and Custom, Challenges to Executive Action, and the Influence of South African Constitutionalism

Eswatini maintains close relations with its largest neighbour, South Africa, and both countries are members of the Southern African Development Community, which allows for the seamless movement of people and goods across their borders.[67]

The vast majority of Swazi people live under and are subject to Swazi law and custom.[68] Swazi law and custom has been defined by Khumalo, a former judge and academic in Swaziland and South Africa, as

> All legally binding customary practices which are not repugnant to natural justice [and] which have been developed from time immemorial and such proclamations, decrees, orders and other enactments, passed by the *Ngwenyama* [the King] in consultation with his *Libandla* [national council], which are intended to apply to Swazis and to be enforced by Swazi courts.[69]

It is thus both necessary and appropriate that the Constitution recognises and adopts the tenets of Swazi law and custom as part of the law of Eswatini.[70] The challenge that arises with this system of law is that it is unwritten and uncodified, and therefore opens itself to various interpretations. The King and his Advisory Council are interpreters of Swazi law and custom. This has led to interpreters of these laws interpreting them in ways which suit their needs and which often disadvantage groups who are already vulnerable.[71]

Nyane has offered a critique of the Swazi succession to Kingship on the basis that it is not outlined in the Constitution.[72] He states that this has effectively given Swazi law and custom superiority over the Constitution in matters concerning the monarchy. He concludes by stating that it would be more appropriate to codify the Swazi law and custom on the succession of the monarchy in the Constitution, in order to affirm and safeguard the supremacy of the Constitution. This argument is quite persuasive as it would ensure that the rule of law is safeguarded. When the customary rules of succession to the Kingship are known to all, then they can be justiciable, which would allow for their development in a manner that responds to changing social norms. However, codifying customary rules has been challenged in South Africa, and has been critiqued for failing to give expression to changing living laws.[73] The extent to which words written in the Constitution can constrain the monarchy is also questionable when the judiciary is unable or unwilling to hold the monarchy accountable.

[67] 'Member States' (*Southern African Development Community*), www.sadc.int/member-states.

[68] A van Schalkwyk, 'The indigenous law of contract with particular reference to the Swazi in the Kingdom of Swaziland' (PhD thesis, University of South Africa, 2006) 19.

[69] JAM Khumalo, *Swazi customary law courts: a supplement to Civil practice and procedure in all Bantu courts in Southern Africa* (Cape Town, Juta, 1976) 1.

[70] Constitution (n 32) s 252(2).

[71] For example, in South Africa traditional leaders often interpret their power as being above the needs of their communities, which often leads to legal challenges before the courts. See generally *Bakgatla-Ba-Kgafela Communal Property Association v Bakgatla-Ba-Kgafela Tribal Authority and Others* 2015 (6) SA 32 (CC).

[72] H Nyane, 'A critique of the Swazi Constitutional rules on succession to kingship' (2019) 52 *De Jure Law Journal* 65.

[73] R Ozoemena, 'Living Customary Law: A Truly Transformative Tool' (2014) 6 *Constitutional Court Review* 147.

In the *Melusi Simelane N.O. and Others v Minister of Commerce and Industry*[74] case, the Supreme Court of Eswatini reviewed the decision of the Registrar of Companies to refuse the registration of an LGBTI+ association on the basis that the association advocates for what is 'against the order of nature and … actions … traceable to the Bible; as depicted in the destruction of Sodom and Gomorrah by God; in the Book of Genesis'. The Registrar of Companies advanced the argument that the rights to freedom of assembly and association in the Constitution are limited by the rights of others and the public interest. The Court found that 'the approach undertaken by the Registrar in this regard does not meet the legal requirements contained in Section 33 of the Constitution'.[75] Section 33 concerns the right to administrative justice. The Minister of Commerce and Industry, which registers companies, was then directed to consider the application of the LGBTI+ association.[76] This decision by the Court shows the effective use of its judicial review powers in line with the Constitution. The Court enforced the fundamental right to administrative justice guaranteed in the Constitution by directing that the application for registration by the LGBTI+ organisation must be considered even when 'found to be offensive' by the executive. This unanimous judgment also signalled that institutional dynamics within the Court are improving and that the Court is committed to interpreting the Constitution in a just manner.

This progressive decision of the Swazi Supreme Court borrowed significantly from South African administrative law.[77] South African-trained lawyers often appear before Swazi courts, and this, too may have an impact on the constitutional culture being created in Eswatini.[78] Small states with large and influential neighbours sometimes adopt their neighbours' legal culture and jurisprudence.

However, in other recent cases, Swazi judges have also been apprehensive about importing South African jurisprudence to their country. For example, in the *Times of Swaziland v Simelane* case, decided in 2014, when considering some of the comparative jurisprudence on the law of defamation submitted by the applicant, the court stated that 'the *Bogoshi* decision was based on the uniquely liberal constitution of South Africa which exhibits marked difference to our constitution and should be approached with trepidation'.[79] This indicates that while the courts may routinely develop their laws in a

[74] *Melusi Simelane N.O. and Six Others v Minister of Commerce and Industry, Registrar of Companies, and Attorney General* (34/2022) [2022] SZSC 23 (16 June 2023).

[75] ibid para 34.

[76] ibid para 38.

[77] In para 32, the judgment quotes a South African law textbook (M Wiechers, *Administrative Law*, (Durban, Butterworths, 1985)) to explain the quasi-judicial power of the Registrar's powers. It also quotes extensively, in para 36, from another South African law textbook (C Hoexter and G Penfold, *Administrative Law in South Africa*, 3rd edn (Cape Town, Juta, 2022)), which explains South African Constitutional Court jurisprudence on administrative law.

[78] The Legal Practitioners Act 15 of 1964 in Eswatini permits citizens who have legal degrees from either Botswana, Lesotho, Swaziland, Zimbabwe, South Africa or Namibia to be enrolled as legal practitioners of the Swazi High Court. Some of the leading Swazi constitutional and human rights scholars state, in their biographies in academic articles, that they received their legal education from South Africa: for example, Hlengiwe Dlamini, Sabelo Gumedze, Thulani Maseko, Musa Njabulo Shongwe, and Angelo Dube. The current Chief Justice, Bheki Maphalala, along with many other judges in the Swazi High Court, received their legal training in South Africa, see eg, 'Hon. Bheki Maphalala, Chief Justice of Eswatini' (*Southern African Chief Justices Forum*), www.sacjforum.org/biographies/hon-bheki-maphalala.

[79] *African Echo (Pty) Ltd (t/a Times of Swaziland) v Inkhosatana Gelane Simelane* (77/2013) SZSC 83 (3 December 2014) para 34.

similar manner to South Africa due to the proximity of the two countries, South African legal education received by Eswatini's legal professionals, and the shared historical and cultural ties of the two countries, Eswatini's judiciary remains cognisant of the differences between the two countries and the need to interpret its laws in a manner that is consistent with eSwatini's unique context.

South Africa and Eswatini have starkly different legal and political cultures. South Africa is a constitutional democracy where all action taken by the government may be challenged before the courts. It also has built a strong rights consciousness where *everyone* is free to approach the courts to seek the protection or promotion of their rights, including socio-economic rights. However, the influence of South African constitutional jurisprudence on Eswatini cannot be understated. Swazi judges have borrowed from South African judgments in matters including taxation,[80] defamation,[81] and the sentencing of convicted persons.[82]

VI. Conclusion

Eswatini is the smallest country in Southern Africa and the only country in the region to have withstood different waves of democratic change. While most Swazis live in poverty and insecurity, the King has been widely reported to live a life of opulence.[83] This was one of the reasons for the 2021 pro-democracy protests in Eswatini described in section III. However, the small, young and traditional population of the country has struggled to topple, or even restrain, the monarchy. The military capabilities of the monarchy, coupled with respect for the symbol that the monarchy represents among Swazi people, have meant that the King retains his absolutist rule. It is the small, insular and homogenous nature of Eswatini, the dominant socio-economic conditions in the country, and the ambiguities embedded in the country's Constitution regarding the contours of the King's powers and the role of the Constitution that enable the King to behave in authoritarian ways.

The King is able to exercise exclusive and unchecked power over all branches of government despite the existence of a Constitution which nominally provides for a

[80] For example, in *Ntini v Dos Santos* (1564/2022) [2023] SZHC 2 (20 January 2023), the Eswatini High Court used the decision of the South African Eastern Cape High Court, Grahamstown in *Olga v Minister of Safety and Security* 2012 (4) SA 127 (ECG) to conclude that '[w]hat is clear from the authorities in TWK (*supra*) and Olga (*supra*) is that a review brought under rule 48(1) by a party who is not present during the taxation cannot succeed'. No distinction is made between the law in Eswatini and the law in South Africa.

[81] For example, in *Sihlongonyane v African Echo (Pty) Ltd* (269/2015) [2023] SZHC 402 (30 January 2023) the Eswatini High Court uses the South African Supreme Court of Appeal case of *National Medial Ltd v Bogoshi* 1998 (4) SA 1196 (SCA) but states at para 36 that this is a foreign case which established relevant factors for establishing a fair quantum of damages that were cited and approved by the Eswatini High Court in the earlier case of *Dlamini v The Swazi Observer and Others* [2017] SZHC 86, para 19.

[82] For example, in *Rex v Dlamini* [2023] SZHC 549, para 4, the Eswatini High Court cites the South African Appellate Division case of *S v Letsolo* 1970 (3) SA 476 (A) as a 'leading case', then proceeds to outline the factors to be considered as established in the *Letsolo* case when assessing the moral blameworthiness of an accused. The Court does not state that this is a decision of a foreign court, and instead applies the factors to the circumstances of the person before it and then reduces his sentence.

[83] 'Anger mounts against Swazi king' *Al Jazeera* (9 October 2011), www.aljazeera.com/features/2011/10/9/anger-mounts-against-swazi-king.

separation of powers. The size, location and culture of Eswatini enable him to exercise this kind of power despite being surrounded by more liberal and progressive countries like South Africa. The Swazi people are mythologised as being peaceful and cooperative by the monarchy, which creates the perception that any form of resistance to the monarchy is 'unSwazi' and due to a foreign influence.[84] The legal system in Eswatini is influenced by South Africa; however, this influence is limited, as judges are cognisant of the cultural and legal differences between the two countries. In any case, judges are subject to the King, who rules absolutely.

[84] Nyane (n 72) 75.

Part IC
Citizenship, Belonging and Regional Integration

10

The Construction of Constitutional Identity(ies) by the Caribbean Court of Justice

SE-SHAUNA WHEATLE*

I. Introduction

'The Caribbean is the basin with the largest concentration of small states and territories in the world'.[1] The size of the states in the region therefore, unsurprisingly, influences the course of regional and national developments in the Caribbean. The small size of individual Caribbean territories was a significant factor in the justification for the establishment of the West Indies Federation in 1958, a short-lived association of Anglophone Caribbean states which would soon give way to Member States opting for national – rather than regional – independent statehood from 1962 onwards. However, there are wider questions about what it means to be a small state, which engage both scale and power,[2] and the metrics of scale and power are interwoven with themes of colonialism, postcolonialism and decolonisation. The fact that the decline of empires from the mid-twentieth century contributed to an increase in the number of small states indicates that a substantial number of these states are former colonial territories, and necessitates reflection on the dynamics of claiming and practising or performing statehood as a postcolonial entity.

A central part of claiming and practising statehood in the Caribbean region is the enforcement and application of constitutions by state institutions. In this chapter, I consider the construction of constitutional identities in the Commonwealth Caribbean. In particular, I focus on the tools that the Caribbean Court of Justice (CCJ) uses to craft and communicate constitutional identities, and I contemplate the normative status of constitutional identities in the region. As such, this chapter does not centre on the characterisation or description of the constitutional identities of Caribbean states or

* This work was supported by the Economic and Social Research Council [grant reference number: ES/X008185/1], as part of the Open Research Area.

[1] G Baldacchino, 'Island versus region: the politics of small states in the Caribbean' in G Baldacchino and A Wivel (eds), *Handbook on the Politics of Small States* (Cheltenham, Edward Elgar Publishing, 2020) 278.

[2] See definitional analysis of small states in G Baldacchino and A Wivel, 'Small states: concepts and theories' in Baldacchino and Wivel (ibid) 3–7.

the Caribbean region.[3] Instead, I focus on the process surrounding the construction and deployment of that identity (or those identities). In section II of this chapter, I first outline the constitutional history of the Commonwealth Caribbean and the formation of the CCJ as an apex court in the region. The influence of the small size of the states in the region is explored in this analysis, drawing attention to the role that smallness plays in confidence in constitutional institutions. In section III, I reflect on the reasons that sculpting and discerning a constitutional identity is important in Caribbean states, and to whom it is important. I suggest that smallness contributes to the significance of creating and asserting identity within a global landscape dominated by powerful former colonial metropoles and the Global North. I also outline the concept of constitutional identity and connect the discourse on constitutional identity to the wider field of identity studies. Section IV then addresses the roles played by constitutional identity(ies). I suggest that constitutional identity, as used by the CCJ, has both narrative and normative dimensions, with the capacity to communicate the story of the state's constitutional development and to shape that development by exerting substantive effect on constitutional decision-making. In section V, I catalogue and examine the devices that the CCJ uses in forming and reforming constitutional identity. These tools encompass both textual and non-textual norms and speak to both local and ostensibly universal values. I conclude with reflections on the role of a regional court as a driver of new ways of approaching constitutional identity in the Caribbean and on the reach of – and limitations on – the Court's influence. I suggest that smallness influences the formation of constitutional identity by the CCJ, but that smallness cannot be limited to a physical conception; it must encompass smallness as a reflection of (geo)political power. Moreover, size – whether conceived in physical or political terms – only tells part of the story. The region's past – particularly its colonial history – is an integral component of the account of constitutionalism and constitutional identity in the states of the Commonwealth Caribbean.

II. The Commonwealth Caribbean and the Caribbean Court of Justice

The Commonwealth Caribbean comprises 12 states that were formerly under British imperial rule and have secured their independence from the UK. These states are also members of the Commonwealth of Nations, which explains the common use of 'Commonwealth' as a qualifier. The countries in question are Antigua and Barbuda, the Bahamas, Barbados, Belize, Dominica, Grenada, Guyana, Jamaica, St Kitts and Nevis, St Lucia, Trinidad and Tobago, and St Vincent and the Grenadines.[4] These countries were

[3] I have explored this issue in other work: S Wheatle, 'Constitutional Principles: Forging Caribbean Constitutionalism' in R Albert, D O'Brien and S Wheatle (eds), *The Oxford Handbook of Caribbean Constitutions* (Oxford, Oxford University Press, 2020) and S Wheatle and Y Campbell, 'Constitutional Faith and Identity in the Caribbean: Tradition, Politics and the Creolisation of Caribbean Constitutional Law' (2020) 58(3) *Commonwealth & Comparative Politics* 344.

[4] This chapter does not address the British Overseas Territories in the Caribbean region.

subject to British colonial rule for a mean duration of 223.5 years.[5] The colonial period led to the decimation of indigenous populations, slavery and plantation rule, extractive economies, and embedded racial tensions and hierarchies. A gradual formal decolonisation occurred in the region from the mid-twentieth century onward in response to unrest over social and economic conditions, active nationalist movements and changing British attitudes and assessments about the utility of the Caribbean colonies. This decolonisation included increased self-government and widening suffrage, which led to further calls for greater local control and political independence. Waves of independence followed, starting with Jamaica and Trinidad and Tobago in 1962. Each state was founded on a constitution upon independence, and each state's constitution includes a catalogue of fundamental rights that are enforceable by the judiciary.

Yet it is stark reality that 'the legal foundation for all Caribbean constitutions, except in the republic of Guyana and Trinidad and Tobago, and arguably Belize, is a UK Order in Council'.[6] Most of the region's constitutions therefore derive legal status from a statutory instrument made on the advice of the Privy Council, and the respective constitutions are schedules to Orders in Council. There has therefore, unsurprisingly, been debate in the decades since the first independence constitutions about the patriation and indigenisation of Commonwealth Caribbean constitutions. These are, in a fundamental sense, questions about the core identity of these constitutions.

Despite departing from British tradition by adopting codified constitutions, the constitutions of the Commonwealth Caribbean were typified by retention of British constitutional structure, institutions, constitutional conventions and, initially, conservative judicial approaches.[7] Most Commonwealth Caribbean states retain a Westminster-style parliamentary system, whereby the head of state is not the head of government, and in which the Cabinet is derived from, and accountable to, Parliament.[8] This model was adopted by all Commonwealth Caribbean states except Guyana, which subsequently opted for a semi-presidential model in a socialist co-operative republic.[9] In all countries, the head of state is the British monarch, represented by the Governor General, with the exception of Guyana, Trinidad and Tobago, Dominica, and Barbados, which – either on independence (in the case of Dominica) or subsequently (in the case of Guyana, Trinidad and Tobago, and Barbados) – replaced the monarch with a President as head of state. The selection process differs, but the functions and constitutional role of the President in Trinidad and Tobago, Dominica and Barbados are similar

[5] HA Young, 'The Caribbean Court of Justice: Meeting the Challenges of a post-colonial Caribbean' in RM Howard, KA Randazzo and RA Reid (eds), *Research Handbook on Law and Political Systems* (Cheltenham, Edward Elgar Publishing, 2023) 289.

[6] T Robinson, A Bulkan and A Saunders, *Fundamentals of Caribbean Constitutional Law*, 2nd edn (London, Sweet and Maxwell, 2021) 7.

[7] KW Patchett, 'English Law in the West Indies: A Conference Report' (1963) 12 *International and Comparative Law Quarterly* 922, 923; D O'Brien and S Wheatle, 'Post-independence constitutional reform in the Commonwealth Caribbean and a new charter of fundamental rights and freedoms for Jamaica' [2012] *Public Law* 683.

[8] SA de Smith, 'Westminster's export models: The legal framework of responsible government' (1961) 1(1) *Journal of Commonwealth Political Studies* 2, 3.

[9] Constitution of the Co-operative Republic of Guyana 1980 art 1. Under art 89 of the Constitution of Guyana 1980, the President is both head of state and head of government. On the transformation of the Guyanese governmental structure from 1970 onwards, see Hari N Ramkarran, 'Seeking a Democratic Path: Constitutional Reform in Guyana' (2004) 32 *Georgia Journal of International and Comparative Law* 585.

to the functions of the Governor General in the other states, and therefore adhere very closely to the Westminster design.[10] Commonwealth Caribbean constitutions also codify some Westminster prerogative powers and conventions, including the power of the head of state to appoint the Prime Minister and the convention that the person appointed should be the person who is most capable of commanding a majority in the House of Commons.[11] Colonial retentionism was also reflected in the maintenance of the Judicial Committee of the Privy Council as the final court of appeal.

Most states retained the Privy Council upon independence and the vast majority have rejected arguments in favour of replacing the Privy Council with a Caribbean institution. The creation of an autochthonous final appellate court to replace the Judicial Committee of the Privy Council is perceived as part of the process of decolonisation, as a further step towards full independence. The CCJ has therefore been created as a facet of both indigenous Caribbean law and regional integration. It has both appellate jurisdiction as an apex court, in respect of domestic laws, and original jurisdiction as the adjudicator of disputes under the regional legal arrangements for the Caribbean Community (CARICOM).[12] The CCJ was inaugurated in 2005, though at present, only Barbados, Belize, Dominica, Guyana, and St Lucia have acceded to its appellate jurisdiction.

Some of the traditionalist and retentionist impulses reflected in institutional design and constitutional development are at least partly a consequence of the size of the states, both with respect to geography and population size and with respect to political power. Sceptics of the CCJ have pointed to the small size of the communities within the region as a factor that cautions against reliance on a Caribbean court as the final court of appeal. In this line of thought, the small size of the population increases the risk of familiarity between parties and judges, and therefore risks undermining the necessary impartiality of judges adjudicating disputes. As Ezekiel Rediker explains, sceptics of a locally-based apex court pointed to the 'political and social pressures of a small, politically and socially intimate region like the Caribbean'.[13] Roget Bryan outlined the argument in detail in 1998, at a time of ongoing debate about the establishment of a home-grown court:

> jurists from the region, despite their integrity and independence, may find it difficult if not impossible to be uninfluenced, due to the small size of the region and the fact that it proves almost impossible to keep the business of one person private from that of another.[14]

On this construction, the JCPC's distance serves as a counterbalance against the potential disadvantages to judicial impartiality and independence of the small size of Caribbean states. Despite these arguments, the call for further steps towards true independence

[10] D O'Brien, 'The Commonwealth Caribbean and the Westminster Model' in Albert, O'Brien and Wheatle, *Oxford Handbook of Caribbean Constitutions* (n 3) 142.

[11] Robinson, Bulkan and Saunders (n 6) 70–79. See, eg Constitution of Barbados s 65(1).

[12] CARICOM is a regional trade and economic group operating under the Revised Treaty of Chaguaramas Establishing the Caribbean Community Including the CARICOM Single Market and Economy (adopted Bahamas, 5 July 2001, entered into force 1 January 2006) 2259 UNTS 293.

[13] D Rediker, 'Courts of Appeal and Colonialism in the British Caribbean: A Case for the Caribbean Court of Justice' (2013) 35 *Michigan Journal of International Law* 213, 248.

[14] RV Bryan, 'Toward the Development of Caribbean Jurisprudence: The Case for Establishing a Caribbean Court of Appeal' (1998) 7 *Journal of Transnational Law & Policy* 181, 204.

and sovereignty, combined with both emotive and practical considerations such as the cost of accessing the Privy Council, eventually prevailed, leading to the CCJ's establishment. The pooling of judicial resources into a regional court – rather than several national courts – can accordingly be seen as a solution to the concerns around state size and the resulting risk of pressure and influence on judges in each state, as well as part of the pursuit of regional integration[15] and the continuation of the centuries-old practice of a regional court of appeal in the form of the Privy Council.[16]

The entrenchment of fundamental rights also represents a point of departure from traditional British constitutionalism, one adopted at the inception of independence. However, there is substantial evidence that even the adoption of fundamental rights reflected imperialist ideas and priorities. It has been shown that the inclusion of civil and political rights – which dominate the independence constitutions – were motivated by a metropolitan anxiety to protect the capital and property of the mostly foreign, landed and investor class.[17] The rights were also depicted in academic literature as merely replicating 'well recognised rules developed at common law', with the corollary that 'resort will be had to English authorities on these matters'.[18] Colonial retention was also clearly expressed in the 'general savings law clause' inserted in earlier constitutions; these clauses purported to insulate pre-independence laws by providing that colonial era laws cannot be held inconsistent with the rights provisions in the constitution.[19]

Tracy Robinson has referred to the 'status quo bias' and 'the endowment effect, that is the tendency to value more highly what one already "owns"', as influential factors in the retention and claiming of colonial criminal laws.[20] Similar dynamics can be observed in the retention of Eurocentric constitutional architecture and broader features in early Caribbean constitutions. Moreover, those dynamics are perceived in early interpretative approaches and methodological choices in interpreting Caribbean constitutions.[21] In one of the embryonic constitutional cases in the region, Lord Diplock famously characterised the new constitutions as 'evolutionary, not revolutionary',[22] thereby tying the identity of the constitutions to themes of continuity and traditionalism.

However, much of the CCJ's jurisprudence has reflected a rejection of traditionalism and the status quo. The CCJ has issued momentous, sometimes transformative, judgments on a range of constitutional issues. Gabrielle Elliott-Williams convincingly argues that the Court is decolonising Caribbean constitutional law.[23] Indeed, in the course of its

[15] See Agreement Establishing the Caribbean Court of Justice (adopted Barbados, 14 February 2001, entered into force 23 July 2002) 2255 UNTS 319, preamble.

[16] I am grateful to Professor Tracy Robinson for the insight that the long history of a regional court would have influenced the choice to establish a regional final appellate court.

[17] T Munroe, *The Politics of Constitutional Decolonization: Jamaica, 1944–62* (Institute of Social and Economic Research, University of the West Indies, 1972).

[18] Patchett (n 7) 925.

[19] These clauses were included in the first five Caribbean independence Constitutions; that is, those of the Bahamas, Barbados, Belize, Jamaica, and Trinidad and Tobago. See, eg Constitution of Barbados 1966, s 26. The Belizean clause had a timeline of five years and no longer has any effect. The Jamaican clause was substantially redrafted in a 2011 constitutional amendment.

[20] T Robinson, 'Sticky Colonial Criminal Laws' (2020) 75 *University of Miami Law Review Caveat* 58, 63.

[21] Wheatle and Campbell (n 3).

[22] *Hinds v R* [1977] AC 195, 211 (PC Jamaica).

[23] G Elliott-Williams, 'The CCJ Decolonizing Caribbean Constitutionalism' (2019) 45(4) *Commonwealth Law Bulletin* 742.

20 years of operation, the CCJ has been challenging the traditionalism that was prevalent in Caribbean constitutionalism, and moreover, it has been developing more distinct ideas about the identity of the constitutions of the Commonwealth Caribbean.

III. Constitutional Identity and Small States – Constitutional Identity(Ies) in the Region

As a precursor to the examination of the tools used in crafting Caribbean constitutional identity and the functions of that constructed identity, it is useful to first reflect on the salience and importance of the issue of constitutional identity in the Caribbean.

First, there is a dimension of scale that is at play. The difference in size, capacity and power between small and larger states in a global and increasingly globalised setting, may prompt an urge to define and assert small states' own constitutional vision and imperatives: their own sense of the fundamental norms that underpin their nations. The small size of Caribbean states – with respect to geography, population size and (global) political power – triggers anxiety to define and assert the identity of the state and the region.[24] There is an impetus around locating and being located on a map – identifying oneself as a distinct place with its own space and identifying features. As constitutional design and ideas migrate, there is a danger that smaller states will be overawed by their larger counterparts and in the process lose – or fail to assert and project – their own conception of constitutionalism.

Second, the postcolonial context in which Caribbean constitutions emerged and are implemented necessitates consideration of the nature and identities of those constitutions. The issues that emerge include, but are not limited to, the extent to which these constitutions are, and should be, distinguished from the British model.

Third, though most Commonwealth Caribbean states achieved independence between the 1960s and 1980s, among those states there have arguably been further waves of independence which have seen increasingly transformative manifestations of decolonisation. In this twenty-first-century wave of decolonisation, the CCJ was established in 2005, Barbados abolished the position of the monarchy as head of state in 2021[25] and in 2023 Jamaica established a Constitutional Reform Committee to provide guidance on the country's transition from a constitutional monarchy to a republic.[26] These changes reveal the continuing nature of constitution building in the region and the space for ongoing formulation and reformulation of regional and national constitutional identity. The formation of constitutional identity is indeed an ongoing process,[27] and accordingly, there ought to be a continuing re-evaluation of states' constitutional identity, especially in states embarking on significant constitutional changes.

[24] See similar discussion in L Lewis, 'Introduction: Sovereignty, Heterodoxy, and the Last Desperate Shibboleth of Caribbean Nationalism' in L Lewis (ed), *Caribbean Sovereignty, Development and Democracy in an Age of Globalization*, 1st edn (New York, Routledge, 2013) 1.

[25] Constitution (Amendment) (No 2) Act 2021 (Barbados).

[26] C Patterson, 'PM Announces Members of Constitutional Reform Committee' *Jamaica Information Service* (23 March 2023), jis.gov.jm/pm-announces-members-of-constitutional-reform-committee/.

[27] G Jacobsohn, *Constitutional Identity* (Cambridge MA, Harvard University Press, 2010) 13.

Identity has been characterised as 'the anchoring concept for thinking about difference and sameness in our time'.[28] The concept of identity has both internal and external components – the internal cognitive process of making sense of who we are, and synthesising our past with our present, and the external process of both developing and relating our sense of who we are and who we are not to our social and cultural environments. There is undoubtedly a leap from psychosocial development studies to identity in legal studies, but the central themes of identity theories in psychology are vividly mirrored in constitutional identity discourse. The challenge of navigating through sameness, difference, continuity and change looms large across both fields. Gary Jacobsohn, for instance, explains that:

> Much of the aspirational content of a nation's specific constitutional identity consists of goals and principles that are shared by other nations and that are indeed part of a common stock of aspirations we have come to associate more generally with the enterprise of constitutionalism … Such norms need to be reconciled with the particularistic commitments of local traditions and practices; the contours of constitutional identity will to a large extent reflect how these disharmonies get resolved.[29]

For Jacobsohn, constitutional identity 'represents a mix of political aspirations and commitments that is expressive of a nation's past, as well as the determination of those within the society who seek, in some ways, to transcend that past'.[30] Central to Jacobsohn's conception of constitutional identity is that it emerges through experience and dialogue and therefore it is changeable.[31] This view of identity, which this chapter adopts, has consequences in the form of the evidence considered to examine and determine a state's constitutional identity. First, it means that constitutional identity is not fixed at the moment of constituting a state, and secondly, that while the text is an important site for establishing the fundamental commitments of a polity, it is far from the only indicium of the identity of a constitution. Further, judicial precedent can be examined as a source of indicia of a state's constitutional identity. The judiciary is often an important – though not the only – actor in forging a constitutional identity[32] and, accordingly, a study of the judiciary's contribution to shaping a state's constitutional identity is valuable. Caribbean constitutional theorist Simeon McIntosh has similarly expressed the view that '[c]onstitutional interpretation has a great symbolic importance: it is a public act of self-definition'.[33]

In the context of an examination of Caribbean constitutional identity formation, two features of identity studies resonate. First, identity may place more emphasis on 'social and political positioning' than 'intrinsic characteristics'.[34] Accordingly, there is

[28] PL Hammack, 'Theoretical Foundations of Identity' in K C McLean and M Syed (eds), *The Oxford Handbook of Identity Development* (Oxford, Oxford University Press, 2015) 11.

[29] Jacobsohn, *Constitutional Identity* 2010 (n 27) 112–13.

[30] G Jacobsohn, 'Constitutional Identity' (2006) 68 *Review of Politics* 361.

[31] Jacobsohn, 'Constitutional Identity' 2006 (n 30) 363.

[32] Jacobsohn, *Constitutional Identity* 2010 (n 27) 351.

[33] S McIntosh, 'Holding our own Court' *Daily Nation of Barbados* (28 November 1994) p 6A, as cited in H Rawlins, *The Caribbean Court of Justice: the History and Analysis of the Debate* (Georgetown, CARICOM Secretariat, 2000) 46 and 54, fn 48.

[34] 'The postcolonial account of identity, therefore, does not emphasise identity as an intrinsic characteristic so much as social and political positioning in particular locations': RJC Young, *Empire, Colony, Postcolony* (Chichester, Wiley-Blackwell, 2015) 164.

the potential for constitutional identity to evolve, to be reformed, to be impacted by, and impact, changing relationships and changing perceptions of relationships between institutions and between states. Constitutionalism in postcolonial states, including constitutional adjudication, reflects these 'positioning' dynamics through citation practices, judicial approaches and other judicial epistemological choices. Secondly, a compelling and resonant theory on the development of identity is that the defining feature of identity is the construction of personal narratives. Narrative construction assumes a central place as the method of coherently navigating a person's experiences throughout their life cycle – it reflects the themes of sameness, difference and continuity. 'Through narrative identity, people convey to themselves and to others who they are now, how they came to be, and where they think their lives may be going in the future'.[35] The construction of narratives as part of the development of constitutional identity is evident in the jurisprudence of the CCJ.

IV. The Role of Constitutional Identity in CCJ Jurisprudence

Though the CCJ's jurisprudence is still in a relatively early stage, its judgments over the approximately 20 years of its operation provide early indications of the role that constitutional identity plays in constitutional adjudication in the states within the Court's appellate jurisdiction. Constitutional identity can be conceived of and utilised in at least two ways in CCJ judgments – as a means of constructing and communicating a narrative and as a normative standard with substantive legal impact. In the narrative sense, constitutional identity is a story that the Court tells about the history and future of the national constitution(s) it interprets and about constitutionalism in the region and relevant states. The Court has opted for an emancipatory approach that acknowledges the harmful impact of colonialism and perceives the constitutions and their judicial application as part of an ongoing independence project – conditioned by the precise terms and values of each country's constitution. The Court's judgments indicate that it sees its role and the text and values of the region's constitutions as, in part, a means of providing remedies for constitutional harm. In a similar vein, in Lee Cabatingan's extensive study of the CCJ, she observes that 'Caribbeanness represents the CCJ's rereading and recasting of the past–present–future in a hopeful light, rather than one of tragedy'.[36] Thus, the CCJ can at times be observed engaging in the process of 'meaning making'; that is, reflecting on points in the history relevant to the constitutions it interprets and trying to draw conclusions from that past about the character of the respective constitutions. The act of meaning making is a core facet of the narrative construction of identity. This process at times involves adaptation, exploring negative experiences, contemplating their impact and seeking resolution of those negative experiences.[37] The

[35] DP McAdams and KC McLean, 'Narrative Identity' (2013) 22 *Current Directions in Psychological Science* 233, 233.

[36] L Cabatingan, *A Region among States: Law and Non-sovereignty in the Caribbean* (Chicago IL, Chicago University Press, 2023) 36.

[37] McAdams and McLean (n 35).

Court's judgment in *Nervais* perhaps epitomises this narrative process; in interpreting the effect of the savings law clause on constitutionally declared rights, the Court invoked 'the perspective of a former subjected people' who believe in the rights of peoples to personal autonomy and national sovereignty, and 'the aspirations set out in the preamble to the Constitution'.[38]

There is also evidence of constitutional identity playing a normative role in the constitutional adjudication of the CCJ. In this sense, constitutional identity is operationalised as a set of principles and values that have legal impact and, potentially, as a collection of non-derogable principles. At least four forms of normative impact of constitutional identity can be observed in CCJ decisions. The normative purchase of constitutional identity in the jurisprudence of the Court ranges from an interpretive effect on the text of the constitution or impugned statute to the power of a superior norm within the constitutional hierarchy. It is through the medium of the basic structure doctrine that constitutional identity potentially exerts the most powerful effect. The identity of the constitution informs the basic structure of the constitution, but it remains unsettled whether there is a 'basic structure doctrine'; that is, whether the basic structure is protected from annulment or from derogation by constitutional amendment. The normative functions of identity (arguably) employed by the CCJ are as follows:

(a) To condition interpretation of the constitutional text or statutory text;[39]
(b) To condition treatment of interpretative aids such as comparative and international law;[40]
(c) Use as a normatively superior constitutional standard to which other constitutional, statutory and other norms must yield;[41]
(d) Use as a non-derogable constitutional norm that cannot be overturned even by constitutional amendment.[42] This final function differs from, and goes beyond, function (c) by requiring that constitutional amendments that comply with the text and procedure prescribed in the constitution must also clear the additional hurdle of compliance with the non-derogable constitutional norm. However, as stated above, it has not yet been definitively determined whether a doctrine of unconstitutional constitutional amendments exists in the Caribbean.

[38] *Nervais v R; Severin v R* [2018] CCJ 19 (Barbados) [57].

[39] *Attorney General of Guyana v Thomas; Jagdeo v Thomas* [2022] CCJ 15 (Guyana).

[40] *Maya Leaders Alliance v Attorney General of Belize* [2015] CCJ 15.

[41] In *Belize International Services Limited v Attorney General of Belize* (*BISL*) [2020] CCJ 9 (Belize) at [321] Jamadar J reasoned that the general savings law clause in the constitution was subject to 'the (more) supreme constitutional principle' – the rule of law); *Nervais v R* (n 38) [43]–[45] and [59].

[42] In *Bar Association of Belize v Attorney General of Belize* [2017] CCJ 4 (Belize) [44]–[50] the Court left open the question whether the basic structure doctrine applied in the Caribbean, finding that even if the basic structure doctrine was part of Belizean law, the doctrine 'does not fall to be applied in this case' because it was not established that the impugned amendment 'purports to "alter the Constitution in such a way as to limit or destroy" any of the "unwritten principles that represent the ethos" of Belizean society' [46]. In *BISL* (n 41) at [319] Jamadar J characterised 'the basic underlying principles' of a Constitution as part of the 'basic "deep" structure' that is 'foundational and essential to the identity and nature of the state of Belize'. On constitutional identity as the source of the basic structure of the Constitution, see Jacobsohn 'Constitutional Identity' (2006) (n 30) 376–78. On the basic structure doctrine in the Caribbean, see A Bulkan, 'The Limits of Constitution (Re)-Making in the Commonwealth Caribbean: Towards the "Perfect Nation"' (2013) 2 *Canadian Journal of Human Rights* 81.

The normative functions listed above show that constitutional identity operates – in the relevant Caribbean countries – not as a merely defensive concept (as is arguably the case for the majority of its use around the world) but also as a positive and generative one. The CCJ employed the concept in this manner in *McEwan*:

> The Co-operative Republic of Guyana is an indivisible, secular, democratic and sovereign nation. Its most precious civic values are laid out in the country's Constitution. The Constitution's Preamble indicates the determination of the Guyanese people to 'forge a system of governance that promotes concerted effort and broad-based participation in national decision-making in order to develop a viable economy and a harmonious community based on democratic values, social justice, fundamental human rights, and the rule of law'. The Constitution proclaims that the people of Guyana celebrate their 'cultural and racial diversity and strengthen [their] unity by eliminating any and every form of discrimination …' In adjudicating complaints of human rights infringements, this Court must be guided by these statements of fundamental principle.[43]

The Court then used this approach to interpret the rights to equal protection of the law and equality before the law and to non-discrimination in a manner that formally and substantially extended rights, inclusion and equal citizenship to sexual minorities. As the Court's jurisprudence develops, it will be revealing whether the positive use of constitutional identity is advanced and even strengthened. The CCJ's cultivation and operationalisation of constitutional identity merits further study and may be a useful comparator for other apex or constitutional courts, particularly – though not exclusively – courts in postcolonial states.

The following section outlines the tools used in crafting constitutional identity in CCJ judgments.

V. Devices for Crafting Constitutional Identity

Among the tools utilised by the Court in crafting constitutional identity are preambles, implied principles and value-laden textual provisions. These devices are able to speak to the history of the nation and to reveal the animating constitutional values of the state.

A. Preamble

Preambles are helpful indicators of constitutional identity as they elucidate the purposes of the constitution and speak in generalist language that can lend itself to contextual application in interpreting the constitution. Preambles often play an explanatory role in the constitution and constitutional adjudication. As I have stated elsewhere, 'in its explanatory role, the preamble informs the reader of the relevant factual background of the Constitution, including references to consultations preceding the enactment of the

[43] *McEwan v Attorney General of Guyana* [2018] CCJ 30 (Guyana) [61] (Saunders PCCJ, Wit and Barrow JCCJ), footnotes omitted.

document'.[44] It reveals the '*raison d'etre* and eternal ideals' of the constitution.[45] As 'one of the primary goals of the preamble is to articulate the nation's highest values, narrate its history, and express aspirations for the future', it is, as Mila Versteeg argues, 'an obvious place to start' in the search for constitutional identity in the constitutional text.[46] It is unsurprising then, that preambles have been employed in the construction of constitutional identity by the CCJ.

The preambles to many constitutions in the region appear in similar terms. A representative example is the Preamble to the Constitution of Barbados:

> Whereas the love of free institutions and of independence has always strongly characterised the inhabitants of Barbados:
>
> …
>
> Now, therefore, the people of Barbados
>
> *(a)* proclaim that they are a sovereign nation founded upon principles that acknowledge the supremacy of God, the dignity of the human person, their unshakeable faith in fundamental human rights and freedoms and the position of the family in a society of free men and free institutions;
>
> *(b)* affirm their belief that men and institutions remain free only when freedom is founded upon respect for moral and spiritual values and the rule of law …

Robinson, Bulkan and Saunders observe that a 'reference to the rule of law is the most oft-cited part of the preambles'.[47] The preamble to Guyana's more modern and autochthonous Constitution is more expansive and inclusive than the older constitutions, speaking to a 'commitment to protect our natural environment and endowment' and '[c]reate a republican community practically aware that the finances, industry, communications, education, business and technology of the world are global factors affecting all in which all must engage and from which all must benefit', commitments which reflect the country's post-independence transition to socialism.[48]

The importance of preambles in informing the identity of a constitution is shown early in CCJ history, with Wit JCCJ saying, in the 2006 case of *Joseph and Boyce*, that preambles 'fill the Constitution with meaning reflecting the very essence, values and logic of constitutional democracies in general'.[49] Speaking of the preamble to the Constitution of Barbados years later in *Nervais*, the CCJ stated:

> It is a preliminary statement which embodies the fundamental values and the philosophy, on which the Constitution is based, and the aims and objectives, which the founding fathers of the Constitution enjoined the people of Barbados to strive to achieve and recites certain historical facts.[50]

[44] S Wheatle, *Principled Reasoning in Human Rights Adjudication* (Oxford, Hart Publishing, 2017) 15.
[45] L Orgad, 'The preamble in constitutional interpretation' (2010) 8 *International Journal of Constitutional Law* 714, 722.
[46] M Versteeg, 'What Counts as Constitutional Identity?' in R Hirschl and Y Roznai, *Deciphering the Genome of Constitutionalism: The Foundations and Future of Constitutional Identity* (Cambridge, Cambridge University Press, 2024) 314.
[47] Robinson, Bulkan and Saunders (n 6) 298.
[48] Constitution of the Co-operative Republic of Guyana, preamble and s 1.
[49] *Attorney General of Barbados v Joseph and Boyce* [2006] CCJ 3 (Barbados) [18].
[50] *Nervais v R* (n 38) [22] (Sir Dennis Byron JCCJ).

And in more participatory language, the preamble of the Constitution of Belize has been characterised as an expression of 'the People who constituted the Constitution as text', of 'the basic and fundamental features, principles, and values that are constitutive of Belizean constitutionalism'.[51] These conceptions of the preamble speak to a constitutional identity that is informed by both general or universal values of democracy and constitutionalism as well as domestic history, objectives and values.

The constitutional objectives and character projected by the preamble do appear to inform the CCJ's interpretation. The preamble to the Constitution of Belize was utilised by the courts in the Maya land rights litigation, with the CCJ recalling 'the solemn pledge in the preamble to the Constitution to ensure that State policies protect the identity, dignity, and social and cultural values of Belize's indigenous peoples'.[52] The Court endorsed Wit JCCJ's comments in *Joseph and Boyce* on the authority of preambles, emphasising that '[t]he preamble of a Constitution cannot be treated as mere surplusage'.[53] Notably the traditionalist view that Caribbean constitutional bills of rights should regulate post-independence but not colonial era laws, was viewed by the Court in *Nervais* as inconsistent with the aspirations in the preamble to the Constitution of Barbados. The rejection of this traditionalist view then paved the way for judicial modification of pre-independence laws that violate Barbadian constitutional rights.

B. Implied or Unwritten Principles

It is firmly established in the Caribbean that the character of a constitution is informed by fundamental principles, some of which are unwritten. These norms are sometimes referred to simply as unwritten principles but have also been collectively described as the content of the basic structure of the constitution, which 'confers integral identity to' constitutionalism in the state.[54] The first statute invalidated by the Privy Council under a Caribbean independence constitution was struck down for violation of the unwritten principle of separation of powers.[55] And more recently, the CCJ has left open the door for constitutional amendments to also be struck down if they fall foul of fundamental implied constitutional principles.[56] As the CCJ affirmed in *Bar Association of Belize v Attorney General of Belize* in the context of a constitutional challenge to a constitutional amendment,

> Since *Hinds v R* [in 1977], it is possible to imply unwritten constitutional principles in the Constitution in order to declare primary legislation unconstitutional. Therefore, by analogy it is difficult to disagree with obiter dicta of Mendes JA in *Attorney-General of Belize v British Caribbean Bank Limited* that unwritten constitutional principles may likewise limit the power of the National Assembly to amend the Constitution of Belize.[57]

[51] *BISL* (n 41) [303] (Jamadar J).
[52] *Maya Leaders Alliance* (n 40) [75].
[53] *Maya Leaders Alliance* (n 40) [54].
[54] *BISL* (n 41) [299] (Jamadar J).
[55] *Hinds v R* (n 22).
[56] *Bar Association of Belize v Attorney General of Belize* (n 42). See discussion in Robinson, Bulkan and Saunders (n 6) 173–86.
[57] *Bar Association of Belize v Attorney General of Belize* (n 42) [50].

The terms of – and omissions from – the respective constitutions create space for unwritten constitutional principles to shape constitutional change in the region. Some of this space arises from the fact that while savings law clauses expressly insulate pre-independence laws from being struck down for inconsistency with constitutional rights provisions, it has been established that those clauses do not prevent invalidation of legislation for inconsistency with constitutional principles.[58] Unwritten principles thereby occupy a potent position in providing a method of obviating the savings law clauses which remain in the region's older constitutions. With this capacity – combined with the generally flexible nature of principles[59] – unwritten principles are perhaps uniquely positioned to facilitate the negotiation between commitments that are 'expressive of [the] nation's past' and efforts 'to transcend that past'.[60]

The rule of law is at present the most influential unwritten constitutional principle in CCJ jurisprudence. The fundamental character of the principle and its place as part of the core constitutional identity of Barbados was affirmed through the decision in *Nervais* that the savings law clause in the Constitution must yield to the rule of law, as implied through the constitutional right to protection of the law.[61] While the rule of law has been conceived and utilised as central to the identity of Caribbean constitutions, it clearly possesses both an inward and an outward-looking dimension. The domestic facet of the principle requires obedience to local laws, including the rules and principles of the constitution. The outward dimension emerges from several considerations. Firstly, there is an innate universality to the rule of law, as it is a concomitant of constitutionalism, and an appeal to the rule of law cannot therefore be confined to the borders of the state in question; it draws upon values developed and applied across states that subscribe to liberal constitutionalism. As noted by Wit JCCJ, the rule of law is 'closely linked to, and broadly embraces concepts like the principles of natural justice, procedural and substantive "due process of law" and its corollary, the protection of the law'.[62] Secondly, the CCJ perceives compliance with international law as a requirement of the rule of law, with the Court noting in *Maya Leaders Alliance* that 'a recognized sub-set of the rule of law is the obligation of the State to honour its international commitments'.[63] Similarly, the lead judgment of the Court in *OO v BK and Attorney General of Barbados* declared that:

> This Court has pointed out that constitutional democracies function under the rule of law and in the context of constitutional supremacy. Accordingly, where the issue of statutory interpretation is at play, the Court should interpret legislation not only to achieve the objectives of the legislation, and the intention of Parliament but to achieve alignment with (1) fundamental human rights and core constitutional values and principles contained in Commonwealth Caribbean Constitutions, and (2) international treaty obligations and commitments of these States.[64]

[58] *DPP of Jamaica v Mollison* [2003] 2 WLR 1160, [2003] UKPC 6 (PC Jamaica).
[59] Wheatle, *Principled Reasoning* (n 44) 206–7.
[60] Jacobsohn, 'Constitutional Identity' (2006) (n 30) 363.
[61] *Nervais v R* (n 38) [43]–[45] and [59].
[62] *Attorney General of Barbados v Joseph and Boyce* (n 49) [20].
[63] *Maya Leaders Alliance* (n 40) [52] (Byron and Anderson JCCJs).
[64] *OO v BK and Attorney General of Barbados* [2023] CCJ 10 (Barbados) [67] (Rajnauth-Lee J).

The Court's jurisprudence to date affirms that the conception of the rule of law which forms part of constitutional identity – at least in countries within the CCJ's jurisdiction – is one that requires respect for both domestic constitutional norms and international legal obligations. Unwritten constitutional principles therefore have the potential to reflect the internal and external dimensions of identity formation.

This duality is clear in the *Maya Leaders Alliance* case, where the CCJ found that the Government of Belize had violated the constitutional rights of indigenous Mayans by failing to create laws that protect indigenous rights to customary land. The Court held that the Mayans' 'right to protection of the law, founded on the concept of the rule of law', had been breached, and ordered the Government of Belize to create a fund to finance measures to identify and protect Mayan property rights. The judgment combined reasoning that reflected on the local historical context of oppression of indigenous peoples in Belize, the terms and principles of the Belizean Constitution, and engagement with international norms.[65] The judgment was founded on Belize's Constitution but also incorporated references to international legal commitments and documents, including the United Nations Declaration on the Rights of Indigenous Peoples, as well as foreign case law from courts such as the Constitutional Court of Indonesia. In informing constitutional identity, unwritten constitutional principles can, therefore, simultaneously connect the state and the region to liberal constitutionalist objectives while reflecting local 'particularistic' understandings of the constitutionalist project.

C. Value-Laden Text

Finally, textual provisions that are underpinned by deep fundamental values are consulted as indicia of the character of the constitution. Unsurprisingly, fundamental rights provisions are utilised in this manner. Specifically, interpretations of fundamental rights provisions are indicators of constitutional identity in cases that raise deeply contested moral or societal issues.[66] Rights sections in Caribbean constitutions are embedded within the constitutional fabric through entrenchment, which indicates 'the value the constitution-makers attribute'[67] to these provisions. The exalted position of fundamental rights within the constitution is reflected in Saunders JCCJ's evaluation in *McEwan*, interpreting the Constitution of Guyana, that

> If one part of the Constitution appears to run up against an individual fundamental right, then, in interpreting the Constitution as a whole, courts should place a premium on affording the citizen his/her enjoyment of the fundamental right, unless there is some overriding public interest.[68]

[65] See Wheatle and Campbell (n 3) 359.
[66] See, in similar terms, M Polzin, 'Constitutional Identity as a Constructed Reality and a Restless Soul' (2017) 18 *German Law Journal* 1595, 1611.
[67] Robinson, Bulkan and Saunders (n 6) 201, referring to entrenchment in Caribbean Constitutions.
[68] *McEwan* (n 42) [41].

In the Guyanese context, the insertion of new rights into the Constitution in 2003 was perceived as embracing an ethos of participatory democracy and respect for equality and an attempt 'to create a more democratic and inclusive society'.[69] This interpretation influenced the Court's ultimate conclusion in *McEwan* that a colonial era law criminalising cross-dressing, and thereby reinforcing the persecution of a sexual minority, was unconstitutional.

The centrality and value of fundamental rights in the text is most concretely depicted by the CCJ's position that the constitutional rights text embodies values that override the expansive limiting section of the constitution – the general savings law clause. The general savings law clauses' purported temporal freezing of the constitution has been lamented by members of the academy and judiciary.[70] The clauses have stymied rights development in relation to capital punishment by preventing the Court from giving effect to a view that a mandatory death penalty violates constitutional rights to freedom from inhuman and degrading punishment[71] and in relation to same-sex relationships by preventing the invalidation of the crime of sodomy.[72] The limitation therefore stands in stark contrast to the promise and potential of the fundamental rights provisions of the constitutions of those countries in which it features. Sir Denys Byron, for the majority in *Nervais*, decisively resolved the disharmony in the text by finding:

> The general saving clause is an unacceptable diminution of the freedom of newly independent peoples who fought for that freedom with unshakeable faith in fundamental human rights. The idea that even where a provision is inconsistent with a fundamental right a court is prevented from declaring the truth of that inconsistency just because the laws formed part of the inherited laws from the colonial regime must be condemned.[73]

This passage reveals a new vision of the identity of the Constitution of Barbados emerging from the disharmony in the text and the disharmony between the colonial past and the constitutionalised present. In rejecting the previous settlement which accorded priority to the savings law clause in the event of conflict, the Court cemented fundamental rights text as part of the core identity of the Constitution. In this new vision of the Constitution, the values and ideals behind the rights text are recognised, as well as the political labour of the constituent power base of the Constitution. Such is the import and resonance of the Court speaking to the activism of 'newly independent peoples who fought for that freedom with unshakeable faith in fundamental human rights'.[74] The fundamental rights text is thereby used to construct constitutional identity, but these textual prescriptions are accorded such centrality and normative impact because of the ideals that underpin them.

[69] *McEwan* (n 42) [53].

[70] See, eg *Nervais v R* (n 38) [56]–[68]; F Alexis, 'When Is an Existing Law Saved?' [1976] *Public Law* 256; T Robinson, 'A Trace of Law: State building and the criminalization of buggery in Jamaica' in C Schields and D Herzog (eds), *The Routledge Companion to Sexuality and Colonialism* (Oxford, Routledge, 2021).

[71] *Boyce and Joseph v R* [2004] UKPC 32 (PC Barbados) (7 July 2004), [27].

[72] *Maurice Tomlinson v Attorney General of Jamaica* [2023] JMFC Full 5; *Gareth Henry and Simone Carline Edwards v Jamaica*, Case 13.637, Report No 400/20, Inter-American Commission on Human Rights; cf WRA James, 'In Search of Progress: The Implications of *Caleb Orozco v. AG of Belize* for the Commonwealth Caribbean' (2018) 22 *International Journal of Human Rights* 640.

[73] *Nervais v R* (n 38) [58].

[74] *Nervais v R* (n 38) [58].

In the subsequent decision in *Cuffy v Skerrit*, concerning a right to appeal from a judicial decision on an election petition, the Court again highlighted the superior position of fundamental rights text over other provisions of the Dominican Constitution. Accordingly, while the constitutional provisions establishing jurisdiction to hear appeals from election petitions appear to allow no exceptions, 'it is also the case that the Constitution prescribes that every person in Dominica is entitled to a fair hearing within a reasonable time by an independent and impartial tribunal'.[75] Lower courts were accordingly directed by the CCJ to assume jurisdiction where necessary to give effect to the right to a fair hearing, which is a 'provision of the supreme law that is to be accorded a value that is higher' than the jurisdictional provisions.[76] Again, in resolving tension between sections of the constitution, the Court not only indicates the nature of the essential character of the constitution, but the manner in which that character is constructed.

Fundamental rights are not the only category of value-laden text that inform judicially constructed constitutional identity. Constitutional norms that contribute to identity are also commonly linked to 'national, cultural, or historic peculiarities' that also inform a national collective identity.[77] One such provision is Article 1 of the Constitution of the Co-operative Republic of Guyana, passed in 1980, which was highlighted in *Attorney General of Guyana v Thomas*:

> Article 1 states that Guyana is 'an indivisible, secular, democratic sovereign state in the course of transition from capitalism to socialism …' This aspiration, articulated in this form and as the very first statement in the new Constitution, is unlike any other independent former British Caribbean colony. It is intentional, purposeful, and instrumental. It telegraphs *an intention to establish a new identity and a fortiori to break with what may have been normative in the past that may hinder this intent.* Guyana intends to be and become a social democratic republic (emphasis added).[78]

This type of provision is more likely to be found in one of the newer constitutions, such as that of Guyana, which is more experimental and more expressive of the (local) values upon which the Constitution is founded.

VI. Conclusion and Lessons

The dissonance and disharmony that Jacobsohn identifies as part of the process of constructing constitutional identity is a thread that runs through Caribbean constitutional adjudication. The distance between the text on the one hand, and constitutional experience on the other,[79] is acutely revealed in broadly conservative constitutional texts of the region and longstanding traditional norms being interpreted in innovative and arguably revolutionary ways by the CCJ. This dissonance is certainly vivid in the substantive outcomes of landmark cases argued before the CCJ. For instance, invalidation of laws criminalising sexual minorities and imposing a mandatory death penalty

[75] *Cuffy v Skerrit* [2022] CCJ 12 (Dominica) [49].
[76] ibid [49].
[77] Polzin (n 66) 1606.
[78] *Thomas* (n 39) [136] (Jamadar JCCJ).
[79] GJ Jacobsohn, 'The formation of constitutional identities' in T Ginsburg and R Dixon (eds), *Comparativ[e] Constitutional Law* (Cheltenham, Edward Elgar Publishing, 2011) 131–32.

are transformative societal results from constitutional litigation in generally socially conservative societies. However, the dissonance is also evident in the Court's interpretive approach and choices. Through its interpretive methods, the Court reveals its perception of the character of the constitutions that it interprets and enforces, and plays a central role in constructing and communicating the identities of the constitutions within its jurisdiction.

The CCJ is well-placed to develop and articulate constitutional identities that are rooted in the region's law, history and constitutional values. As an institution that, while regional in its reach, must make decisions based on national constitutive texts, the Court is able to navigate a delicate path between the regionalism occasioned by the small size of Caribbean states and the nationalist inclinations that propelled these states to independence. The corollary is that it is sometimes unclear which features of the CCJ's judgments are regional, applicable to a similar subset of constitutions, or national. Moreover, despite the Court's favourable positioning, a crucial unresolved issue is the scope of impact of the CCJ's approach to constitutional identity in the Caribbean more broadly. The pooling of resources and expertise that is designed to counteract some of the risks and disadvantages of the smallness of the states and societies in the region has not yet convinced the majority of Commonwealth Caribbean states; as noted in section II, only five Caribbean countries have acceded to the appellate jurisdiction of the CCJ. Certainly, there is the potential that the powerful narrative and normative force given to constitutional identity by the CCJ will have an impact that outstrips expectations for a Court with such a small jurisdictional scope and such limited time to develop its jurisprudence. However, the extent to which this approach will nonetheless filter into lower courts in the remaining countries and into the Caribbean jurisprudence of the Judicial Committee of the Privy Council remains to be seen.[80] Ultimately, then, the construction and progression of constitutional identity within the Commonwealth Caribbean is influenced and conditioned by *smallness*, but also by *time* as a reflection of both the region's past and the limited time that the CCJ has had to construct an identity that respects that history and honours the future that the region's constitutions envision.

Finally, however, the borders of the Caribbean are not the limit of potential influence of the CCJ's approach to constitutional identity. The tools employed by the Court, and the manner in which the Court weaves those tools into a narrative about the history and meaning of the constitution, ought to resonate in other jurisdictions. Certainly, the commonality of preambles, unwritten principles and value-laden text suggests that such tools probably play – or should play – a meaningful role in formulating constitutional identity in a range of countries. The Court's positive operationalisation of constitutional identity also offers intriguing prospects for the functions that the concept may play in adjudication; constitutional identity, as shown by the CCJ, has the potential to work as a positive and generative – rather than merely a defensive – concept. The 'agile thinking and innovation'[81] of small states can thereby influence constitutionalism in other states grappling with the definition and assertion of constitutional identity.

[80] On comparative practices within CCJ jurisprudence, see T Robinson and A Bulkan, 'Constitutional Comparisons by a Supranational Court in Flux: The Privy Council and Caribbean Bills of Rights' (2017) 80 *Modern Law Review* 379.

[81] C Morris, 'Navigating Law-Making and Law Reform in Small Jurisdictions' in C Morris (ed), *Making and Changing Law in Small Jurisdictions* (Cham, Springer, 2024) 6.

11

A European Union Style Pacific Common Market?

PETRA BUTLER AND SAM MACINTOSH

I. Introduction

The Pacific islands occupy a vast oceanic region. The region is home to oceans covering almost 20 per cent of the Earth's surface, and the largest global concentration of microstates.[1] While Pacific countries vary widely in population, economic circumstances, development, political status, and stability, they share common socio-cultural values,[2] and face common regional challenges.[3] These include pursuit of deeper regional integration, economic development, and geopolitical security, and addressing the impacts of climate change.[4]

With that in mind, comments made in 2023 by the Honourable Fiamē Naomi Mata'afa, Prime Minister of Samoa, that Australia and New Zealand should make good on their rhetoric of being part of a Pacific family by creating a European Union (EU)-style 'common market' take on particular significance.

The Hon Mata'afa's emphasis was on the creation of a framework that would allow people to move and work freely across the region,[5] and reflected areas of tension in the Pacific region regarding seasonal labour mobility.[6]

To create a common market in the Pacific akin to that in the EU would require further development of intra-regional economic, political, and institutional links,

[1] Hon Fiamē Naomi Mata'afa, '2023 FDC Pacific Lecture' (Old Parliament House, Canberra, March 2023).

[2] H Chen, 'Pacific Island Countries: Trade Integration in a Changing Global Economy' in HE Khor, RP Kronenburg and P Tumbarello (eds), *Resilience and Growth in the Small States of the Pacific* (Washington DC, International Monetary Fund, 2016) 290.

[3] Hon Mata'afa, '2023 FDC Pacific Lecture' (n 1).

[4] ibid.

[5] M Knott, 'Pacific leader calls for European Union-style free movement across the region', *The Sydney Morning Herald* (online ed, Australia, 21 March 2023), www.smh.com.au/politics/federal/pacific-leader-calls-for-european-union-style-free-movement-across-the-region-20230321-p5ctvp.html.

[6] Hon Mata'afa (n 1); Knott (n 5); S Sachdeva, 'Solomons PM joins Pacific push for NZ visa waiver access', *Newsroom* (online ed, New Zealand, 22 March 2023), newsroom.co.nz/2023/03/22/solomons-pm-joins-pacific-push-for-nz-visa-waiver-access/.

alongside potential changes to domestic constitutions. The feasibility of such a common market is far from certain, and the process is complex, particularly in light of existing frameworks and regional bodies.

This chapter explores the question whether the creation of an economic-centred common market in the Pacific would be sufficient to achieve the level of integration that the Hon Mata'afa is striving for, or whether a more fulsome union, and the sovereignty devolution it would entail, is necessary.

Accordingly, section II of the chapter presents a summary of potential 'templates' for common market frameworks, focusing on the EU, but also giving consideration to the structures set out by the Association of Southeast Asian Nations (ASEAN) and the Southern Common Market (MERCOSUR). Section III of this chapter provides an outline of the current picture in the Pacific as it concerns trade and the mobility of labour, before section IV concludes with an evaluation of what the regional integration of a Pacific family might look like.

II. Common Market Frameworks

A. Introduction

Economic theory has developed a series of labels to describe different levels of market integration.[7] The initial economic bonds of free trade agreements (FTAs) result in the removal of all impediments to the movement of goods between signatories, while each retains their complete national sovereignty, autonomy to regulate ulterior trading relations and indeed the movement of other capital and persons.[8] Each subsequent level of integration, up to the creation of a full union, requires increasingly closer ties between states. These can range from cooperation on common external policies in respect of non-Member States (a customs union), to a political union capable of setting policy on non-economic issues (eg foreign policy) through a supranational Parliament.[9]

Theorists argue that integration by states in one area leads to a 'spillover' into integration in other areas of increasing complexity.[10] The development of the EU is a strong example of this. Through initial economic integration, Member States gradually moved to harmonise other policy areas in more politically charged areas. The ultimate result was a shift from total legislative power being held by individual Member States, to the creation of (and commensurate increase in power being held by) supranational institutions acting with collective authority.[11]

Accordingly, the principle underpinning the EU, and indeed all multilateral trading blocs, is that by reducing trade barriers, Member States' economies prosper (boosting

[7] C Barnard, *The Substantive Law of the EU: The Four Freedoms*, 7th edn (Oxford, Oxford University Press, 2022) 8.
[8] ibid 9.
[9] ibid 9.
[10] ibid 20.
[11] ibid 21.

peace domestically) through the free flow of goods, but in doing so states become dependent on one another, making conflict between trading nations uneconomic.[12]

However, there is an inherent trade-off between liberalising trade and the exercise of sovereignty. In the context of the EU, ASEAN and MERCOSUR there is the trade-off of preferential access to Member States' markets and the benefits of trading externally as a bloc, against the devolution of national sovereignty.[13] As is clear, that trade-off can be viewed as a sliding scale, adjusted according to the collective will of a bloc's Member States.

B. European Union

(i) Freedoms of the EU and Single Market

The EU is fundamentally rooted in the pursuit of preventing the outbreak of conflict in Europe.[14] After a history of frequent wars, and in the wake of the destruction wrought by World War II, there arose a need for peace, stability, and economic development in Europe, in addition to a desire to counterbalance the emerging Soviet Union. As a result, the emergence of a European community was finally brought into reality.[15]

Political integration in the European community was achieved with the Treaty of Maastricht in 1992,[16] which was effectively the establishment of the EU as we perceive the organisation today,[17] complete with EU membership for nationals of the Member States, while also creating the foundation for a common currency.[18] The conclusion of the Treaties of Amsterdam, Nice, and Lisbon sought to simplify, enlarge and democratise the EU to its current state.[19]

The EU operates on the founding principles of the 'four freedoms',[20] which establish the framework for the internal single market and provide the basis of the EU's integration.[21] The European Single Market means a unified economic zone across all Member States where goods, services, capital, and labour can move freely without barriers such as tariffs or border controls. It aims to create a seamless economic environment, fostering trade, competition, and economic growth among EU countries while

[12] ibid 6.

[13] Barnard (n 7) 34.

[14] European Union, 'History of the European Union – 1945–59', european-union.europa.eu/principles-countries-history/history-eu/1945-59_en.

[15] T Koh, 'ASEAN and EU: Similarities and Differences' in T Koh and LH Yeo (eds), *ASEAN-EU Partnership. The Untold Story* (Singapore, World Scientific Publishing Co, 2020) 94.

[16] European Parliament, 'Treaty on European Union (TEU)/Maastricht', europarl.europa.eu/about-parliament/en/in-the-past/the-parliament-and-the-treaties/maastricht-treaty.

[17] A Duff, J Pinder and R Pryce, *Maastricht and Beyond: Building a European Union* (Routledge, 1994) 19–20; P Craig and G de Búrca, *EU Law Text, Cases, and Materials*, 8th edn (Oxford, Oxford University Press, 2024) 13.

[18] Duff, Pinder and Pryce (n 17) 20–21.

[19] Craig and de Búrca (n 17) 17–28.

[20] Freedom of movement, freedom of establishment and to provide services, free movement of capital, free movement of workers.

[21] European Union, 'Single Market', european-union.europa.eu/priorities-and-actions/actions-topic/single-market_en.

harmonising regulations and standards to ensure a level playing-field for businesses and consumers.[22]

The Single Market initially focused on eliminating internal trade restrictions such as quantitative limitations and measures with equivalent effects, and establishing a common external tariff. Over time, however, these efforts laid the groundwork for adopting federal models of market governance and implementing the principle of mutual recognition.[23]

Today the EU is a highly integrated supra-national organisation that consists of 27 Member States and speaks with one voice.[24] In this way, the EU has fulfilled its initial objective of pursuing peace among Member States through the harmonisation of economic activity, and eventually crystallisation of political integration.[25] Nonetheless, issues of sovereignty remain, particularly given the innate tensions in preserving national sovereignty as between the Member States and supra-national institutions, which have increasingly sought for the EU to act internationally as an entity with its own principle and values.[26]

(ii) Fundamental Legal Framework of the EU

The EU as an organisation is a 'community of law'. As such, actions taken by EU are based on the principle of the rule of law,[27] and on treaties that have been voluntarily and democratically adopted by all EU Member States and are binding between them.[28]

The primary treaties relating to the function of the EU are the Treaty on the European Union (TEU) and the Treaty on the Functioning of the European Union (TFEU). The TEU forms the basis of EU law, by setting out the EU's purpose and the governance of its central institutions.[29] Conversely, the TFEU sets out in far greater detail the basis of EU law by defining the principles and objectives of the EU and the scope for action within its policy area. It also includes a number of fundamental provisions such as the types and areas of competence of the EU.[30]

[22] EUR-Lex, 'Internal Market', eur-lex.europa.eu/summary/chapter/internal_market.html?root_default=SUM_1_CODED%3D24&locale=en.

[23] M Maciejewski and C Ratcliff, 'Fact Sheets on the European Parliament' (European Parliament, April 2019).

[24] European Union, 'Principles, countries, history' (European Union), european-union.europa.eu/principles-countries-history_en.

[25] Duff, Pinder and Pryce (n 17) 20–21.

[26] T Karakamisheva-Jovanovska, 'The Challenges of the "Ever Closer Union" Concept and the Protection of the Sovereignty and Constitutional Identity of EU Member States – The Role of National Constitutional Courts and the EU Court of Justice in the Post-Westphalian Order of the Union' (2023) 4(2) *Central European Journal of Comparative Law* 69, 74.

[27] Consolidated Version of the Treaty on European Union [2016] OJ C 202, art 6; Case 294/83 *Parti écologiste 'Les Verts' v European Parliament* ECLI:EU:C:1986:166, [1986] ECR 1339, [23]; R Mańko, 'Briefing: The EU as a community of law' (European Parliamentary Research Service, March 2017).

[28] European Union, 'Founding agreements', european-union.europa.eu/principles-countries-history/principles-and-values/founding-agreements_en.

[29] European Union, 'Treaty on the European Union', eur-lex.europa.eu/EN/legal-content/summary/treaty-on-european-union.html.

[30] Mańko (n 27).

(iii) Competences

The EU legislature (comprising the Parliament and the Council of Ministers) is bound by the will of the constituent Member States as expressed in the Treaties, which set out the fields of potential EU legislative activity. Those limitations are expressed as the principle of conferral,[31] according to which the EU has only those competences conferred upon it by the Member States.[32]

Exclusive competences allow the EU to act with sole power in certain areas, such as the functioning of the customs union and establishment of competition policy.[33] However, 'shared' competences allow the EU and the Member States to act in the same field at the same time.[34] Such fields include the internal market and its various freedoms, and certain aspects of social policy.[35]

To grant the EU exclusive or shared competence the Member States have to relinquish a degree of national sovereignty. The relinquishment of sovereignty must conform with the Member States' constitutions. Particularly instructive is the jurisprudence of the German Federal Constitutional Court (*Bundesverfassungsgericht*) regarding the relationship of the German Basic Law and EU law.[36] In *Solange I* the Court determined that it would refrain from closely scrutinising EU actions as long as the protection of fundamental rights was ensured.[37] The Court went on to hold that in the case at hand Community law was not congruent with the Basic Law since

> the Community still does not have a democratically elected Parliament with full legislative powers, chosen by general suffrage, to which the legislative bodies of the Community are politically accountable. Additionally, it lacks a codified catalogue of fundamental rights, with their content clearly and reliably established for the future, much like the provisions of a Constitution.[38]

In *Solange II* the Court held that the EU human rights protection has since evolved to a level on par with the protection afforded by the Basic Law.[39] The Court has, on numerous occasions since then, tested the compatibility of EU law with the German Basic Law.[40] The Court found the key constitutional consideration to be whether the EU had acted outside the bounds of the competences conferred on it by the primary treaties of the EU. If such actions had occurred, the EU will be taken to have directly breached citizens' fundamental rights. The Court went on to note that it retained a responsibility

[31] Consolidated Version of the Treaty on the Functioning of the European Union [2016] OJ C 202. Article 5(2).

[32] Mańko (n 27).

[33] TFEU, art 3(1); R Schütze, 'EU Competences: Existence and Exercise' in D Chalmers and A Arnull (eds), *The Oxford Handbook of European Union Law* (Oxford, Oxford University Press, February 2016) 85.

[34] Schütze, ibid, 86.

[35] EUR-Lex, 'Division of competences within the European Union' (EUR-Lex, 24 February 2022).

[36] The term EU law encompasses the different stages of integration, eg The Treaty of Rome (1958), Maastricht Treaty (1993), and the Treaty of Lisbon (2009).

[37] BVerfGE 37, 271 B-I para 4.

[38] BVerfGE 37, 271 B-I para 7c.

[39] BVerfGE 73, 339.

[40] See, for example, Maastricht-Urteil BVerfGE 89, 155; Bundesverfassungsgericht 2 BvR 547/21, 2 BvR 798/21 (6 December 2022).

to review the actions of the EU, and to police actions taken ultra vires.[41] The German Constitutional Court approaches issues of EU competence from the position that the Member States are 'Masters of the Treaties', and remain fundamentally sovereign entities.[42] That approach has been echoed by the constitutional courts of other Member States.[43]

(iv) Summary

The EU is a supranational political and economic union. Member States have relinquished a degree of sovereignty and bestowed regulatory power on the EU. The force of the EU's regulatory power is such that it causes unilateral regulatory globalisation, called the Brussels effect.[44] However, as the *Solange* jurisprudence makes clear, the conditions upon which national sovereignty is bestowed remain an open issue.

The German Constitutional Court (and others) view Member State sovereignty and its devolution as questions of supranationalism and constitutional identity.[45] On the other hand, commentators have suggested that one of the core principles of the EU, as set out in Article 4(2) TEU, call on it to respect *national* identity rather than conceptions of sovereignty, or specific constitutional identity.[46] Resultantly, the Court of Justice of the EU (CJEU) and other supranational bodies should seek to uphold the exclusive competence of Member States to act in areas unique to their own national identities such as areas involving the state's official language.[47]

C. Association of Southeast Asian Nations (ASEAN)

ASEAN is the poster child for South-East Asia's economic integration, and it also plays a central role in the area's regional cooperation.[48] In 1967 Indonesia, Malaysia, the Philippines, Singapore and Thailand, through the Bangkok Declaration, founded ASEAN as a forum for economic cooperation between these developing countries. They were later joined by Brunei Darussalam, Vietnam, Lao PDR, Myanmar and Cambodia.[49] These nations later founded the ASEAN Free Trade Agreement (AFTA) in 1993.[50]

In 2003, through agreement to the Bali Concord II, ASEAN announced the formation of the ASEAN Community pursuant to three pillars: the ASEAN Economic

[41] Bundesverfassungsgericht 2 BvR 547/21, 2 BvR 798/21 (6 December 2022) I-1.
[42] E Cloots, 'National Identity, Constitutional Identity, and Sovereignty in the EU' (2016) 45(2) *Netherlands Journal of Legal Philosophy* 93.
[43] ibid, 92–93.
[44] A Bradford, '*The Brussels Effect: How the European Union Rules the World* (Oxford, Oxford University Press, 2020) 1–2.
[45] ibid 92.
[46] ibid 92.
[47] ibid 86.
[48] K Ishikawa, 'The ASEAN Economic Community and ASEAN economic integration' (2021) 10(1) *Journal of Contemporary East Asia Studies* 24.
[49] ASEAN, 'History', asean.org/the-founding-of-asean/.
[50] Ishikawa (n 48) 24.

Community (AEC); the ASEAN Security Community (ASC); and the ASEAN Socio-Cultural Community (ASCC).

Importantly, the evolution of ASEAN integration began as, and has remained, a state-led project. ASEAN's flexible organisational set-up pursuant to the Bangkok Declaration demonstrates that it is fundamentally concerned with cooperation rather than integration.[51]

While the practical driver of ASEAN is often viewed as economic cooperation,[52] commentators have suggested that the growth of ASEAN as an economic community is a comparatively recent development, and was preceded by a desire for socio-political stability within the region.[53] That objective remains embedded in the political, security, and socio-cultural pillars underpinning ASEAN to this day.[54]

While the AFTA proved successful in reducing intra-ASEAN tariffs, the AEC was established with the objective of deepening economic integration through the free movement of services, investment, capital and skilled workers.[55]

To achieve that goal, measures were developed to attract foreign capital, including the conclusion of FTAs with countries outside the region. To make the region more attractive as a foreign investment destination, ASEAN created an integrated market and promoted economic integration with countries outside the region through FTAs.[56]

(i) Regional Integration

ASEAN economic integration has intensified over the years, with roughly 23 per cent of regional trade occurring between ASEAN countries in 2016.[57] Further, intra-ASEAN investments provided the largest contributor to Foreign Direct Investment flows in the region and reached a record high of US$27 billion in 2017, contributing 19 per cent to the total inflows, mostly from Singapore, Malaysia, and Thailand.[58]

The bloc's approach to *trade* integration is, in some ways, similar to the approach taken by the EU. ASEAN has adopted a product- and sector-specific methodology to address non-trade barriers (NTB) and harmonise non-trade measures (NTM) extant between Member States.[59] However, unlike the EU, reduction of NTBs and harmonisation of NTMs were initially left as a self-assessment task to be undertaken by Member States individually and, accordingly, compliance with the implementation of

[51] I Deinla, 'The Development of the Rule of Law in ASEAN' (PhD Thesis, University of New South Wales, 2009) 40.

[52] D Park, C Castillejos-Petalcorin and J Kim, 'Analysis of Brexit and its Policy Lessons for Asian Integration' (2020) Asia Development Bank Institute Working Paper 1189, www.adb.org/sites/default/files/publication/637991/adbi-wp1189.pdf.

[53] Deinla (n 51) 38.

[54] Park, Castillejos-Petalcorin and Kim (n 52) 7.

[55] Ishikawa (n 48) 25; F Jurje and S Lavenex, 'ASEAN Economic Community: what model for labour mobility?' (January 2015) NCCR Working Paper 2015/2, p 2, https://www.wti.org/media/filer_public/24/f2/24f2c553-c4cc-4cc2-b670-6144e31d453c/nccr_working_paper_asean_jurje_lavenex__.pdf.

[56] Ishikawa (n 48) 38; Park, Castillejos-Petalcorin and Kim (n 52) 7.

[57] Park, Castillejos-Petalcorin and Kim (n 52) 8.

[58] Park, Castillejos-Petalcorin and Kim (n 52) 8.

[59] J Kean, J Kennan, S Page and C Stevens, 'Dealing with Non-tariff Barriers in South Asia' in M Razzaque and Y Basnett (eds), *Regional Integration in South Asia: Trends, Challenges, and Prospects* (Commonwealth Secretariat, 2014) 126.

an intra-bloc common tariff was left to individual states.[60] Limited cooperation was facilitated through a collective definition of NTBs, and through working groups set up at the ASEAN secretariat level.[61]

As a result, the harmonisation of standards has proceeded in a largely ad hoc manner and has meant that harmonisation of regional standards for products in key sectors, such as agriculture, remains a work in progress.[62]

(ii) Freedom of Movement

The ASEAN Agreement on the Movement of Natural Persons was concluded in 2012 to promote the mobility of skilled labour.[63] Mutual Recognition Agreements (MRAs) concluded in relation to eight professional services further facilitate sector-specific mobility.[64] Labour rights were further integrated through the 2007 ASEAN Declaration on Protection and Promotion of the Rights of Migrant Workers. This declaration gives a framework for employment protection, payment of wages, access to decent working and living conditions, and anti-trafficking. However, as a Declaration, it does not, in and of itself require ratification at the national level, with the result that Member State implementation has been haphazard at best.[65]

ASEAN has separately sought to liberalise trade in services through the implementation of the ASEAN Framework Agreement on Services (AFAS).[66] However, the measures have largely failed to live up to expectations.[67] Practically, AFAS serves only to facilitate the mobility of business visitors (30 to 90 days) and intra-corporate transferees, such as professionals, managers and qualified staff (between two and up to five / eight years).[68] Further, domestic immigration procedures, quotas, economic needs tests, pre-employment requirements as well as technological transfer conditions continue to hinder free movement.[69]

(iii) The ASEAN Way

Southeast Asian leaders saw ASEAN as a framework for providing a platform for the tailoring of 'regional solutions to regional problems'.[70] Its establishment was in part born

[60] ibid.
[61] ibid.
[62] ibid.
[63] ASEAN Agreement on the Movement of Natural Persons (Phnom Penh, 19 November 2012); Ishikawa (n 48), 30; Jurje and Lavenex (n 55) 9.
[64] Ishikawa (n 48) 30; Jurje and Lavenex (n 55) 3.
[65] Jurje and Lavenex (n 55) 9.
[66] ASEAN Framework Agreement on Services (AFAS) (Bangkok, 15 December 1995).
[67] Ishikawa (n 48) 29; Jurje and Lavenex (n 55) 4.
[68] D Nikomborirak and J Supunnavadee, 'ASEAN Trade in Services' in S Basu Das, J Menon, R Severino and OL Shrestha (eds), *The ASEAN Economic Community: A Work in Progress* (Singapore, Asia Development Bank, 2013) 103; Jurje and Lavenex (n 55) 5.
[69] Jurje and Lavenex (n 55) 5.
[70] Deinla (n 51) 41.

out of the fear that regional issues, left unmanaged, would invite unwelcome intervention by outside powers at a national and regional level.[71]

With that in mind, while ASEAN has achieved the highest level of regional integration within Asia,[72] its brand of regionalism is fundamentally based on consensus and informality[73] rather than the presence of binding rules and formal institutions characteristic of the EU. Further, ASEAN Member States remain firmly committed to classical tenets of sovereignty and non-intervention.[74]

Non-interference has been a core principle in ASEAN since its founding in 1967 and has remained embedded in its institutions to the present day. Initially, non-interference was upheld in order to prioritise regional integration, irrespective of undemocratic regimes in Member States.[75] However, the continuation of non-interference in present-day ASEAN can be attributed largely to the individual strength of Member States, and their shared understanding that they can or should rely on their state strength to handle domestic issues.[76]

Despite ASEAN institutions having the technical capacity to act more intrusively in the domestic issues of the bloc's Member States,[77] the principle of non-interference continues as an effective block to deeper institutional and political integration and remains part of the 'ASEAN Way'.[78] Other principles falling within ASEAN's particular method of cooperation include recognition of national sovereignty and state equality, peaceful settlement of disputes, and effective inter-state cooperation.[79]

However, even if further integration was pursued, commentators have suggested that significant obstacles remain through economic disparities between Member States and the extreme diversity of political, social, and cultural values in the region.[80]

D. Southern Common Market (MERCOSUR)

In 1991 Argentina, Brazil, Paraguay and Uruguay established MERCOSUR by signing the Treaty of Asunción with the objective of creating a common market, inducing development and strengthening democracy in its Member States.[81] The four countries agreed to eliminate customs duties, implement a common external tariff (CET) of 35 per cent on certain imports from outside the bloc, and adopt a common trade policy toward outside countries and blocs. In a similar vein to the original purpose of the precursor

[71] Deinla (n 51) 9.
[72] Park, Castillejos-Petalcorin and Kim (n 52) 2.
[73] Deinla (n 51) 1.
[74] Deinla (n 51) 291.
[75] S Suzuki, 'Why is ASEAN not intrusive? Non-interference meets state strength' (2019) 8(2) *Journal of Contemporary East Asia Studies* 157.
[76] ibid.
[77] ibid.
[78] Deinla (n 51) 7.
[79] Deinla (n 51) 7.
[80] Ishikawa (n 48) 25.
[81] Treaty establishing a Common Market (Asunción Treaty) between the Argentine Republic, the Federative Republic of Brazil, the Republic of Paraguay and the Eastern Republic of Uruguay (Asunción, 26 March 1991); 'H Simoes, 'MERCOSUR: Challenges and Opportunities in the Regional and Global Order' (2024) 15(1) *cience and Public Administration Journal* 57.

to the EU, the bloc was initially created as an instrument to improve relations between regional rivals Argentina and Brazil.

The founding states were subsequently joined by Venezuela in 2012, although since 2016 that country has suspended its adherence to the economic, human rights and immigration agreements that govern MERCOSUR. Venezuela nonetheless remains a full member of MERCOSUR, even in suspension.[82] As of 2024, Bolivia has been accepted as a new permanent member subject to its completion of the entry process.[83] Other MERCOSUR States have pledged technical support to Bolivia in conforming its national legislation to fulfil bloc requirements.[84] Chile, Colombia, Ecuador, Guyana, Peru, and Suriname are associate members of MERCOSUR. They receive tariff reductions when trading with the full members but do not enjoy full voting rights or free access to members' markets.

Following the Treaty of Asunción, in 1994 MERCOSUR's Member States entered into the Ouro Preto Protocol, which gave MERCOSUR international legal personality, and outlined its institutional framework.[85] The Protocol consolidated Member States' commitment to a consensus-based decision-making process, and to the adoption of a CET.[86]

The Protocol established a MERCOSUR trade commission, and a Parliament – known as Parlasur – which serves in an advisory role.[87] The Protocol also served to further define the role of the bloc's two decision-making bodies: the Common Market Council, which provides a high-level forum for coordinating foreign and economic policy; and the Common Market Group, which coordinates macroeconomic policy.[88]

(i) Regional Integration

MERCOSUR resisted supranational integration, preferring instead to rely on a form of intergovernmental integration, whereby any norms or resolutions formulated by MERCOSUR's institutions still require ratification and internalisation by Member States' governments.[89] In practice, the views of MERCOSUR's institutions therefore receive scant political priority by the national governments of the bloc's Member States, especially Brazil.[90]

[82] ibid.

[83] MERCOSUR, 'MERCOSUR In Brief', mercosur.int/en/about-mercosur/mercosur-in-brief/; Simoes (n 81) 57.

[84] Simoes (n 81) 57.

[85] Additional Protocol to the Asunción Treaty on the institutional structure of Mercosur (Ouro Preto Protocol) (Ouro Preto, Brazil, 17 December 1994); BT Luciano and A Campos, 'Supranationalism as a taboo: analysing the 30 years of Mercosur's institutional development' (2021) 10 *Brazilian Journal of International Relations* 105.

[86] ibid.

[87] Chapter 1, Ouro Preto Protocol.

[88] Articles 9–15 of Asunción Treaty (n 81).

[89] Luciano and Campos (n 85); P Veiga and S Rios, 'MERCOSUR experience in regional integration: what could Africa learn from it?' (June 2019) Policy Center for the New South, Policy Paper PP-19/07, 21, https://www.policycenter.ma/sites/default/files/PCNS-PP1907.pdf.

[90] Simoes (n 81) 57; Veiga and Rios (n 89) 20.

This is at least in part owing to the theory that larger countries have less incentive than smaller ones to negotiate on themes perceived as hindering their economic sovereignty in policy areas where they value their national autonomy.[91] In doing so, larger economies preserve their status, and ability to influence strategies for regional integration, while simultaneously pursuing their own global ambitions.[92] Putting that principle into practice, Brazil has historically pursued national autonomy and sovereignty in the implementation of its own broad trade and industrial policy in areas favourable to the state, and to the detriment of deeper regional integration.[93]

Further, given their original non-executive advisory roles, MERCOSUR's institutions have never possessed significant institutional means to demand or gain additional competences over time, which has, in practice, hindered the transformation of these non-executive institutions into supranational bodies.[94]

(ii) Permanent Review Tribunal (PRT)

The need for a dispute resolution mechanism was recognised at the outset of MERCOSUR, and in its first meeting in 1991 the Common Market Group agreed that disputes would be dealt with by tiered resolution, beginning with negotiation and culminating in ad hoc arbitration.[95]

However, in 2002 MERCOSUR approved the Protocol of Olivos,[96] which provided for the creation of the Permanent Review Tribunal (PRT).[97] The PRT is the highest adjudicatory body in MERCOSUR and its awards are binding on the parties before it.[98] Its implementation was a watershed moment in allowing for consistent interpretations of MERCOSUR law, and in its inaugural decision the PRT found the nature of MERCOSUR law to be 'integration law', which consequently takes precedence over international law typically at play in the resolution of Member States' disputes.[99] In making its findings, the PRT relied heavily on CJEU jurisprudence, opening the door to suggestions that the PRT would take up a supranational mantle in a similar way to the CJEU.

Nonetheless, the primary distinction between the PRT and the CJEU remains that there is an absence of a recognised supreme 'integration law' of general application in MERCOSUR.[100] The award of the PRT in *Laudo No 1/2005*, while binding on the parties, did not require adherence by other Member States. By eschewing the development of a supranational legal system, principles formulated at an intergovernmental level remain subject to the process of incorporation into national legal systems, and in the manner defined by national constitutions.[101]

[91] Veiga and Rios (n 89) 18.
[92] Luciano and Campos (n 85) 108.
[93] Veiga and Rios (n 89) 18.
[94] Luciano and Campos (n 85) 109.
[95] Luciano and Campos (n 85) 111.
[96] Olivos Protocol for the Settlement of Disputes in MERCOSUR (Olivos, 18 February 2002).
[97] ibid 112.
[98] Deinla (n 51) 147.
[99] *Laudo* [Award] No 1/2005 of 20 December 2005 (*Import Ban on Remolded Tires (Uruguay v Argentina)*; Deinla (n 51) 147.
[100] Luciano and Campos (n 85) 112.
[101] ibid.

(iii) Freedom of Movement

In brief, MERCOSUR'S Residence Agreement, which entered into force in 2009,[102] regulates the free movement of peoples within the bloc. Under the Agreement, MERCOSUR offers free movement of MERCOSUR citizens, as well as Bolivian and Chilean nationals, within the bloc provided that they have no criminal record within the past five years.[103] In particular, it allows for the renewable duration of one to two years for independent professionals, intra-corporate transferees and contractual service suppliers and, in Argentina, even an indefinite period for the duration of the relevant working contract.[104] That is granted through a right of residency and work which may be transformed into permanent residency.[105] Nevertheless, domestic labour legislation continues to hinder true free movement, such as the Brazilian requirement for economic need tests for foreign service providers. Notably, the Residence Agreement also lacks the implementation of MRAs.[106]

(iv) Summary

From the models set out above it is clear that inter-state integration will be heavily influenced by the economic, socio-cultural, and political environment in which it arises. In the case of ASEAN, lingering concerns around external party interference, coupled with a drive to foster broad cooperation, has provided an excellent foundation for the development of an informal, state-based forum to aid resolution of regional issues.

Conversely, MERCOSUR and the EU sought to implement more rigid structures to govern the process of integration, and to foster deeper integration. However, MERCOSUR took a slightly different approach, and while establishing regional bodies to guide the bloc, it retained a fundamentally intergovernmental position towards integration. In doing so it retained the sovereignty of Member States, but at the expense of conferring powers to regional bodies. The EU on the other hand involved far more sovereignty conferred by individual Member States on the Union, which while leading to questions around the extent of the EU's powers vis-à-vis individual Members, has resulted in the most integrated model.

III. The Pacific Islands

A. Introduction

Pacific Island Countries (PICs) face unique domestic developmental challenges, such as small domestic markets, accessibility to global production networks, lack of

[102] The Residence Agreement for Nationals of the Member States of MERCOSUR and Associated States (Bolivia and Chile) (signed 2002, entered into force 2009).
[103] Jurje and Lavenex (n 55) 19.
[104] ibid 14.
[105] ibid 19.
[106] ibid 20.

investment, and the impact of their geographically isolated location on trade costs and opportunities.[107] While significant progress has been made by PICs towards regional integration and trade liberalisation, existing preferential market access arrangements have been substantially reduced, leading Pacific Island exports to lose their competitiveness and market share in international markets.[108]

Recently, PIC leaders have developed and advanced the concept of the 'Blue Pacific'. This formulation is intended to encourage PICs to act as a 'Blue Continent' based on a shared stewardship of the ocean.[109] The narrative sees PICs exercising stronger strategic autonomy,[110] and provides renewed impetus to deepening Pacific regionalism.[111]

Further, the future of regionalism within the Pacific Islands is likely to be influenced heavily by geography, geopolitics, and economics. While economic considerations will also continue to affect patterns of integration much as they always have, it will be wider geopolitical concerns and regional climate issues that will likely provide the greatest incentive for future integration.

B. Existing Frameworks

(i) Socio-political Framework

The establishment of the Pacific Islands Forum (PIF), in 1971, provided for the creation of cooperative institutions, and gave shape to a new Pacific voice and regional identity.[112] It has subsequently become the primary agency for regionalism in Oceania,[113] and gives Pacific Islanders a stronger presence in international affairs.[114] Notably, the PIF has the most diverse membership of any current regional grouping, comprising 18 members ranging from OECD nations to Pacific Small Island Developing States (PSIDS).[115]

Further sub-regional integration has also been pursued through groups such as the Polynesian Leaders Group, the Micronesian Chief Executives' Summit, and the Melanesian Spearhead Group (MSG – to which Papua New Guinea, the Solomon Islands, Vanuatu and Fiji are parties),[116] among others.[117] As a result, while sub-regional

[107] K Tavola, 'Towards a New Regional Diplomacy Architecture' in G Fry and S Tarte (eds), *The New Pacific Diplomacy* (Canberra, ANU Press, 2015) 30.
[108] Chen (n 2) 289; MB Malua, 'Case Study: The Pacific Islands' in *Turning losses into gains: SIDS and multilateral trade liberalisation in agriculture* (UNCTAD, June 2003) 175, unctad.org/system/files/official-document/ditctncd20031p5_en.pdf.
[109] J Wallis, 'Submission – Strengthening Australia's relationships with countries in the Pacific region' (Canberra, Australian National University, July 2020) 2, aph.gov.au/DocumentStore.ashx?id=3e5c73e9-4a1 2-462d-b809-3fa047fa8ec1&subId=679921.
[110] Mata'afa (n 1).
[111] Wallis (n 109) 2.
[112] M Pöllath, 'Revisiting island decolonization: The pursuit of self-government in Pacific island polities under US hegemony' (2018) 13(1) *Island Studies Journal* 235, 239.
[113] D Canyon, 'Time for the Pacific Islands Forum to Step-Back and Heal' (Daniel K. Inouye Asia-Pacific Center for Security Studies, 2021) https://apcss.org/nexus_articles/time-for-the-pacific-islands-forum-to-step-back-and-heal/.
[114] Pöllath (n 112) 239.
[115] Canyon (n 113) 1.
[116] Chen (n 2) 290.
[117] Tavola (n 107) 34.

bodies provide valuable guidance within their own communities, regional architecture as a whole remains fragmented.

That fragmentation has been recognised by the PIF, and its resolution is outlined as an objective in the organisation's 2050 Blue Pacific Continent Strategy.

(ii) Economic Framework

Pursuit of economic liberalisation and integration in the Pacific has been primarily pursued through overlapping multilateral FTAs; most notable are the Pacific Agreement on Closer Economic Relations (PACER Plus) and Pacific Island Countries Trade Agreement (PICTA), both of which are intended to encourage trade liberalisation and deepen regional integration.

In 2001, PICTA was opened for signature by PICs in Nauru.[118] The multilateral agreement is the first and only FTA between 14 of the Pacific Island Forum countries, but excludes Australia and New Zealand (which are also PIF members).[119] The Agreement has the broad objective of promoting regional integration among signatories[120] by progressively eliminating tariffs and other barriers to trade with the ultimate goal of eventually creating a 'single regional market among the Pacific Island economies'.[121] However, while PICTA was initially seen as a stepping stone to further integration of signatories with Australia and New Zealand, and trade liberalisation generally, only the Cook Islands, Fiji, Niue, Samoa, the Solomon Islands, Tuvalu and Vanuatu have actively pursued its implementation.[122]

PACER Plus was launched in Tonga on 14 June 2017, covering goods, services, investment, labour, sanitary and phytosanitary (SPS) measures, aid and other issues. The Agreement brought closure to eight years of negotiations between Australia, New Zealand and eight PICs:[123] the Cook Islands, Kiribati, Niue, Samoa, the Solomon Islands, Tonga, Tuvalu, and Vanuatu. Further, a ninth PIC, Nauru, has signed but has not yet ratified the Agreement.[124] Papua New Guinea and Fiji chose not to sign up.

[118] S Chand, 'Shaping New Regionalism in the Pacific Islands: Back to the Future?' ADB Working Paper Series on Regional Economic Integration No 61 (Manila, Asian Development Bank, October 2010), 16 www.econstor.eu/bitstream/10419/109573/1/wp-061.pdf.

[119] 'Pacific Island Countries Trade Agreement (PICTA)' (Samoa Ministry of Foreign Affairs and Trade), www.mfat.gov.ws/pacific-island-countries-trade-agreement-picta/.

[120] ILO Office for Pacific Island Countries, *Labour Mobility in Pacific Island Countries* (International Labour Organization, November 2019) 22, www.ilo.org/sites/default/files/wcmsp5/groups/public/@asia/@ro-bangkok/@ilo-suva/documents/publication/wcms_712549.pdf.

[121] Article 1, Clause [e] of the Pacific Island Countries Trade Agreement (Nauru, 18 August 2001); see also Chand (n 118) 16.

[122] B Natens and R Kumar, 'The Pacific Islands and Trade in Services: One Step Back to Take Two Steps Forward' (2015) 12(1) *Transnational Dispute Management* (Special Issue: 'The Pacific Rim and International Economic Law: Opportunities and Risks of the Pacific Century').

[123] 'Pacific Agreement on Closer Economic Cooperation (PACER) Plus' (*UN LDC Portal – International Support Measures for Least Developed Countries*), www.un.org/ldcportal/content/pacific-agreement-closer-economic-cooperation-pacer-plus.

[124] New Zealand Ministry of Foreign Affairs and Trade, 'PACER Plus Overview: The Agreement', www.mfat.govt.nz/en/trade/free-trade-agreements/free-trade-agreements-in-force/pacer-plus/overview.

PACER Plus, while operating as a multilateral FTA between PICs, Australia, and New Zealand,[125] was primarily negotiated for the purpose of facilitating the gradual and progressive integration of PICs into the international economy and bringing them into line with international rules developed by the World Trade Organization.[126]

The structure of PACER Plus accelerated PICs' integration with the rest of the world by facilitating capacity building, fiscal reform and structural adjustment between signatories,[127] but the trade-off was that Australia and New Zealand received most-favoured nation (MFN) treatment.[128] In doing so, Australia and New Zealand were provided with similar low-tariff access to PIC markets as had been set out in PICTA. Practically, this is problematic for PIC producers, who may struggle to compete with goods manufactured in Australia or New Zealand, then sold at comparative prices.

Intra-regional trade between PICs is relatively low, with most registering significant trade deficits, particularly among non-resource-rich states.[129] However, rather than being the product of non-performing trade policy, low trade volumes among PICs could be attributed to the fact that while PICs may share common socio-cultural features, they are not 'natural' trade partners.[130] This is particularly the case among smaller PICs with fewer goods and services to offer, and results in significantly lower trade complementarities.[131] Notably, and as will be explored below, the absence of strong economic ties militates against the applicability of EU-centric theories of 'spillover', and the growth of integration from mercantile underpinnings.

(iii) Economics of Labour Mobility

One exception to the intra-PIC trade deficits is temporary migration.[132] This is illustrated by the fact that in 2023, 16,144 temporary PIC workers from PACER Plus signatory states worked in New Zealand's agriculture and horticulture sectors through the New Zealand Recognised Seasonal Employer (RSE) programme, and remitted over NZ$116 million to their home states[133] (an amount equivalent to approximately 16 per cent of the total import value from PACER Plus signatories to New Zealand for that year).

Australia's Pacific Australia Labour Mobility (PALM) scheme is also a significant provider of employment to PIC workers, with 35,494 people recorded as having

[125] Chand (n 118) 16.
[126] New Zealand Ministry of Foreign Affairs and Trade (n 124); Chand (n 118) 16.
[127] Pacific Network on Globalisation, 'A Critical Response to PICTA, PACER and the Pacific Islands Forum's Social Impact Assessment' (Press Release, 19 February 2002), www.scoop.co.nz/stories/WO0202/S00068/a-critical-response-to-picta-pacer.htm; I Sandford, 'Expanding the trade litigator's toolkit: Developing tools to achieve effective and legitimate resolution or disputes under PACER Plus and other trade agreements' in S Frankel & MK Lewis (eds) *Trade Agreements at the Crossroads* (London, Routledge, 2014) 36.
[128] New Zealand Ministry of Foreign Affairs and Trade New Zealand (n 124); Chand (n 118) 16.
[129] Chen (n 2) 293.
[130] ibid 290.
[131] ibid.
[132] ibid 292.
[133] New Zealand Ministry of Foreign Affairs and Trade (n 124).

participated in various iterations of the scheme between 2008 and 2023.[134] The PIF has reported that in Samoa, remittances from Samoan migrant workers in Australia make up around 18 per cent of GDP, the equivalent percentage to the manufacturing, agriculture, and mining industries combined in Australia. In Tonga, remittances make up 40 per cent of GDP.[135] Remittances provide a powerful economic force which contributes to economic growth, improved living standards and increasing imports and consumption in PICs.[136]

In the era of climate change, labour mobility has also helped provide insurance against negative domestic market shocks,[137] and a safety net for instances where resource-based livelihoods are less productive, due to extreme weather events or longer-term climate trends.[138] The importance of promoting labour mobility has been recognised by the PIF, and has been underscored in Forum meetings as a source of revenue, knowledge transfer, and employment opportunities, especially for Pacific youth.[139] However, PICs also recognise the unintended consequences of labour mobility, which can include social issues such as the breakdown of family structures, and risks to physical wellbeing,[140] alongside economic issues around domestic PIC labour and skill shortages.[141]

Accordingly, in negotiating PACER Plus in 2009, PICs sought a broader agreement than the rights offered through the PALM and RSE schemes, envisaging an agreement similar to the Australia–New Zealand Closer Economic Relationship Trade Agreement,[142] which allows unrestricted labour migration between those two countries. PICs also sought stronger commitments to safeguard the benefits the region gains from labour mobility.[143]

While these aims did not come to fruition, negotiations were successful in agreeing a non-legally binding engagement platform alongside PACER Plus: the Arrangement on Labour Mobility (ALM).[144] This Arrangement enhances regional cooperation on labour mobility through the creation of institutions such as the Pacific Labour Mobility Annual Meeting (PLMAM).[145] The PLMAM is funded by the governments of Australia and New Zealand, with facilitation provided by the PACER Plus Implementation Unit, in its role as the Labour Mobility Secretariat.[146] The Meeting provides PICs an opportunity

[134] Australian Department of Employment and Workplace Relations, 'Consultations on PALM scheme deed of Agreement and Guidelines: Expanding and improving the PALM scheme' (2023) Document D23/370219.

[135] Pacific Islands Forum Secretariat, 'Comprehensive Assessment of Regional and Sub-Regional Labour Mobility Arrangements in the Pacific' (December 2022) 10, forumsec.org/publications/comprehensive-assessment-regional-and-sub-regional-labour-mobility-arrangements.

[136] ibid.

[137] ibid 10.

[138] ibid 7.

[139] 'Labour Mobility' (*Pacific Islands Forum*), forumsec.org/labour-mobility.

[140] ibid.

[141] C Bedford, 'Growing pains: Samoa's participation in New Zealand and Australia's Pacific labour schemes' (*DevPolicy Blog*, 7 November 2022), devpolicy.org/samoas-participation-in-nz-and-australias-pacific-labour-schemes-20221107.

[142] Australia–New Zealand Closer Economic Relationship Trade Agreement (Canberra, 28 March 1983).

[143] A Kautoke-Holani, 'Labour Mobility in the PACER Plus' (2018) 5(1) *Asia & the Pacific Policy Studies* 90–93.

[144] Arrangement on Labour Mobility (July 2017).

[145] ILO Office for Pacific Island Countries (n 120) 22.

[146] PACER Plus Implementation Unit, 'Seventh Pacific Annual Labour Mobility Meeting Taking Regional Labour Mobility Cooperation to the Next Level' (Press Release, 24 November 2023) pacerplus.org/resources

to foster high-level regional cooperation regarding both existing mobility schemes and new initiatives with Australia and New Zealand.[147] The PLMAM also seeks to strengthen the legislative, regulatory and institutional frameworks for labour mobility in the participating countries.[148]

Accordingly, given its existing regional and economic importance, increased freedom of movement and labour may provide a founding pillar for further Pacific integration, rather than being a consequent step in a traditional integration process initiated through trade.

IV. Building a 'Pacific Family'

A. Blue Pacific Continent

Potential pillars aside, the starting point for deeper Pacific integration is naturally the regional framework proposed by the PIF in the '2050 Strategy for the Blue Pacific Continent'.[149] The framework is broken down into seven thematic areas, of which this chapter will focus on one – 'Political Leadership and Regionalism'.[150]

Notably, the framework suggested by the Blue Pacific strategy is reminiscent of ASEAN in a number of ways, in that it provides for a state-centric approach; calling for respect of national sovereignty, non-interference, and consensus-based decision-making, while urging states to remain mindful of 'collective regional priorities'.[151] Further, the Strategy also urges states to resolve challenges and disputes in 'our own unique Pacific Way[152] – a statement reminiscent of commitments made about an 'ASEAN Way'.

As the ASEAN experience demonstrates, non-interference comes with its own unique set of opportunities and challenges, but at its core the principle impedes organic integration at a deeper level, particularly where states are left to 'self-enforce' their commitments. Indeed, reticence on behalf of PICS to adopt regional initiatives can be seen in the responses of PICs to the PICTA Trade in Services Protocol,[153] which while being signed by 10 PICs, has only been ratified by four (the Marshall Islands, Nauru, Samoa, and Tuvalu).[154] Partly in response, expectations of fostering the free movement of temporary and seasonal workers between PICTA Member States never quite materialised.[155]

media-portal/press-releases/seventh-pacific-annual-labour-mobility-meeting-taking-regional-labour-mobility-cooperation-to-the-next-level.

[147] ILO Office for Pacific Island Countries (n 120) 22.

[148] Pacific Islands Forum Secretariat, 'Comprehensive Assessment' (n 135) 16.

[149] Pacific Islands Forum Secretariat, '2050 Strategy for the Blue Pacific Continent' (Pacific Islands Forum Secretariat, 2022), forumsec.org/sites/default/files/2023-11/PIFS-2050-Strategy-Blue-Pacific-Continent-WEB-5Aug2022-1.pdf.

[150] ibid 15.

[151] ibid 17.

[152] ibid 10.

[153] PICTA Trade in Services Protocol (28 August 2012).

[154] ILO Office for Pacific Island Countries (n 120) 22.

[155] ibid.

Further, as the MERCOSUR experience shows, small states have a strong interest in the establishment of legally-binding measures securing regional compliance and limiting the adoption by larger states of policies that could distort relationships within the bloc. In effect, the disparity of economic sizes between countries generates 'asymmetric interdependence' between them,[156] meaning that larger members in an integration project have less incentive than smaller ones to remain 'mindful of collective regional priorities' insofar as those priorities arise in high value domestic policy areas.[157]

With that in mind, the framework set out in the Blue Pacific Strategy lends itself to implementation by a subset of PIF Member States; a regional organisation of PICs, but excluding Australia and New Zealand. The reasoning for this is the asymmetry in size and issue prioritisation between PICs and Australia and New Zealand. Commentators have suggested that a PIC-only forum would protect the integrity and coherence of its critical issues, and avoid instances in which critical issues become deprioritised or compromised as a result of pressures from Australia and New Zealand.[158] Instead, the PIC-only forum would arguably increase commonality and similarity of policy aspirations and developmental status.[159] In doing so, the risks of a MERCOSUR-esque scenario, whereby the largest players control the game, are likewise reduced.

However, given the currently low levels of intra-PIC trade, and the existing framework providing Australia and New Zealand access to PIC markets and labour, in practice the efficacy of such a forum is fraught, particularly given that funding for the forum, at least in its initial stages, would still likely be sought from Australia and New Zealand.[160]

Returning to the PIF as it stands, the Blue Pacific Strategy is helpful in how it frames the wider Pacific identity, through reference to embracing cultural diversities, and strengthening regional partnerships.[161] Building a strong regional identity will be significant when looking beyond the loose framework of the Blue Pacific Strategy, toward the possibility of a common market along the lines of the Hon Mata'afa's comments.

B. What Could a Pacific Common Market Look Like?

(i) Institutions

Regional integration, in its broadest terms, can be regarded as a process by which Member States agree to form regional institutions that promote the attainment of common goals.[162] The EU demonstrates the opportunities to be gained where Member States are united by ties deeper than pure economics, and form part of a broader arrangement seeking political and socio-cultural integration.[163] Accordingly, existing cultural and

[156] Veiga and Rios (n 89) 18.
[157] ibid.
[158] Tavola (n 107) 29.
[159] ibid 30.
[160] ibid 36.
[161] Pacific Islands Forum Secretariat, '2050 Strategy for the Blue Pacific Continent' (n 149) 10.
[162] Deinla (n 51) 11.
[163] Veiga and Rios (n 89) 21.

istorical ties between Pacific nations, including Australia and New Zealand, present a strong factor in the development of a potential common market.

However, to be successful, more robust institutions and greater devolution of Member tate sovereignty would be required than is proposed in the Blue Pacific Strategy. As is demonstrated by the institutions of MERCOSUR, where regional bodies are created to fulfil an advisory role only, there is a significant risk that they will lack the institutional means to gain scope or demand further competences over time.[164]

Further, the importance of a functioning adjudicatory body is illustrated by the role of both the PRT in MERCOSUR, and the CJEU in the EU. In both cases, the institutions are tasked with ensuring the correct interpretation and application of broader community law'.[165] Without this, Member States cannot ensure the consistency of their egislation with sources of regional law.

Practically, establishing mechanisms for the consistent production and enforcement of regional rules provides predictability for economic players – particularly in the private sector – and generates incentives for further cooperation among Member tates.[166] Elements of this principle can already be seen in the modernisation of Papua New Guinea's arbitration legislation for the express purpose of seeking to attract foreign investment and trade by aligning the state's legal system with global arbitration tandards.[167]

A key difference between the legal environment of MERCOSUR and the EU remains the hierarchy of regional and domestic law. Whereas the doctrines of supremacy and direct effect developed by CJEU have underpinned the development of a constitutional order in Europe,[168] there remains an absence of uniform application of MERCOSUR norms within Member States' domestic laws.[169] There is no equivalent obligation to nforce the norms issued by MERCOSUR, as there is with EU instruments operating with direct effect.

In determining the feasibility of the Pacific adopting 'community law' and granting it imilar levels of primacy as is seen in the EU, consideration must be had to the asic principle that Member States' acceptance of a community law (either in the Pacific or EU), must stem from authorisation by their national constitutions.[170] As the *Solange* decisions demonstrate, different national courts' may accept primacy on different conditions. For the German Constitutional Court, acceptance was conditional on community law providing sufficient protections for individual rights, and the retention of the Court's power to review certain acts of the EU.

What conditions may be required from individual PIC constitutions remains an open question. However, it is instructive that recent changes to Tuvalu's Constitution included explicit reference to the threat posed to Tuvalu by climate change and sea-level rise,[171] while other PIC constitutions have recognised indigenous customary law,

[164] Luciano and Campos (n 85) 109.
[165] Luciano and Campos (n 85) 112.
[166] Veiga and Rios (n 89) 22.
[167] A Latu, 'Pacific Islands Review (2021–24)' [2025] *New Zealand Law Review* (forthcoming) p 28.
[168] Deinla (n 51) 97.
[169] Luciano and Campos (n 85) 114.
[170] Deinla (n 51) 99.
[171] Latu (n 167) 12.

inclusive of its own unique set of constitutional rights.[172] Accordingly, these issues around PICs' national identities would probably require a provision in any proposed 'community law', similar to Article 4(2) TEU, discussed above, expressly respecting PICs' competence to legislate on matters unique to them. Of course, questions immediately arise in the context of regional challenges, such as climate change, which while having unique effects on PSIDS such as Tuvalu, nonetheless would affect the broader bloc.

(ii) Trade Integration

While current Regional Trade Agreements such as PICTA and PACER Plus have provided some measure of trade liberalisation among PICs within the Pacific region, there nonetheless remains an ingrained belief in mercantilism and protection of national industry among smaller, non-resource-heavy PICs.[173] Other arguments objecting to trade liberalisation stem from concerns that there is not a level playing-field in international trade and thus that economically small PICs have little to gain from liberalisation.[174]

With that in mind, developing a common market would require openness and compromise from Australia and New Zealand as the region's leading economies in developing legitimate and accessible regional institutions. To avoid the trajectory of MERCOSUR, and given the economic asymmetries, Australia and New Zealand would need to put aside domestic incentives to exempt certain policy areas where they value their national autonomy, in favour of establishing regional cohesion.

Accordingly, the implementation of non-discrimination practices would be key, particularly when looking at reciprocal trade barriers in Australia and New Zealand, since ensuring that PIC exports are granted barrier-free entry to larger, sophisticated markets will be important in building trust and community between prospective Member States.

As the MERCOSUR experience highlights, rather than excepting certain areas of domestic policy from negotiated integration rules, or setting exceptions whose validity tends to be repeatedly kept in force, a better course may be to implement longer timetables for prospective Member States to conform with negotiated requirements.[175] For PICs, longer timeframes would assist in developing national legislation and institutions for integration, whereas for Australia and New Zealand timeframes would likely be required in order to identify relevant non-tariff barriers and a means of possible harmonisation with PIC domestic policy. Where exceptions are required, their definitions will need to be carefully assessed to avoid hindering the expected positive impacts of reciprocal liberalisation.[176]

The development and implementation of new policy initiatives require substantial resources, which many PICs often struggle to afford.[177] This challenge of securing funding for PICs to implement these regulations and foster development could be addressed

[172] ibid 11–12.
[173] Chand (n 118) 23.
[174] ibid; Pacific Network on Globalisation (n 127).
[175] Veiga and Rios (n 89) 7.
[176] ibid.
[177] A Kautoke-Holani (n 143) 97.

by aligning common market objectives with sufficient development assistance. This approach can help secure necessary resources for change.[178]

Moreover, the reduction of barriers to investment and capital would likely aid in the development of projects that are compatible with PIC community structures, and reflect cultural nuances, such as property investments via land trusts and lease arrangements structured in such a way as to respect customary land tenure and laws.[179] Reduction of intra-regional investment barriers would require significant technical consultation and harmonisation of intra-regional regulations; however, a free flow of investment and capital represents a significant opportunity for PSIDS to improve standards of living, and for larger economies to invest capital and expertise in potentially profitable markets.[180]

(iii) Freedom of Movement

As set out above, the importance of labour mobility to the Pacific region is widely recognised and should therefore be seen as a necessary pillar on which to build a common market. In developing cooperation in this area, action could be pursued through existing institutions such as the PLMAM, which in conjunction with facilitation support provided by the PACER Plus Implementation Unit, could provide a platform for PICs (and Australia and New Zealand) to move forward in harmonising labour legislation and reducing barriers to labour mobility.

In terms of fostering effective movement of workers, the implementation of MRAs and formal recognition of qualifications will likely be a useful first step towards integration. While New Zealand has previously announced that qualification recognition projects are ongoing under the umbrella of PACER Plus,[181] no firm progress appears to have been made to date.[182] Notably, a similar principle has been successfully implemented by other Small Island Developing States (SIDS) regional bodies, eg CARICOM.[183]

Further, cooperation and development of MRAs may provide a stepping stone to further labour-centric integration, on the basis that MRAs and harmonised standards still depend for their implementation on the political will of Member States. Accordingly, they do not impugn Member States' sovereignty particularly in the area of rule-making, as the right to regulate professions would still fall within the domestic jurisdiction of Member States.[184]

Beyond the narrow parameters of labour mobility, Pacific leaders have raised concerns regarding differences in the time required for visas to be processed for PIC

[178] ibid.
[179] Wallis (n 109) 3.
[180] E Annis, 'Climate Change and Trade in the Pacific Island Countries: The PACER plus Agreement' (2016) 47 *Georgetown Journal of International Law* 1497, 1504.
[181] P Twyford, 'Speech to PACER Plus one year anniversary reception' (13 December 2021), www.beehive.govt.nz/speech/speech-pacer-plus-one-year-anniversary-reception.
[182] 'How New Zealand supports qualification recognition in the Pacific' (*New Zealand Qualifications Authority*, 2024), www2.nzqa.govt.nz/about-us/why-we-are-here/international-role/qualification-recognition-in-the-pacific/.
[183] Chand (n 118) 23.
[184] Deinla (n 51) 247.

migrants depending on the purpose of their travel.[185] In suggesting the creation of common market including freedom of movement, the Hon Mata'afa noted that doing would allow people to live in smaller PICs while still visiting family and doing busine in the larger countries as needed.[186] In that respect, for true freedom of movement to achieved, models from the EU and MERCOSUR should be considered.

(iv) Geopolitical Incentives

Modern regional concerns include the finite nature of the Pacific's natural resources, t region's geostrategic importance, and the effects of climate change. Sustainably managi these issues necessitates a regional approach, and their ultimate resolution necessitat a global response.[187] Notably, Tuvalu's explicit reference to existential climate chan risks in its Constitution highlights the vulnerability of PICs to challenges that cannot overcome through unilateral action.

This is particularly true given the size of the Pacific Ocean as a global asset, bo in terms of the commons, and as a resource supply. However, due to their geograph cal isolation and economic size, PICs benefit from acting collectively to drive action global forums on climate change. While existing groupings exist, such as SIDS, whi include PICs among other climate-vulnerable states, there remains a case for a collecti voice specific to the Pacific region, and facilitated by strong regional institutions.[188] Th role is currently filled by PIF, and under a common market this would likely continue

Separately, within the broader pillar of geopolitics, the creation of a Pacific comm market would require consideration of the security risks posed to the bloc as a who Accordingly, Member States would need to ensure consistency of strategic positioni to avoid undermining the bloc's geopolitical influence. For example, Australia and Ne Zealand continue to frame regional geostrategy in terms of power competition and t need to counterbalance China. However, to date, PICs have developed their own 'tact cal, shrewd and calculating approaches' toward prospective regional partners. So have welcomed China's increased activity in the region,[189] in some cases, going so far to end diplomatic relations with Taiwan in favour of a 'One China Principle'.[190]

The result is that either PICs will face increased pressure to conform with the str tegic position of Australia and New Zealand (which to some extent already occurs or definitive boundaries will need to be drawn as to the scope of the common mark However, even then economic partnerships may give rise to security or geostrateg concerns, for example the increasingly strong economic ties between the Solomo Islands and China.[191]

[185] T Mika 'Consul-General clears air on N.Z. visa process' *The Samoa Observer* (online ed, Samo 24 August 2023), www.samoaobserver.ws/category/samoa/105126.
[186] Knott (n 5).
[187] Chand (n 118) 22.
[188] ibid.
[189] Wallis (n 109) 2.
[190] Latu (n 167) 18.
[191] ibid.

V. Conclusion

In 2023, the Hon Fiamē Naomi Mataʻafa raised the possibility of a Pacific Family styled on the EU common market. Her conception went beyond economic integration and provided also for freedom of movement of goods, services, capital, and workers.

As the above analysis makes clear, there is no one-size-fits-all approach to regional integration. Each of the EU, ASEAN, and MERCOSUR incorporate their own unique characteristics and, understandably, involve their own strengths and weakness. Nonetheless, if a common market along the lines of the Hon Mataʻafa's conception was to be implemented, experience from the EU and the other trade blocs would be fundamental.

What is also clear is that pursuing an EU-style common market would require more than what is possible from existing frameworks in the Pacific. Integration would, at a base level, require Member States to devolve far greater amounts of sovereignty to regional institutions than what is currently envisaged under the Pacific Islands Forum's Blue Pacific Continent Strategy.

Further, a common market would require the implementation of a regional adjudicatory body, exercising its jurisdiction over a 'community law'. States must be ready to devolve sovereignty to institutions so that the latter may interpret and enforce the bargain struck between Member States independently of state governments.

Incentives to create such a market do exist. Previous efforts to liberalise intra-Pacific trade have been successful in removing tariff barriers and building trade capabilities for PICs. Further, there is a region-wide recognition of the importance of labour mobility within the Pacific. Increasing the openness of this market may be a substantial source of growth for PICs, and for Australia and New Zealand.

On the other hand, geopolitical issues in the Pacific region present both opportunities and challenges for the Pacific region, and its aspirations for integration. While PICs face existential threats as a result of climate change, opening barrier-free movement of capital and goods may facilitate further foreign sustainable investment in PIC economies, which could in turn be used to invest in climate resilience. However, open questions remain regarding the direction of a regional foreign policy given existing divergences between some PICs and Australia and New Zealand.

The question may ultimately come down to whether, as the Samoan saying suggests, *e manaʻo I le vao ae o loʻo mamalu mai le aitu I le aoa* (we want the trees in the forest but are afraid of their spirits') Are the benefits of a truly integrated Pacific Family worth the inevitable compromises and devolution of state sovereignty to regional institutions?

12

Freeing Up the Movement of People

An Incremental Strategy for African Citizenship

ADA ORDOR AND VICTOR T AMADI

I. Introduction

Citizenship is primarily understood by reference to constitutional provisions in domestic legal systems. In relation to membership of the geo-economic bloc which Africa spires to grow into, citizenship becomes a continental construct, advanced through the free movement of people and ultimately consolidated by means of a continental passport. As currently articulated in Agenda 2063, the 50-year development plan of the African Union (AU), the African passport is primarily about freeing up the movement of African citizens around the continent through the dismantling of visa requirements.[1] The idea of a continental passport is to ease travel around the continent, with the associted rights of entry, residence and establishment in another Member State of the AU.[2] It is, however, not inconceivable that with time and increased engagement, other rights may be negotiated to accrue to this continental passport.

The desirability or necessity of greater ease of mobility on the African continent is not in contention by State parties. The challenge is how to achieve this in ways that re actually and perceptually beneficial and not detrimental for individual countries nd sub-regions. Both the adoption of an instrument by a regional bloc, as well as the domestic response to it are indicative of issues identified by that bloc as pertinent enough to demand action. By adopting the Free Movement of Persons Protocol (AU-FMP Protocol), AU State parties acknowledge its importance, but by not subsequently ratifying this Protocol in their individual countries, they have signalled a hesitancy in their internal processes to commit to its far-reaching provisions.

[1] See African Union Commission, 'Agenda 2063: The Africa We Want (Popular Version)' (September 2015) 7.

[2] The Protocol to the Treaty Establishing the African Economic Community Relating to Free Movement of Persons, the Right of Residence and Right of Establishment (adopted 29 January 2018) (AU-FMP Protocol) art 5.

So far, the goal of the free movement initiative has mostly been put forward as an all-inclusive process where every African is conceptually entitled to access the length and breadth of the continent. However, in simple terms, what seems to be happening is a progressive approach to *freer* movement, undertaken by each country in line with its own prerogatives and that is worth paying attention to.

Every indication points to the fact that while their heads of state may have participated in the adoption of the AU-FMP Protocol, states and regions prefer to handle the free movement issue in their own way, evidently by advancing national and regional imperatives already underway in a tempered, considered, graduated way – placing domestic priorities at the forefront of decision-making. These national imperatives may have to do with a host of factors, including size, economic health, geo-political stability, religious, cultural and ethno-linguistic affinities, as well as the positioning of host countries in relation to surrounding regions. The first and last of these variables are particularly key for island nations, which often have to manage a small size and a confined, delicately placed location while juggling for balance between their partial dependence on other economies and their need to preserve their collective identity within the web of meanings constructed by the concept of citizenship.

Central to this web is Marshall's view of citizenship as a status bestowed on those who are full community members, conferring equality in respect of rights and duties with which the status is endowed.[3] Heywood emphasises the relationship between the individual and the state, in which reciprocal rights and obligations bind the two.[4] Iija describes citizenship in terms of legal status, political recognition, and rights and obligations attaching to members of a community as a result of that membership – all within a state-centred world where the state confers benefits in return for certain obligations on its citizens.[5]

The predominant theme in these reflections on citizenship is that of a defined sphere within which a citizen enjoys rights and performs duties. It is, therefore, to be expected that for citizens of small states, this 'defined sphere' is perceived as a limited space, making the safeguarding of this space from outsider influx or even influence paramount at any given time. Not to be left out is Adotey's observation flagging members of border communities in Africa as a hybrid who often exercise trans-national citizenship.[6] This is dependent on a number of factors, including the actual or perceived benefits of alternative citizenship regimes on either side of land borders irrespective of country size. This makes the movement of people as an expression of citizenship in Africa, seen through the lenses of small states, a pertinent subject of study.

This chapter starts by describing continental frameworks constructed to advance citizenship by way of the AU-FMP Protocol. This is followed by an overview of initiatives of Member States, not strictly within the sequence or pattern envisaged by the AU-FMP Protocol but complementary or supplemental to it. Much of this approach is

[3] See BS Turner, 'Marshall and Dahrendorf: Theories of Citizenship 1945–2022' (2022) 26 *Citizenship Studies* 702, 703.

[4] A Heywood, *Political ideas and concepts: An introduction* (New York, St Martin's Press, 1994) 155.

[5] VI Iija, 'An Analysis of the Concept of Citizenship: Legal, Political and Social Dimensions' (Master's Thesis, University of Helsinki, 2011) 9.

[6] See E Adotey, 'Transnational Citizenship on the Borderlands: Towards Making (non)sense of National Borders in Africa' (2023) 10 *Contemporary Journal of African Studies* 74, 81.

by way of rational policy, retaining state autonomy and the prerogative to move at a pace responsive to domestic needs and constraints rather than having to bend over backwards to accommodate supranational directives often perceived by state legislatures as an overreach of regional authority structures. In other words, *this is what the AU-FMP Protocol proposes, but here's what states are doing*, and this is where attention needs to be paid since enhanced movement will be activated at the state level. In this respect, the experience and perspectives of small states are particularly relevant, because small states readily present a functional prism for a strategic view of the impact of demographic shifts, changes and shocks.

Africa's small states, as defined in this volume, are mostly island states. Five of its six island nations are small states. Geographically dispersed across the Atlantic and Indian Oceans, Africa's island nations and State parties to the AU are Cape Verde, Comoros, Madagascar, Mauritius, São Tomé and Príncipe, and Seychelles. Located in the Atlantic Ocean, Cape Verde and São Tomé and Príncipe have populations of 562,000 and 223,000, respectively. Situated in the Indian Ocean, Comoros has a population of 850,000, Mauritius 1.2 million and Seychelles approximately 102,612. Except for Madagascar, which has approximately 30 million people, the other five island states, together with Guinea-Bissau, which has a mainland and several islands, constitute the African members of the Small Island Developing States (SIDS), a group of low-lying island nations with a combined population of over 4 million people.[7] It is also noteworthy that these small island states are members of various regional blocs. Cape Verde is a member of the Economic Community of West African States (ECOWAS),[8] while São Tomé and Príncipe is a member of the Economic Community of Central African States (ECCAS).[9] Comoros, Madagascar, Seychelles and Mauritius are members of both the Southern African Development Community (SADC) and the Common Market for Eastern and Southern Africa (COMESA).[10]

Table 1 African small island states, population and regional memberships

	Estimated population	**Regional Economic Blocs**
Seychelles	102,612	SADC and COMESA
Cape Verde	562,000	ECOWAS
Mauritius	1,200,000	SADC and COMESA
Comoros	850,000	SADC and COMESA
Madagascar	30,000,000	SADC and COMESA
São Tomé and Príncipe	223,000	ECCAS

[7] 'List of SIDS' (United Nations Office of the High Representative for the Least Developed Countries, Landlocked Developing Countries and Small Islands Developing States), www.un.org/ohrlls/content/list-sids.
[8] Cape Verde joined ECOWAS in 1976.
[9] São Tomé and Príncipe joined ECCAS in 1983.
[10] Comoros joined COMESA in 1981 and became a SADC member in 2018. Madagascar joined COMESA in 2000 and became a SADC member in 2005. Having withdrawn from the SADC in 2004, Seychelles was readmitted in 2008 and has been party to COMESA since 2001. Mauritius joined COMESA in 1981 and joined the SADC in 1995.

Other small states on the African continent include Equatorial Guinea, with a population of 1.6 million, Eswatini, with 1.2 million people, and Botswana, Lesotho and Namibia, with populations of less than 3 million each. African states, big and small, have, for the most part, displayed tempered responses to the AU-FMP Protocol, and the next section concisely considers why this is the case.

II. The African Union Free Movement of Persons Protocol

Following the adoption of the AU Agenda 2063 in 2015, two complementary legal instruments were further adopted at the 2018 Kigali Summit, namely, the AU-FMP Protocol[11] and the African Continental Free Trade Area Agreement (AfCFTA). The main objective of the AfCFTA is to create a single market for goods and services, facilitated by the movement of persons, to deepen economic integration on the continent.[12] The AU-FMP Protocol complements the AfCFTA with its definitive aim of facilitating the free movement of people (capital, goods, and services) and promoting integration, all of which are envisaged to herald many other benefits, including improved science, technology, education, research, and tourism.[13] The adoption of these two instruments simultaneously was, therefore, the outcome of efforts to ultimately advance the exercise of socio-economic citizenship on the continent. The AU-FMP Protocol sets out a three-phase approach to its implementation, with phase one focusing on the right of entry and abolition of visa requirements. Phase two defines the right of residence, while phase three advances the right of establishment.[14] Further actions outlined in the Protocol include the provision of valid travel documents by Member States to their nationals to facilitate free movement, the adoption of the African passport as a travel document, and the harmonisation of laws, policies and systems of regional economic communities and states relating to the free movement of persons.[15]

As of August 2025, 32 AU Member States have signed the AU-FMP Protocol, while only four have ratified it, namely Mali, Niger, Rwanda, and São Tomé and Príncipe.[16] Except for São Tomé and Príncipe, the other three ratifying countries are relatively big, with populations ranging from 14 million to over 20 million. However, they share the common feature of being classified as least developed countries (LDCs),[17] which arguably contributes to a predisposition towards liberal migration policies, envisaged to have positive developmental impact. However, this is still a far cry from the 15 ratifications

[11] See n 2.

[12] Agreement Establishing the African Continental Free Trade Area (adopted 21 March 2018, entered into force 30 May 2019) (2018) 58 ILM 1028 (AfCFTA) art 3(1).

[13] See Preamble of the AU-FMP Protocol (n 2).

[14] AU-FMP Protocol (n 2) art 5.

[15] AU-FMP Protocol (n 2) arts 9, 10 and 26.

[16] See the status list at 'Protocol to the Treaty Establishing the African Economic Community Relating to Free Movement of Persons, Right of Residence and Right of Establishment' (*African Union*), au.int/en/treaties/protocol-treaty-establishing-african-economic-community-relating-free-movement-persons.

[17] 'LDCs at a Glance' (*United Nations Department of Economic and Social Affairs – Economic Analysis*), www.un.org/development/desa/dpad/least-developed-country-category/ldcs-at-a-glance.html.

required for the Protocol to come into force.[18] This raises the question of why most African governments have hesitated to ratify the AU-FMP Protocol.

Several explanations have been advanced for the AU-FMP Protocol's slow and delayed ratification, including lack of knowledge and appreciation of the benefits of free movement of persons, lack of awareness of the AU-FMP Protocol among states, lack of institutional, procedural and technical capacities, and absence of a strong political will.[19] Another factor contributing to the slow rate of ratification of the AU-FMP Protocol is the lack of legal identity systems caused by inadequate civil registration systems in many African countries. An October 2023 policy report by the United Nations Economic Commission for Africa (UNECA) notes concerns about inadequate migration management systems and infrastructure as a factor affecting the ratification of the AU-FMP Protocol.[20] This concern stems from the lack of effective national civil registration systems, reliable movement control systems, and machine-readable passports compliant with international standards.[21] Therefore, building institutional and technical capacities towards civil registration and identity document systems, and having a common standard of travel documentation, should reduce the current lack of trust between countries and help expedite ratifications of the AU-FMP Protocol.[22]

Additionally, concerns about national security and perceptions of a loss of control over national migration policy are cited as reasons for the slow implementation of the AU-FMP Protocol. As noted by Hirsch and Amadi, this stems from a misunderstanding of countries' obligations and the timing of the Protocol's implementation.[23] For instance, through a *note verbale*, South Africa advised its Cabinet not to support the Protocol on several grounds, including concerns that it did not adopt a phased approach.[24] There was also broader discomfort on the part of South Africa, Algeria, Egypt, Kenya, Tunisia, and Uganda over the fact that both the Protocol and the implementation roadmap were to be adopted at the January 2018 AU summit.[25] This contradicted the AU-FMP Protocol prescription for a progressive realisation of the free movement of persons in phases, with a requirement of 15 ratifications for its implementation.[26]

Further, domestic political and social narratives also play a role, primarily where high unemployment fuels concerns about jobs for nationals, where security issues are

[18] AU-FMP Protocol (n 2) art 33.

[19] See R Adeola, 'The African Union Protocol on the free movement of persons in Africa: development, provisions and implementation challenges' (2019) 3 *African Human Rights Yearbook* 260; A Hirsch, 'The AU Free Movement of Persons Protocol: Why has it faltered and how can its objectives be achieved?' (2021) *South African Journal of International Affairs* 497.

[20] UNECA, 'Free Movement of Persons for Trade: Towards an accelerated ratification of the African Union Protocol to the Treaty Establishing the African Economic Community Relating to Free Movement of Persons, Right of Residence and Right of Establishment, in support of the Implementation of the African Continental Free Trade Area' (Policy Research Paper, October 2023) 48.

[21] ibid.

[22] ibid.

[23] A Hirsch and V Amadi, 'Can Africa Accelerate Initiatives towards the Freer Movement of Africans in Africa?' in F Mangeni and J Atta-Mensah (eds), *Existential Priorities for the African Continental Free Trade Area* (Addis Ababa, UNECA, 2022) 123–24.

[24] Hirsch (n 19) 508.

[25] ibid.

[26] AU-FMP Protocol (n 2) art 32.

prominent, or where the possibilities to exchange information between countries are considered inadequate.[27] Whatever the socio-economic and political sentiments at the domestic level, the regional legal frameworks for mobility on the continent reflect a more liberal tone, perhaps because regional mobility has been in place for decades and is less daunting than the continental initiative. It is therefore important to consider the current regional provisions for the movement of people in a number of regions, and the next section of this chapter focuses on this subject in relation to the East, West and Southern Africa regions.

III. Regional Initiatives

Detailed provisions on citizenship at the national level and earlier conceptualisations of regional citizenship work together to relieve the concept of African citizenship, in relation to the movement of people, from traditional citizenship demands. Traditionally understood as a legal status within a nation-state, citizenship is increasingly viewed through the lens of regional integration in Africa.[28] This broader conceptualisation redefines citizenship not only as a set of rights and responsibilities tied to a nation but also as a dynamic transnational status that intersects with and is enabled by the movement of people across borders. The movement of people, in this context, can be viewed as a catalyst for reimagining citizenship and a necessary mechanism for economic growth and cooperation, essential to the vision of an increasingly integrated Africa. This is demonstrated in the regional initiatives described in this section, which provide for freer movement with careful management of migration flows to promote the benefits of integration without threatening national sovereignty and identity.

Three regions present instructive examples, and this section starts by discussing the region with the oldest mobility framework in the contemporary era, namely, West Africa, and thereafter, the East African and Southern African regions.

A. West Africa

In the West African region, the Authority of Heads of State and Government of ECOWAS[29] adopted the Protocol relating to the Free Movement of Persons, the Right of Residence and Establishment in 1979. Examining citizenship in ECOWAS shows that regional citizenship has developed in steps. The first step was abolishing visas and providing a 90-day visa-free stay in all Member States for ECOWAS citizens with a valid travel document[30]

[27] ibid.

[28] See Turner (n 3) 703; Adotey (n 6) 81.

[29] The Authority comprised Heads of State and Government from 15 countries: Benin, Burkina Faso, Cape Verde, Côte d'Ivoire, the Gambia, Ghana, Guinea, Guinea Bissau, Liberia, Mali, Niger, Nigeria, Senegal, Sierra Leone and Togo.

[30] Notably, during the 45th ECOWAS Ordinary Summit in 2014, the ECOWAS Authority adopted Supplementary Act A/SA.1/07/14 (Act 1) and Supplementary Act A/SA.2/07/14 (Act 2) amending some provisions in the 1979 and 1985 Protocols, respectively (see below nn 31 and 32). These Acts come into force upon signature by a Member State, and the respective Acts have 14 signatures, with Cape Verde being the outstanding signatory. However, a notable amendment under *Act 1* is the revision of a definition of a trave

and international health certificate, followed by the right to residence and establishment as outlined in the 1979 Protocol.[31] This Protocol came before the legal definition of the ECOWAS community citizenship, which followed in 1982.[32] However, this right to move freely under the 1979 Protocol is not absolute. Member States reserve the right to refuse admission into their territories to any citizen who comes within the category of inadmissible immigrants under their laws.[33] Further, members can expel illegal migrants under Article 11 of the 1979 Protocol. That notwithstanding, several measures have subsequently been adopted to ensure the implementation of the free movement initiative to ease cross-border movement and further entrench the ECOWAS citizenship narrative. These include the adoption of an ECOWAS passport in 2000 and an ECOWAS national biometric identity card in 2014, which is currently utilised by six[34] out of the 12 members of the ECOWAS.

The ECOWAS passport, introduced to facilitate the free movement of people across Member States, serves as a tangible symbol of regional identity and belonging. The passport allows for more accessible travel within the region, potentially strengthening the Member States' economic ties and social cohesion. Similarly, the ECOWAS national biometric identity card complementing the passport provides a secure and standardised form of identification for ECOWAS citizens. A standardised legal identity document can help streamline border controls and assuage some security concerns around free movement. However, the effectiveness of these instruments in enhancing a regional citizenship narrative and achieving the broader goals of ECOWAS faces implementation issues, varying commitment levels among Member States, and infrastructural deficiencies.[35] Furthermore, as may be inferred from Article 4 of the 1979 Protocol, the ECOWAS regional citizenship is fundamentally limited by mutual respect for state sovereignty, as Member States can refuse admission into their territories to any citizen within the inadmissible category of the particular host state. Moreover, political will, cooperation among Member States, and capacity-building of domestic civil registries are critical for ensuring that the benefits of such measures are fully realised.

For clarity, the 1979 ECOWAS Protocol on free movement of persons defines a 'community citizen' as a citizen of any Member State of the ECOWAS.[36] Further to this, the 1982 Protocol Relating to the Definition of Community Citizen defines community citizenship to include citizenship by descent, birth, adoption and naturalisation.

Thus, the criteria which must be met by an ECOWAS citizen are that such a person must:

(a) be a national by birth, descent or naturalisation of any of the Member States;
(b) not be a national of any state that is not a member of the ECOWAS;

document, which the Act currently defines as a passport, other official biometric national identity card or a laissez-passer issued by a Member State or any other ECOWAS Institution.

[31] See ECOWAS Protocol Relating to Free Movement of Persons, Residence and Establishment (signed 29 May 1979, entered into force 8 April 1980) 1906 UNTS 56 arts 2 and 3.

[32] See ECOWAS Protocol Relating to the Definition of Community Citizen (adopted 29 May 1982, entered into force 10 July 1984) 1690 UNTS 77 art 1.

[33] ibid art 4.

[34] Guinea Bissau, Ghana, Senegal, Benin, the Gambia, and Sierra Leone.

[35] JO Bolarinwa, 'The ECOWAS Free Movement Protocol: Obstacle or Driver of Regional Integration' (2015) 7(2) *Insight on Africa* 154, 160–64.

[36] ECOWAS Protocol Relating to Free Movement of Persons, Residence and Establishment (n 31) art 1.

(c) if a naturalised citizen, must have resided permanently in a Member State of the ECOWAS for a continuous period of at least 15 years;
(d) not jeopardise the fundamental interests of any Member State.[37]

Conversely, ECOWAS community citizenship may be lost by citizens from birth, in case of loss of nationality of country of origin, permanent settlement in a state outside the ECOWAS, or voluntary acquisition of the nationality of a state outside the ECOWAS.[38] For naturalised citizens, citizenship can be lost by involvement in activities incompatible with the status of an ECOWAS citizen and prejudicial to the fundamental interests of one or more Member States of the ECOWAS, conviction for a crime (ie they have been sentenced for a crime in any Member State), or ECOWAS citizenship obtained by fraud.[39] A summation of these provisions indicates that proof of nationality of an ECOWAS Member State is a prerequisite to obtaining ECOWAS citizenship. This means that ECOWAS citizenship is not automatic or foundational but is intended to complement and enhance domestic citizenship rights by securing benefits such as the right to free movement.

This may not be the place for an analysis of these provisions, but it is sufficient to say that the ECOWAS Protocol on free movement of persons, which was adopted in 1979, was ratified by 14 out of the then 15 ECOWAS states within three years of adoption, with the last ratification by Cape Verde coming in 1984. These provisions have, therefore, been in operation for at least 40 years. Cape Verde became an independent nation in 1975, the same year ECOWAS was established, and joined ECOWAS in 1976. While there may be no particular significance to the timing of Cape Verde's ratification, it signalled a willingness to align with the broader goals and objectives of ECOWAS.

B. East Africa

As with the ECOWAS bloc, the East African Community (EAC) has been progressing towards the free movement of people in the East African region. Under Article 104 of the 1999 Treaty reestablishing the EAC, Partner States agreed to adopt measures to achieve the free movement of persons, labour and services and to ensure the enjoyment of the right of establishment and residence of their citizens with the community. Like the ECOWAS regional bloc, several measures have been adopted by the EAC to implement its treaty objectives. Notable is the adoption and progressive implementation of the Common Market Protocol in 2010, which under Article 8 prescribes that the EAC Partner States[40] should commit to working progressively towards establishing a 'common standard system of issuing national identification documents to their nationals'.[41] Further,

[37] ECOWAS Protocol Relating to the Definition of Community Citizen (n 32) art 1.
[38] ibid art 2, para 2.
[39] ibid art 2, para 3.
[40] With the recent admission of Somalia on 24 November 2023, the EAC is an 8-Member State organisation comprising Burundi, the Democratic Republic of Congo, Kenya, Rwanda, Somalia, South Sudan, Uganda, and Tanzania.
[41] Protocol on the Establishment of the East African Community Common Market (signed 20 November 2009, entered into force 1 July 2010) (EAC Common Market Protocol) art 8.

Article 9 prescribes that citizens of a Partner State who wish to travel to another Partner State shall use a valid common standard travel document. Partner States may agree to use machine-readable passports and electronic national identity cards as travel documents.[42] Kenya, Rwanda, and Uganda recognise each other's national idetity cards as valid travel documents instead of solely passports to facilitate travel. Also, in 2017, against the backdrop of the 17th Ordinary Summit of the EAC Heads of State in 2016, the Summit directed the Partner States to start issuing new regional passports in the form of the EAC e-passport.[43] This is clearly rapid progress.

C. Southern Africa

The Southern African Development Community (SADC)[44] has attempted to develop a legal framework to facilitate and ensure the free movement of persons. First, in 1995, the SADC adopted the draft Protocol on the Free Movement of Persons. This arrangement was not enforced due to resistance from South Africa, Namibia and Botswana on the presumption that a regional arrangement would compromise national sovereignty and cause an influx of migrants.[45] Afterward, a Protocol on Facilitation of the Movement of Persons (Facilitation Protocol) was adopted in 2005.[46] This Protocol is not in force as the minimum ratification threshold of two-thirds of Member States prescribed by Article 36 has not been met.[47] With no enforced regional law, the governance and management of the movement of persons depends on bilateral agreements focused on visa exemptions, and also depends on national laws which are often restrictive.[48]

The Facilitation Protocol envisages a phased approach to achieving visa-free travel for SADC citizens.[49] This would apply to a 'visit for a maximum period of ninety (90) days' per year[50] with a gradual extension to longer stays through provisions on residence and establishment. Notably, the obligation on Member States to afford visa-free entry to persons under Article 14 is subject to an exemption, valid for no more than 12 months, in instances where an entry visa can be applied for at a border post at no cost.[51] Residence, in

[42] ibid art 9.

[43] 'EAC to start issuing EA e-passport in January 2018' (*East African Community*, 7 April 2017), www.eac.int/press-releases/148-immigration-and-labour/754-eac-to-start-issuing-ea-e-passport-january-2018%20=.

[44] The SADC Member States are Angola, Botswana, Comoros, the Democratic Republic of Congo, Eswatini, Lesotho, Madagascar, Malawi, Mauritius, Mozambique, Namibia, Seychelles, South Africa, Tanzania, Zambia, and Zimbabwe.

[45] J Oucho and J Crush, 'Contra Free Movement: South Africa and the SADC Migration Protocols' (2001) 48 *Africa Today* 139, 143.

[46] V Amadi and P Lenaghan, 'Advancing Regional Integration through the Free Movement of Persons in the Southern African Development Community (SADC)' (2020) 34 *Speculum Juris* 51, 53.

[47] The Protocol has been signed by 13 Member States and ratified by six members, including Botswana, South Africa, Mozambique, Namibia, Lesotho, and Eswatini. See C Nshimbi, I Moyo, and T Gumbo, 'Between Neoliberal Orthodoxy and Securitisation, Prospects and Challenges for a Borderless Southern African Development Community' in MH Hangwelani et al (eds), *Crisis, Identity and Migration in Post-Colonial Southern Africa* (Cham, Springer, 2018).

[48] ibid 179. See also V Amadi, 'A flexible approach to enabling the free movement of people in Southern Africa' (2023) 56 *Comparative and International Law Journal of Southern Africa* 1, 9.

[49] SADC Protocol on the Facilitation of Movement of Persons (adopted 18 August 2005) art 5.

[50] ibid art 14(2)(a).

[51] ibid art 15(2). This is specific to the State Party that applies for the exemption.

the Protocol, shall mean permission to live in a State party's territory granted by the State party's legislative and administrative provisions.[52] To reside in a Member State, a citizen must apply to the appropriate authorities of the host state for a residence permit.[53] The Protocol offers some certainty around administering residence permits by prescribing for the processing of residence permits without undue delay.[54] A definition of undue delay is missing in the Protocol, and this is an aspect that can be concretised to enhance the efficacy of national authorities responsible for issuing these permits. Article 19 states that 'each State Party shall in terms of its national laws grant permission for the establishment to citizens of other State Parties'. Establishment means permission granted by a State party under its national laws to a citizen of another State party to exercise an economic activity and profession either as an employee or self-employed person and establish and manage a profession, trade, business or other kind of livelihood.[55]

IV. State Initiatives

At national levels, African countries are adopting more liberal travel regimes for citizens of other African countries, albeit unilaterally or bilaterally. In 2023, based on the African Development Bank (AfDB) 'Visa Openness Report', 50 of 55 African countries either improved their openness to travel or maintained their status from 2022.[56] Visa openness solutions include visa-free regional blocs, as discussed earlier, visa on arrival for Africans, and simplifying visa processes through e-visas. In recent times, African countries have made significant advances towards free movement, unilaterally abolishing visa requirements for the continent or negotiating bilateral agreements allowing for visa waivers. For instance, President William Ruto of Kenya announced in October 2023 that Kenya's borders would be open to African visitors, with no visas required, by the end of 2023.[57] This announcement came after several bilateral agreements with, for instance, South Africa, which enabled visa-free travel to South Africa for 90 days in a year for Kenyan citizens,[58] and agreements with Eritrea,[59] Comoros,[60] Senegal,[61] and Djibouti[62] allowing for a visa-free regime with these countries. Just as President Ruto

[52] ibid art 16.
[53] ibid art 17(1) and (2).
[54] ibid art 17(3).
[55] ibid art 18(a) and (b).
[56] 'Africa Visa Openness Report 2023' (African Development Bank and African Union Commission, 2023) 9.
[57] 'Kenya to become visa-free to African visitors' *BBC* (30 October 2023), www.bbc.com/news/world-africa-67254349.
[58] L Ndebele 'Kenyans can now visit SA without a visa for three months', *news24* (3 January 2023), www.news24.com/news24/africa/news/kenyans-can-now-visit-sa-without-a-visa-for-three-months-20230103.
[59] 'Kenya-Eritrea permanently abolishes visa requirements for their citizens' (*Republic of Kenya*, 9 February 2023), www.president.go.ke/kenya-eritrea-permanently-abolish-visa-requirements-for-their-citizens/.
[60] 'Kenya and Comoros agree to abolish visa requirements' *CGTN Africa* (6 July 2023), africa.cgtn.com/kenya-and-comoros-agree-to-abolish-visa-requirements/.
[61] 'Kenya, Senegal agree to champion the Integration of Africa' (*Republic of Kenya*, 26 January 2023), president.go.ke/kenya-senegal-agree-to-champion-the-integration-of-africa/.
[62] 'Kenya and Djibouti agree on a visa-free regime to boost trade' (*Republic of Kenya*, 11 June 2023), www.president.go.ke/kenya-and-djibouti-agree-on-a-visa-free-regime-to-boost-trade/.

afforded visa-free travel to Kenya, President Paul Kagame of Rwanda followed with a similar announcement in November 2023, saying all Africans could enter Rwanda without visas.[63] Further, Botswana and Namibia, in March 2023, signed a bilateral agreement on the movement of persons affording access to the respective countries using national identity cards.[64] Similarly, the governments of Ghana and South Africa reached a visa waiver agreement to allow citizens of both countries to travel to each other visa-free.[65]

None of the countries mentioned above is the first to implement liberal measures in the cross-border movement of people. According to the AfDB visa openness index in 2023, a range of visa-openness solutions have been adopted and maintained, with most leading countries being relatively low-income and small island states. For example, as highlighted earlier, Rwanda, Benin, the Gambia, and Seychelles offer visa-free access to all African visitors with appropriate travel documents.

Further, island countries Cape Verde, Comoros and Madagascar have a combination of visa-free access and visa-on-arrival policies for citizens of most African countries. In Cape Verde, no visa is required for citizens of 16 African countries and 36 African countries are eligible for visa on arrival access, while a visa is required for one African country: Morocco. Meanwhile, in Comoros, Africans from 53 countries in the continent are granted a visa on arrival. Similarly, in Madagascar, a visa on arrival is afforded to citizens of 52 African countries. However, a visa is required from one African country: Burundi. For the least performing island nation in the 2023 AfDB index, São Tomé and Príncipe, a visa is required for 46 African countries, with no visa required for seven African countries, primarily lusophone (Portuguese-speaking) countries such as Angola, Cape Verde, Equatorial Guinea, Gabon, Guinea-Bissau, and Mozambique, as well as Gabon and Morocco.[66] See the table below for a summary of these initiatives and the visa openness ranking of the respective African island states.

Table 2 Visa openness ranking and national approaches to the free movement of people in African small island states from 2016 to 2023

	2016	**2017**	**2018**	**2019**	**2020**	**2021**	**2022**	**2023**	**National Initiative**
Seychelles	1	1	1	1	1	1	1	1	No visa
Cape Verde	4	5	8	8	10	10	8	8	No visa; visa on arrival
Mauritius	9	9	12	12	15	13	11	11	No visa; visa on arrival

(continued)

[63] E Igunza 'Rwanda announces visa-free travel for all Africans as continent opens up to free movement of people' *Independent* (6 November 2023), www.independent.co.uk/travel/news-and-advice/rwanda-travel-visa-free-africa-schengen-b2442207.html.

[64] G Erasmus and T Hartzenberg, 'Botswana and Namibia concluded an agreement on the movement of persons' (*tralacBlog*, 8 March 2023) www.tralac.org/blog/article/15940-botswana-and-namibia-concluded-an-agreement-on-the-movement-of-persons.html.

[65] 'Ghana, South Africa sign visa waiver deal' *africanews* (13 August 2024), www.africanews.com/2023/10/16/ghana-south-africa-sign-visa-waiver-deal/.

[66] See 'Africa Visa Openness Report 2023' (n 56).

Table 2 ***(Continued)***

	2016	2017	2018	2019	2020	2021	2022	2023	National Initiative
Comoros	12	11	14	14	17	15	14	14	Visa on arrival
Madagascar	12	11	14	14	19	16	15	17	Visa on arrival
São Tomé and Príncipe	52	36	42	43	43	40	44	45	No visa; visa required

Authors' construction based on the AfDB visa openness reports (2016–23).[67]

The table suggests a mixed approach and varying levels of commitment to enabling and facilitating the movement of people in Africa. Seychelles consistently ranks as the most open, holding the top position with no visa requirements. Cape Verde, Mauritius, Comoros and Madagascar have improved steadily, indicating moderate openness. São Tomé and Príncipe remain the least open; despite some improvement in ranking from 52 in 2016 to 40 in 2021, it subsequently declined to 45 in 2023.

Several factors may account for the more liberal approach adopted by small island states in their individual capacities towards the movement of people. Generally, island states are limited in population size and economy, and face labour shortages, relying on skilled and unskilled labour to sustain economic growth. For instance, in Seychelles, the most liberal of all African small islands, the economy is limited by its small size, with few opportunities for economic diversity and high production costs. The economy depends on tourism and fishing, which represent 35 per cent of GDP, and relies on foreign labour in crucial sectors.[68] Tourism generated an estimated annual revenue of US$960 million as of 31 December 2023.[69]

Evidently, the reticence of African states to ratify the AU-FMP Protocol is not a display of a lack of political will but an indication of a preference to address the matter at the individual country level, particularly in the case of small island states who want to retain control of mobility flows in and out of their territories. The examples of Seychelles and Mauritius, discussed in the next segment, demonstrate this point.

V. Perspectives from Two Small Island Nations

The discussion at this point describes the position in two island states, namely Seychelles and Mauritius. The population dynamics of both island nations in the Indian Ocean present a unique case study of the interplay of historical, cultural and environmental factors shaping human demographics.

[67] See the 2023 AfDB Visa Openness Report (n 56).

[68] Seychelles Ministry of Employment, Immigration and Civil Status, *Seychelles National Labour Migration Policy* (October 2019), https://www.ics.gov.sc/downloads/policies/labour-migration-policy/viewdocument 9–11.

[69] 'Tourism Seychelles' (*Tourism Seychelles*), tourism.gov.sc/ (8 October 2024).

Seychelles, an archipelago of about 115 islands, has a smaller population than Mauritius, mainly owing to its dispersed geographic nature and limited landmass, which impacts its capacity for extensive population growth. As of 2022, Seychelles had a population of 102,612, characterised by a diverse ethnic mix.[70] In contrast, Mauritius, which is made up of one main island surrounded by other smaller islands presents a more heterogeneous demography with a population of over 1.2 million people as of December 2023.[71] The island's larger land area and resource base have supported a denser population. Additionally, Mauritius has experienced significant urbanisation and industrialisation, contributing to its larger population and more diverse economic structure.[72] Both island states' population trends and demographic structures are closely tied to environmental constraints and opportunities. The populations of both Seychelles and Mauritius exemplify how small island states navigate the complexities of modern development ideas, such as migration within the constraints of limited natural resources and environmental vulnerability.

Seychelles and Mauritius approach migration and citizenship with a delicate balance of openness and caution. In Seychelles, the government promotes a relatively open policy towards immigration, mainly for economic purposes such as tourism and attracting skilled migrants, while maintaining controls on long-term residency and citizenship.[73] Similarly, Mauritius, a multi-ethnic society, actively encourages skilled immigration and investment-based immigration schemes to bolster its economy while strictly governing temporary residence.[74]

Constitutionally, Mauritius and Seychelles primarily provide the right to nationality for all, and every child has the right to a name and nationality. Both countries feature birthright citizenship (*jus soli*) and the right of blood citizenship (*jus sanguinis*). In the Mauritian and Seychellois context, the principle of *jus soli* covers people born in Mauritius before and after 12 March 1968, when Mauritius became independent and those born in Seychelles on or after the coming into force of the Constitution.[75] However, the respective Constitutions of Mauritius and Seychelles provide for certain qualifications or exceptions to this principle. For instance, even though a person born in Mauritius after 1968 can become a citizen on the date of their birth, such an exception applies if neither parent is a citizen of Mauritius or either parent is an enemy alien, and the birth occurs in a place under occupation by the enemy.[76] In Seychelles, a similar exception applies if neither parent is a citizen of Seychelles and the father possesses such immunity from suit and legal process as is accorded to an envoy of a foreign sovereign power accredited to Seychelles, or the father is a citizen of a country with which

[70] National Bureau of Statistics Seychelles, *The Seychelles Population and Housing Census 2022* (21 March 2024) 11.

[71] 'Population and Vital Statistics – Republic of Mauritius – January – June 2024' (*Statistics Mauritius*, 29 August 2024) statsmauritius.govmu.org/Pages/Statistics/ESI/Population/Pop_Vital_Jan-Jun24.aspx.

[72] PS Narrainen 'Industrialisation: The Mauritian Model' in JE Stiglitz, JL Yifu and E Patel (eds), *The Industrial Policy Revolution II* (Houndmills, Palgrave Macmillan, 2013) 569–70.

[73] *Seychelles National Labour Migration Policy* (n 68) 10–16.

[74] J Crush and V Williams, 'Mauritius: Labour Migration Review' (Southern African Migration Management Project, 2024) 1–3.

[75] See ss 20 to 22 of the Constitution of Mauritius, 1968. See arts 7 and 8 of the Constitution of the Republic of Seychelles, 1993 (as amended).

[76] Section 22(a) and (b) of the Constitution of Mauritius, 1968.

Seychelles is at war, and the birth occurs in a place under occupation by that country.[77] Under these provisions, the principle of *jus soli* does not apply to individuals born in either country to foreign citizens.

Besides obtaining citizenship by birth, a person born outside Mauritius can be a citizen of Mauritius if either parent is a citizen of Mauritius by birth.[78] However, citizenship by descent is only applicable for one generation. Essentially, one cannot claim citizenship by descent based on a grandparent's citizenship. A limitation of this provision is the lack of recognition of individuals of unknown parents, an omission of particular importance in countries currently or previously affected by conflict.[79]

Seychelles and Mauritius have neither signed nor ratified the AU-FMP Protocol. That notwithstanding, both island nations have made definitive progress in enabling the free movement of persons into their respective territories, especially for tourism purposes. As noted earlier, according to the AfDB visa openness index of 2023, Seychelles ranks first, alongside Benin, the Gambia and Rwanda as countries that offer visa-free access to all African nations and citizens with appropriate travel documents.[80] Tourism is said to be one of the pillars of the economy of Seychelles.[81] Conversely, Mauritius offers visa-free access to citizens of 27 countries,[82] visas on arrival to those of 21 countries[83] and requires a visa from five countries[84] on the continent.[85]

Small island states such as Seychelles and Mauritius possess unique vulnerabilities in relation to the free movement of people, primarily due to their geographic and economic characteristics. For example, Seychelles and Mauritius have limited land resources and are susceptible to environmental risks such as rising sea levels and hurricanes. This geographic reality makes controlling population density critical, as excessive immigration could strain infrastructure, natural resources, and environmental sustainability. Moreover, these islands often have specialised economies predominantly reliant on migrant labour. An unregulated influx of people can lead to challenges for both the host economy and the migrant, including human- and drug-trafficking, forced labour, migrant smuggling, and exploitation.[86]

This often leaves countries with no option than to take drastic measures to protect their borders, making it necessary, from this point of view, to revisit and reconstruct the 'free movement' rhetoric into a more feasible 'freer movement' rubric.

[77] Art 9(2) of the Constitution of the Republic of Seychelles, 1993 (as amended).
[78] Section 20(3) of the Constitution of Mauritius, 1968.
[79] B Manby, 'Citizenship Law in Africa: A Comparative Study' (Open Society Foundations, 2016) 5.
[80] See 'Africa Visa Openness Report 2023' (n 56).
[81] 'Tourism Seychelles' (n 69).
[82] Angola, Benin, Botswana, Burundi, Cape Verde, Chad, Democratic Republic of Congo, Egypt, Eswatini, Gabon, Kenya, Lesotho, Malawi, Mozambique, Namibia, Republic of Congo, Rwanda, Seychelles, Sierra Leone, South Africa, Tanzania, The Gambia, Tunisia, Uganda, Zambia, and Zimbabwe.
[83] Algeria, Burkina Faso, Cameroon, Central African Republic, Comoros, Côte d'Ivoire, Djibouti, Equatorial Guinea, Eritrea, Ethiopia, Guinea, Guinea-Bissau, Liberia, Madagascar, Mauritania, Morocco, Niger, Nigeria, São Tomé and Príncipe, Senegal, and Togo.
[84] Libya, Mali, Somalia, South Sudan, and Sudan.
[85] See 'Africa Visa Openness Report 2023' (n 56).
[86] See eg *Seychelles National Labour Migration Policy* (n 68) 28–29.

VI. From Free to Freer Movement

The concepts of the 'free' and 'freer' movement of people in Africa hold similar but distinct implications. Free movement of people refers to the unimpeded ability of individuals to move across borders without restrictions, as envisioned by the AU-FMP Protocol, which expressly defines it as:

> The right of nationals of a Member State to enter, move freely and reside in another Member State under the laws of the host Member State and to exit the host Member State under the laws and procedures for exiting that Member State.[87]

In contrast, 'freer' movement suggests a gradual, progressive, easing of barriers, allowing for increased mobility across the continent. This difference shapes policy design and implementation. Whereas the AU-FMP Protocol provides in blanket terms for the right of entry, residence and establishment, subject to the domestic laws of the receiving country, the concept of freer movement proposes an incremental process that first relaxes restrictions on entry for tourism, business, study and other temporary visits and gives the reins to the receiving country to determine when to progress to a right to reside and establish, including the applicable criteria and conditions. The idea of freer movement is conceptually less imposing and should, therefore, be more feasible and acceptable to states wary of sovereignty erosion as well as states located at challenging levels of development. The freer movement concept presents a feasible incremental approach toward achieving the ultimate goal of the free movement of people on the continent.

Secondly, the freer movement concept can build on the regional mobility achieved in the regions. As discussed in section III, citizens of regional blocs across Africa already enjoy free movement within their regions, and this could be extended to citizens of other regional blocs through regional visas, much like the Schengen visa, which allows unimpeded movement around most European Union Member States.

Thirdly, given the breadth of access which the continental passport is expected to provide, strict eligibility requirements must be put in place to ensure that the grantee is demonstrably trustworthy and does not present a risk to any country. Simply being a citizen of an African country does not hold the assurance which domestic populations need in order to open their doors.

Fourthly, the free movement rights attaching to the first issue of a continental passport could be limited to a short duration, serving as a probationary period of sorts, guaranteeing a visa-on-arrival in all participating countries with visa requirements for the visitor's nationality. A reissue for a longer term would be predicated on satisfactory use of the first issue. In other words, this continental citizenship by way of a continental passport to ease mobility may be more beneficially construed as an incremental privilege rather than a blanket right.

However, as the framework currently stands, it is conveyed in the parlance of rights. People are beneficiaries of various fundamental human rights protection within an AU State party. From an African perspective, the African Charter on Human and Peoples'

[87] AU-FMP Protocol (n 2) art 1.

Rights (AfCHPR) enshrines several human rights protections. Article 12 explicitly protects all people, emphasising the right to freedom of movement and residence within one's state, as well as the right to leave.[88] This provision, as with other international human rights provisions relating to free movement,[89] does not bestow on a person a right to enter or remain in a country of which they are not a citizen. From an international law and human rights perspective, freedom of movement as a legal entitlement is much narrower in scope.

The right to enter and stay in another country is subject to the laws of the host state, any law imposed on the host state by a supranational or intergovernmental organisation (such as the AU), or any bilateral agreement that a particular host state may have concluded which allows for free or liberalised movement. In essence, the free movement of people is closely linked to regional economic integration processes and models, given the focus on supporting the pan-African objective of an integrated and unified Africa. The establishment of a common market, the gradual removal of obstacles to the free movement of persons, goods, services and capital, and the right of residence and establishment are key steps towards this goal.[90]

This notion of 'free' has proved to be a misnomer as it conveys the expectation of borders flung wide open in a way that often presents a stumbling block to an improved mobility regime.[91] The free movement of people in Africa represents a strategy for promoting and facilitating the cross-border movement of people within the African continent. At its foundation, the free movement of people in Africa is an effort to remove barriers that prevent people from travelling, working, and settling in different African countries, thereby facilitating economic, cultural, and social integration.[92] Generally, visa liberalisation, which entails reducing or abolishing visa rules, is central to this concept.[93] Furthermore, the idea of free movement of people should emphasise the importance of improved and coordinated border management, underlining the need and relevance for standardised travel documents and processes. Fundamentally, it is essential to the success of this initiative that the free movement of people is viewed from the perspective of a 'freer, facilitated or graduated movement', and it is important that the appropriate terminology be utilised to capture the intended objectives and outcomes.

Given how the continent is developing, regional agreements play a crucial role in enabling and facilitating cross-border movement, as part of a broader ethos of fostering collective geographic identity, and this needs to become the reference point in formulating and fine-tuning the policies around African citizenship through the activation of freer movement.

[88] African Charter on Human and Peoples' Rights (adopted 27 June 1981, entered into force 21 October 1986) (1982) 21 ILM 58 (AfCHPR) art 12(2).

[89] See Universal Declaration of Human Rights (adopted 10 December 1948) UNGA Res 217 A(III) art 13(2) and International Covenant on Civil and Political Rights (adopted 16 December 1966, entered into force 23 March 1976) 999 UNTS 171, art 12.

[90] Treaty Establishing the African Economic Community (signed 3 June 1991, entered into force 12 May 1994) (1991) 30 ILM 1241, art 4(2)(h)–(i).

[91] See Oucho and Crush (n 45) 143–44 for a discussion on the decline of the SADC Draft Protocol on Free Movement of Persons and the development of the Protocol on the Facilitation of the Movement of Persons.

[92] AU-FMP (n 2) art 5(1)(a).

[93] AU-FMP (n 2) art 6.

VII. Reflections on Africa's Small States and Constitutionalism

As earlier mentioned, five of Africa's six island nations constitute the majority of the continent's small states; hence the focus on island states in this chapter. Applying a stratified view of Africa's legal systems, constitutionalism constitutes only one layer of the multi-strata of normative sources, others being customary law, variants of colonial-era laws, post-independence constitutional systems and domestic laws, as well as regional legal frameworks. These are all embedded within dominant legal traditions, principally common law and civil law, as well as religious law. This plural legal environment makes it compelling for the constitutional ethos to be evaluated against its multi-normative environment, as the latter shapes states' responses to both internal and external stimuli in supplementary ways to the constitution.

This chapter has therefore used regional law and policy imperatives presented by the AU-FMP Protocol to demonstrate how small states find alternative but complementary ways, not necessarily stipulated in their constitutions, to address regional law imperatives.[94]

VIII. Conclusion

Central to this chapter's discussion is the concept of citizenship, explored in the context of enabling freer movement across Africa. Traditionally tied to the nation-state, citizenship is increasingly reimagined as a transnational status, enabled by the movement of people across borders, through regional and continental integration aspirations. An effective freer movement regime requires complementary regional and national initiatives as critical steps toward a shared African identity. This chapter highlights various regional initiatives and national strategies to advance freer movement, including those of small island nations.

The transformative potential of African citizenship by way of a continental passport includes enhanced cross-border movements for various purposes, and certain essential enablers need to be in place for an effective cross-border process, principally legal identity and border management infrastructure. This twin mechanism is foundational to orderly and secure movement across borders, which is where the delicate balance between integration and national security interests typically plays out. The United Nations (UN) frames the legal identity imperative as a

> holistic approach to the civil registration of all vital events, the production of vital statistics, the establishment and maintenance of population registers and identity management apparatus from birth to death, with full interoperability between these functions simultaneously,

[94] The Constitutions of Mauritius and Seychelles are silent on participation in regional schemes; nor do they outline the status of engagement in international or regional laws domestically. However, in Seychelles, art 64(4) of the Constitution of the Republic of Seychelles, 1993 (as amended) provides that for Seychelles to be bound by a Treaty, such Treaty must be ratified by Parliament.

> according to international standards and recommendations and in compliance with human rights of all people concerned, including the right to privacy.[95]

Taking this framework into consideration, a concerted effort to educate and build capacity is essential, focusing on strengthening civil registration systems to ensure that all citizens possess the legal identity documents necessary for seamless cross-border movement. Additionally, harmonising legal, procedural, and technical standards across the continent is critical. Adopting common standards for biometric data collection and ensuring interoperable systems would streamline the verification processes at borders, enhancing security without sacrificing efficiency. This harmonisation should extend to security measures, emphasising investing in advanced technologies for border management and establishing robust data-sharing mechanisms that respect individual privacy and data protection laws.

Further, an incremental implementation strategy, prioritising regions with strong regional ties and frameworks would be useful. This means, in other words, integrating regional mobility systems that are already in operation as eligibility indicators for the African passport in ways that ease the transition towards a continent-wide freer movement regime. Incremental options such as regional visas, with appropriate eligibility requirements, can drive regional mobility while countries retain their prerogative to legislate for visa-free travel for citizens of their preferred countries, visas on arrival, right of residence and right of establishment. The key thing is to deploy a gradual and manageable process which allows for real-time monitoring of the impacts of mobility policy changes, accommodates the diverse levels of development on the continent, and enables each country to preserve its ability to achieve its national imperatives.

Importantly, establishing a robust monitoring and evaluation framework is indispensable for enabling the free movement regime and making necessary policy adjustments. This framework should include feedback mechanisms allowing for a grounded assessment of each implementation phase of the freer movement programme.

Implementing the free movement of people initiative has had mixed results. On one hand, several regional blocs and countries have made strides in easing visa restrictions for African nationals, thereby increasing intra-continental travel. On the other hand, the full realisation of unrestricted movement faces significant hurdles, including disparities in economic development, security concerns, and the protectionism of national labour markets. If there has been reluctance on the part of mainland African states to the AU-FMP Protocol, the reticence from island nations is even more pronounced and for good cause, as discussed in earlier sections of this chapter. Small island nations, such as Seychelles and Mauritius, must balance the potential benefits of increased mobility with the need to preserve their unique cultural and geographic landscapes. This chapter underscores the importance of carefully calibrating free movement policies to align with the domestic needs and settings of small states. Ultimately, the path toward freer movement will require a flexible, incremental approach that respects the sovereignty of all African nations.

[95] UNECA, AU Commission, and AfDB 'United Nations Legal Identity Agenda: fulfilling the promise to leave no one behind' (Report from UNECA Conference of African Ministers Responsible for Civil Registration, Lusaka, 14–18 October 2019) 3.

On the other hand, there is a gradual but definite transition from a portfolio of visas to a less obstructive and restrictive visa regime, cautiously steered through domestic and regional policies, intent on avoiding the tipping-point potential of the worrisome, blanket free movement construct.

As much as it necessitates a delicate balancing act between advancing regional integration and respecting national sovereignty, the African visa-free movement duet is a resoundingly bold step towards continental citizenship, and the movement of people across borders is envisaged to catalyse economic, cultural and social integration. While there are challenges, the potential benefits are perceived as immense; hence the commitment of states, at domestic levels, to implement it at varying incremental levels.

PART II

State Design and Operation

Part IIA
Separation of Powers, and Checks and Balances

13

Multitasked Office in Pacific Constitutions

ANNA DZIEDZIC*

I. Introduction

Multitasking is a fact of life in small states. Limited human resources mean that nearly everybody is called upon to perform multiple roles.[1] This accumulation of overlapping roles and responsibilities occurs within government administration but also expands beyond it, across business, professions and community institutions.[2]

This chapter explores multitasked office as a constitutional design response to conditions of smallness. Multitasked offices are created and mandated by the constitution. In this, they are distinct from the conferral of multiple offices on the one individual through an exercise of political discretion[3] or the accumulation of various roles and functions over time.[4] Multitasked office, as explored in this chapter, is a matter of constitutional design in the creation of constitutional offices and the allocation of powers and functions to them.

Multitasked office takes two broad forms. The first is combined office, which arises when constitutional offices and functions which in larger states would usually be held by separate officials are combined into the one office. The main example pursued here is where the head of state is combined with the head of government in a parliamentary system. The second instantiation of multitasked office is double hatting. This occurs when the constitution confers additional offices on a constitutional office-holder.

* I am grateful to the editors and all participants at the Small States Constitutionalism Workshop at University of New South Wales, 11–12 December 2023 for their generous engagement with the ideas presented in this chapter. Archival research on constitution making in the three states featured here was facilitated by the award of a National Library of Australia Fellowship supported by the Stokes Family in 2021.

[1] J Corbett, '"Everybody Knows Everybody": Practising Politics in the Pacific' (2015) 22 *Democratization* 51, 61.

[2] M Jugl, *Country Size and Public Administration* (Cambridge, Cambridge University Press, 2022) 15–16, 20–24.

[3] SG Calabresi and JL Larsen, 'One Person One Office: Separation of Powers or Separation of Personnel' (1993) 79 *Cornell Law Review* 1045.

[4] I use the term 'multitasking' to capture this phenomenon. The term 'polyvalence' is also sometimes used in the literature: Jugl (n 2) 15.

An example is a constitutional provision making the Chief Justice the Supervisor of Elections.

Ideas of multitasked office circulated around the Pacific region as states were making new constitutions to mark their independence in the 1960s and 1970s. This chapter focuses on three Pacific states: Kiribati, the Marshall Islands and Nauru, which are briefly introduced in section II below. Each of these states adopted a parliamentary system in which the president is both head of state and head of government, a departure from the more typical design of a parliamentary system where those two offices are separated. They also explored innovations to multitask other offices, including the Speaker of Parliament and the Chief Justice. Section III presents examples of the different forms of multitasking in the three constitutional systems.

Drawing on the discussions of constitution-makers, section IV examines the motivations behind the constitutional design choice to mandate multitasked office. Multitasked office was frequently characterised as a response to the small size of the state. It was seen as a solution to issues arising from a shortage of qualified personnel (a result of both smallness and colonisation) and reflected a desire to minimise the costs of government. Multitasked office was also seen to offer some continuity with forms of government adopted under colonial rule, and to resonate with the cultural context of the small island states.

Multitasked office comes with some risks, however. Combined office risks concentrating a great deal of power in the one office, a particular concern in small states, where the personalisation of politics can contribute to the accumulation of political power by individual leaders. Double hatting, meanwhile, raises concerns about conflict of interest and 'trading off' the prestige and independence of one office to enhance another. In section V, I present some examples of these risks, but also show that they are not inevitable and can be countered by constitutional design and practice.

II. The Constitutions of Three Small States

Many small states utilise forms of multitasking. This chapter focuses on three small states in the Pacific: Kiribati, the Marshall Islands, and Nauru. The peoples of these neighbouring countries are classified as Micronesian, although the arbitrariness of that classification should be acknowledged.[5] The peoples and cultures of each country, and communities within each country, are varied and distinctive. The islands and atolls that now form these three small states share long-standing interconnections, through ancestry, marriage and the movement of peoples for education, work and business.[6] Other connections were created through shared colonial histories under German, British,

[5] D Hanlon, 'The "Sea of Little Lands": Examining Micronesia's Place in "Our Sea of Islands"' (2009) *The Contemporary Pacific* 91.

[6] N Meller, 'Bankroll Instead of Bullets: Nauru's Role in the Birth of the Marshall Islands Republic' (1988) 23 *The Journal of Pacific History* 200, 200. Smith notes that many Micronesians and I-Kiribati had worked in Nauru, while De Jonge highlights the education and business links between Nauru and the Marshall Islands: J Smith, *An Island in the Autumn* (Kinloss, Librario Publishing, 2011) 188; A De Jonge, *The Constitution of the Marshall Islands: Its Drafting and Current Operation* (Sydney, Centre for South Pacific Studies, University of New South Wales, 1993) 20.

Australian and American administration, war-time occupation by Japan, and the continuing effects of colonial exploitation through mining and nuclear testing. Inter-country connections also informed constitutions and constitution-making processes. This section sets out the constitutional stories of each of the three countries, following the chronological order in which their independence constitutions were made.

A. Nauru

Nauru is a single island of 21 square kilometres in the western Pacific. It has a current population of 12,000 mostly Indigenous peoples who trace their heritage to 12 clans or tribes.[7]

In 1888, Germany annexed Nauru and administered it together with the Marshall Islands. From 1920, Nauru was a League of Nations Mandate and then, from 1947, a United Nations Trust Territory administered by Australia with Britain and New Zealand as co-trustees. The three joint administering countries ran the British Phosphate Commission, which mined the phosphate reserves of the island. This period was interrupted by three years of Japanese occupation during the Pacific war, during which 1200 Nauruans were taken to Chuuk in the present-day Federated States of Micronesia and nearly a quarter of the Nauruan population died.

Pressure for Nauru's independence grew over the 1960s. Negotiations focused on the phosphate industry as Nauruan leaders advocated for a fair share of profits, the transfer of assets and rehabilitation of lands.[8] Only once the issues relating to the phosphate industry had been agreed did attention turn to constitution making. The basic structure for the Constitution was proposed by Nauruan leaders and discussed and substantially drafted at meetings in Canberra between Nauruan leaders, Australian government officials and representatives of New Zealand and the United Kingdom.[9] Jim Davidson, a professor of history at the Australian National University who had advised leaders in Samoa and the Cook Islands on their independence constitutions, was an adviser to the Nauruan government throughout, and had a 'profound' influence on the constitutional text.[10] The draft was debated and adopted by a Constitutional Convention. All in all, the constitution-making process took less than 12 months.

The Constitution established Nauru as a republic with a parliamentary system of government, led by a President who is both head of government and head of state.[11]

[7] 'Population Projection Table 2024' (*Pacific Community Pacific Data Hub*), sdd.spc.int/topic/population.

[8] C Storr, *International Status in the Shadow of Empire: Nauru and the Histories of International Law* Cambridge, Cambridge University Press, 2020) chapter 5. The issue of rehabilitation was not resolved until Nauru took a case against Australia to the International Court of Justice: Certain Phosphate Lands in Nauru *Nauru v Australia)* [1992] ICJ 240 (26 June 1992) (*Phosphate Lands Case*).

[9] 'Statement of Nauruan Delegation on Political and Constitutional Changes', 15 June 1967, Papers of W Davidson, National Library of Australia, MS 5105/42, Box 22; JW Davidson, 'The Republic of Nauru' 1968) 3 *The Journal of Pacific History* 145.

[10] K McDowell, 'The Factors behind the Constitutional Arrangements in Nauru' in PG Sack (ed), *Pacific Constitutions* (Canberra, Australian National University, 1982) 73.

[11] The Constitution does not explicitly state that the President is head of state and head of government. It is inferred from other provisions and the accepted understanding at the time of drafting: Nauru Constitutional Review Committee, *Naoero Ituga: Report* (2007) 44.

The Parliament elects the President from among its members by majority vote. The President then appoints a Cabinet of five to six members, drawn from the 19-member Parliament. The Parliament can remove the President by a vote of no confidence, again by majority vote. Changes in the composition of Parliament due to vacancies, shifting allegiances and suspensions have resulted in periods of political instability.[12]

B. Marshall Islands

The Marshall Islands is an independent state in free association with the United States. It consists of five islands and 29 coral atolls, across two island chains. Its current population is 54,000 people, the majority of whom are Indigenous.[13] An estimated 27,000 Marshallese live in the United States.

The Marshall Islands was subject to German and then Japanese rule before it was occupied by the United States military in 1944. From 1947, the Marshall Islands was administered by the United States as part of the Trust Territory of the Pacific Islands, which also covered what is now the Federated States of Micronesia, Palau and the Northern Mariana Islands. During this time, from 1946 to 1958 the United States used the Marshall Islands as the site for 67 nuclear tests. The health and environmental impacts of nuclear testing continue today.

Advocacy for self-determination in the late 1960s led the Congress of Micronesia (representing the whole Trust Territory) to begin negotiations with the United States. The Congress established the Future Political Status Commission to consider options for self-determination. In 1975 delegates from all parts of the Trust Territory participated in a Constitutional Convention to draft a constitution. The Convention proceeded on the basis that all the island groups would join together in a federation.

However, the Marshall Islands sought a separate path.[14] Its legislature formed its own Political Status Commission in 1973 to negotiate separately with the United States. In 1977 it convened its own Constitutional Convention to draft a constitution for the Marshall Islands. By mid-1978, the first draft of the Constitution had been publicly released, the plebiscite for joining the Micronesian federation was pending, and negotiations with the United States were at a crucial stage. At this critical point, the government of Nauru loaned a substantial sum to the Constitutional Convention, 'for purposes connected with self-determination of the Marshallese people', effectively 'bankrolling the birth of a new Marshallese Republic'.[15]

The Constitution of the Marshall Islands was adopted by the Constitutional Convention on 21 December 1978 and recognised by the United States on 1 May 1979. The Trusteeship Arrangement was terminated in 1986, when a Compact of Free Association with the United States entered into force. The Compact gives the

[12] M Quanchi, 'Nauru' in SI Levine (ed), *Pacific Ways: Government and Politics in the Pacific Islands*, 2nd edn (Wellington, Victoria University Press, 2016) 148, 154–55.

[13] Population Projection Table 2024 (*Pacific Community – Pacific Data Hub*), sdd.spc.int/topic/population.

[14] For detailed analysis of constitution making in the Marshall Islands see De Jonge (n 6); A Quentin-Baxter, 'Making Constitutions, from the Perspective of Constitutional Adviser' (2002) 33 *Victoria University of Wellington Law Review* 274.

[15] Meller (n 6).

United States full authority and responsibility for the security and defence of the Marshall Islands. Under the Compact, the United States provides funding to the Marshall Islands and permits Marshallese citizens to access United States programmes and services and gives them rights of entry and residence in the United States.[16]

The Marshall Islands did not follow the United States and the other Micronesian countries that were formerly part of the Trust Territory in adopting a presidential system of government. It instead chose a parliamentary system, with a President who is both head of state and head of government. The Marshall Islands' leaders selected a constitutional adviser with this in mind. New Zealand lawyer and academic, Alison Quentin-Baxter, who with her husband, Robert Quentin Quentin-Baxter, had provided constitutional advice on the Constitution of Niue, was appointed counsel to the Constitutional Convention in 1977.[17]

Under the Marshall Islands Constitution, the President is elected by the *Nitijela* (the parliament) from among its members, using a secret ballot and absolute majority vote. The President then appoints a Cabinet from among the members of parliament. The *Nitijela* may remove the President and Cabinet by a no confidence vote, although if it fails to elect a new President within 14 days, the removal lapses.[18] The Council of Iroij – a body composed of traditional chiefs from each district in the country – has an advisory role to the Parliament and the Cabinet.

C. Kiribati

Kiribati comprises 32 atolls and one island, Banaba, spread across the centre of the Pacific Ocean. Its population is 126,000, the majority Indigenous.[19] Kiribati – formerly called the Gilbert Islands – was a protectorate and then a colony of Britain, administered together with what is now Tuvalu, then called the Ellice Islands. Like Nauru, Kiribati's island of Banaba had phosphate reserves which were mined by the British Phosphate Commission resulting in the displacement of peoples and environmental destruction.[20]

Kiribati became an independent state in 1979. Several factors shaped its path to independence. The Ellice Islands separated from the Gilbert Islands in 1975 and became the independent state of Tuvalu in 1978. The people of Banaba also called for separation. The concerns of Banaban people were partially addressed through the constitution-making process, with constitutional guarantees for the rights and special status of Banabans living in Kiribati and in Fiji.[21]

[16] Compact of Free Association, Agreement between the United States of America and the Marshall Islands, 25 June 1983, amended 30 April 2003.

[17] Although the influence of the United States Constitution informed the choice of Laurence Tribe, from Harvard University, to provide advice on the constitutional rights provisions: Quentin-Baxter (n 14) 240–41.

[18] Constitution of the Marshall Islands, art V, s 7.

[19] Population Projection Table 2024 (*Pacific Community Pacific Data Hub*), sdd.spc.int/topic/population.

[20] KM Teaiwa, *Consuming Ocean Island: Stories of People and Phosphate from Banaba* (Bloomington IN, Indiana University Press, 2015).

[21] J McAdam, 'Self-Determination and Self-Governance for Communities Relocated across International Borders: The Quest for Banaban Independence' (2017) 24 *International Journal on Minority and Group Rights* 428.

In 1976, the Gilbert Islands Council of Ministers agreed to a proposal from the colonial Governor, John Smith, to establish a Constitutional Convention to make recommendations for the independence Constitution of Kiribati. The Convention was broadly representative and inclusive. All members of the Convention were Gilbertese, with the exception of academic David Murray, who served as adviser. The Convention included all elected members of the House of Assembly, Gilbertese senior civil servants, and representatives of the churches and unions. Also in attendance were the presidents of each Island Council and representatives of the cooperative society, the women's club and the *Unimane* (male elders) from each of the 21 island groups.[22] The rules of procedure for the Constitutional Convention were based on *maneaba* (meeting house) traditions. Discussions were in Gilbertese and decision making aimed for consensus.[23] The recommendations made by the Convention were reviewed by the House of Assembly[24] and a constitutional conference in London.[25] The Constitution was approved by the House of Assembly on 1 May 1979 and adopted upon independence on 12 July 1979. Formally, the Constitution was made as a schedule to an Order in Council of the British monarch.

Kiribati also adopted a parliamentary system in which the *Beretitenti* (president) is both head of government and head of state. In contrast to the Marshall Islands and Nauru, the *Beretitenti* is directly elected. Following parliamentary elections, up to four candidates are nominated by the parliament from among its membership, who then contest a national election for the presidency. The *Beretitenti* may be removed by the parliament through a vote of no confidence. A successful vote of no confidence leads automatically to the dissolution of parliament. A Council of State, composed of the Speaker of Parliament, the Chief Justice and the Chair of the Public Service Commission, is the caretaker government until a new parliament is elected and new government formed.

III. Multitasked Office

Multitasking is not unique to small states. In one sense, the Westminster parliamentary system involves multitasking ministers with executive and legislative functions. Even in presidential systems with a stricter separation of powers, such as the United States, the idea that one person should not hold multiple offices across the different branches of government became a binding constitutional principle only relatively recently.[26]

Constitution makers in the Pacific experimented with various forms of multitasking. This section outlines the features of three such innovations that made it into the written Constitutions of Kiribati, the Marshall Islands and Nauru, namely: the combined head

[22] Gilbert Islands, *Report of the Constitutional Convention 1977*, April 21–May 9 (Tarawa, 1977) Appendix B; D Murray, 'Constitutional Instruments in Kiribati and Tuvalu: A Case Study of Impact and Influence' in H Hiery and J MacKenzie (eds), *European Impact and Pacific Influence* (London, IB Tauris, 1997) 259, 265.

[23] Murray (n 22) 263–65.

[24] *Report of the Select Committee on the Recommendations of the Constitutional Convention*, 13 May 1977 (Tarawa, 1977).

[25] *Report of the Gilbert Islands Constitutional Conference:* London, November/December 1978 (HMSO 1979).

[26] Calabresi and Larsen (n 3).

of state and head of government; multitasking the Speaker of Parliament; and double hatting the Chief Justice.[27]

A. Head of the Executive

A combined head of state and head of government is a standard feature of presidential systems of government, in which the legislature and the president are separately elected and each serves for a fixed term. It is much less common in parliamentary systems of government, in which the head of government is drawn from the parliament and holds office only while his or her government has the confidence of the parliament. In addition to Kiribati, the Marshall Islands and Nauru, other examples of parliamentary systems in which the head of state and head of government are combined include Botswana and South Africa. Various terms have been coined for this system, including 'parliamentary president'[28] and 'executive president'.[29]

The Constitutions of Kiribati, the Marshall Islands and Nauru demonstrate how this multitasked head of the executive works. First, their systems of government are clearly parliamentary. The president and Cabinet ministers are selected from among the members of parliament and serve in both executive and legislative roles. The president and his or her government hold office only as long they have the confidence of the parliament.

Second, the combined office multitasks at least three distinct roles: the head of state in the exercise of formal or ceremonial powers and some 'reserve' powers; the head of government with the support of the majority of the parliament; and the head of the Cabinet. Yet more roles might be added beyond those constitutionally mandated: the president might assign him or herself ministerial portfolios; while as an elected member of the parliament, the president is also a representative and legislator. Importantly, however, all three Constitutions explicitly vest executive power in the *Cabinet*, not the president or head of state.[30] It is in the role as head of the Cabinet that the multitasked head of the executive exercises the most significant executive powers.[31] Although the president depends on Cabinet for most of these powers, the president's powers to appoint and dismiss ministers, allocate portfolios and preside over meetings of Cabinet give the president significant control over the Cabinet.[32]

[27] Other forms of multitasking were discussed but not adopted. The committee system of government, in which the assembly of elected representatives exercises legislative authority as a whole and executive authority amongst committees, was proposed by the Canberra-based Working Group on Nauruan Constitutional Arrangements as an alternative to the combined head of state and head of government: 'Committee Systems of Executive Government', 9 June 1967, and 'A Committee System of Executive Government for Nauru', 30 August 1967, Papers of JW Davidson, National Library of Australia, MS 5105/42, Box 22.

[28] YP Ghai and J Cottrell, *Heads of State in the Pacific: A Legal and Constitutional Analysis* (Suva, Institute of Pacific Studies of the University of the South Pacific, 1990) 7.

[29] Smith (n 6) 188.

[30] Constitution of Kiribati art 45; Constitution of Nauru art 17; Constitution of the Marshall Islands art V, s 1.

[31] CJ Lynch, 'Draftsman's Notes on the Executive Government of Kiribati' 1979, Papers of CJ Lynch, National Library of Australia, MS Acc11.076, Box 9, File 7/2, 21; Ghai and Cottrell (n 28) 7; Nauru Constitutional Review Committee (n 11) 45.

[32] Constitution of Kiribati arts 41, 47(1); Constitution of Nauru arts 19, 20(c), 23; Constitution of the Marshall Islands art V, ss 4–6.

Third, the decision to combine the office of the head of state and head of government informs the kind of detail that needs to be included in the written Constitution. Because executive power is vested in the Cabinet, the president cannot exercise executive power in his or her own right except where authority to do so is expressly conferred by law. Constitutional provisions which confer specific powers on the president tend to define whether the power is exercised in the president's own discretion or in accordance with advice.

It is tempting to try to organise the presidential powers of a combined office against the three different offices that have been combined. This has been done in South Africa, where, broadly speaking the President is understood to be acting as Head of State when he or she formalises a decision made elsewhere; as Head of Government when the support of the Cabinet is required; and as Head of Cabinet when acting alone to make political decisions about the composition of Cabinet.[33] However, the three Pacific constitutions do not present a standard pattern, and the Constitutions of Kiribati, the Marshall Islands, and Nauru confer and regulate the exercise of presidential powers in their own ways.

Kiribati's Constitution provides that the *Beretitenti* shall 'act in his [or her] own deliberate judgment and shall not be obliged to follow the advice tendered by any other person or authority', unless otherwise provided by the Constitution.[34] The Constitution requires the *Beretitenti* to act in accordance with the advice of the Cabinet when making a declaration of a state of emergency,[35] exercising the prerogative of mercy,[36] and appointing senior independent constitutional office-holders (such as Electoral Commissioners, the Chief Justice and the Commissioner of Police).[37] The Constitution also specifies that some powers of the *Beretitenti* must be exercised in accordance with advice from other bodies, such as the Public Service Commission.[38] These powers resonate with the formal role performed by a separate head of state in other parliamentary systems, where the head of state acts on the advice of the elected government. The *Beretitenti* also has head of state-type powers to act as a brake or check on the exercise of power. The *Beretitenti*'s power to assent to legislation is not exercised on advice, and so is an act in the 'deliberate judgment' of the *Beretitenti*. The Constitution regulates this judgment by permitting the *Beretitenti* to withhold assent only on the ground that the Bill is inconsistent with the Constitution. The *Beretitenti* may then refer the Bill back to parliament once and then to the High Court. If the Court declares the Bill is constitutional, the *Beretitenti* must give his or her assent.[39] When the *Beretitenti* is required to act on advice, the *Beretitenti* may also refer a matter back to the advising authority for reconsideration before acting in accordance with the advice.[40] Other powers and functions conferred on the *Beretitenti* to be exercised in his or her 'deliberate judgment' align with

[33] C Murray and R Stacey, 'The President and the National Executive' in S Woolman and M Bishop (eds), *Constitutional Law of South Africa*, 2nd edn (Cape Town, Juta & Co, 2013) chapter 18.

[34] Constitution of Kiribati art 46(1).

[35] ibid art 16(2).

[36] ibid art 50.

[37] ibid arts 62(2), 81(1), 100.

[38] eg, ibid arts 100, 105.

[39] ibid art 66.

[40] ibid art 46(2).

those political powers exercised by the Head of Cabinet, such as the appointment and removal of Ministers and summoning meetings of Cabinet.[41]

Nauru's Constitution grants significant powers to the President which can be exercised without the advice or approval of the Cabinet. These include the power to declare an emergency and make orders during an emergency,[42] grant a pardon,[43] and appoint judges.[44] Head of state-type functions to summon, prorogue and dissolve parliament are vested in the Speaker of Parliament, who must act on the advice of the President.[45] The only time the President is required by the Constitution to act with the approval of Cabinet is when referring a question of constitutional interpretation to the Supreme Court,[46] and, by implication, when exercising any of the executive powers vested in the Cabinet. Nauru's Constitution contains fewer requirements that the President exercise his or her powers on advice than Kiribati's Constitution.

In the Marshall Islands, as in Kiribati and Nauru, the President's powers as Head of Cabinet, such as the selection of ministers and assignment of portfolios, are relatively unfettered.[47] In contrast to the other two states, however, many formal head of state-type functions and some head of government-type functions are conferred on other offices and institutions. The Speaker of Parliament formally appoints Ministers and performs a range of other head of state-like functions (outlined below). The President has limited powers to summon and dissolve parliament in specified circumstances.[48] The formalities of appointment tend to be performed by the President when the appointment relates to the parliament, the Speaker when the appointment relates to the executive, and the Cabinet for judicial appointments. Substantively, the President has few appointment powers outside the ministry and for most appointments is bound to act on the advice of bodies such as the parliament, the Public Service Commission and the Judicial Services Commission. In this way, the Marshall Islands Constitution spreads executive powers across multiple multitasked offices and institutions, preserving checks and balances across the branches of government.

This discussion of the detail of constitutional provisions demonstrates the variety of approaches to conferring and regulating the powers of a combined head of executive. The common thread is that arrangements for a multitasked head of the executive require that written constitutions prescribe not only the matters over which the President may exercise powers, but also the extent of the President's discretion in exercising those powers. The *sui generis* nature of combined office limits the usefulness of conventions and precedents inherited from Westminster and other parliamentary systems. Instead, constitutional provisions relating to executive power are more detailed and not always systematic, and new conventions must be worked out between the various actors in the system of government over time.

[41] ibid arts 41, 47(1), 48.
[42] Constitution of Nauru arts 77, 78.
[43] ibid art 80.
[44] ibid arts 49, 57A.
[45] ibid arts 39, 40, 41.
[46] ibid art 55.
[47] Constitution of the Marshall Islands art V, ss 4–6.
[48] ibid art IV, ss 10(2), 13.

B. Speaker of Parliament

Combining the offices of the head of government and the head of state has consequences for how other constitutional offices are defined. Here, too, multitasking is apparent. A prominent example is the Speaker of Parliament, who in all three jurisdictions takes on functions in addition to the Speaker's role as the presiding officer of the parliament.[49] Some of these functions are akin to those of a separate head of state.[50] For example, in the Marshall Islands and Nauru, the Speaker formally 'assents' to Bills by certifying that they have been validly passed by the Parliament.[51] In Nauru, the Speaker formally summons, prorogues and dissolves parliament on the advice of the President.[52] In the Marshall Islands, the Speaker formally appoints the President and the Ministers and receives their resignations,[53] and when necessary selects and appoints an acting President.[54] In these examples, the multitasking tends towards combined office.

In Kiribati, the directly elected *Beretitenti* assents to laws,[55] while the Speaker and the parliament are responsible for summoning and dissolving parliament.[56] In contrast to the Marshall Islands and Nauru, in Kiribati the office of the Speaker tends to be multitasked by way of double hatting. For example, the Speaker is *ex officio* a member of the Council of State.[57] The Council of State is a non-partisan body which acts in the place of the government after the President has lost a vote of confidence and new elections are pending.[58] The Speaker, together with the Chief Justice, also decides on appointments to the Public Service Commission.[59] In these roles, double hatting takes advantage of the independence of the Speaker, who in Kiribati is elected by the parliament from persons outside the parliament.[60]

C. Chief Justice

Multitasking in judicial office is a common phenomenon. Judges in many jurisdictions perform non-judicial functions, ranging from those closely adjacent to judicial

[49] For brief discussion of the multitasked Speaker in other Pacific jurisdictions, see CJ Lynch, 'Legislatures in Some Pacific Constitutions' in PG Sack (ed), *Pacific Constitutions* (Canberra, Australian National University, 1982) 153, 166–67.

[50] Indeed, discussions of the Working Group on Nauruan Constitutional Arrangements, which met in Canberra to develop the Nauruan Constitution, considered whether the Speaker could be head of state or 'exercise safeguarding powers of summoning and dissolution of [the] legislature': Summary of Matters discussed by Working Party on Nauruan Constitutional Arrangements' undated, Papers of JW Davidson, National Library of Australia, MS 5105/42, Boxes 22 and 24.

[51] Constitution of the Marshall Islands art IV, s 21; Constitution of Nauru art 47.

[52] Constitution of Nauru arts 40, 41.

[53] Constitution of the Marshall Islands art V, ss 3(4), 4(2), 6.

[54] The power to select an acting President arises only where the Cabinet fails to do so within a specified time: ibid art V, s 9(2).

[55] Constitution of Kiribati art 66.

[56] ibid arts 77, 78.

[57] ibid art 49(1).

[58] In Kiribati, a vote of no confidence in the President and government automatically results in the dissolution of parliament: ibid art 78.

[59] ibid art 98(1).

[60] ibid art 71(2).

functions, such as arbitration or adjudicating electoral matters, to roles closer to legislative and executive functions, such as serving in law reform commissions or diplomatic roles.[61] In many of these cases, the additional roles are taken up by judges or bestowed upon them as a matter of choice.

In some small states, however, multitasked judicial office is mandated by the Constitution. This is most often done by double hatting, by which the Chief Justice serves, *ex officio*, in other offices or institutions. For example, in Kiribati the Chief Justice is a member of the Council of State.[62] The Chief Justice, acting jointly with the Speaker of Parliament, advises the *Beretitenti* on the appointment and removal of the members of the Public Service Commission.[63] The Chief Justice is responsible for appointing the tribunal of medical practitioners as part of the process for the removal of the President on grounds of incapacity.[64] The Chief Justice is also supervisor of presidential elections.[65]

Notably, the Constitutions of Nauru and the Marshall Islands do not confer any additional non-judicial functions on the Chief Justice, which suggests that constitutionally multitasked judicial office is not widespread, even among small states.

On occasion, there have been proposals to multitask the office of Chief Justice in ways that resemble combined office, rather than double hatting. The Working Group on Nauruan Constitutional Arrangements proposed to confer a range of additional duties on judges, including law reform and legal drafting.[66] These proposals were perhaps inspired by provisions in the Constitution of Niue 1974, which gave the Chief Justice a role in legislative review and law reform, as a way to take advantage of scarce legal expertise.[67] An unnamed reviewer of a draft of the Nauru Constitution raised concerns that the judge responsible for interpreting the law should not also be the one drafting it,[68] and the provisions were removed from the draft.

IV. Motivations for Multitasking

The provisions for multitasked office in the Constitutions of Kiribati, the Marshall Islands and Nauru demonstrate innovation and experimentation in constitutional design in small states. Constitution makers were prepared to adapt the Westminster parliamentary template to the distinctive conditions of their newly independent states. Multitasked office was often explained as an adaptation to suit the small size of the jurisdiction. This section draws on the discussions and writings by constitution makers

[61] N Garoupa and T Ginsburg, 'Judicial Roles in Nonjudicial Functions' (2013) 12 *Washington University Global Studies Law Review* 755.

[62] Constitution of Kiribati art 49(1).

[63] ibid art 98(1).

[64] ibid art 34(1).

[65] ibid arts 38(1), 63(2).

[66] 'Summary of Matters discussed by Working Party on Nauruan Constitutional Arrangements' undated, Papers of JW Davidson, National Library of Australia, MS 5105/42, Boxes 22 and 24.

[67] These provisions of Niue's Constitution were repealed in 1992: Quentin-Baxter (n 14) 265.

[68] Note to Jim Davidson signed David, 1 May 1967, Papers of JW Davidson, National Library of Australia, MS 5105/42, Box 24.

and their advisers in each of the three countries to identify the motivations for creating multitasked offices. The discussion in this section focuses on the rationales for the combined head of state and head of government, as the example of multitasking that received the most attention by constitution makers in the three states.

Constitution makers and their advisers preparing for independence expressed concern about the shortage of qualified personnel with experience in government. The shortage was partially a result of small populations, but also the result of the policies and practices of the colonial administrations, which were very slow to involve Indigenous peoples in governmental decision making. At the time of constitution making, many felt there was a need to take advantage of the skills of a few to the greatest extent possible.[69] Multitasked office was seen as a desirable way to do this.[70]

Multitasking was also seen as a way of managing potential conflicts between eminent people in a small state. In the Marshall Islands, the central constitutional debate was not about combining the head of state and head of government in one office but rather about the choice between a parliamentary and presidential system of government. In this debate, parliamentary government was framed as a kind of multitasked institution which combined the legislature and executive, as opposed to the stricter separation of the two branches under a presidential system. It was argued that the strict application of the doctrine of separation of powers (of the kind in the United States' presidential system) would create a rivalry between the executive and the legislature, and preclude participation in government by members of the legislature.[71] In a similar vein, John Smith, Governor of the Gilbert Islands at the time of constitution making, noted that a combined head of state and head of government was preferred because of the 'concern that an eminent person with little to do other than preside at the occasional ceremony might well be tempted to interfere in matters not the responsibility of a Governor General'.[72] By facilitating the participation of as many officials as possible in government, multitasking not only took advantage of scarce human resources, but also mitigated political competition and division.

Multitasked office was also justified as a way to reduce the costs of government. Combining the head of state and head of government in one office was seen as a way to remove the need to fund a Governor General or other largely ceremonial figurehead.[73] In the Marshall Islands it was argued that a parliamentary system was less expensive than funding wholly separate executive and legislative branches of government.[74] This was not merely a question of the financial costs of running institutions of government. Under the Trust Territory Administration, the legislature composed of Marshallese

[69] eg Territory of Nauru, 'Record of the Proceedings of the Constitutional Convention' (10 January 1968) 43, noting the 'need to use qualified people to the greatest possible extent, both in the government and the legislature'.

[70] Lynch (n 49) 166.

[71] 'Report of the United Nations Visiting Mission to the Trust Territory of the Pacific Islands, 1964', T/1628, paras 196–198.

[72] Smith (n 6) 188.

[73] ibid.

[74] De Jonge (n 6) 25; A Quentin-Baxter, 'The Constitutions of Niue and the Marshall Islands: Common Traits and Points of Difference' in Peter G Sack (ed), *Pacific Constitutions* (Canberra, Australian National University, 1982) 104.

members operated as an advisory body to the Trust Territory Administrator appointed by and accountable to the United States government. Building the new government from the existing legislature took advantage of Marshallese legislators' experience under the colonial administration, reducing the need for (and cost of) foreign experts to assist in running the new system.[75] It was also thought that other states would be more likely to recognise the Marshall Islands' independence if its government emerged from an existing body, minimising the political costs of international diplomacy.[76] In this, multi-tasked office was valued for its continuity with the form of government under colonial administration. Such continuity had a dark side, however, as colonial administrators had a great deal of concentrated and largely unchecked executive power.[77]

Another motivation for multitasking was that it resonated with the cultural context and values of the peoples of the islands. In his observations on Kiribati's Constitutional Convention of 1977, Roniti Teiwaki notes that the recommendation to combine the head of state and head of government 'was not made because of costs or economy'. Rather, it reflected 'a traditional issue of *tabiteuea*' (a prohibition on chiefs that applied in some parts of Kiribati) in the face of the 'widespread misconception that a head of state in the form of a governor-general was synonymous with a monarchy for the islands'.[78] Several external advisers to constitution-making processes across the Pacific noted that the idea of a king, president or governor was a foreign idea in the region. Governor John Smith also considered that a figurehead head of state was not compatible with Kiribati's egalitarian communal culture.[79] Jill Cottrell and Yash Ghai expressed a concern that a separate head of state and head of government might create confusion in the minds of the public about where power lay.[80] Alison Quentin-Baxter, counsel to the Marshall Islands Constitutional Convention, noted that the idea of a ceremonial President who could only act on advice was foreign to Marshallese experience.[81] It was felt that a combined head of state and head of government, representing and advised by the Cabinet, was more consistent with traditions of leadership and group decision making.[82]

Considerations of smallness therefore played a role in constitutional design and in the creation of multitasked office. The small size of the states was seen to limit the number of personnel and the resources to operate new governments. Smallness might also, in some contexts, have contributed to a culture of egalitarianism, which is one way to maintain personal relationships and social harmony in a small community, which in turn influenced the decision to reject separate and potentially competitive executive offices.

[75] De Jonge (n 6) 25, 27.

[76] ibid 25–26; DC Smith, 'Marshall Islands: Tradition and Dependence' in R Crocombe and A Ali (eds), *Politics in Micronesia* (Suva, Institute of Pacific Studies of the University of the South Pacific, 1983) 57, 59.

[77] In Nauru, see Storr (n 8) 242, 245.

[78] R Teiwake, 'The Constitutional Convention and Gilbertese Culture' (1977) 6(2) *Pacific Perspectives* 6, 7.

[79] H Van Trease, 'From Colony to Independence' in H Van Trease (ed), *Atoll politics: the Republic of Kiribati* Christchurch, Macmillan Brown Centre for Pacific Studies, 1993) 3, 12.

[80] Ghai and Cottrell (n 28) 18.

[81] Quentin-Baxter (n 74) 104.

[82] De Jonge (n 6) 24.

V. Risks of Multitasked Office

Multitasked office presents some risks to accountable government. One significant concern is that multitasking leads to the concentration of power in a single office, a problem that can be compounded in small states by the personalisation of politics. Another set of problems for accountability can arise when multitasking seeks to borrow from the prestige of one (usually independent) office to enhance another. This section examines these risks, drawing on examples from the three states.

A. Concentration of Power

Literature on small states identifies the dominance of the executive over parliament, the courts and the public service as a potential effect of smallness. This is attributed to the personalisation of politics, whereby power comes to be concentrated not just in the office, but in the individual office-holder. In small states, individual leaders accumulate power not just by virtue of their office, but because of their status in other institutions and the community.[83] The first Presidents of the Marshall Islands and Nauru provide examples. Amata Kabua, the Marshall Islands' first President, was an *iroijlaplap* or paramount chief, with *iroij* or chiefly status from both the *Ralik* (western) and *Ratak* (eastern) chains of the Marshall Islands. He served as President for five consecutive terms, a period of 17 years, until his death in 1996.[84] In Nauru, Hammer DeRoburt led Nauru's negotiations for independence as Head Chief of the Nauru Local Government Council, an elected position that he held from 1955 to 1992, alongside terms as President of Nauru for most of the first 20 years of independence. Kabua and DeRoburt, like Kiribati's first President, Ieremia Tabai, held office for a long time, although this likely reflects their status as the leaders who negotiated independence as much as the personalisation of politics. Many Presidents in the years since have also held chiefly and other high status in the community but have not served for such long periods.[85]

Personalisation of politics provides 'mixed blessings' in small states.[86] It means that those holding leadership and constitutional office are closer to the community, with family, clan, church, business and other ties. These connections can enhance representation, participation, and – importantly – social or relational accountability. Because they are close to the community, those in public office are often under great pressure, as they are personally identified with the decisions they make in government. However, personalisation also presents risks of patronage, polarisation and the accumulation of unchecked power.[87]

[83] W Veenendaal, *Politics and Democracy in Microstates* (Oxford, Routledge, 2015) 50.

[84] DW Kupferman, 'Marshall Islands' in SI Levine (ed), *Pacific Ways: Government and Politics in the Pacific Islands*, 2nd edn (Wellington, Victoria University Press, 2016) 132, 133.

[85] Term limits apply in Kiribati: Constitution of Kiribati art 32(5).

[86] J Corbett and W Veenendaal, 'Why Small States are Beautiful' (2019) 10(1) *Political Insight* 4, 8.

[87] J Corbett and W Veenendaal, *Democracy in Small States: Persisting Against All Odds* (Oxford, Oxford University Press, 2018) chapter 7.

Combined office, which vests one office with multiple powers and functions, risks further concentration of power, particularly in small states. This gives rise to a range of potential problems. At a practical level, it imposes a high workload and responsibility on a single individual. President Hammer DeRoburt, for example, had a reputation for handling a high volume of work and decision-making responsibilities which in other countries would be delegated to lower levels of government, a workload which came with personal costs to his health.[88] The scope and complexity of a multitasked role can also make the transfer of power from one office-holder to another more difficult, especially where some powers and prestige remain with the individual rather than the office.

The most significant constitutional concern, however, is the increased risk of abuse of power and corruption when powers are concentrated in one office.[89] Nauru's experiences provide a cautionary lesson. Nauru's economy, initially strong as a result of mining revenue, collapsed in the late 1990s due to declining phosphate prices and reserves and the mismanagement of government investments. Since the revival of Australia's offshore processing centre for refugees in Nauru, Nauru has experienced significant declines in the rule of law.[90] The Cabinet dismissed senior government officials and judges when they made decisions against the interests of the government.[91] A majority in the Parliament voted to suspend members of the opposition, sparking protests that led to charges against 19 protesters who were found guilty of criminal offences after long delayed and unfair trials.[92] Recent events in Kiribati also give cause for concern about the personalisation of politics and concentration of power. Beginning in August 2022, government officials made several attempts to remove High Court Justice David Lambourne by cancelling his visa and suspending him from office. Justice Lambourne, an Australian citizen, is married to the leader of the opposition, which has made him the target of political attention. After Kiribati's courts upheld Justice Lambourne's judicial appointment, the Chief Justice and three Judges of Appeal were also targeted for removal. As in Nauru, the President's powers over the appointment and suspension of judges, and indirectly over immigration, have been used in ways that undermine checks on government by an independent judiciary.[93] As these examples show, the concentration of power in a multitasked office increases the opportunities for leaders to extend significant influence across all institutions of government.[94]

The key checks on executive power in a parliamentary system are the vote of no confidence and judicial review. Both, however, can have limited effectiveness as a check on multitasked heads of the executive. The vote of no confidence provides a mechanism for the parliament to remove an executive government. However, in many parliamentary

[88] R Crocombe and C Giese, 'Nauru: The Politics of Phosphate' in R Crocombe and A Ali (eds), *Politics in Micronesia* (Suva, Institute of Pacific Studies of the University of the South Pacific, 1983) 31, 45, 48.

[89] De Jonge (n 6) 45; Ghai and Cottrell (n 28) 7.

[90] Quanchi (n 12) 154, 157.

[91] G Eames, 'The Rule of Law in Nauru: An Evolving Concept?' (Paper presented at Law Society of South Australia Criminal Law Conference, McLaren Vale, 24 October 2014).

[92] M Swanson, 'Trial of the "Nauru 19"' [2018] *Bar News: Journal of the NSW Bar Association* 83.

[93] Special Rapporteur on the Independence of Judges and Lawyers, Letters to Government of Kiribati 17 August 2022, AL KIR 1/2022 and 14 September 2023, AL KIR1/2023; A Dziedzic, 'Judiciaries Upholding Judicial Independence in Pacific Island States' (2022) 96 *Australian Law Journal* 621, 622–24.

[94] E Perham, M De Visser and R Dixon, 'On Small State Constitutionalism', Chapter 1, section IV in this volume.

systems, the close partisan relationship between the executive and parliament inhibits the parliament's capacity to hold the executive to account. This can be especially true in small states, where a significant proportion of the parliament are likely to be ministers in the Cabinet. The Parliament of Nauru, for example, has been described as a 'rubber stamp' for government.[95] The personalisation of politics adds another layer of influence and connection: for example in the Marshall Islands, the authority of President Amata Kabua was such to amount to an effective veto power; without his support a Bill would not pass.[96]

The capacity of the courts to check a multitasked head of the executive may also be limited. The Constitutions of Kiribati, the Marshall Islands and Nauru all provide the superior courts with jurisdiction to review the actions of parliament and the executive for compliance with the constitution and courts have exercised this jurisdiction on many occasions. However, the expectation at the time of independence that most judges would be foreign made constitution makers reticent to confer more specific powers on courts. For example, the main concern of the Working Group on Constitutional Arrangements for Nauru, led by the Australian government, was that if the multitasked President refused to resign after a vote of no confidence, there was no head of state to step in to dismiss the President. The Working Group examined the possibility of conferring the power to dismiss the President in such circumstances on the Supreme Court, but rejected the idea on the basis 'such procedure would … be unlikely to be favoured by the Nauruans, since the Judge will be an expatriate'.[97] The fact of foreignness was seen to affect how a judge might engage with politically sensitive questions, and how that judge's decisions might be received in a country that is not their own.[98]

Judiciaries can also be vulnerable to influence and interference, particularly when the multitasked head of the executive has a direct role in the appointment of judges. In Nauru, the President appoints all judges, with no requirement to act on the advice of Cabinet or any other body.[99] In Kiribati, the Chief Justice is appointed by the *Beretitenti* acting on the advice of Cabinet, and all other judges are appointed by the *Beretitenti* on the advice of the Chief Justice and Public Service Commission. This introduces a greater degree of separation from the executive in judicial appointments than in Nauru.[100] However, the *Beretitenti* also has powers 'in his own deliberate judgment' to suspend a judge and commence the formal process for removal.[101] In Nauru, the formal process to remove judges has not been used; instead foreign judicial officers with whom the executive has disagreed have had their visas cancelled and have been deported through an exercise of executive power over immigration.[102] In these jurisdictions, the multitasked head of the executive has greater opportunity to influence the judiciary through

[95] Ruben Kun, W Togomae and Roland Kun, 'Country Study Report: Nauru' in *National Integrity System* (Transparency International, 2004).

[96] KE Stege, 'Marshall Islands' in SI Levine (ed), *Pacific Ways: Government and Politics in the Pacific Island* (Wellington, Victoria University Press, 2009) 116.

[97] 'The Executive Head' undated, Papers of JW Davidson, National Library of Australia, MS 5105/42 Box 25.

[98] A Dziedzic, *Foreign Judges in the Pacific* (Oxford, Hart Publishing, 2021) chapter 5.

[99] Constitution of Nauru art 49(2).

[100] Constitution of Kiribati art 81.

[101] ibid art 83.

[102] Eames (n 91).

appointments and removal, potentially undermining the courts' role as an independent check on executive power.

The concentration of executive power in a multitasked office is not inevitable, however. In the Marshall Islands, constitution makers were alive to the issue and addressed the concern through three features of constitutional design. First, the Constitution provides that most significant government decisions are to be made by the Cabinet or the President on the advice of the Cabinet.[103] Of course, because in the Marshall Islands, as in Kiribati and Nauru, the President appoints, dismisses and assigns portfolios to members of Cabinet, the President has a significant degree of authority over Cabinet decision making. However, in contrast to Kiribati and Nauru, the President of the Marshall Islands cannot take office unless at least six members of parliament accept the invitation to serve in the Cabinet. This requirement has in the past determined the presidency: in 2016, the newly elected President was removed by a vote of no confidence after two members of parliament refused to accept their nominations to the Cabinet.[104] This requirement provides an additional layer of 'confidence' from the ministry as well as the parliament. Second, as discussed in section III and again in contrast to Kiribati and Nauru, powers over the appointment of judges and public servants are spread across many institutions rather than in the hands of one, which safeguards them from political influence.[105] Third, in the Marshall Islands the Speaker of Parliament is itself a combined office with significant constitutional powers, providing a counterweight to the powers of the President and Cabinet.[106]

Looking beyond constitutional design, cultural values and context can also be influential checks on power. Kiribati's constitution makers cited its egalitarian culture in support of multitasking. This might appear counter-intuitive: how can the concentration of power in one office be squared with egalitarianism? In Kiribati, however, egalitarianism refers to the sense in which individual interests should not be put before collective interests. It does not mean that power is shared horizontally, but rather that no individual – including the powerful President – is considered above reproach.[107] This, together with the close social bonds that arise as a consequence of smallness, can create an 'accountability ecosystem' of formal and informal checks and balances on those in power.[108]

B. Continuity, Conflict of Interest and Compromised Independence

In May 1994, the government of Kiribati lost a vote of confidence. As required by the Constitution, the parliament was dissolved, elections called and the Council of State was

[103] CJ Lynch, 'The 1979 Constitution of the Marshall Islands: A Hybrid?' (1980) 61 *The Parliamentarian* 230, 232, 234.

[104] Kupferman (n 84) 144.

[105] 'Report of the United Nations Visiting Mission to Observe the Referendum in the Marshall Islands Trust Territory of the Pacific Islands March 1979', T/1805, para 166.

[106] De Jonge (n 6) 48; Stege (n 96) 116–17.

[107] A Craney and T Tanielu, *Accountability Ecosystems Political Economy Analysis: Kiribati Country Study* Melbourne, La Trobe University Centre for Human Security and Social Change, 2024) 16, 25.

[108] ibid 16.

formed as caretaker government. The Council of State was chaired by the Chair of the Public Service Commission, Tekire Tameura, with Chief Justice Faqir Muhammed (a foreign judge) and the Speaker of Parliament, Beretitara Neeti, as members. However, during the caretaker period, Mr Tameura's term of appointment as the Chair of the Public Service Commission expired. The Speaker and Chief Justice named a new successor and removed Tameura from the Council of State, over his strong objections. Mr Tameura sought to clarify the powers of the Council of State to regulate its own membership in this way, but because the Chief Justice – Kiribati's only permanent judge at the time – was himself a member of the Council of State, a legal challenge before the courts was not practical by reason of conflict of interests.[109]

This incident highlights a range of issues that can arise when independent offices are double hatted with other roles and functions. First, it shows how double hatting depends on stability in the appointments to *ex officio* positions. The expiry of the term of appointment of the Chair of the Public Service Commission had serious consequences for the composition of the Council of State, which it was not equipped to deal with, exposing a gap in the law. Vacancies in constitutional offices and disputes over appointments are disruptive, but the disruption is multiplied when that office is a multitasked one.

Second, it demonstrates the potential for conflicts of interest. The rule against bias prevented the Chief Justice from hearing a legal challenge to the actions of the Council of State. In practice, this precluded judicial review because in Kiribati at the time there were no other permanent judges. It might have been possible for a temporary foreign judge to hear the case; however, they would need to be appointed and sworn in, presumably by the Council of State, raising again the prospect of conflict of interest.

Third, this example illustrates the intersection of multitasking with reliance on foreign personnel in small states. Multitasking and the importation of foreign expertise are both responses to limited human resources in small states. However, the appointment of foreign citizens to constitutional office can raise concerns about sovereignty, which centre on individual office-holders' allegiance to the state.[110] The appointment of foreign judges, including chief justices, has been common in the Pacific. However, the justifications for appointing a foreign citizen as a judge will not necessarily also justify the appointment of a foreign citizen to other constitutional offices, such as the Council of State. A review of the Constitution conducted following these events in Kiribati considered proposals that only a citizen Chief Justice should be a member of the Council of State, but no formal constitutional amendment was pursued.[111]

Finally, the incident demonstrates the risks when double hatting borrows from the prestige of one office to confer credibility on another. The independence and impartiality of some constitutional offices, such as judicial office, make them attractive offices to multitask with other functions that benefit from distance and independence. This is especially the case in small states, where the prevailing sense that 'everyone knows everyone' places a premium on independence. In designing the Council of State,

[109] R Kaplan (ed), *Freedom in the World 1995–1996* (New York, Freedom House, 1996) 291.
[110] On foreign judges and sovereignty, see Dziedzic (n 98) 93–99.
[111] B Macdonald, *Governance and Political Process in Kiribati* (Canberra, Australian National University Research School of Pacific and Asian Studies, 1996) 44–45.

Kiribati's constitution makers sought to take advantage of existing independent offices, drawing on three existing independent offices for its members.

However, conferring additional roles on independent office-holders, and political roles in particular, comes with the risk of undermining independence and politicising these offices.[112] The risk of politicisation arises most starkly when additional functions are conferred on judges or other independent office-holders at the discretion of political actors, which raises concerns about patronage and the offer of office as an incentive or reward.[113] But even where double hatting is mandated by the constitution, the deployment of an independent officeholder to a politically-charged role can place confidence in the independence, impartiality and non-partisanship of the original office at risk.

There is evidence of political and public loss of confidence in the Chief Justice in Kiribati following the events in the Council of State described above. The newly-elected government suspended Chief Justice Faqir and established a tribunal to investigate allegations of misconduct. The suspension was set aside by the High Court pending a legal challenge and the government then encouraged the Chief Justice to take leave, bringing forward the end of his term of appointment.[114] A range of concerns had been raised about the performance of the Chief Justice, including extensive delays in hearing cases in the outer islands, his tendency to refer cases back to lower courts rather than determine appeals, and allegations that he interfered in politics.[115] The allegations were never investigated and substantiated, but the political role played by the Chief Justice in the Council of State appears to have been the last straw, compelling the government to begin the rare process (at that time) for the formal removal of a judge.

VI. Conclusion

Multitasked office is a constitutional design response to conditions of smallness. It is a way to take advantage of scarce human and financial resources and specialist expertise. Multitasking is also a way to adapt the Westminster parliamentary system – which is built around a separate ceremonial head of state – to contexts where a separate and purely ceremonial executive role does not have cultural purchase.

A range of different constitutional offices may be multitasked, from the head of the executive, to the Speaker of Parliament and Chief Justice. There is great variety in the kinds of powers and functions that are conferred on a multitasked office and how those powers are regulated. Some general conclusions can be drawn, however, about double hatting on the one hand, and combined office on the other, to inform choices in constitutional design and the operation of multitasked office in practice.

Double hatting captures the sense that there is a primary constitutional office to which is added other, separate, tasks and roles. The appointment of the Chief Justice, *ex officio*, to an appointment body or caretaker government maintains the sense that the primary role of the Chief Justice is his or her judicial role. For this reason, double

[112] Garoupa and Ginsburg (n 61) 764.
[113] Calabresi and Larsen (n 3).
[114] *Muhammad v Attorney-General* [1995] KIHC 1.
[115] Macdonald (n 111) 47–48.

hatting tends to be used when multitasking independent offices, such as judges and (in Kiribati) the independent Speaker. Framing multitasking as double hatting can be helpful from a constitutional design perspective. It prompts the question whether the additional offices or tasks that are to be conferred on the office-holder are compatible with the primary function of the independent office, and the need for that office, by definition, to be impartial and independent from government. Careful consideration of the compatibility of the offices conferred on one individual can help to address the risks that the independence of the primary office will be compromised by multitasking.

In combined office, it is more difficult to distinguish and separate out the functions associated with the different offices. It is sometimes tempting to try to characterise elements of combined office as primary and incidental, as CJ Lynch does when he writes that in Kiribati the *Beretitenti* is 'primarily a Prime Minister who incidentally carries out functions as head of state'.[116] A better view may be that rather than divide the functions of combined multitasked office by reference to the offices that have been combined, the office should be taken *sui generis* in context. This means that the design choices about the nature of the office, the kinds of powers and functions conferred on it, the manner in which those powers and functions are exercised, and the avenues for review and accountability are constructed around the combined office, not its constituent parts. As the discussion of the combined head of state and head of government in each of the three jurisdictions shows, there may be significant variation across countries, even within the small category of those with multitasked heads of executive.

One of the perils of combining the office of the head of state and head of government is concentration of executive power. However, as the example of the Constitution of the Marshall Islands shows, one potential solution is not to avoid multitasking, but to expand it such that there are many multitasked offices across all institutions of government which each provide a check and balance on the other. The closeness between officials and the community in small states can foster social or relational forms of accountability, with the effect that accountability functions are spread across a range of formal as well as informal societal institutions. Rather than suppressing multitasking – which is, after all, a fact of life in small states – the constitutional system might embrace multiple sites of multitasking, building a system of accountable government that is responsive to the conditions of smallness.

[116] Lynch (n 31).

14

Niue: The Constitutional Journey

TONY ANGELO AND JENNIFER CORRIN

I. Introduction

The Constitution of Niue projects executive power and political status but not size. In fact, since it was changed in 1992, the Constitution has aspired to the indicia of greater size, in spite of its diminishing population. Nevertheless, closer examination reveals that smallness was a significant factor, both in the making of the Constitution and its content. Size also presents particular challenges for the operation of constitutionally enshrined aspirations, such as the separation of powers.

The chapter commences with some context on Niue and its historical journey to the present constitutional position. It proceeds to discuss the move to self-government and the form and process by which the Constitution was made. This is followed by a detailed discussion of the challenges presented by the small size of the country and its population and the impact of this on the separation of powers. The chapter concludes with some comparisons with Tuvalu, another Pacific island country, which has many similarities with Niue but illustrates how different such countries can be constitutionally.

II. Niue and Historical Features

Niue is a single island of about 2663 square kilometres. Whilst being one of the world's smallest countries, it is one of the largest raised coral atolls. It lies in the South Pacific Ocean, 2,400 kilometres northeast of New Zealand, in the middle of the triangle created by the other Polynesian countries of Samoa to the north, Tonga to the south and the Cook Islands to the east. It is a village-based community, with a population hovering around 1,500, spread among its 14 villages. Most residents are Polynesian, more specifically, Niuean or part-Niuean, with a small number of European, Chinese, Indian and Pacific islanders from other Pacific countries. There is a large diaspora in New Zealand, principally in Auckland.[1] It is not resource rich or strategically located like, for instance, Brunei or Singapore; nor is it populous like Mauritius.

[1] There is a population of about 30,000 Niuean in New Zealand. 'Niuean ethnic group' (*Stats NZ | Tatauranga Aoteoroa)*, www.stats.govt.nz/tools/2018-census-ethnic-group-summaries/niuean/.

The constitutional journey of Niue could start at many points: the time of arrival of human inhabitants on the island; the inclusion of Niue as a Protectorate in the British Empire (1900); the incorporation of Niue into the colony of New Zealand (and therefore into the New Zealand territory of the Cook Islands) (1901); the severance of Niue from the Cook Islands (1967);[2] or the accession by Niue to the position of being a self-governing state in free association with New Zealand in 1974.

The present constitutional situation can be seen clearly to begin in 1966 with the separation of Niue from the Cook Islands and the coming into force of the Niue Act 1966 – an Act of the Parliament of New Zealand.[3] That Act was compendious – 735 sections – and like the Cook Islands Act 1915 and the 1920 Samoa Constitution Order before it, it provided the framework for government at Niue island level. The Act provided a system of courts for land matters, a criminal code, family law rules, and the extension of specific New Zealand legislation to Niue. All was subject to the powers of the sovereign, and of the New Zealand government:[4]

> Section 4
>
> The executive government of Niue is hereby declared to be vested in Her Majesty the Queen in right of the Government of New Zealand.
>
> Section 5
>
> …
>
> (2) The Resident Commissioner shall, in the exercise of his powers and the discharge of his functions, be subject to the control of the Minister, exercised through instructions or otherwise.
>
> (3) The Resident Commissioner shall be charged with the executive government of Niue.
>
> …
>
> (5) The Resident Commissioner shall be stationed in Niue.

The executive government was entrusted to a Resident Commissioner and an Executive Committee (sections 9, 15) and to the New Zealand government Minister for Island Territories. The State Services Commission of New Zealand was the employer of public servants in Niue.[5]

Legislative power lay with the Niue Island Assembly, a body which had been continued from Cook Islands times.[6] The Niue Island Assembly was composed of the Resident Commissioner and the elected representative of each of the 14 villages of Niue. The Niue Island Assembly could enact Ordinances (section 37) subject to the requirement of non-repugnancy[7] to the 1966 Act and a number of New Zealand Acts,[8] which related principally to external affairs matters. The backstop provided was section 672, which

[2] Niue Act 1966 (NZ).
[3] The Act came into force on 1 January 1967.
[4] Niue Act 1966 (NZ).
[5] State Services Commission Act 1962 (NZ).
[6] The Cook Islands had the status, from 6 August 1965, of a self-governing state in free association with New Zealand.
[7] On the origins of the doctrine of repugnancy see E Campbell, 'Colonial Legislation and the Laws of England' (1965) *University of Tasmania Law Review* 148, 149.
[8] Extended to Niue (First Schedule to the Niue Act 1966 (NZ)).

applied the law of England existing on 14 January 1840 to Niue, unless it was inconsistent with the Act or inapplicable to the circumstances of Niue.

There were several amendments to the Niue Act by the New Zealand Parliament between 1967 and 1974. Most related to land matters. The Niue Amendment Act 1971 (NZ) (in force from 4 March 1972) saw significant amendments to the Act of 1966, which were steps to advance local self-government and were a clear prelude to Niue's act of self-determination and to the Niue Constitution Act 1974 (NZ) which came into force on 19 October 1974.[9]

III. The Constitution of Niue

The Constitution of Niue is found in three basic documents. The first is the Niue Constitution Act 1974 of New Zealand, which came into force on 19 October 1974. The second is the Constitution of Niue, which had its original form as Schedules to the Niue Constitution Act 1974 (NZ)–(the First Schedule had the Constitution in *Vagahau Niue* – the Niuean language – and the Second had it in English). Many of the provisions of the 1966 Act are to be found in recognisable form in this document. The third document is the Letters Patent Constituting the Office of the Governor-General of New Zealand of 1983.[10]

The Niue Constitution Act 1974 (NZ) is the law that marks the end of Niue's status as a colony. At the time it was made the population was 4,272. The economy and public service were controlled by New Zealand. As discussed below, there was no 'Realm' until 1983. Transport in and out of Niue was limited. The boundaries were then, and remain, as established in the 1901 Order in Council altering the Boundaries of the Colony of New Zealand.[11] There was no representation of a foreign country in Niue other than of New Zealand. The Act has nine sections and those sections deal with the relationship of Niue to New Zealand; that is to say, that Act, which is also law for Niue, deals with the nature of 'free association'.

Free association is the international law description of the current status of Niue. The significance of the expression is that Niue retains a special relationship with the state of New Zealand even though Niue is independent of New Zealand.[12] The fact of being 'free' means that Niue can, at any time, change its status with New Zealand and become a fully independent state at international law.[13]

[9] The impetus for self-determination of Niue came from the act of self-determination of the Cook Islands. The New Zealand government had the experience of dealing with Western Samoa and the Cook Islands; the next on its decolonisation list was Niue.

[10] Letters Patent SR 1983/225.

[11] Order in Council 1901, No 531.

[12] For further information on the Letters Patent see A Quentin-Baxter and J McLean, *This Realm of New Zealand: The Sovereign, the Governor-General and the Crown* (Auckland, Auckland University Press, 2017). See also A Quentin-Baxter, 'The Cook Islands, Niue and Tokelau as Parts of the Realm of New Zealand' (2021) 52 *Victoria University of Wellington Law Review* 579. For further discussion of the Niue experience see C McDonald, 'Decolonisation and Free Association: The Relationships of the Cook Islands and Niue with New Zealand' (PhD Thesis, Victoria University of Wellington, 2018).

[13] UN General Assembly, 'Factors which should be taken into account in deciding whether a Territory is or is not a Territory whose people have not yet attained a full measure of self-government' GA Res 742 (27 November 1953) Annex, third part, para 2.

The Niue Constitution Act 1974 states that it and the Schedules to it, are the supreme law of Niue (section 4),[14] that New Zealand has specific duties to Niue in respect of external affairs and defence (section 6), and that New Zealand also has specific responsibilities to provide economic and administrative assistance to Niue (section 7). Most importantly, the Act states that Niueans have a right to New Zealand citizenship (section 5).[15]

The relationship to New Zealand is supported by a provision which requires cooperation between the heads of government of New Zealand and Niue (section 8), and also that the state of New Zealand must maintain a physical diplomatic representation in Niue (section 9).

The 'Constitution of Niue' as defined in the Act (section 4) has 82 articles. Those articles relate to the domestic government structures of Niue. In other words, the 82 articles are a domestic national complement to the six sections of the Act which deal with Niue's association with New Zealand.

The Letters Patent Constituting the Office of Governor-General of New Zealand establish and describe a particular construct called the 'Realm of New Zealand'.[16] That Realm is the Kingdom of New Zealand. Charles III is the King of the Realm of New Zealand, of which Niue is a part; he is not the King of Niue.[17]

The first clause of the Letters Patent declares that the Realm of New Zealand is made up of the state of New Zealand, the self-governing state of the Cook Islands, the self-governing state of Niue, and Tokelau, and the Ross Dependency. The Governor-General of New Zealand is therefore the representative of the Sovereign in the Realm. The powers of the Governor-General are set out in the Letters Patent. It is important, however, to note that those powers are subject to any such powers given to anybody else in a country of the Realm.[18] This means that where there is a power given in the law of Niue which is different from that given to the Governor-General in the Letters Patent, the Niue power takes precedence. The Governor-General must exercise his or her powers in accordance with the Letters Patent and in accordance with laws in force in Niue. That limitation is emphasised by the Oath that is taken by the Governor-General. It reads, among other things:

> 'I will faithfully and impartially serve His Majesty King Charles III, King of New Zealand, His heirs and successors, and the people of the Realm of New Zealand, in accordance with their respective laws and customs. So help me God'.[19]

To summarise: the sections of the Constitution Act 1974 relate to the relationship of Niue to New Zealand, the Constitution of Niue (the document originally in the Schedules to the Act) deals with the government of Niue, and the Letters Patent place Niue within the Realm of New Zealand (which includes both New Zealand and Niue).

[14] Article 82(1) of the Constitution of Niue includes in its definition of 'Constitution', the Niue Constitution Act 1974 (NZ).

[15] E Perham, 'Citizenship Laws in the Realm of New Zealand' (2011) 9 *New Zealand Yearbook of Internationa[l] Law* 219.

[16] Letters Patent SR 1983/225, cl 1. See further Quentin-Baxter and McLean (n 12).

[17] This is of some constitutional significance to the relationship between the state of New Zealand and th[e] state of Niue. There was in historic times a customary ruler designated as King of Niue but that tradition ha[s] not been continued. A strong sense of fealty to the monarchy was engendered by the significant contributio[n] by Niue of troops in World War II.

[18] Letters Patent SR 1983/225, cl 1.

[19] Letters Patent SR 1983/225, cl 6.

The architects of the Constitution were Professor RQ Quentin-Baxter and his wife, Alison Quentin-Baxter. They discussed self-determination and the future Constitution extensively in Niue with the local leaders and the village communities in the leadup to the act of self-determination. They had a particular concern for the economic and social well-being of Niue after self-determination and pressed upon the New Zealand government the need to maintain economic and administrative support for Niue in the event that it voted for a status of free association with New Zealand – which Niue did on 3 September 1974.

Smallness was a matter about which Professor Quentin-Baxter was much concerned. This is reflected in the constitutional provisions for the 'continuing responsibility of the Government of New Zealand to provide necessary economic and administrative assistance to Niue' (section 7), the requirement for permanent New Zealand government representation in Niue (section 9) and the link to New Zealand 'employment opportunities and levels of remuneration available in New Zealand' (article 69).[20]

That fact that Niue is a village-based community is reflected in the strong position of the villages in the Constitution,[21] in social life generally and in the absence of political parties and of a constitutional office of Leader of the Opposition. Recognising that enabled the acceptance of a unicameral legislature. In 2024, village affiliation is still strong but there has been a significant societal change since 1974. The population in 1974 was 4,272 with 1,600 electors, but has dwindled to around 1,800 with 1,167 electors. In 1974, it was anticipated that the sizes of the villages would be maintained at approximately the same level for electoral purposes. That has not happened. In the 2023 elections there was a significant disparity between the number of electors in each village; in one village for instance the number of voters was in single figures. To balance the size of the constituencies would be a matter of great cultural difficulty, given the close affiliation of Niueans to their village. The outflow of people to New Zealand has left many villages practically deserted.[22] Constitutionally, this is significant because of the key role of the villages in the operation of government.

The strength of the villages can be gleaned from contemporaneous statements made or recorded by Terry Chapman in *The Decolonisation of Niue*.[23] For instance, Professor Quentin-Baxter is quoted as saying:

> Democracy in Niue is close to the classical ideal. Each of the 14 villages has its own Assemblyman who is known to every villager. It is customary for public affairs to be discussed at weekly village meetings; and – as the special meetings on constitutional development have shown – the extent of public interest and involvement is greater than could be achieved in larger, more affluent societies.[24]

Terry Chapman stated:

> Theoretically, the disparity in size between electorates could be rationalised by reconstituting the village boundaries. However, this would have been totally unacceptable to the Niuean

[20] RQ Quentin-Baxter, 'Second Report to the Niue Assembly on the Constitutional Development of Niue' 1999) 30 *Victoria University of Wellington Law Review* 577.

[21] See art 16.

[22] The basis for voting in legislative elections is set out in art 17 of the Constitution. Effectively there are no bsentee votes.

[23] TM Chapman, *The Decolonisation of Niue* (Wellington, Victoria University Press, 1976). Terry Chapman as a Niuean and a high official in the public service of Niue at the time of the referendum on decolonisation.

[24] ibid 53.

> people, as it would have struck at the very roots of the Niuean society, in which every village jealously guarded its individual identity.[25]

In relation to the entrenching provisions of article 35 of the Constitution,[26] it was said:

> Article 35 was also consistent with the traditionally republican nature of Niuean society where tribalism or a chiefly structure was absent and where, in the decision-making process, the Niuean character was as overtly and absolutely egalitarian as it was individualistic.[27]

The post-1974 history is one of establishing the identity of Niue. The record is one of striving for greater economic independence, and the establishment of an international identity separate from that of the state of New Zealand. Notwithstanding, the falling population and continual financial challenges, Niue is concerned with regaining or at least retaining its own identity. This is demonstrated by the contents of the first Act amending the Constitution, passed in 1992.[28] This made several changes to the Constitution, which were all approved by a single poll – that is to say, a voter either approved them all, or rejected them all. In terms of the subject matter of this chapter, those amendments were about patriation, not size. The overall goal of the amendments was to bring home the power.[29] The 1992 amendment also terminated the link that there had been between the Niue Public Service Commission and the New Zealand State Services Commission.[30] The small size of Niue and the consequent level of human capital and resources accounts for the fact that the Constitution is not an autochthonous one. However, it had a creation process which reflected that sort of approach and its small size demanded unique approaches, which amount to a document in the nature of an autochthonous Constitution.

In a comment in the United Nations Fourth Committee, the Swedish delegate stated:[31] 'It seemed to me an excellent example of how to decolonize a small non-self-governing territory, in constant touch with the people, without too sudden a rupture in the past and with a faith in the future preserved'.

IV. Separation of Powers, Checks and Balances, and Closeness

The Niue Constitution is built on the idea of the separation of powers. The Constitution begins with 15 articles relating to the Executive (the Premier and Cabinet Ministers). That is followed by 21 articles on the Legislature (the Niue Assembly) and 22 articles

[25] ibid 73.

[26] Article 35 of the Constitution requires qualified majorities for any Bill amending the Constitution, and i[f] that Bill is passed by the Niue Assembly it is then required to receive the support of electors either by a majority or, in the case of particular articles, two-thirds of the votes validly cast.

[27] Chapman (n 23) 71.

[28] Constitution Amendment Act (No 1) 1992 (No 162 of 1992) NZ. In August 2024, four further proposals for constitutional change were presented to the people of Niue. None related expressly or apparently t[o] the size of Niue. Two of the proposals became law under art 35 of the Constitution. One is of constitutiona[l] significance: in the articles of the Constitution 'Premier' is now 'Prime Minister'.

[29] An example of this is the change from the Constitution of 1974 which provided for appeals from the Niu[e] High Court to the Court of Appeal of New Zealand (art 51); the 1992 amendment repealed the former art 5[1] and in art 52 established a Niue Court of Appeal.

[30] Arts 64 and 65.

[31] Chapman (n 23) 56.

relating to the Judiciary (the Courts). Those provisions are followed by articles relating to the finances of Niue, which concern both executive and legislative matters. Then there are provisions on social services and importantly, on the Niue Public Service. The latter are executive matters, but are dealt with separately in the Constitution to emphasise the importance of maintaining the independence of the Niue Public Service from political influence, an importance highlighted by the fact that before 1974 the Niue Public Service was under the control of the New Zealand State Services Commission.

The notion of separation of powers is one that needs to be understood if it is to function well. That means for those in a non-European cultural environment, there needs to be information, education and examples to demonstrate the meaning of the phrase. Even with that done, there is a degree of flexibility in the term itself. For instance, which version of separation of powers is to be understood: the English or the French? And if the easiest example for Niue would be that of the state of New Zealand, then it is to be noted that in New Zealand it is both possible and indeed not remarkable if the head of the executive, as an essential part of the legislature, is also the Chief Justice. To the extent that there are limits in that scenario, they are there by constitutional convention and not by law.

Closeness can lead to dysfunction in purely legal terms or, more seriously, to discord which leads to societal collapse or violent contestation. Closeness, especially of a small number of people in a small physical space, may produce more tension and difficulty in the maintaining of any separation of powers arrangement than in a country with a larger population and more space.

The fact that there is a clear statement of separation of powers in Niue has merit in the interests of accuracy even if in practice the boundaries are not always respected.

Elections, democracy and the power of the people can reset the standards of practice at the time of each election. This provides some protection against a dictatorship.

A lack of practice of the entrenched constitutional principles in a small state is indicative of a general tolerance or nonchalance in the community. As a result, constitutional litigation to strengthen the system would probably be unhelpful because enforcement of a judgment may be neglected or be weak; lack of respect for the letter of the law would permeate the institutions of government in such a case.

If a small state has constitutionally separated governmental powers but the practice of strong political direction, an election could change attitudes towards the separation of powers. Alternatively, where an unconstitutional practice is engrained, the Constitution could be changed to reflect the pattern of government that the state enjoys. A difficulty in doing that would be that constitutional change can be difficult to reverse. Falling short in terms of separation of powers is just that. While the principles remain as guiding rules, they can be followed in a fulsome way at any time.

The less formal the form of separation of powers is, the more elaborate the checks and balances that are required to maintain the integrity of the system. By definition, a very small state may lack the capacity to operate an extensive web of checks and balances.

The leader of government of Niue, in July 1974, said that the arrangements set out in the draft Niue Constitution Act and in the Constitution provided:[32]

> a system of checks and balances, with the broad outlines of policy making and administration of policy. A bad thing in any government is the abuse of power and each of the component

[32] Chapman (n 23), 83.

> parts is therefore a check against the abuse of power and a balance against bad government. Each of the component parts so to speak, is a 'watching brief' on the other.

Indicative of the pressures of closeness in a small state is the case of *Ex parte Niue Public Service Commission.*[33] In that case, the head of government conveyed 'a message of his feelings' on a public service employment matter to the Public Service Commission which by article 69 of the Constitution 'shall not receive any direction from the Cabinet but shall act independently'. The High Court accepted the Premier's statement that he had no intention to interfere with the independence of the Commission.

In summary form, the Niue system is the following –

Authority	Checks on	Checked by
Executive (Cabinet)	Provides direction for the operation of the public service (articles 2, 62, 68) Appoints the Chief Justice, Judges and other judicial officers of the High Court and Court of Appeal (Part III)	*The Niue Assembly* enacts or approves legislation (article 28) *Audit*: 'The Auditor-General of New Zealand shall be the auditor of the Niue Government account and of all other public funds or accounts'. (article 60) *The Judiciary* (article 37) Issues prerogative orders Makes declarations
Legislature (Niue Assembly)	*The Executive* Budget Legislation (including Regulations) Surveys reports (article 68) Votes of confidence	*The People* (article 22) Elections *The Judiciary* Compliance with the Constitution (section 2 and article 71) Vires (article 37)
Judiciary	*The lower courts* (articles 48 and 51) Appeal system *The Executive* Prerogative orders Declarations Vires *Legislature* Vires	*The superior courts* (articles 37(2), 55 and 55A) *The Governor-General* (article 45) *The Assembly* By legislation

A. Executive

The power is vested in the Cabinet of four Ministers by article 2. The effect of article is to confer on the Premier the powers not only of head of government but also c

[33] *Ex parte Niue Public Service Commission* (2002) 4 Niue Law Reports 35.

head of state. This type of 'multi-tasking', which can also be observed in the Speaker's duties (discussed below), reflects the size of the population and is not unusual in small states.

B. Legislature

The Speaker of the Niue Assembly is a principal officer under the Constitution. The role is dealt with primarily in article 20 of the Constitution and elaborated on in the Standing Orders of the Niue Assembly.[34]

The first thing to occur after a general election is for the Assembly to elect a Speaker. If the person elected as Speaker is, at the time of that election, a member of the Assembly, he or she must vacate the seat as member upon taking up the duties of Speaker. The Speaker is part of the Niue Assembly but is not a voting member. The Speaker is, in other words, a neutral figure politically.

The Speaker has a number of significant duties set out in the Constitution: receipt of resignation of the Premier (article 4), the appointment and revocation of Ministers (articles 5 and 7), the appointment of temporary Ministers and of acting Premier (articles 8 and 9), the administration of the oath (articles 10, 21 and 55C), custodianship of the Seal (article 15), the calling of Assembly meetings (usually on advice – article 22), the dissolution of the Assembly (article 26), and the certification of legislative Acts (articles 34 and 35). Many of the duties reflect the size of the state and might, in other circumstances, have been performed by a head of state. This type of multi-tasking is discussed in detail in Anna Dziedzic's Chapter thirteen in this book.

C. Judiciary

The Constitution of Niue provides a complex system of courts for a country with a resident population of about 1,800 people. Part III, which is headed 'The Judiciary', comprises 19 of the 82 articles of the Constitution. These articles are in addition to those dealing more directly with the sources of law of Niue, which are dealt with in articles 28, 34, 35 and 36, and article 71 (existing law – 1974 – a transitional provision).

Part III of the Constitution was replaced in 1992 by the current Part which provides for a four-tier system of courts.[35] In descending order, these are the Judicial Committee of the Privy Council; the Court of Appeal; the High Court constituted by a judge sitting as a superior court; and the High Court constituted by a Commissioner of the High Court[36] or by two Justices of the Peace sitting as an inferior court.[37] When constituted by a Commissioner resident in Niue or two Justices of the Peace, the High Court has jurisdiction to deal with actions for the recovery of debt or damages or chattels not exceeding $1,500 and in specified minor criminal cases,[38] and in effect acts as a

[34] These are rules made by the Assembly under art 22(10) of the Constitution.
[35] Constitution Amendment (No 1) Act 1992, s 4. The Act came into force on 1 July 1992.
[36] Constitution of Niue, art 46.
[37] Constitution of Niue, art 51(2).
[38] Rules of the High Court 1916, r 83A.

subordinate court. In practice, the Commissioners and Justices of the Peace sit as a panel of three (one Commissioner and two Justices of the Peace).[39] Commissioners of the High Court and Justices of the Peace are appointed by the Cabinet of Ministers of Niue.[40] For the period 2019–22 there were two Civil and Criminal Commissioners, eight Land Commissioners and four Justices of the Peace.[41]

The 1992 amendment patriated the Court of Appeal and the High Court.[42] It replaced the Land Court of Niue and the Land Appellate Court of Niue with the High Court of Niue as the superior court,[43] and the Court of Appeal of New Zealand with the Court of Appeal of Niue as the appeal court,[44] and added a prerogative right of appeal to 'Her Majesty in Council'. Of legal interest is the fact that the Niue Land Court operated in inquisitorial mode. As a consequence of the closing of the land forums this process has been lost; the High Court operates in adversarial mode in all divisions, including when exercising the jurisdiction of the former Land Courts.

When constituted by a judge, the High Court has unlimited first instance jurisdiction.[45] It is divided into three divisions: a Civil Division, a Criminal Division and a Land Division.[46] In practice these superior courts are staffed entirely by Māori Land Court judges of New Zealand.[47] In the majority of cases heard by a judge, the High Court sits as the Land Division. The Niue High Court convenes twice a year and the judges usually travel to Niue for these sittings.[48] The Court of Appeal sits as required;[49] in the period ending December 2023, the Niue Law Reports record that the Court of Appeal delivered five judgments in 2019 and two in 2020. The size of the population and the small number of legally qualified residents explains the appointment of foreign judges. However, this poses a challenge for the development of a Niuean jurisprudence that is responsive to local culture. This is well illustrated by *Nelisi v Niue Public Service Commission*,[50] which it may be argued has limited value as a precedent. There, the Court not only decided the dispute on the basis of New Zealand law, but also failed to contextualise the challenged local decision.

Unlike Commissioners and Justices of the Peace, Judges, of whom there were four in 2023, are not appointed by a body within Niue. Instead, appointment is by the

[39] PJ Savage CJ of Niue, 'Message from the Chief Justice' in T Tukuniu and D Tohovaka, *Niue High Court Annual Report 2013–2014* (November 2014), paclii.austlii.edu.au/nu/court-annual-reports/2013-2014-hcar.html.

[40] Constitution of Niue, arts 46(1) and 51(1).

[41] T Tukuniu, *Niue Courts Annual Report July 2019 – June 2022.*

[42] Constitution Amendment (No 1) Act 1992.

[43] Constitution of Niue, art 37(1).

[44] Constitution of Niue, art 52(1).

[45] Constitution of Niue, art 37(2).

[46] Constitution of Niue, art 38.

[47] Since about the year 2000 all the judges have been appointed from among the Māori Land Court Judges of New Zealand. The fact that all senior court judges are not Niue-based judges is perhaps inevitable, given the population size.

[48] 'Government and Political System' (*Government of Niue*), www.gov.nu/government-and-political-system/

[49] T Tukuniu, *Niue High Court Annual Report July 2015/2016 – June 2018/2019*, paclii.austlii.edu.au/nu court-annual-reports/niuecourtsannualreport2015_2019.pdf, 7.

[50] *Nelisi v Niue Public Service Commission* (2004) Niue Law Reports 153, [2004] NUHC 2 (4 April 2004) https://www.paclii.org/nu/cases/NUHC/2004/2.html.

Governor-General of New Zealand, although he or she must act on the advice of the Cabinet of Ministers of Niue.[51] Appointees' names are tendered by the Premier of Niue in the case of judges of the Court of Appeal of Niue who are not High Court judges, and by the Chief Justice and the Minister of Justice in the case of other judges.[52] The Chief Justice and puisne judges of the High Court are *ex officio* members of the Court of Appeal.[53]

Apart from the complexity, there is also the continuing possibility of appeals to a foreign tribunal, in the form of the Judicial Committee of the Privy Council.[54] The relevant provision of the Constitution is noticeably brief and stated in the form of a proviso rather than a direct conferral of jurisdiction.[55] Article 55(2) states:

> Nothing in this Article shall limit the right of Her Majesty in Council, upon the petition of any person aggrieved by any decision of the Court of Appeal to admit that person's appeal therefrom upon such conditions as Her Majesty in Council shall think fit to impose.

This raises two issues, which although not arising directly from the size of the country, reflect the fact that it is still burdened with problems rooted in colonialism, which a larger country might have had the means to shed. The first is the fact that article 55(2) refers expressly to 'Her Majesty'.[56] With the accession of King Charles, this could be taken to require a constitutional amendment in order for this provision to operate. On the other hand, the Oath of Allegiance, which is set out in article 55C, clearly anticipates a change of the reigning sovereign, providing the following form of words:[57]

> 'I, … … …… …… …… …… … …., swear by Almighty God that I will be faithful and bear true allegiance to Her (or His) Majesty [Specify the name of the reigning Sovereign, as thus: Queen Elizabeth the Second] as the Head of State of Niue, Her (or His) heirs, and successors, in accordance with the Constitution and the law. So help me God'.

The Judicial Oath is in a similar form. Further, King Charles III is clearly the King of the Realm of New Zealand, of which Niue is a part. Unlike the Cook Islands, where it is arguable that Charles III is its King, neither the Bill of Rights 1688 nor the Act of Settlement 1701 applies in Niue. However, there may be an argument that the common law rules of succession, which encompass rules of primogeniture, are part of the common law of Niue.[58]

The second issue is that in the absence of any statutory elaboration, the process is opaque. Assuming that the provision can now be read as referring to the King, the King of the Realm of New Zealand does not have a Privy Council. He is advised by an

[51] Constitution of Niue, arts 42(a) and 52(2)(b).

[52] Constitution of Niue, art 42(b).

[53] Constitution of Niue, art 52(2)(a). No Act prescribes the necessary qualifications. In 2023 there were no other Court of Appeal judges.

[54] The right to appeal from New Zealand courts to the Privy Council was brought to an end in 2004, but only in respect of the New Zealand metropolitan courts: Supreme Court Act 2003, s 42. See now Senior Courts Act 2016, Part 1.

[55] There is no other relevant legislation. This is in contrast to the position, eg, in the Cook Islands: the Privy Council (Judicial Committee) Act 1984.

[56] See also art 1, which vests executive authority in 'Her Majesty the Queen in right of New Zealand'.

[57] The oath of allegiance to be taken by the Governor-General is in similar terms. See above, text at n 19 (Letters Patent SR 1983/225, cl 6).

[58] Interpretation Act 2004 (Niue), s 37(4).

Executive Council,[59] which in practice means the New Zealand Cabinet. It seems highly unlikely that article 55(2) or clause 7 of the Letters Patent was intended to allow an appeal to that body;[60] rather, it was intended to allow appeals to the Judicial Committee of the Privy Council. This is the view of the Judicial Committee itself, which states on its website that it has jurisdiction to entertain appeals from Niue.[61] This view does not confer jurisdiction in Niue law.[62]

The failure to fully patriate the courts could be seen as out of step with attempts, made in 2004, to patriate the law itself. This included the repeal of section 672 of the Niue Act 1966, which had applied the law of England in force in New Zealand on 14 January 1840 to Niue. It was replaced in 2004 with the following sources of law:[63]

The sources of Niuean law are, in order of priority –

(a) The Constitution;
(b) Acts of the Assembly;
(c) Regulations;
(d) Niuean custom;
(e) The common law of Niue.

This makes it clear that Niuean custom is superior to the common law of Niue, a factor of particular significance in land disputes given that customary land is governed by the custom and usage of Niueans.[64] This patriation paves the way for the development of a uniquely Niuean jurisprudence. However, as mentioned above, the appointment by the Governor-General of New Zealand of Judges currently from and resident in New Zealand presents a hurdle to this endeavour; that is, the common law of Niue will often in practice be the current law of New Zealand, as demonstrated by, for example *Koligi v Iakopo*,[65] *Tahega v Niue Police*,[66] and *Nelisi v Niue Public Service Commission*.[67] There is a significant role for the Chief Justice of New Zealand here, because the appointment of New Zealand judges to the High Court of Niue requires his or her consent.

This extensive hierarchy of courts seems extravagant viewed in the light of the smallness of the country and its population. The size of the country is reflected in the fact that there is only one law firm – one lawyer in private practice – in Niue.[68] The amount of business conducted by the Court of Appeal and by the High Court constituted by

[59] Letters Patent SR 1983/225, cl 7.

[60] If it were, the mechanism used may be expected to be similar to that indicated in *Rigg v University of Waikato* [1984] 1 NZLR 149.

[61] 'Role of JCPC' (*Judicial Committee of the Privy Council*), www.jcpc.uk/about/role-of-the-jcpc.html#Commonwealth.

[62] If the Judicial Committee of the Privy Council has jurisdiction, this would make Niue one of four countries in the Pacific region which still allow an appeal from its superior court to the Judicial Committee of the Privy Council. The others are the Cook Islands, Kiribati and Tuvalu.

[63] Interpretation Act 2004, s 4.

[64] Niue Amendment Act (No 2) 1968 (NZ), s 23.

[65] *Koligi v Iakopo* (2017) Niue Law Reports 1003, [2017] NUHC 1 (12 October 2017), https://www.worldlii.org/cgi-bin/sinodisp/paclii/nu/cases/NUHC/2017/1.html.

[66] *Tahega v Niue Police* (2012) Niue Law Reports 555, [2012] NUHC 6 (16 February 2012), https://www.worldlii.org/cgi-bin/sinodisp/paclii/nu/cases/NUHC/2012/6.html.

[67] *Nelisi v Niue Public Service Commission* (2004) Niue Law Reports 153, [2004] NUHC 2 (4 April 2004).

[68] KS Hekau, 'Niue' in J Corrin and T Angelo (eds), *Legal Systems of the Pacific: Introducing Sixteen Gem* (Cambridge, Intersentia, 2021) 165, 169.

a Judge is modest. In the 2021–22 period, the number of cases finalised in the Land Division of the High Court was 61; 20 cases were finalised in the Criminal Division of the High Court. In that same period, 35 cases were finalised by Land Commissioners and 45 cases were finalised by a Commissioner with two Justices of the Peace.

The court system of Niue has no doubt been influenced by the Cook Islands, which has a very similar system.[69] However, there is no necessary reason (i) why Niue should follow the three-tier hierarchy consisting of inferior court, superior court, and court of appeal, favoured by larger countries, or (ii) for a further appeal to a foreign court. Courts that are disconnected from the country for which they dispense justice can only exacerbate their remoteness from members of the society which they are intended to serve.

The current structure also puts a strain on resources. There is currently no dedicated court building and most land files are stored in a shipping container. Given the prevalence of land cases, a more practical approach might include the re-institution of a land tribunal. Alternatively, a village-based system might be considered, as in Tokelau.[70] There, land disputes, which cannot be informally mediated and resolved by the family are within the exclusive jurisdiction of the *Taupulega* (Council of Elders) of the village on each atoll.

V. Conclusion with Comparisons

The Niue Constitution is not written in the conveyancing document style of so many of the colonial constitutions that came out of the UK Colonial Office, although necessarily, because of the common law heritage, it has much in common with Colonial Office constitutions.

The current Constitution came into force in October 1974. The situation at that time was an interesting one. Niue had been split from the Cook Islands by Act of the New Zealand Parliament in 1966. The Niue Act 1966 provided a basic code of legislation on many topics, including a significant number of sections on matters that are now entrenched in the 1974 Constitution. If Niue could have been regarded as small at the time, the matter is beyond doubt now.

The Constitution of 1974 may be regarded as having reasonably addressed the then small size of the country. Sections 4–9 of the Niue Constitution Act 1974 can all be seen to reflect the small size and remoteness of Niue: the guarantee of New Zealand government department help; New Zealand citizenship; defence by New Zealand; economic and financial assistance by New Zealand; inter-government cooperation; and permanent physical representation of the New Zealand government in Niue.

Small size is also reflected in many of the articles of the Constitution. Cabinet has executive authority in the state; the 14 traditional villages are reflected in the Niue Assembly; special provision is made for public servants who wish to become members

[69] See M Lilly-Howe and M Mitchell, 'The Cook Islands' in J Corrin and A Angelo (eds), *Legal Systems of the Pacific: Introducing Sixteen Gems* (Cambridge, Intersentia, 2021) 7, 14.
[70] Constitution of Tokelau, r 15.

of the Niue Assembly; there is a distinctive role for the Speaker of the Niue Assembly; a constitutional change system exists that requires popular endorsement;[71] there is provision for New Zealand to legislate for Niue on request;[72] and the audit of Niue government finances is by the Audit Office of New Zealand.

The environment in 1974 was one in which there was a Realm of New Zealand which embraced metropolitan New Zealand and its associated countries. It was not until 1983 that the current Realm of New Zealand was clearly articulated in the Letters Patent for the Governor-General of New Zealand.

Comparison with Tuvalu is informative and illustrates how states that have many similarities can be very different constitutionally. As for the similarities, the Constitutions of Niue and Tuvalu both date from the 1970s, both island countries are in Polynesia, both are resource-poor, and both rely heavily on external economic support. The differences are that Tuvalu with 11,425 people and eight inhabited atolls, each mutually separated by the high seas, has had a standard British Colonial Office Constitution. It began life in difficulty because it had, to the chagrin of the UK, rejected the proposal by the UK that it continue life with Kiribati because the countries had been together as the Gilbert and Ellice Islands Colony.

Tuvalu refused to be part of Kiribati. As a result, Tuvalu acceded to independence under something of a cloud and essentially was ill-equipped in economic and infrastructure terms to succeed as an independent state. The Constitution that Tuvalu received in 1978 was not suited to its needs and especially not to its culture.[73] At the time of independence, the island government in Tuvalu was essentially customary government. That resolved itself in part in the promulgation of a revised Constitution in 1986 which principally effected the key cultural adjustments deemed necessary.[74]

The government, immediately after independence, had to find ways to address its economic dilemma. This it has done with the establishment and development of trust funds (eg the Tuvalu Trust Fund 1987), the Tuvalu Maritime Training Institute, and the commercial assignment of its top domain name '.tv' (1998).

Tuvalu is low-lying. That fact is reflected in the 2023 Constitution.[75] Niue is a raised, single island where a centralised national government was in place at the time of self-determination.

Tuvalu had human rights law (the European Convention model) from day one. Niue, undoubtedly influenced by New Zealand practice, has no Bill of Rights and, since self-determination, has made positive decisions not to entrench human rights. At the time of the 1992 constitutional amendments, not only was the decision clear but minor repeals of the original Constitution reinforced that decision.[76]

[71] Constitution of Niue, art 35.

[72] Constitution of Niue, art 36.

[73] Constitution of Tuvalu 1978.

[74] The cultural consequences of this were played out in *Teonea v Kaupule* [2005] TVHC 5 and *Teonea v Pu o Kaupule of Nanumaga* [2009] TVCA 2; in the Constitution (Recognition of Traditional Standards, Value and Practices) Amendment Act 2010; and more recently in the Constitution of Tuvalu 2023, Principles 3 to

[75] Constitution of Tuvalu 2023, s 2(5) and (6); the preamble expresses a deep concern for 'the immine existential threat of Climate Change'.

[76] See Constitution Amendment Act (No 1) 1992, s 3.

The Constitution of Niue projects executive power and political status but not size. The post-1974 constitutional history of Niue shows a generally strong executive, but in the Niue Assembly a legislature which is much weaker than might have been expected. There is no evidence that the state of Niue has chafed under the burden of its small size. On the contrary, Niue has in many ways and noticeably in population size, got smaller. Nonetheless, the Constitution was changed in 1992 and aspired in succeeding years to the indicia of greater size; that is to say, not to better accommodate smallness but arguably, at a constitutional level, to ignore it.

15

Not the Usual Suspects – Executive Dominance in Seychelles and the Developing Institutions that could Counter it

JOELLE BARNES*

I. Introduction

Seychelles' history until 1993 told a tale of domination by the ruling power. The small island state experienced two centuries of French and British colonisation followed by years of brutal autocratic rule under President Albert René who took power by coup d'état in 1977. However, in 1993, Seychelles adopted a new Constitution and transitioned from one-party rule to multiparty democracy. This Constitution commits to implementing a liberal democracy which adopts pluralism, tolerance, respect for human rights, the rule of law and the separation of powers.[1]

Thirty years later there is still an authoritarian culture despite Seychelles' democratic trappings. However, with the slow development of constitutional institutions, a constitutional culture can be seen taking root in this small state, and with it the promise of the development of a meaningful separation of powers. The most recent developments in the forming of a meaningful separation of powers are, however, not found in the usual suspects of the National Assembly or the judiciary, but rather in the recent strengthening of the 'guarantor' institutions which fortify specific constitutional norms.[2] In time, these institutions could work with the other branches to effectively counter the dominance of the executive in Seychelles.

* I am indebted to Elisabeth Perham, Rosalind Dixon and Maartje De Visser for their thoughtful comments which have vastly improved the drafts of this chapter, and for the input of the participants at the workshop held in December 2023. I am also grateful to Justice Mathilda Twomey-Woods, former Chief Justice of the Supreme Court of Seychelles and current Justice of Appeal on the Court of Appeal, for her wealth of knowledge about the development of the law in Seychelles and for always fact-checking my assumptions.

[1] Constitution of the Republic of Seychelles 1993 (1993 Constitution), art 49.

[2] See T Khaitan, 'Guarantor Institutions' (2021) 16 (Supplement S1) *Asian Journal of Comparative Law* S40 for a conceptual overview of the term 'guarantor institution'.

René had turned Seychelles into a one-party 'Sovereign Socialist Republic'[3] in which he held all executive power and appointment power,[4] supported by the military, police and a People's Assembly constituted entirely from his own party, the Seychelles People's Progressive Front (SPPF).[5] René's rule was characterised by an 'overreach of executive power, resulting in state oppression and numerous human rights abuses', including disappearances, killings, arbitrary detention, and direct and indirect political persecution, much of which has only recently been documented in the work of the Truth, Reconciliation and National Unity Commission.[6] Under René's rule, power was consolidated in the President, who controlled the media and the People's Assembly. Moreover, the courts' powers of judicial review were narrowly construed and, with a few notable exceptions, were ineffective safeguards against the abuse of executive power.[7]

Coming out of this era, the 1993 Constitution is laden with provisions that promote the restriction of the power of the executive. The 1993 Constitution introduces a separation of powers between the branches of state and subordinates all power-bearing under its provisions.[8] It includes enforceable human rights,[9] a role for the judiciary as the watchdog of the Constitution through judicial review of legislation and executive action,[10] and a role for the National Assembly to oversee executive conduct.[11] Moreover, it establishes independent bodies to take over responsibilities previously monopolised by the executive and to ensure independent consideration of complaints against the government. These bodies are the Advisory Committee on the Presidential Power of Pardon (Pardon Committee),[12] the Electoral Commission,[13] the Constitutional Appointments Authority (CAA),[14] the Ombudsman,[15] the Public Service Appeal Board (PSAB),[16] and the Auditor-General.[17]

The constitutional entrenchment of such independent bodies was an invention of late-twentieth-century constitutional design.[18] This invention is often attributed to the

[3] Constitution of the Republic of Seychelles 1979 (1979 Constitution), s 1.

[4] Including the appointment of judges: 1979 Constitution, s 26.

[5] 1979 Constitution, s 37(b). The SPPF later changed its name to the People's Party (*Parti LePep*) and the United Seychelles. For ease of discussion, it is simply referred to as SPPF throughout this chapter.

[6] Truth, Reconciliation and National Unity Commission, *Final Report Volume II: Historical Context and Overview of Main Evidence* (9 August 2022) (TRNUC Report) 69, available at: https://www.statehouse.gov.sc/. Indirect persecution or victimisation included lawful, but targeted government behaviour such as the denial of licences or permits, the re-zoning of land, or the compulsory acquisition of property.

[7] See, eg *R v Passport Officer, ex parte Kathleen Pillay* (1990) SLR 250 and *Michael & Co (Pty) Ltd v Rassool* (1990) SLR 243.

[8] 1993 Constitution, art 5. The courts have held that the separation of powers is implicit in the provisions of the Constitution, see *Hackl v Financial Intelligence Unit and Another* (2012) SLR 225.

[9] 1993 Constitution, chapter III.

[10] ibid arts 5, 46, 125(1)(a) and 130.

[11] ibid arts 53, 56, 64, 69, 73–74, 93, 160.

[12] ibid art 61.

[13] ibid art 115.

[14] ibid chapter IX.

[15] ibid arts 143–144, sch 5.

[16] ibid art 146.

[17] ibid art 158.

[18] M Tushnet, 'Institutions Protecting Constitutional Democracy' (2020) 70(2) *The University of Toronto Law Journal* 95, 96.

South African Constitution drafters;[19] however, it is worth noting that the Seychelles Constitution drafting process was contemporaneous with the South African process, and the Seychelles Constitution was completed in May 1993 before the completion of the South African Interim Constitution.[20] The International Ombudsman Institute consulted with Seychellois Constitution drafters during the drafting process, influencing the decision to include an Ombudsman.[21] Moreover, both Constitutions were likely influenced by the 1990 Namibian Constitution, which had already included an Ombudsman, Public Service Commission and Auditor-General.[22] Furthermore, such institutions are broadly described as 'integrity' institutions,[23] 'fourth branch institutions'[24] or 'institutions protecting constitutional democracy'.[25] In this chapter I am using Khaitan's terminology of 'guarantor institution' which he defines as: 'a tailor-made constitutional institution, vested with material as well as expressive capacities, whose function is to provide a credible and enduring guarantee to a specific non-self-enforcing constitutional norm (or any aspect thereof)'.[26]

The identified institutions fall neatly within this definition. The Seychelles Constitution also requires that the government provides independent, state-funded broadcasting media.[27] However, no institution with material and expressive capacities is created by the provision, and so it will not be discussed.

The separation of powers in Seychelles has struggled to take root in practice, and executive dominance has continued to characterise governance in Seychelles in the 30 years since the adoption of the 1993 Constitution. This chapter considers Seychelles' constitutionalism and how the mechanisms designed to place executive power under constitutional control have worked in practice over three decades. It plots a narrative of the development of constitutionalism through slow, incremental progress and identifies factors which persist in frustrating the imposition of effective mechanisms of accountability on the executive. These factors are exacerbated by Seychelles' smallness, including its small political elite, its limited resources and personnel constraints, as well as an underdeveloped civil society. Some tentative solutions are suggested to assist with the development of a constitutional culture of executive accountability that may have relevance to the constitutional design discussions of larger states as well as of other small states.

[19] CM Fombad, 'The Diffusion of South African-Style Institutions? A Study in Comparative Constitutionalism' in R Dixon and T Roux (eds), *Constitutional Triumphs, Constitutional Disappointments* (Cambridge, Cambridge University Press, 2018) 359.

[20] Constitution of the Republic of South Africa 1993.

[21] Personal communication with Mathilda Twomey-Woods and Pesi Pardiwalla, former members of Constitutional Assembly (4 September 2024).

[22] Constitution of the Republic of Namibia 1990, chapters 10, 13 and art 127.

[23] B Ackerman, 'The New Separation of Powers' (2000) 113 *Harvard Law Review* 633, 694; AJ Brown, 'The Integrity Branch: A "System", An "Industry", Or a Sensible Emerging Fourth Arm of Government?' in M Groves (ed), *Modern Administrative Law in Australia: Concepts and Context* (Cambridge, Cambridge University Press, 2014) 302.

[24] Fombad (n 19) 362.

[25] Tushnet 'Institutions Protecting Constitutional Democracy' (n 18) 96.

[26] Khaitan (n 2) S40.

[27] 1993 Constitution, art 168.

II. Presidential Exceptionalism and Delayed Changeover

The development of the separation of powers under the 1993 Constitution has faced several challenges. An important factor is that the position of the President remains a powerful one in the Constitution, the existing law and the public perception. The President is the 'Head of State, Head of Government and Commander-in-Chief of the Defence Forces of Seychelles'.[28] Article 66 vests executive authority in the President individually, whereas legislative and judicial power is vested in the National Assembly and the judiciary respectively as institutions.[29] As the leader of the executive, the President's powers over the executive are almost unrestricted, and the Vice-President and Ministers are hand-picked by the President and perform their functions under the *direction* of the President.[30]

Moreover, the President may establish and abolish government offices and departments without restriction.[31] Currently President Ramkalawan is responsible for three significant ministerial portfolios in addition to his responsibilities as President. These are Defence, Legal Affairs, and the Public Administration. This makes him the cabinet member responsible for the most portfolios. Holding the portfolio of Minister for Legal Affairs also means that the Office of the Prosecutor (housed in the Attorney General's chambers) and the judiciary rely on the President in matters relating to their resourcing.

In addition to these powers, there is a pervasive exceptionalism in the Constitution regarding the President. The National Assembly may question Ministers regarding their portfolios but is not empowered to question the President directly on matters which fall within his responsibility.[32] This affects the ability of the Assembly to scrutinise decision-making in these ministries. The President, however, may choose to attend and address the National Assembly at any time, and may send a message to the Assembly which must be read out by the Speaker.[33] Money Bills may only be tabled before the National Assembly if recommended by the President, represented by the Minister of Finance, and the President plays a role in determining the order of priority for the presentation of Bills in the Assembly.[34] The President's power to summon and prorogue the National Assembly seems incongruous in a constitutional democracy where the legislature is directly elected and the Cabinet and President are not members of the Assembly, however this vestige of the colonial Parliament remains.[35] Moreover, many Acts, pre- and post-1993, vest unfettered discretionary powers in the President – even in relation to portfolios which are not handled by the President.[36] The President is still responsible

[28] ibid art 50.

[29] ibid arts 85, 119.

[30] ibid arts 70–71. Ministers are not permitted to be members of the National Assembly, under art 81.

[31] ibid arts 62, 71.

[32] ibid art 93(2).

[33] ibid art 92.

[34] ibid arts 90, 93(3).

[35] ibid arts 107, 109, 110. This power has survived from the first post-independence 1976 Seychell Constitution, through the one-party state, to be incorporated in the 1993 Constitution.

[36] See, eg: s 5(1) of the Citizenship Act, cap 30 enables the President to grant citizenship to a person who, his/ her opinion, 'has done signal honour or rendered distinguished service to Seychelles'. The Children A cap 28, requires the President's consent in certain adoption cases: ss 37–38.

for appointing magistrates, commissioners, boards and committees under most Acts.[37] These provisions, taken together, create a President who is empowered to direct all of the branches of state and who is above answering Assembly questions regarding his or her actions or policies except through deputies.

The breadth of presidential power could possibly be attributed to the constitutional drafting process. The elected Constitutional Commission was dominated by two parties, each led by charismatic leaders both expecting to become President after the Constitution was adopted, and thus both disinclined to restrict or limit the role. However, some protections have been introduced by the Constitution to protect against abuse of this office, including restrictions on terms of office,[38] the introduction of the Pardon Committee,[39] and the appointment of certain officials subject to the approval of the National Assembly.[40] One of the most important innovations of the new Constitution is the creation of the CAA to assist with the appointment and discipline of certain high-level public officials.[41]

Despite these protections, the balance of powers still tilts in favour of the presidency.[42] This is exacerbated by Seychelles' smallness. The President can influence all aspects of society and governance because of the smallness of the bureaucracy in Seychelles. A President can be directly involved in ways which would not be feasible in larger administrations. Individuals regularly bring all kinds of complaints directly to the Office of the President, and these are sometimes dealt with by the President personally.[43] This involvement would simply not be possible in a larger country.

Seychelles' constitutionalism has also been stunted by its enduring linkages to its autocratic past. René won the first and second multiparty elections under the new Constitution and his political party remained in power until 2020, when Wavel Ramkalawan became the first President elected from an opposition party since the coup in 1977. For 43 years, executive power had been vested in the hands of the same party which had illegitimately come to power in 1977. Baker describes this as 'a lost opportunity for democracy'.[44] The legacy of the pre-1993 René regime, with its intimidation, victimisation and oppression has had a chilling effect on the development of a

[37] See, eg: Courts Act 1964, cap 52, s 25; Seychelles Heritage Foundation Act 2006, s 5(2); Seychelles Revenue Commission Act 2009, s 4(1); Seychelles Energy Commission Act 2010, ss 7(1), 15(3); Seychelles Pension Fund Act 2005.

[38] 1993 Constitution, art 52. The number of terms was reduced from three terms to two terms in the Constitution of the Republic of Seychelles (Seventh Amendment) Act 2016.

[39] 1993 Constitution, art 60.

[40] The appointment of diplomats and representatives (art 64), the appointment of Ministers (art 69), and the appointment of the Commissioner of Police (art 160).

[41] 1993 Constitution, arts 61, 115A, 123, 127, 134, 143(1), 158, 165.

[42] ibid art 49.

[43] *The Ombudsman – Righting Wrongs* (Annual Report of the Ombudsman, 2022), www.nationalassembly.sc/publications/reports/annual-report-ombudsman-2022-ombudsman-righting-wrongs (Ombudsman Report 2022) p 3 lists this as an official form of dispute resolution. This is consistent with academic findings in other countries where matters can be addressed personally without utilising official institutional channels. WP Veenendaal, 'Democracy in Microstates: Why Smallness Does Not Produce a Democratic Political System' (2015) 22(1) *Democratization* 92, 100.

[44] B Baker, 'Seychelles: Democratising in the Shadows of the Past' (2008) 26(3) *Journal of Contemporary African Studies* 278, 280–81.

constitutional culture and meaningful challenge to executive overreach even after the introduction of checks and balances.

The exceptionalism ascribed to the President by the Constitution itself makes it easy for incumbents to begin to believe that they can rule by will rather than according to the law. The 2022 Truth, Reconciliation and National Unity Commission Report documents executive domination, human rights abuses by security forces, as well as violent and systemic discrimination against opposition supporters well into the democratic regime.[45]

Concerningly, in its first four years, the new *Linyon Demokratik Seselwa* (LDS) Government has exhibited hints of executive abuse of power.[46] An example is the Tenth Amendment to the Constitution proposed by the executive, passed by the LDS by a two-thirds majority vote in the National Assembly and assented to by the President. This amendment enlarges the powers of the Defence Forces to permit operations alongside the police outside of a state of emergency. It is currently subject to a constitutional challenge.[47] However, it has been vigorously defended by the Government. The Truth, Reconciliation and National Unity Commissioner noted that the introduction of such an amendment is indicative of a fundamental constitutional regression and concentrates immense power in the hands of the President in a manner which harks back to the René days.[48]

Although this power imbalance in favour of the executive is still present 30 years after the introduction of constitutionalism, it is important to consider whether the other actors in the Constitution have begun to play a role in developing a constitutionalism that checks the wide executive powers, as envisaged by the introduction of a separation of powers. The remainder of this chapter turns to consider the accountability roles played by the other institutions in the Constitution.

III. The National Assembly

The National Assembly is a unicameral body elected in a separate vote from the President. It consists of 35 members – with an elected representative for each of the 26 voting districts, and nine members appointed by parties in proportion to the overall vote in the legislative election. The 1993 Constitution vested legislative authority in the National Assembly, and it also expanded the Assembly's role as an accountability mechanism with oversight of the use of executive power. For example, the appointment

[45] TRNUC Report (n 6) chapter 7.

[46] Rumours abound of political favouritism and victimisation of political adversaries. For example, the government granted the Chief Justice a 'favour' by permitting him to purchase land from the Ministry for Lands and Housing Land Bank despite his not being legally eligible, and at a significantly below-market rate on discretionary 'compassionate' grounds. P Joubert, 'Minister clarifies land allocation to Chief Justice' *Seychelles Nation* (4 October 2022), www.nation.sc/articles/15291/minister-clarifies-land-allocation-to-chief-justice. Journalists also described being chastised by the President personally after critically reporting on the conduct of a Minister. US Department of State Bureau of Democracy, Human Rights and Labor, '2022 Country Reports on Human Rights Practices: Seychelles', www.state.gov/reports/2022-country-reports-on-human-rights-practices/seychelles, s 2A.

[47] *Seychelles Human Rights Commission and Others v Speaker of the National Assembly of Seychelles and Others* (CP7 of 2022) [2024] SCCA 14 (3 May 2024).

[48] TRNUC Report (n 6) 132.

of certain officials is subject to the approval of the Assembly.[49] The Assembly may also initiate investigations into the President's ability to perform and may pass a vote of censure in respect of a Minister. These powers have never been exercised to date.[50] It is the Assembly which delegates legislative authority to the executive and exercises oversight over the use thereof.[51] The Assembly enjoys the privilege of unrestricted speech and can summons Ministers to attend to answer questions related to 'dealing with any matter arising in the Assembly'.[52] Moreover, committees can be set up for any purpose necessary for the efficient discharge of its functions.[53]

However, the strength of the National Assembly as an accountability mechanism against executive power is directly related to whether the President's political party controls most of the seats in the Assembly. After 23 years of the Assembly acquiescing to the executive, in 2016, an opposition coalition led by Ramkalawan secured control of the Assembly. During the next five years the National Assembly was active in opposing the mere *use* of executive power, let alone its abuse. The Assembly refused to approve the nomination of three Ministers in April 2018, and Ramkalawan stated that this was 'for the simple reason that LDS is demanding … fresh presidential and even parliamentary elections'.[54] Similarly, the National Assembly defeated a government Bill to increase the salaries of the public service, and when similar measures were introduced by statutory instrument, these were annulled by the Assembly.

The opposition-dominated Assembly also set up an extra-judicial committee to investigate 'victimisation' within the government's administration. The committee took complaints, summonsed witnesses and made findings in this extra-judicial space without applying the rules of fair procedure. A challenge was brought to the constitutionality of this manner of exercising the accountability function in the case of *Herminie v Pillay*, where it was argued that the Assembly was usurping the judicial function.[55] The committee was later disbanded.

During this period of power-sharing, some important laws were introduced which furthered the interests of Seychelles as a whole, including the establishment of a human rights body[56] and the setting up of the Truth, Reconciliation and National Unity Commission.[57] Otherwise, it was a period characterised by political point-scoring, particularly as National Assembly deliberations are aired live on radio and YouTube and

[49] The appointment of diplomats and representatives (art 64), Ministers (art 69), and the Commissioner of Police (art 160).

[50] 1993 Constitution, arts 53, 56, 73–74.

[51] ibid art 89. Section 64 of the Interpretation and General Provisions Act, cap 103 requires all subsidiary legislation to be laid before the Assembly, which has the power to annul the subsidiary legislation within three months.

[52] 1993 Constitution, arts 93, 102.

[53] ibid art 104.

[54] 'LDS Blocks Nomination of Three New Ministers' *Seychelles Nation* (12 April 2018), www.nation.sc/archive/258440/lds-blocks-nomination-of-three-new-ministers. Two years later, Ramkalawan would later appoint one of those same persons, Mr Billy Rangasamy, as a Minister in his cabinet.

[55] Rulings were given in preliminary matters in *Herminie and Another v Pillay and Others* (CP02/2017; CP06/2017; CP07/2017) [2018] SCCC 6 (12 March 2018) and in *Herminie and Another v Pillay and Others* (MA 149/2017) [2017] SCCC 5 (26 May 2017). The final disposition of the case is not available online; it is presumed to have been discontinued.

[56] Seychelles Human Rights Commission Act 2018.

[57] Truth, Reconciliation and National Unity Commission Act 2018.

the members are immune to prosecution for statements made in the Assembly, even if they are false or misleading.

In 2020, Ramkalawan's party won the two-thirds supermajority in the Assembly required to amend the Constitution, giving the party control over the executive, the Assembly and the Constitution. The ruling party's policy of strict party loyalty weakens the Assembly's likelihood of being an effective mechanism to prevent executive overreach during this political term.

IV. The Judiciary

The third branch of government and primary guardian of the constitutional structure is the judiciary, which functions subject only to the Constitution and the other laws of Seychelles.[58] The courts' jurisdiction includes the 'application, contravention, enforcement or interpretation' of the Constitution, which creates a constitutional review power for the courts over the constitutionality of legislation as well as executive conduct.[59] Furthermore the courts have 'supervisory jurisdiction', originating from the English common law, to judicially review the exercise of public power.[60] The Constitutional Court may hear and determine election petitions, and the President may refer a Bill passed by the National Assembly to the Constitutional Court to determine its constitutionality.[61] Moreover, the Constitutional Court may, on the reference by a supermajority of the National Assembly, investigate allegations that the President has committed a violation of the Constitution or gross misconduct which would be grounds for removal from office as President.[62]

From 1993 to approximately 2007 – the years when René was in power and the first few years of his chosen successor, James Michel – there were few cases engaging with politically sensitive matters involving the exercise of presidential conduct or ministerial discretion. Those that were brought were unsuccessful, as judges appeared reluctant to determine the merits of the cases.[63] However, around 2007 there was a shift in judicial attitudes and a deeper engagement with the judicial role under the new Constitution.[64] In judicial review cases, the judges began applying the common law standards of fairness to ministerial decisions and requiring that the 'exercise of executive power [was] within

[58] 1993 Constitution, art 119.

[59] ibid arts 66, 125(1)(a).

[60] ibid art 125(1)(c) and ss 4–6 of the Courts Act 1964 which vests common law judicial review powers in the courts.

[61] 1993 Constitution, arts 51(2), 82(1), 87.

[62] ibid art 54.

[63] See, for example, *Benker v Government of Seychelles and Another* (CS 58/1996) (1999) SLR 48, [1999] SCSC 13 (1 December 1999); *Omaghomi Believe v Government of Seychelles* (CS 141/2003) (2003) SLR 140, [2003] SCSC 14 (12 June 2003); *Timonina v Government of Seychelles* (CS 173/2007) [2007] SCSC 13 (12 December 2007).

[64] It is difficult to pinpoint the cause of this shift, although it may have been the fading of René's legacy of control. Changes to the bench also may have affected the jurisprudence with the retirement of a controversial Chief Justice and the appointment of new judges to the Court of Appeal bench including Seychellois judge Jacques Hodoul (appointed 2005) and Mauritian academic and judge Dr Satyabhooshun Gupt Domah (appointed 2006). See Baker (n 44) 282.

the parameters of the law and the Constitution'.[65] Furthermore, the Constitutional Court in *Brioche v Attorney General* held that the standards expected of administrative decision-makers in common law judicial review – legality, rationality, procedural fairness and proportionality – would apply to the review of the exercise of powers originating in the Constitution.[66] These common law standards provide robust standards for the review of the exercise of executive powers.

However, in the past 10 years there has been a backsliding, with the courts deferring to the President or again finding technical reasons to avoid determining politically sensitive matters (such as dismissals on the grounds of standing or on the grounds of bringing proceedings out of time, or at the leave to review stage).[67] There have also been cases which could be examples of what Landau and Dixon term 'weak form abusive judicial review'.[68]

In the 2018 case of *Volcere v Felix and others*, for example, the Constitutional Court overturned existing jurisprudence on standing to avoid determining the constitutionality of the President's appointment of members of the CAA.[69] Furthermore, in a 2015 election petition, the Constitutional Court found that the leader of the opposition party, Ramkalawan, had committed an electoral offence and struck him off the electoral role for five years as required under the law.[70] On appeal, the Court of Appeal reversed this politically difficult result on the grounds that Ramkalawan had not had an opportunity to be heard on the allegations against him prior to the finding. Rather than remitting the matter to the Constitutional Court, as would be the ordinary procedure, the Court of Appeal allowed Ramkalawan an opportunity to provide reasons for his misconduct in open court room, after the matter had been heard and during the sitting of the Court to hand down judgment in the case. The Court of Appeal then adjourned for a short period and returned to overturn the decision of the Constitutional Court and replace the decision with its own, exonerating Ramkalawan of all wrongdoing.[71]

When determining the lawfulness of the use of power by elected officials, judges in Seychelles appear self-conscious of their democratic credentials.[72] In *Michel and Others*

[65] *Raihl v Ministry of National Development* (2010) SLR 66, 69, [2010] SCCA 3 (20 May 2010). See also *Seychelles Ports Authority v Desaubin* [2015] SCCA 13 (17 April 2015); *Trajter v Morgan* [2013] SCCA 17; *Chow v Attorney General and Others* [2007] SCCA 2, [18]; and *Poonoo v Attorney General* [2011] SCCA 30.

[66] *Brioche v Attorney General* (2013) SLR 425.

[67] See, eg *Karunakaran v Constitutional Appointment Authority* [2017] SCCA 9 (refusal to grant leave to review the decision to suspend a judge pending disciplinary matters against him because matter not ripe); *Assemblies of God v Attorney General* [2020] SCCC 975 (Constitutional Court dismissed constitutional petition regarding petitioner's right to property, stating that petitioner could have sought alternative relief by means of judicial review and not constitutional review).

[68] The authors define weak abusive judicial review as 'when courts uphold legislation or executive action that significantly undermines the democratic minimum core, thus legitimating damaging moves undertaken by political actors.' D Landau and R Dixon, 'Abusive Judicial Review: Courts Against Democracy' (2020) 53 *UC Davis Law Review* 1313, 1345.

[69] *Volcere v Felix and others* [2018] SCCC 4.

[70] *Ramkalawan v Electoral Commission and Others (Election Non-compliance and Illegal Practices)* (CP 1 of 2016) [2016] SCCC 11 (30 May 2016).

[71] *Ramkalawan v Electoral Commission and Others* (SCA 1 of 2016) [2016] SCCA 17 (12 August 2016).

[72] M Twomey, *Legal Metissage in a Micro-Jurisdiction: The Mixing of Common Law and Civil Law in Seychelles* (Wellington, City Print, 2017) 120.

v Dhanjee and Others,[73] a case concerning a challenge to the reappointment of Domah JA to the Court of Appeal by the President, the Court of Appeal held that:

> In cases such as the present one, an unelected body (the Judiciary) tells an elected body – either the [legislature] (the National Assembly) or the executive (The President), who are elected by the people, that their will is incompatible with the fundamental aspirations of the people as formulated in the Constitution of the Seychelles. It is for this reason that the law has developed procedural and substantive safeguards to control the boundaries of judicial authority (and to prevent what Sedley J … called 'the direct withering fire on the executive').

However, the courts' perceived democratic deficit may not be the only factor that judges weigh when exercising their accountability function over the use of executive powers. The courts remain constrained by several factors which affect their ability to perform their function. The first of these is their lack of financial autonomy.[74] The judiciary relies on the executive and the National Assembly for budget and is subject to a performance-based budgeting process which includes Ministry of Finance involvement in setting financial priorities for the judiciary. The judiciary has been subjected to spontaneous budget cuts which affect its independence and ability to perform its mandate.[75] The judiciary must go, cap-in-hand, to the executive, specifically to the Minister of Justice (as noted above, currently the President) to secure funding for its needs, be they infrastructure upgrades, salary increases, adequate staffing or facilities.[76] This reliance creates a power imbalance between the two branches and arguably affects the courage of individual judges.

Twomey argues that foreign judges in Seychelles have historically shown bravery against the executive in Seychelles and that they may be less susceptible to influence from the executive due to being appointed on fixed-term contracts.[77] She argues that this is because their tenure and promotion is not linked to executive favour. In the past decade, the CAA has prioritised appointing Seychellois judges over foreign judges, with nine of the 10 most recent appointees to the Supreme Court all being Seychellois.[78] This broadly correlates to the increased judicial reticence in determining political cases evident from the case law in the same period, which may confirm Twomey's theory. It is possible that local judges are concerned that strictly enforcing the Constitution against the interests of political individuals would have negative impacts on their own ambitions.

An additional inhibiting factor is the lack of foundational legal training in Seychellois constitutional law. To date, all judges and lawyers have received their foundational legal training in foreign law. The University of Seychelles began teaching Seychellois law in its post-graduate Bar Course programmes from 2014 onwards and its Seychelles LLB

[73] *Michel and Others v Dhanjee and Others* (2012) SLR 258, [2012] SCCA 10 (31 August 2012).

[74] See The Judiciary of Seychelles 'Vision 2021-2025: Judiciary Strategic Plan' www.judiciary.sc/wp-content/uploads/2022/01/judiciary-strategic-plan-2021.pdf, 8.

[75] ibid 13.

[76] S Nicette and B Bonnelame, 'Seychelles judges meet with President Ramkalawan to discuss future plans and challenges' *Seychelles News Agency* (5 December 2023), www.seychellesnewsagency.com/articles/1973 Seychelles%27+judges+meet+with+President+Ramkalawan+to+discuss+future+plans+and+challenges.

[77] M Twomey, 'Impartial Adjudicators? The Role of Foreign Judges in Seychelles' in A Dziedzic and SNM Young (eds), *The Cambridge Handbook of Foreign Judges on Domestic Courts* (Cambridge, Cambridge University Press, 2023) 197–98.

[78] ibid 186–88.

law degree only launched in 2022. There are no legal textbooks specifically addressing Seychellois public law. The courts rely on cases being brought properly and according to the correct procedure, and the lack of legal resources and training could certainly impact on the ability of lawyers to bring such cases to court. The lack of development in the field of legal education and academia is directly related to the small size of Seychelles, and the University has struggled to develop and staff a full-time four-year law course that will only attract a cohort of about 10 students per year. Developing the materials for this course will also take time.

There is also a culture of not challenging the executive even when a challenge could stand. This applies particularly to the actions of the President.[79] This might be a result of a lack of knowledge of the law, lack of resources to bring litigation, or a fear of executive reprisal based on historical conditioning. It may also be a direct result of social proximity in a small state, where matters can often be resolved politically without recourse to the courts. However, without cases being brought the judiciary cannot effectively perform its role as bulwark of the Constitution.

Seychelles also has a small, undeveloped civil society.[80] Although there is a Citizen Engagement Platform that operates as a national platform for civil society in Seychelles, with around 200 registered organisations, very few such organisations engage actively with legal and governance topics.[81] The Bar Association has occasionally brought cases to the courts; however this is rare, and no other organisations have intervened or brought cases in the 30 years since the Constitution was adopted.[82] A mobilised civil society is an important factor in ensuring the durability of a constitutional framework and in its absence the checking interrelationship between the constitutional institutions, including the guarantor institutions, becomes all the more important.[83]

Overall, although the judiciary has developed standards by which to determine the lawfulness of the use of executive power, there appears to be some recent reticence to determine cases concerning the President and high executive. Moreover, as just outlined, the courts face significant challenges which are exacerbated by the context of operating within a small country. The independence of the judiciary ought to be strengthened to

[79] For example, the President placed restrictions on citizens' rights of freedom of movement, association, education and work during the Covid-19 pandemic and invoked the assistance of the military in policing. This was done without invoking the constitutional State of Emergency provisions which permit derogation from rights and the deployment of the military domestically (1993 Constitution, chapter III, part III). This did not lead to a single legal challenge despite negatively impacting individuals and businesses across the country.

[80] L Briguglio, M Briguglio, S Bunwaree and C Slatter, *Handbook of Civil Society and Social Movements in Small States* (New York, Routledge, 2023) 1, define civil society as 'organized groups operating in the interests of citizens, independently of government and commercial businesses, including various forms of non-governmental organizations (NGOs)' and 'social movements which are considered to be loosely organized collective campaigns in pursuit of social goals'.

[81] D Benoit, 'The role of civil society actors in responding to gender-based violence in Seychelles' in L Briguglio, M Briguglio, S Bunwaree and C Slatter, *Handbook of Civil Society and Social Movements in Small States* (New York, Routledge, 2023) 151, 154.

[82] See, eg *Bar Association of Seychelles v President of Republic* [2004] SCCA 2 and more recently in the challenge to the Tenth Amendment of the Constitution: *Seychelles Human Rights Commissions and Others v The Speaker of National Assembly and Others* Constitutional Petition 7 of 2023, ongoing (n 47).

[83] See M Bernard, A Hicken, C Reenock and S Lindberg, 'Parties, Civil Society, and the Deterrence of Democratic Defection' (2020) 55 *Studies in Comparative International Development* 1 and the citations therein.

enable them to exercise their role through creating mechanisms to ensure greater financial autonomy and less direct involvement by the executive.

But this alone will not address the variety of factors affecting the judiciary, and the success of its role is also closely linked to the capacity of the guarantor institutions, particularly the CAA, which is responsible for the appointments and removal of judges, and the Ombudsman, which has a role to play in bringing cases to court. I turn now to those institutions.

V. The Slow Strengthening of the Guarantor Institutions

The guarantor institutions set up by the Constitution have been plagued by under-resourcing, political apathy and political interference, but a closer look at them reveals that each institution is developing incrementally despite early difficulties. However, as the discussion will show, despite their constitutionalisation, the guarantor institutions remain vulnerable to the whims of the executive. As such, I argue that they require reinforcement and protection from stakeholder interference.

Writing in 2008 and reviewing the institutions under the post-1993 René regime, Baker concluded:

> It was not that the new institutions were abolished; they were neutered. They were permeated by partisanship; manipulated to serve the interests of the SPPF. They functioned, but only in as much as they did not threaten the government-SPPF interests. President René did not prove to have any interest in allowing democracy to flourish.[84]

This 'neutering' was largely achieved through the political capture of one very important institution: the CAA, which multitasks as the appointment committee for the members of most of the other guarantor institutions, including the Electoral Commission, the Ombudsman, the Auditor-General, the Pardons Committee, the Anti-Corruption Commissioner and the Human Rights Commissioner, as well as the President of the Court of Appeal, the Justices of Appeal, the Judges and Masters of the Supreme Court.[85] The CAA also determines whether other officials of the judiciary or fourth branch ought to be investigated or disciplined.[86]

A. The Constitutional Appointments Authority

The CAA was designed to protect the norm of independent, non-partisan appointment of non-elected members to important constitutional and statutory bodies. The 1993 Constitution states that the CAA should not be subject to the direction or control of any person or authority;[87] however, manipulation of the membership of the CAA makes

[84] Baker (n 44) 280–81.
[85] 1993 Constitution, arts 115A, 123, 127, 143(1), 158; Anti-Corruption Act 2016, s 6(1); and Seychelles Human Rights Commission Act 2018, s 5(1).
[86] 1993 Constitution, arts 134 and 165.
[87] ibid art 139.

it possible for the CAA to be influenced. The influencing of the membership of the CAA occurs through the inherently political appointment process. The President and the Leader of the Opposition party in the Assembly each appoint two persons to be on the CAA, and the fifth member, the chairperson of the CAA, is appointed by the members themselves.[88] This process is intended to balance the influence of the political parties; however, it in fact ensures that the appointment is intrinsically political and the members feel bound to represent the political parties which appointed them to secure reappointment or curry political favour. Also, in a country as small and as politically polarised as Seychelles, the political nature of their appointment gives the perception that they will not exercise their mandate independently.

The inherently political nature of the appointment of the CAA members was intended to be tempered by the qualification requirements of the members.[89] Article 141 of the 1993 Constitution provides that:

> A person is qualified to be a member of the Constitutional Appointments Authority if the person is a citizen of Seychelles who—
>
> (a) has held judicial office in a court of unlimited original jurisdiction; or
> (b) is of proven integrity and impartiality who has served with distinction in a high office in the Government of Seychelles or under this Constitution or in a profession or vocation.

Article 141 was drafted at a time when the judicial bench was small, and most judicial positions were held by foreign judges. As such there was a need for sub-clause (b) to supplement sub-clause (a). The requirements of 'proven integrity and impartiality' were presumably intended to encompass individuals with 'judicial probitas'.[90] However, these are particularly malleable concepts and, to date, not a single member of the CAA has been a former judge. Almost all CAA members appointed to date lack knowledge of the workings of the judiciary or the requirements of judicial appointments and discipline. This undermines the ability of the CAA to perform its role – particularly with regards to judicial appointments,[91] and the same criticism remains true for the appointment to the guarantor institutions. The members who have been appointed to the CAA have regularly been active politicians and cronies of the appointors, which has attracted criticism.[92] Of course, it cannot be said that all the members of the CAA have been politically active, but rather that the appointment of those members who are career politicians is problematic. It undermines their impartiality and the perception of their impartiality in the course of their work. Furthermore, the failure to appoint members who accord with the provisions of the Constitution undermines the legitimacy of the institution.

As mentioned above, the only legal challenge to the constitutionality of the appointment of the CAA's members (in the late 2010s) was dismissed by the Constitutional Court on technical grounds without determination of the merits.[93] In that case, it was

[88] ibid art 140. The number of members was increased from three to five in 2017.
[89] M Twomey, 'Judicial Appointment in Seychelles – a study in what not to do' (Address at the South African Chief Justices Forum Annual Meeting, Seychelles, October 2019), www.judiciary.sc/wp-content/uploads/2020/09/sacjf-judicial-appointments-in-seychelles-october-2019.pdf.
[90] ibid. See also Twomey 'Impartial adjudicators?' (n 77) 181.
[91] Twomey 'Judicial Appointment' (n 89) 3.
[92] Baker (n 44) 283 and Twomey 'Judicial Appointment' (n 89).
[93] *Volcere v Felix and others* [2018] SCCC 4.

argued by the petitioners that recently appointed members of the CAA were not of proven integrity and impartiality, in violation of article 141(b) of the Constitution. The members whose appointment was being challenged consisted of a businessman and two career politicians, one of whom was the Secretary General of the party controlling the National Assembly. The case was dismissed at a preliminary stage on grounds of standing, with the Court narrowing its previous definition of standing to exclude challenges brought by a concerned citizen who 'could not demonstrate that his personal interest is being or is likely to be affected'.[94] This finding was upheld on appeal, with the Court of Appeal stating that 'public interest litigation is alien to our jurisdiction'.[95]

The Constitutional Court bench hearing the matter consisted of two judges appointed by the CAA shortly before the matter came to court, one of whom was appointed Chief Justice by the same CAA two years later. The Court of Appeal was unusually constituted for the hearing of the appeal – with three instead of the normal five Justices of Appeal for a constitutional appeal. Two of these Justices of Appeal were appointed by the same CAA under challenge, and the third was later appointed as the President of the Court of Appeal by the CAA in 2020.

Following this challenge, and other criticisms of the CAA, it has taken steps to reinforce its transparency through the adoption of standard operating procedures and rules for the appointment and investigation of complaints against constitutional appointees.[96] These have been developed in line with the Lilongwe principles for judicial appointment.[97] The CAA had operated based on internal policies with no publicised criteria, rules or operating procedures since 1993, and so increased transparency and an apparently meritorious appointment process is welcomed. However, it is regrettable that the publication of these operating processes has not led to meaningful change in the functioning of the CAA, and Twomey notes that the CAA fails to appoint the best qualified and experienced candidates despite 'lip service application of the Lilongwe Principles and cynical distortion of the rules of transparency and accountability'.[98]

Reform of, or improved adherence to, the constitutional provisions relating to the CAA is key for the enhancement of Seychelles' democracy. Its improved independence can only serve to enhance the independence of the judiciary and the guarantor institutions whose members it nominates.

Regarding the remaining guarantor institutions: across the board, it is noted that they continue to struggle with lack of legal infrastructure, under-resourcing, and a poor

[94] ibid. Previous cases such as *Bar Association of Seychelles v President of Republic* [2004] SCCA 2; *Chow v Gappy* (2006–2007) SCAR 93; and *Michel and Others v Dhanjee and Others* [2012] SCCA 10 had adopted a liberal approach to standing and permitted constitutional cases being brought by bodies as well as concerned citizens.

[95] *Volcere v Georges and Others* [2018] SCCA 43, [51].

[96] Rules and Guidelines on the Selection and Appointment of Constitutional Appointees (Other than Judicial Officers) and Appointees under the Laws of Seychelles, 2019 (adopted by the Constitutional Appointments Authority on 16 August 2019); and Constitutional Appointments Authority (Complaints And Removal) Rules 2020. Both sets of rules are available at 'CAA Rules' (*Constitutional Appointments Authority*) caaseychelles.com/constitutional-authority-rules.

[97] Lilongwe Principles and Guidelines on the Selection and Appointment of Judicial Officers (adopted by the Southern African Chief Justices Forum Conference and Annual General Meeting, Lilongwe, 2018) available at: law.uct.ac.za/sites/default/files/media/documents/law_uct_ac_za/2353/lilongwe_principles_and_guidelines_on_the_selection_and_appointment_of_judicial_officers.pdf.

[98] Twomey, 'Judicial Appointment' (n 89) 188.

response from the government. However, each of these institutions has shown a gradual strengthening in its ability to act as an accountability mechanism for the use of executive power, as will be explored in the next sections of this chapter.

B. The Advisory Committee on the Power of Pardon

The Pardon Committee was set up in 1993 under the provisions of the Constitution to provide a measure of transparency in respect of the exercise of the President's article 60 power to pardon offenders.[99] The Committee recently noted that in the 30 years since the Committee was created by the Constitution, there has been no legislative framework enacted to enable it to formalise its operations.[100] There are currently no clearly defined criteria to determine which offenders are eligible for pardon, and the system has been discretionary and based on perceived merit or other ad hoc reasons. For example, in 2016, President Faure pardoned 78 prisoners 'who have completed at least three-quarters of their sentence and have also exhibited good behaviour' based on having received a letter from the Pope 'in which world leaders were invited to show forgiveness and mercy'.[101] More recently, in July 2024, President Ramkalawan pardoned only one of the many individuals convicted annually of drug-related offences. No explanation was given for the pardon, but it is noteworthy that the individual is the son of a prominent businesswoman and the Dutch honorary consul to Seychelles.[102] Over the years, opposition parties have regularly alleged that offenders were offered pardons in return for their or their families' political loyalty to the President.[103] The continued lack of clarity on procedures and processes for obtaining a pardon does nothing to dispel these rumours.

In December 2021, four new members were appointed to the five-member Committee by the President following recommendation by the CAA. They have taken steps to professionalise the Committee's work.[104] The newly-constituted Committee has adopted a strategic plan and begun lobbying the government for the adoption of a Parole and Pardon Act in line with comparative practice.[105] However, the Pardon Committee depends on the executive and legislature to work together to create and adopt legislation within which it can operate.[106]

[99] 1993 Constitution, art 61. The power to pardon is, of course, a powerful discretionary prerogative power raditionally exercised by the Crown in the British public law system and introduced to Seychelles during the ritish colonial period.

[100] M Bertin, 'Paving the Way Forward for a Parole and Pardon System' *Seychelles Nation* (24 November 2023), ww.nation.sc/articles/20213/paving-the-way-forward-for-a-parole-and-pardon-system.

[101] 'President Pardons 78 Prisoners' *Seychelles Nation* (29 December 2016), www.nation.sc/archive/252377/ resident-pardons-78-prisoners.

[102] 'Alexander Geers granted presidential pardon' *Seychelles Nation* (19 July 2024), www.nation.sc/ ticles/22875/alexander-geers-granted-presidential-pardon.

[103] 'Presidential Pardon: Flossel Francois' Liberation Controversy' *Seychelles Weekly* (1 August 2016), www. ychellesweekly.com/2016/January%204,%202016/pol1a_presidential_pardon_flossel.html.

[104] Office of the President of the Republic of Seychelles 'New Advisory Committee on the Power of rdon appointed' (21 December 2021), statehouse.gov.sc/news/5413/new-advisory-committee-on-the-wer-of-pardon-appointed.

[105] Bertin (n 100).

[106] ibid.

C. The Ombudsman

The Ombudsman has similarly called for government support in creating a stand-alone Ombudsman Act, as required by the Constitution, to provide for matters not addressed in the provisions which establish it.[107] For 30 years this institution has operated without the legislation anticipated by the Constitution to empower it to do its work.[108]

Under articles 143 and 144 of the Constitution, the Ombudsman is appointed by the President from candidates proposed by the CAA, and has extensive powers and duties, as described in schedule 5. The Constitution gives the Ombudsman a wide role to investigate actions taken by a public authority, including the President and Cabinet members; to investigate allegations of fraud or corruption by a person in a public authority; to assist with bringing legal proceedings in relation to a contravention of human rights; and to join or initiate proceedings relating to a breach of the Charter of Human Rights or the constitutionality of a law. Given the historical context of executive abuse of power, the role of the Ombudsman is particularly vital. Furthermore, in the absence of an active civil society in Seychelles, a proactive Ombudsman can serve as a crucial counterbalance, helping to address the challenges posed by the country's small size and limited resources.

The former Ombudsman described her powers as 'soft power' and stated that the Ombudsman role is to act as 'an independent, apolitical and impartial' entity looking to work with parties to resolve problems within the administration.[109] Perhaps because the Ombudsman plays an 'informal, extra judicial' function, it is sometimes difficult to identify tangible signs of the Ombudsman's work.[110]

For the first years of multiparty democracy, any work done by the Office of the Ombudsman remained out of the public record. It was only with the appointment of Nichole Tirant-Gherardi in 2017 that this office became better known and the number of complaints brought to the Office consistently increased.[111] Since her appointment, Ombudsman reports have been produced in courts to assist with court cases[112] and in 2022 the Ombudsman joined the petition to challenge the constitutionality of the Tenth Amendment to the Constitution which expanded the powers of the Defence Force in non-emergency times (mentioned above in section II).[113]

In her 2022 Annual Report, the Ombudsman described the challenges and difficulties she faces. These include a lack of understanding of the role of the Ombudsman, a failure by the government to respond to her inquiries and a resistance to her intervention by 'denying liability, seeking legal advice and raising legal concepts to reject .. [her] recommendations'.[114] She cites lack of adequate human and financial resourc ing and significant budget cuts as major challenges and describes being exclude

[107] Ombudsman Report 2022 (n 43) 21.
[108] 1993 Constitution, art 143(6).
[109] Ombudsman Report 2022 (n 43) 3.
[110] ibid 4.
[111] ibid 15.
[112] See, eg *Mellie v Government of Seychelles and Another* [2019] SCCC 1 and *Faure v Government of Seychell* [2021] SCSC 987.
[113] *Seychelles Human Rights Commission and Others v Speaker of the National Assembly of Seychelles a Others* CP7/2022, ongoing (n 47).
[114] Ombudsman Report 2022 (n 43) 2, 4.

from the National Assembly budget deliberations.[115] Furthermore, the government's performance-based budgeting process is ill-suited to the Ombudsman's work, is time consuming for a staff with limited resources, and the imposition of government audits as part of the process creates an obstacle to the autonomy and independence of the Office of the Ombudsman.[116] In 2021, the Ombudsman noted that her 'annual budget, reduced each year at the whim of the executive, continues to negatively impact … [her] service delivery. It directly affects the Ombudsman's independence and autonomy'.[117] Moreover, the reports of the Ombudsman submitted to the executive and the National Assembly have been disregarded and the recommendations to remedy wrongs against complainants are ignored by the respondent public authorities.[118] This list of executive pushback and budgetary interference portrays an attitude of flagrant disregard of the constitutional role of the Ombudsman by the legislative and executive branches.

D. The Human Rights Commission and the Anti-Corruption Commission

Two new statutory bodies, the Human Rights Commission and the Anti-Corruption Commission, have overlapping responsibilities with the mandate of the Ombudsman, and since their creation, the Ombudsman has begun working with these bodies to refer relevant complaints to them for further investigation. It should be noted, however, that both the Human Rights Commission and the Anti-Corruption Commission report directly to the President who has oversight of their budget, makes regulations for carrying into effect the purposes of their respective Acts, and receives their annual reports.[119] These institutions, thus, cannot be classed as 'guarantor' by Khaitan's definition, despite their role in protecting constitutional norms, because they are the creatures of statute whose mandates may be changed in the ordinary political process. The creation of these parallel institutions undermines the constitutional role of the Ombudsman by diverting responsibility and budget from the Office. Further, the involvement of the executive in these fundamental aspects of these Commissions potentially undermines their independence.

Like the Ombudsman, the Human Rights Commission reports a lack of understanding of its role and mandate by other stakeholders, a lack of financial and human resources to effectively meet its investigative mandate, and a sad lack of cooperation by public authorities with its inquiries.[120] It, too, reports a failure on the part of the legislature and the executive to respond to its recommendations or to engage with the Commission in its work.[121]

[115] ibid 7, 9.
[116] ibid 14.
[117] *The Ombudsman – An Institution in Jeopardy* (Annual Report of the Ombudsman, 2021), www.nationalassembly.sc/publications/reports/annual-report-ombudsman-2021-ombudsman-institution-jeopardy, 5.
[118] ibid 25, 36–42.
[119] See Anti-Corruption Act 2016, ss 2, 80(4), 81 and 85; and Human Rights Commission Act, ss 2, 21, 22, 24, and 27(1).
[120] Seychelles Human Rights Commission Annual Report 2022, nationalassembly.sc/publications/reports/seychelles-human-rights-commission-annual-report-2022, 40–41.
[121] ibid 41.

E. The Public Service Appeal Board

The PSAB is an independent constitutional body set up to consider employment matters and maladministration within the public service. During the one-party state, René had total power over the government bureaucracy and promotions were rewards in the same way that terminations, disciplinary measures and dismissals were weapons. During this period, members of the civil service 'were expected to show allegiance to the regime and its political party in order to obtain a position, retain their jobs and get promotion within the service'.[122] The introduction of the PSAB in the 1993 Constitution was intended to provide an independent body to review employment matters within the public service. Two of the three members of the Board appointed in 1993 by René served four consecutive seven-year terms until 2021. In May 2022, the newly-configured Board procured a proper office area from which to operate and four support staff after 'many years of struggle'.[123] The new Chairperson reported resource constraints which affected its ability to secure office space and equipment.[124] Furthermore, it reported difficulties with the government departments not obeying the orders of the Board despite the quasi-judicial powers of the Board to compel the departments to 'take appropriate action as specified in the order'.[125]

F. The Electoral Commission

The 1993 Constitution first created the role of the Electoral Commissioner to conduct elections and make proposals for electoral reform.[126] In 2011 the Constitution was amended to introduce an independently appointed Commission of five persons in place of an individual Commissioner.[127] The Chairman of the Commission and the four commissioners are appointed by the President upon recommendation by the CAA for a renewable seven-year term.

The Electoral Commission came under scrutiny following the 2015 presidential election and since then has successfully introduced regulations to address deficits in the elections process.[128] In the election petition arising out of the 2015 presidential elections, the Constitutional Court bemoaned the lack of adequate procedural regulations under the Elections Act to guide the Chief Electoral Officer in his/ her duties and the

[122] TRNUC Report (n 6) 83–84.
[123] V Gappy, 'Public Services Appeal Board launched' *Seychelles Nation* (21 May 2022), www.nation.sc/articles/13675/public-service-appeal-board-launched.
[124] ibid.
[125] ibid. See also 1993 Constitution, art 146(4).
[126] See 1993 Constitution, chapter VII.
[127] Constitution of the Republic of Seychelles (Sixth Amendment) Act 2011.
[128] See *Ramkalawan v Electoral Commission and Others (Election Non-compliance and Illegal Practices* [2016] SCCC 11 [516]–[527]. Recent regulations include Elections (Procedures) Regulations 2016, SI 5 of 2016; Elections (Code of Conduct of Election Observers) Regulations 2020, SI 131 of 2020; Elections (Code of Conduct of Polling and Counting Agents) Regulations 2020, SI 133 of 2020; Elections (Conduct of Registered Political Parties and Candidates during Election) Regulations 2020, SI 141 of 2020; and Elections (Procedures) (Amendment) Regulations 2020, SI 140 of 2020.

lack of rules and procedures for the operations of the Commission.[129] The new regulations were passed in 2016 following this public criticism by the Court and improve the transparency of and systems for elections. The Electoral Commission reports difficulties with finding adequate and permanent office space, which is indicative of poor resourcing.[130] It does not publicly indicate other difficulties with its relationship with the executive.

G. The Auditor-General

One body which appears to enjoy certain autonomy and government support is the Auditor-General, a constitutional office created by article 158 to audit the accounts of all ministries, departments, offices and statutory bodies and authorities and to ensure the accountability for expenditure of public funds. Additionally, it operates under the Auditor-General Act 2010 under which it enjoys certain financial and administrative autonomy, and which requires it to issue annual reports to the National Assembly. The Auditor-General appears to enjoy a good working relationship with the National Assembly and reports that many matters it raises in audit management letters are dealt with satisfactorily by the government entities involved.[131] The Annual Report for 2021 does report that the Ministry of Finance has failed to roll out the new Accounting Manual as had been agreed, and that some amendments to the Procurement Act were still required to achieve 'a more standardized, modern and practical approach to accounting function'.[132]

H. Concluding Thoughts on the Guarantor Institutions in Seychelles

Tushnet argues that Institutions for Protecting Constitutional Democracy (IPDs) can supplement constitutional courts in safeguarding democracy and mitigate any deficiencies of the courts.[133] However, he notes that while IPDs can promote democracy, they can also 'make no difference to a democracy's performance, and they can impede or undermine democracy'.[134]

A review of the guarantor institutions in Seychelles reveals a constitutional framework that creates and empowers institutions which already add valuable support to the country's constitutionalism. These institutions protect the integrity of elections, ensure

[129] *Ramkalawan v Electoral Commission* (n 128) [494]–[495].

[130] Electoral Commission, *Report on the Conduct of the 2020 Presidential and National Assembly Elections* (January 2021), www.ecs.sc/index.php/8-news/36-2020-election-report-january-2021, 31.

[131] Office of the Auditor-General, *Report of the Auditor General 2021* (submitted to the National Assembly on 20 November 2022), www.nationalassembly.sc/publications/reports/annual-report-office-auditor-general-year-2021, 6.

[132] ibid 7.

[133] M Tushnet, *The New Fourth Branch: Institutions for Protecting Constitutional Democracy* (Cambridge, Cambridge University Press, 2021) 20–21.

[134] ibid 6.

non-partisan appointments, demand transparency in public finances and remedy misconduct in public employment. Furthermore, they investigate and report on abuse of public power, and advise on presidential pardons. Therefore, the Seychelles guarantor institutions may certainly supplement the courts in protecting constitutional norms, by exerting extra-judicial pressure on the government.

However, the survey also tells a tale of the practical struggle of these institutions to ensure that the government (both previous and current) commits to enabling their meaningful transition from the law into reality. For these institutions to succeed, the government must respect their reports and findings and provide adequate financial resources to enable the guarantor institutions to fulfil their mandate. The Seychelles' narrative reflects this ongoing struggle, but nevertheless, reveals each institution showing signs of development in its role, albeit slowly.

VI. Conclusion

The Seychelles narrative is one of slow development and deepening of constitutionalism despite many setbacks and challenges. This brief survey shows a small state with an ambitious Constitution that envisaged a sophisticated separation of powers relying on the National Assembly, the judiciary and the guarantor institutions, each with their part to play in ensuring that the executive dominance of the René years would never be repeated. However, the appointment of the same government following the first elections and its continued dominance over the National Assembly and the CAA hamstrung the development of these institutions. As discussed in section III, to date the National Assembly has failed to play a meaningful role in balancing executive power, even when it was controlled by a different party from that of the Presidency. And as discussed in section IV, the judiciary has the power and the jurisprudential standards to enable it to effectively hold the executive to account for its use of power and enable citizens to find redress for breaches of their rights. However, the judiciary is not consistent and recently has shown signs of democracy-undermining 'abusive' judicial review when the CAA and the high-level politicians are involved in litigation. Moreover, the number of cases brought challenging the executive has reduced significantly in recent years.

It is, surprisingly, the 'fourth branch' or guarantor institutions that have shown the most development in the past decade with various institutions showing a deepening of the understanding of their constitutional role and lessening political control over them. They are, in general, more active than in the early years of constitutionalism. The introduction of published procedures and the regular publication of annual reports also creates greater transparency in these institutions. However, it is concerning to note the reports of the executive ignoring their recommendations, reducing their budgets and restricting their resources.

A key takeaway from this chapter is that there is a pressing need for greater public awareness regarding the accountability roles of guarantor institutions and the potential that they hold for deepening Seychelles' constitutionalism. A key benefit of smallness is the ability to harness the active political climate and create dialogue between those who vot and those who are elected.[135] In Seychelles, the National Assembly debates are broadcast on radio and a dedicated Youtube channel, with significant debates also aired on television. This accessibility means the public is well-informed about the Assembly's activities.

If citizens were better educated on the Constitution's content and norms and the institutions which protect these norms, the reduced distance between the National Assembly members and the electorate could empower citizens to demand that their representatives more effectively support the guarantor institutions. Increased public awareness could encourage civilians to advocate for stronger executive support and adherence to the institutions' recommendations.

Seychelles' experience with the separation of powers and the struggle to establish effective checks and balances against executive power can offer other valuable lessons for small states facing similar challenges in governance. The first is the need to take measures to address the perception of presidential exceptionalism. Academics and the courts could play a role in unbundling the approach to formal, symbolic presidential powers (such as appointing and pardoning) from those that are inherently political in nature (such as foreign policy and appointing Ministers, directing Cabinet). The bundling of these powers occurred when the role of head of the government was combined with the head of state, making the President concurrently the Monarch and the Prime Minister. Democratically, a President does not require the same amount of deference when acting in a head of state capacity as would perhaps be appropriate when performing the role as the head of the elected government. This unbundling could have rule of law benefits and could assist judges with feeling more comfortable when holding the President to account for their conduct.

Secondly, it is fundamentally important that the appointment of members of the CAA is consistent with the constitutional provisions. This would increase the legitimacy of the body and reduce the likelihood of politicisation of the institution by ensuring the inherent impartiality of the members. As local capacity increases, it would also be beneficial to reconsider the option to appoint non-former judges, under article 141(b). It is hoped that when the next members are appointed, the increased number of Seychellois retired judges and the criticism of previous appointments will encourage appointment in line with the constitutional standards.

Thirdly, the Seychellois experience underscores the need for continuous efforts to strengthen the judiciary's independence and capacity and the significance of nurturing and empowering guarantor institutions. Establishing and protecting such institutions is critical for promoting transparency and addressing governance challenges. The Ombudsman could play a more important role in bringing constitutional cases, including cases that relate to the functioning of the separation of powers. In this way it could mitigate the absence of a developed civil society. However, the Ombudsman's capacity is limited, and it would require strengthening and support – ideally from international non-governmental organisations with expertise in constitutional litigation until such time as local expertise is developed.

[35] G Baldacchino, 'Islands and despots' (2012) 50(1) *Commonwealth & Comparative Politics* 103, 106.

Fourthly, a model that provides financial autonomy for the judiciary and the guarantor institutions is required. Budgeting processes should be inclusive, enable long-term planning and once budget is allocated, it should not be alterable at the whim of the executive. Innovative legal provisions could be sought from comparative jurisdictions.[136]

Seychelles' journey suggests that the path towards effective governance is often gradual and requires sustained commitment from stakeholders. Incremental progress in strengthening democratic institutions, though slow, can be transformative over time. Some of Seychelles' challenges are exacerbated by its smallness, such as the ability of the executive to be omnipresent due to the increased social proximity. However, Seychelles' smallness also enables small changes that seek to develop constitutional culture to take effect quicker.

The separation of powers in Seychelles has struggled to take root in practice, and executive dominance has continued to characterise its governance. While this may be a product of Seychelles' history of presidentialism, it is also consistent with findings in research into democratic small states.[137] Political science scholars studying democracy in microstates have noted that there is often a disparity between the presence of formal, democratic institutions and the implementation of democratic political practices.[138] Thus, while the 1993 Constitution established the institutions of a liberal democracy, constitutionalism has not grown deep roots in the years since. This has been exacerbated by constitutional design that endorses presidential exceptionalism. However, in the past decade we see promising developments in the guarantor institutions, which suggests that it may be too early to write off Seychelles' separation of powers as a failure. At this time, it is important for the guarantor institutions in Seychelles to be strengthened by focusing on institutional resilience, promoting understanding of their role, and investing in their independence.

[136] For example, the 2014 Third Amendment to the Namibian Constitution amended art 78 to introduc constitutional provisions providing for financial autonomy of the judiciary, which could be modelled for a guarantor institutions. Ackerman suggested ensuring high salaries and guaranteeing the branch a budget th equals a minimum percentage of the total government revenues: see Ackerman (n 23) 694.

[137] See J Erk and WP Veenendaal, 'Is Small Really Beautiful? The Microstate Mistake' (2014) 25(4) *Journal Democracy* 135; Veenendaal (n 43) 92.

[138] Veenendaal (n 43); WP Veenendaal and J Corbett, 'Why Small States Offer Important Answers to Lar Questions' (2015) 48(4) *Comparative Political Studies* 527; Erk and Veenendaal (n 137); J Corbett, '"Everybo Knows Everybody": Practising Politics in the Pacific Islands (2015) 22(1) *Democratization* 51.

16

And 'At His Majesty's Pleasure'

The Constitution, Law and Ideology in the Small Sultanate of Brunei Darussalam

ANN BLACK

I. Introduction

'At his Majesty's pleasure' is a phrase used throughout the Constitution of Brunei Darussalam.[1] It encapsulates the Sultan's pivotal role in every aspect of governance.

By way of background, Brunei Darussalam[2] is a small Southeast Asian Sultanate situated on the much larger island of Borneo. As Brunei comprises just one per cent of Borneo, it is tiny in comparison to the neighbouring East Malaysian states of Sabah and Sarawak (36 per cent) and Indonesia's Kalimantan province (63 per cent). In Brunei's 'Golden Era' in the fifteenth century, all of Borneo and the southern Philippines were under Bruneian suzerainty.[3] However, a conflation of events including economic mismanagement, succession disputes, and incursions by the white Rajas of Sarawak,[4] resulted in Brunei contracting to its current size. When Sarawak annexed Brunei's Limbang section in 1890, Brunei was further divided into two enclaves with a total land area of 5,770 square kilometres. With a population of 452,524, Brunei is, in terms of people, Asia's smallest nation.[5] By contrast, its petro-carbon resources and international investments have given Bruneians one of the highest standards of living in Asia with a

[1] Constitution of Brunei Darussalam 1959 (Revised edition 2011). Arts 3A(1), 8A(4), 12, 22(1), 31, 37(2), 50, 66(3), 70, 71(3), 72, 81(6), 84(2), 86(7).

[2] *Darussalam* means 'Abode of Peace'.

[3] In the 15th and 16th centuries Brunei (from the Sanskrit meaning 'region of seafaring traders') was a prosperous thalassocracy based on sea and river, rather than land, domination.

[4] See A Black, '"Brunei Darussalam": Small by Choice but Great in the Eyes of Allah' in T Angelo and Corrin (eds), 'Small States: a Collection of Essays' (2019) XXIII *Comparative Law Journal of the Pacific* (Hors eries Special Issue) 84–86.

[5] 'Asian Countries by Population (2023)' (*Worldometer*), www.worldometers.info/population/countries-in-sia-by-population/.

GDP per capita PPP of US$58,669.[6] Brunei is a classic rentier state,[7] in which citizens pay no income or sales taxes but receive generous welfare and public sector employment. The steady flow of income from petro-carbon resources has made Brunei's 29th Sultan and *Yang Di-Pertuan*[8] – Haji Hassanal Bolkiah Mu'izzaddin Waddaulah (the Sultan) – one of the world's wealthiest rulers.[9]

Although there is not one definition of a small state,[10] the following four factors show the ways in which Brunei qualifies. First, in terms of area and population (set out above), Brunei is comparatively small. Second, Brunei is small by choice. During the mid-twentieth century, Brunei's Sultan Omar Ali Saifuddien III resisted two opportunities to join as a State in a larger federal nation. In 1962, the citizens of Brunei voted in favour of joining a democratic federation with other Bornean colonies in a Greater Borneo (*Negara Kalimantan Utara*). Sultan Omar ignored their vote.[11] It was the only election ever held in Brunei and served as the turning point in Brunei's brief experiment with democracy. Despite the urging of Great Britain, Sultan Omar again refused in 1963 to join the larger Malay Federation, which was to be comprised of nine neighbouring Malay Sultanates and former British Malay colonies. As a federation would involve revenue- and power-sharing, including a rotating five-year Kingship, Sultan Omar knew that going it alone, albeit as a small Sultanate, would allow Brunei to keep its petro-carbon wealth, remain an absolute monarchy, and put an end to democracy. The third small state qualification comes from Brunei's reliance on 'smallness' to justify illiberal restrictive practices and systemic breaches of human rights.[12] This is a recurring theme throughout this chapter. Size also has been a factor in allowing Brunei to fly 'under the international radar'.[13] Lastly, Brunei draws on its size to showcase achievements vis-à-vis larger nations, one of which is its Islamic credentials. Brunei's Mufti summarised the latter: 'Brunei may be small but in the sight of Allah it is great, because as a nation, it does not doubt, it does not hesitate, to implement the Laws of Allah'.[14]

[6] 'Brunei GDP per capita' (*Trading Economics*), www.tradingeconomics.com/brunei/gdp-per-capita. GDP per capita PPP (purchasing power parity) includes an adjustment for differences in the cost of living in different countries.

[7] A rentier state receives most revenue through 'rents' exploiting natural resources (90 per cent of Brunei's state revenues) not domestic taxation. Rentier arrangements stabilise undemocratic authoritarian regimes. See AT Kuru, 'Authoritarianism and Democracy in Muslims Countries: Rentier States and Regional Diffusion' (2014) 129(3) *Political Science Quarterly* 399, 400.

[8] *Yang Di-Pertuan* means 'He who is made Lord'. It is the Sanskrit title for king used during a period of Hindu rule which Malay Sultans in Brunei and Malaysia continue to use.

[9] See A Black, 'Marching to the Beat of a Different Drum: Royalty, Women, and Ideology in the Sultanate of Brunei Darussalam' (2020) 7(2) *Royal Studies Journal* 84, 107.

[10] AK Henrikson, 'A Coming "Magnesian" Age? Small States, the Global System, and the International Community' (2001) 6(3) *Geopolitics* 49, 56.

[11] Discussed later at section II.B.

[12] For example, despite not holding elections, Brunei has remained a continuing member of the Commonwealth of Nations, unlike Fiji whose membership was fully suspended (2006–2009) when 'democracy' ceased, and elections were not held in accordance with the Constitution. Also, Brunei response to international criticism on enacting stoning as a penalty for same-sex intimacy. See A Black 'Brunei's Stoning for Gay-sex law flies under the Radar', *Asia Views*, 27 April 2020, www.asiaviews.net/brunei-bruneis-stoning-for-gay-sex-law-flies-under-the-radar/.

[13] ibid.

[14] Bin Juned, *The Shari'ah Penal Code: An Introduction* (Brunei, State Mufti's Office, 2013) 71.

Today, Brunei is one of only two remaining independent national Sultanates:[15] an Islamic form of monarchy in which the Sultan serves as Allah's vice regent on earth. As Islam came to Brunei in either the fourteenth or the sixteenth century,[16] when Raja Awang Alak Betatar converted to Islam, adopting the Islamic title of Sultan Muhammad, it is a grafted rather than an indigenous form of rule. This is acknowledged today as the Sultan retains the Indic co-title of *Yang Di-Pertuan*. As Sultan, his mandate to rule comes from Allah and it is Allah, not the people or a parliament, to whom he is accountable. The Sultan's connection with the divine is a crucial concept in legitimising his rule. Conceptually, Islam and the Sultan are indivisible and to criticise the Sultan is to criticise Islam. He claims descendance from the Prophet Mohammad, which adds 'to his charismatic aura of sacred leadership'.[17] Sultan Bolkiah explained: '*Beraja* (absolute monarchy) is 'God's Will: not a choice, it is *anugerah* (an honour) from Allah'.[18] There are also legal consequences because as Head of Islam, the Sultan determines jurisprudential interpretation, Islamic practices, and the implementation of *Syariah* (Islamic law). He holds the monopoly on the interpretation of Islamic truth. Whilst the Islamic dimension is important, it is not applicable just to small states as there are close parallels with large states for whom Islam is the state religion.[19] For this reason Islam is not a focus of this chapter. Instead, this chapter considers how one-man rule (the Constitution excludes female rule)[20] operates and is justified, legitimised and accepted by Bruneians and the extent to which 'smallness' makes each viable. The first part argues that Brunei's smallness allows for a personalised style of rule through a special ruler–subject bond: '*Sentiasa Bersama Rakyat*' meaning the Sultan is 'always together with his subjects'.[21] Democracy and rule of law are rejected as Western, unsuitable, or inferior. The government explains that *Sentiasa Bersama Rakyat* is:

> a central, cardinal element in His Majesty's rule. It is a *living democracy* in the context of the daily political and social lives of Bruneians, which those outside the country may find difficult to fathom much less understand.

[15] The other is the Sultanate of Oman.

[16] Brunei's official narrative is that the first Raja's conversion to Islam was in 1368; however, historians (from outside Brunei) established that Islam was not adopted until 1514–21. See MB Bishku, 'Brunei, Islam, and the Muslim Middle East: A Malay State Defining its Purpose and Preserving the Maintenance of an Independent Dynastic Line' (2024) 47(2) *Journal of South Asian and Middle Eastern Studies* 72, 75.

[17] Human Rights Resource Centre, *Keeping the Faith: A Study of Freedom of Thought, Conscience and Religion in ASEAN* (Jakarta, HRRC, 2016) 87.

[18] *Titah* commemorating the Sultan's 64th Birthday, 26 July 2010. *Titah* are royal speeches in which the Sultan announces policy and new Orders. Most *titah* can be accessed in Malay, with some translated into English, from the Government of Brunei's website: www.rtb.gov.bn/Titah/.

[19] The Federation of Malaysia with a population of 33.4 million and a land area of 330,803 km^2 has similar issues arising from constitutional prioritisation of Islam. See A Black, 'Assessing Religious Freedom in Muslim Majority Brunei and Malaysia' in Md Jahid Bhuiyan and A Black (eds), *Freedom of Religion and Religious Diversity: State Accommodation of Religious Minorities across Europe and Asia* (London, Routledge, 2024) chapter 13.

[20] 'No person shall be considered a lawful Heir or a lawful Successor unless *he* professes the Islamic Religion and is a *male* lawfully begotten descendant in the *male* line of the common ancestor' (emphasis added). Constitutional Matters II: Succession and Regency Proclamation 1959, s 4. In the Sultanate's 650 years, there has not been a female ruler, although Sultanas have ruled in other parts of Asia, as discussed in A Black, 'The Sultanate of Brunei's Gender Paradox' (2022) 23 *Australian Journal of Asian Laws* 45.

[21] 'His Majesty attends get-together ceremony with residents of Brunei Muara District' (Brunei Government Website, 18 July 2005), www.sultanate.com/news_server/18_jul_2.html.

> At the same time, the element '*Sentiasa Bersama Rakyat*' provides the *rakyat* (subjects) with access to the highest order of government between the ruled and their ruler (emphasis added).[22]

The second dimension considered in this chapter is how 'smallness' justifies recourse to illiberal practices, most of which are now constitutionally entrenched. Unlike the Constitutions of neighbouring Muslim-majority Malaysia and Indonesia, Brunei's does not protect rights and liberties but cements the supreme authority of its Sultan. Although censorship, silencing of opposition, and use of nationalistic ideology are claimed to be necessary for social cohesion in a small state, not unexpectedly, the main beneficiaries are the Sultan, his family, and Brunei's elites.

II. Cementing One-Man Rule in the Constitution

The Sultan is the pivot of the Constitution. Revolving around him are six consultative Councils whose members can give advice, but whose advice he need not take.[23] Each member is appointed by him to serve for the duration of His Majesty's 'pleasure'.[24] Brunei's Constitution does not contain any guarantee of judicial independence,[25] nor references to any personal status matters. It provides for one human right: namely, that religion 'can be practised in peace and harmony by those professing' it.[26] There are no guarantees of 'equality of all before the law' even though it is a fundamental liberty in neighbouring Asian Constitutions.[27] Equality is seen through an Islamic lens in which men and women have complementary, but different, rights and responsibilities,[28] and non-Muslims are not the equals of Muslims. Schedule 3, together with article 84A(1) of the Constitution sets out 10 offices of State from which non-Muslims and non-Malays are excluded, including the office of Attorney-General. There are also race and religion requirements for Ministers and Deputy Ministers: article 4(5) of the Constitution states: 'the appointment of Ministers and Deputy Ministers shall be made from among the Malay race professing the Islamic Religion', 'save where His Majesty the Sultan … otherwise decides'. By preferencing the 65 per cent of Bruneians who are Muslim Malays, it locks out a third of the population, including Chinese citizens, who are the second largest ethnic group, and the 10 per cent indigenous animist Borneans. It signifies that Muslim Malays are trusted citizens and links Islam and the Malay race as the core of Bruneian identity. In a small nation, the benefits that accrue to the Muslim Malays

[22] ibid.

[23] Constitution, art 19: 'His Majesty the Sultan and Yang Di-Pertuan is not bound to act in accordance wit[h] the advice of the Council of Ministers but in any such case, he shall record in writing, for inclusion in th[e] minutes, the reasons for his decision'.

[24] For example, art 12: 'Subject to this Constitution, every Minister shall hold his seat in the Council o[f] Ministers during His Majesty the Sultan and Yang Di-Pertuan's pleasure'.

[25] A Black, 'Judicial Independence in Brunei Darussalam' in HP Lee and M Prittard (eds), *Asia-Pacifi[c] Judiciaries: Independence, Impartiality and Integrity* (Cambridge, Cambridge University Press, 2018) 57.

[26] The implementation of this freedom is problematic as it has been interpreted to favour Brunei's religiou[s] majority, not as a protection for minorities.

[27] Constitution of Malaysia, arts 8, 27(1); Constitution of Indonesia, art 27(1).

[28] For example, s 106 of the Islamic Evidence Order 2001 outlines that the testimony of a woman is wor[th] less than that of a man (two for one principle) and excluded for certain matters.

loyally bind them to the Sultan. Human rights are similarly seen through an Islamic lens, with Islamic human rights held as superior to 'man-made' rights. The Sultan explains that 'as Muslims, we uphold human rights with the Quran as our foothold'.[29] Only when international rights instruments accord with Brunei's interpretation of Islam and Malay tradition will Brunei be a signatory. Brunei has a general reservation in both the Convention on the Rights of the Child and the Convention on the Elimination of Discrimination against Women for any provision 'contrary to the Constitution of Brunei Darussalam and the beliefs and principles of Islam'.[30]

In 2004, a series of constitutional amendments 'doubly fortified'[31] and entrenched illiberal one-man rule. One amendment clarified that no court, including the Supreme Court, has authority to conduct judicial review.[32] The Ministry of Justice was abolished. The judiciary became formally subordinate to the executive within the office of the Prime Minister. At the same time, the Sultan gained discretionary powers over adjudication in all courts, including power to direct a court to hear a case in camera;[33] or to hold proceedings at a time and venue of his ordering.[34] Exercise of these powers cannot be appealed or reviewed.[35] The Sultan cannot be compelled to attend any court proceeding[36] and importantly can exempt 'any person required by the court to attend'.[37] From 2004, publishing a judgment that might lower or adversely affect the 'position, dignity, standing, honour, eminence or sovereignty' of the Sultan was prohibited.[38] Prior to 2004, the Constitution stated that the Sultan's 'power to make laws' was 'with the advice and consent of the Legislative Council' but from 2004 the 'advice and consent' requirement was deleted.

Furthermore, by his Proclamation, the Sultan can amend or revoke any part of the Constitution.[39] Interpretation of the 'meaning, purpose, construction, ambit or effect' of the Constitution is the remit of an ad hoc Interpretation Tribunal whose members the Sultan may appoint should he so decide.[40] There are no reports of the Tribunal being constituted. There is no separation of powers. In a small country, it is administratively feasible for the Monarch to assume governmental roles in addition to that of head of state. He is the Prime Minister,[41] a position held since independence, but, from 2004 became constitutionally entrenched. He is head of the Council of Ministers[42] (the executive), by which he allocated himself three additional ministerial portfolios – Defence, Finance

[29] *Titah* cited in 'Laws of Islam Seek Blessings not Oppression' (*Borneo Bulletin*, 5 November 2013).
[30] eg, 'CEDAW Declaration and Reservations, as at May 2024' (United Nations Treaty Collection) www.treaties.un.org/pages/viewdetails.aspx?src=ind&mtdsg_no=iv-8&chapter=4&clang=_en#EndDec.
[31] T Hang Tey, 'Brunei's Revamped Constitution: The Sultan as the Grundnorm?' (2007) 9(2) *Australian Journal of Asian Law* 264.
[32] Constitution, art 84C(1).
[33] Supreme Court Act (Cap 5), s 15(5).
[34] ibid s 15(6).
[35] ibid s 15(7).
[36] ibid s 34(1); Constitutional Matters II: Succession and Regency Proclamation 1959 (n 20), s 25(b).
[37] Supreme Court Act (Cap 5), s 34(2).
[38] ibid s 15(8).
[39] Constitution, art 85.
[40] ibid art 86.
[41] ibid art 4(1A).
[42] ibid part III.

and Economy, and Foreign Affairs and Trade. He is the nation's legislator[43] (discussed below); head of religion[44] (Islam, the state religion);[45] and Supreme Commander of the Armed Forces.[46] Cumulatively, the 2004 constitutional amendments made the Constitution subservient to the Sultan, which Tsun Hang Tey argues makes him the nation's '*Grundnorm*'[47] from whom all norms and laws derive validity.[48]

Bruneians were reassured by their Attorney-General that such concentration of power in one man is desirable, as their Sultan will 'always have the best interest of his subjects at heart' and what 'is considered to be the best policy in other jurisdictions may not be suitable for Brunei Darussalam and vice versa'.[49] Müller describes the Sultan's authority as 'uncontested' royal power, not seen elsewhere in maritime Southeast Asia.[50]

A. A Model for Consultation: Brunei's Six Councils

The imprint for the 1959 Constitution lies in pre-colonial history when the Sultan was advised by senior nobles known as *wazirs*, and in the colonial era, where the British Resident had exclusive power (except over Islam which remained with the Sultan) with Councils to advise him but whose advice he need not take. Advisory councils are also in keeping with both the Islamic concept of *shura* (consultation),[51] as well as the Bruneian (and Indonesian) notion of working through differences to find agreement (*musyawarah mufakat*),[52] through cooperation based on duty and obligation (*memucang-mucang*).[53] It is claimed that 'since time immemorial'[54] these concepts have been synonymous with communal life in Brunei and continue today in rural villages, especially for traditional dispute resolution.[55] It goes some way to understanding how in a small state, the traditional model of one-man rule supported by advisory councils can resonate. Brunei's Councils reflect a division of powers with Western and Asian components. There is the Legislative Council[56] (legislature); Council of Ministers[57] (executive); and Religious Council[58] (Islam and *fatwas*) with the other three Councils intrinsically Bruneian: the

[43] The Sultan can enact legislation through four constitutional provisions: ss 83, 47(1), 84(2) and 43.

[44] Constitution, art 2.

[45] ibid art 3(1).

[46] ibid art 4(1B).

[47] *Grundnorm* is a term used by Austrian jurist Hans Kelsen (1881–1973) for the norm, or rule, that form an underlying basis for a legal system. It signifies the source of legitimacy for the Constitution and laws.

[48] Hang Tey (n 31) 264.

[49] Attorney-General Hayati, *Speech for the Opening of the Legal Year* (4 February 2016), www.agc.gov.bn.

[50] Namely the region contining Brunei, Indonesia, Malaysia, the Philippines, Singapore, and East Timo See DM Müller, 'Beyond the Sharia State: Public Celebration and Everyday State-Making in the Malay Islami Monarchy of Brunei Darussalam' (2022) 9(3) *Asian Journal of Law and Society* 418.

[51] Used in other absolute Islamic monarchies such as the Sultanate of Oman and Kingdom of Saudi Arabi

[52] A traditional decision-making approach for meetings in rural communities and villages in Brunei an Indonesia.

[53] M bin Omar, 'The making of a National Culture: Brunei's Experience' in E Thumboo (ed), *Cultures ASEAN and the 21st Century* (Singapore, UniPress, 1996) 14.

[54] RBT News, 6 December 2012.

[55] A Black, 'Alternative Dispute Resolution in Brunei Darussalam: the Blending of Imported and Tradition Processes' (2001) 13(2) *Bond Law Review* 7.

[56] Constitution part VII.

[57] ibid part III.

[58] ibid part II, with more details in the Religious Council and Kadis Courts Act (Cap 77).

Privy Council[59] (rank and honours); the *Adat Istidat* Council[60] (state customs); and the Council of Succession and Regency[61] (Royal matters).

Although consensus is lauded, it is doubtful whether consensus and cooperative decision-making does occur in any of the six Councils. Several factors cast doubt on the extent to which it does. First, as the head of each Council, the Sultan appoints all members to serve during 'His Majesty's pleasure',[62] including authority to dismiss or suspend. As he can remove a member for any reason that may appear 'good and sufficient' to him, without reasons,[63] it would be counter-intuitive to take a contrary stance. When making appointments, the Sultan's practice is to turn to people he knows and trusts, like his family. For example, membership of the Privy Council includes Sultan Bolkiah's three brothers,[64] Crown Prince Muhtadee and his other three adult sons[65] (no daughters), prominent nobles, aristocrats, and cabinet ministers. In a small, socially stratified society, the Sultan relies on personal connections with family, nobility, and the aristocracy. This leads to the second factor.

By tradition, Brunei was a socially stratified society with the royal family at the apex, descending to hereditary nobility, aristocrats, commoners, and the now abolished slave class.[66] Social ranking remains important today and as a person's name comes with titles, honorifics, and family connections, one's place in the hierarchy is immediately apparent. In a small society, a class system impacts appointments to office and employment generally, as well as marriage. Haque notes that 'individuals with titles such as *Pehin, Dato, Datin Paduka, Pengrin, Awangku, Dayangku*, are looked up [to], by [the] majority of the people' and, 'unfortunately', she argues, this overrides merit in Brunei's workforce.[67] This is true also for the Council membership. Because high status individuals directly benefit from the Sultan's grace and favour, it ensures their full loyalty to him, thereby negating the likelihood of policy opposition from powerful Bruneians.

Thirdly, patriarchal views are re-enforced by the domination of Muslim Malay men of social standing in each Council. It took 60 years before a woman was appointed as a full Minister. In 2022, Hajah Romaizah[68] became Minister of Education in the 25-person Executive Council. In contrast to the article 4(5) requirements on race and religion, the Constitution does not expressly specify male membership (except for membership of the Religious Council) so the gender barrier is historical and cultural.[69] It reflects the Sultan's own practice of allocating senior positions to his sons, whilst his daughters perform community engagement tasks. In 2011, the Sultan appointed the first women to the Legislative Council (LegCo) and a decade later in 2021 appointed three women to the 33-member LegCo. The importance of female input was seen when Khairunnisa Ash'ari

[59] ibid part 1V.
[60] ibid part II.
[61] Constitutional Matters II: Succession and Regency Proclamation 1959 (n 20) part II.
[62] Constitution, arts 55, 11.
[63] ibid art 31(5).
[64] HRH Princes Mohamed, Sufri and Jefri Bolkiah.
[65] HRH Princes Abdul Azim, Abdul Malik and Abdul Mateen.
[66] Black, 'Marching' (n 9) 99–102.
[67] F Haque, 'The Position of Women in Brunei: Both in Private and Public Spheres' (2020) 3(5) *Sumerianz Journal of Education, Linguistics and Literature* 68.
[68] Datin Seri Paduka Dr Romaizah Mohd Salleh.
[69] See Black, 'Brunei's Gender Paradox' (n 20) 48–50.

called for the government to address sexual harassment of women in the workplace[70] and for de-gendering the regulations that allowed only men to become village heads. She argued for a more open 'democratic process' in which the best candidate is chosen, regardless of gender.[71] The relevant (male) Ministers agreed to consider these issues, but to date there have not been changes. Although Khairunnisa's appointment ended in 2022, three new women replaced them in the 2023 LegCo.

Fourthly, even where the Constitution requires consultation with Council members, attaining consensus is not necessary. For example, article 19 states that the Sultan 'is not bound to act in accordance with the advice of the (Legislative) Council' and article 85, on Constitutional amendment, requires consultation with his Privy Council but again, the Sultan is not bound to act on it. It falls short of the tradition of finding agreement (*musyawarah*).

Fifthly, 'His Majesty's pleasure', was bolstered by another 2004 amendment that provides that LegCo members can lose their seats, or be suspended,[72] if 'disloyal' or 'disaffected' towards to the Sultan.[73] What amounts to 'disloyalty' or 'disaffection' is undefined, but like all state matters it is for His Majesty to decide. Article 53(1A) states that every LegCo member can 'express his opinion freely' but no member 'shall speak or make any comments' that are

> directly or indirectly derogatory of the rights, status, position, powers, privileges, sovereignty or prerogatives of His Majesty and Yang Di-Pertuan, his Successors, His Consort or other members of the Royal Family or the National Philosophy of Malay Islamic Monarchy.

With every aspect of government under the Sultan's control, only minor matters are left for comment or discussion. Acquiescence to government policy prevails rather than any genuine debate with opposing as well as supportive views from which consensus may be reached. The Sultan affirmed this by telling members in 2006 not to be afraid to express their views, providing their views were 'positive and led to consensus'.[74] Commentators note that 'debates are rarely heard'[75] in the LegCo; it functions as a rubber-stamp for government policy under the 'living democracy' guise.

B. Emergency Powers Override the One Constitutional Check on the Sultan's Power

One check on the Sultan's power in the 1959 Constitution was the provision for 16 popularly elected members to sit with 17 appointed members (ex officio, official, and nominated)[76] in a 33-seat Legislative Council. In the 1962 election, at which more

[70] N Haris, 'PMO: Sexual Harassment Framework to be Ready in July' (*The Scoop*, 26 March 2021), thescoop.co/2021/03/26/pmo-sexual-harassment-framework-to-be-ready-in-july/.

[71] N Haris, 'Women Should be Able to Become Village Heads' (*The Scoop*, 8 February 2021), thescoop.co/2021/03/19/women-should-be-able-to-become-village-heads/.

[72] Constitution, art 31(4).

[73] ibid art 30a.

[74] HMY Damit, 'Brunei Darussalam: Towards a New Era' in D Singh and L Salazar (eds), *Southeast Asian Affairs* (Singapore, ISEAS, 2007) 101, 104.

[75] SCY Ku, 'Brunei in 2009. Maturity in Doubt?' (2009) 50 *Asian Survey* 263.

[76] Constitution part V1 allowed for eight ex officio, six official and three nominated members. The Sultan could remove official and nominated members at will (art 31(1)).

than 90 per cent of Bruneians voted,[77] the *Parti Rakyat Brunei* (PRB) or Brunei People's Party secured all 16 elected seats. As the PRB was pro-democracy and anti-monarchy, the results were an anathema for Sultan Omar. That gave rise to royal distrust of elections and democratic principles. He refused to have the 16 elected members take their places in the LegCo. Thwarted and angered, a small armed revolt took place. The Sultan declared a state of emergency. Although the revolt was quickly supressed by British troops from Singapore,[78] the state of emergency did not end then, nor at the two-year automatic expiry period in the Constitution. Instead, a new Emergency Proclamation has been issued every two years since.[79] Despite the absence of the constitutional pre-conditions (public danger, internal unrest, war or external aggression, as set out in article 83), Sultan Bolkiah continues to use Emergency Proclamations for enacting laws known as (Emergency) Orders on 'whatsoever he considers desirable in the public interest'.[80] He justifies this as 'in keeping with tradition and values' of Brunei, and necessary 'for the country's peace and stability'.[81] It has proved useful in enacting contentious legislation, such as the Syariah Penal Code Order 2013 (SPCO), without LegCo scrutiny or media commentary. There are over 100 Orders listed on Brunei's website. Neocleous argues that the continuation of Emergency Powers not only normalises their use but also gives them 'formal legal grounding', which has a discernible effect on wider political culture, including creating 'dependency' in the general population.[82]

Sultan Bolkiah claims he has not yet seen 'evidence of a genuine interest in politics on the part of the responsible majority of Bruneians'.[83] In place of LegCo elections, the government offers '*Sentiasa Bersama Rakyat*' as a 'living democracy' in which a 'close relationship between His Majesty and his *rakyat* (citizenry) spontaneously and naturally comes to life whenever His Majesty mingles with his subjects, [creating] a mutual expression of utmost satisfaction, happiness and respect'.[84]

C. The Special Ruler–Subject Relationship '*Sentiasa Bersama Rakyat*'

The Sultan and his government assert that in a small traditional Malay kingdom, the special ruler–subject bond is superior to participatory democracy, separation of powers, and rule of law. They claim that the 'unique and very special bond between the ruler

[77] Hang Tey (n 31) 267.

[78] Coup leaders fled or were tried and convicted of treason and imprisoned. The PRB was declared illegal and remains so.

[79] Constitution, art 83A.

[80] ibid art 83.

[81] 2004 birthday *titah* cited in A Othman, 'His Majesty Announces Big Changes for Brunei' (*Borneo Bulletin*, 6 July 2004).

[82] M Neocleous, 'The Problem with Normality: Taking Exception to Permanent Emergency' (2006) 31(2) *Alternatives: Global, Local, Political* 191.

[83] Sultan Bolkiah in an interview reported in C Neher and R Marley, *Democracy and Development in Southeast Asia* (Boulder CO, Westview Press, 1995) 145. Note the 90 per cent voter turnout, however, in the one election held.

[84] 'His Majesty attends' (n 21).

and his *rakyat*' creates a 'society of harmony, stability, prosperity and peace'.[85] The relationship requires loyalty from his subjects, which the Sultan reciprocates with a generous welfare system with free education, healthcare, training, and government employment. As citizens pay no taxes, they are grateful to His Majesty for taking care of them 'from cradle to grave'.[86] Davies argues that 'without taxation it is possible to do without formal representation altogether'.[87] The 'special relationship' means the Sultan, whilst exalted and revered, needs a connection with his subjects and not to be too distant or remote. A small kingdom makes this achievable. The Sultan is seen, and, with help from compliant media, recorded at events, large and small, in every corner of the Sultanate. Accompanied by a contingent of photographers and reporters, he opens buildings, business ventures and conferences; visits ministries, departments, schools, hospitals, and sports venues; he regularly tours the villages in all four districts where citizens pledge him their allegiance;[88] and each week he prays with the men at different local mosques for the compulsory communal Friday prayer. The Sultan connects with his subjects in a three-day 'open house' at the world's largest palace, his *Istana Nurul Iman* ('The Light of Faith Palace') during Ramadan's *Hari Raya* celebration. Annually over 100,000 people (a quarter of the population) come to personally pay their respects to the Sultan and his family at the palace.[89] At the end of Ramadan, he gives thousands of personal gifts (*kurnia peribadi*) to his subjects[90] and on other celebratory state occasions adds B$1000 to each citizen's bank account. He is present at graduations to congratulate and give diplomas[91] (as University Chancellor) and hands over the keys to converts to Islam who, on conversion, receive new homes under the National Housing Scheme.[92] Müller gives a detailed and fascinating account of the political and symbolic significance of three grand, lavish, and lengthy annual celebrations,[93] which create a 'personality cult' for the Sultan: the Royal Birthday, National day and the Prophet's birthday. Each contributes to the 'endurance and enhancement of Royal power'.[94] This is seen in the 'spectacular mass choreographies[,] some loosely resembling the choreographies of synchronized bodies and colours in more internationally well-known propaganda events, such as those in China or North Korea'.[95]

Sultan Bolkiah is a visible ever-present ruler who is cheered by seemingly adoring flag-waving throngs whenever he ventures into public, with Brunei's media, academia and officials unanimous in their praise of their 'caring Monarch' and his 'generosity'. Yet, visibility and popularity, whether genuine or manufactured, are not consultation, or representation. Waving and having photographs taken with your subjects does not equate to hearing their needs or listening to their views on the laws and policies that

[85] ibid.
[86] M de Vienne, *Brunei: From Age of Commerce to Rentier State* (Singapore, NUS Press, 2015) 258.
[87] J Davies, *Libyan Politics: Tribe and Revolution* (London, IB Tauris, 1987) 18.
[88] 'His Majesty attends' (n 21).
[89] A Othman, 'Istana Open House from 2nd Day of Raya' (*Borneo Bulletin*, 8 September 2010).
[90] L Mohamad and R Mahmud, 'Thousands get more Kurnia' (*Borneo Bulletin*, 12 June 2018); D Müller, 'Paradoxical Normativities in Brunei Darussalam and Malaysia' (2016) 56(3) *Asian Survey* 415, 422.
[91] ibid.
[92] Black, 'Marching' (n 9) 108.
[93] Müller, 'Beyond the Sharia State' (n 50) 431–37.
[94] ibid 437.
[95] ibid 436.

impact their lives, including for Brunei's minorities. It is unlikely, even for the majority Muslim Malays, that real grievances will be raised, or could be, given the culturally ingrained deference to superiors in this socially hierarchical society. De Vienne suggests that 'celebrating over and over again the cohesiveness of society' does not compensate for the absence of representation[96] and ponders whether the 'interminable public celebrations' prevent 'subversive inaction'.[97]

III. Small State Cohesion: Ideology, Opposition and Censorship

Brunei is the only ASEAN nation not to hold national elections. To justify and deflect criticism from undemocratic autocratic governance, Brunei employs a three-pillar national ideology of MIB – *Malay Islam Beraja* (Malay Islamic Monarchy). At home and abroad, MIB is a tool for legitimisation. After World War II, many newly independent Asian nations[98] adopted nationalistic ideologies as compasses for building an idealised social and political order. MIB, 'which must be honoured and practised by all the people of Brunei',[99] was first announced and explained in the Sultan's independence *titah* of 1984.[100] Outside Brunei, debate exists about whether MIB was an existing but unarticulated ideology for over 600 years, as Brunei's government asserts, or was in reality a 'fictitious'[101] 'invention'[102] to legitimise royal absolutism. Braighlinn (pseudonym) argues that MIB's architects devised the ideology to legitimise the present, based on a continuum from the past – an artificially recreated past[103] pretending to be traditional and 'time-honoured'.[104] Either way, MIB today is sacrosanct and is constitutionally protected from criticism.[105] MIB is inculcated in every aspect of government[106] and society – it has its own bureaucracy,[107] and other departments and media 'tirelessly

[96] de Vienne (n 86) 286.
[97] ibid.
[98] *Pancasila* (Indonesia); *Rukun Negara* (Malaysia); Thai Trinity – Nation, King and Buddhism (Thailand).
[99] Independence *Titah* 1984.
[100] Scholars, such as Muhammad Melayong from the MIB Council, claim the ideology commenced in 1360 upon the conversion of the first Sultan. It was not articulated until 1984. See 'Brunei's golden period of expansion' (*Borneo Bulletin*, 24 October 2016).
[101] NS Talib, 'A Resilient Monarchy: the Sultanate of Brunei and Regime Legitimacy in an Era of Democratic Nation-States' (2003) 4(2) *New Zealand Journal of Asian Studies* 134, 144.
[102] ibid 142; de Vienne (n 86) 286; G Saunders, *A History of Brunei* (Oxford, Oxford University Press, 1994) 87–90.
[103] G Braighlinn, *Ideological Innovation under Monarchy: Aspects of Legitimation Activity in Contemporary Brunei* (Amsterdam, VU University Press, 1992) 29.
[104] R Kershaw, 'Constraints of History: the eliciting of Modern Brunei' (1998) 29 *Asian Affairs* 312, 315.
[105] Constitution, s 53(1A)(a) links 'directly or indirectly lower or adversely affect the standing or prominence' of the State ideology to sedition.
[106] Vehicles for indoctrination of MIB include the Departments of Justice, Education, and Radio and Television, Information, Office of Prime Minister's Office, Office of State Customs, Ministry of Religious Affairs, Ministry of Culture, Youth and Sport, Language and Literature Bureau, History Centre, and the University of Brunei Darussalam, in particular its Academy of Brunei Studies.
[107] MIB Supreme Council and the Academy of Brunei Studies propagates MIB through mandatory courses the three levels of education, in all government institutions and departments, and in the private sector.

emphasise how anything they do is in support of and rooted in MIB'.[108] Without MIB's legitimisation, it would be difficult to rationalise Brunei's medieval political structure at home or internationally, and to justify legalised racial, religious, gender and sexual orientation discrimination. If it accords with MIB then it is not considered discriminatory but is simply upholding Islamic or Malay values. The Sultan secures his position as MIB's centrepiece, bolstered by the Malay and Islam support pillars. MIB's beneficiaries, the Brunei Malays, reap the economic benefits and social rewards which ensure the continued support from Brunei's Muslim Malay majority.

A. Censorship

The limits on what can be expressed by members in the six advisory Councils have been covered but censorship and the corollary of self-censorship pervades all the Sultanate. Criminal laws censor speech, publications, and visual content, including documentaries[109] and satirical videos[110] if critical or demeaning of the Sultan, the Royal family, Islam, the government, or MIB. For example, the Sedition Act (Cap 24) criminalises as seditious any statement 'derogatory of the Sultan, the Royal family, Islam or MIB'.[111] The Internal Security Act (Cap 133) criminalises any act, 'speech or publication done with the intention of inciting disaffection for the Sultan'.[112] The SPCO criminalises 'printing, disseminating, importing, broadcasting, and distributing publications contrary to Islamic law',[113] which specifically includes 'any person who in any manner contempts, neglects, contravenes, opposes or insults any *titah* of His Majesty'. As *titahs* are the mode for announcing policies and commencement of (Emergency) Orders, this prevents public and media commentary – unless it constitutes a glowing endorsement – of new laws and policies after and before coming into force.

The Newspaper Act (Cap 105) gives the Minister of Home Affairs discretion to grant or revoke a publishing licence, to shut down a newspaper, and to bar distribution of foreign publications. There is no avenue for appeal from, or judicial review of the Minister's decisions. Brunei's only television station is state-run. The country's main daily newspaper, the *Borneo Bulletin*, is controlled by the Sultan's family and its journalists practise self-censorship. They give obsequious coverage to the Sultan and his government. Ensuring nothing dents the wholesome

[108] D Müller, 'Sharia Law and the Politics of Faith Control in Brunei Darussalam' (2015) *Internationale Asienforum* 313, 317.

[109] For example, 'Sex, lies and Sharia Law: The secret life of the Sultan of Brunei' (*Sixty Minutes Australia* 23 April 2015).

[110] Distributing a satirical video depicting the Royal family via mobile phone resulted in one year's impri onment for three Bruneians. Reported in Amnesty International, 'Brunei Darussalam: Submission to tl UN Periodic Review: Sixth Session of the UPR Working Group of the Human Rights Council, November December 2009' (13 April 2009), www.amnesty.org/en/documents/asa15/001/2009/en/. Also, Undesirab Publications Act (Cap 25), Censorship of Films and Public Entertainments Act (Cap 69).

[111] Sedition Act (Cap 24) Revised edition 2019, s 4.

[112] Sedition Act (Cap 24) Revised edition 2019, s 3(1)(i). The Internal Security Act (Cap 133) allows f detention without trial for up to two years with indeterminate extensions.

[113] Syariah Penal Code Order (2013), ss 213, 214 and 215.

image of the Sultan and his family requires shutting out reports of scandals involving Royal family members, especially the Sultan's brother Jefri's profligacy, salacious lifestyle, and alleged past sexual indiscretions. The government uses an 'informant system to monitor suspected dissidents, and online communications are monitored for subversive content'.[114] The internet[115] is government-owned and -monitored. Senior Counsel in the Attorney-General's Department explained that whilst there are laws protecting freedom of expression in many Western countries, in Brunei 'there are no such rights of freedom of expression as the likes of in the US and in the UK … censorship in more conservative countries like Brunei is crucial' in preventing 'the community from being exposed to negative information'.[116]

International organisations such as Freedom House categorise Brunei as 'not free'.[117] In 2023 Brunei was 142nd on the World Press Freedom Index.[118] In an affluent nation with high literacy and a well-educated population, the extent of paternalistic censorship is difficult to justify, except to ensure that nothing tarnishes the Sultan's image or permits questioning of the state's illiberal practices.

B. Silencing Opposition

Whilst censorship silences individuals, the government wants to prevent groups who might come together to undermine royal authority, oppose government policy, advocate for reform, or engage in 'undesirable' activities. To thwart threats to social cohesion, any group gathering of five or more requires registration. Under the Societies Order 2005 any group – whether commercial, professional, business, religious, political, service-focused, support, advocacy, or community-based – must be registered. To be a member of an un-registered group/ organisation is a criminal offence. Registration is refused if the purpose is 'unlawful'; for example, one in support of LGBTIQ+ rights,[119] or 'incompatible with the peace, public order, security or public interest', for example a political party or nightclub. Once approved, a group can be de-registered. When the Brunei National Democratic Party (BNDP), with a membership of 3,000, announced a policy calling for parliamentary democracy, elections, repeal of emergency laws, and a constitutional monarchy, it was de-registered and its leader arrested under the Internal Security Act.[120] The mission statement of Brunei's only currently registered political party, the National Development Party (NDP) gives unequivocal endorsement of

[114] 'Freedom in the World 2023: Brunei' (*Freedom House*), freedomhouse.org/country/brunei/freedom-world/2023.

[115] The Internet practice code stipulates that content must not be subversive, promote illegitimate reform, incite disharmony or instability, or fall out of line with Brunei's religious values, social and societal mores': from Y Yahya, 'Censorship is still important' (*The Brunei Times*, 19 November 2007).

[116] R Alai Zin, 'Rights, social responsibilities of bloggers' (*The Brunei Times*, 26 September 2010).

[117] Freedom House (n 114).

[118] 'Index: 2023' (*Reporters Without Borders*), rsf.org/en/index?year=2023.

[119] Same-sex intimacy is criminalised in the SPCO and Brunei's Penal Code (Cap 22) which makes any LGBTIQ+ support group against the 'public interest' and 'unlawful'.

[120] A Mani, 'Brunei' in W Sachsenroder and U Frings (eds), *Political Party Systems and Democratic Development in East and Southeast Asia*, Vol 1 (Aldershot, Ashgate, 1998) 85.

MIB, pledging to 'serve and support the Sultan and his descendants in upholding and defending Malay-Muslim primacy' as a 'just and benevolent government is more excellent and universal compared to the various western concepts of governance which are only meant to benefit their proponents'.[121] Despite its sworn allegiance to the Sultan and support for MIB, the Sultan has never appointed an NDP representative to the LegCo.[122]

IV. Conclusion

> Without the Sultan there would be no *rakyat* (people) and without the *rakyat* there would be no Sultan. The two cannot exist independently.
>
> Pengiran Haji Mohamad Yusof (Noble and former Government Minister)[123]

Brunei's current Sultan is the linchpin around which all aspects of life, religion, and governance revolve. As a small state, it has been possible to craft an alternative model to democracy as Mohamad Yusof noted above, based on a symbiotic alignment of a 'caring Monarch' with an unquestioningly loyal *rakyat*. The government reminds citizens that they owe an 'undivided and unconditional loyalty to His Majesty the Sultan and *Yang Di Pertuan*'.[124] For the domestic and international audience, the Bruneian model draws on traditional Islamic and historical Malay concepts[125] of consultation. However, this chapter argues that many factors indicate acquiescence to the Sultan rather than meaningful consultation.[126]

After using state revenues to ensure a decadent lavish lifestyle for the Royal family, Brunei's small population makes it is feasible for the Sultan to distribute a portion of Brunei's vast petro-carbon wealth to give Bruneians an enviable comparatively high standard of living in Asia. Doing so serves to demonstrate the Sultan's 'caring' nature and buys acquiescence to 'illiberal' autocratic rule. The latter is legitimised and re-enforced by MIB, which is constitutionally immune from criticism and inculcated at school, university, the mosque, and workplace.

Smallness also facilitates acceptance of 'personalised' rule. In a population of 452,500, Sultan Bolkiah is visible and ever-present in the lives of citizens. He is not a mere photographed image but is seen in person on village tours, at mosques, graduations, open days at the palace and at the many lavish celebratory events, including his three-week birthday extravaganza. The ruler–*rakyat* connection is bolstered by compliant media and censorship laws. Each published account from within Brunei declares that his Majesty's subjects love him and endorse rule at his 'pleasure'.

[121] Abdul Ghani Bujang, 'Education for Nationhood' (1987) 24 *Southeast Asian Journal of Educational Studies* 39, 43.
[122] Freedom House (n 114).
[123] J Falconer, *Abode of Peace: Brunei Darussalam* (Singapore, Éditions Didier Millet, 1993) 19.
[124] Information Department, Government of Brunei, www.information.gov.bn/VER2/content/view/448/54
[125] Discussed in sections II.A and II.C.
[126] Discussed in section II.A. and sections III.A. and B.

This chapter does not deny the sincerity and success in the promotion of '*Sentiasa Bersama Rakyat*' but questions whether it is as genuine and spontaneous as claimed: if so, why does the Sultan and his hand-picked government need to silence all opposition, control the media, prevent groups with common interests from forming, dictate what cannot be said in the six consultative Councils, stop elections, maintain a state of emergency for six decades, allow discrimination against non-Muslim, non-Malay and LGBTIQ+ minorities, abolish judicial review in the courts of law, and make constitutional amendments during Sultan Bolkiah's reign which fortify his powers at the expense of the rights and freedoms of Bruneian citizens?

17

The Struggle for Democratic Government in Malta

JOHN STANTON*

I. Introduction

Malta is an archipelago of five islands,[1] situated 100 km south of Sicily, in the middle of the Mediterranean Sea. Covering just 316 km^2 and with a population of over 550,000,[2] Malta is the most densely populated member of the European Union (EU). Over the centuries, the country has been colonised by a range of global powers.[3] Sammut explains:

> Malta … has been inhabited for 7000 years. In the ninth century BC, the Phoenicians colonised the Maltese islands. A succession of other rulers followed[,] notably Carthaginians, Romans, Byzantines, Arabs and then Spanish. In 1530 Malta was ceded by the Emperor Charles V of Spain to the Knights of the Order of St John. During the next 250 years, Malta functioned as a *de facto* independent state ruled by the Knights. After the departure of the Order in 1798, the French forces briefly occupied Malta. Then at the request of the Maltese, the … islands were placed under British protection in 1799 and formally became part of the British Empire from 1814 under the Treaty of Paris. Malta gained its independence on 21 September 1964 and became a democratic constitutional monarchy. The Constitution was amended on 13 December 1974 turning Malta into a Republic.[4]

n the context of this historical development, this chapter examines the way in which overnment in Malta has evolved. It briefly explains the administrative models employed re-1800, before then setting out the governmental systems that were imposed on Malta uring its time as a British colony. This period can be described as one in which there

* I am grateful to Tonio Borg, Hillary Briffa, Mark Sammut Sassi, and David Zammit for their comments d input. A version of this chapter was presented at the Global Summit on Constitutionalism, held at the niversity of Texas at Austin, 16–18 March 2023.

[1] The five islands are Malta, Gozo, Comino, Comminotto, and Filfla.

[2] World Bank Group, 'Population, total – Malta' (*World Bank Group*), data.worldbank.org/indicator/.POP.TOTL?locations=MT.

[3] For a deeper discussion of Malta's history, see B Blouet, *The Story of Malta*, 9th edn (San Gwann, BDL blishing, 2022); JS Abela, *Malta: A Brief History* (San Gwann, BDL Publishing, 2014).

[4] I Sammut, 'Introduction – The Maltese Legal System and the EU' in I Sammut and J Agranovska (eds), *e Implementation and Enforcement of European Union Law in Small Member States: A Case Study of Malta* asingstoke, Palgrave Macmillan, 2021) 1, 1–2.

was a struggle for democracy on the islands, with various attempts made to establish representative institutions thwarted by continuous tendencies towards autocracy. Whilst the 1964 Independence Constitution established the Westminster model of government on the islands, autocratic practices have continued to feature in Maltese politics. This chapter argues that this reality is linked to Malta's small size, and the political climate that is prevalent on the islands as a consequence. These factors, in turn, undermine the operation of the Westminster model, leaving space for these autocratic practices to continue.

II. Maltese Constitutional History and Autocratic Experiences

A. Malta under the Knights of the Order of St John

When the Knights of the Order of St John arrived in Malta in 1530, the *Università* and the *Consiglio Popolare* were the prevailing form of government, these being rooted very much within the 'medieval fiefdom tradition'.[5] It did not take long, however, for a new approach to be established. As Pirotta observes, 'the government of the Order in Malta was deeply influenced by Spanish and French ideals of absolutism … Autocracy was the dominant form of government to be found throughout Europe at the time'.[6] In addition:

> [T]he religious character of the Order … explain[s] its readiness to extend and add to the paternalistic structures it found in Malta. However, as a consequence of the Order's never-ending feud with Muslim princes, within the administrative system adopted in Malta by the Knights, autocracy and paternalism overlapped significantly with the requirements of military security.[7]

The autocratic rule of the Knights was compounded by the reality that 'it was politically inconceivable for the Order to allow a rival administration to exist side by side with its own'.[8] The displeasure that the Maltese people experienced – at least latterly – under the Order of St John is reflected in the fact that, following the expulsion of the French in 1800, and contrary to the 1802 Treaty of Amiens, the local population petitioned to become a British protectorate rather than for the islands to be returned to the Order.

[5] Abela, *Malta* (n 3) 131. The *Consiglio Popolare*, or Popular Council, was the representative assembly mad up of 'influential people in the islands along with the mayors and representatives of each parish or village . [together] they deliberated about the taxes to be imposed; [and] the safeguarding of long-held privilege established customs and sacred traditions' (Abela, *Malta* (n 3) 112). The *Università* was more an admini trative or governmental entity and was made up, in part, of four jurats chosen annually from the *Consigl Popolare* (see G Rapinet, *Lectures on the British Constitution and on the Government of Malta* (Valletta, Aquilina & Co, 1883) 158). I am grateful to Mark Sammut Sassi for his clarification on these institutions.

[6] GA Pirotta, *The Maltese Public Service 1800–1940: The Administrative Politics of a Micro-State* (Msid Mireva Publications, 1996) 25, citing C Price, *Malta and the Maltese: A Study in Nineteenth Century Migrati* (Melbourne, Georgian House, 1954) 1–2.

[7] ibid 25.

[8] ibid 26.

[9] Treaty of Amiens 1802, art 10 provided: '[t]he islands of Malta, Gozo, Comino, shall be restored to Order of St John of Jerusalem, to be held on the same conditions on which they possessed them before war'. See J Stanton, 'In Search of Constitutional Supremacy in Malta' (2024) 30(1) *European Public Law* 23,

They 'presumed that the King of Britain would reign, not rule, over the Maltese'.[10] In the event, and despite calls for protectorate status, Malta became a British colony in 1813 and it was, at this point, granted the first of its 11 colonial constitutions. This document, along with its successors, would come to shape the system of government across the archipelago for the next 150 years.

B. Malta as a British Colony I – The Emergence of a Council of Government

The form of government initially adopted by the British was an autocratic, gubernatorial one. The 1813 Constitution provided that:

> The chief authority is vested in the person of the Governor … The authority of the Governor is limited only by the orders of the King. He is responsible to His Majesty and to his country for his conduct; but his discretion is not to be shackled by any person or by any body of persons resident in Malta.[11]

Whilst the Constitution empowered the Governor 'to form a Council for the investigation and discussion of such matters relating to the civil interests of the Island' if he saw fit,[12] neither the first Governor, Sir Thomas Maitland, nor his immediate successors adopted such a Council, opting instead to rule alone. In its most simple form, autocracy equates with a 'form of government in which absolute power is concentrated in the hands of an individual, whose decisions are not subject to popular control or external legal constraints'.[13] Maitland's governorship of Malta typified this class of leadership. He was 'a dour but benevolent autocrat. His was a one-man rule … he could take anything but opposition. His system was aptly described as driving and kicking mankind into obedience … he believed in ruling unaided and unhampered'.[14] In this vein, Maitland 'put himself in charge of all branches of the state. He introduced jury trials, but there was no independent judiciary. There was no elected legislature. There was only Maitland'.[15]

[10] C Cassar, *A Concise History of Malta* (Msida, Mireva Publications, 2000) 146. See also Stanton, 'In search of constitutional supremacy in Malta' ibid; P Caruana Galizia, *A Death in Malta: An assassination and a family's quest for justice* (London, Hutchinson Heinemann, 2023) 20–21.

[11] Constitution of Malta, 1813. The text of this Constitution is reproduced in W Hardman, *A History of Malta during the period of the French and British occupations, 1798–1815* (Uckfield, The Naval and Military Press Ltd, 1909) 527.

[12] ibid.

[13] N Dasandi, *Is Democracy Failing? A primer for the 21st century* (London, Thomas & Hudson, 2018) 27.

[14] JJ Cremona, *The Maltese Constitution and Constitutional History since 1813*, 2nd edn (San Gwann, PEG Ltd, 1997) 2, citing *Letters of the Rt Hon George Cornewall Lewis Bart to Various Friends* (London, Longmans, Green & Co, 1870) 69.

[15] Caruana Galizia, *A Death in Malta* (n 10) 21. The extent of Maitland's autocracy was evidenced by the way he dealt with opposition. In 1821, a petition was submitted by British and Maltese merchants to the House of Commons, complaining of the concentration of power in the Governor, and the lack of any form of check or opposition that might enhance his rule (see JJ Cremona, *Malta and Britain: The Early Constitutions* (San Gwann, PEG Ltd, 1996) 34). The petition requested, inter alia, the 'formation of a Council or Colonial Assembly, without whose sanction no laws could be promulgated and no taxes imposed' (G Mitrovich, *The Cause of the People of Malta* (London, Effingham Wilson, Royal Exchange, 1836) 36). In response to this petition, Maitland 'met a deputation of the merchants' and 'cunningly alternated bullying with appeasement tactics', ultimately causing the petition to be withdrawn (Cremona, ibid 34).

Though, under Maitland's successors,[16] '[t]he power of the Governor remained more absolute than ever',[17] there was an acceptance that the system needed to change. The Constitution of 1835, therefore, established an unelected, seven-member Council of Government to assist the Governor in the exercise of his responsibilities.[18] This did not have the power to raise matters for discussion; it only met when instructed by the Governor. Moreover, the Governor was only required to resort to the Council for advice on matters of significant importance, and 'retained his absolute power and had the freedom to go against the recommendations of the Council'.[19] Even after the creation of this Council, therefore, autocracy remained in Malta, leading to vociferous calls for a more meaningful, democratic model.

This came under the Constitution of 1849, which increased the size of the Council to 18 members, eight of whom would be locally elected for five-year terms.[20] The powers of the Council also became more established. The Constitution granted

> to the Governor … with the advice and consent of the … Council of Government, full power and authority to make, ordain and establish Laws not being repugnant to the Law of England or to any Statute of the United Kingdom, or to any Order in Council made or to be made by our Royal Predecessors.[21]

Though any member of the Council could propose new laws, all were 'to be enacted with the approval of the Governor, who had the right to reject or reserve a law for consideration by the Home Government even if he had initially voted in favour.[22]

The importance of the 1849 Constitution, on paper at least, cannot be overstated. The Maltese had 'succeeded in persuading the Imperial government … [to grant] some form of popular elective representation in the Council of Government, which had only been previously conceded to New South Wales among the colonies'.[23] This said, the new arrangements appeared to keep 'the Governor in total control of public administration', with the elected representatives in the minority on the Council.[24] Moreover, from 1881, an Executive Council was created to 'assist the Governor in the administration of the government'.[25] The Governor 'was required in all cases to consult this Council', though he remained free to depart from their advice, provided he explained to the Secretary of State his reason(s).[26]

[16] Maitland (1813–24) was succeeded as Governor by Francis Hastings (1824–26) and Frederic Ponsonby (1827–36). After Hastings, Alexander Woodford served as Acting Governor for three months before Ponsonby took office.

[17] Cremona, *Malta and Britain* (n 15) 35.

[18] 'Four of these [members] were to be official members (the Senior Officer in command of the Land Forces … the Chief Justice, the Bishop of Malta and the Chief Secretary to the Government) and the rest were to be unofficial members (two Maltese and one British)' (Cremona, *Maltese Constitution and Constitutional History since 1813* (n 14) 3–4).

[19] S Portelli, 'The 1849 Constitution: Actions and reactions concerning the beginnings of popular representation in Malta' in Central Bank of Malta, *Landmarks in Maltese Constitutional History 1849–1974: The Central Bank of Malta Symposium – June 2011* (23 June 2011) 11, 12.

[20] ibid 19.

[21] Constitution of Malta, 1849. The text of this Constitution is reproduced in *Laws, Letters Patent and Other Papers in relation to the Constitution of the Council of Government of Malta* (Malta, Government Printing Office, 1889) 13. The provision here quoted is at 16–17.

[22] Portelli, 'The 1849 Constitution' (n 19) 19.

[23] ibid 21–22.

[24] ibid 20.

[25] Cremona, *Maltese Constitution and Constitutional History since 1813* (n 14) 10.

[26] ibid 10.

Majority democratic governance finally came under the 1887 Constitution, which made provision for 14 of the 21-member Council of Government to be locally elected.[27] Whilst this was seen as a significant step in affording the Maltese greater autonomy over questions of local concern, the model *still* fell far short of meaningful representative government. Not only did the Governor retain his power of veto over the Council, but the British Government also retained its ability to exercise full power over the Maltese through exercise of the prerogative. Problems also soon emerged, however, with the way in which the different branches of the Maltese Government related to one another. Three members of the Executive Council were also members of the Council of Government, generating a potential conflict of interest and 'a feeling … that their freedom of action in the legislature might be impaired by the decisions of policy previously taken in the Executive Council'.[28] After 1891, members of the Executive Council would no longer sit on the Council of Government; this separated legislative and executive powers, the former being predominantly local, and the latter being predominantly imperial.

Concerns about the system put in place in 1887 were addressed by a reversion back to a system with an unelected majority. The 1903 Constitution retained the 21-strong Council established in 1887, but reduced the number of elected members to eight.[29] This was criticised, and described by the elected members as 'one of the narrowest and most oppressive oligarchies that ever mocked the form of free government'.[30] Consequently, elected members would frequently abstain from the Council.[31] The model established in 1903 remained in place throughout the First World War, after which shifts in imperial aspirations motivated significant change. In the more than 80 years since the first Council of Government had been established, the Maltese had not yet achieved a system that was truly – and satisfactorily – representative of local needs. The various models that had been introduced had remained inherently imperial, even in the face of attempts to increase local democratic representation.

C. Malta as a British Colony II – Experiments in Self-government

After the First World War, desire for a stronger sense of home rule grew across the British Empire.[32] Malta was no exception: after the war, 'a general dissatisfaction against

[27] See E Dobie, *Malta's Road to Independence* (Norman OK, University of Oklahoma Press, 1967) 37. This made the body a representative legislature under section 1 of the Colonial Laws Validity Act 1865, which defined such an institution as 'any colonial legislature which shall comprise a legislative body of which one half are elected by inhabitants of the colony' (see further ibid 16).

[28] JJ Cremona, *An Outline of the Constitutional Development of Malta under British Rule* (Malta, Malta University Press, 1963) 17.

[29] The new Council of Government was made up 'of the Governor as President, a Vice-President, the holder of the office of Lieutenant Governor and Chief Secretary to the Government and seventeen other members. Of these, nine were official members (the Crown Advocate and eight other public officers to be nominated) and the rest were unofficial members elected by eight electoral districts, one of which consisted of Gozo' Cremona, *Maltese Constitution and Constitutional History since 1813* (n 14) 21).

[30] *Parliamentary Papers 1903*, xliv (Cd. 5217) 1, cited at ibid 22.

[31] See Cremona, *Maltese Constitution and Constitutional History since 1813* (n 14) 22.

[32] Including, for example, in Ireland, Egypt, India, Pakistan, Malta. See JM Pirotta, *1919 Consequences of Imperial Conceit: Four Case Studies* (Valletta, Midsea Books, 2022).

the British Imperial Administration began to emerge'.[33] Widespread unemployment and 'a high rate of illiteracy ran parallel to a general low standard of living and poor educational provision'.[34] Though emigration schemes were introduced to help tackle these challenges, they did little to suppress a tense political environment, which reached its height on 7 June 1919 when riots broke out amid protests that called for stronger political autonomy for the Maltese.

As a consequence of these various factors, the 1921 Constitution established self-government in Malta.[35] This came in the form of a diarchy. Two Governments were created. The first, which had responsibility for purely local matters, was a Maltese Government that was accountable to a bicameral legislature, comprising the Legislative Assembly and the Senate.[36] Seven of the 15 Senate Members were elected, as were all 32 members of the Legislative Assembly. Elections took place through the single transferable vote model and established a system based on the Westminster model. Government itself was still exercised by an Executive Council, which 'consisted of the Head of the Ministry and not more than six other members'.[37] The second form of government was

> a Maltese Imperial Government … [This was led by the Governor, and it] administered the so-called reserved matters which included the defence of Malta, all the British forces of the Crown, foreign, security and defence policy, coinage and currency, to mention but a few.[38]

This experiment in self-government was short-lived and was abandoned after just 12 years. Though it had initially worked well, 'with few matters being referred to London',[39] the Constitution was suspended in 1930 amid a political crisis triggered by efforts to replace Italian with Maltese as the language of the courts and exacerbated by the tension that this created between the Maltese Government and the (Catholic) Church. Following settlement of the language question,[40] the Constitution was reinstated in 1932. However, when the governing Nationalist Party 'immediately started to enhance the place of Italian in [Maltese] education',[41] the British suspended the Constitution again in November 1933. It was never reinstated.

D. Malta as a British Colony III – The Final Steps to Independence

An interim system of government was established under the 1936 Constitution. This comprised a fully appointed Executive Council with no fewer than eight members

[33] A Cutajar, *Remembering Sette Giugno 1919* (Ħamrun, Kite Group, 2019) 12.
[34] ibid 13.
[35] See, for further discussion on the 1921 Constitution, D Fenech, *1921 Self-Government in Malta: 1921 1933* (Valletta, Midsea Books, 2021).
[36] See T Borg, *A Commentary on the Constitution of Malta*, 2nd edn (Ħamrun, Kite Group, 2022) 1.
[37] JM Pirotta, 'The 1921 Self-Government Constitution' in Central Bank of Malta, *Landmarks in Maltese Constitutional History 1849–1974: The Central Bank of Malta Symposium – June 2011* (23 June 2011) 33, 38.
[38] Borg, *Commentary on the Constitution of Malta* (n 36) 1.
[39] Blouet, *Story of Malta* (n 3) 212.
[40] 'Maltese became the language of the courts, English and Maltese were to be taught at the elementary school level, and Italian not introduced until the secondary level' (ibid 212).
[41] ibid 213.

'The Governor legislated by means of Ordinances, but power of concurrent legislation by Order in Council was expressly reserved to the Crown, as also [was] power to revoke, alter or amend the Letters Patent'.[42] A more permanent form of government was introduced under the 1939 Constitution. This kept the 1936 iteration of the Executive Council and re-established a Council of Government made up of 10 elected members, five *ex officio* members, and five members appointed by the Governor.

After the end of the Second World War, local desire for – and imperial willingness to introduce – a new Constitution were prominent. The subsequent 1947 Constitution bore close resemblance to that granted in 1921, creating a diarchic system of self-government, albeit with a unicameral legislature. This experiment in self-government, however, would be as short-lived as the first. Amid a broader trend of decolonisation across the Empire, significant discussions throughout the 1950s regarding Malta's relationship with Britain defined the next chapter of its history. The Nationalists favoured – and sought, unsuccessfully – dominion status within the Empire, whilst the Labour Party pursued the idea of integration.[43] This initially found favour both with the Maltese – who endorsed it in a referendum – and the British Government, which went so far as to set the finer details of the arrangement and propose legislation that would give it legal effect. However, '[i]n October 1957 … differences arose … connected with the proposed change in British defence policy and its deleterious effects on Malta's economy'.[44] This led to the resignation of the Maltese Labour Government and, in a drastic reversal in aspirations, calls for independence. Following Labour's resignation, responsible government was again suspended and an absolute gubernatorial system operated for a while before another Executive Council was established under the 1959 Constitution.[45] This system was also short lived, with the 1961 Constitution establishing self-government for a third time.

The system in place under the 1961 Constitution was the most significant to date, not least because of its departure from the diarchic system that had previously operated. The 1961 Constitution 'provided for a [unicameral] Legislative Assembly of fifty members with full legislative and executive powers'.[46] The Governor retained power to appoint judges, as well as a power of veto, whilst the British Government continued its broad oversight of Malta, and the Crown preserved the power to amend or revoke the Constitution by Order in Council.[47] Despite the significance of the system put in place in 1961, 'it was made abundantly clear that this Constitution did not represent the final word so far as the constitutional development of Malta was concerned'.[48] Amid the broader trend towards decolonisation across the Empire, in August 1962, Nationalist Prime Minister, George Borg Olivier, wrote to the Secretary of State

[42] Cremona, *Maltese Constitution and Constitutional History since 1813* (n 14) 39.
[43] '[T]hat is to say, the gradual incorporation of Malta into the political, financial and social structure of the United Kingdom whilst retaining its local autonomy and legislature' (ibid 53).
[44] ibid 55.
[45] See R Mangion, *Constitutions and Legislation in Malta 1914–1964*, Volume 2: 1933–1964 (Oxford, Whitelocke Publications, 2017) 167.
[46] Cassar, *Concise History of Malta* (n 10) 230. Powers over defence and external affairs were exercised concurrently with the British Government.
[47] See Cremona, *Maltese Constitution and Constitutional History since 1813* (n 14) 64 and 69–70.
[48] ibid 72.

'to invoke … the right [of Malta] to be an independent state'.[49] This was granted on 21 September 1964 by virtue of the Malta Independence Order 1964 and the Malta Independence Act 1964. The Constitution that came into effect upon independence was granted by the UK Government and was set out in a Schedule to the 1964 Order. Though the Constitution bore many similarities to other such texts granted to former colonies seeking independence at this time, there was an element of local involvement. The Maltese Attorney General at the time, JJ Cremona, played a central role in the drafting of the Constitution, whilst the finished text was approved by the Maltese people in a referendum.[50]

This section of the chapter, then, has explored the development of government in Malta, with a particular focus on its time as a British colony. During this period, Malta's system evolved from a gubernatorial autocracy to one that gradually accepted a democratic element in its Council of Government, finally reaching its height in the – ultimately unsuccessful – attempts at self-government. Whilst increasingly democratic models were established on the islands, the mixed success with which these were met nevertheless ultimately meant that an element of autocracy featured consistently during Malta's time as a British colony. The next section now explores the evolution of government post-independence.

III. Independent Malta – The Persistence of Autocracy

The 1964 Constitution of Malta, granted to the islands upon independence, establishes the Westminster model of government on the archipelago. The unicameral Maltese Parliament, comprising a base-level 65 MPs (though capable of being made up of as many as 81 MPs) is elected every five years through the single transferable vote (STV) mechanism. The precise number of MPs will depend on the operation of two electoral corrective mechanisms. The first, introduced in 1987, and subsequently amended,[51] ensures that the political party that wins the most votes is able to secure a parliamentary majority. Following the election result, additional MPs from the winning party are elected to ensure that it has a majority of seats in the House. The second mechanism introduced ahead of the 2022 General Election, 'means that, if one gender is represente by less than 40 per cent of the House, then up to 12 seats can be assigned to MPs of tha gender, the allocation being split equally between the parties'.[52]

For the first decade of independence, Malta was a constitutional monarchy, wit Queen Elizabeth II as head of state. Since 1974, it has been a republic. The Constitutio

[49] Cited in H Frendo, *The Origins of Maltese Statehood: A Case Study of Decolonization in the Mediterrane* (San Gwann, BDL Publishing, 2000) 7.

[50] Though the referendum passed with a 51.5 per cent majority (on a turnout of just 74 per cent – low Maltese standards), the fact that the Nationalists had won the 1962 election with pursuit of independen central to their manifesto further legitimised its realisation.

[51] The procedure was amended in 1996 and 2007. See A Bencini, *Malta's Hybrid Electoral System: Constitutional Review*, 2nd edn (Ħamrun, Kite Group, 2022) 163.

[52] J Stanton, 'Maltese independence and the 1964 Constitution' in T Borg and J Stanton (eds), *Constitution of Malta at Sixty* (Ħamrun, Kite Group, 2024) 43, 59.

formally vests executive power in the President, who is appointed by a two-thirds majority in Parliament for a non-renewable five-year term.[53] In reality, the President is largely a ceremonial figurehead, with the exercise of executive power lying with the Prime Minister and the Government. Consistently with the Westminster model, the political party that commands a majority of the seats in the House of Representatives is appointed to Government by the President, though the legitimacy of that Government is predicated on it maintaining the confidence of a majority of the legislature, this being ensured through constant scrutiny and accountability.[54]

A fundamental feature of the Westminster model, one that is particularly pertinent in the context of this chapter's focus on autocracy, is that it observes a diffusion of power across the three main constitutional actors – the legislature, the executive, and the judiciary. Whilst this diffusion of power does not result in a clear and total separation of authority, it is nonetheless

> concerned with the avoidance of concentrations of power. What it requires above all is that each branch of government … is able to check the exercise of power by the others, either by participating in the functions conferred on them, or by subsequently reviewing the exercise of that power.[55]

In this way, the Westminster model is the antithesis of autocracy: a diffusion of power and interactions that foster accountability, as opposed to a consolidation of authority and a rejection or dismissal of opposition and criticism. This said, and despite the introduction of the Westminster model in Malta, a tendency towards autocracy has been allowed to continue post-independence, as this section now illustrates.

A. Mintoff, the Early Years, and Polarised Politics

During the first 40 years after independence, Maltese politics became increasingly polarised with the two parties, the Nationalists and Labour, adopting contrasting stances with respect to the way in which Malta would develop post-independence. Nationalist Governments[56] tended to pursue agendas that were more neo-liberal, facilitating Malta's engagement with the wider world and stronger alignment with the West. It was the Nationalists, for example, who incorporated the European Convention on Human Rights into Maltese law,[57] and who oversaw Malta's accession to the EU in 2004

[53] See Constitution of Malta, art 78(1).
[54] The effectiveness of this scrutiny and accountability is arguably compromised 'by the fact that there is no 'mit on the number of MPs who can be appointed to the Government' (Stanton, 'Maltese independence and ne 1964 Constitution' (n 52) 59). Consequently, there is 'potentially little scope for backbench rebellion and he opportunity to achieve majority support with relative ease' (J Stanton, 'Small States and Constitutional eform: Democracy in Malta' in C Morris (ed), *Making and Changing Law in Small Jurisdictions* (Cham, pringer, 2024) 31, 39).
[55] E Barendt, *An Introduction to Constitutional Law* (Oxford, Oxford University Press, 1998) 15.
[56] Post-independence, Nationalist Governments were in office in Malta from 1964–71, 1987–96, ad 1998–2013.
[57] See European Convention Act 1987.

and adoption of the Euro in 2008. By contrast, Labour Governments[58] have adopted an approach that sought to prioritise Malta's own interests. Labour favoured close ties with Gaddafi's Libyan regime;[59] they negotiated the closure of the British naval base in 1979; and even attempted to halt the process of EU accession during their two years in Government from 1996 to 1998. Prominent during Labour's early periods in office was Dom Mintoff, Prime Minister between 1955 and 1958 and between 1971 and 1984, and it is with him that our identification of post-independence autocracy starts. The former Prime Minister was invariably described as an 'autocrat', 'authoritarian', and as 'harbouring dictatorial tendencies'.[60] Indeed, in an obituary, published the day after Mintoff's death in 2012, Maltese journalist, Debono, opined that

> [o]n an international level, Dom Mintoff … cross[ed] the line several times by courting dictators like North Korea's Kim Il Sung and Romania's Nikolai Ceauşescu, while earning a certain notoriety for his brinkmanship in dealing with a Western world pitted against the eastern bloc at the height of the Cold War.[61]

Mintoff displayed these autocratic tendencies in myriad ways. One example is shown by the 'excesses of overzealous "Mintoffjani" thugs, as emblemized by the attacks on the Opposition leader's Birkirkara home, as well as the Times building in Valletta, in October 1979'.[62] Mintoff was notoriously sensitive to criticism and intolerant of opposition. Earlier in the 1970s, he took action that hindered the work of judges, most notably by suspending the operation of the Constitutional Court amid a dispute with the Opposition Party regarding constitutional reform. Moreover, in 1973, Mintoff forcibly took over the shares of the National Bank of Malta, violating the owners' rights.[63] Mintoff is by no means, though, the only post-independence leader to demonstrate autocratic practices. Recent leaders have also shown similar tendencies, as the next subsection now discusses.

B. Autocracy Today

Autocracy can take many forms and display varying characteristics. From a broad perspective, it entails the 'undermining of democratic institutions' and a disregard for established processes and systems, this taking place 'through a series of discrete changes in the rules and informal procedures that shape' the various elements of a working liberal

[58] Post-independence, Labour Governments were in office in Malta from 1971–87, 1996–98, and 2013 – present.

[59] E Saliba, 'Gaddafi and Malta-Libya relations' *Times of Malta* (1 September 2011), timesofmalta.com/article/Gaddafi-and-Malta-Libya-relations.382747.

[60] J Debono, 'Death of a patriarch: Dom Mintoff' *Malta Today* (21 August 2012), www.maltatoday.com.mt/news/national/20450/death-of-a-patriarch-dom-mintoff-20120821.

[61] ibid.

[62] ibid.

[63] C Mangion, 'Mintoff's forcible take-over violated National Bank shareholders' rights' *Malta Today* (6 February 2014), www.maltatoday.com.mt/news/court_and_police/35759/mintoff-s-forcible-take-over-violated-national-bank-shareholders-rights-20140206. Also see Caruana Galizia, *A Death in Malta* (n 10) 3

constitutional democracy.[64] In addition, it is not uncommon in the process of autocratisation to see an 'increasing power of actors that do not have electoral accountability'.[65]

With regard to this last characteristic, there are examples of clientelism[66] and cronyism[67] in Malta, these practices empowering leaders to use their authority to the advantage of professional and personal allies, and these allies, in turn, being potentially allowed to influence government activity. Observation of cronyism and clientelism in Malta is not novel,[68] and some instances of these practices are – or, at least, have been – enabled by the Constitution. Prior to reforms passed in 2020, for instance, the Prime Minister of Malta had the power to appoint judges, magistrates, the Attorney-General, and the Police Commissioner. Whilst, on paper, such appointments were made by the President, this was done in accordance with the binding advice of the Prime Minister.[69] Even following the 2016 creation of a Judicial Appointments Committee, which makes an evaluation of potential judicial candidates before an appointment is made, '[t]he choice and ultimate decision … remained in the hands of the Prime Minister'.[70] That the retention of this power by the Prime Minister potentially fostered a culture 'of … nepotism, discrimination in treatment, elitism and favouritism',[71] is evidenced by the fact that in 2019, a magistrate was appointed by then Prime Minister, Joseph Muscat, who was the daughter-in-law of 'the Prime Minister's personal lawyer … [and] the Labour Party's main legal advisor'.[72] In 2018, the Venice Commission criticised Malta's judicial appointments process, stressing that:

> The principle of independence of the judiciary requires that the selection of judges and magistrates be made upon merit and any undue political influence should be excluded. The Prime Minister should not have the power to influence the appointment of Justices and Judges-Magistrates. This would open the door to potential political influence, which is not compatible with modern notions of independence of the judiciary.[73]

These views contributed directly to the introduction of the 2020 reforms, following which 'the government can now no longer exercise discretion in the appointment

[64] N Lindstaedt, *Democratic Decay and Authoritarian Resurgence* (Bristol, Bristol University Press, 2021) 22.

[65] ibid 22.

[66] Clientelism typically permits leaders to sustain relationships 'involving mutual benefits' and 'the exchange of favours' with non-political actors who are, in turn, able to influence government decisions and are often permitted to collect an unequal share of wealth (ibid 64).

[67] Cronyism is 'the practice of appointing known acquaintances or allies to given positions' (Stanton, 'Small States and Constitutional Reform' (n 54) 35).

[68] See W Veenendaal, 'How smallness fosters clientelism: a case study of Malta' (2019) 67(4) *Political Studies* 1034; Stanton, 'Small States and Constitutional Reform' (n 54) 31.

[69] See Constitution of Malta, arts 96(1) and 100(1) (prior to reforms introduced in 2020).

[70] Borg, *Commentary on the Constitution of Malta* (n 36) 521. If the Prime Minister chose to go against the evaluation of the Committee, he was required to explain his reasons to Parliament (see Constitution of Malta, art 96(4) (repealed in 2020)).

[71] K Aquilina, *The Rule of Law à la Maltaise* (University of Malta Press, 2017) 50.

[72] N Camilleri, 'Lawyers might boycott Nadina Lia if she is made a magistrate' *Malta Independent* (3 March 2019), www.independent.com.mt/articles/2019-03-03/local-news/Lawyers-might-boycott-rumoure-new-magistrate-Nadine-Lia-6736204432.

[73] European Commission for Democracy Through Law (Venice Commission), 'Malta – opinion on constitutional arrangements and separation of powers and the independence of the judiciary and law enforcement' (Opinion No 940 / 2018, 17 December 2018) [43].

of judges, with appointment now by the President on the advice of the Judicial Appointments Committee'.[74]

Clientelism and cronyism are even more prominent when we examine the more informal government interactions in Malta. Delia, for example, in cataloguing myriad perceived scandals during the early days of Muscat's 2013–20 Government, opines that the new Prime Minister,

> decapitated the public service, firing nearly all euphemistically-called permanent secretaries and replaced them with people who owed their careers to him. Within weeks, all major and most middle-ranking positions of influence in Malta's administration were filled by hand-picked cronies, sycophants and hangers on.[75]

Muscat resigned from office in January 2020 amid accusations of government corruption and alleged government involvement in the 2017 murder of investigative journalist Daphne Caruana Galizia. Despite this, and other scandals that punctuated Muscat's tenure at Castille,[76] the new (and currently serving) Prime Minister, Robert Abela, did not deny Muscat the opportunity of standing as a Labour candidate in European parliamentary elections, asking rhetorically 'Why should I say no to Muscat?'.[77]

Another element of autocracy is reflected in a disregard for established procedures and due process. In 2022, the Prime Minister told 'self-employed people and business-people … [that] if you feel terrorised by an institution … [c]ome directly to me so that I can defend you and so that you can keep on working and investing in the country'.[78]

This encouragement 'to circumvent due process and resort to … [Abela's] merciful benevolence[, b]ypass[ing] the courts, the police, [and] the tax department',[79] would appear to undermine existing avenues of due process, and compromise executive separation from the courts, also jeopardising the independence of certain executive institutions, such as those pertaining to tax and the police. In a similar vein, in October 2023, Abela endorsed the actions of the Transport Minister, Ian Borg, in his efforts 'to help certain candidates with their driving test applications', saying that such practices were 'part of Malta's political system'.[80] Explaining the broader concern with such practices, the Malta Employer's Association noted that:

> The Prime Minister's pronouncement … is a radical invitation to anarchy which encourages individuals and businesses to bypass what should be established and trusted structures to either get fast-tracked to obtain what they are eligible for, or worse, to acquire entitlements which they should never have at the expense of others.[81]

[74] Stanton, 'Small States and Constitutional Reform' (n 54) 45.

[75] M Delia, 'Which scandal will do it?' *Times of Malta* (8 October 2023), timesofmalta.com/article which-scandal-it.1059636.

[76] Castille refers to the Auberge de Castille in Valletta, the 18th-century building – constructed by th Knights of the Order of St John – that serves as the office of the Prime Minister.

[77] J Arena, '"Why should I say no to Muscat?" – PM' *Times of Malta* (27 January 2024) 1.

[78] T Diacono, '"Complain directly to me" Robert Abela urges Maltese businesses "terrorised" by institution *Lovin Malta* (24 January 2022), lovinmalta.com/news/complain-directly-to-me-robert-abela-urges-maltes businesses-terrorised-by-institutions/.

[79] K Cassar, 'The language of autocracy' *Malta Independent* (30 January 2022), www.independent.com.m articles/2022-01-30/blogs-opinions/The-language-of-autocracy-6736240197.

[80] 'Driving test scandal: Employers slam Abela's "invitation to anarchy"' *Times of Malta* (3 October 202 timesofmalta.com/article/driving-test-scandal-employers-slam-abela-invitation-anarchy.1058859.

[81] ibid.

Autocrats across the world are also typically dismissive of criticism and opposition, and often avoid challenge or scrutiny. This enables them to galvanise their positions by undermining, discrediting or dismissing views that are critical of or in opposition to their own. As Gessen notes, '[a]utocracy is incompatible with free and open media because autocracy does not brook transparency and accountability'.[82] For example, amid ongoing contentions concerning abortion laws in Malta, Abela 'didn't hesitate to denigrate and vilify one of Labour's own icons, [former President] Marie Louise Coleiro Preca, for daring to contradict him. He unscrupulously dug up her views on divorce from a decade earlier to discredit her'.[83] Abela's intolerance of criticism and opposition extends to the Government's regard for the press. In January 2023, for instance, Maltese journalist Kevin Cassar reported that

> [a] whole army of lawyers paid through public funds is currently engaged in stopping us from finding out what Abela and his government are up to … [and] he's embarked on a mission to suppress the free press and extinguish the public's right to information … [Abela] is now brazenly and ruthlessly pursuing journalists for asking basic questions. He is determined to cripple truly independent media houses filing Freedom of Information requests with multiple financially ruinous lawsuits.[84]

Criticism of international organisations is a further sign of autocracy. In 2022, Abela offered an 'open attack on the European Parliament' and openly criticised the Maltese President of the Strasbourg legislature, Roberta Metsola, for 'swiftly removing [the] Vice President'.[85] This, says Cassar, places

> him firmly in the camp of autocrats. His hostility towards the European Parliament matches that of Hungarian Prime Minister Viktor Orbán. Orbán uploaded a mocking tweet attempting to ridicule the European Parliament. Abela and Orbán's approaches are perfectly aligned.[86]

The effect of this criticism of those offering opposing or critical views is exacerbated in Malta by the lack of challenge by those close to the Government and the Prime Minister. In 2021, for instance, Labour MP, Rosianne Cutajar, was found to have taken money and had dealings with the businessman standing trial for orchestrating the 2017 assassination of journalist Caruana Galizia. This, however, did not stop her from being appointed by Abela as chair of the parliamentary health committee. It has been suggested that this trend has permeated the Labour Party more broadly, as one journalist reports:

> For Labour, the Leader is God. Nobody challenges him. Nobody disputes his decisions, no matter how malignant. Nobody criticises him, no matter how atrocious his behaviour. Party unity and cohesion override national interest. Partisan interests override morality.[87]

This section, therefore, has identified numerous examples of autocracy in post-independence Malta. These examples can broadly be categorised as relating, firstly, to clientelism and cronyism, and, secondly, a deeply polarised and personalised political

[82] M Gessen, *Surviving Autocracy* (London, Granta, 2020) 134.
[83] K Cassar, 'Malta's New Year Resolution' *Sunday Times of Malta* (1 January 2023) 19.
[84] ibid 19.
[85] ibid 19.
[86] ibid 19.
[87] K Cassar, 'What separated the parties?' *Malta Independent* (6 February 2022), www.independent.com.mt/articles/2022-02-06/blogs-opinions/What-separated-the-parties-6736240387.

climate, within which leaders are often dismissive of, and sometimes hostile towards, challenge, opposition and criticism. The final section of the chapter now discusses how these practices are linked to state size, before then going on to explain how they undermine the Maltese system.

IV. Small States, Autocracy, and Malta

A. Small States and Autocracy

There is a wealth of literature on the relationship between state size and democracy. With regard to small states, work here observes that small states tend to be more democratic than their larger counterparts.[88] Whilst there is much evidence to support these claims, the reality is that '[s]mall states … can look formally liberal-democratic [from the outside] but might be rather illiberal in their actual workings'.[89] Identification and examination of this trend in Malta has already been carried out, and it is not for this chapter to replicate those discussions.[90] In brief, though, the view holds that, from the outside, frequent and regular elections, an ostensibly free press, human rights, institutions upholding the text of the Constitution and the rule of law, all exemplify ways in which Malta appears to be democratic. Closer examination, though, of the way in which the Maltese Government operates, the allegations of corruption, manipulation of the press, and concerns for the rule of law on the islands, reveals 'an imperfect democracy'.[91]

Where studies have shown concerns for the state of democracy in small states, clientelism and cronyism, as well as a deeply polarised and personalised political climate, often feature.[92] With regard to the relationship between small size and clientelism, for example, Veenendaal observes that 'small settings have high levels of social intimacy and cohesion, and politicians and citizens are likely to know and interact with each other in multiple social roles'.[93] This fosters the potential for a 'blurring of professional and private relationships … [meaning] that politicians have a stronger temptation tc favor their personal relations, while constituents might exert greater social pressures or politicians to provide them with material largesse'.[94] In the Maltese context, the close and densely populated nature of the Maltese community means that it is not only eas

[88] See, for example, RA Dahl and ER Tufte, *Size and Democracy* (Stanford CA, Stanford University Pres 1973) 4–8; G Baldacchino, 'Islands and despots' (2012) 50(1) *Commonwealth and Comparative Politics* 103.

[89] J Erk and W Veenendaal, 'Is small really beautiful? The microstate mistake' (2014) 25(3) *Journal Democracy* 135, 136. Also see C Morris, 'Attempting constitutional reform on the island micro jurisdiction Alderney' (2018) 47(2) *Common Law World Review* 105; Stanton, 'Small States and Constitutional Refor (n 54) 31.

[90] See Stanton, 'Small States and Constitutional Reform' (n 54).

[91] ibid 37.

[92] See Veenendaal, 'How smallness fosters clientelism' (n 68).

[93] ibid 1037, citing D Ott, *Small is Democratic: An Examination of State Size and Democratic Developme* (New York, Garland, 2000); L Tsai, *Accountability without Democracy: Solidary Groups and Public Goo Provision in Rural China* (Cambridge, Cambridge University Press, 2007); W Veenendaal, *Politics a Democracy in Microstates* (Abingdon, Routledge, 2014); DPJ Wood, 'The Smaller Territories: Some Politi Considerations' in B Benedict (ed), *Problems of Smaller Territories* (London, Athlone Press, 1967).

[94] Veenendaal, 'How smallness fosters clientelism (n 68) 1037.

to engage with those in power, but also that it is easier for those in power to connect with the electorate, with businesses, and with other organisations. As Veenendaal states, 'clientelistic relationships are particularly likely to emerge and persist in small societies, due to the direct, face-to-face contacts between citizens and politicians'.[95] In Malta, these factors can be seen in the aforementioned example of the Prime Minister appointing as Magistrate, the daughter-in-law of 'the Prime Minister's personal lawyer … [and] the Labour Party's main legal advisor',[96] as well as by the appointment of – what Delia labels – 'handpicked cronies, sycophants and hangers on'.[97] Such appointments were made easier due to the small nature of Malta and the intimate political communities that are fostered as a result.

Another factor underpinning the link between small states and clientelism is 'the increased value of individual votes in small societies … [which] provide a powerful incentive for the establishment of patron-client linkages'.[98] This is undoubtedly true in Malta, where voter turnouts are consistently high, and seats are closely contested, meaning that 'there are greater incentives for politicians to allocate targeted benefits to individual voters'.[99] More than this, though, the particular form of STV at work in Malta itself fosters the increased potential for clientelistic relationships to be established. For the purposes of general elections, the Maltese islands are divided into 13 districts, with each district returning five MPs to Parliament. In a two-party system, it is inevitable that candidates from the same party will be contesting the same seats. Consequently, and since political or ideological arguments between competing candidates from the same party will be unlikely to differ to any great degree, political campaigns and inter-candidate competitions are likely to be strengthened by the additional, individual values and incentives that particular politicians might offer their constituents. As Boissevain comments, the

> [p]ressure on … [parliamentary candidates] to perform services for both voters and for civil servants, who must provide the prizes [their] electors seek, is intense. The immense pressure on civil servants to provide the contracts, jobs, transfers, licences, scholarships, and so on that competing politicians from the governing party require to satisfy their constituents must not be underestimated.[100]

This, says Boissevain, 'strongly fosters patronage, subversion of civil servants, internal rivalry and factionalism within the parties',[101] factors directly contributing to the maintenance of clientelistic relationships.

A polarised and personalistic political climate is another feature not uncommon in small states. Corbett and Veenendaal observe that '[d]ue to the close personal links and social intimacy that follow from small population size, people are generally aware of each other's political affiliations, resulting in the almost complete absence of political

[95] ibid 1035.
[96] Camilleri, 'Lawyers might boycott Nadina Lia if she is made a magistrate' (n 72).
[97] Delia, 'Which scandal will do it?' (n 75).
[98] Veenendaal, 'How smallness fosters clientelism' (n 68) 1037.
[99] ibid 1037.
[100] J Boissevain, 'Proportional Representation and Development: Some Critical Thoughts' (1974) 3 *Economic and Social Studies* 1, 14.
[101] ibid 14.

anonymity for individual citizens'.[102] In Malta, this is deeply rooted. 'Polarization has centred on issues like language, religion, and ideology, … [though] regardless … Malta has a penchant for tribal politics'.[103] This is most profoundly reflected in the oft-quoted words of Dom Mintoff, who once claimed that 'whoever is not with us is against us'.[104] This polarisation is evidenced by the aforementioned examples of ways in which the Nationalist Party and the Labour Party pursued different agendas post-independence, and by the way in which politicians – particularly in recent years – have been openly critical of challenge and opposition. The two-party system in Malta exacerbates this polarisation since there are only two broad political camps. Consequently, the system is further defined by 'antagonism, and longstanding rivalries between individual politicians'.[105]

The practices of clientelism and cronyism, and the polarised and personalised political climate, both evident in Malta, are linked to its small size. Given the gradual democratisation of Malta, particularly by the 1964 Independence Constitution, however, it is important to ask how and why these autocratic practices have continued to be a feature of government on the islands.

B. The Westminster Model in Malta

The full democratic potential of the Westminster model of government has not been realised in Malta, meaning that historic tendencies towards autocracy have been allowed to continue. There are a number of reasons why this is the case. Some of these reasons are linked to Malta's small size, such as the polarised and personalised nature of Maltese politics, whilst others relate to the absence or the inadequacy of political and constitutional features that elsewhere serve to sustain the Westminster model.

The polarised and personalised nature of Maltese politics is particularly problematic in the context of the Westminster model that prevails in Malta. This is because there are instances when cross-party consensus is needed for certain decisions to be made, this being harder to achieve where politicians are so divided. For example, following reforms introduced in 2020, appointments to various official positions, including that of the President of Malta, the Chief Justice, the Ombudsman, and the Chairman of the Permanent Commission Against Corruption, require approval by two-thirds of the House of Representatives. Such appointments are more difficult where political consensus is harder to achieve and predicated upon politically distant parties agreeing on the individuals to appoint.[106]

Moreover, and with regard to the broader working of government, the personalised and polarised nature of Maltese politics also 'means that the supposedly impartia

[102] J Corbett and W Veenendaal, 'Westminster in Small States: Comparing the Caribbean and Pacifi Experience' (2016) 22(4) *Contemporary Politics* 432, 443.

[103] Veenendaal, 'How smallness fosters clientelism' (n 68) 1045.

[104] Cited, for example, at: Debono, 'Death of a patriarch' (n 60).

[105] J Corbett and W Veenendaal, 'The personalisation of democratic leadership? Evidence from small state (2017) 36(3) *Social Alternatives* 31, 33.

[106] This said, the first President appointed under the new procedure in 2024, Myriam Spiteri Debono, w approved by the two parliamentary parties relatively quickly.

and neutral functioning of Westminster institutions like the civil service, the electoral commission, the ombudsman, and the judiciary is virtually impossible to realize'.[107] In Malta, this concern is exemplified by the reality that the Constitution permits the Government to choose who chairs the Broadcasting Authority, meaning that the party in power can use this to their advantage. During the COVID-19 pandemic, for example, the Prime Minister used a 90-minute press conference on lockdown rules to promote Government reforms on various matters. When the opposition protested, it took three and a half months for them to be given a right to reply. This state of affairs highlights the importance of having non-partisan public service institutions, which serve 'as an important handbrake on executive domination in Westminster systems'.[108]

Beyond the political climate in Malta, there are further factors that contribute to the issues affecting the working of the Westminster model on the islands. In this regard, there is a disparity between the clear, legal framework of the system, and the conventions and political norms that are designed to sustain it. The Westminster model, in the context of the UK at least, is allowed to function because of myriad conventions, political principles, and legal remedies that have developed and evolved over the centuries to deliver a system that is workable and democratic, and that is capable of keeping the executive branch of government in check. Reflecting this, Bulmer observes:

> History, tradition, fortuitous circumstance … produced a system [in Britain] without theory or grand design. Incremental and pragmatic change, managed by 'good chaps' with a clear sense of what was 'done' and 'not done', resulted in a living constitution, consisting of an elaborate patchwork of statutes, conventions, rules of common law, institutional traditions and ingrained habits.[109]

The conventions of ministerial responsibility, for example, ensure that Government, both as a collective entity and as exercised by individual ministers, is held accountable to the elected Parliament. Judicial review of administrative action permits the High Court to assess the lawfulness of Government action, where a particular application to the Court has been made. And, finally, supporting the Government of the day is an impersonal, impartial, and professional bureaucracy, carrying out the day-to-day business of running the country.

Whilst Britain's own constitutional arrangements have always permitted the gradual evolution of these conventional and political principles, this was not always the case in many former colonies. Certainly, the colonies that became Dominions experienced a more gradual path to independence,[110] permitting an easier inheritance of conventions and principles relevant to the working of the Westminster model. Other colonies, though, for whom independence was a singular event, such as Malta, did not inherit such conventions and principles as easily.[111] Consequently, upon adoption, the model

[107] Corbett and Veenendaal, 'Westminster in Small States' (n 102) 443.

[108] ibid 443, citing RAW Rhodes, J Wanna, and P Weller, *Comparing Westminster* (Oxford, Oxford University Press, 2009).

[109] WE Bulmer, *Westminster and the World* (Bristol, Bristol University Press, 2020) 17.

[110] For example, Australia, Canada, and New Zealand.

[111] See H Kumarasingham, 'Eastminster – decolonisation and state-building in British Asia' in H Kumarasingham (ed), *Constitution-making in Asia: Decolonisation and state-building in the aftermath of the British Empire* (Abingdon, Routledge, 2016) 1, https://ukconstitutionallaw.org/2016/09/29/harshan-kumarasingham-eastminster-the-westminster-model-in-british-asia/.

could be adapted or manipulated to accommodate local factors. Writing in the context of 'Eastminster',[112] Kumarasingham observes that:

> Asian nations did not have centuries to interpret and adjust in order to develop their constitution as the British had. Instead within months they needed to formulate and design a constitution and therefore invariably drew upon the system of their imperial master. The local elites with the involvement of external actors like Sir Ivor Jennings determined that Westminster could work in the East. Since the Westminster system is based on convention and ambiguity and not rigid rules and clarity the same Westminster system could be adopted and manipulated to produce diverse results and reactions that would shape their countries forever.[113]

In Malta, whilst certain British constitutional conventions accompanied the Westminster model into the 1964 Independence Constitution in written form,[114] others did not. As a consequence, certain features designed to sustain a parliamentary democracy are lacking, leaving space for historic constitutional practices potentially to continue. One such principle is categorised in the 'good chap theory of government'.[115] Blick and Hennessy explain:

> A key characteristic of the British constitution is the degree to which the good governance of the United Kingdom … has relied on the self-restraint of those who carry it out … we have trusted politicians to behave themselves. We have long assumed that those who rise to high office will be 'good chaps', knowing what the unwritten rules are and wanting to adhere to them, even if doing so might frustrate the attainment of their policy objectives, party political goals, or personal ambitions – the argument being that 'good chaps' … know where the undrawn lines lie and come nowhere near to crossing them … The 'good chap' principle emerged over a long period of time. Its existence was assumed rather than expressly defined. As [Prime Minister, William] Gladstone put it in 1879, the British constitution 'presumes more boldly than any other the good sense and good faith of those who work it'.[116]

[112] 'Eastminster' is a term used by Kumarasingham to refer to the adoption of the Westminster model in certain Asian former colonies (see ibid 1–2).

[113] ibid 1.

[114] For example, the appointment of a Prime Minister. In the UK, the position, and the method of appointment are purely matters of convention. There is no legal provision requiring that the UK have a Prime Ministe and, as a matter of convention, an individual is appointed to the position where they can be said to commanc the confidence of a majority of the House of Commons. Reflecting a translation in written form into th Maltese system, art 79(1) of the Constitution of Malta provides that there will be a Prime Minister, and art 8 makes clear provision for the President's appointment of an individual to the office of Prime Minister.

[115] A phrase coined by Clive Priestley, a member of Margaret Thatcher's 'Efficiency Unit' in the 1980 (see C Priestley, 'Promoting the efficiency of central government' in A Shenfield et al (eds), *Managing th Bureaucracy* (London, Adam Smith Institute, 1986) 117)). Peter Hennessy has further explored the notio He states that the theory can be explained as 'being that a good chap knows what a good chap has to do an doesn't need to be told' (P Hennessy, '"Harvesting the cupboards": Why Britain has produced no administra tive theory or ideology in the Twentieth Century' (1994) 4 *Transactions of the Royal Historical Society* 20 205).

[116] A Blick and P Hennessy, 'Good Chaps No More? Safeguarding the Constitution in Stressful Times' *Th Constitution Society* (18 November 2019), consoc.org.uk/publications/good-chaps-no-more-safeguardin the-constitution-in-stressful-times-by-andrew-blick-and-peter-hennessy/, citing Cabinet Office, 'T Cabinet Manual: A guide to the laws, conventions and rules on the operation of government' *Cabinet Offi* (October 2011) 2, assets.publishing.service.gov.uk/media/5a79d5d7e5274a18ba50f2b6/cabinet-manual.p WE Gladstone, *Gleanings of Past Years 1843-1878* Volume 1 (London, John Murray, 1879) 243.

In short, the sustainability of the Westminster model in the UK has been attributed, in part, to the 'good chap theory of government'.[117] This theory, though, is a political rule that was not transplanted into post-colonial constitutions due to the unwritten, almost unacknowledged, role that it plays. In Malta, without a reliance on this self-restraint and presumption that government is practised by 'good chaps', there is a void in which local political practices have been allowed to develop and continue. Chief amongst these is a tendency toward autocracy. In the absence of this unspoken reliance on the notion that governing officials are 'good chaps' and can be presumed to act with 'good sense and [in] good faith', the space exists for the deeply embedded practice of autocratic government to continue.

V. Concluding Remarks

Historic and recent tendencies towards autocracy in Malta have been catalogued throughout this chapter. These are linked to the islands' small size and population, and they undermine the working of the Westminster model of government. Prevalent concerns in this regard are a lack – or inadequacy – of conventions and political rules designed to sustain the Westminster model, as well as the polarised and personalised nature of Maltese politics. All this has contributed to what can be described as a struggle for genuinely democratic government on the islands.

[117] Whilst not for discussion here, Blick and Hennessy explore the extent to which the theory no longer applies in the UK itself.

Part IIB
Mediating Division

18

Mauritius and Constitutionalism

The Interplay of Smallness, Constitutional Dynamics, and International Relations

TONY ANGELO AND SABIR KADEL

I. Introduction

As a small island nation with diverse ethnic, linguistic, and religious characteristics, Mauritius presents an exemplary case study for understanding the role of smallness in constitution-making processes and constitutional operation. This chapter examines how the nation's size has influenced its constitutional framework, with an emphasis on the 'Best Loser System', which is a unique component of the political structure of Mauritius designed to maintain multi-ethnic representation in the National Assembly. Established in the Constitution at independence in 1968, it ensures that if any of the country's major ethnic communities (Hindus, Muslims, Sino-Mauritians, and General Population (including Franco-Mauritians, other European immigrants, Indo-Mauritians of the Christian faith, and Creoles – see section III.A. below) are underrepresented following a general election, additional seats (up to a maximum of eight in total) will be awarded to the 'best losers' among candidates from that community.

Furthermore, the chapter will highlight the significant role played by international nteractions because of the country's size. The chapter looks at the way these external nfluences have shaped constitutional amendments, including through constitutional ights jurisprudence, and contributed to the evolution of Mauritius' post-independence onstitutional identity.

In section II, we offer some information on the Mauritius context and examine ow the smallness of the country influences its constitutional framework in general. ection III then focuses on some constitutional specificities of Mauritius and assesses hether and how these are linked to smallness. It first considers the Best Loser System, nd then turns to international relations and influences and their relationship with auritius' constitutional identity – both with respect to constitutional rights, and with spect of territorial disputes

II. Background and Smallness

A. The Mauritian Context

Mauritius is a small state. It has a population of one and a half million persons, most of whom live on the island of Mauritius, which is geologically a volcanic crater with an area of 1756 square kilometres. The establishment of a Dutch outpost and eventually French and British colonial rule saw the importation of slaves, indentured labourers, and settlers, which created a demographic tapestry that continues to characterise Mauritian society.[1] The divisions within society aligned historically with the economic and political stratifications instituted during colonial times. The French brought African slaves to work on sugar plantations. This period laid the groundwork for the socio-economic hierarchy that would persist for the descendants of slaves, commonly referred to as Creoles, often occupying the lower socio-economic strata. After the abolition of slavery in 1835, the British administration brought indentured labourers, primarily from India. This significantly altered the island's demographics, with Indo-Mauritians coming to form the majority. This migration introduced further complexity, as these labourers brought with them diverse languages, cultures, and religions. Ethnic groups in Mauritius are commonly classified into several categories: Indo-Mauritians, Creoles, Sino-Mauritians, and Franco-Mauritians, with the latter historically being the landowners and part of the economic elite due to their colonial ties.[2]

At the time of independence from the United Kingdom in 1968 the Mauritian economy was dominated by sugar production.[3] The official language of the Mauritian Parliament and Government was English. There were few English people living in Mauritius in 1968; the lingua franca was Mauritian Creole; and the majority of the population were of Indian ethnicity, speaking a variety of languages from the Indian sub-continent which reflected their area of origin or religion. In that context, English levelled the playing-field because it was the first language of very few citizens.[4]

The road to independence for Mauritius was the standard British colonial route.[5] In the years immediately preceding independence, there were two constitutional documents which moved Mauritius from a purely colonial organisation to 'a sovereign democratic State' (section 1 of the Constitution). The first of those steps along the way was the Mauritius (Constitution) Order 1964 (UK). It provided for a Legislative Assembly with a life of five years. That Assembly had a Speaker, a Chief Secretary, 40 elected members and 15 members appointed by the Governor. That constitutional document included a Bill of Rights modelled on the European Convention on Human

[1] See B Benedict, *Mauritius: The Problems of a Plural Society* (New York, Praeger, 1965) 9–21 for an overview of the 'peopling of Mauritius'.

[2] For further discussion, see eg, TH Eriksen, 'Nationalism, Mauritian Style: Cultural Unity and Ethnic Diversity' (1994) 36 *Comparative Studies in Society and History* 549; AS Simmons, *Modern Mauritius: The Politics of Decolonization* (Bloomington, Indiana University Press, 1982) 5–7 and chapters 2 and 3.

[3] Simmons (n 2) 7–9.

[4] SA de Smith, 'Mauritius: Constitutionalism in a Plural Society' (1968) 31 *Modern Law Review* 601, 602.

[5] See generally, DG Boyce, *Decolonization and the British Empire, 1775–1997* (Basingstoke, MacMillan Press, 1999).

Rights,[6] a Public Service Commission, a Police Service Commission, a Judicial and Legal Service Commission, an Attorney-General and a Director of Public Prosecutions (DPP). There was a power of disallowance by the British Sovereign of legislation passed by the Assembly.

The second document in this progression was the Mauritius Constitution Order 1966 (UK). It continued the pattern of the 1964 Order but extended the Assembly to one of 70 elected members, which included 62 elected members and eight 'best losers'. The inclusion of the 'Best Loser System' in the Mauritius Constitution Order of 1966 was primarily motivated by the need to ensure fair representation across Mauritius' diverse ethnic communities, a measure aimed at promoting political stability in a multi-ethnic society.[7] This system is discussed further in section III of this chapter. This constitutional document included special financial provisions, and provided for a Leader of the Opposition, and an Ombudsman. The 1966 Order was the springboard for the Mauritius Independence Order 1968 (UK) which came into force on 6 March 1968. Independence from the UK, sanctioned by the Mauritius Act 1968 (UK), was celebrated on 12 March 1968. Recognising the transition from colonial status to independence resulted in the addition to the Constitution of a definition of the state (section 1), the declaration of the supremacy of the Constitution (section 2), and the change of status of the Governor to that of Governor-General.

The existing law, which included some French codes from French colonial times, reflected English tradition. The Governor-General appointed by the British monarch was the Head of State. During French colonial rule (1715–1810), Mauritius adopted the Code Napoléon (now the Civil Code), which governed areas such as personal status, property law, and contractual relations. This legal framework, deeply rooted in European civil law traditions, provided a stable and comprehensive system for regulating private matters. After the British captured Mauritius in 1810, they chose to retain the French legal framework in private law while introducing common law principles in areas such as public administration, criminal law, and procedural rules.[8] This pragmatic decision avoided disrupting the existing societal and legal order, illustrating an early instance of Mauritius' ability to adapt to dual colonial influences. Retaining elements of both French and British systems ensured a degree of stability and familiarity during the transition to independence. This continuity is essential in understanding how Mauritius voided the disruptions that often accompany decolonisation.

Since gaining independence from British colonial rule in 1968, Mauritius has ndergone significant political and constitutional changes. Two of the most notable evelopments in its post-independence era include its transition to a republic and the stablishment of a degree of self-government for Rodrigues, a semi-autonomous island ithin Mauritius' territory.

[6] MJN Meetarbhan, 'The Constitution at 50' in R Ramtohul and HT Eriksen (eds), *The Mauritian Paradox: ty years of Development, Diversity and Democracy* (Port Louis, University of Mauritius Press, 2018) 15, 19.

[7] See SS Sookrajowa, 'The Paradox of Power-Sharing in Mauritius' in EW Aboultaif, S Keil and A McCulloch ds), *Power-Sharing in the Global South: Patterns, Practices and Potentials* (Cham, Springer, 2024) 189, 192–1 for a discussion of the development of the Best Loser System. See also Simmons (n 2) chapter 10; de Smith 4) 607–11.

[8] T Angelo, 'Mauritius: Capitulation, Consolidation, Creation' in S Farran, E Örücü and SP Donlan (eds), *tudy of Mixed Legal Systems: Endangered, Entrenched or Blended* (Farnham, Ashgate, 2014) 115, 118–24.

Upon independence, Mauritius retained its status as a Commonwealth realm, with the British monarch as the head of state represented by a Governor-General. The decision to become a republic was part of a broader trend of decolonisation. On 12 March 1992, Mauritius officially became a republic within the Commonwealth, severing its constitutional ties with the British monarchy. This transition required amendments to the 1968 Constitution to establish the President of Mauritius as the ceremonial head of state while retaining the original parliamentary system of governance. Becoming a republic symbolised the full attainment of national sovereignty and the maturity of Mauritius' democracy. The change to a republic did not significantly alter the functioning of the government, as the role of the head of state remained largely ceremonial.[9]

Rodrigues, located about 560 kilometres east of mainland Mauritius, has a distinct geographical, cultural, and social identity. There had been long-standing calls from the people of Rodrigues for greater autonomy to manage their own affairs, recognising their unique needs and aspirations. In 2001, the Mauritian Parliament passed the Rodrigues Regional Assembly Act which established the Rodrigues Regional Assembly (RRA).[10] The RRA is composed of elected members and is responsible for the administration of local affairs, including education, health, environment, and agriculture.[11] The establishment of the RRA marked a significant step in empowering the people of Rodrigues, and allowing them greater control over their development. While self-government has brought many benefits, Rodrigues continues to face challenges including economic development, connectivity with mainland Mauritius, and resource management.

B. Some General Observations about the Constitution of Mauritius and Smallness

This section examines key features of the constitutional design of Mauritius, with a particular focus on how these elements respond to the unique challenges and opportunities associated with the small size of the nation, including its capacity for adaptability, inclusivity, and efficient governance within a limited geographic and demographic context.

The Constitution establishes Mauritius as a 'sovereign democratic State', known as the Republic of Mauritius (section 1). This foundational declaration emphasises commitment to self-governance and national sovereignty. For a nation that emerged from centuries of colonial rule – first under the Dutch, then the French, and finally the British – declaring itself a sovereign democratic state is an essential repudiation of its colonial past and an assertion of its independence. This proclamation underscores Mauritius' right to self-determination, marking a decisive break from the external control and exploitation that characterised its history. As the supreme law (section 2) the Constitution provides a stable and predictable legal framework to ensure that a

[9] See R Mathur, 'The Republican Model of Mauritius: A Short Comparative Study' (1997) 24 *The Afric Review* 180 for a discussion of the choice of republican model.

[10] See F Berry and T Angelo, 'From Pirate's Lair to Federal Partner …' (2004) *Revue Juridique Polynésie Hors Series Volume IV* 308, 317–20 for a discussion of the development of this Act.

[11] ibid 321–27.

other laws are consistent with it. The Constitution recognises and declares the existence of fundamental human rights and freedoms without discrimination (section 3). These include the right to life, liberty, security of the person, freedom of conscience, expression, assembly, association, and the right to establish schools. The Constitution allows for a responsive governance structure to ensure that governance remains closely aligned with the needs and aspirations of the Mauritian population. In the opinion of the authors, such constitutional provisions are essential in small state contexts, where the impact of policies is often immediate and visible and where social cohesion and the protection of minority rights are paramount.

Small states often experience a concentration of power, with a limited number of political actors. This can pose challenges to constitutionalism, particularly in maintaining checks and balances and preventing abuses of power.[12] In Mauritius, the small scale of politics means that political processes are often more personalised, with greater emphasis on individual relationships and community ties.[13] This can impact on the impartiality and objectivity essential to constitutional governance. Mauritius has demonstrated adaptability in its legal system, blending elements from its colonial past (French and British) with local realities. This adaptability is crucial in small jurisdictions where legal systems must be efficient yet comprehensive. For example, the country's legal system allows for the co-existence of civil law principles with elements of customary and religious laws that govern personal matters such as marriage, divorce, and inheritance among certain communities. While the general law of marriage and divorce in Mauritius is governed by the Civil Code, provisions exist that respect the religious and customary practices of various communities, including the Waqf Act.[14] The Muslim Family Council, although not a formal court, plays a role in mediating and advising on matters of marriage, divorce, and inheritance according to Islamic principles.[15] Labour law in Mauritius also demonstrates the blend of colonial legal influences with local adaptations that address the unique socio-economic context of the island. The Industrial Court, established under the Industrial Relations Act 1973, is an example of how Mauritius has developed a hybrid system that combines common law procedural aspects with civil law principles to adjudicate on labour disputes.[16]

Furthermore, the potential for close political and personal connections in small states can significantly impact the fairness of legal proceedings. In particular, the concentration of power and the often-personalised nature of politics, mentioned in the last paragraph, may threaten the independence and impartiality that are essential for upholding the rule of law. In response to these challenges, certain aspects of Mauritius' constitutional framework are designed to safeguard against such risks. One notable example is the role of the DPP, as provided for in section 72 of the Mauritian Constitution. Section 72 establishes the office, appointment qualifications, and powers of the DPP, ensuring the independence of prosecutorial decisions from undue political interference. This

[12] See eg, discussion in J Stanton, 'The Struggle for Democratic Government in Malta', Chapter 17 in this volume.
[13] See eg, discussion in Simmons (n 2) 13–14.
[14] See Angelo (n 8) 121.
[15] Established by s 29 of the Civil Status Act 1991.
[16] See Angelo (n 8) 130–33 for a discussion of the development of labour law in Mauritius.

section is particularly significant due to the unique challenges and dynamics inherent in jurisdictions like Mauritius. Subsection (1) sets up the DPP as a public office appointed by the Judicial and Legal Service Commission, ensuring independence and impartiality. Subsection (2) specifies that the DPP must be qualified for appointment as a Judge of the Supreme Court. This high qualification threshold ensures that the DPP possesses the necessary legal acumen and integrity; in small states where the legal community is often small, fulfilling these requirements can be difficult.[17] Subsection (3) outlines the broad powers of the DPP, including instituting, taking over, and discontinuing criminal proceedings. In small states, this level of discretion must be balanced with a high degree of accountability and transparency to maintain public trust in the justice system. Subsections (5) and (6) emphasise the DPP's exclusive powers and independence.

Section 47 of the Mauritian Constitution outlines the procedures and requirements for altering the Constitution. This section is important due to the intimate interplay between legal frameworks, governance, and societal dynamics. Subsections (1) and (4) allow for constitutional amendments, but with significant thresholds (a two-thirds or three-quarters majority in the National Assembly). This balance between flexibility and rigidity is vital to ensuring stability while allowing adaptation to evolving circumstances. Subsection (3) stipulates that any amendment to section 1 (the establishment of the Republic) or section 57(2) of the Constitution (the term of Parliament) requires not only a unanimous National Assembly vote but also a referendum attracting approval of not less than three-quarters of the electorate. This underscores the significance of direct public participation in decisions which impact on the nation's fundamental identity and governance, particularly important matters in nations with a small population.[18]

The various amendments to the Constitution reflect Mauritius' ability to adapt its fundamental legal framework to changing circumstances,[19] such as in matters relating to the powers and discretion of the Public Service Commission, or to provide for the offices of President and Vice-President, their election and removal, privileges and immunities, and for changes relating to the establishment of these offices.

In some cases, foreign imports into the Mauritius constitutional system have been continued successfully without amendment: for example, the Judicial Committee of Privy Council (JCPC) was retained as Mauritius' highest appellate court post-independence and has been widely regarded as a successful element of the Mauritian constitutional system. As a foreign appellate body, the JCPC operates independently of local political or social pressures, ensuring impartial adjudication. This is particularly valuable in small states like Mauritius, where the size of the legal and political community can result in closer interpersonal relationships that might inadvertently affec

[17] There are around 900 barristers in Mauritius, more than 200 attorneys, and around 60 notaries. In orde to be admitted as a law practitioner in Mauritius, one has to complete three distinct stages. The first stage i to obtain a qualifying law degree or equivalent. The second stage is to pass approved bar examinations. Upo passing approved bar examinations, one must then finally commence pupillage under the supervision of a approved pupil master. Pupillage is accordingly the final stage to the route to qualification at the Bar. Se *Report of the Committee on the Review of the Law Practitioners Act* (10 March 2020), attorneygeneral.govm org/Documents/ReportCommiteeLawPractitionersAct/FinalReportofCommittee.pdf.

[18] See further discussion of constitutional identity and size in Se-Shauna Wheatle's 'The Construction Constitutional Identity(ies) by the Caribbean Court of Justice', Chapter 10 in this volume.

[19] There have been 32 amendments to the Mauritian Constitution, as well as 72 Regulations made under since 1968.

judicial impartiality. Retaining the JCPC ensured legal continuity during the transition to independence, avoiding abrupt changes to the judicial framework. This stability has been instrumental in fostering trust in the legal system; particularly in a multiethnic society like Mauritius where communal sensitivities can influence perceptions of local institutions, the external nature of the JCPC adds an additional layer of credibility and fairness to its decisions.

Other imported entities, such as the Ombudsman, have been less successful. Unlike courts, the Ombudsman's role and powers are not widely understood or utilised by the public. In the view of the authors, this lack of awareness diminishes the institution's ability to serve as an effective channel for addressing grievances against government administration.

As can be seen, the smallness of Mauritius significantly influences its approach to constitutionalism. While it presents unique challenges in terms of governance, political concentration, and economic vulnerability, it also offers opportunities for closer community engagement, responsive governance, and a sense of shared national identity. The key for Mauritius lies in leveraging its smallness to enhance its constitutional framework, ensuring that it remains adaptable, responsive, and resilient in the face of both internal and external challenges. The Constitution of Mauritius is not just a legal document but a living framework that reflects and adapts to the realities of its small island context.

III. Selected Constitutional Specificities – Responses to Smallness?

A. Divided Society

A defining feature of the Mauritius Constitution is its electoral system – the Best Loser System – which provides for representation for the 'best losers' in order to ensure the accommodation of ethnic minorities. Whether this system was devised, and is continued, because of the small size of the state of Mauritius or because of the extreme diversity of the population or out of political necessity, may be debated. Political necessity rather than smallness was probably the reason.[20] There had been a history of discrimination and segregation in practice since the times of slavery and that continued through the period of indentured labour and then into the political system of a Mauritius preparing for independence.[21]

The fabric of Mauritian society is intricately woven with strands of various ethnic, cultural, and religious identities, a mosaic formed through the complex history of settlement, colonialism, and trade briefly explained in section II. The historical applications of this diversity and its contemporary ramifications and implications for the politics

[20] See eg, Sookrajowa (n 7) 201; Y Fessha and N Ho Tu Nam, 'Is it time to let go? The Best Loser System in Mauritius' (2015) 28 *Afrika Focus* 63, 65–66.

[21] Simmons (n 2) chapters 2–9; R Boswell, *Le Malaise Creole: Ethnic Identity in Mauritius* (New York, Berghahn Books, 2006).

of Mauritius reflect a dialogue between unity and division, between a shared national identity and distinct communal groupings.

Paragraph 3(1) of the First Schedule of the Mauritian Constitution provides that every candidate for election at any general election of members of the National Assembly shall declare in such manner as may be prescribed which community they belong to and that community shall be stated in a published notice of their nomination. Paragraph 3(4) adds that the population of Mauritius shall be regarded as including a Hindu community, a Muslim community and a Sino-Mauritian community; and every person who does not appear, from his way of life, to belong to one or other of those three communities shall be regarded as belonging to the General Population, which shall itself be regarded as a fourth community. In *Carrimkhan v Lew Chin*, the Judge, DB Seetulsingh, declared that:

> Way of life may depend on a series of factors – the way one dresses, the food one eats, the religion one practises, the music one listens to, the films one watches. External appearance and the name one bears are also pointers as to the community to which one may belong. The expression 'way of life' used in the First Schedule has never been put to the test and some 33 years after the Constitution was drafted one cannot escape the conclusion that a common way of Mauritian life has gradually and steadily developed in Mauritius which cuts across communal barriers.[22]

The Best Loser System in Mauritius holds significant relevance in the context of small states, providing a framework for ensuring ethnic representation, political stability, and democracy in a multiethnic society. The Best Loser System was crafted to address the deeply ingrained ethnic diversity of Mauritius, where significant communities – Hindus, Muslims, Sino-Mauritians, and the General Population – possess distinct social, cultural, and historical identities. In a conventional first-past-the-post electoral model, minority communities might find themselves consistently underrepresented, as political majorities could more easily dominate constituency-based elections. Under the Best Loser System, however, seats are allocated to candidates who rank as the 'best losers' within their communities if these communities are underrepresented in the election results. Specifically, following a general election, up to eight additional seats in the National Assembly are allocated by the Electoral Service Commission to the highest-ranking unsuccessful candidates from the underrepresented ethnic groups. This guarantees a minimum level of representation for each major community, ensuring that even if an ethnic minority fares poorly in the regular constituency elections, it still has a voice in the legislature. Consequently, the Best Loser System mitigates the risk of any community being entirely excluded from the legislative process, which the authors believe is essential for a fair and representative democracy in Mauritius.

However, it also reflects the challenges that small states face in balancing historical mechanisms with the need for modernisation and inclusivity in their political systems. The Best Loser System, despite its unique and somewhat unconventional design, has largely been successful in Mauritius. This success is evident in the stability and inclusivity it has brought to the Mauritian political landscape, a notable achievement in a multi-ethnic society where social cohesion could be easily strained by disparities in politic

[22] *Carrimkhan v Lew Chin* [2000] SCJ 264.

representation. One of the primary successes of the Best Loser System is its role in ensuring that all major ethnic communities feel represented within the Mauritian legislature. By reserving a limited number of parliamentary seats for the highest-ranking unsuccessful candidates from underrepresented ethnic communities, the system mitigates the effects of alternative electoral approaches that could skew representation toward more populous or geographically concentrated groups. This inclusivity has helped to foster a sense of belonging and mutual respect across Mauritius' diverse communities, allowing for peaceful co-existence and minimising the risk of inter-community conflicts. Moreover, political stability is crucial in any state, but particularly in small states where governance systems can be more vulnerable to polarisation. The Best Loser System has helped create a stable political environment by accommodating ethnic diversity within formal political structures. By giving each community a stake in the legislature, the system has reduced the perception of political disenfranchisement and has helped to consolidate a shared national identity that transcends individual community lines. This balance between community representation and national unity, the authors suggest, has been instrumental in Mauritius' stability since independence.[23]

B. International Relations and Identity

(i) Overview

The international relationships of Mauritius following its independence in 1968 have been characterised by a strategic alignment that balances its historical ties, regional cooperation, and broader global engagements. As an island nation situated in the Indian Ocean, Mauritius has navigated a complex geopolitical landscape, leveraging its strategic position to foster diverse international relations. Mauritius' independence marked a significant shift in its international relations. Initially, Mauritius maintained strong ties with its former colonising powers, notably the UK and France. These relationships were underpinned by historical, cultural, and economic links, including continued reliance on these nations for economic support and development aid.

Mauritius is an active member of the African Union and the Southern African Development Community. Its engagement in these regional bodies underscores its commitment to African solidarity and regional integration. Mauritius has played a pivotal role in various regional initiatives, focusing on sustainable development, maritime security, and economic cooperation. Mauritius has also cultivated strategic partnerships beyond its immediate region, notably with India, China, the European Union, and the US. These relationships are multifaceted, encompassing trade, investment, defence, and cultural exchanges. The partnership with India, in particular, is deep-rooted, drawing on shared historical and cultural ties. The relationship with China has been growing, evident in increased Chinese investment in Mauritian infrastructure projects. Moreover, Mauritius has actively participated in the United Nations and other

[23] There have been criticisms made of the Best Loser System – in particular that it crystallises ethnic identity communalism in Mauritius, and that it has lost its relevance. These criticisms are outlined, though not necessarily agreed with, by Fessha and Ho Tu Nam (n 20) 69–75.

international forums, advocating for small island developing states' interests. It has been vocal on issues like climate change, maritime security, and sustainable development, reflecting its vulnerabilities and strengths as an island nation.

Mauritius' international relations have a strong economic dimension. The country has successfully positioned itself as a gateway for investment into Africa, leveraging its political stability and business-friendly environment. It has entered into several Free Trade Agreements and Double Taxation Avoidance Agreements, enhancing its attractiveness as an investment destination.

As a small state, reliant on outside investment and trade with the outside world, Mauritius is careful to maintain its international standing, and – as just described – to work with like-minded states to advocate for issues of shared interest. In the rest of this section, we focus on recent developments in the spheres of constitutional human rights (relating to the rights of LGBTQ+ people) and international territorial disputes (particularly relating to the Chagos Islands), and consider what they tell us about Mauritius' evolving constitutional identity as a small state.

(ii) Smallness, Constitutional Human Rights and International Standing

As a small state, Mauritius faces distinctive challenges and opportunities in embedding human rights within its constitutional framework. This sub-section explores how Mauritius has used its constitutional commitment to human rights as a mechanism to enhance its international standing and align with global norms. The key points highlighted in this section include the adaptability of Mauritius' Constitution in responding to evolving human rights standards, the integration of international human rights principles into domestic law, and the role of these commitments in shaping Mauritius' identity as a progressive and rule-of-law-based state.

In two judgments of 2023,[24] the Supreme Court of Mauritius ruled that the criminalisation of sodomy between consenting adult males was unconstitutional. In those cases,[25] the Supreme Court declared that section 250(1) of the Criminal Code was unconstitutional and violated section 16 of the Constitution (protection from discrimination) insofar as it prohibited consensual acts of sodomy between adult males in private, and must therefore be interpreted in such a way as to exclude such consensual acts from the scope of section 250(1).

In its reasoning,[26] the Supreme Court defined 'sex', for the purposes of section 16 constitutional prohibition of discrimination on the basis of sex, as including 'sexu orientation' by relying on various foreign and international cases such as the UN Huma

[24] *Ah Seek v State of Mauritius* [2023] SCJ 399 and *Fokeerbux and Others v State of Mauritius* [2023] SCJ 4
[25] On 6 September 2019, four young LGBTQ Mauritians, from different strata of Mauritian socie approached the Supreme Court of Mauritius to seek permission to apply for constitutional redress on the ba that s 250(1) of the Criminal Code Act 1838 violated their fundamental rights and freedoms and was unco stitutional. The plaintiffs, from Hindu, Christian, and Muslim backgrounds, were all members of the You Queer Alliance, a youth-led NGO dedicated to promoting the human rights of LGBTQ people in Mauriti Three of the four plaintiffs were the first public officials to have openly declared that they were homosex the fourth plaintiff was a graphic designer.
[26] See *Ah Seek v State of Mauritius* (n 24) 6–13.

Rights Committee's communication in *Toonen v Australia*,[27] the Canadian Supreme Court's decision in *Vriend v Alberta*,[28] the Belize Supreme Court's decision in *Orozco v Attorney-General of Belize*,[29] the Indian Supreme Court's decision in *Navtej Singh Johar v Union of India*[30] and the High Court of Botswana's decision in *Motshidiemang v Attorney-General*.[31] The Supreme Court reiterated that the Constitution is an evolving document and must be given a generous and teleological interpretation. Consequently, the Supreme Court held that for Mauritius – having acceded to the International Covenant on Civil and Political Rights (ICCPR) and having agreed to adhere to the international norms and standards concerning the fundamental rights and freedoms guaranteed by the ICCPR – interpreting the term 'sex' to include 'sexual orientation' in section 16 of the Constitution would be consistent with the standard canon of constitutional interpretation.[32]

This ruling is a landmark step in recognising and protecting the human rights of the LGBTQ+ community in Mauritius. In minimally populated countries where societal norms and legal systems are often tightly interwoven, such progressive legal decisions play a crucial role in advancing human rights and equality. By aligning its legal framework with international human rights treaties such as the ICCPR, Mauritius bolsters its international standing. For small states, adherence to international norms is crucial for maintaining a positive global image and for international relations. The ruling indicates a shift in societal attitudes towards greater acceptance and understanding of diversity. The Supreme Court's 2023 ruling in *Ah Seek* signifies not merely an affirmation of fundamental rights but, crucially, a judicial acknowledgment of evolving societal values toward the LGBTQ+ community in Mauritius. The decision underscores a broader, though nuanced, societal shift towards greater acceptance and recognition of sexual orientation as an aspect of individual identity deserving of legal protection. The ruling appears to embody a judicial response to an already-shifting social discourse rather than being the sole catalyst for change. Mauritius has gradually aligned itself more closely with international human rights standards, and its reliance on international precedents signals that the judiciary is increasingly sensitive to the progressive norms surrounding sexual orientation in international human rights law.

(iii) *International Issues Faced by Decolonising Small States*

Decolonising small states like Mauritius often face unique challenges as they navigate the transition to independence, particularly in reconciling their newfound sovereignty with external pressures and geopolitical realities. In Mauritius, these challenges manifest in disputes over sovereignty, the initial presence of foreign military bases at independence,

[27] *Toonen v Australia*, UN Human Rights Committee Communication No 488/1992, UN Doc CCPR//50/D/488/1992 (1994).
[28] *Vriend v Alberta* [1998] 1 SCR 493.
[29] *Orozco v Attorney-General of Belize* (no 668/2010) (2016) 90 WIR 161.
[30] *Navtej Singh Johar v Union of India* [2018] 7 SCR 379, *AIR* (2018) SC 4321.
[31] *Motshidiemang v Attorney-General* (2019) MAHGB-000591-16, https://globalfreedomofexpression.lumbia.edu/wp-content/uploads/2020/01/legabibo.pdf.
[32] ibid 17.

and the vulnerabilities posed by global geopolitical shifts. The dispute over who holds sovereignty over the Chagos Islands is a good illustration of this.[33]

The excision of the Chagos Archipelago of 60 islands, including Diego Garcia, from Mauritius prior to its independence in 1968, remains a contentious issue in international law and relations. The events surrounding this excision and the subsequent developments, including numerous court cases and an advisory opinion by the International Court of Justice (ICJ), highlight the complex interplay of geopolitics, human rights, and colonial legacies. In the early 1960s, during the decolonisation process, the UK excised the Chagos Archipelago from Mauritius, creating the British Indian Ocean Territory (BIOT), and between 1967 and 1973, expelled the native population. This move was primarily to facilitate the establishment of a military base by the US on Diego Garcia.[34] Mauritius claims this was done under duress, making it illegal under international law.

The *Bancoult* cases, spearheaded by Chagossian leader Olivier Bancoult, represented a significant legal challenge against the British Government's actions in the Chagos Archipelago. These cases are central to understanding the struggle of the Chagossians for their right to return and the broader human rights implications. The first major case, often referred to as *Bancoult (No 1)*, was initiated in 1998. Bancoult challenged the 1971 Immigration Ordinance of the BIOT which prohibited Chagossians from returning to the archipelago. In 2000, the High Court of Justice in London ruled this Ordinance illegal.[35] The decision was hailed as a significant victory for the Chagossians. However, the UK government issued a new Order in Council in 2004 to effectively overturn this decision, leading to *Bancoult (No 2)*. In 2008, the House of Lords, by a narrow majority, upheld the government's right to legislate by Order in Council, thereby preventing the return of Chagossians to their islands.[36] Bancoult also took his case to the European Court of Human Rights, which in 2012 declared the case inadmissible, stating that the matter had been resolved by British courts.[37] Despite these setbacks, Bancoult and other Chagossian activists continued to advocate for their right to return, highlighting issues of displacement, cultural erosion, and human rights.[38]

In February 2019, the ICJ delivered a landmark advisory opinion regarding the legal status of the Chagos Archipelago.[39] The opinion was requested by the United Nations General Assembly (UNGA) in 2017, seeking clarity on the legal consequences of the separation of the Chagos Archipelago from Mauritius before independence.[40] The ICJ

[33] See generally, C Monaghan, 'The fight to achieve full decolonization: Mauritius versus the Unite Kingdom' in G Baldacchino (ed), *The Success of Small States in International Relations: Mice That Roar?* (Nev York, Routledge, 2023) 148.

[34] See eg, Simmons (n 2) 172–73.

[35] *R (Bancoult) v Secretary of State for Foreign and Commonwealth Affairs* [2000] EWHC 413 (Admin [2001] QB 1067.

[36] *R (Bancoult) v Secretary of State for Foreign and Commonwealth Affairs (No 2)* [2008] UKHL 81, [200 AC 453.

[37] *Chagos Islanders v United Kingdom* App no 35622/04 (ECtHR, 11 December 2012).

[38] For a discussion of the effects of the displacement of the Chagossians as a result of the actions of th UK and the US, see generally L Jeffery, *Chagos Islanders in Mauritius and the UK: Forced Displacement a Onward Migration* (Manchester, Manchester University Press, 2011).

[39] *Legal Consequences of the Separation of the Chagos Archipelago from Mauritius in 1965 (Advisory Opinio* [2019] ICJ Rep 95 (ICJ, 25 February 2019).

[40] UNGA Res 71/292 (22 June 2017) UN Doc A/RES/71/292. The catalyst for engaging the ICJ was a comb nation of persistent Mauritian advocacy, evolving international support for decolonisation, and a growi

found that the process of decolonisation of Mauritius had not been lawfully completed when Mauritius was granted independence in 1968, as the Chagos Archipelago had been wrongfully separated from Mauritius by the UK. The ICJ stated that the UK's continued administration of the Chagos Archipelago constituted an unlawful act of a continuing character, and urged the UK to end its administration of the archipelago as rapidly as possible. The opinion placed significant international pressure on the UK, with many viewing it as a step towards rectifying a historical injustice. Though the ICJ's advisory opinions are not binding, they carry considerable moral and legal weight in international law and diplomacy.

Following the ICJ opinion, the UNGA passed a resolution affirming Mauritius' sovereignty over the Chagos Archipelago and demanding that the UK withdraw.[41] Initially, the UK and US largely resisted these international calls, citing strategic and security reasons for maintaining the military base on Diego Garcia. The African Union and Non-Aligned Movement supported Mauritius' claim, reflecting broader issues of decolonisation and sovereignty. Ultimately, in October 2024, the UK announced it would hand sovereignty over the Chagos Islands back to Mauritius following finalisation of a treaty between the two states, but the US–UK base would remain. A formal agreement on the transfer of the islands was signed by the UK Prime Minister in May 2025.[42]

The excision of Diego Garcia and the ICJ's advisory opinion are emblematic of the challenges and opportunities faced by small states in the international arena. They highlight the importance of international law, the need for historical justice, and the ability of small states to assert their rights and interests on the global stage. Small states like Mauritius can utilise international legal mechanisms, such as the ICJ or arbitration tribunals, to assert their rights and seek justice in disputes with larger, more powerful nations. These mechanisms offer a level playing-field where legal arguments, rather than power dynamics, take precedence.[43] Moreover, small states often form alliances with like-minded nations or international bodies to amplify their voices. They can draw upon shared interests, historical experiences, or thematic causes – such as decolonisation, human rights, or climate change – to gain broad-based support. These states also often command significant moral authority by presenting their claims as cases of historical injustice or systemic inequity, resonating with the broader international community. Success in such disputes can galvanise national unity and pride, strengthening a small state's internal cohesion and fostering a collective sense of identity.

Mauritius has also encountered several border disputes since independence, including a territorial dispute with France over the uninhabited island of Tromelin and a

cognition of the Chagos issue as emblematic of broader questions of historical injustice and the legitimacy f post-colonial territorial arrangements. Mauritius engaged in persistent diplomatic lobbying within the frican Union (AU), Commonwealth, and UN to secure support for its claims. By framing the separation f the Chagos Archipelago as an incomplete decolonisation process, Mauritius positioned its case within the ell-established international legal principles on self-determination and territorial integrity. This approach sonated with a wide array of states, many of which had also experienced colonial rule.

[41] UNGA Res 31/295 (22 May 2019) UN Doc A/RES/73/295.

[42] A Harding, 'UK will give sovereignty of Chagos Islands to Mauritius' *BBC* (4 October 2024), www.bbc.m/news/articles/c98ynejg4l5o; 'UK signs Chagos deal with Mauritius to seal future of US-UK air base' *uters* (22 May 2025), https://www.reuters.com/world/uk/uk-set-sign-deal-ceding-sovereignty-chagos-ands-mauritius-2025-05-22/.

[43] See discussion in Monaghan (n 33).

dispute with India over the leave and use of the two-island dependency of Agaléga. Notably, both Tromelin and Agaléga occupy strategic positions in the Indian Ocean. For Mauritius, these disputes are not only about territorial integrity but also about asserting its political position in a strategically significant region. The resolution of these issues involves navigating historical claims, international law, diplomatic negotiations, and the balancing of regional and global geopolitical interests.

As Mauritius continues to assert itself on the international stage, these border issues remain crucial elements of its foreign policy and national identity. Indeed, border disputes often serve as a unifying issue, allowing a nation to rally diverse groups around a shared cause. In Mauritius, the claim over the Chagos Archipelago has resonated across ethnic and political lines, reinforcing a sense of collective national purpose. The narrative of Mauritius as a small state overcoming colonial subjugation is central to its national identity. Its sovereignty claims over the Chagos Archipelago and Tromelin Island are framed as extensions of its decolonisation journey, making these disputes emblematic of its right to self-determination and territorial integrity. Furthermore, national identity is intrinsically tied to territorial sovereignty. The reclamation of the Chagos Archipelago has been portrayed as a moral and legal imperative that affirms Mauritius' identity as an independent and self-determined state. The Chagos Archipelago dispute is deeply embedded in the narrative of Mauritius' struggle for decolonisation. By linking the issue to the unfinished business of colonialism, Mauritius has presented itself as a small but determined nation committed to rectifying historical wrongs, a critical element of its national identity.

IV. Conclusion

To what extent can the appropriateness in relation to governance and stability and in fostering social cohesion of an independence Constitution be judged by the number and nature of post-independence amendments to the Constitution? They could be developmental changes, or they could be purely political changes. Have they been motivated by the size of the state? There is a possibility that that may have been the case, but the more obvious factors have been nation building and the strengthening of government.

The journey of Mauritius, from a small island state to a thriving democracy with an influential role in international affairs, exemplifies the unique interplay of size geopolitics, and legal governance. In the realm of international relations, Mauritiu has 'punched above its weight', leveraging its strategic location and diplomatic savvy Mauritius' involvement in international legal disputes, such as those concerning th Chagos Archipelago, has demonstrated its commitment to upholding constitutiona principles and international law, even against much larger adversaries. Mauritiu Constitution lays the legal and institutional groundwork for its international relations. establishes the principles of governance, rule of law, and human rights, which are funda mental in shaping the country's foreign policy and international commitments. For small nation, the Constitution acts as a cornerstone in its dealings with other nation showcasing its commitment to democratic values and legal standards.

The constitutional evolution of Mauritius is a testament to the island's ability adapt and grow in response to both internal and external pressures. The dynamic natu of its Constitution has allowed Mauritius to address the complexities of a small island state while laying the groundwork for a stable, prosperous, and equitable society. Thus, the experience of Mauritius offers valuable insights into how small states can navigate the complexities of modern governance and international relations.

Several other small states around the world exhibit dynamics similar to those of Mauritius, particularly in terms of constitutional governance, political structures, and the challenges of managing a small, often close-knit society. These include Seychelles, another small island nation in the Indian Ocean, which shares historical, cultural, and political similarities with Mauritius, including the challenges of managing a society within a limited geographical space. Fiji too faces challenges similar to Mauritius in terms of balancing traditional communal structures with modern democratic governance.[44] Fiji has historically grappled with tensions between Indigenous Fijians and Indo-Fijians. Its Constitutions (such as the 1997 Constitution) have attempted to balance these groups through mechanisms like communal voting systems. However, periodic coups (in 1987, 2000 and 2006) have demonstrated the fragility of these arrangements when perceived ethnic imbalances in political power arise. Unlike Mauritius and Fiji, Seychelles has a relatively homogenous Creole population, reducing the ethnic or communal dimensions of governance. Instead, its constitutional challenges have revolved around centralisation of power and political pluralism.[45] Mauritius' use of the Best Loser System shows that institutional mechanisms can provide stability and inclusivity, but they may also entrench communal identities. While Seychelles, Fiji, and Mauritius share challenges as small states, their divergent strategies illustrate the importance of tailoring governance systems to specific historical, cultural, and political contexts. Mauritius stands out for its ability to balance inclusivity, stability, and adaptability, offering lessons for other small states. The experiences of Fiji and Seychelles, however, caution against over-reliance on nstitutional mechanisms without broader efforts to foster national unity and trust. By xamining these states together, we gain valuable insights into the dynamic interplay of onstitutional governance and societal diversity in small states.

Mauritius' smallness, often perceived as a limitation, has instead been harnessed s a strength, fostering a close-knit society and a responsive governance model. The oncentration of power, typical of small states, has been counterbalanced by robust onstitutional mechanisms ensuring checks and balances, transparency, and the rotection of minority rights. The personalised nature of Mauritian politics discussed bove, stemming from its small size, has contributed to a political culture that is deeply oted in community values and direct engagement. Mauritius, with a population of proximately 1.3 million, is a quintessential small state where social, economic, and litical spheres are interconnected. This interconnectedness means that politicians d constituents often share familial, communal, or professional ties, fostering a politil culture of direct engagement and accessibility. The geographical and demographic

[44] It is worth noting that when Fiji was reconsidering its Constitution after its first military coup, it sent its nstitutional Commission on a field study to Mauritius to discuss Mauritius' Best Loser System: P Larmour, troduction' in BV Lal and P Larmour (eds), *Electoral systems in divided societies: the Fiji constitution* nberra, ANU E Press, 2012) 1, 7.

[45] See for example, discussion in J Barnes' 'Not the Usual Suspects – Executive Dominance in Seychelles and Developing Institutions that Could Counter it', Chapter 15 in this volume.

compactness of Mauritius enables citizens to engage with political figures more directly than in larger states. This fosters a sense of closeness between leaders and the electorate but can also blur the boundaries between public office and personal relationships. The Mauritian model underscores the importance of institutional mechanisms that accommodate personalisation while safeguarding against its excesses, ensuring that community values enrich rather than undermine democratic governance.

Despite the rather stark picture painted in the mid-twentieth century by Burton Benedict of Mauritius as an overpopulated country dependent on one export crop (sugar)[46] and the unflattering picture presented by VS Naipaul of Mauritius as an 'Overcrowded Barracoon',[47] Mauritius persisted in its nation-building and as an advertisement in *The Times* said in the immediate post-independence period: 'In the land of the dodo, we are up and doing'.

[46] B Benedict, *Indians in a Plural Society: A Report on Mauritius* (London, HMSO, 1961).

[47] VS Naipaul, *The Overcrowded Barracoon* (London, Andre Deutsch, 1972). A 'barracoon' was a type enclosure used for the internment of African slaves prior to transportation by ship in the Atlantic slave tra

19

A Tale of Self-Fulfilling Constitutional Failure

The Role of 'Smallness' in the Cyprus Constitutional Breakdown of 1963

CHRISTOS PAPASTYLIANOS

I. Is Cyprus a Small State?

Considering its population and territory, Cyprus is clearly a small state.[1] However, the accuracy of these criteria for determining 'smallness' has been challenged in the relevant literature. Instead of focusing on these, a growing body of literature looks for a more composite definition of smallness.[2] Such a definition focuses on two characteristics: the extent of a state's capacity to operate its political, economic and administrative systems; and its limited capacity to exercise in external relations the full range of options that such capacity entails.[3] Thus, size is linked to capability and influence.[4] Furthermore, the literature emphasises that size affects the way political affairs are run in a polity. Smallness is associated with a personalised style of politics in which intermediate institutions like political parties play a limited role. It fuels political dynamics that destruct democracy despite the formal characteristics of a political regime,[5] and often 'results in personalistic politics, polarization and victimization, disproportionate executive dominance, patron–client linkages, and particularistic forms of political participation'.[6]

[1] Cyprus has a territory of 9,251 km^2 (167th in the world in terms of area) and a population of nearly 1,000,000 people. However, since the Turkish invasion of 1974, the Republic of Cyprus has exercised effective control over only 58 per cent of the island's territory and roughly 75 per cent of the population.

[2] G Baldacchino and A Wivel, 'Small States: Concepts and Theories' in G Baldacchino and A Wivel, *Handbook on the Politics of Small States* (Cheltenham, Edward Elgar, 2020) 2, 6–7.

[3] ibid 7.

[4] C Browing, 'Small, Smart and Salient? Rethinking Identity in the Small States Literature' (2006) 19 *Cambridge Review of International Affairs* 669.

[5] WP Veenendaal, 'Democracy in Microstates: Why Smallness does not Produce a Democratic Political System' (2015) 22 *Democratization* 92, 106.

[6] ibid 106.

Another feature of small-scale societies is that there tends to be an overlapping and coincidence of roles compared with larger, more structurally differentiated societies.[7]

Cyprus exhibits most of these characteristics, although their impact on the way political affairs are run has abated since the early 1960s. Cypriot independence has been subject to extensive constitutional and treaty limitations in the form of the unamendability of the constitutional provisions that define the structure of governance, the presence of foreign troops and sovereign military bases in its territory, and the right of intervention reserved to the guarantor powers: Greece Turkey, and the United Kingdom. Formally, Cyprus is an independent state but as Costas Constantinou has observed, it is in fact an 'in-dependent' state.[8] Certain constitutional provisions (see below, section IV) left major issues related to the administrative structure of Cyprus, such as the collection of taxes and the running of municipalities, open to negotiations between the two communities, thus impairing the state's capacity to fully operate its economic and administrative system. Furthermore, the administration of justice has been provided either by hybrid courts or by courts the composition of which was based on defined ethnic quotas of judges, depending on the nationality of the litigants (Article 159 of the Constitution).[9]

In light of all this, the Republic of Cyprus has never fully possessed the autonomy and authority to make decisions independently that are hallmarks of a formally independent state, since other states were legally able to infiltrate (directly or indirectly) certain sectors of state operation.[10] The formal transfer of power through the independence Act of the British Parliament (Cyprus Act 1960 section 1, which authorised the Queen to issue an Order in Council that would bring the Cypriot Constitution into force) did not preclude the dominion of other states over Cyprus' territory and sovereignty (internal or external).[11]

Although the traditional 'motherlands' (Greece and Turkey) have abandoned their respective discourses of unification or partition, and Cyprus' accession to the EU has bolstered Cypriot statehood and sovereignty,[12] subsequent plans to settle the Cyprus

[7] J Richards, 'Politics in Small Independent Communities: Conflict or Consensus' (1982) 20 *The Journal o* *Commonwealth and Comparative Politics* 155, 157. Cyprus is an exemplar of such features, especially in the early '60s. Archbishop Makarios maintained both his religious and political office from 1960 until his death in 1977, as he was concurrently the Head of the Orthodox Church and the Head of the state.

[8] CM Constantinou, 'Cypriot In-dependence and the Problem of Sovereignty' (2010) 22 *The Cypru* *Review* 17.

[9] Hybrid courts are courts in which foreign nationals serve as judges. On the composition of th Constitutional and the Supreme Court of Cyprus under the 1960 Constitution, see n 38 below. On hybri courts generally, see R Dixon and V Jackson, 'Hybrid Courts: Foreign Judges on National Constitutiona Courts' (2019) 57 *Columbia Journal of Transnational Law* 283.

[10] Constantinou (n 8) 20–21.

[11] James Crawford considers Cyprus an example reminiscent of internationalised territories, ie territori that constitute autonomous entities under a form of international protection, supervision or guarantee. Eve if Cyprus is an independent state and not an internationalised territory, the Constitution and treaty limit tions introduce a form of dependent sovereignty that shares elements with the status of internationalis territories. See J Crawford, *The Creation of States in International Law*, 2nd edn (Oxford University Pres Oxford, 2011) 241–44.

[12] In terms of offering security and a framework for re-unification, and especially of its recognition as unitary state by international actors, since the recognition of the Turkish–Cypriot entity as a state wou certainly impact relations between the EU and the recognising state: see JK Linsday, 'Shifting Alignments: T External Orientations of Cyprus Since Independence' (2010) 22 *Cyprus Review* 67 72–73.

question nevertheless leave intact the role of the guarantor powers and the ethnic segregation between the two communities.[13] There are still different perceptions between the communities about the form of the state that will be established after an agreement (unitary but federal or confederal) and the role of the guarantor powers.

Thus, among the factors which led to the 1963 constitutional breakdown was one of the main characteristics of small states: their limited capacity to act as fully sovereign states. In Cyprus, from the very beginning, crucial issues related to the constitutional design and the form of government were not decided by the local agents. The following analysis will show that there were also other factors, similarly characteristic of small states, such as the personification of politics, which hastened the breakdown, but that these were not the primary cause of it. The 'externality' of the constitution-making and amendment process not only caused a legitimacy deficit to the Constitution; it entirely subordinated the structure of governance the Constitution provided for to foreign powers, namely the two motherlands, Greece and Turkey.

Nevertheless, we should consider that the current situation presents a rather different picture from that of the early years of independence when, due to the lack of organised political parties, each community seemed to reflect its own perception about what a viable solution to the co-existence of the two communities in a unified state could be.[14]

Since 'smallness' in the Cypriot case severely impacted the constitutional breakdown, the analysis will be limited to the first three years of independence. After the withdrawal of all Turkish-Cypriot officials from their offices in December 1963 and the inability of state organs to function, the constitutional provisions which provide for the bi-communal structure of governance were suspended. According to the doctrine of necessity, which was first implemented by the Supreme Court in the *Ibrahim* case,[15] the provisions which provided for the bi-communal structure of Parliament were sidelined, thus enabling Parliament to enact laws by simple majority of the members who belonged to the Greek-Cypriot community.[16]

Furthermore, the role of external powers (the guarantor powers) and the personalisation of politics – characteristics of 'smallness' – have tapered since 1963. Since the events of July 1974 (a coup d'état backed by the Greek Junta and the subsequent Turkish military intervention, resulting in de facto Turkish control of 37 per cent of Cypriot

[13] VK Fouskas, 'The Realism of Utopia: Towards an Anti-Nationalist Critique of Imperial Policy in Cyprus' (2010) 22 *Cyprus Review* 75, 83–84.

[14] However, it is worth noting that until 1973, within the Greek community there were various groups that exercised covert forms of politics, but which remained unable to challenge the politics expressed by President/ Archbishop Makarios and his political allies, including AKEL (the communist party). The main characteristic of such politics was the emphasis on Cypriot independence instead of unification with Greece or partition of the island. However, their perception about this principle also encompassed the exclusion of power-sharing as a system of governance because they considered the principle of majority rule a detriment to self-determination. However, the Cypriot case is not unique. In small societies, conformity very often co-exists with what can be at times a very deep factionalism see, eg: Richards (n 7) 170. The peculiarity of Cyprus is that for each community the outside world encompasses not only external powers but also the other community and the 'motherland' affiliated with that community.

[15] *Attorney General of the Republic v Ibrahim* [1964] CLR 195.

[16] In subsequent rulings, the Supreme Court would go on to extend the suspension to all constitutional provisions which provide for the bi-communal composition of key state organs. For a discussion of the doctrine of necessity see: C Kombos, *The Doctrine of Necessity in Constitutional Law* (Athens, Sakkoulas Publications, 2015) 151–239.

territory), all efforts towards a new constitutional settlement between the two communities rely on bilateral negotiations under the auspices of the UN.[17] Additionally, as mentioned above, the establishment of political parties and the infrastructures of civil society lessened the single-minded self-perception of each community.

II. Historical Background[18]

The bi-communal structure of the Republic of Cyprus was designed by the signatories to the Zurich Agreement, which is cited in Article 182(1) of the Cypriot Constitution. This Agreement was negotiated by the governments of Greece and Turkey in December 1958 and January 1959, during a series of top-secret meetings and diplomatic exchanges between the respective Ministers of Foreign Affairs.[19] The negotiations were predicated upon the intention of the two governments to support the establishment of a formally independent state of Cyprus, precluding both *Enosis* (the union of the island with Greece), and *Taksim* (the partition of the island).

Greece and Turkey, with the consent of the UK, finally reached an agreement that excluded *Enosis* or partition, and provided for independence. Nevertheless, the Greek-Cypriot community continued to harbour a pro-*Enosis*, anti-independence sentiment, which continued to influence the political landscape.[20] Indeed, in the first presidential elections, the pro-*Enosis* political forces which were cordially anti-communists established a contradictory alliance with AKEL (the communist party) and stood by a common delegate against the future President Makarios, who gained almost 33 per cent of the Greek-Cypriot vote.

The bargaining which gave birth to the Republic of Cyprus was concluded under conditions of secrecy – no official records were kept – at the Zurich summit of 5–11 February 1959, where Prime Ministers Konstantinos Karamanlis and Adnan Menderes approved the documents of the Zurich Agreement.[21] The first of these,

[17] Two additional factors reduced the role of external powers. First, as the events between 1964 and 197 have shown, *all three guarantor powers failed to discharge the obligations they had undertaken* under the guar antee treaty they had signed. Second, the accession of Cyprus to the EU enabled EU involvement in th negotiations, even in the pre-accession stage. Furthermore, UNSC Resolution 367 (12 March 1975) UN Do S/RES/367, stated that intercommunal negotiations under the auspices of the UN General Secretary wer recognised as the only legitimate process of negotiations. While the guarantor powers have ceased to be exter nal agents in the resolution of the conflict since 1975, this has not eliminated the presence of external agent as such.

[18] For a very succinct and balanced introduction to the Greek-Turkish conflict over Cyprus, see e GD Camp, 'The Greek-Turkish Conflict over Cyprus' (1980) 95(1) *Political Science Quarterly* 43.

[19] For a detailed account, see SG Xydis, *Cyprus: The Reluctant Republic* (Berlin, De Gruyter, 1973) 342–5 359–85, 388–408. See also R Holland, *Britain and the Revolt in Cyprus, 1954–1959*, (Oxford, Clarendon Pres 1999) 293–305; A Suat Bilge, *Le Conflict De Chypre et les Cypriotes Turks* (Ankara, Ajans-Türk Matbaas 1961) 247–51.

[20] On EOKA's (EOKA, National Organisation of Cypriot Combatants) struggle, see Holland (n 19). C the issue of separate municipalities, see D Weston Markides, *Cyprus 1957–1963, From Colonial Conflict Constitutional Crisis: The Key Role of the Municipal Issue* (Minneapolis MN, Minnesota University Pre 2001).

[21] The original documents of the Zurich Agreement were drafted in French. They are reprinted in S Soulic *Fettered Independence – Cyprus, 1878–1964, Volume 2: The Documents* (Minneapolis MN, Minnes University Press, 2006) 225–33.

entitled '*Structure de base de la République de Chypre*', prescribed in great detail the bi-communal structure of the nascent state and stipulated that all the points therein would become basic and thus unamendable articles of the Constitution.[22] The second was a draft Treaty of Guarantee between Cyprus, on the one hand, and Greece, the UK and Turkey, on the other.[23] Under this treaty, the Republic of Cyprus undertook 'to ensure the maintenance of its independence, territorial integrity and security, as well as respect for its Constitution'.[24] The Republic also undertook 'not to participate, in whole or in part, in any political or economic union with any State whatsoever', and with this intent, to prohibit 'all activity likely to promote, directly or indirectly, either union with any other State or partition of the Island'.[25] Pursuant to Article II of the Treaty of Guarantee, the three external powers guaranteed not only the independence, territorial integrity and security of the Republic of Cyprus, but also 'the state of affairs established by the basic articles of its Constitution'.[26] Furthermore, Article IV of the Treaty stipulated that, 'in the event of a breach of its provisions', the three external powers would 'consult together with respect to the representation or measures necessary to ensure observance' of the provisions of the Treaty.[27] Besides, 'in so far as common or concerted action may not prove possible', each of the three powers reserved 'the right to take action with the sole aim of re-establishing the state of affairs created by the present Treaty'.[28] Another component of the Zurich Agreement was the Treaty of Alliance between Cyprus, Greece and Turkey.[29] Both the Treaty of Guarantee and the Treaty of Alliance are accorded constitutional status.[30]

A few days after the Zurich Agreement, the documents that compose it were approved by the UK government and by the leaders of the two Cypriot communities, Archbishop Makarios and Dr Fazil Küçük respectively, at the Lancaster House Conference in London.[31] The signatories to the London Agreement assigned the drafting of the Constitution to a Joint Constitutional Commission consisting of four members – representatives of Greece, Turkey, and the two Cypriot communities – each heading a delegation composed of a small number of experts.[32] Although its work proved arduous, in no way could the Joint Commission be compared to a constituent assembly, not least

22 Point 27 in conjunction with point 7.
23 Treaty of Guarantee (signed 16 August 1960) 382 UNTS 3.
24 ibid art 1.
25 ibid.
26 ibid art 2. When the British Foreign Secretary inquired about the precise meaning of this, the Greek and the Turkish Ministers of Foreign Affairs confirmed that the term 'basic articles' referred to the provisions set out in the document that prescribed the basic structure of the Republic of Cyprus. The record of this meeting is reproduced in Soulioti (n 21) 235–40, 236.
27 Including those which provide for the basic structure of the Constitution, see Treaty of Guarantee (n 23) 4.
28 ibid.
29 Treaty of Alliance (with Additional Protocols) (signed 16 August 1960) 397 UNTS 287.
30 Constitution of Cyprus, art 181.
31 'Conference on Cyprus: Signed and Initialled at Lancaster House on February 19, 1959', reproduced in Soulioti (n 21) 218–21.
32 For a brief introduction to the drafting process, see TW Adams, 'The First Republic of Cyprus: A Review of an Unworkable Costitution' (1966) 19 *The Western Politics Quarterly* 475, 475–76.

because – as was agreed in London – its competence was strictly limited to scrupulously observing the points contained in the documents of the Zurich Conference.[33]

The Cypriot conflict, and the constitution-making process which can be viewed as a post-conflict constitution-making process, exhibited certain features which Hanna Lerner ascribes to deeply divided societies. First, the conflict could be described as an 'ideational dispute that touched upon citizens' deepest beliefs and commitments'; and, as it turned out, this dispute could not 'be taken off the political agenda'.[34] However, the 'ideational' element in the dispute was not centred on particular political or other philosophies embedded in different values. Instead, it was different perceptions of the constitutive features of the nascent state – a truly independent and unitary, even if bi-communal, state favoured by Greece and for Greek Cypriots; a partnership state which could also be taken as a functional federation, made up of two separate national entities whose policies should be aligned with the national interests of the two motherlands favoured by Turkey and for the Turkish Cypriots.

III. The Basic Structure of the Cypriot Constitution

The establishment of a constitution in a divided society serves a dual function. The constitution creates institutions and procedures that allow or prevent decision-making by the organs of the state like any other constitution (regulatory function). However, in deeply divided societies this dimension serves a different purpose. While in the constitutions of non-divided societies the permissive and deterrent rules of decision-making are intended to allow the organs of one power to prevent excesses/ abuses by the organs of another power, in those of divided societies the purpose of the corresponding rules is to prevent excesses/ abuses of the state organs controlled by one community at the expense of the organs controlled by the other communities. In other words, the purpose is to prevent the majority community from exploiting its demographic dominance to achieve political dominance over the other communities. At the same time, the constitution of a divided society must also perform a constitutive function. It creates th conditions for the development of a political identity, which, by surpassing individua ethnic, linguistic or religious identities, allows the established constitutional order t operate smoothly.[35] The constitution of these states must contribute to both the legit macy and the stability of the constitutional order.[36] The constitutions of deeply divide societies are usually the result of negotiations after war or civil conflict and aim promote the stability and durability of state institutions by negotiating for the distrib tion of power between formerly belligerent communities. The negotiations reflected

[33] This was stipulated by para 2 of the 'Agreed Measures to Prepare for the New Arrangements in Cypr one of the documents signed at Lancaster House (reproduced in Soulioti (n 21) 221–22).

[34] H Lerner, *Making Constitutions in Deeply Divided Societies* (Cambridge, Cambridge University Pre 2013) 38.

[35] S Choudhry, 'Bridging comparative politics and comparative constitutional law: Constitutio design for divided societies' in S Choudhry (ed), *Constitutional Design for Divided Societies: Integration Accommodation?* (Oxford, Oxford University Press, 2008) 5–6.

[36] ibid 6.

the constitution are intended to prevent an abusive use of majority rule that would hold the minority communities 'hostage' to the disposition of the demographically dominant community.[37] Lack of inter-communal trust renders ineffective the conflict-resolution mechanisms charged with fostering conditions of stability and trust towards the institutions, such as the judiciary, which perform this role in non-divided states with relative success.[38] Nor is the enshrinement of a list of rights through the constitution sufficient to create conditions for overcoming partiality and creating a framework for resolving conflicts by reference to claims of a universal nature.[39] In deeply divided societies individual self-determination is synonymous with the collective self-determination of the group to which the individual belongs.[40] Without the achievement of collective self-determination and its accompanying guarantees (arrangements for the distribution of political power), individual self-determination is unattainable. The collective dimension of self-determination is a concept that attributes to communities an intrinsic value separate from the individuals who compose them and therefore considers communities as actors with a distinct status, which requires the protection not only of their members, but of communities themselves, from arbitrary acts of political power.[41]

Constitutions of deeply divided societies have two main hallmarks: (a) the sharing of power between the constituent peoples/ communities that constitute the peoplehood of the state; and (b) the level of autonomy of the peoples/ communities.[42] The constitutional structure of a deeply divided society aims to achieve legitimacy and stability based on these characteristics. However, the fulfilment of the associated objectives does not require only a single, exclusive model of constitutional structure but instead may be achieved through a number of different models. A key distinction is between models that promote the self-determination of communities and those that take for granted the predetermination of communities by specific identities. It is evident from the provisions

[37] ibid 18.

[38] For this reason, in divided societies the Supreme Courts are often constituted either according to specific quotas between representatives of the various communities, or by persons not belonging to the communities, or by a combination of both. See further: S Choudhry and R Stacey, 'Independent or Dependent? Constitutional Courts in Divided Societies' in C Harvey and A Schwartz (eds), *Rights in Divided Societies* (Oxford, Hart Publishing, 2012) 87–123.

The Constitutional Court and Supreme Court of Cyprus established by the 1960 Constitution were constituted as follows: (a) the Constitutional Court was composed of three judges, two of whom belonged to each of the two communities while the third was neutral; and (b) the Supreme Court was composed of four judges: two Greek Cypriots, one Turkish Cypriot and one neutral judge. Cases beyond the jurisdiction of the Supreme and the Constitutional Court were heard only by courts composed of members of each community separately, if the parties belonged to the same community, or by courts composed of judges from both communities if persons from both communities were involved in the dispute to be settled (Constitution of Cyprus, art 159).

[39] This is for two main reasons: (a) the violation of rights and its review by authorities constitutes a form of persistent review of acts or omissions that may affect minority demographic groups; and (b) an important part of this review is based on the way in which courts interpret abstract concepts in the specific context, which is charged by established relations between communities, and therefore the recipients of judicial decisions have no confidence that these interpretations are impartial and not biased by the communal background of the judges, see, eg Choudhry (n 35) 11, and Choudhry and Stacey (n 38) 88–89.

[40] S Tierney, 'Rights v Democracy' in C Harvey and A Schwartz (eds), *Rights in Divided Societies* (Oxford, Hart Publishing, 2012) 11, 16.

[41] P Jones, 'Group Rights and Group Oppression' (1999) 7 *The Journal of Political Philosophy* 353, 363.

[42] See especially: A Lijphart, 'Constitutional Design for Divided Societies' in A Lijphart, *Thinking about Democracy* (London, Routledge, 2008) 75, 75–76.

concerning the composition of the state bodies that the 1960 Cypriot Constitution provided for the latter model.

The 1960 Constitution establishes the Cypriot state according to the bi-communal model with full power-sharing between the two communities (Greek Cypriots and Turkish Cypriots). Notably, the Constitution completely omits the concept of people from its text. The citizens of Cyprus are not members of the Cypriot people, but members of two separate communities (Greek and Turkish), to which they belong according to certain criteria, such as descent, language, cultural traditions and religion. Citizens who could not be affiliated with one of the two communities according to the above criteria were invited to choose individually which community they would join. This dual structure is also followed in determining the executive bodies (President from the Greek community, Vice-President from the Turkish community), and their powers were distinguished between those exercised jointly and those exercised exclusively by each of them individually (see Articles 47–49 of the Constitution). As regards the Council of Ministers, its composition is determined by a specific ratio between the Ministers belonging to the two groups (7:3). This dual structure is also evident in the legislative function, as MPs are elected only by the members of their respective communities. The Constitution also makes similar provisions regarding the composition of other basic state organs, such as the Supreme and Constitutional Courts, and the staffing of the positions of Attorney-General, Auditor-General, Governor of the Central Bank and their assistants. In all cases, the assistants must belong to a different community from that to which the head belongs. Quotas also exist for the composition of the public service (7:3). This is a model of constitutional state structure which takes the identities of the two communities for granted and is limited to a conciliatory distribution of power between the two groups to ensure stability. It does not, however, provide the means to transcend these identities. As such, the Constitution has remained 'incomplete' in its constitutive function, failing to establish a new common identity.

Furthermore, the 1960 Constitution of Cyprus contains 31 articles blocking decisions or processes without both communities' consent. Sixteen of these provisions give veto power to officers from each community, and the remaining ones require the involvement of members from both communities in decision-making or process completion. These provisions apply to the composition of almost all state bodies.

The Cypriot Constitution is a typical example of constitutional design in deeply divided societies. Such societies are understood as those in which ethnic, religious, or linguistic identities dominate political identity, resulting in political conflicts determined not by political divisions between political subjects but by the subjects' integration in a group with ethnic, linguistic, or religious characteristics.[43] For a state to be considered divided, such identities must be the determining factor in the political mobilisation and identity formation of the politically active agents (political parties, trade unions, political associations).[44]

[43] Choudhry (n 35) 3–5.
[44] ibid 9.

IV. The Inability of Parliament to Enact Organic Laws[45] and The Collapse of the Constitutional Order

The inability of the two communities to cooperate reveals the lack of trust between the two communities in three main issues: the creation of separate municipalities for Turkish Cypriots; the establishment of the Cypriot military; and the composition of the civil service based on the quotas provided for in the Constitution (70:30). The corollary was that three fundamental articles of the Constitution (Articles 173(1), 129 and 78(2)) were dead letters from the outset. They were not implemented because their implementation required the cooperation of the two communities: something that was desirable under the Constitution but not possible in practice.

Soon, however, the lack of cooperation of both communities, which was required for the enactment of the relevant laws, led to a type-three constitutional crisis. Such a constitutional crisis occurs when each side claims that the opponents are violating the constitution and the dispute between the two sides goes beyond the limits set by the constitution for resolving disagreements. Each side becomes willing to resort to means that overstep the bounds of political disagreement and attempt to eliminate the opponent.[46] In Cyprus, the failure to implement the constitutional requirement for quotas in the composition of the civil service (70:30) resulted in marked disagreement between the two communities.[47] A heated dispute over the application of a constitutional provision in which each side accused the other of practices that were contrary to the Constitution (composition of the civil service) led to the non-application of another constitutional provision through the non-cooperation of the two communities in passing tax laws, ie the Turkish Cypriots refused to vote on a number of bills related to the imposition of taxes, which according to Article 78(2) of the Constitution required separate majority votes from both communities.[48]

The second case in which a constitutional provision was rendered ineffective by lack of cooperation between the two communities is the provision concerning the establishment of the military (Article 129 of the Constitution). This provision did not provide for how the armed forces were to be constituted but only their composition (2,000 men, 60 per cent Greek Cypriots and 40 per cent Turkish Cypriots). The two communities had conflicting views on the issue because of different pre-conceptions about the role of the military. For the Turkish Cypriots, it was a means of securing the guarantees of the bi-communal structure, while the Greek Cypriots viewed it as a threat to the unity of the state, as 40 per cent of its personnel would be composed of members of a community

[45] Laws the enactment of which is provided for by the Constitution and which specify, complete or apply the constitutional provisions.

[46] On the characteristics of a type-three constitutional crisis, see especially S Levinson and JM Balkin, 'Constitutional Crises' (2009) 157 *University of Pennsylvania Law Review* 707, 739–40.

[47] The issue was resolved with the adoption of tax laws by the two communities separately in accordance with art 87(1)(f) of the Constitution, which states that each community assembly may pass taxes and levies on the members of the respective community for the purpose of serving the needs of the members of each community. These laws were found to be in conformity with the Constitution by the Constitutional Court. See further AC Emilianides, *Beyond the Constitution of Cyprus* (Athens, Sakkoulas Publications, 2006) 74–80.

[48] ibid 79.

which, during the anti-colonial struggle, had staffed the forces of repression and had supported partition as a solution.[49]

The third issue of disagreement between the two communities concerned the establishment of separate municipalities for Turkish Cypriots. Article 173 of the Constitution envisaged the establishment of separate municipalities for Turkish Cypriots in the five largest cities of Cyprus, on the condition that the decision would be reviewed jointly by the President and the Vice-President within four years from the entry into force of the Constitution. However, Article 78(2) of the Constitution required separate majorities to enact laws on the creation of municipalities, while the transitional provisions of Article 188 stipulated that the pre-existing provisions of the Constitution on municipalities would expire on 15 February 1961. This expiration date was eventually extended to 31 December 1962. However, a second attempt by the Turkish-Cypriot MPs to extend the validity of the laws for an additional year was voted down by the Greek-Cypriot MPs and, in light of the separate majority requirement of Article 78(2), no decision was reached. The Greek-Cypriot MPs refused to vote for the relevant proposal based upon arguments about the interpretation of Article 173(1) and, in particular, whether the establishment of separate municipalities was compulsory or optional. Similarly, the Turkish-Cypriot MPs who tabled the proposal for a law to extend the validity of the previous laws referred to the need for a solution that would not undermine the constitutional order.[50]

The case of the separate municipalities is typical of how the operation of a constitution may be undermined by its own design. Many constitutions contain clauses which entrust the legislator with the regulation of matters that could have been regulated by the constitution. This is partly because, in designing a constitution, existing 'passions' may render decision-making on a given issue impossible.[51] Entrusting the legislature with the relevant regulation is intended to give the parties involved the opportunity to decide calmly in the future. However, this option can only be effective if there are no factors that prevent strategic behaviour of the actors involved in the legislative process.

The fierce disagreement between the two communities also caused collateral damage: the President of the Constitutional Court resigned, since he realised that the Constitutional Court could no longer be considered a neutral mediator by the two communities and as such could not function. In November 1963, President Makarios submitted a 13-point proposal for the revision of the Constitution, the adoption of which would have significantly changed the structure of the system of government, with the elimination of most of the power-sharing elements. Turkish-Cypriot Vice-President Küçük refused to discuss the proposal[52] and Turkey threatened to intervene if the proposal was implemented unilaterally by the Greek Cypriots. Meanwhile, riots broke out in December 1963 with hundreds of casualties on both sides, and in the last 10 days of December Turkish-Cypriot officials resigned from all state institutions. Subsequently

[49] ibid 79.

[50] S Soulioti, *Fettered Independence – Cyprus, 1878–1964, Volume 1: The Narrative* (Minneapolis MN, Minnesota University Press, 2006) 180.

[51] R Dixon and T Ginsburg, 'Deciding not to Decide: Deferral in Constitutional Design' (2011) *International Journal of Constitutional Law* 636, 638.

[52] Turkish Vice-President Küçük stated in his reply that the Greek Cypriots had not applied the pro-Turkish Cypriot provisions of the Constitution until then.

in January 1964, the Turkish-Cypriot Vice-President and MPs declared that they did not recognise the legitimacy of the Cypriot government, and many Turkish Cypriots who were serving in public services or the police stopped coming to work.[53] Thus, all state organs which, according to the Constitution, should have a bicommunal composition could not operate any longer.

V. State Size and Constitutional Breakdown in Cyprus

The crucial question for this chapter is whether the smallness of the Cypriot state affected the outbreak of the crises which led to the constitutional breakdown. The above analysis demonstrates that the drafting of the Cypriot Constitution, its inherent resistance to change via amendment, and the lack of cooperation between the two communities, rendered it completely inapplicable. If we take into account that the constitutional design did not provide any incentives for the cooperation of the two communities, and the change of the Constitution presupposed in fact the consent of external actors, then the constitutional breakdown could be considered a self-fulfilling prophecy. In this section I examine the contingent influence of smallness upon these factors.

A. The Drafting of the Cypriot Constitution

The negotiations which led to the agreement and the drafting of the Constitution were he outcome of an elite-driven process. As already mentioned, the leaders of both ommunities were each accompanied by a group of consultants with whom they deliberated before signing the agreement. These consultants were not representatives elected y the people of the two communities, but instead were appointed by the leaders of the ommunities: Archbishop Makarios and Dr Küçük. The drafting of the Constitution as also the outcome of an elite-driven process. As described above, the signatoies to the London Agreement assigned the drafting of the Constitution to a Joint onstitutional Commission consisting of four members, representatives of Greece, urkey, and the two Cypriot communities, each heading a delegation composed of a nall number of experts, mostly lawyers and/ or politicians. Furthermore, the members f the joint commission had been appointed by the leaders of the Greek-Cypriot and urkish-Cypriot communities.

Notwithstanding the composition of the Joint Constitutional Commission which afted the Constitution, and despite the fact that the Constitution was not the product a constituent assembly, the process followed was nevertheless constituent, at least as as the parts of the Constitution which were drafted originally by the joint commit-, are concerned. However, the consent of the two communities to the Constitution nnot be disputed given that Makarios and Küçük signed the Agreements in London their capacities as leaders of the respective communities, and that in Nicosia, on lependence Day, they signed the Agreements, as well as the Constitution, acting in

Soulioti (n 50) 316–84.

concert under the heading 'Republic of Cyprus'.[54] However, ex-post consensus cannot replace a lack of public participation during the drafting process. The relevant literature notes that some sort of local ownership and self-enforcement of the new constitutional settlement is necessary for its endurance in the long run. A constitution may only play its enabling role – by establishing devices which enable reflection, deliberation and collective learning – to the degree that it is a self-binding mechanism.[55]

Thus, Cyprus may be considered a case of a small state the population of which, regardless of size, had no participatory or inclusive impact on the constitution-making process. Instead, other variables common to small states affected the character of the process.[56] Among these factors in the Cypriot case are elite stewardship and ethnic/religious heterogeneity.[57] One of the forms through which political elites can influence the outcome of a constitution-making process is consultation. However, consultation can take the form of a top-down input to the drafting process, which reflects not the participation of single individuals whose representatives are the consultants, but the community as a whole.[58] Consultation in such cases is not part of a deliberative process; rather the representatives of the people play only an informative role.[59] Another variable related to the constitution-making process in some small states and relevant to the Cypriot case is ethnic and religious heterogeneity.[60] The lack of a common sense of belonging or of a common vision for the future among the ethnic and religious groups in a small state, if they dominate the constitution-making process, would hinder the efforts of the drafters to create a functional constitution.[61]

Both variables are present in the Cypriot case. As for the former, the island had been home to two distinct communities since the early twentieth century. Throughout the first half of that century, they remained distinct in many respects: religion

[54] See 'Photocopies of Signatures to the Treaties and Other Documents Signed on 16 August 1960, excep[t] for the Treaty of Guarantee and the Statements and Exchanges of Notes', reproduced in Soulioti (n 21) 30[7]. The Cypriot case indicates that there is a spectrum between heteronomous and autochthonous constitution[-] making processes, since imposition does not always imply the alienation of the people who will be th[e] addressees of the Constitution: R Albert, 'Constitutions imposed with Consent?' in R Albert, X Contiades an[d] A Fotiadou (eds), *The Law and Legitimacy of imposed Constitutions* (London, Routledge, 2020) 103. It is wort[h] pointing out, as Albert notes at 119 of the chapter, that in such cases the imposition is the outcome of the loc[al] actors' reluctance to agree on the terms of an autochthonous constitution-making process.

[55] U Preuss, 'Perspectives on Post-Conflict Constitutionalism: Reflections on Regime Change throu[gh] External Constitutionalisation' (2006–07) 51(3) *New York Law School Law Review* 467, 472.

[56] On such variables, see M De Visser and E Perham, 'Variables shaping participatory constitution makin[g]: Insights from the experiences of small states' (2022) 20 *International Journal of Constitutional Law* 1216.

[57] ibid 1238–40, 1242–43.

[58] The highly personalised form that politics assume in small states is a variable which complica[tes] immensely the distinction between individual and community. On the personalisation of politics in sm[all] states see, eg D Peters, *The Democratic System of Eastern Caribbean* (Westport CT, Greenwood Press, 19[9…]) 38–40, W Veenendaal and J Corbett, 'Clientelism in Small States: How Smallness Influences Patron-Cli[ent] Networks in the Caribbean and the Pacific' (2020) 27 *Democratization* 61, 68–71. President/ Archbish[op] Makarios is a salient example of the personalisation of politics in Cyprus: according to the relevant literatu[re] he allegedly knew one-third of Greek Cypriots by their first names and acted as a mediator even in dispu[tes] not normally handled by a leader of a state, such as disputes between two soccer clubs over the outcom[e of] a match or family disputes: K Markides, *The Rise and the Fall of the Cyprus Republic* (New Haven CT, Y[ale] University Press, 1977) 44–45.

[59] De Visser and Perham (n 56) 1239.

[60] ibid 1242.

[61] ibid 1242.

educational systems, languages, laws and customs regarding personal status, the rarity of intermarriage,[62] and, finally, their very strong emotional ties with the two 'motherlands', Greece and Turkey. The crystallisation of national identities took place in the larger context of the modernisation process. In Cyprus this manifested through the emergence of a Greek-Cypriot urban elite who promoted the cause of *Enosis*;[63] through 'the rise to prominence of young intellectuals in Nicosia who took their cue from New Turkey and opposed the traditional religious and collaborationist elite';[64] through the unequal spread of the growth in income and in property ownership;[65] and, on a deeper level, through the development of diverging attitudes towards the issue of moral and material progress.[66] As for the latter, the division of Cypriot society into two communities reflected the features of the drafting process. The most fascinating feature of the Joint Constitutional Commission was, of course, its Zurich straitjacket, ie the obligation of the drafters of the Constitution to abide strictly by certain points agreed upon in Zurich. Thus, one could speak of a two-track constitution-making process, with the second being subordinate to the first. The drafting of the Constitution remained a difficult and markedly complex task. This was so not only because there were still important issues to be settled apart from the Zurich points, such as the problem of how community members would be defined,[67] or the list of fundamental rights,[68] but also because adhering to the Zurich points while elaborating on them so as to establish functional institutions and understandable provisions turned out to be a very complex exercise. This was all the more so because decisions had to be made unanimously; that is, all four parties – Greece, Turkey, and the Greek Cypriot and Turkish-Cypriot communities – had to agree on each and every constitutional provision, which also had to be compatible not only with the letter but also with the spirit of the Zurich Agreement.[69]

[62] On this issue see, eg J Asmussen, 'Life and Strife in Mixed Villages: Some Aspects of Inter-Ethnic Relations in Cyprus under British Rule' in E Solomou and H Faustmann (eds), *Colonial Cyprus: Selected Readings*, vol 2 (Nicosia, University of Nicosia Publishing, 2010) 335, 337–39.

[63] See, eg J Choisi, 'The Greek Cypriot Elite – Its Social Function and Legitimization' in E Solomou and H Faustmann (eds), *Colonial Cyprus: Selected Readings*, vol 2 (Nicosia, University of Nicosia Publishing, 2010) 301.

[64] N Kızılyürek and R Denktaş, 'Fear and Nationalism in the Turkish Cypriot Community' in A Aktar, N Kızılyürek and U Özkırımlı, *Nationalism in the Troubled Triangle: Cyprus, Greece and Turkey* (Basingstoke, Palgrave Macmillan, 2010) 175, 177. See also E Apeyitou, 'Turkish Cypriot Nationalism: Its History and Development (1571–1960)' in E Solomou and H Faustmann (eds), *Colonial Cyprus: Selected Readings*, vol 2 (Nicosia, University of Nicosia Publishing, 2010); J Choisi, 'The Turkish Cypriot Elite – its Social Function and Legitimisation' in E Solomou and H Faustmann (eds), *Colonial Cyprus: Selected Readings*, vol 2 (Nicosia, University of Nicosia Publishing, 2010).

[65] See Holland (n 19) and Markides (n 20).

[66] R Bryant, 'On the Condition of Postcoloniality in Cyprus' in Y Papadakis, N Peristianis and G Welz (eds), *Divided Cyprus: Modernity, History and an Island in Conflict* (Bloomington IN, Indiana University Press, 2006) 47.

[67] On the handling of this issue by the Joint Commission, see Xydis (n 19) 490–92.

[68] The Declaration of the Government of the UK whereby it accepted the Zurich and London Agreements required that provision be made 'for the protection of the fundamental human rights of the various communities on Cyprus'. See 'Conference on Cyprus', as reproduced in Soulioti (n 21) 219.

[69] Thus, the issue of the criteria that would determine the composition of the two communities, combined with the presence of small minorities of Armenians, Latins (Catholics) and Maronites on the island, was tied up with Turkish-Cypriot insistence on securing their status as one of the two – and only – communities which would participate in the sharing of political power. The other minorities were eventually titled 'religious groups'. See Xydis (n 19) 492.

The drafting of the Cypriot Constitution thus resembles cases in which the small size of the country acted as an obstacle to, and not as a vehicle for, more participatory forms of constitution-making due to ethnic and religious heterogeneity and the peculiarities of elite stewardship. Furthermore, the constitutional design did not address the fragmentation between the two communities. Additionally, the lack of mechanisms that would prevent the strategic action of constitutional actors[70] created a context which allowed factors related to the smallness of Cyprus, such as those discussed below (in sections V.B. and C.) to catalyse the constitutional breakdown.

B. Limited Capacity of Small States to Act as Fully Sovereign States

Another common aspect of small states relevant to the Cypriot case is their limited capacity to self-define in relation to external forces. In this respect, they usually act as the 'weaker party in asymmetric relations'. They are legally sovereign but not fully autonomous in terms of the control they are able to exert over external relations and even over internal affairs. Particularly indicative of this is the drafting and the unamendability of the Cypriot Constitution.

Furthermore, the influence of external factors upon the drafting extended to the life span of the Constitution, according to a formula for external unamendability. The term 'external unamendability' indicates three factors. The first is that the unamendable provisions of the Constitution of Cyprus, and their status as unamendable, were determined by an international agreement. Secondly, this agreement was negotiated without the direct participation of the people(s) of Cyprus, and was only approved ex post facto by their – at the time unelected but nevertheless undisputed – leaders, without room for negotiation or even for deliberation. The third feature of external unamendability in Cyprus is related to the founding treaties and to the fact that the entrenchment of the basic structure of the Republic, as established in Zurich, was equipped with a set of iron-clad guarantees that secured the military presence of the former colonial ruler and of the two 'motherlands' on the island. These treaties became the legal grounds – according to more or less plausible legal constructions – for the channelling of external influences into the constitutional order of Cyprus, not only on the part of the three external powers but also on the part of the other powers that were involved in the Cold-War struggle for mastery over the wider Middle East and Eastern Mediterranean. More broadly, the term 'external unamendability' is meant to connote situations in which the the constitutional actors' control over constitutional affairs and the development of the Constitution, its amendment included, is (severely) curtailed by external factors.

[70] The Constitution of Cyprus, by giving both the President and Vice-President a veto regarding issues of vital interest of each community (a side effect of the power-sharing system of governance), without any mechanism to resolve the impasses that mutual vetoing could lead to, does not preclude a constitutional deadlock. The result is that a mechanism intended to limit the consequences of disagreement between the two communities caused intensified disagreements, as the Constitution of Cyprus offers no incentive to cooperate rather than clash. On the issue of mechanisms which make the lack of cooperation unattractive as a factor for the successful implementation of consociational models of government, see G Tsebelis, 'Elite Interaction and Constitution Building in Consociational Democracies' (1990) 2 *Journal of Theoretical Politics* 22.

As Stanley Kyriakides indicates, the three guarantor powers could 'act as philosopher Kings in the constitutional development of the republic'.[71] In cases like Cyprus, the internationalisation of the constitution-making process and the reasonable expectation that the external framers of the constitution would continue to be interested in the endurance of their project, can be taken as adequate substitutes for unamendability; or, on the flip side: the fear that continuous involvement by the framers in constitutional affairs, combined with other circumstances (eg the constitutional granting of wide autonomy to the confederated entities), would render unamendability irrelevant, especially if all parties involved were aware of its limited effectiveness in practice.[72] The common ground, then, which made possible the Zurich and London settlements was the bilateral intention to create a formally – though not necessarily – independent state of Cyprus. Such a lack of ability of the constitutional agents to operate at their full capacity, which characterises small states, regarding not only the implementation of the Constitution but also its amendment, contributed to the constitutional breakdown.

C. The Role of the Electoral System and the Lack of Political Parties in the Constitutional Breakdown

According to the relevant literature, two other variables that affect the quality of democracy in small states are the lack of political parties, due to the personalised way local politics function, and their tendency to follow majoritarian variants of democracy, even if a strong consensual framework of political activity exists.[73] Cyprus exhibited both variables in the first years after independence,[74] and this fuelled the inability of the two communities to work together in the House of Representatives and ultimately led to the collapse of the constitutional order. The literature highlights the importance of the applicable electoral system for the achievement of consensus between diverging communities in deeply divided societies.[75] For example, majority electoral systems in which the candidate who receives a relative majority is elected in each constituency (so-called 'first-past-the-post') do not favour the electoral representation of minority

[71] S Kyriakides, *Constitutionalism and Crisis Government* (Philadelphia PA, University of Pennsylvania Press, 1968) 55.

[72] S Suteu, 'Eternity Clauses in Post-Conflict and Post-Authoritarian Constitution-Making: Promise and Limits' (2017) 6 *Global Constitutionalism* 63, 66: In part because eternity clauses are a fairly common constitutional feature, constitution-makers in post-conflict settings may not always be aware of the full array of implications flowing from the inclusion of such clauses in constitutions, or of how these provisions fit within the broader constitutional architecture – notably with mechanisms for constitutional openness (such as legislative initiative provisions) and for constitutional enforcement (such as constitutional review).'

[73] On these variants, see D Anckar, 'Small Polities Tyrannized by Majorities?' (2009) 2 *The Open Political Science Journal* 35; D Anckar and C Anckar, 'Democracies without Parties' (2000) 33 *Comparative Political Studies* 225; W Veenendaal, 'Size and Personalistic Politics: Characteristics of Political Competition in four Microstates' (2013) 102 *The Round Table* 245.

[74] The first Greek-Cypriot political parties were established in 1969. The first sign that political divisions of a traditional ideological kind were re-emerging among the members of the Turkish community was the founding of the opposition Republican Turkish Party (CTP) in 1970.

[75] See, eg Lijphart (n 1) 78–79. See also I O'Flynn, 'Democratic Theory and Practice in Deeply Divided Societies' (2010) 46 *Representations* 281 and B Reilly, *Democracy in Divided Societies: Electoral Engineering for Conflict Management* (Cambridge, Cambridge University Press, 2001).

'voices' within each community and thus give rise to a unidimensional representation of the minority in Parliament.[76]

The first parliamentary elections in Cyprus were held under the electoral law of the colonial administration, since neither community proposed any changes to the law when the issue of the elections was raised.[77] Cyprus was divided into six constituencies, which would elect the 35 Greek-Cypriot and 15 Turkish-Cypriot MPs. In each constituency, the deputies from each community who received the most votes were elected until the number of seats corresponding to each constituency was reached. In other words, MPs would not be elected proportionally based on the number of votes each party received, but all seats could be awarded to a single party if its candidates won a majority in all six constituencies.[78]

This led to the election of predetermined deputies from both communities, as both communities presented electoral lists in each constituency which represented the whole community, leaving no room for the election of deputies who were not included in these lists. In the constituencies of Larnaca, Nicosia, and Keryneia the Turkish-Cypriot MPs entered Parliament without elections, as there was only a single list, that of the National Turkish Union of Cyprus, a political association that represented the majority of Turkish Cypriots. This was mirrored for the Greek-Cypriot MPs in the Paphos constituency, where four MPs also entered Parliament without elections.[79] The deputies of the Greek-Cypriot community corresponded to a coalition of two parties (Patriotic Front-AKEL), but they were elected based on a prior agreement which determined the proportion of MPs between the members of the alliance (30 MPs for the Patriotic Front and five for AKEL). In other words, there was no competition within either community based on different electoral programmes on how the two communities should cooperate and implement the aims of the constitutional settlement that determined the relations between them.[80]

The rigidity of the dividing lines between the two communities was also intensified by the lack of organised political parties (apart from AKEL). This impacted the way the two communities were represented. Intermediary institutions, like political parties structure conflicts in such a way as to allow the political system to absorb tensions. They disconnect politics from any 'absolute truth', by enabling public debate and challenging monolithic approaches to facts. The electoral pact and alignment between AKEL and

[76] The majority model is not always synonymous with the strengthening of extreme 'voices' in a community however. According to the relevant literature, if the majority model is combined with the alternative voting system, which favours the election of moderate candidates, then candidates may be elected who transcend the boundaries of their community, see D Horowitz, 'Encouraging electoral accommodation in divided societies' in B Lal and P Larmour, *Electoral Systems in Divided Societies: The Fiji Constitution Review* (Canberra Research School of Pacific and Asian Studies, 1997) 21.

[77] AC Emilianides, *The Secret Negotiations: The Birth of the Republic of Cyprus (1959–1960)* (Athens Papazisis, 2021, in Greek) 142.

[78] The electoral system was a decisive factor in AKEL's decision to form a coalition with the Patriotic Front see Kyriakides (n 71) 73–74.

[79] On the parliamentary elections of 1960, see C Christophorou, 'The first Parliamentary Election 31 July 1960' (*Eklektor*, 2 July 2019), www.eklektor.org/parliamentary-elections-1960-analysis.

[80] The election of candidates who can adopt policies that transcend communal identity is a prerequisite the success of power-sharing systems in deeply divided societies. See, eg O'Flynn (n 75) 287–88.

the pro-Makarios political forces during the first years of independence, which were critical for the consolidation of the Cypriot Republic, precluded a possible alternative to a unified and rigid Greek-Cypriot approach to intercommunal relations. On the other hand, the Turkish-Cypriot community also failed to give rise to such an alternative, due to the absolute control of its political life by those who considered that its 'survival' depended upon its solidification vis-a-vis the Greek majority.[81]

The dearth of political parties in both communities[82] meant that no competitive processes of political agency were in place to prevent all-or-nothing politics. The existence of a legitimate opposition guarantees that 'more than one outcome can be pursued without being subject to coercion'.[83] Lack of such opposition makes the outcome of political processes not a matter of horizontally acting collective agency but instead one of unidimensional agency represented by the head of the collective body, who acts top-down. Tellingly, this is also a characteristic of the structure of governance in small states. Even if they are democratic, a considerable number of small states exhibit the dominance of the executive over the other branches of government.[84] Furthermore, this executive dominance in small states is not always the outcome of the structure of governance that the Constitution provides for, but of informal patterns in the way political actors perceive their role.

The lack of political parties is also a strong indicator of high dispositional homogeneity, which also reflects political competition (or lack thereof) in small states. Small states tend to be more homogenous in terms of disposition, regardless of the electoral system.[85] The outcomes of political processes may thus be much more consensus-oriented, but this consensus is achieved not through deliberation but through compliance with social norms.

81 The AKEL-Patriotic Front coalition and their common perception about the nature of the Cypriot state ıd the structure of governance in the first years after independence nullified their ideological and programatic contestation over the major issues, which was the source of the constitutional breakdown. Thus, there as no expression of alternative views within the Greek-Cypriot community which might lead to a mitigan of the confrontation between the two communities regarding the relevant constitutional issues. On the rkish-Cypriot side, the outbreak of the Greek-Cypriot revolt gradually led to the suffocation of any leftist ganisation: N Kızılyürek, 'Turkish-Cypriot left: A Historical Overview' in N Trimikliniotis and U Bozkurt, *yond a Divided Cyprus: A State and Society in Transformation* (Cham, Springer, 2012) 169. The insignificance of ideological and programmatic contestation is one of the characteristics of politics in small states: enendaal and Corbett (n 58) 61.

82 On the homogeneity of Turkish-Cypriot political expression during 1950–1960, see M Hamit, 'Critical flections on Universal Human Rights Discourses in the Context of National Conflicts over Cyprus' (PhD sis, University of East London, 2022). The solidification of the two communities in the first years after lependence is obvious in the way that their parliamentary representatives voted on the issues which led the constitutional breakdown. The sole exception was the matter of tax laws, where, however, the different aviour of four Turkish-Cypriot MPs did not affect the outcome of the dispute, see, eg Emilianides (n 46) 37.

83 AS Kirshner, *Legitimate Opposition* (New Haven CT, Yale University Press, 2022) 64–65.

84 J Gerring and G Zarecki (April 2011) 'Size and Democracy Revisited' available at: www.bu.edu/polisci/ /2011/04/SizeandDemocracyRevisited.pdf, 8–12; Veenendaal and Corbett (n 58) 70–71.

85 D Anckar, 'Homogeneity and Size: Dahl and Tuft revisited' (1999) 22 *Scandinavian Political Studies* 29, 40.

VI. Concluding Remarks

The preceding analysis demonstrates that the Constitution of Cyprus itself, due to its design and the provisions for state institutions, contributed to the constitutional crisis and the collapse of the constitutional order in 1963. Some of these deficiencies, however, are interlinked with the smallness of Cyprus.

The process of constitution-making and the enactment of the Constitution relied heavily on external powers. The constitutional provisions which formed the basic structure of governance were drafted exclusively by external agents, and the Constitution itself was enacted by an Act of the British Parliament. Thus, the Constitution was drafted and entered into force without any participation by the local agents. If ratification 'means the confirmation of a constitution by a duly legitimated power',[86] then in Cyprus there was no confirmation by such power. Peoplehood was completely absent, even as a fiction. The 'externality' of the Cypriot Constitution is also reflected in the provisions which render certain sections of it unamendable. Such provisions do not express the Cypriot will but instead reflect the interests of the external powers which formulated these sections of the Constitution. It is obvious, then, that an aspect of small states, namely the inability of their state organs to operate at their full capacity due to external factors, contributed to the constitutional breakdown. In Cyprus, the externality in the constitution-making and amendment processes drastically curtailed the ability of all the internal constitutional agents to formulate the agenda on crucial issues, either in the making of the Constitution or its amendment/ replacement.[87] We should bear in mind that the major premise of the Zurich Agreement was to forestall both *Enosis* and *Taksim* The independence of Cyprus, ie the very foundation of its constitutional order, merely reflected the outcome of this zero-sum game. Such territorial settlement, which was the result of an agreement between the guarantor (external) powers, preceded the drafting of the Constitution. It is the foundation of the political pact on which the Constitution is based, and the constitutional structures are locked into it in the form of unamendabl provisions.

Additionally, as shown, the crisis that led to the deadlock and the constitution breakdown was catalysed by both the constitutional design and the small size of Cypru The lack of intermediate institutions, the personification of politics, and consensu building through the informal acceptance of social norms that characterise politics i several small states, all characterised Cyprus in its first years as an independent sta and defined how both communities behaved as institutional actors. Thus, they all b precluded the emergence of competing visions for the co-existence of both comm nities. In essence, they left the communities with no alternative other than zero-su competition.

The detailed prescription of the constitutional institutions in the Zurich Agreeme left precious little space for incrementalism – an essential strategy for overcoming passio

[86] F Becker, *Ratification of Constitutions* (Oxford, Oxford University Press, 2018) 1.

[87] Richard Albert rightly points out that 'Where those choices are made by persons or bodies external to state, it is right to ask whether the state is sovereign': Albert (n 54) 119.

in divided societies – as a matter of the constitution-making process. Furthermore, the same issues which occupied the drafters of the Zurich Basic Structure and then the members of the Joint Constitutional Commission remained central and were to dominate the political life of the new Republic, blurring the distinction between constitutional and ordinary politics, to a certain extent due to the smallness of Cyprus, and making consensus on constitutional matters almost impossible.

www.ingramcontent.com/pod-product-compliance
Ingram Content Group UK Ltd.
Pitfield, Milton Keynes, MK11 3LW, UK
UKHW020232290926
15470UKWH00002B/504

9 781509 979